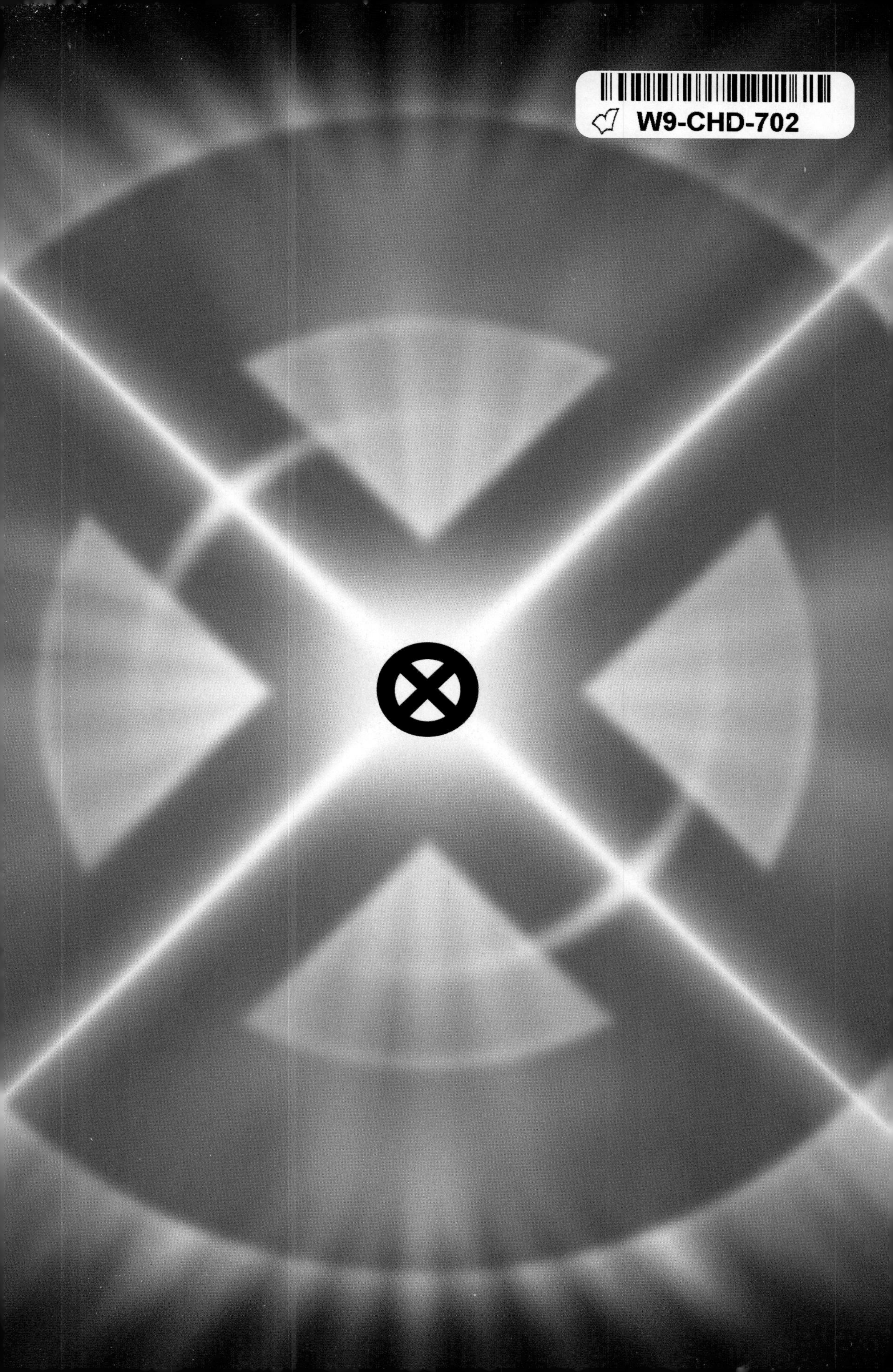

ASTONISHING X-MEN BY JOSS WHEDON & JOHN CASSADAY ULTIMATE COLLECTION BOOK 1. Contains material originally published in magazine form as ASTONISHING X-MEN #1-12. Third printing 2015. ISBN# 978-0-7851-6194-3. Published by MARVEL WORLDWIDE, INC., a subsidiary of MARVEL ENTERTAINMENT, LLC. OFFICE OF PUBLICATION: 135 West 50th Street, New York, NY 10020.
Printed in the U.S.A. ALAN FINE, President, Marvel Entertainment; DAN BUCKLEY, President, TV, Publishing and Brand Management; JOE QUESADA, Chief Creative Officer; TOM BREVOORT, SVP of Publishing; DAVID BOGART, SVP of Operations & Procurement, Publishing; C.B. CEBULSKI, VP of International Development & Brand Management; DAVID GABRIEL, SVP Print, Sales & Marketing; JIM O'KEEFE, VP of Operations & Logistics; DAN CARR, Executive Director of Publishing Technology; SUSAN CRESPI, Editorial Operations Manager; ALEX MORALES, Publishing Operations Manager; STAN LEE, Chairman Emeritus. For information regarding advertising in Marvel Comics or on Marvel.com, please contact Jonathan Rheingold, VP of Custom Solutions & Ad Sales, at jrheingold@marvel.com. For Marvel subscription inquiries, please call 800-217-9158. **Manufactured between 6/24/2015 and 7/27/2015 by R.R. DONNELLEY, INC., SALEM, VA, US.**

10 9 8 7 6 5 4 3

ISHING

EN

WRITER JOSS WHEDON

ARTIST JOHN CASSADAY

COLORIST LAURA MARTIN
LETTERER CHRIS ELIOPOULOS

ASSISTANT EDITORS STEPHANIE MOORE,
SEAN RYAN & CORY SEDLMEIER
ASSOCIATE EDITOR NICK LOWE
EDITOR MIKE MARTS

COLLECTION EDITOR JENNIFER GRÜNWALD
ASSISTANT EDITOR SARAH BRUNSTAD
ASSOCIATE MANAGING EDITOR ALEX STARBUCK
EDITOR, SPECIAL PROJECTS MARK D. BEAZLEY
SENIOR EDITOR, SPECIAL PROJECTS JEFF YOUNGQUIST
SVP PRINT, SALES & MARKETING DAVID GABRIEL

EDITOR IN CHIEF AXEL ALONSO
CHIEF CREATIVE OFFICER JOE QUESADA
PUBLISHER DAN BUCKLEY
EXECUTIVE PRODUCER ALAN FINE

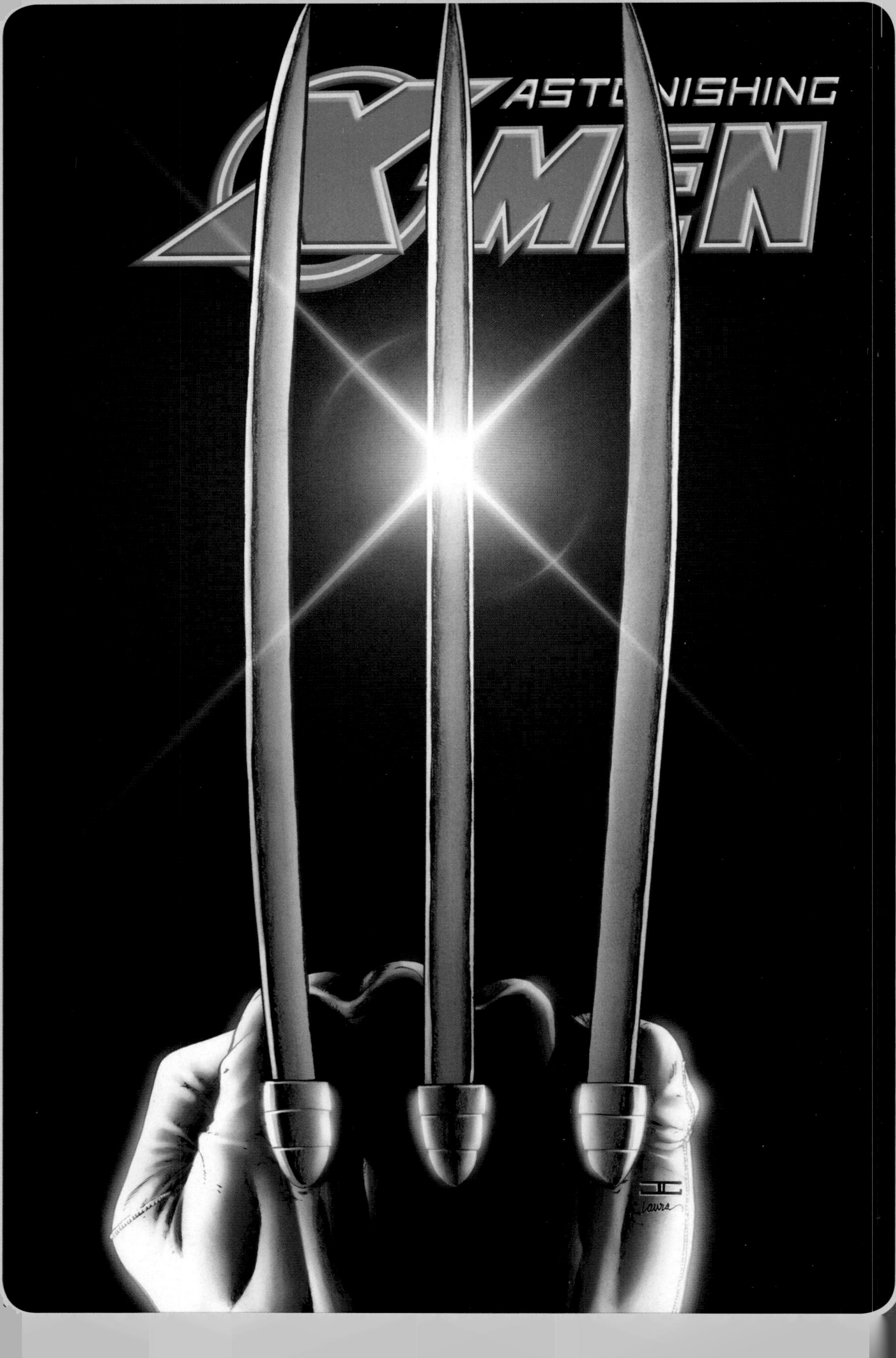
ASTONISHING
X-MEN

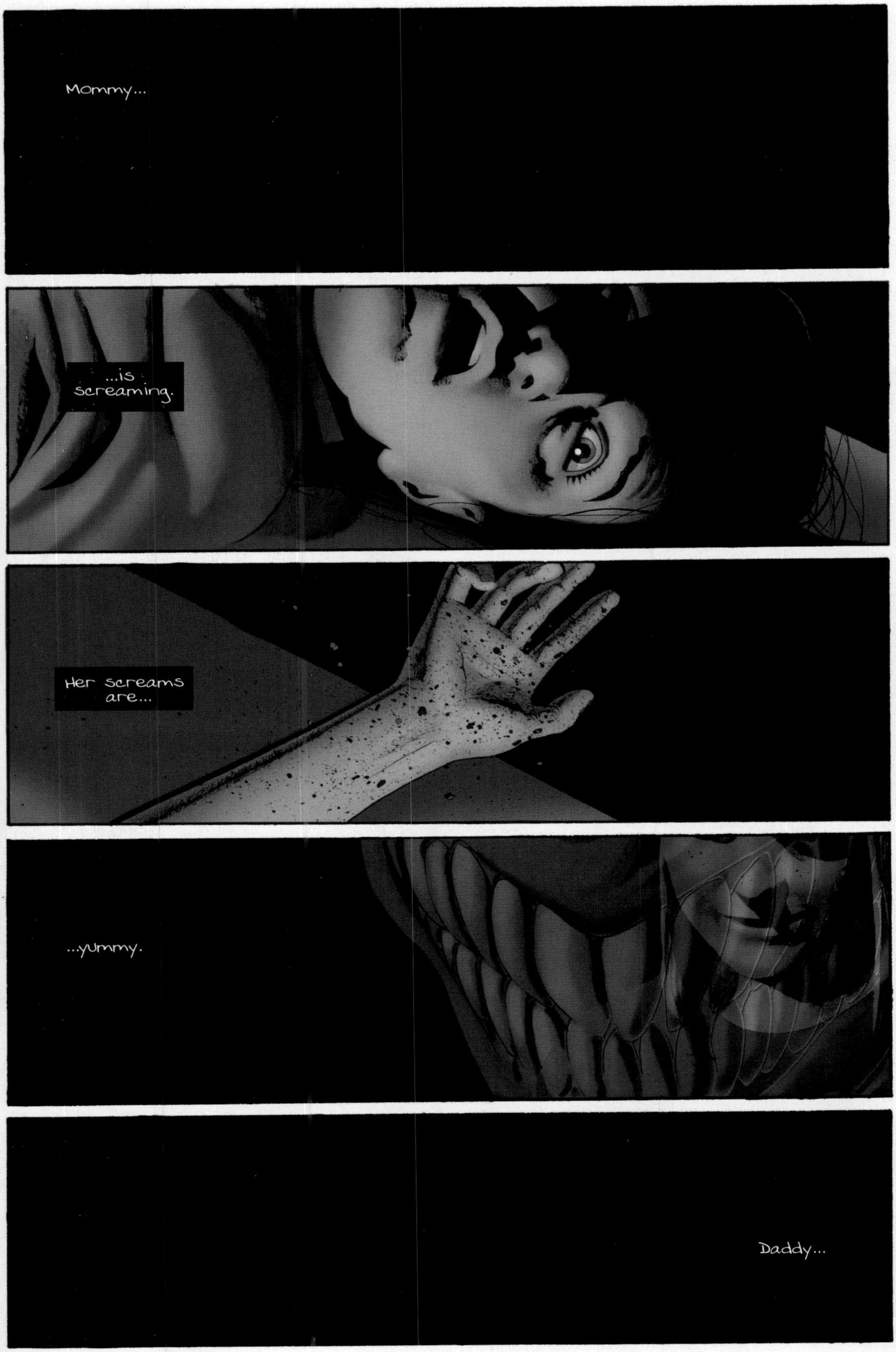
Mommy...
...is screaming.
Her screams are...
...yummy.
Daddy...

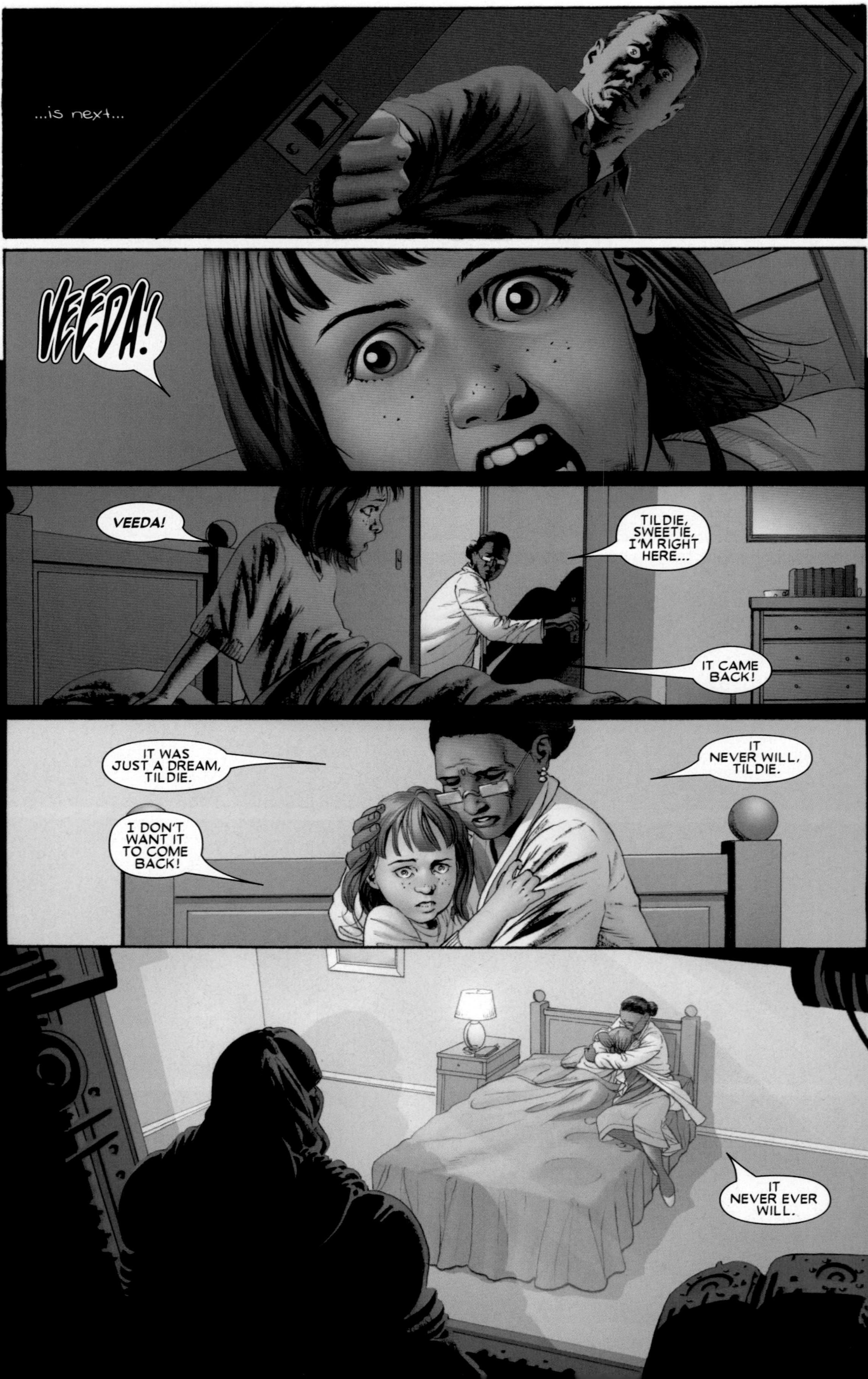
...is next...
VEEDA!
VEEDA!
TILDIE, SWEETIE, I'M RIGHT HERE...
IT CAME BACK!
IT WAS JUST A DREAM, TILDIE.
IT NEVER WILL, TILDIE.
I DON'T WANT IT TO COME BACK!
IT NEVER EVER WILL.

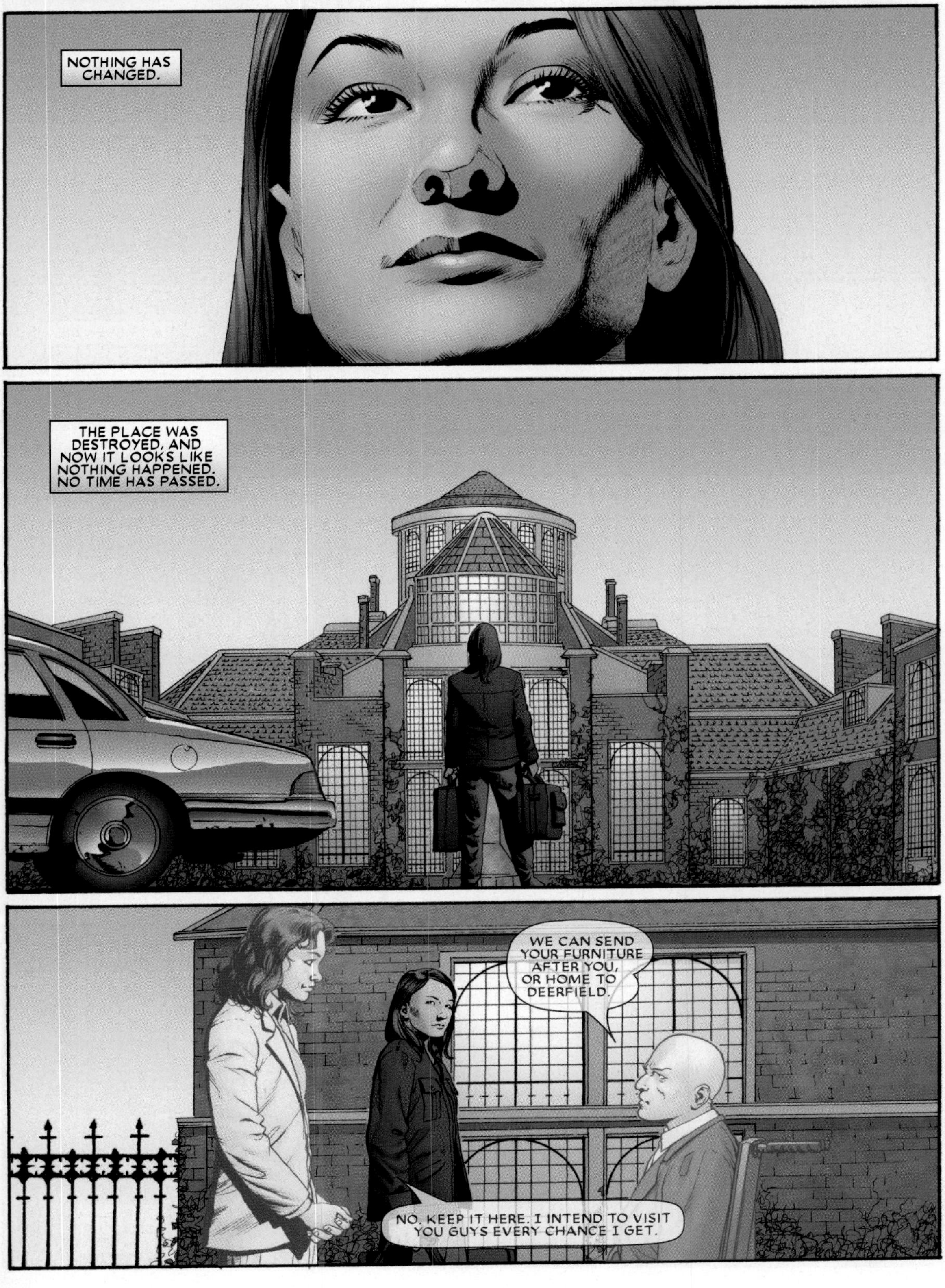
NOTHING HAS CHANGED.
THE PLACE WAS DESTROYED, AND NOW IT LOOKS LIKE NOTHING HAPPENED. NO TIME HAS PASSED.
WE CAN SEND YOUR FURNITURE AFTER YOU, OR HOME TO DEERFIELD.
NO. KEEP IT HERE. I INTEND TO VISIT YOU GUYS EVERY CHANCE I GET.

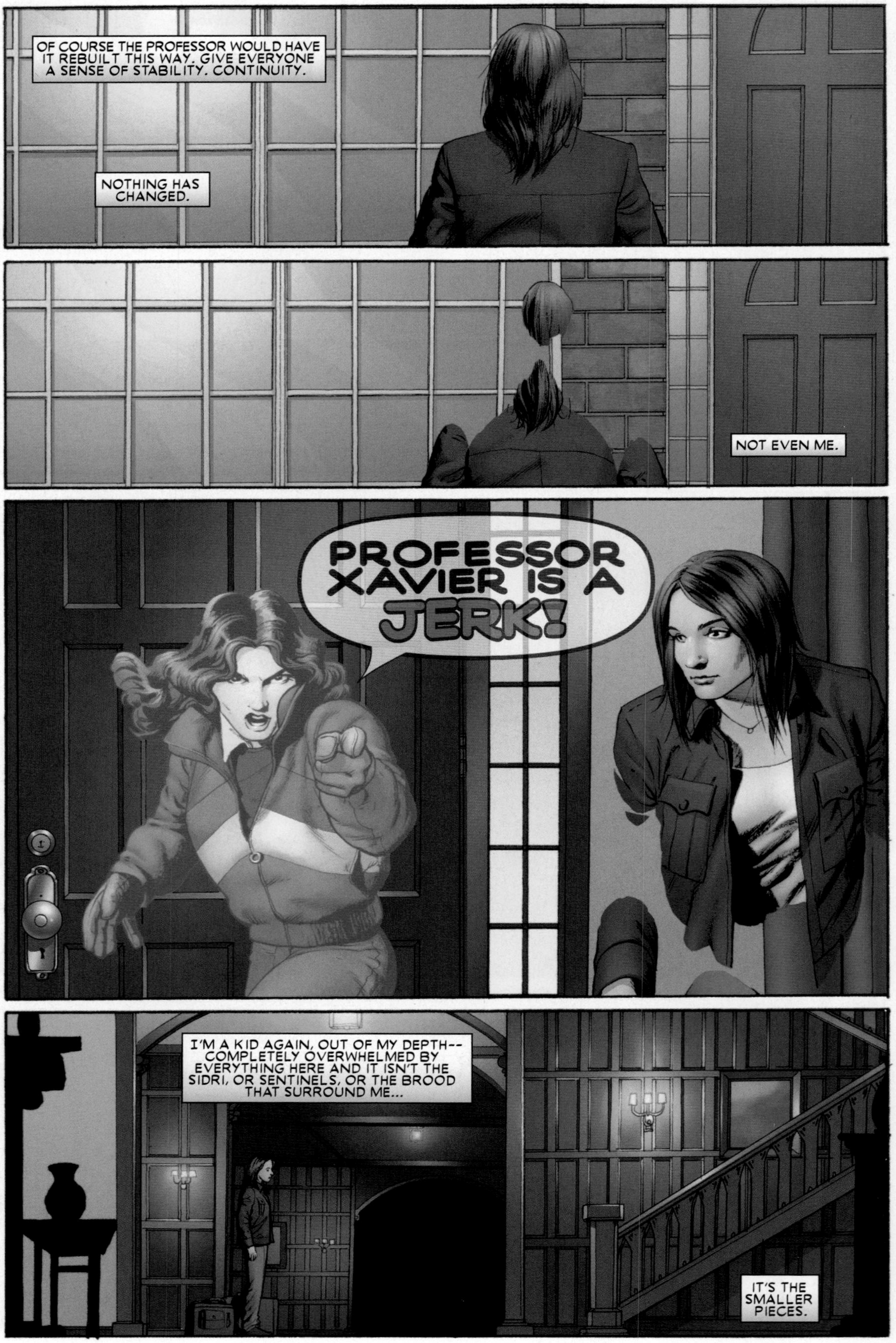
OF COURSE THE PROFESSOR WOULD HAVE IT REBUILT THIS WAY. GIVE EVERYONE A SENSE OF STABILITY. CONTINUITY.
NOTHING HAS CHANGED.
NOT EVEN ME.
PROFESSOR XAVIER IS A JERK!
I'M A KID AGAIN, OUT OF MY DEPTH-- COMPLETELY OVERWHELMED BY EVERYTHING HERE AND IT ISN'T THE SIDRI, OR SENTINELS, OR THE BROOD THAT SURROUND ME...
IT'S THE SMALLER PIECES.

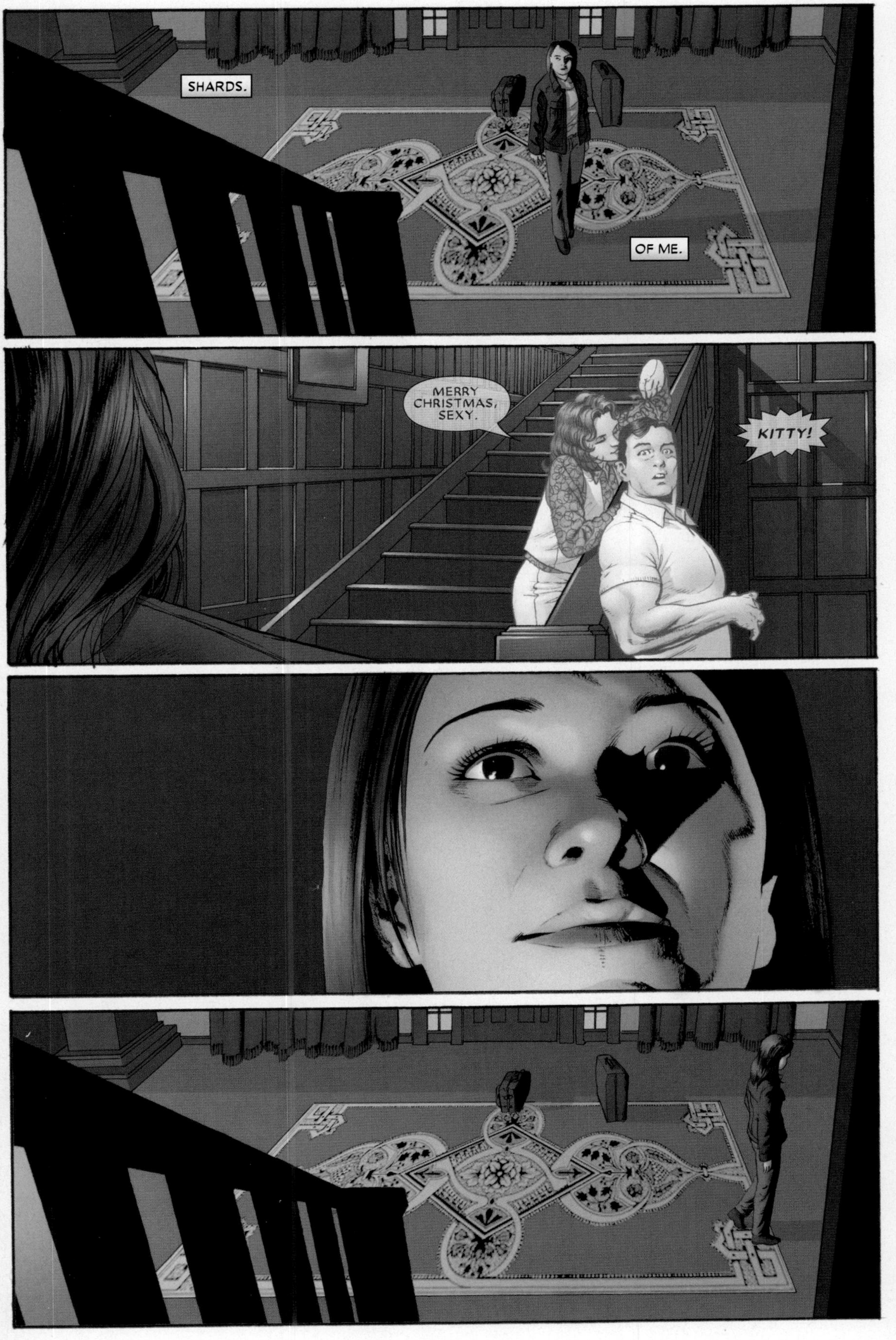
SHARDS.
OF ME.
MERRY CHRISTMAS, SEXY.
KITTY!

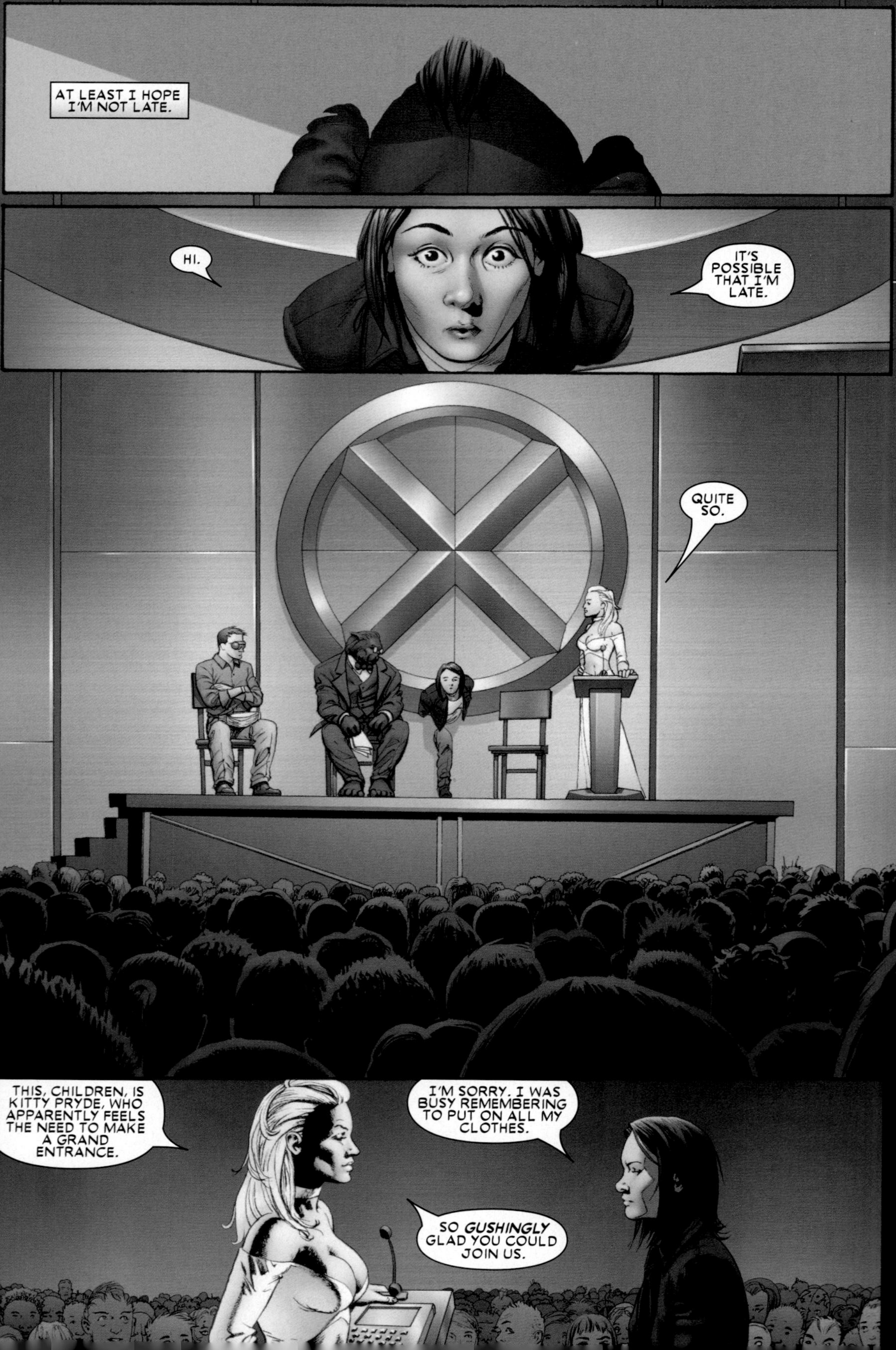
AT LEAST I HOPE I'M NOT LATE.
HI.
IT'S POSSIBLE THAT I'M LATE.
QUITE SO.
THIS, CHILDREN, IS KITTY PRYDE, WHO APPARENTLY FEELS THE NEED TO MAKE A GRAND ENTRANCE.
I'M SORRY. I WAS BUSY REMEMBERING TO PUT ON ALL MY CLOTHES.
SO *GUSHINGLY* GLAD YOU COULD JOIN US.

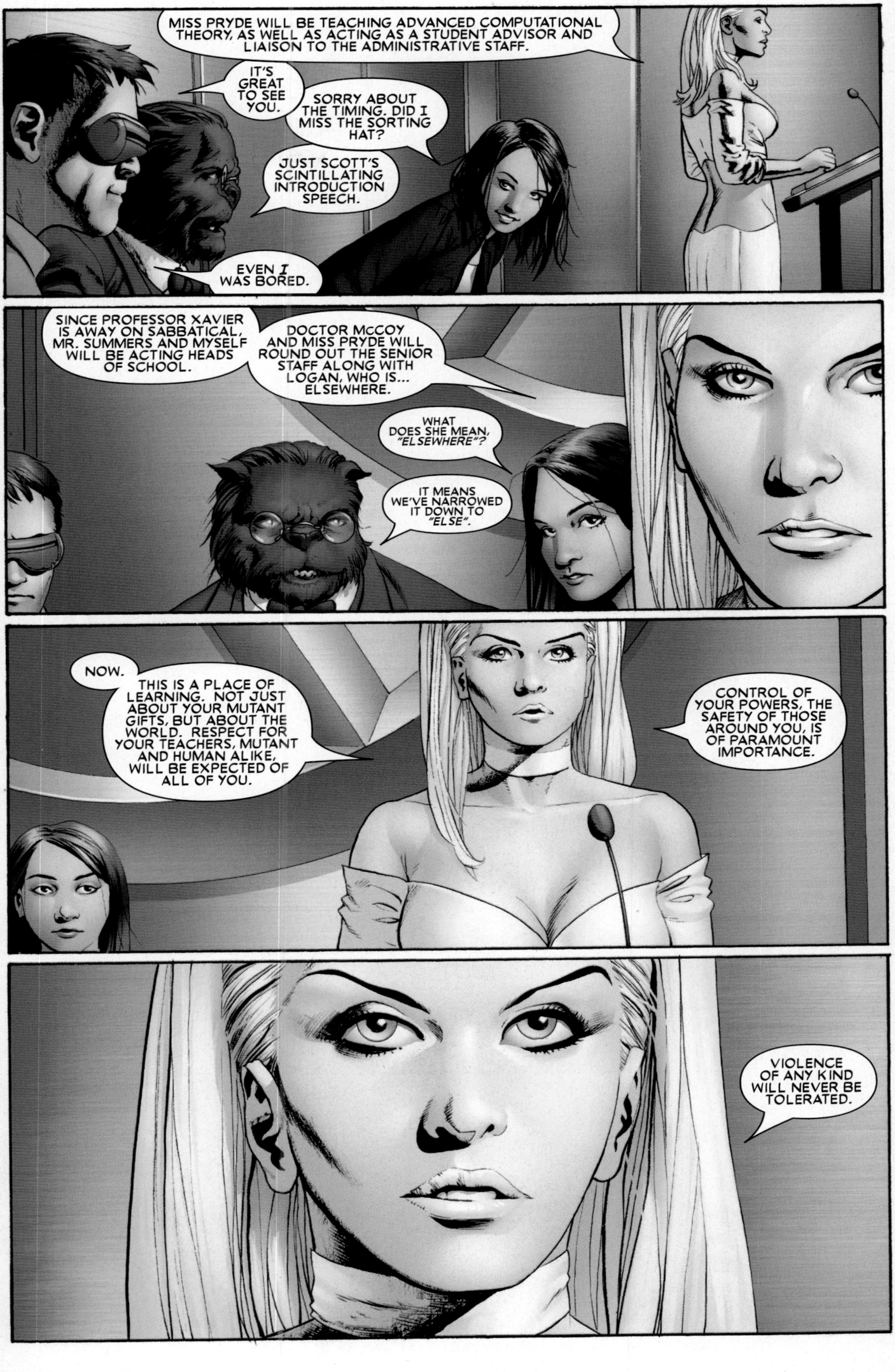
MISS PRYDE WILL BE TEACHING ADVANCED COMPUTATIONAL THEORY, AS WELL AS ACTING AS A STUDENT ADVISOR AND LIAISON TO THE ADMINISTRATIVE STAFF.
IT'S GREAT TO SEE YOU.
SORRY ABOUT THE TIMING. DID I MISS THE SORTING HAT?
JUST SCOTT'S SCINTILLATING INTRODUCTION SPEECH.
EVEN *I* WAS BORED.
SINCE PROFESSOR XAVIER IS AWAY ON SABBATICAL, MR. SUMMERS AND MYSELF WILL BE ACTING HEADS OF SCHOOL.
DOCTOR McCOY AND MISS PRYDE WILL ROUND OUT THE SENIOR STAFF ALONG WITH LOGAN, WHO IS... ELSEWHERE.
WHAT DOES SHE MEAN, *"ELSEWHERE"*?
IT MEANS WE'VE NARROWED IT DOWN TO *"ELSE"*.
NOW.
THIS IS A PLACE OF LEARNING. NOT JUST ABOUT YOUR MUTANT GIFTS, BUT ABOUT THE WORLD. RESPECT FOR YOUR TEACHERS, MUTANT AND HUMAN ALIKE, WILL BE EXPECTED OF ALL OF YOU.
CONTROL OF YOUR POWERS, THE SAFETY OF THOSE AROUND YOU, IS OF PARAMOUNT IMPORTANCE.
VIOLENCE OF ANY KIND WILL NEVER BE TOLERATED.

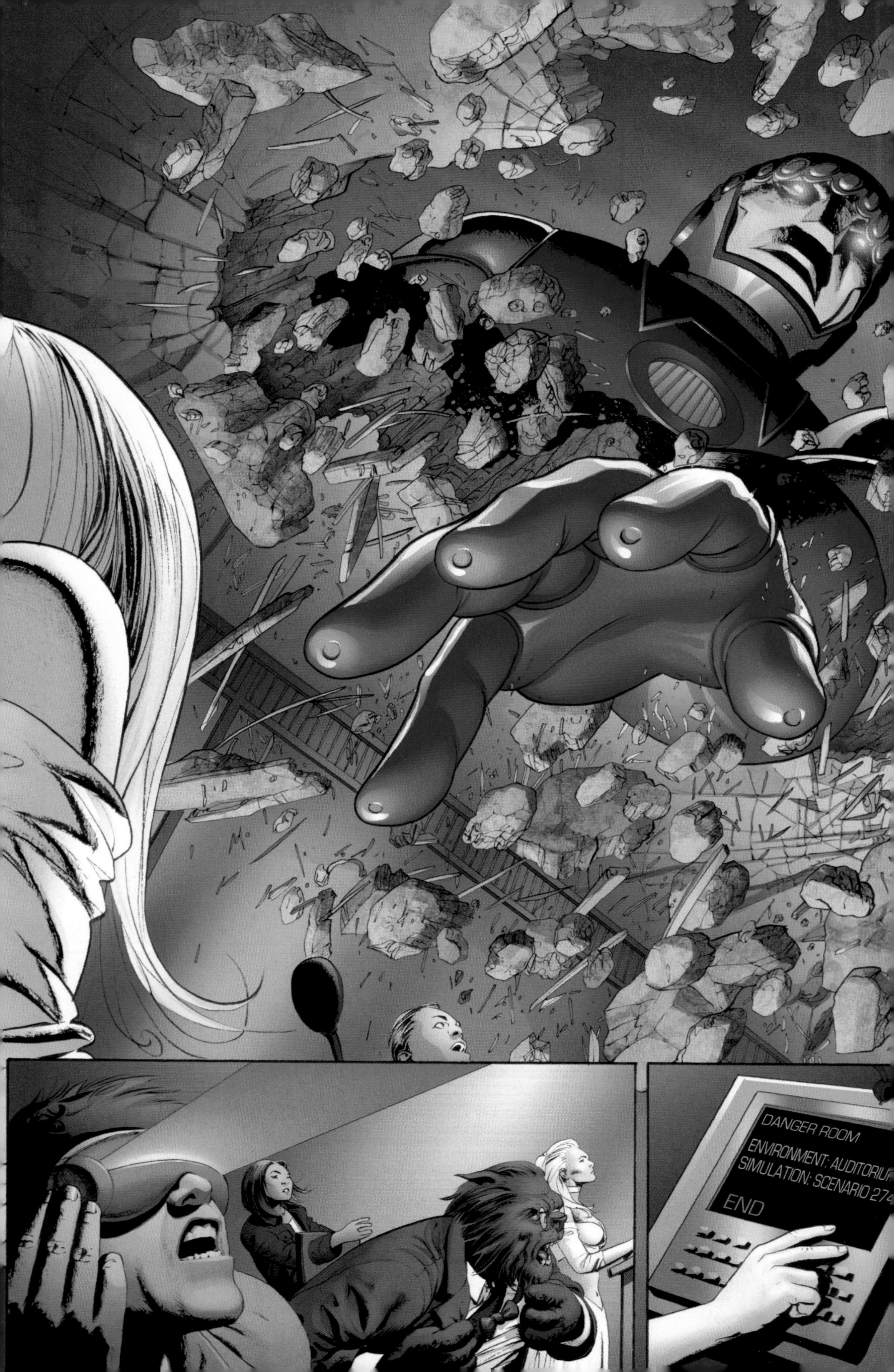
DANGER ROOM
ENVIRONMENT: AUDITORIU
SIMULATION: SCENARIO 274
END

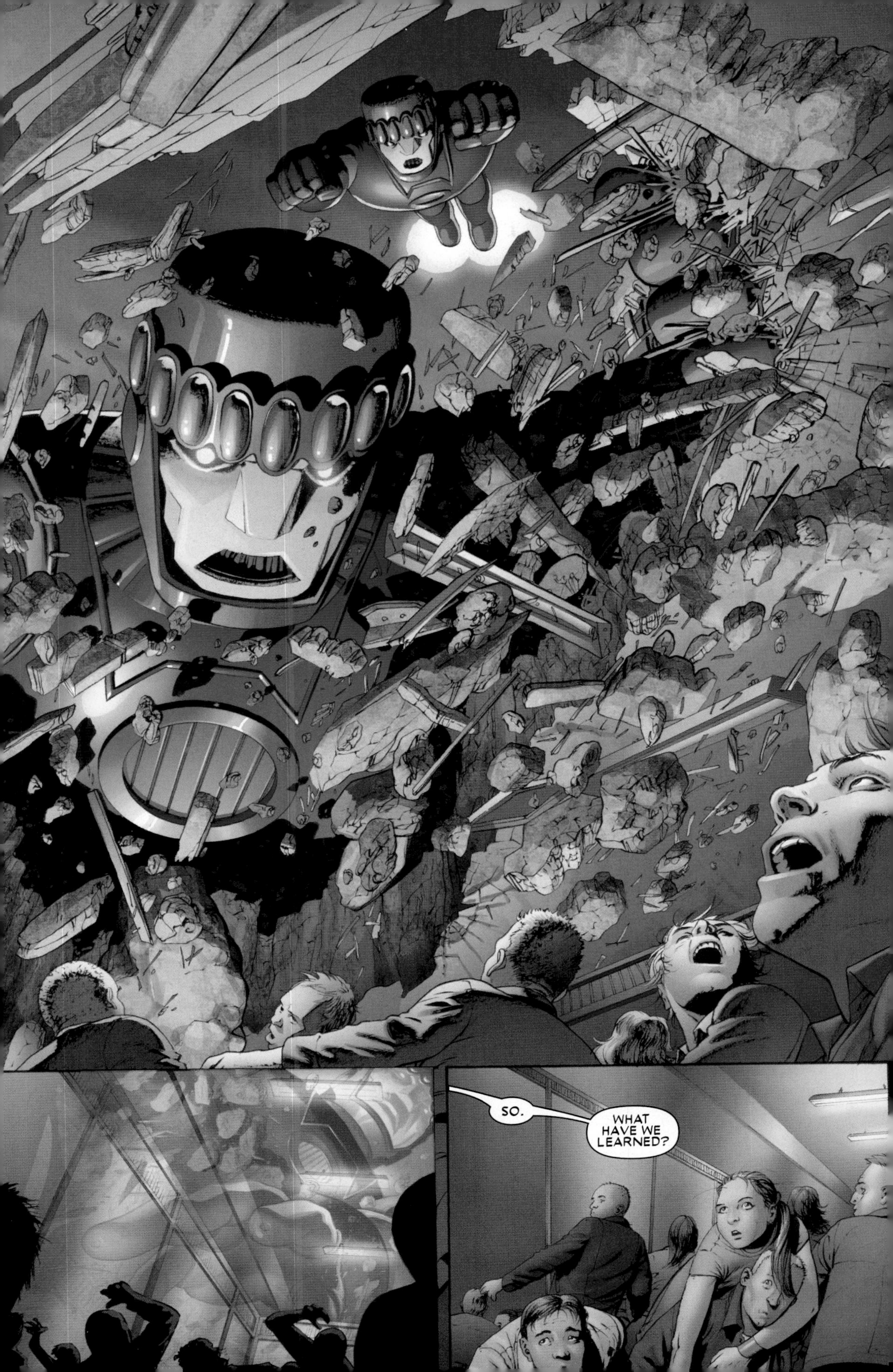
SO.
WHAT HAVE WE LEARNED?

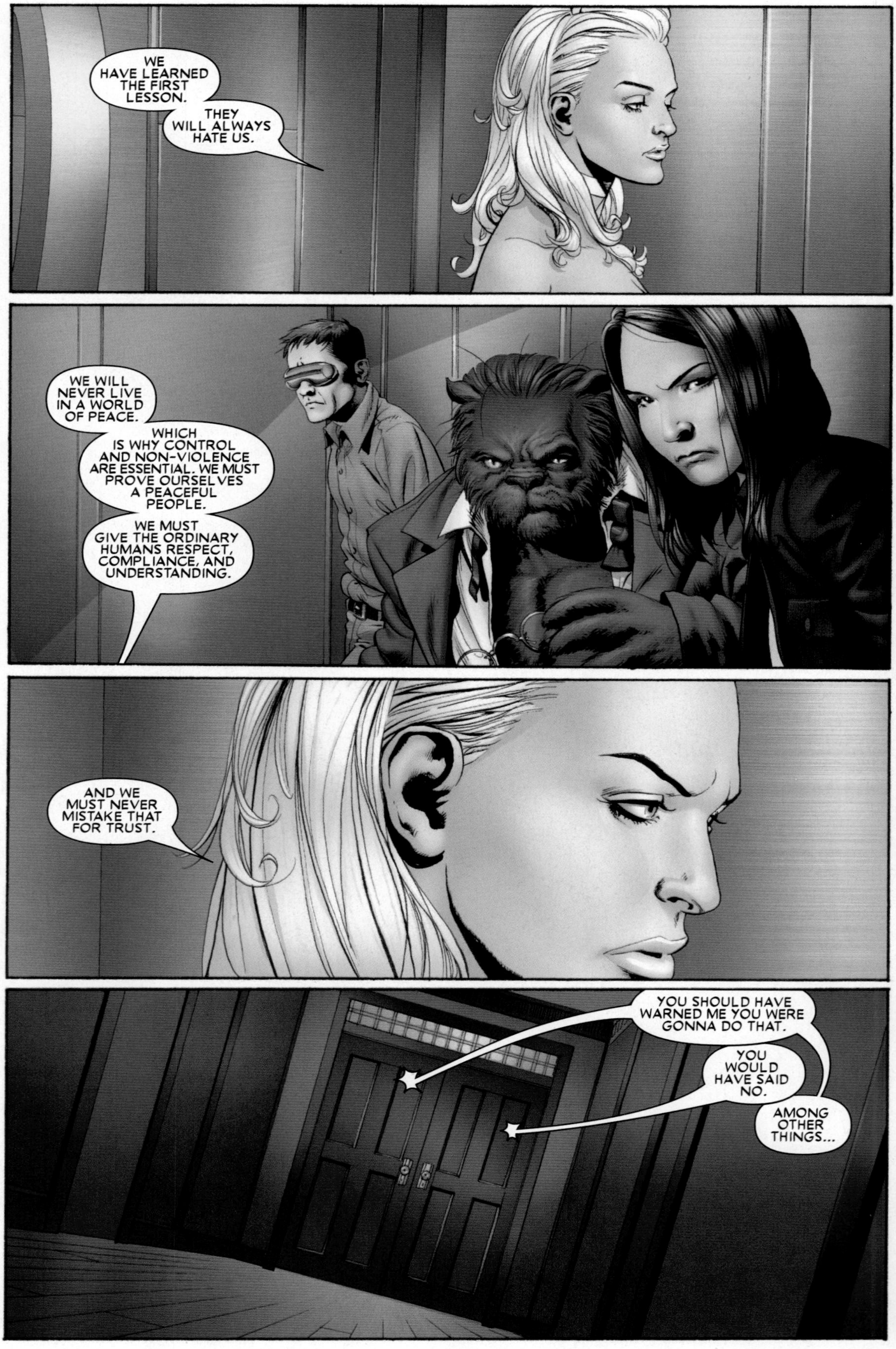
WE HAVE LEARNED THE FIRST LESSON.
THEY WILL ALWAYS HATE US.
WE WILL NEVER LIVE IN A WORLD OF PEACE.
WHICH IS WHY CONTROL AND NON-VIOLENCE ARE ESSENTIAL. WE MUST PROVE OURSELVES A PEACEFUL PEOPLE.
WE MUST GIVE THE ORDINARY HUMANS RESPECT, COMPLIANCE, AND UNDERSTANDING.
AND WE MUST NEVER MISTAKE THAT FOR TRUST.
YOU SHOULD HAVE WARNED ME YOU WERE GONNA DO THAT.
YOU WOULD HAVE SAID NO.
AMONG OTHER THINGS...

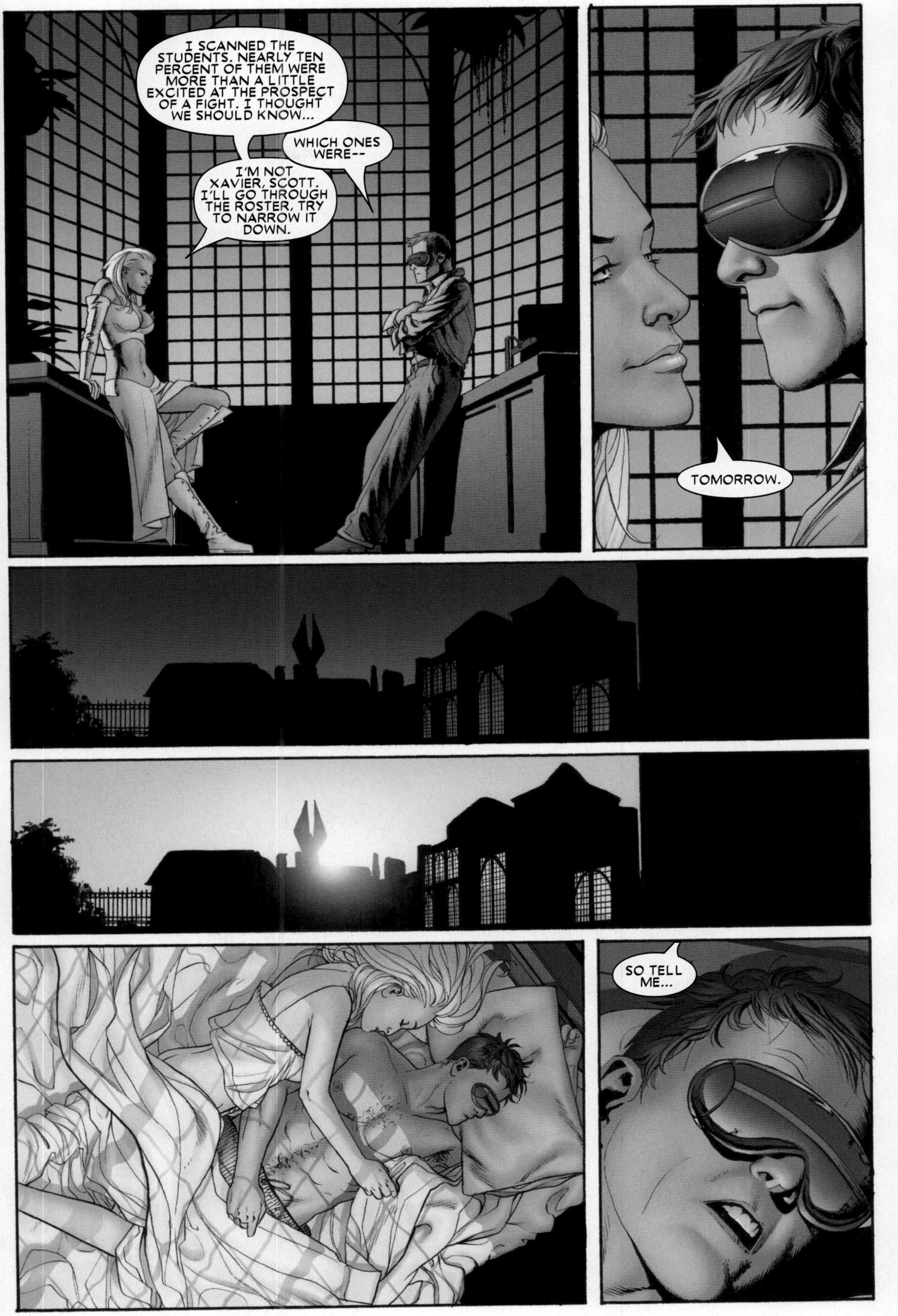
I SCANNED THE STUDENTS. NEARLY TEN PERCENT OF THEM WERE MORE THAN A LITTLE EXCITED AT THE PROSPECT OF A FIGHT. I THOUGHT WE SHOULD KNOW...
WHICH ONES WERE--
I'M NOT XAVIER, SCOTT. I'LL GO THROUGH THE ROSTER, TRY TO NARROW IT DOWN.
TOMORROW.
SO TELL ME...

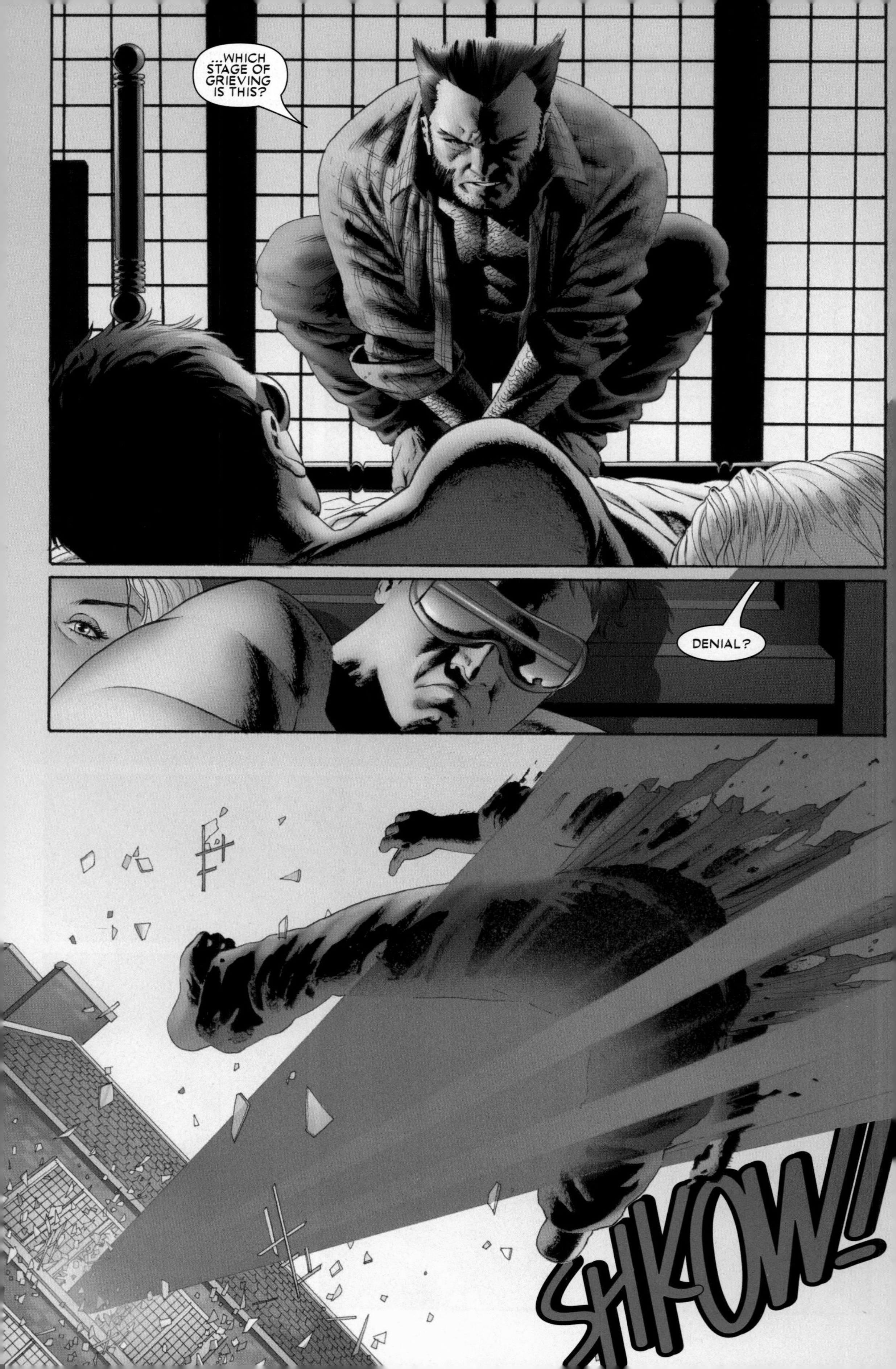
...WHICH STAGE OF GRIEVING IS THIS?
DENIAL?
SHKOW!!

STRIKE A NERVE, SUMMERS?

THIS IS GOOD.

THE GUY WHO'S TRIED TO STEAL MY WIFE SINCE THE DAY HE MET US IS GONNA TELL ME ALL ABOUT WHAT'S *PROPER*.

ONLY REASON JEAN AND YOU STAYED TOGETHER AT ALL IS SHE WAS TOO STRONG TO GIVE IN TO WHAT SHE REALLY WANTED...

...AND YOU WERE TOO SCARED.

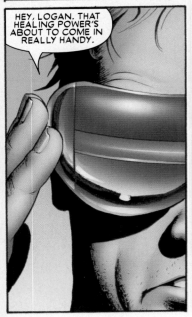

HEY, LOGAN. THAT HEALING POWER'S ABOUT TO COME IN REALLY HANDY.

SHKOW!

WHAT'S THIS ALL ABOUT?

WHAT DO YOU THINK?

SUPERPOWERS, A SCINTILLATING WIT AND THE BEST BODY MONEY CAN BUY...

...AND I STILL RATE BELOW A CORPSE.

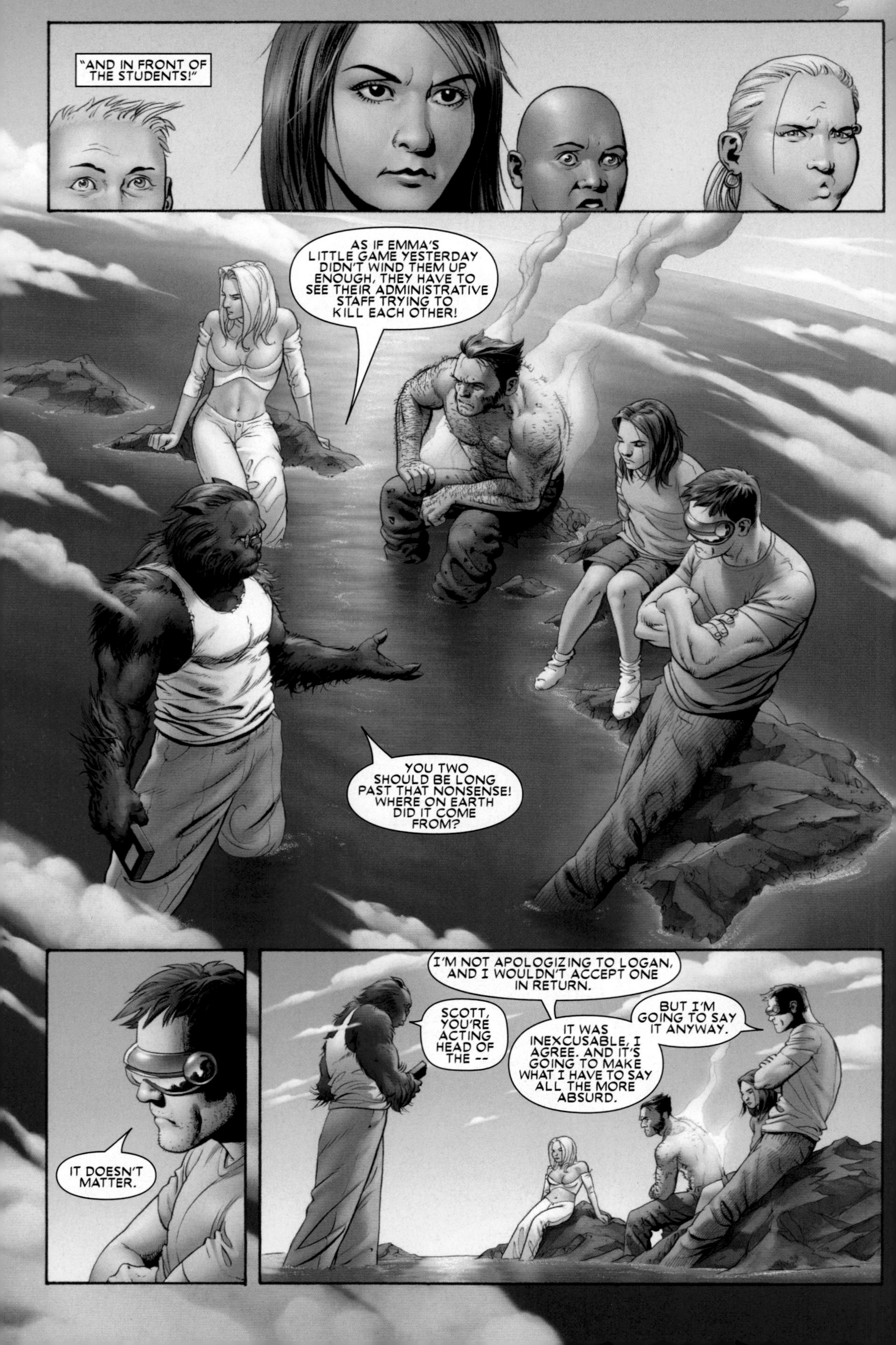
"AND IN FRONT OF THE STUDENTS!"
AS IF EMMA'S LITTLE GAME YESTERDAY DIDN'T WIND THEM UP ENOUGH, THEY HAVE TO SEE THEIR ADMINISTRATIVE STAFF TRYING TO KILL EACH OTHER!
YOU TWO SHOULD BE LONG PAST THAT NONSENSE! WHERE ON EARTH DID IT COME FROM?
IT DOESN'T MATTER.
SCOTT, YOU'RE ACTING HEAD OF THE --
I'M NOT APOLOGIZING TO LOGAN, AND I WOULDN'T ACCEPT ONE IN RETURN.
IT WAS INEXCUSABLE, I AGREE. AND IT'S GOING TO MAKE WHAT I HAVE TO SAY ALL THE MORE ABSURD.
BUT I'M GOING TO SAY IT ANYWAY.

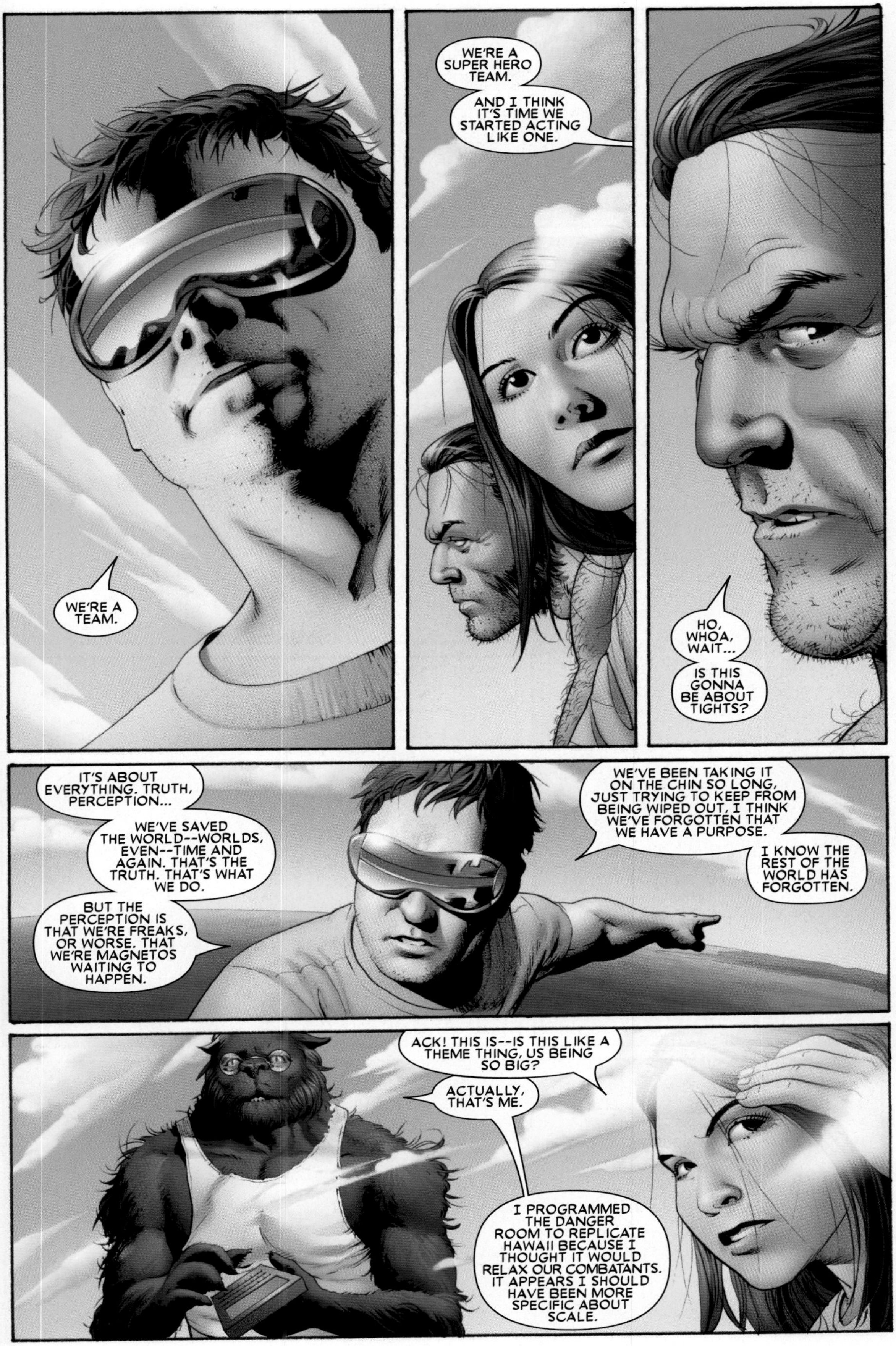
WE'RE A TEAM.
WE'RE A SUPER HERO TEAM.
AND I THINK IT'S TIME WE STARTED ACTING LIKE ONE.
HO, WHOA, WAIT...
IS THIS GONNA BE ABOUT TIGHTS?
IT'S ABOUT EVERYTHING. TRUTH, PERCEPTION...
WE'VE SAVED THE WORLD--WORLDS, EVEN--TIME AND AGAIN. THAT'S THE TRUTH. THAT'S WHAT WE DO.
BUT THE PERCEPTION IS THAT WE'RE FREAKS, OR WORSE. THAT WE'RE MAGNETOS WAITING TO HAPPEN.
WE'VE BEEN TAKING IT ON THE CHIN SO LONG, JUST TRYING TO KEEP FROM BEING WIPED OUT, I THINK WE'VE FORGOTTEN THAT WE HAVE A PURPOSE.
I KNOW THE REST OF THE WORLD HAS FORGOTTEN.
ACK! THIS IS--IS THIS LIKE A THEME THING, US BEING SO BIG?
ACTUALLY, THAT'S ME.
I PROGRAMMED THE DANGER ROOM TO REPLICATE HAWAII BECAUSE I THOUGHT IT WOULD RELAX OUR COMBATANTS. IT APPEARS I SHOULD HAVE BEEN MORE SPECIFIC ABOUT SCALE.

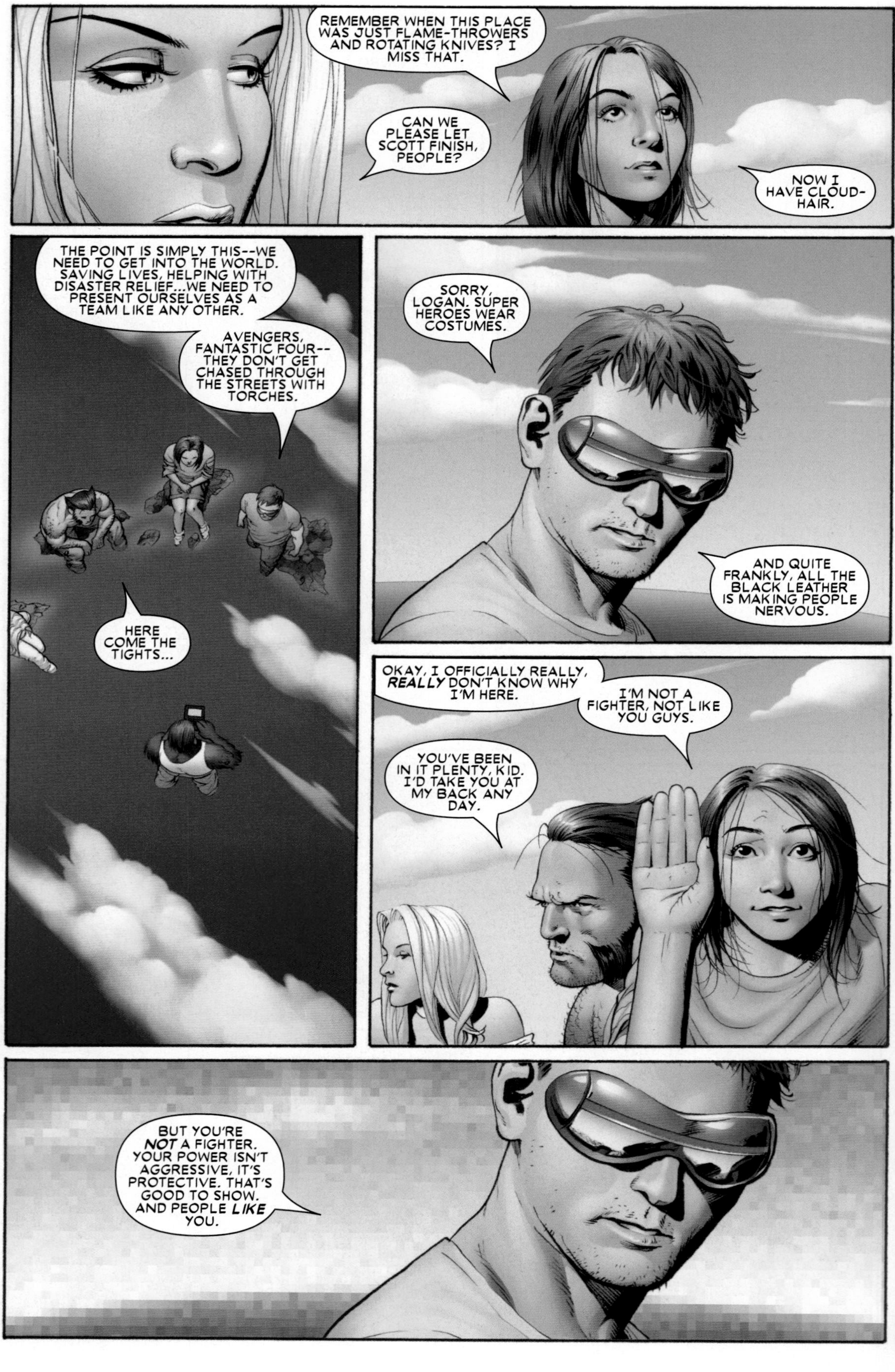
REMEMBER WHEN THIS PLACE WAS JUST FLAME-THROWERS AND ROTATING KNIVES? I MISS THAT.
CAN WE PLEASE LET SCOTT FINISH, PEOPLE?
NOW I HAVE CLOUD-HAIR.
THE POINT IS SIMPLY THIS--WE NEED TO GET INTO THE WORLD. SAVING LIVES, HELPING WITH DISASTER RELIEF...WE NEED TO PRESENT OURSELVES AS A TEAM LIKE ANY OTHER.
AVENGERS, FANTASTIC FOUR--THEY DON'T GET CHASED THROUGH THE STREETS WITH TORCHES.
HERE COME THE TIGHTS...
SORRY, LOGAN. SUPER HEROES WEAR COSTUMES.
AND QUITE FRANKLY, ALL THE BLACK LEATHER IS MAKING PEOPLE NERVOUS.
OKAY, I OFFICIALLY REALLY, ***REALLY*** DON'T KNOW WHY I'M HERE.
I'M NOT A FIGHTER, NOT LIKE YOU GUYS.
YOU'VE BEEN IN IT PLENTY, KID. I'D TAKE YOU AT MY BACK ANY DAY.
BUT YOU'RE ***NOT*** A FIGHTER. YOUR POWER ISN'T AGGRESSIVE, IT'S PROTECTIVE. THAT'S GOOD TO SHOW. AND PEOPLE ***LIKE*** YOU.

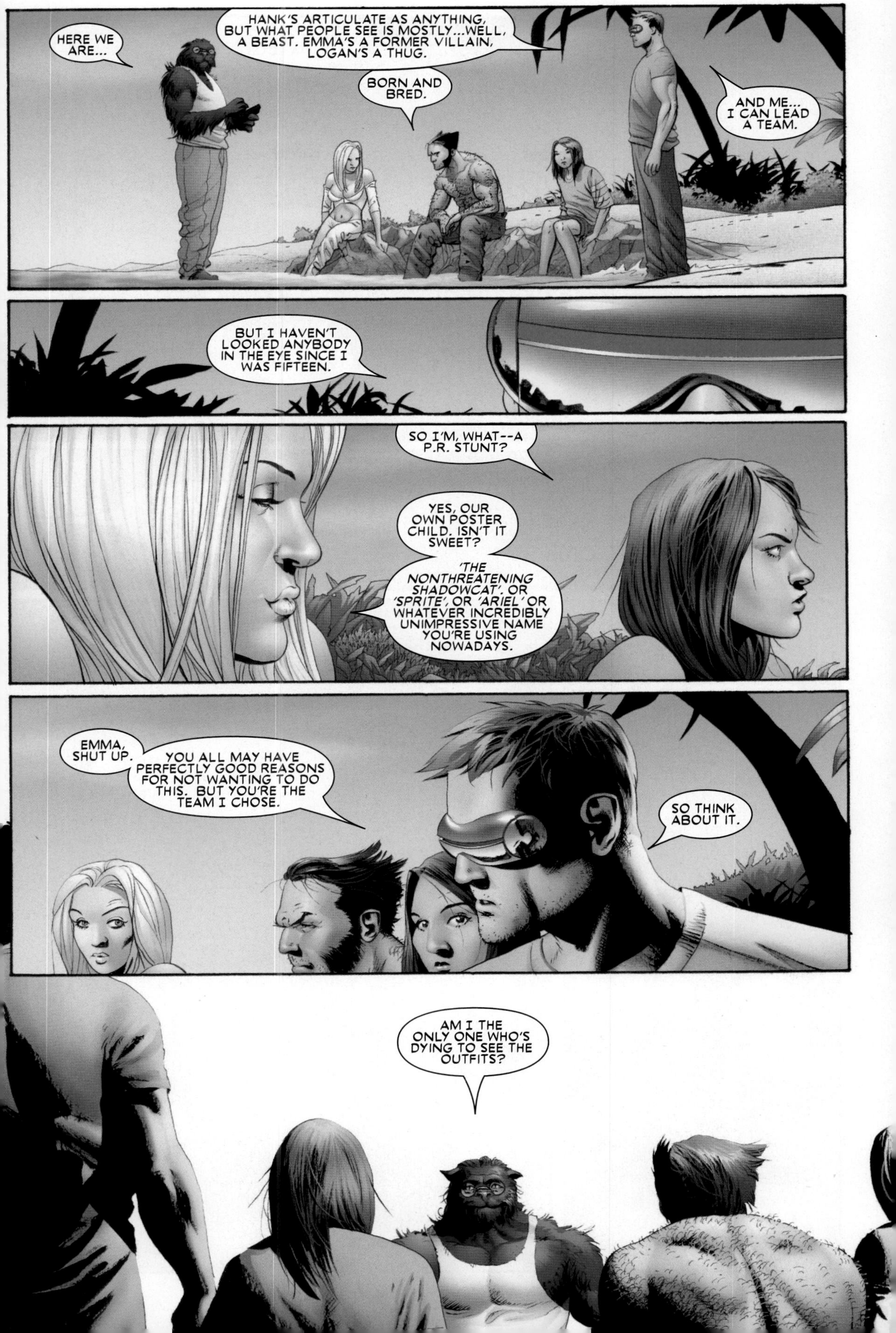
HERE WE ARE...
HANK'S ARTICULATE AS ANYTHING, BUT WHAT PEOPLE SEE IS MOSTLY...WELL, A BEAST. EMMA'S A FORMER VILLAIN, LOGAN'S A THUG.
BORN AND BRED.
AND ME... I CAN LEAD A TEAM.
BUT I HAVEN'T LOOKED ANYBODY IN THE EYE SINCE I WAS FIFTEEN.
SO I'M, WHAT--A P.R. STUNT?
YES, OUR OWN POSTER CHILD. ISN'T IT SWEET?
'THE NONTHREATENING SHADOWCAT'. OR 'SPRITE', OR 'ARIEL' OR WHATEVER INCREDIBLY UNIMPRESSIVE NAME YOU'RE USING NOWADAYS.
EMMA, SHUT UP.
YOU ALL MAY HAVE PERFECTLY GOOD REASONS FOR NOT WANTING TO DO THIS. BUT YOU'RE THE TEAM I CHOSE.
SO THINK ABOUT IT.
AM I THE ONLY ONE WHO'S DYING TO SEE THE OUTFITS?

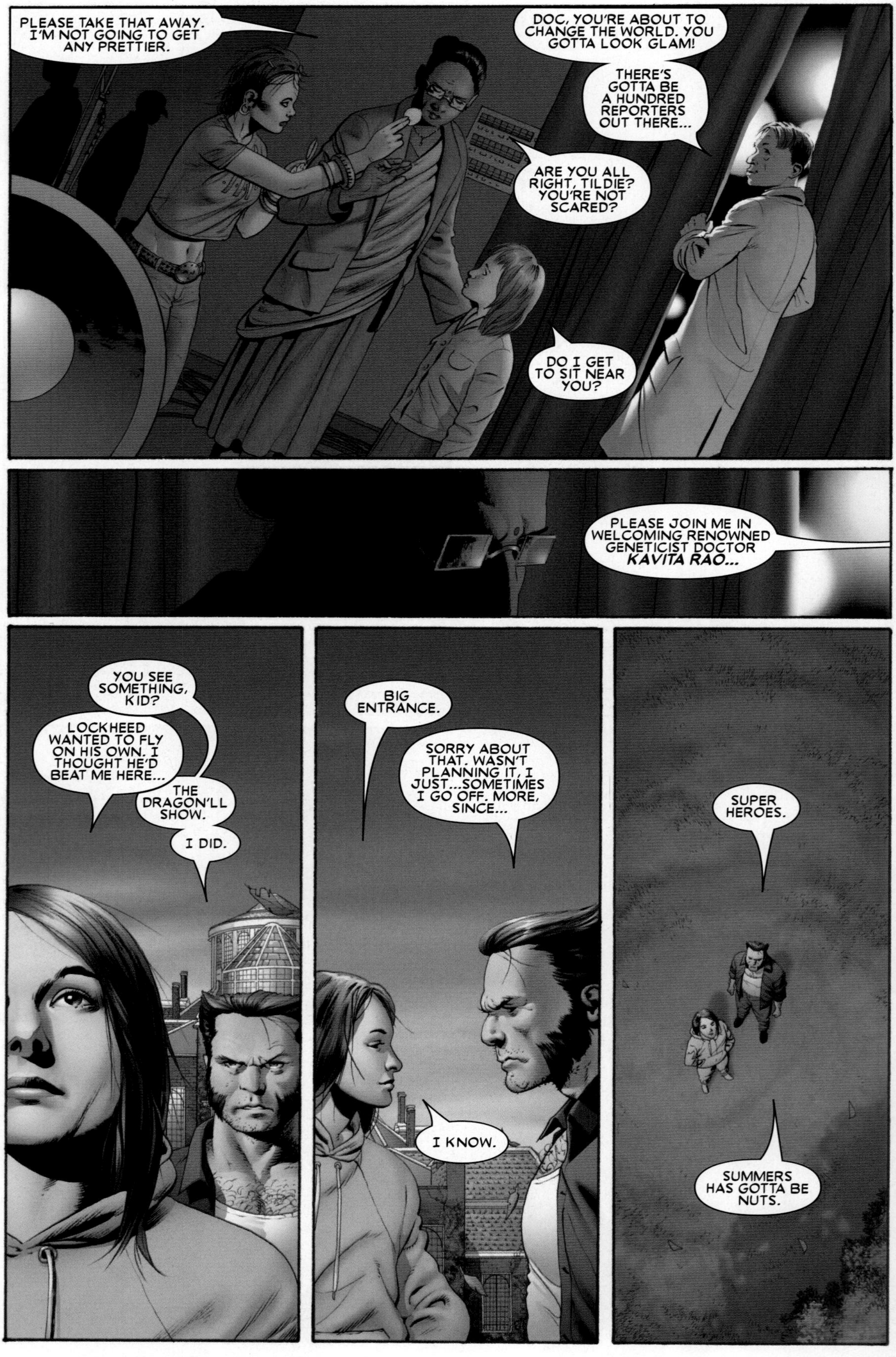
PLEASE TAKE THAT AWAY. I'M NOT GOING TO GET ANY PRETTIER.
DOC, YOU'RE ABOUT TO CHANGE THE WORLD. YOU GOTTA LOOK GLAM!
THERE'S GOTTA BE A HUNDRED REPORTERS OUT THERE...
ARE YOU ALL RIGHT, TILDIE? YOU'RE NOT SCARED?
DO I GET TO SIT NEAR YOU?
PLEASE JOIN ME IN WELCOMING RENOWNED GENETICIST DOCTOR *KAVITA RAO...*
YOU SEE SOMETHING, KID?
LOCKHEED WANTED TO FLY ON HIS OWN. I THOUGHT HE'D BEAT ME HERE...
THE DRAGON'LL SHOW.
I DID.
BIG ENTRANCE.
SORRY ABOUT THAT. WASN'T PLANNING IT, I JUST...SOMETIMES I GO OFF. MORE, SINCE...
I KNOW.
SUPER HEROES.
SUMMERS HAS GOTTA BE NUTS.

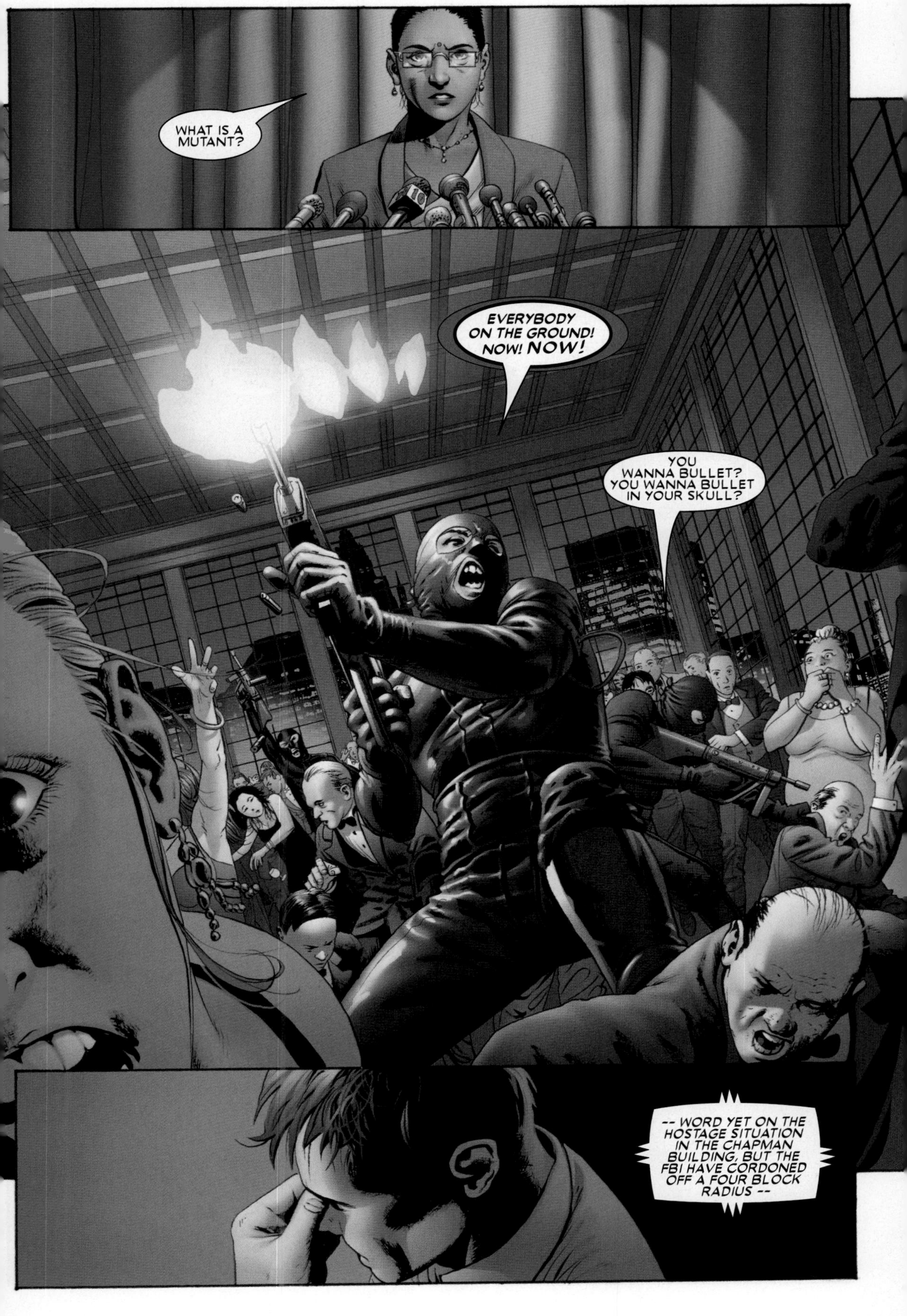
WHAT IS A MUTANT?
EVERYBODY ON THE GROUND! NOW! NOW!
YOU WANNA BULLET? YOU WANNA BULLET IN YOUR SKULL?
-- WORD YET ON THE HOSTAGE SITUATION IN THE CHAPMAN BUILDING, BUT THE FBI HAVE CORDONED OFF A FOUR BLOCK RADIUS --

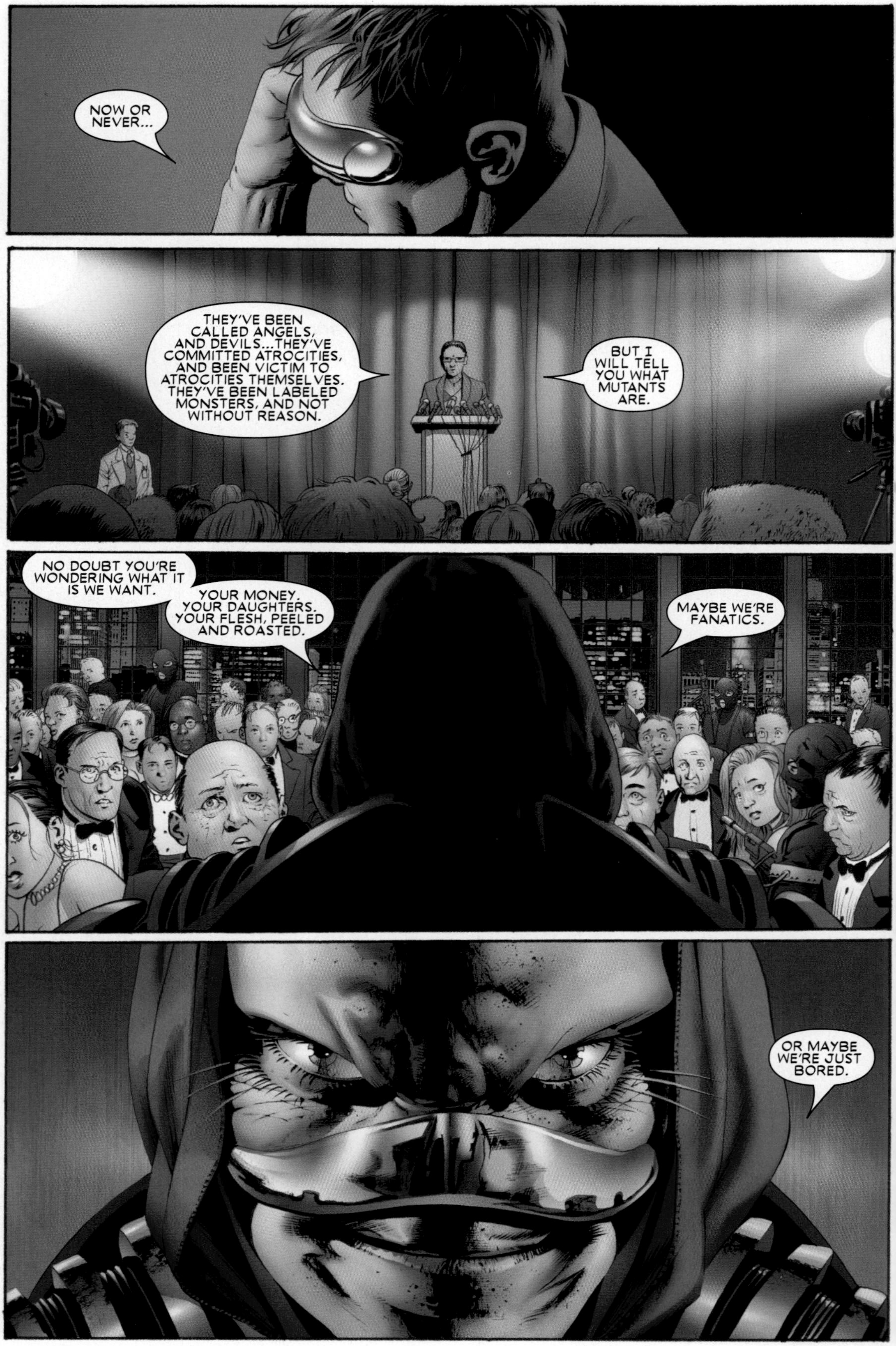
NOW OR NEVER...
THEY'VE BEEN CALLED ANGELS, AND DEVILS...THEY'VE COMMITTED ATROCITIES, AND BEEN VICTIM TO ATROCITIES THEMSELVES. THEY'VE BEEN LABELED MONSTERS, AND NOT WITHOUT REASON.
BUT I WILL TELL YOU WHAT MUTANTS ARE.
NO DOUBT YOU'RE WONDERING WHAT IT IS WE WANT.
YOUR MONEY. YOUR DAUGHTERS. YOUR FLESH, PEELED AND ROASTED.
MAYBE WE'RE FANATICS.
OR MAYBE WE'RE JUST BORED.

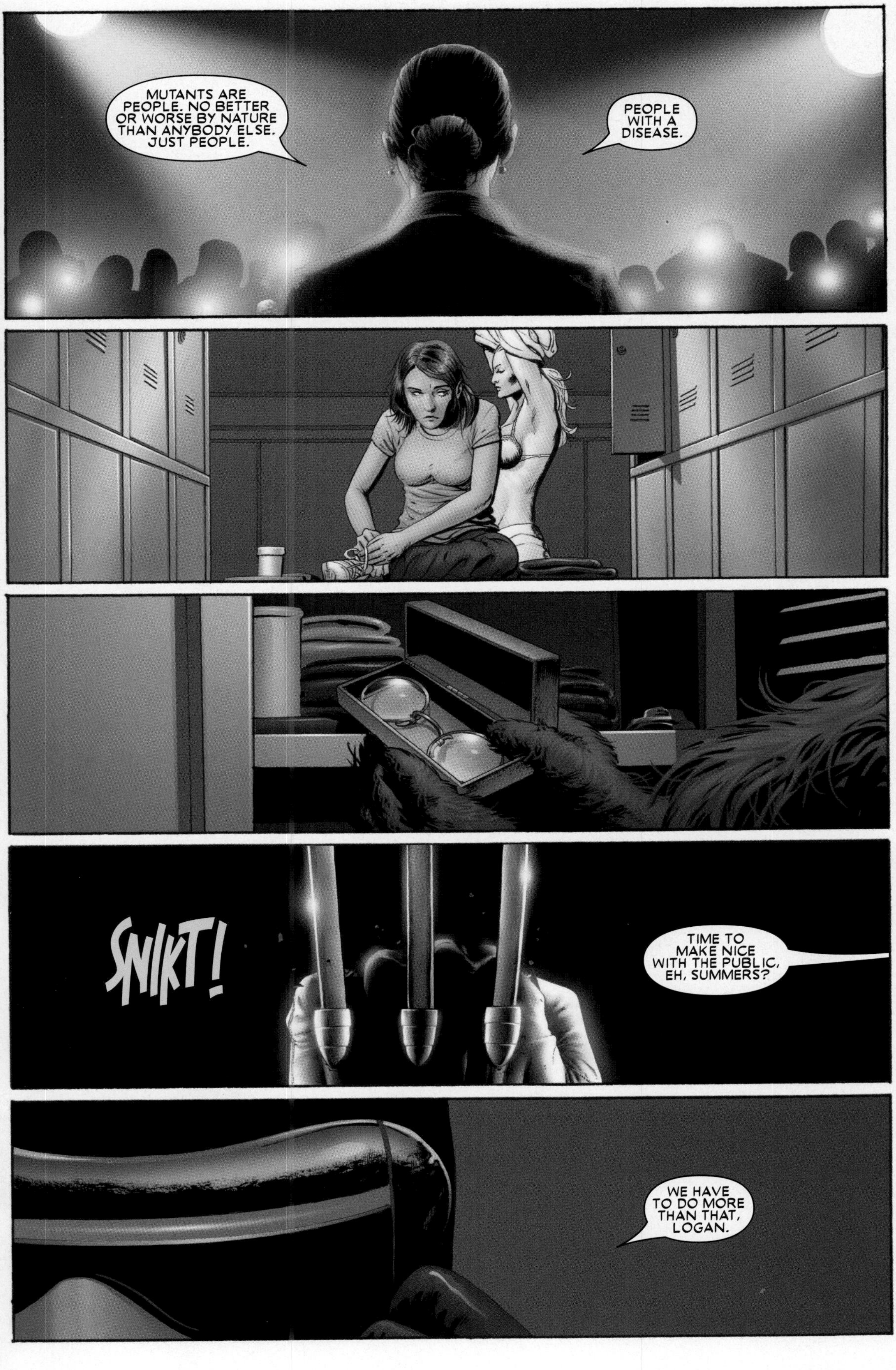
MUTANTS ARE PEOPLE. NO BETTER OR WORSE BY NATURE THAN ANYBODY ELSE. JUST PEOPLE.
PEOPLE WITH A DISEASE.
SNIKT!
TIME TO MAKE NICE WITH THE PUBLIC, EH, SUMMERS?
WE HAVE TO DO MORE THAN THAT, LOGAN.

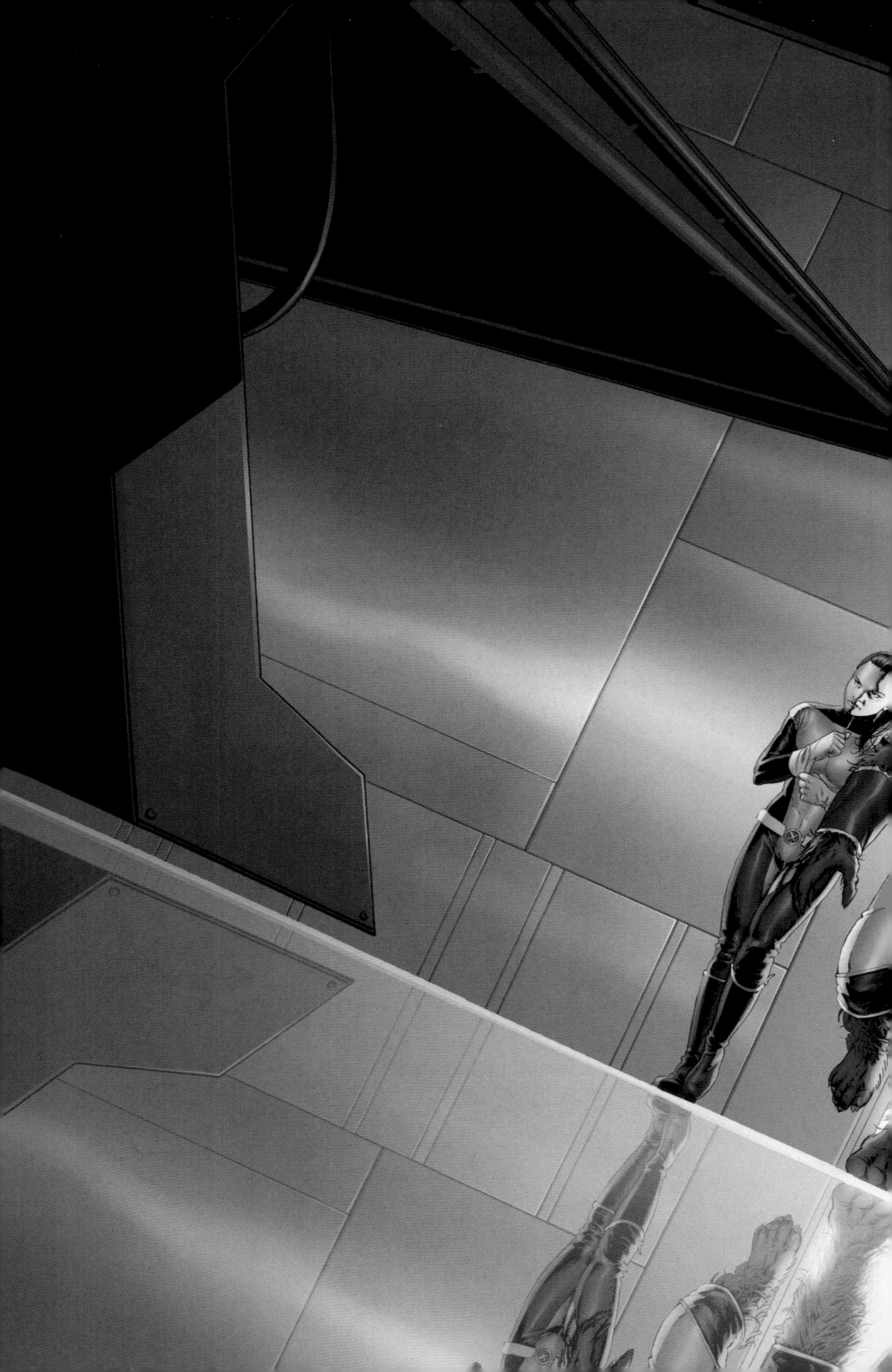

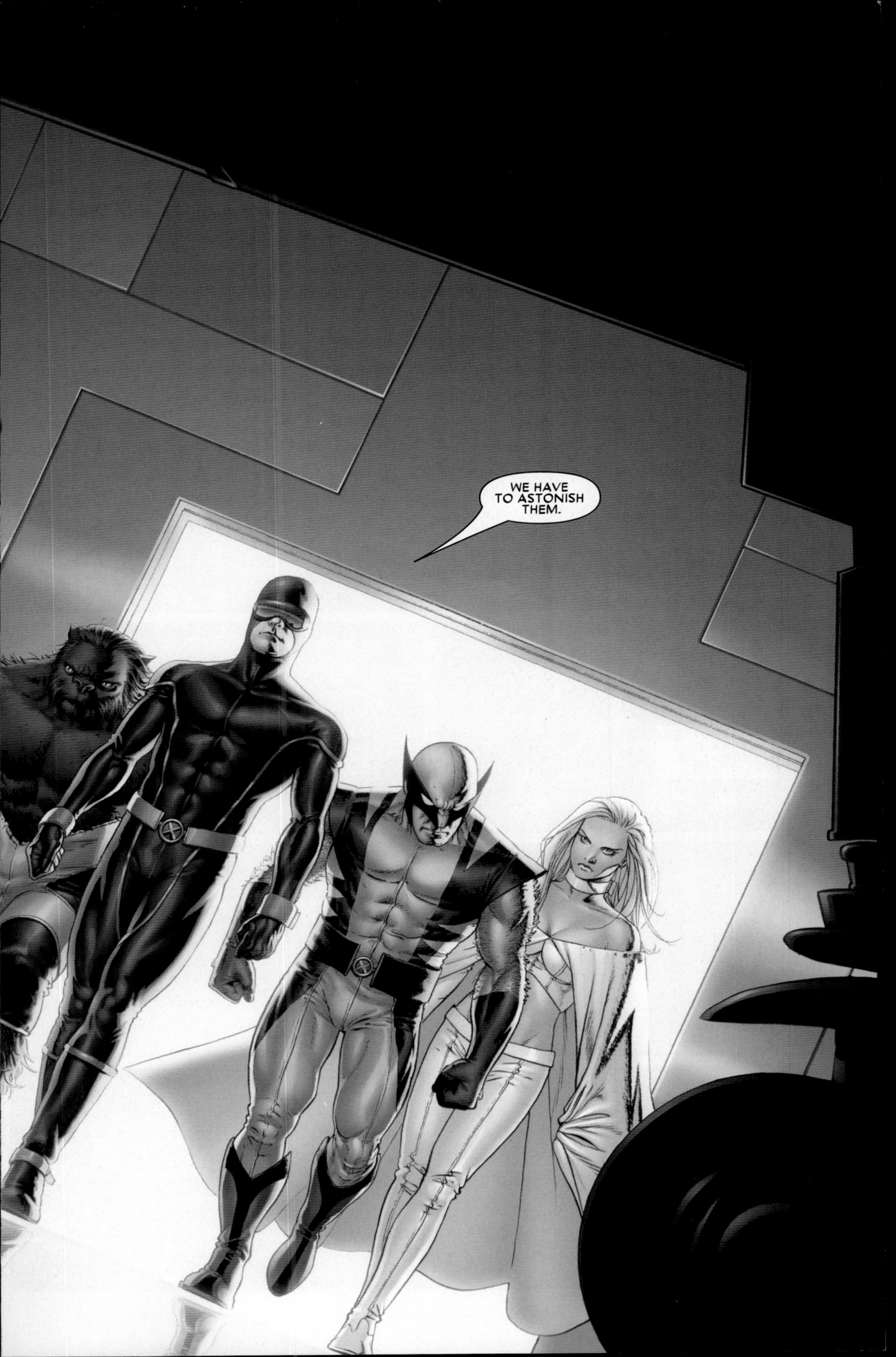
WE HAVE TO ASTONISH THEM.

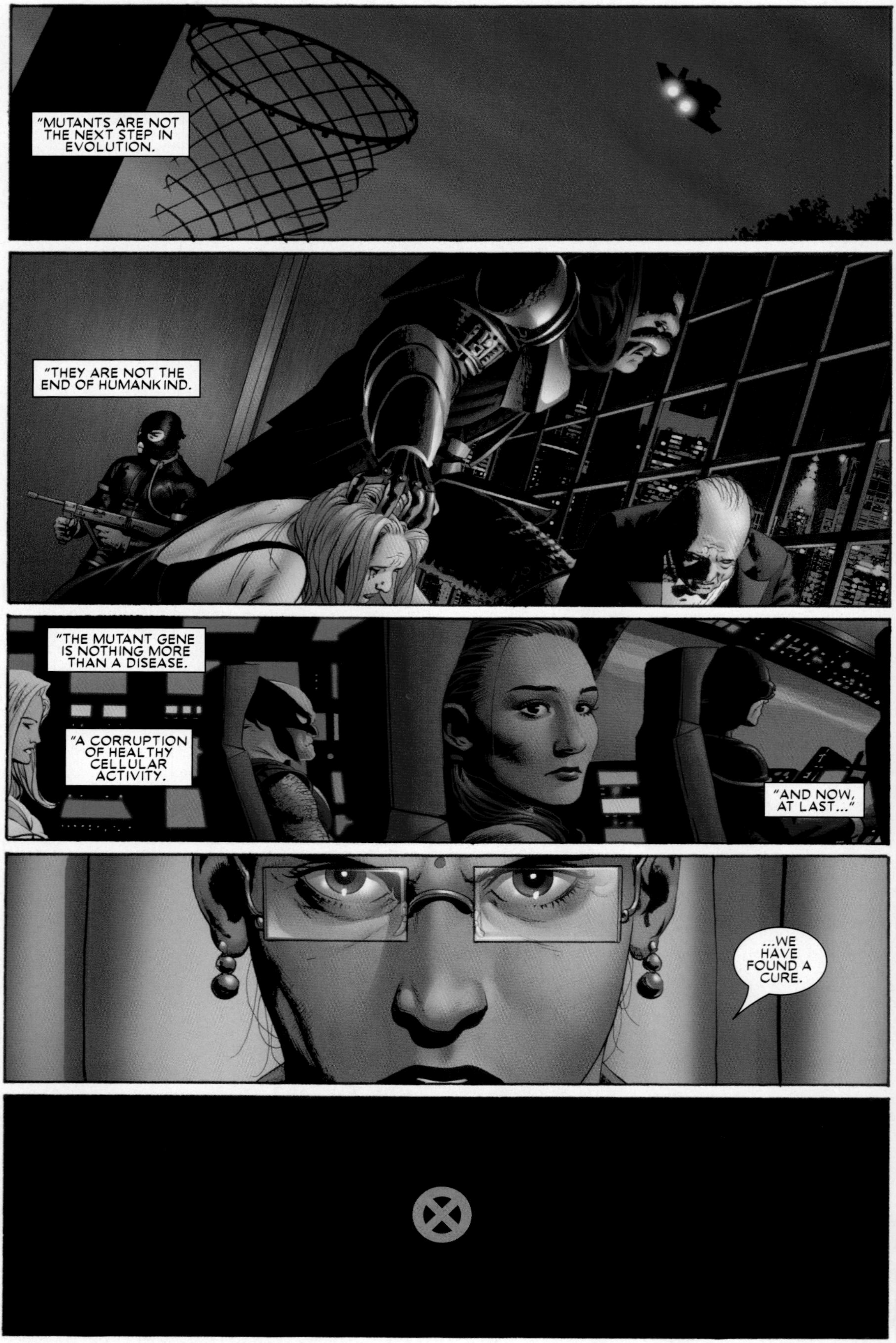

"MUTANTS ARE NOT THE NEXT STEP IN EVOLUTION.
"THEY ARE NOT THE END OF HUMANKIND.
"THE MUTANT GENE IS NOTHING MORE THAN A DISEASE.
"A CORRUPTION OF HEALTHY CELLULAR ACTIVITY.
"AND NOW, AT LAST..."
...WE HAVE FOUND A CURE.

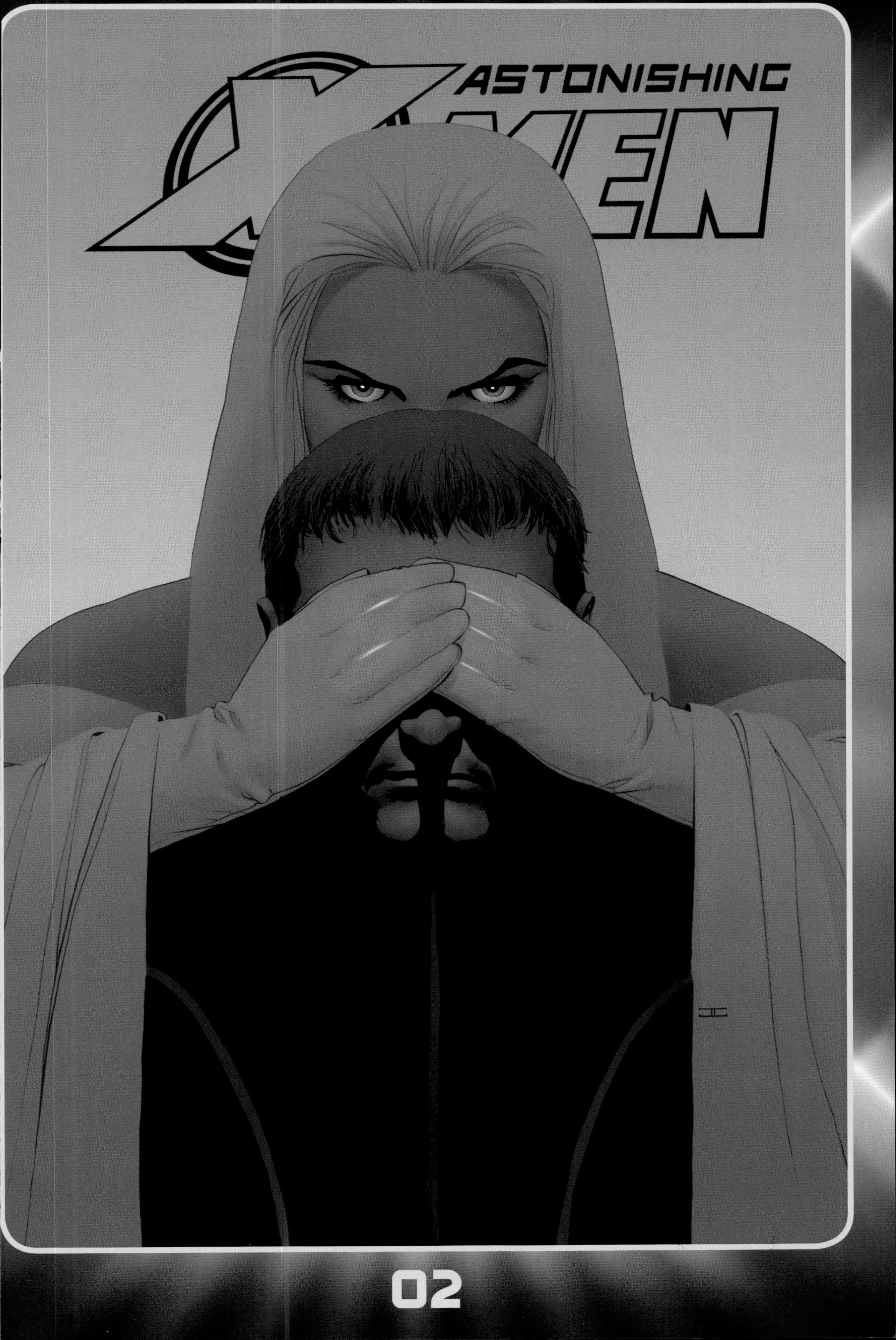
ASTONISHING
X-MEN

02

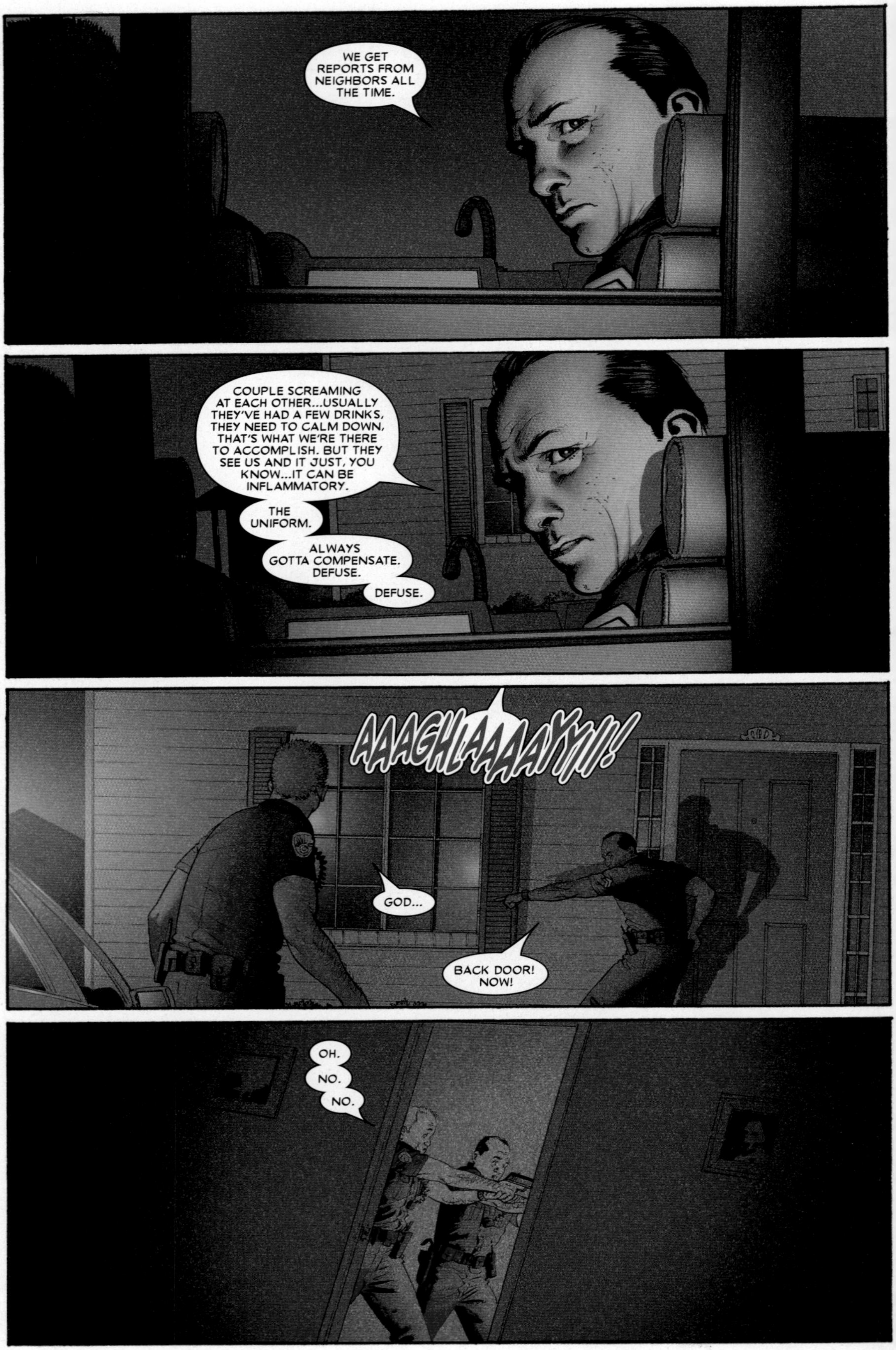
WE GET REPORTS FROM NEIGHBORS ALL THE TIME.
COUPLE SCREAMING AT EACH OTHER...USUALLY THEY'VE HAD A FEW DRINKS, THEY NEED TO CALM DOWN, THAT'S WHAT WE'RE THERE TO ACCOMPLISH. BUT THEY SEE US AND IT JUST, YOU KNOW...IT CAN BE INFLAMMATORY.
THE UNIFORM.
ALWAYS GOTTA COMPENSATE. DEFUSE.
DEFUSE.
AAAGHLAAAAAYYIII!
GOD...
BACK DOOR! NOW!
OH.
NO.
NO.

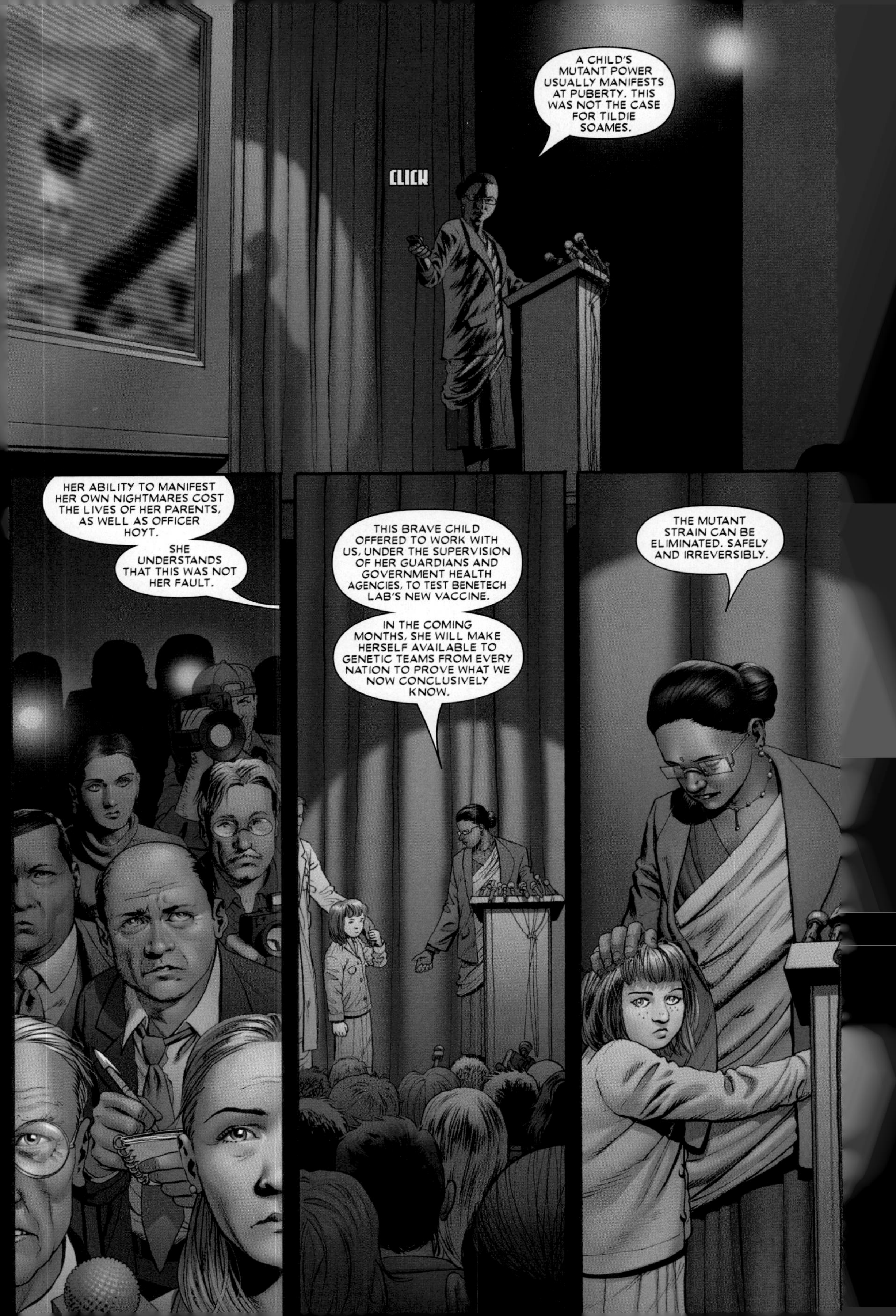
A CHILD'S MUTANT POWER USUALLY MANIFESTS AT PUBERTY. THIS WAS NOT THE CASE FOR TILDIE SOAMES.
CLICK
HER ABILITY TO MANIFEST HER OWN NIGHTMARES COST THE LIVES OF HER PARENTS, AS WELL AS OFFICER HOYT.
SHE UNDERSTANDS THAT THIS WAS NOT HER FAULT.
THIS BRAVE CHILD OFFERED TO WORK WITH US, UNDER THE SUPERVISION OF HER GUARDIANS AND GOVERNMENT HEALTH AGENCIES, TO TEST BENETECH LAB'S NEW VACCINE.
IN THE COMING MONTHS, SHE WILL MAKE HERSELF AVAILABLE TO GENETIC TEAMS FROM EVERY NATION TO PROVE WHAT WE NOW CONCLUSIVELY KNOW.
THE MUTANT STRAIN CAN BE ELIMINATED. SAFELY AND IRREVERSIBLY.

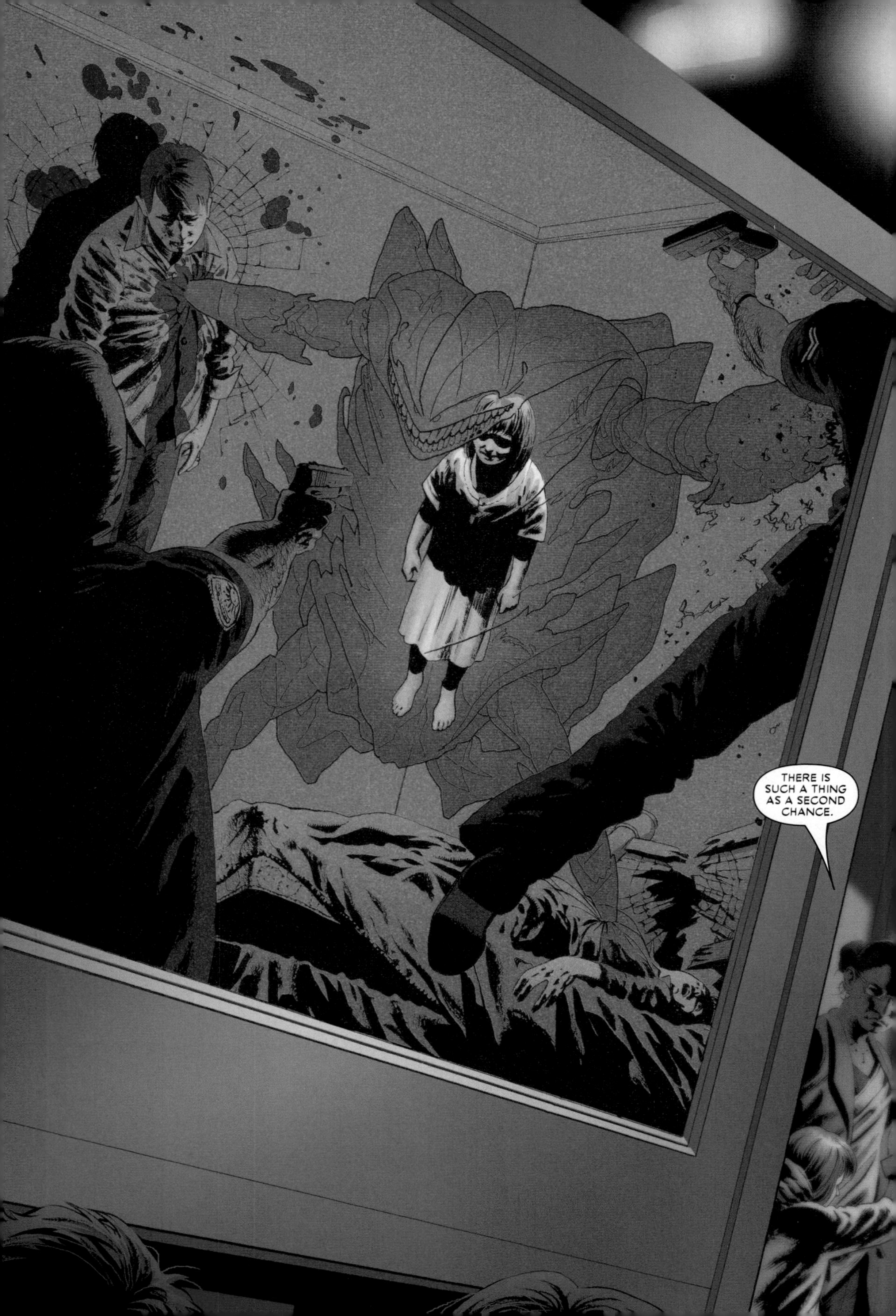
THERE IS SUCH A THING AS A SECOND CHANCE.

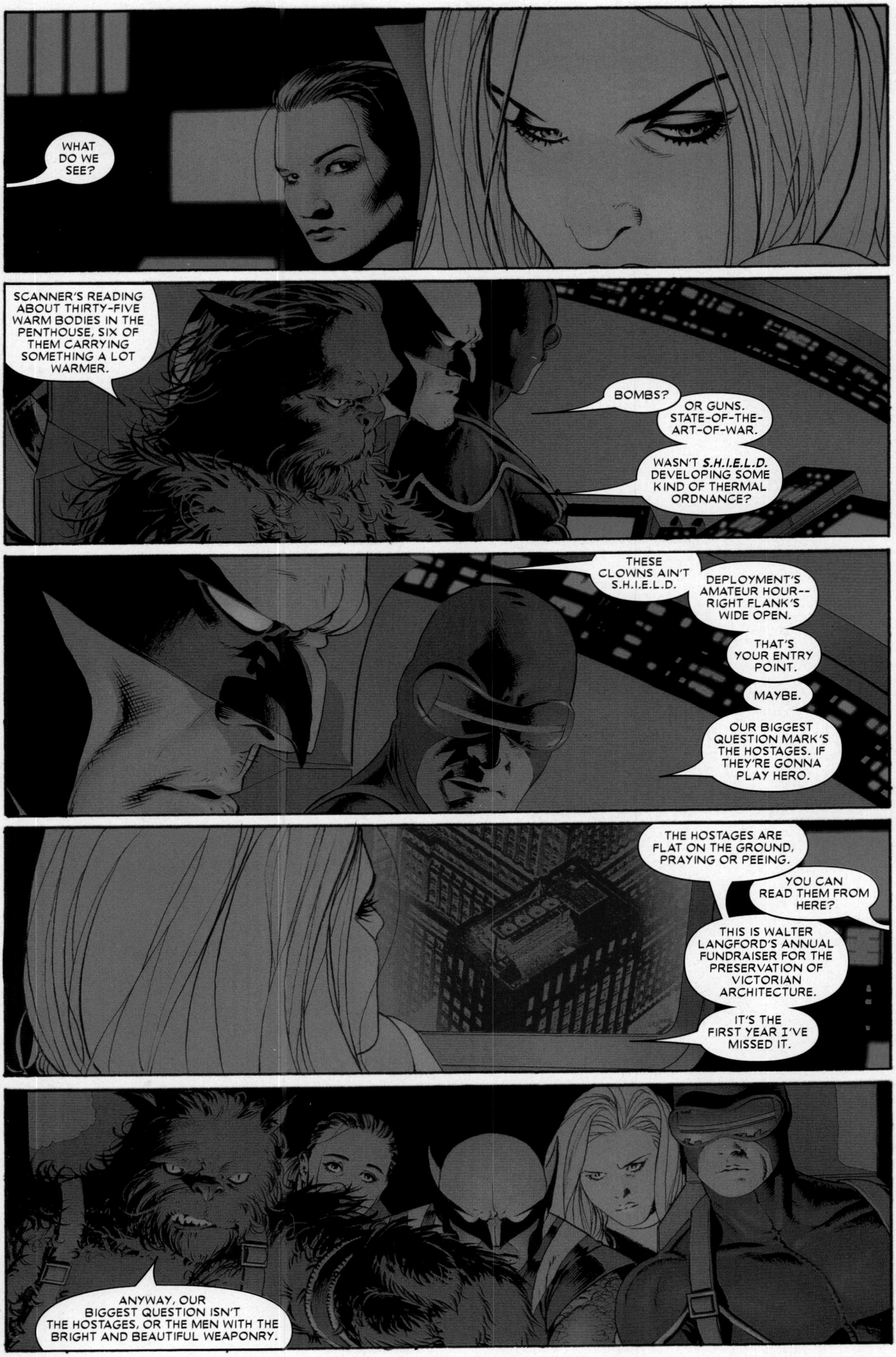
WHAT DO WE SEE?
SCANNER'S READING ABOUT THIRTY-FIVE WARM BODIES IN THE PENTHOUSE, SIX OF THEM CARRYING SOMETHING A LOT WARMER.
BOMBS?
OR GUNS. STATE-OF-THE-ART-OF-WAR.
WASN'T S.H.I.E.L.D. DEVELOPING SOME KIND OF THERMAL ORDNANCE?
THESE CLOWNS AIN'T S.H.I.E.L.D.
DEPLOYMENT'S AMATEUR HOUR-- RIGHT FLANK'S WIDE OPEN.
THAT'S YOUR ENTRY POINT.
MAYBE.
OUR BIGGEST QUESTION MARK'S THE HOSTAGES. IF THEY'RE GONNA PLAY HERO.
THE HOSTAGES ARE FLAT ON THE GROUND, PRAYING OR PEEING.
YOU CAN READ THEM FROM HERE?
THIS IS WALTER LANGFORD'S ANNUAL FUNDRAISER FOR THE PRESERVATION OF VICTORIAN ARCHITECTURE.
IT'S THE FIRST YEAR I'VE MISSED IT.
ANYWAY, OUR BIGGEST QUESTION ISN'T THE HOSTAGES, OR THE MEN WITH THE BRIGHT AND BEAUTIFUL WEAPONRY.

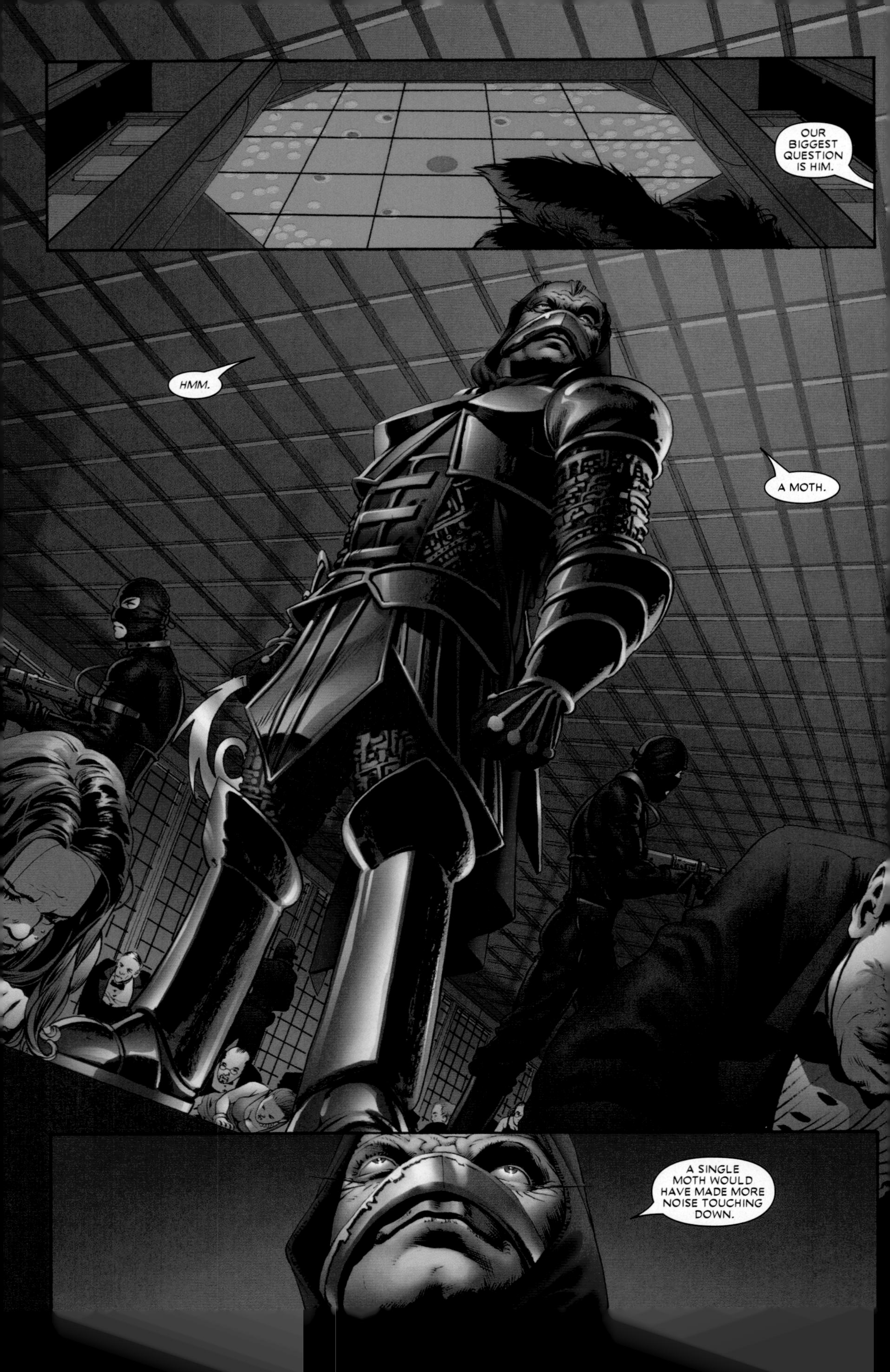
OUR BIGGEST QUESTION IS HIM.
HMM.
A MOTH.
A SINGLE MOTH WOULD HAVE MADE MORE NOISE TOUCHING DOWN.

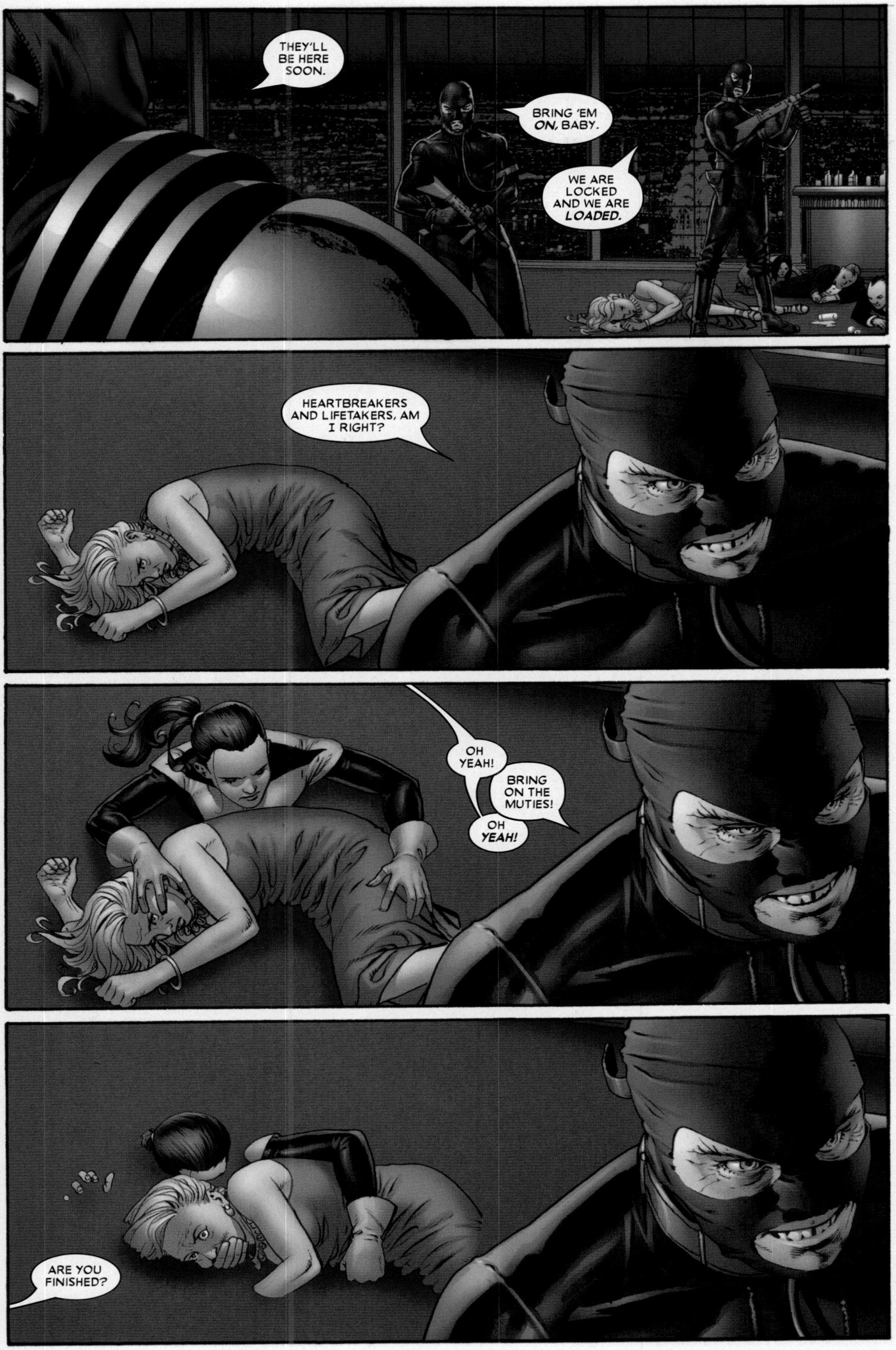
THEY'LL BE HERE SOON.
BRING 'EM ON, BABY.
WE ARE LOCKED AND WE ARE LOADED.
HEARTBREAKERS AND LIFETAKERS, AM I RIGHT?
OH YEAH!
BRING ON THE MUTIES!
OH YEAH!
ARE YOU FINISHED?

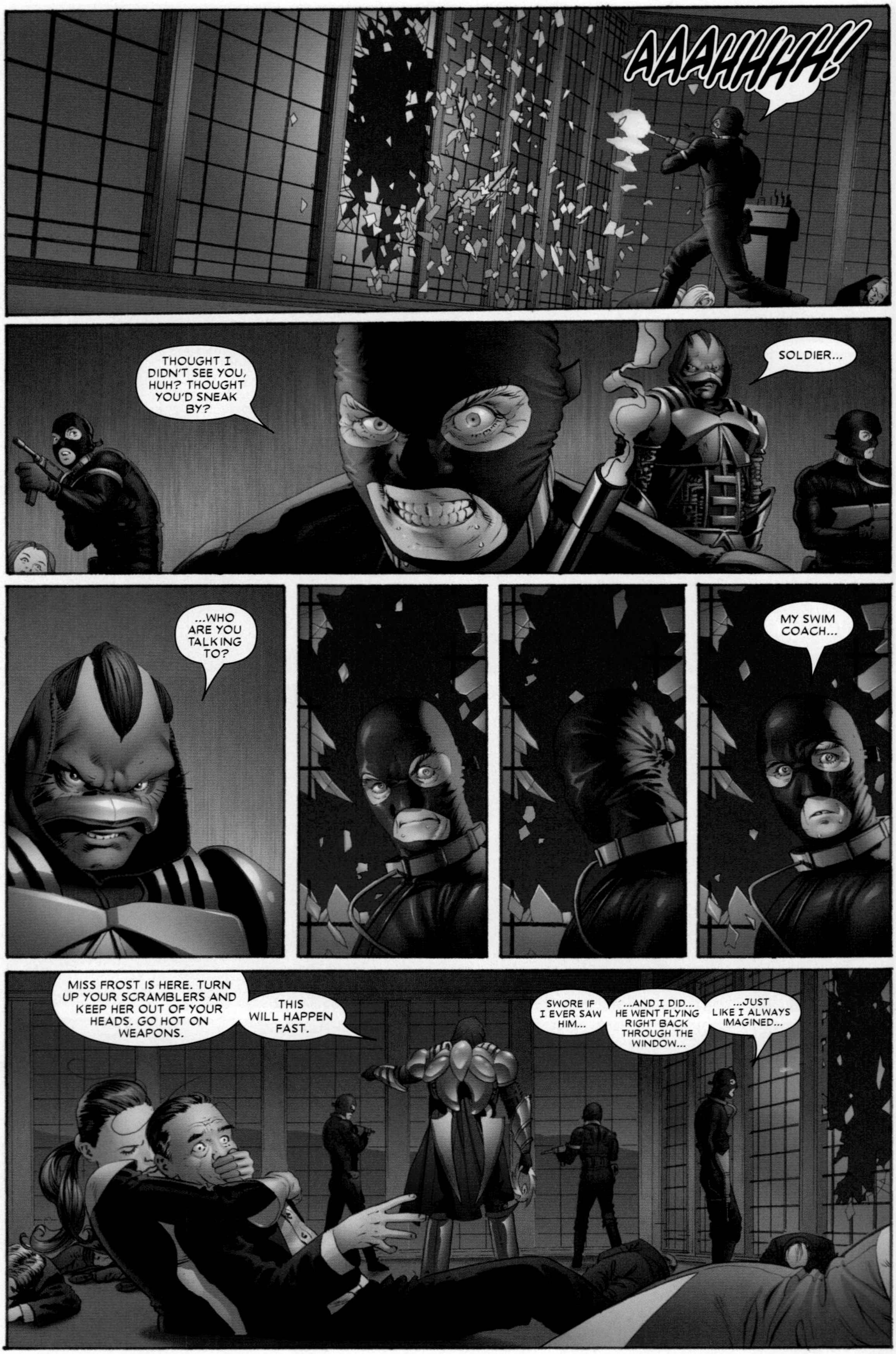
AAAHHHH!
THOUGHT I DIDN'T SEE YOU, HUH? THOUGHT YOU'D SNEAK BY?
SOLDIER...
...WHO ARE YOU TALKING TO?
MY SWIM COACH...
MISS FROST IS HERE. TURN UP YOUR SCRAMBLERS AND KEEP HER OUT OF YOUR HEADS. GO HOT ON WEAPONS.
THIS WILL HAPPEN FAST.
SWORE IF I EVER SAW HIM...
...AND I DID... HE WENT FLYING RIGHT BACK THROUGH THE WINDOW...
...JUST LIKE I ALWAYS IMAGINED...

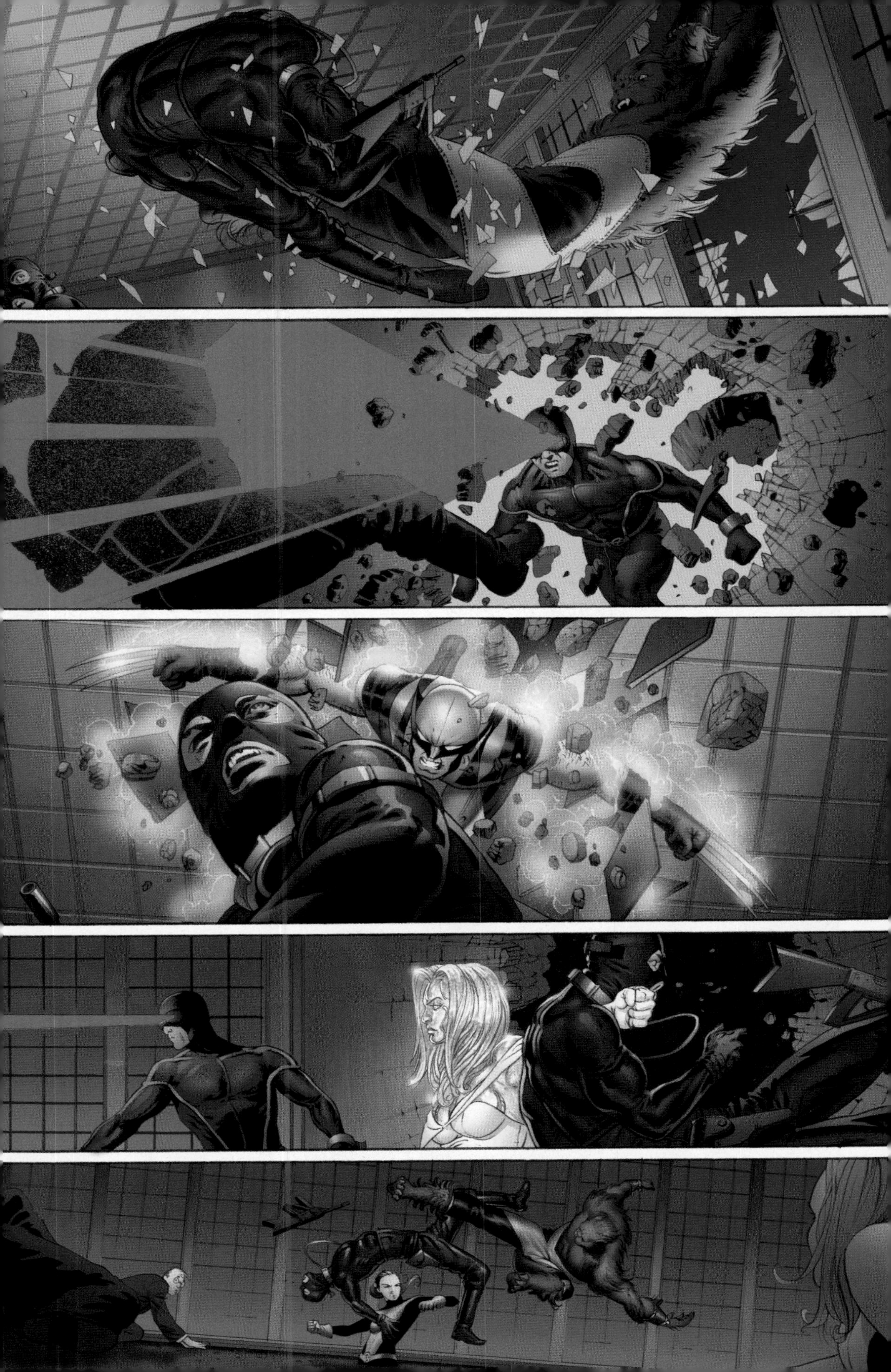

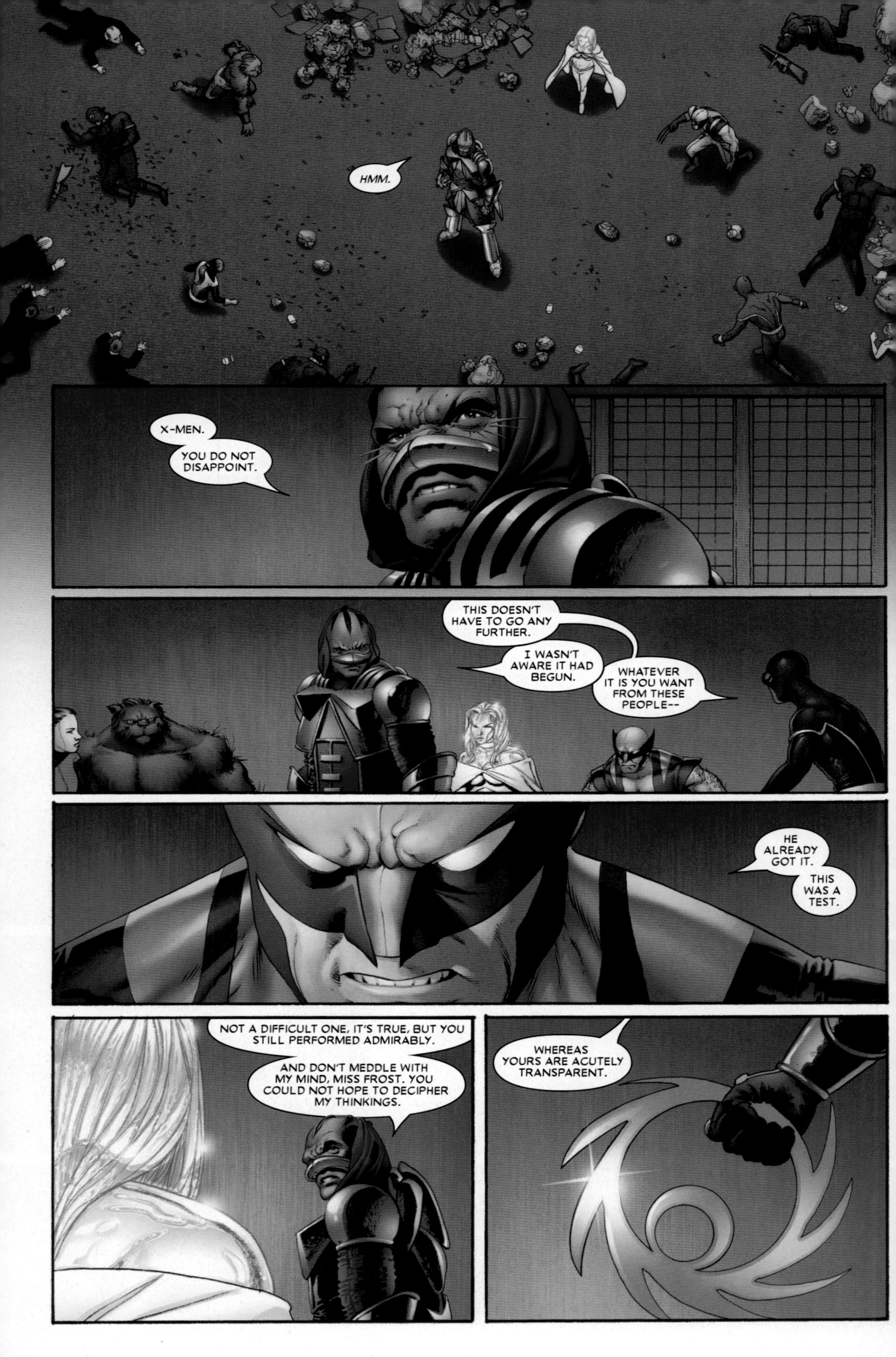
HMM.
X-MEN.
YOU DO NOT DISAPPOINT.
THIS DOESN'T HAVE TO GO ANY FURTHER.
I WASN'T AWARE IT HAD BEGUN.
WHATEVER IT IS YOU WANT FROM THESE PEOPLE--
HE ALREADY GOT IT.
THIS WAS A TEST.
NOT A DIFFICULT ONE, IT'S TRUE, BUT YOU STILL PERFORMED ADMIRABLY.
AND DON'T MEDDLE WITH MY MIND, MISS FROST. YOU COULD NOT HOPE TO DECIPHER MY THINKINGS.
WHEREAS YOURS ARE ACUTELY TRANSPARENT.

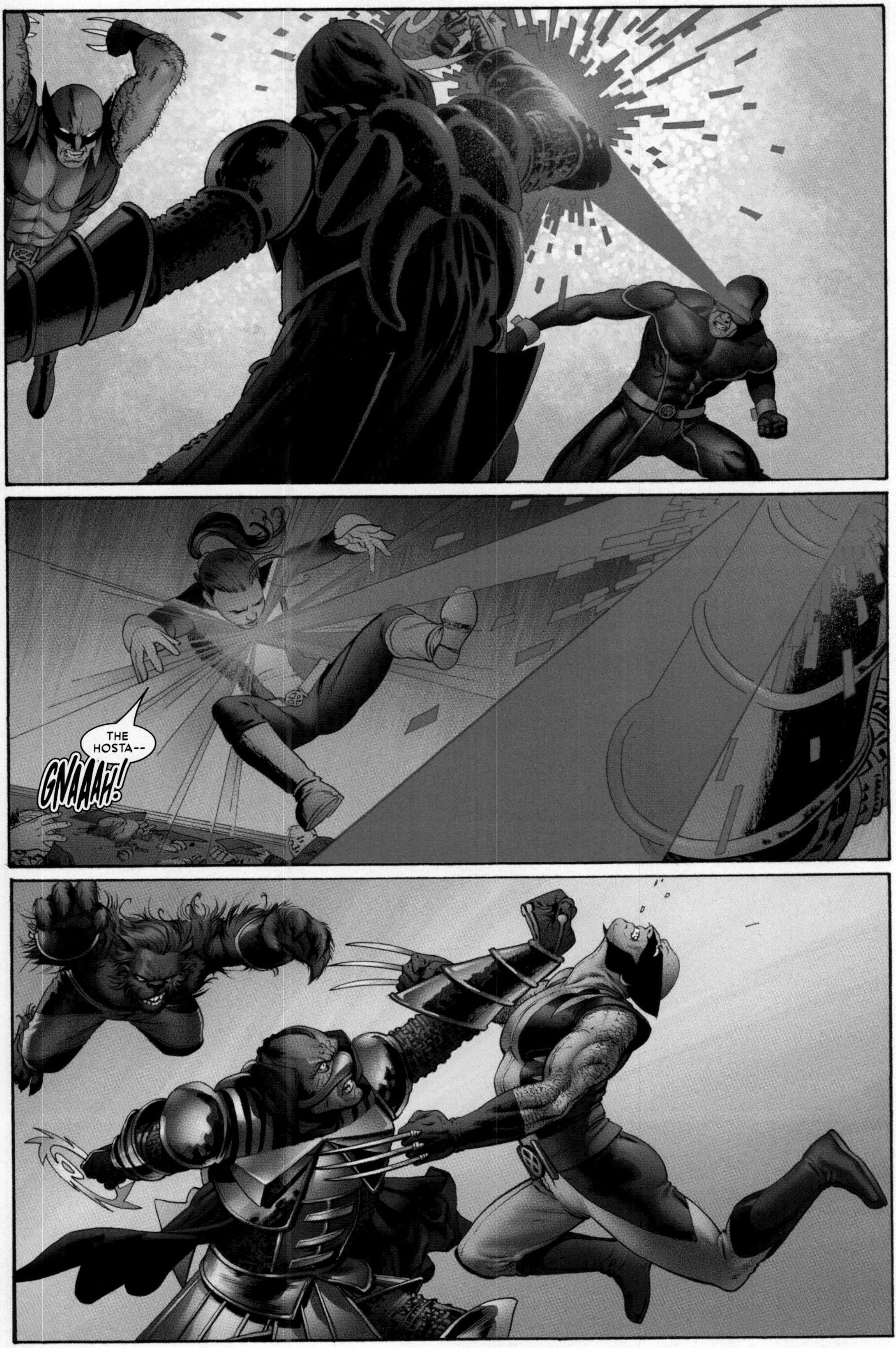
THE HOSTA--
GNAAAH!

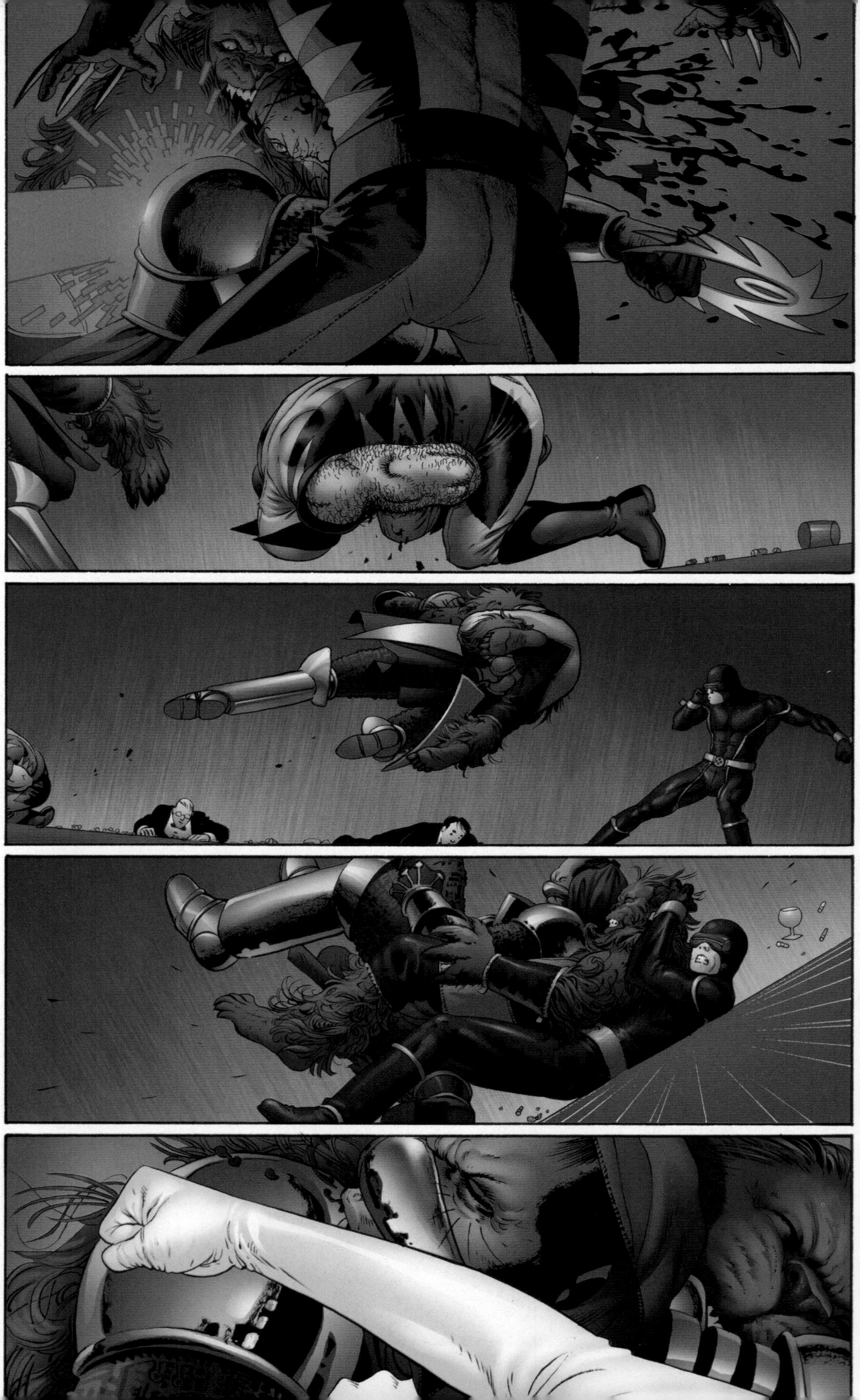

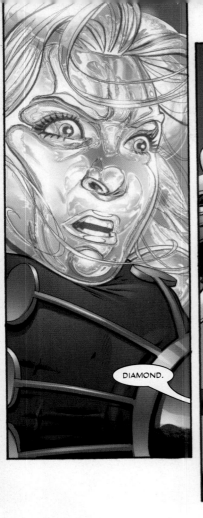

DIAMOND.

I AM ORD, OF THE BREAKWORLD.

WE STUFF OUR PILLOWS WITH DIAMONDS.

I WAS WRONG. I *AM* DISAPPOINTED.

THE MIGHTY X-MEN. AND NOT ONE OF THEM STRONG ENOUGH TO...

WAIT--

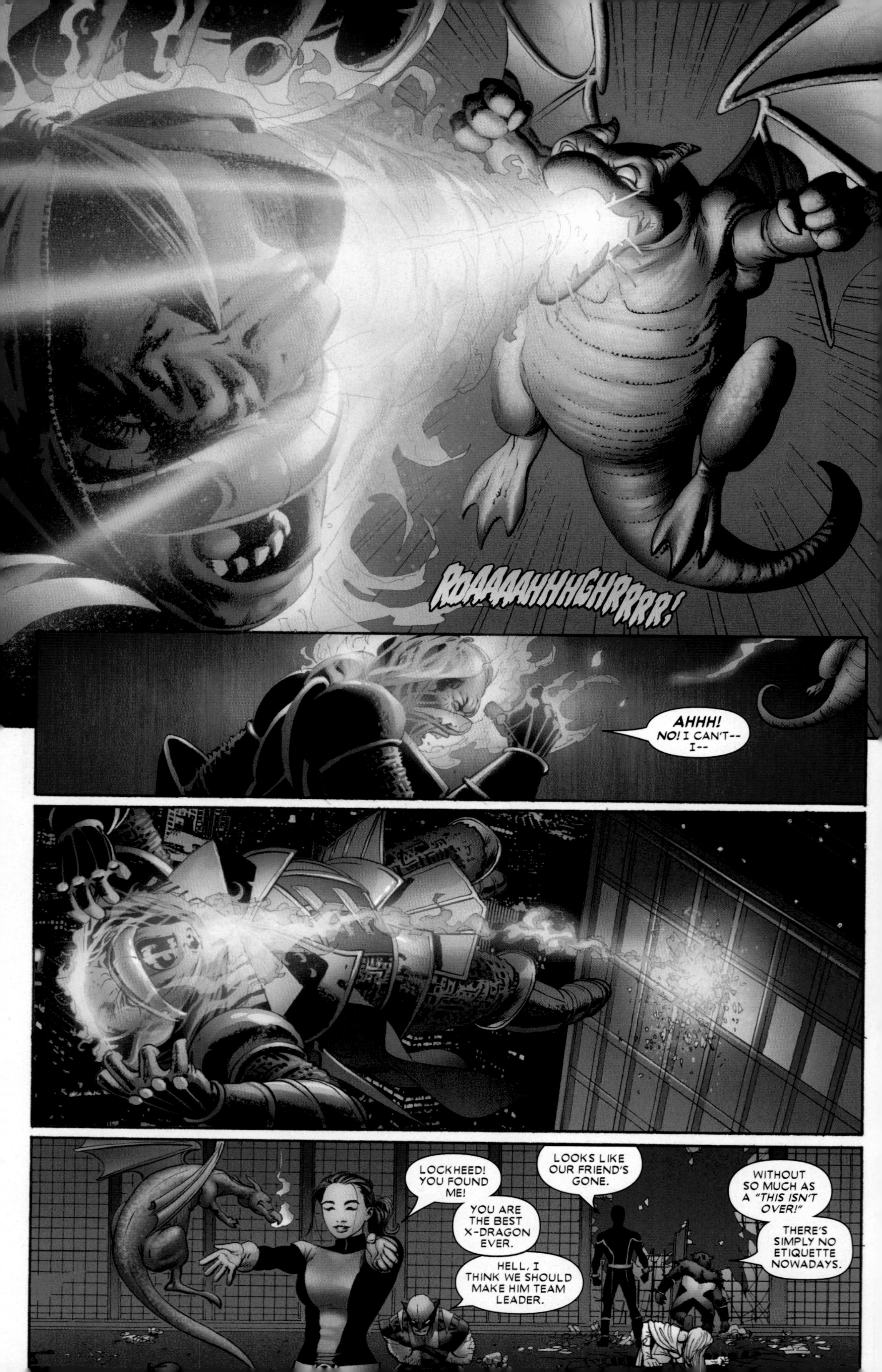
ROAAAAHHHGHRRRR!
AHHH! NO! I CAN'T-- I--
LOCKHEED! YOU FOUND ME!
YOU ARE THE BEST X-DRAGON EVER.
HELL, I THINK WE SHOULD MAKE HIM TEAM LEADER.
LOOKS LIKE OUR FRIEND'S GONE.
WITHOUT SO MUCH AS A "THIS ISN'T OVER!"
THERE'S SIMPLY NO ETIQUETTE NOWADAYS.

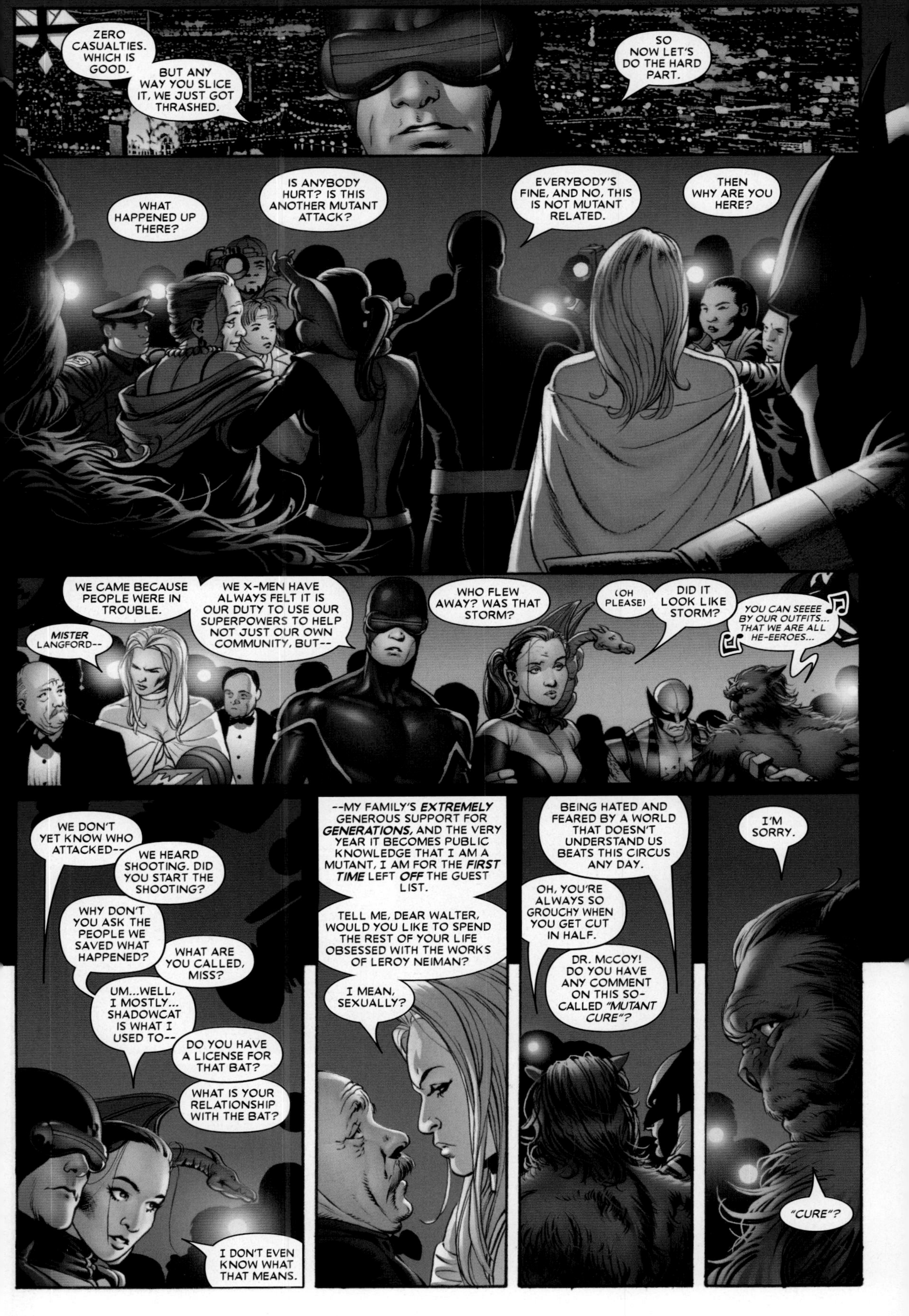
ZERO CASUALTIES. WHICH IS GOOD.
BUT ANY WAY YOU SLICE IT, WE JUST GOT THRASHED.
SO NOW LET'S DO THE HARD PART.
WHAT HAPPENED UP THERE?
IS ANYBODY HURT? IS THIS ANOTHER MUTANT ATTACK?
EVERYBODY'S FINE, AND NO, THIS IS NOT MUTANT RELATED.
THEN WHY ARE YOU HERE?
WE CAME BECAUSE PEOPLE WERE IN TROUBLE.
WE X-MEN HAVE ALWAYS FELT IT IS OUR DUTY TO USE OUR SUPERPOWERS TO HELP NOT JUST OUR OWN COMMUNITY, BUT--
MISTER LANGFORD--
WHO FLEW AWAY? WAS THAT STORM?
(OH PLEASE)
DID IT LOOK LIKE STORM?
YOU CAN SEEEE BY OUR OUTFITS... THAT WE ARE ALL HE-EEROES...
WE DON'T YET KNOW WHO ATTACKED--
WE HEARD SHOOTING. DID YOU START THE SHOOTING?
WHY DON'T YOU ASK THE PEOPLE WE SAVED WHAT HAPPENED?
WHAT ARE YOU CALLED, MISS?
UM...WELL, I MOSTLY... SHADOWCAT IS WHAT I USED TO--
DO YOU HAVE A LICENSE FOR THAT BAT?
WHAT IS YOUR RELATIONSHIP WITH THE BAT?
I DON'T EVEN KNOW WHAT THAT MEANS.
--MY FAMILY'S EXTREMELY GENEROUS SUPPORT FOR GENERATIONS, AND THE VERY YEAR IT BECOMES PUBLIC KNOWLEDGE THAT I AM A MUTANT, I AM FOR THE FIRST TIME LEFT OFF THE GUEST LIST.
TELL ME, DEAR WALTER, WOULD YOU LIKE TO SPEND THE REST OF YOUR LIFE OBSESSED WITH THE WORKS OF LEROY NEIMAN?
I MEAN, SEXUALLY?
BEING HATED AND FEARED BY A WORLD THAT DOESN'T UNDERSTAND US BEATS THIS CIRCUS ANY DAY.
OH, YOU'RE ALWAYS SO GROUCHY WHEN YOU GET CUT IN HALF.
DR. McCOY! DO YOU HAVE ANY COMMENT ON THIS SO-CALLED "MUTANT CURE"?
I'M SORRY.
"CURE"?

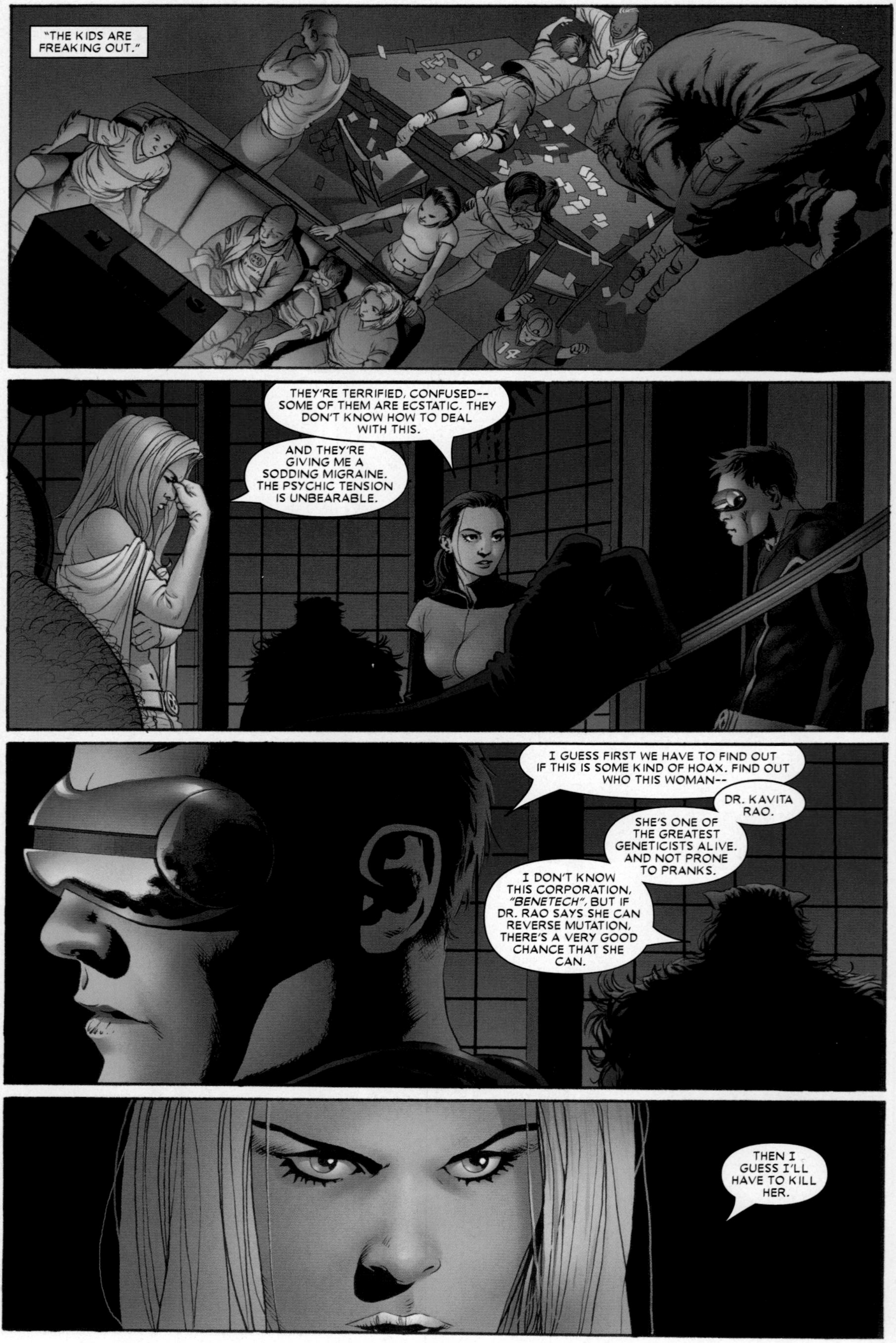
"THE KIDS ARE FREAKING OUT."
THEY'RE TERRIFIED, CONFUSED-- SOME OF THEM ARE ECSTATIC. THEY DON'T KNOW HOW TO DEAL WITH THIS.
AND THEY'RE GIVING ME A SODDING MIGRAINE. THE PSYCHIC TENSION IS UNBEARABLE.
I GUESS FIRST WE HAVE TO FIND OUT IF THIS IS SOME KIND OF HOAX. FIND OUT WHO THIS WOMAN--
DR. KAVITA RAO.
SHE'S ONE OF THE GREATEST GENETICISTS ALIVE. AND NOT PRONE TO PRANKS.
I DON'T KNOW THIS CORPORATION, "BENETECH", BUT IF DR. RAO SAYS SHE CAN REVERSE MUTATION, THERE'S A VERY GOOD CHANCE THAT SHE CAN.
THEN I GUESS I'LL HAVE TO KILL HER.

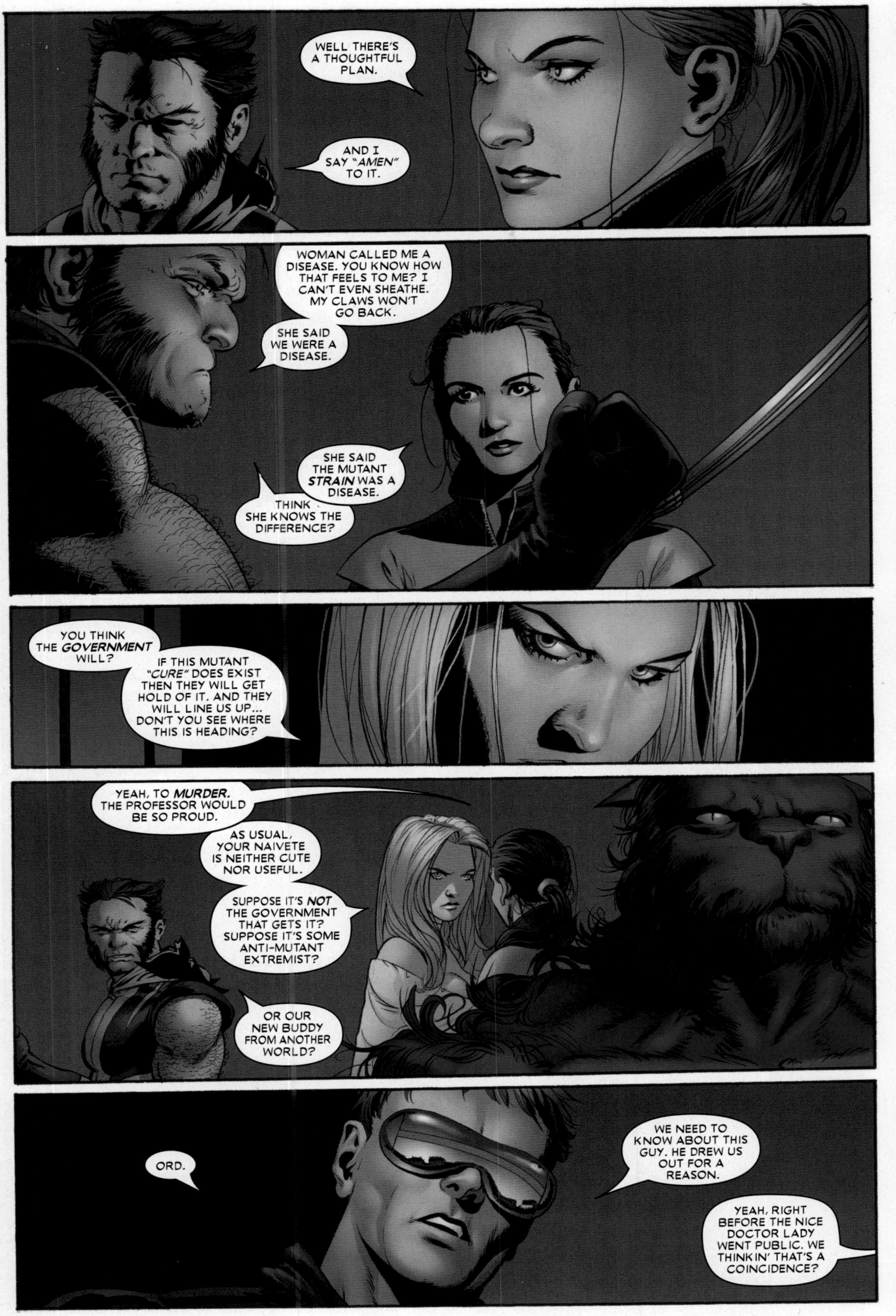
WELL THERE'S A THOUGHTFUL PLAN.
AND I SAY "AMEN" TO IT.
WOMAN CALLED ME A DISEASE. YOU KNOW HOW THAT FEELS TO ME? I CAN'T EVEN SHEATHE. MY CLAWS WON'T GO BACK.
SHE SAID WE WERE A DISEASE.
SHE SAID THE MUTANT STRAIN WAS A DISEASE.
THINK SHE KNOWS THE DIFFERENCE?
YOU THINK THE GOVERNMENT WILL?
IF THIS MUTANT "CURE" DOES EXIST THEN THEY WILL GET HOLD OF IT. AND THEY WILL LINE US UP... DON'T YOU SEE WHERE THIS IS HEADING?
YEAH, TO MURDER. THE PROFESSOR WOULD BE SO PROUD.
AS USUAL, YOUR NAIVETE IS NEITHER CUTE NOR USEFUL.
SUPPOSE IT'S NOT THE GOVERNMENT THAT GETS IT? SUPPOSE IT'S SOME ANTI-MUTANT EXTREMIST?
OR OUR NEW BUDDY FROM ANOTHER WORLD?
ORD.
WE NEED TO KNOW ABOUT THIS GUY. HE DREW US OUT FOR A REASON.
YEAH, RIGHT BEFORE THE NICE DOCTOR LADY WENT PUBLIC. WE THINKIN' THAT'S A COINCIDENCE?

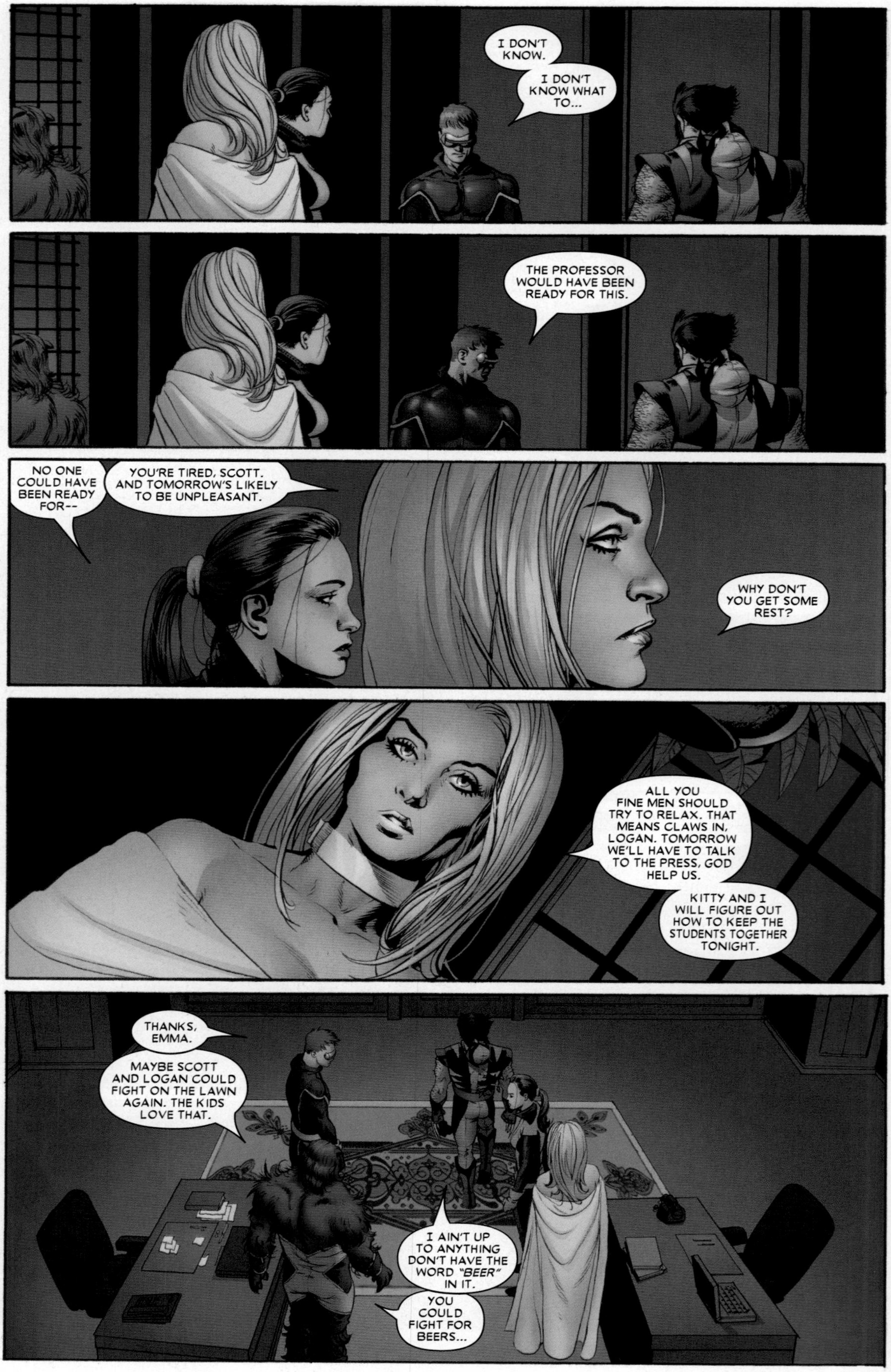
I DON'T KNOW.
I DON'T KNOW WHAT TO...
THE PROFESSOR WOULD HAVE BEEN READY FOR THIS.
NO ONE COULD HAVE BEEN READY FOR--
YOU'RE TIRED, SCOTT. AND TOMORROW'S LIKELY TO BE UNPLEASANT.
WHY DON'T YOU GET SOME REST?
ALL YOU FINE MEN SHOULD TRY TO RELAX. THAT MEANS CLAWS IN, LOGAN. TOMORROW WE'LL HAVE TO TALK TO THE PRESS, GOD HELP US.
KITTY AND I WILL FIGURE OUT HOW TO KEEP THE STUDENTS TOGETHER TONIGHT.
THANKS, EMMA.
MAYBE SCOTT AND LOGAN COULD FIGHT ON THE LAWN AGAIN. THE KIDS LOVE THAT.
I AIN'T UP TO ANYTHING DON'T HAVE THE WORD "BEER" IN IT.
YOU COULD FIGHT FOR BEERS...

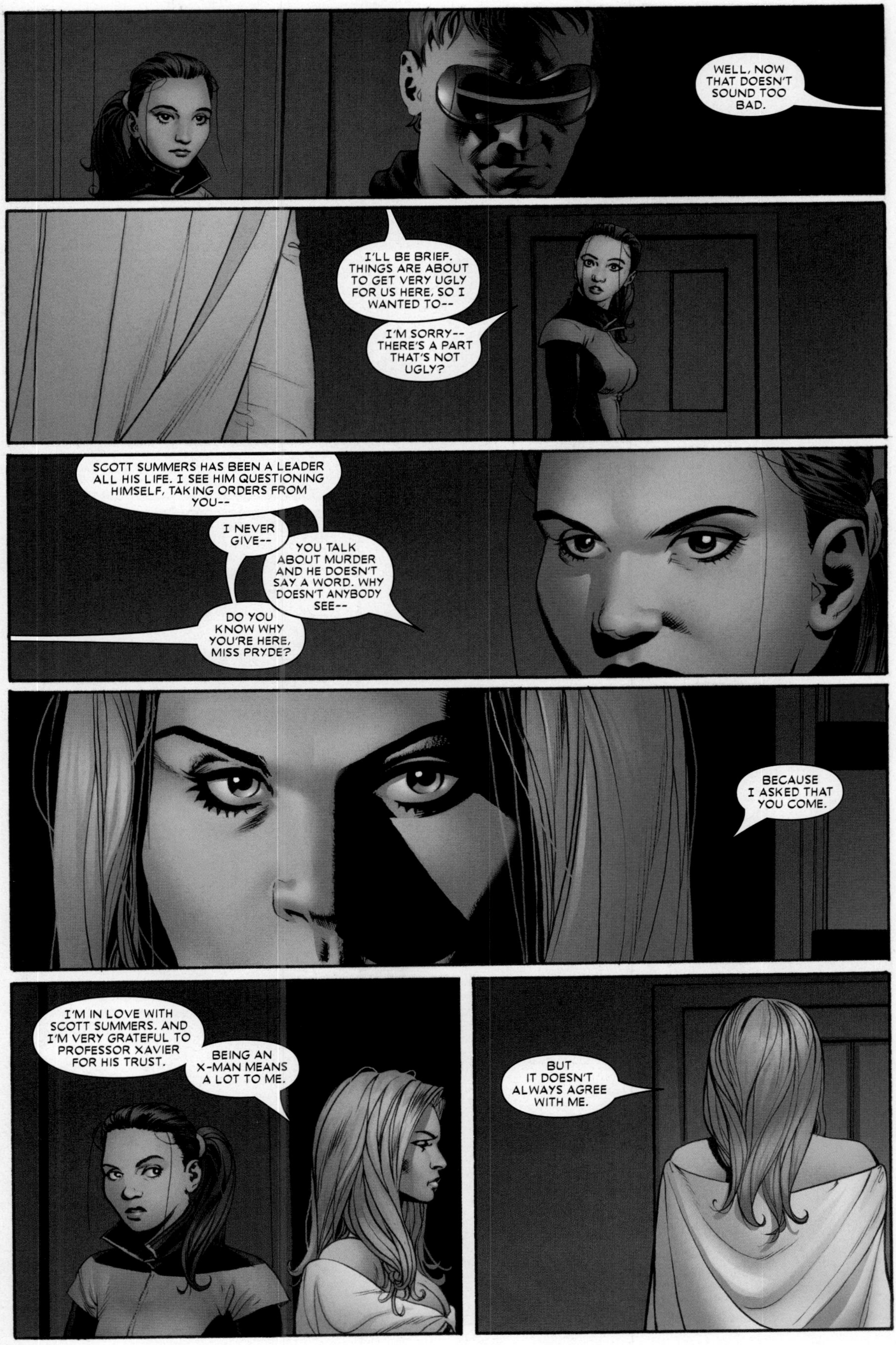
WELL, NOW THAT DOESN'T SOUND TOO BAD.
I'LL BE BRIEF. THINGS ARE ABOUT TO GET VERY UGLY FOR US HERE, SO I WANTED TO--
I'M SORRY-- THERE'S A PART THAT'S NOT UGLY?
SCOTT SUMMERS HAS BEEN A LEADER ALL HIS LIFE. I SEE HIM QUESTIONING HIMSELF, TAKING ORDERS FROM YOU--
I NEVER GIVE--
YOU TALK ABOUT MURDER AND HE DOESN'T SAY A WORD. WHY DOESN'T ANYBODY SEE--
DO YOU KNOW WHY YOU'RE HERE, MISS PRYDE?
BECAUSE I ASKED THAT YOU COME.
I'M IN LOVE WITH SCOTT SUMMERS. AND I'M VERY GRATEFUL TO PROFESSOR XAVIER FOR HIS TRUST.
BEING AN X-MAN MEANS A LOT TO ME.
BUT IT DOESN'T ALWAYS AGREE WITH ME.

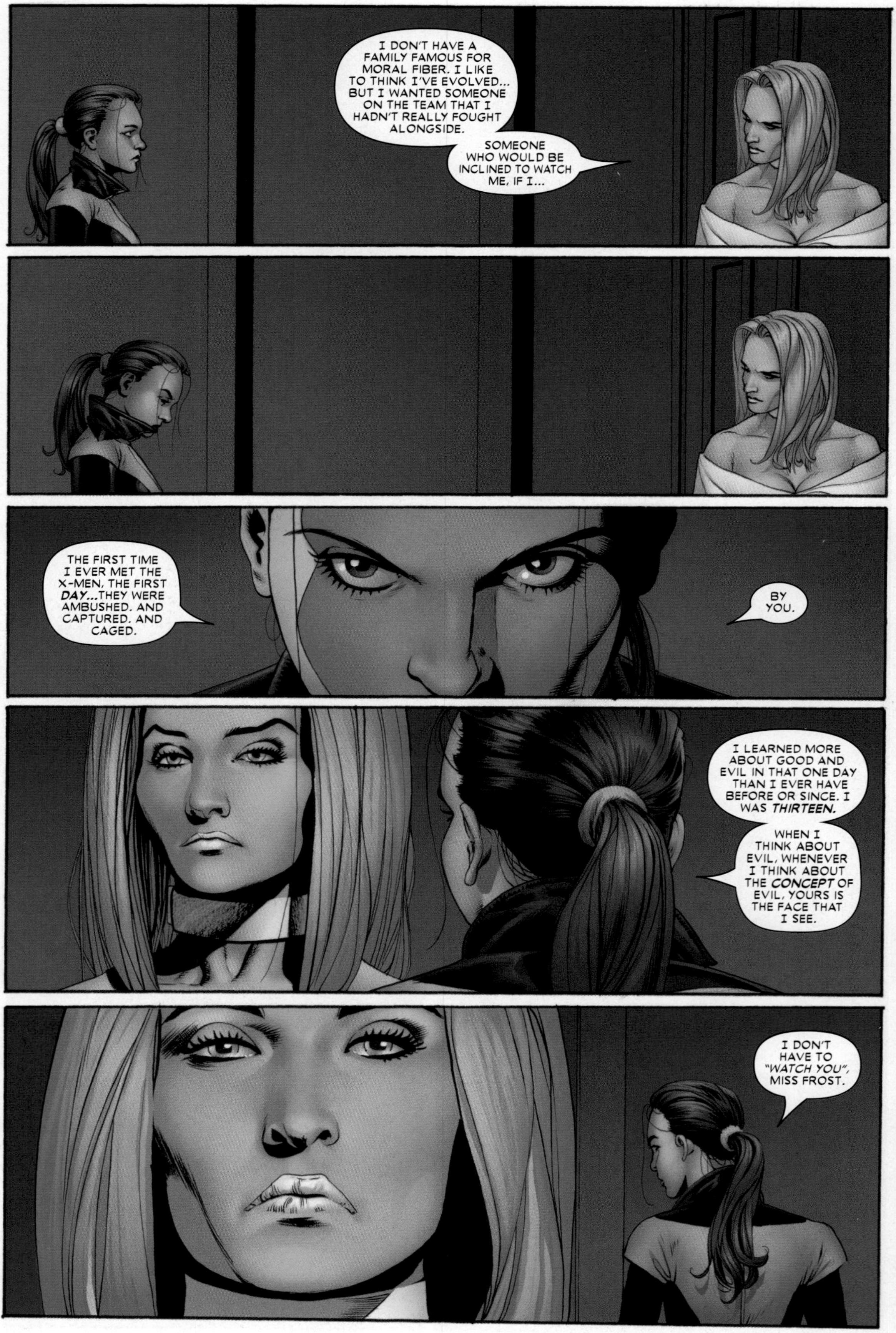
I DON'T HAVE A FAMILY FAMOUS FOR MORAL FIBER. I LIKE TO THINK I'VE EVOLVED... BUT I WANTED SOMEONE ON THE TEAM THAT I HADN'T REALLY FOUGHT ALONGSIDE.
SOMEONE WHO WOULD BE INCLINED TO WATCH ME, IF I...
THE FIRST TIME I EVER MET THE X-MEN, THE FIRST DAY...THEY WERE AMBUSHED. AND CAPTURED. AND CAGED.
BY YOU.
I LEARNED MORE ABOUT GOOD AND EVIL IN THAT ONE DAY THAN I EVER HAVE BEFORE OR SINCE. I WAS THIRTEEN.
WHEN I THINK ABOUT EVIL, WHENEVER I THINK ABOUT THE CONCEPT OF EVIL, YOURS IS THE FACE THAT I SEE.
I DON'T HAVE TO "WATCH YOU", MISS FROST.

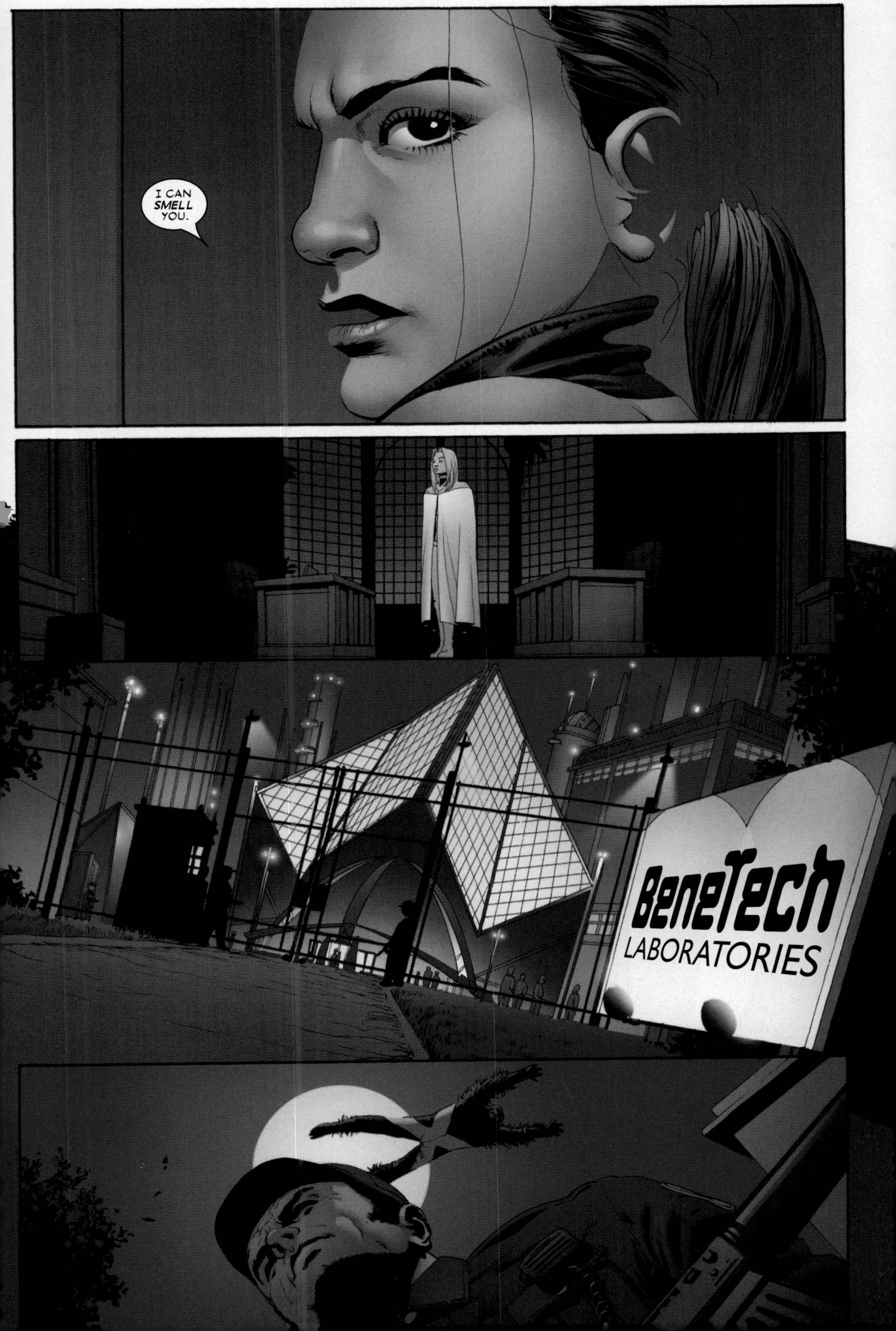
I CAN SMELL YOU.
BeneTech
LABORATORIES

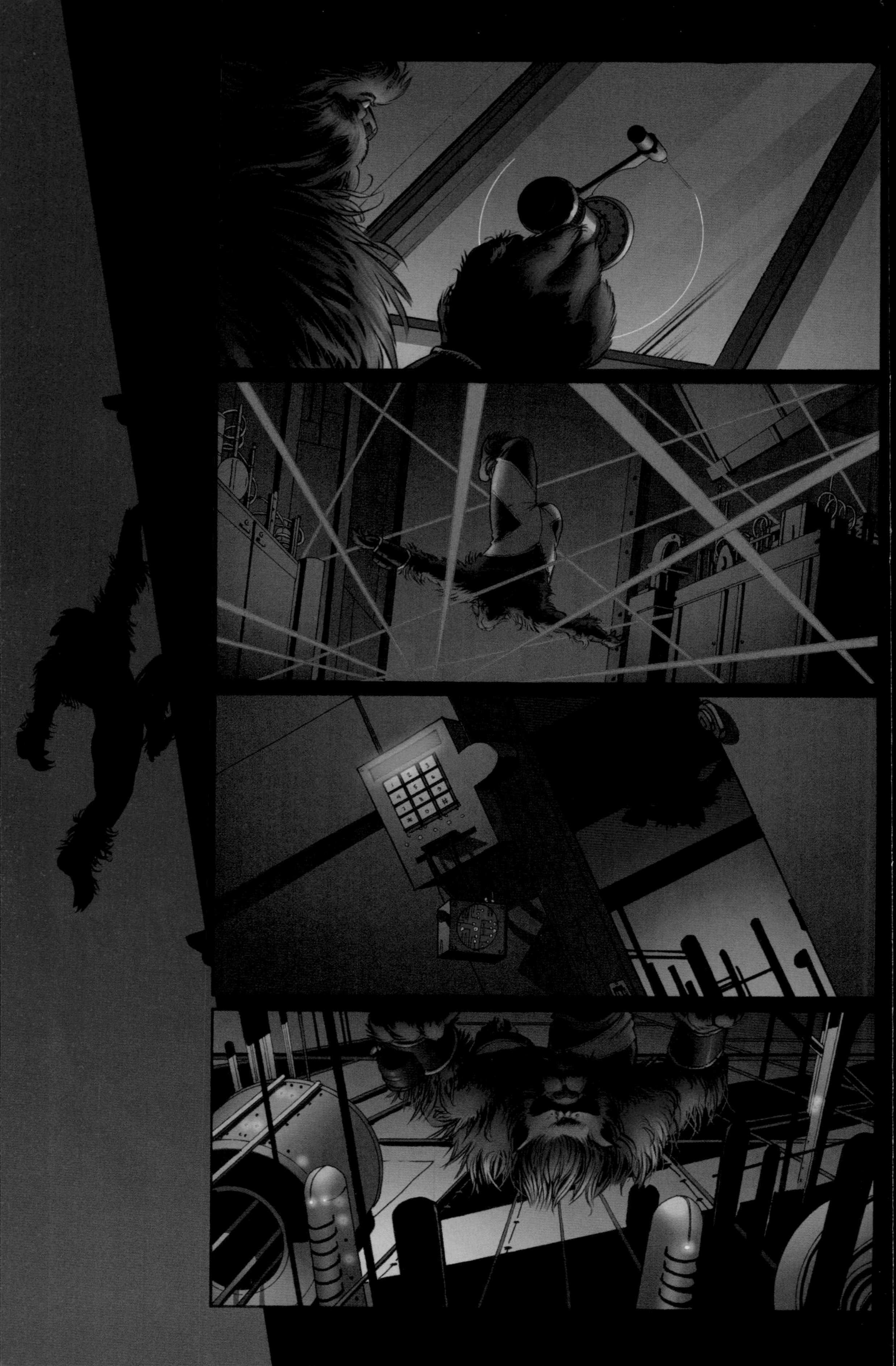

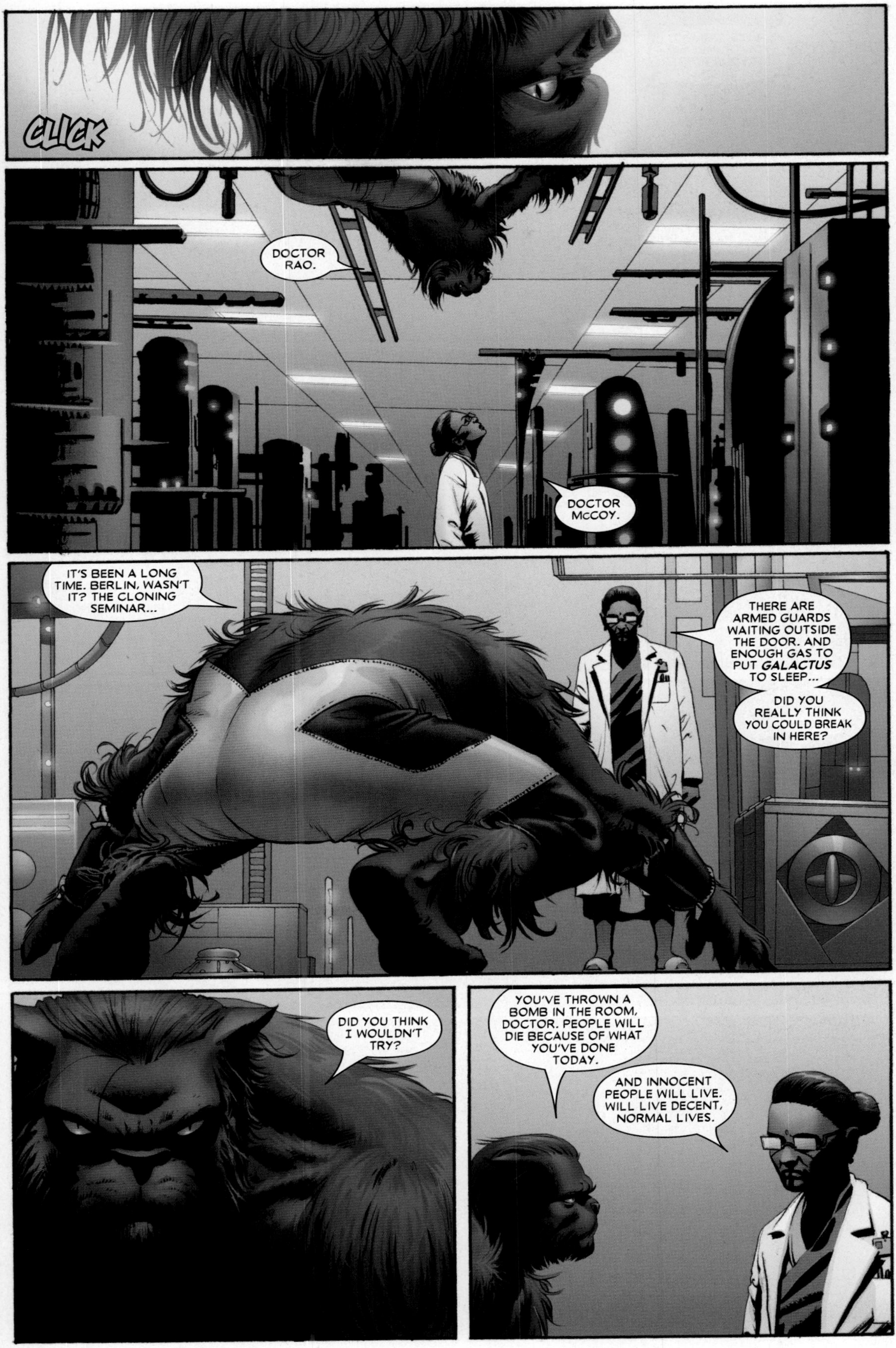
CLICK
DOCTOR RAO.
DOCTOR McCOY.
IT'S BEEN A LONG TIME. BERLIN, WASN'T IT? THE CLONING SEMINAR...
THERE ARE ARMED GUARDS WAITING OUTSIDE THE DOOR. AND ENOUGH GAS TO PUT GALACTUS TO SLEEP...
DID YOU REALLY THINK YOU COULD BREAK IN HERE?
DID YOU THINK I WOULDN'T TRY?
YOU'VE THROWN A BOMB IN THE ROOM, DOCTOR. PEOPLE WILL DIE BECAUSE OF WHAT YOU'VE DONE TODAY.
AND INNOCENT PEOPLE WILL LIVE. WILL LIVE DECENT, NORMAL LIVES.

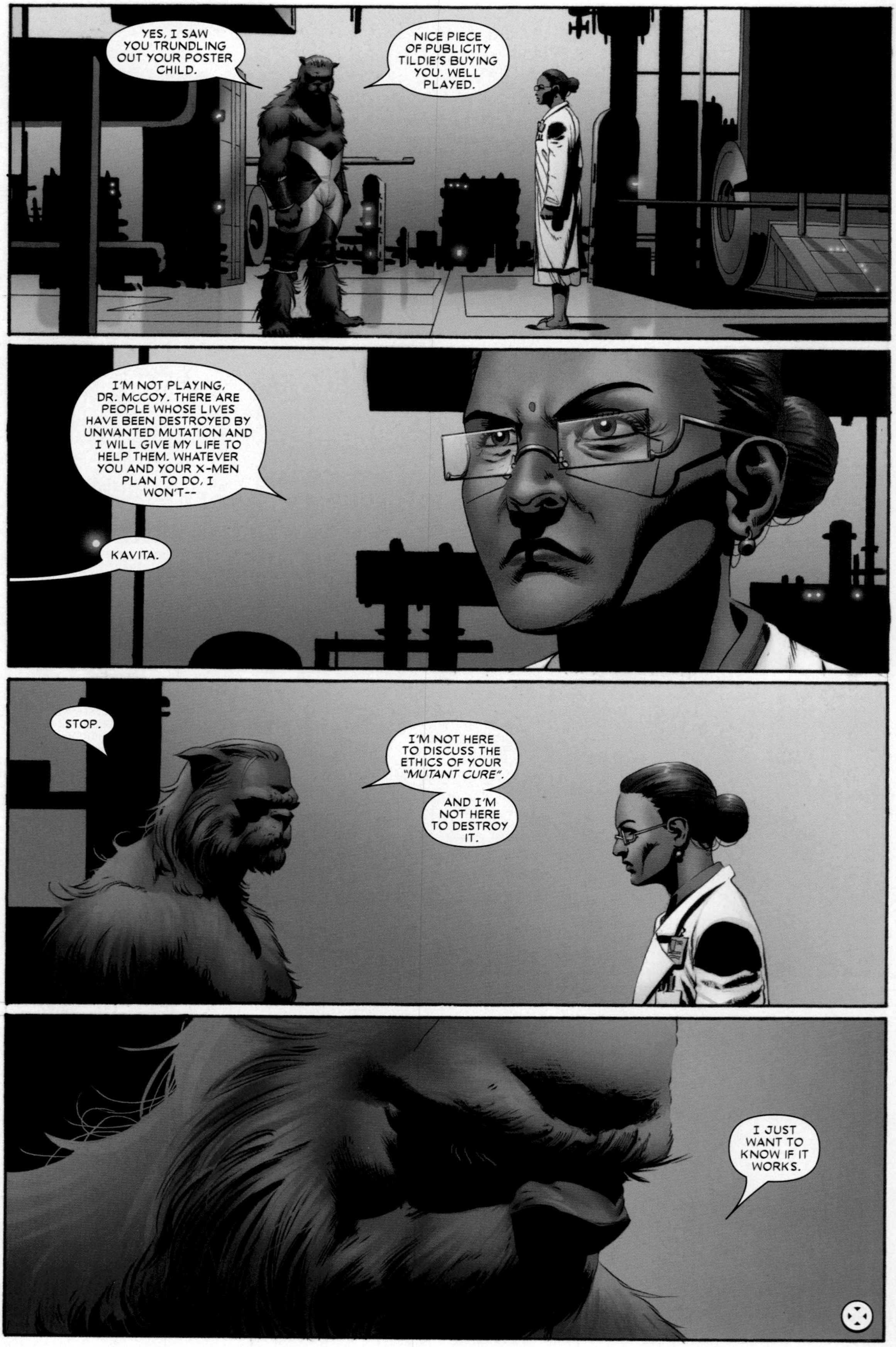
YES, I SAW YOU TRUNDLING OUT YOUR POSTER CHILD.
NICE PIECE OF PUBLICITY TILDIE'S BUYING YOU. WELL PLAYED.
I'M NOT PLAYING, DR. McCOY. THERE ARE PEOPLE WHOSE LIVES HAVE BEEN DESTROYED BY UNWANTED MUTATION AND I WILL GIVE MY LIFE TO HELP THEM. WHATEVER YOU AND YOUR X-MEN PLAN TO DO, I WON'T--
KAVITA.
STOP.
I'M NOT HERE TO DISCUSS THE ETHICS OF YOUR *"MUTANT CURE"*.
AND I'M NOT HERE TO DESTROY IT.
I JUST WANT TO KNOW IF IT WORKS.

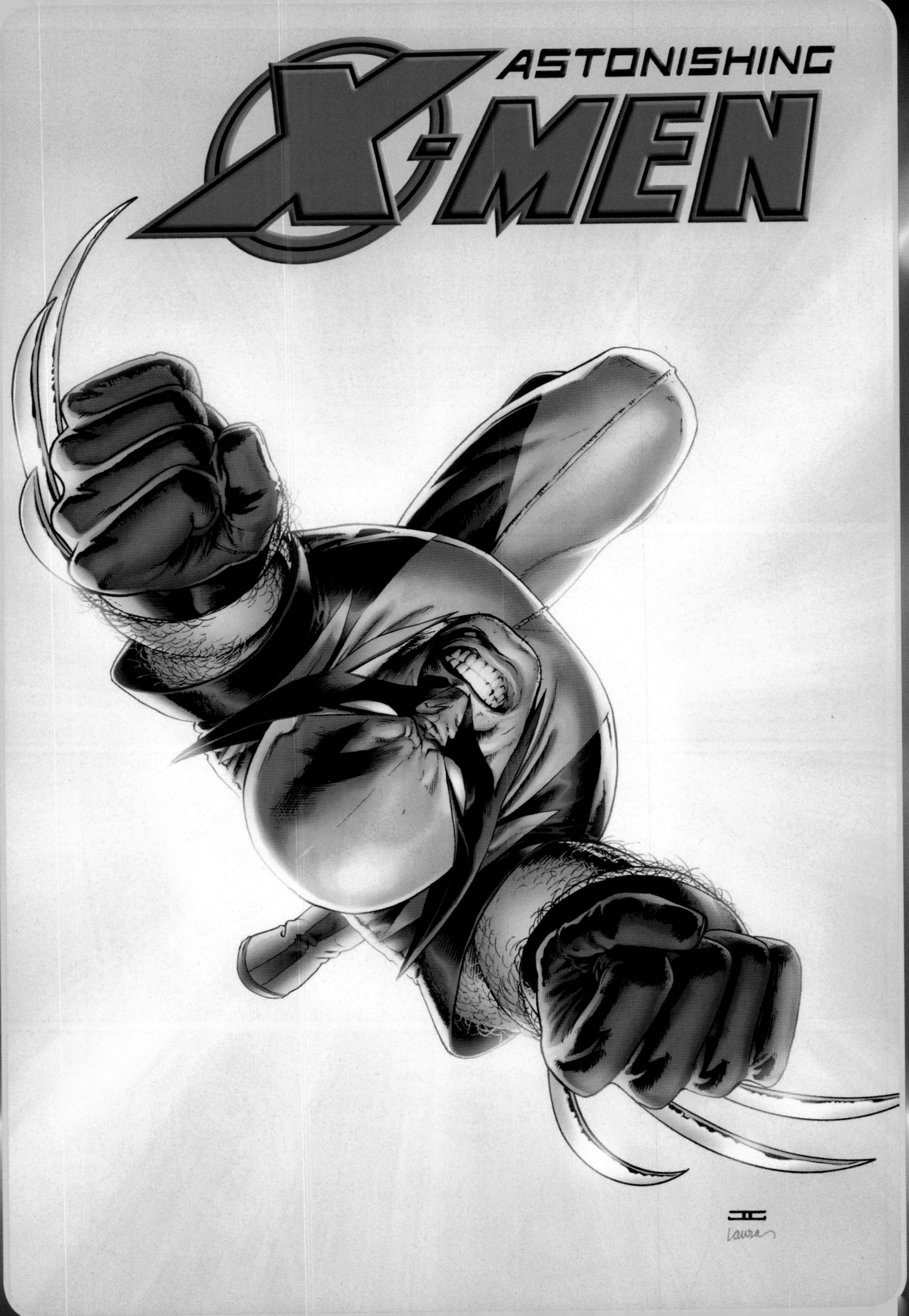
ASTONISHING
X-MEN

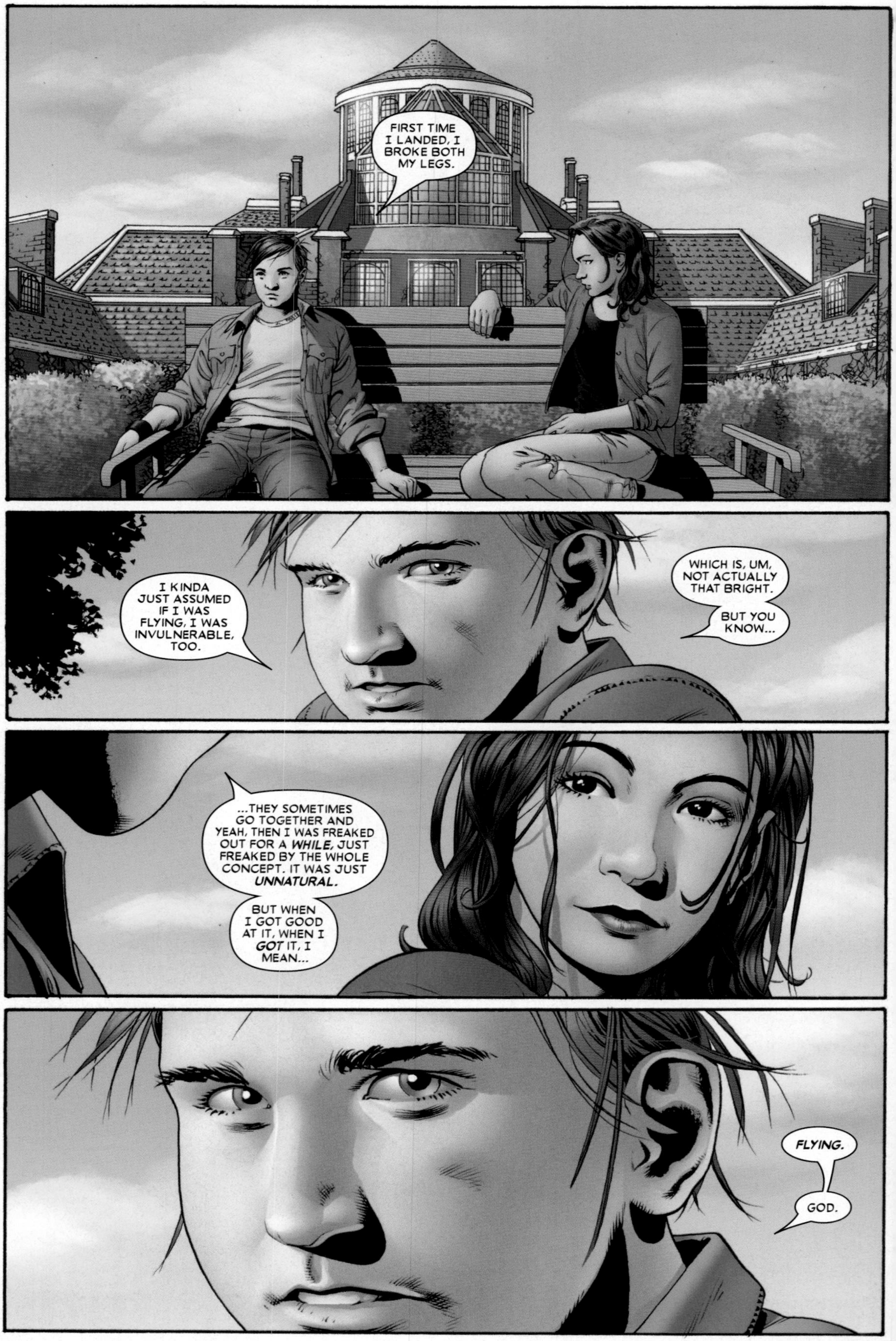
FIRST TIME I LANDED, I BROKE BOTH MY LEGS.
I KINDA JUST ASSUMED IF I WAS FLYING, I WAS INVULNERABLE, TOO.
WHICH IS, UM, NOT ACTUALLY THAT BRIGHT.
BUT YOU KNOW...
...THEY SOMETIMES GO TOGETHER AND YEAH, THEN I WAS FREAKED OUT FOR A *WHILE*, JUST FREAKED BY THE WHOLE CONCEPT. IT WAS JUST *UNNATURAL*.
BUT WHEN I GOT GOOD AT IT, WHEN I *GOT* IT, I MEAN...
FLYING.
GOD.

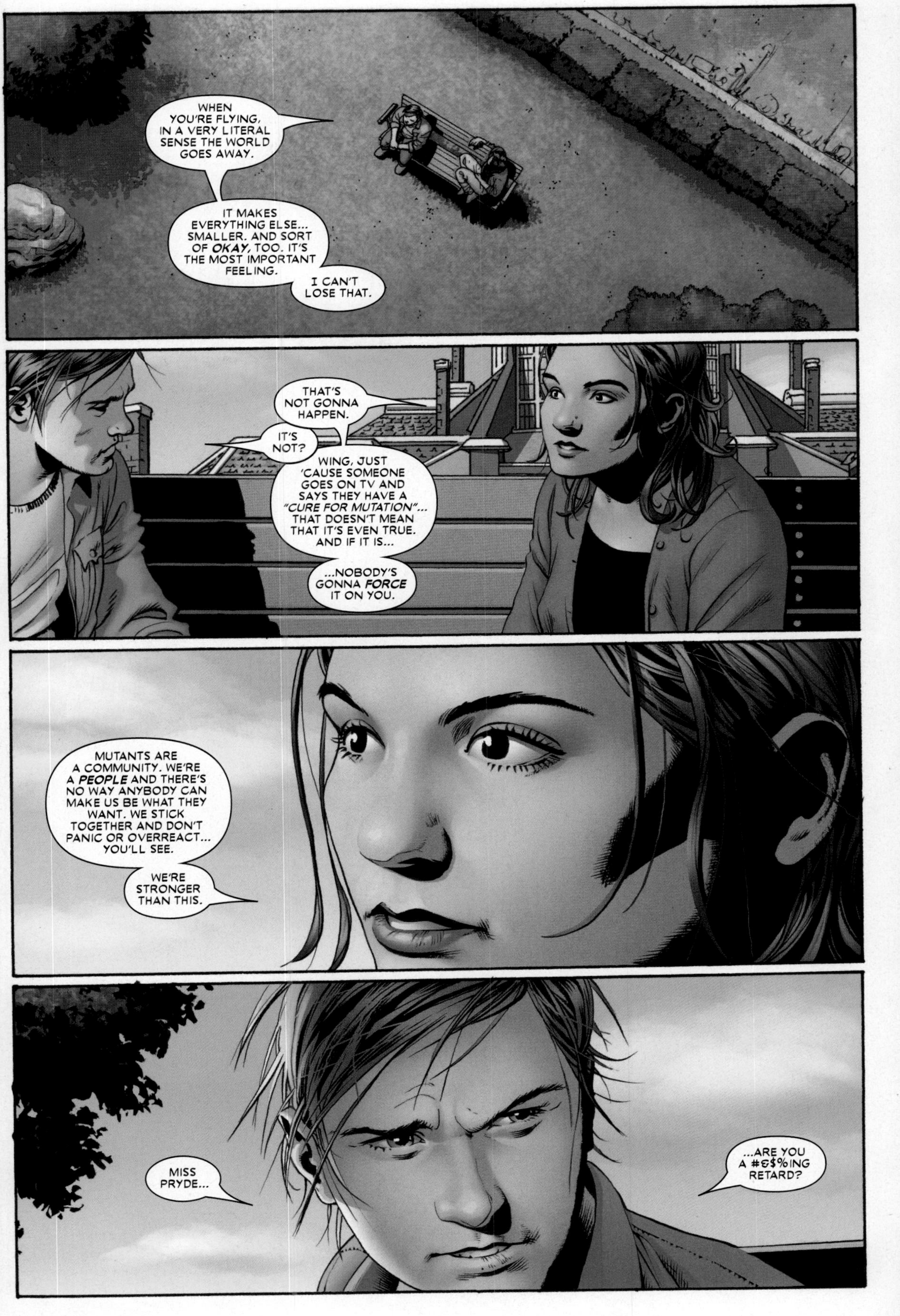
WHEN YOU'RE FLYING, IN A VERY LITERAL SENSE THE WORLD GOES AWAY.
IT MAKES EVERYTHING ELSE... SMALLER. AND SORT OF OKAY, TOO. IT'S THE MOST IMPORTANT FEELING.
I CAN'T LOSE THAT.
THAT'S NOT GONNA HAPPEN.
IT'S NOT?
WING, JUST 'CAUSE SOMEONE GOES ON TV AND SAYS THEY HAVE A "CURE FOR MUTATION"... THAT DOESN'T MEAN THAT IT'S EVEN TRUE. AND IF IT IS...
...NOBODY'S GONNA FORCE IT ON YOU.
MUTANTS ARE A COMMUNITY. WE'RE A PEOPLE AND THERE'S NO WAY ANYBODY CAN MAKE US BE WHAT THEY WANT. WE STICK TOGETHER AND DON'T PANIC OR OVERREACT... YOU'LL SEE.
WE'RE STRONGER THAN THIS.
MISS PRYDE...
...ARE YOU A #&$%ING RETARD?

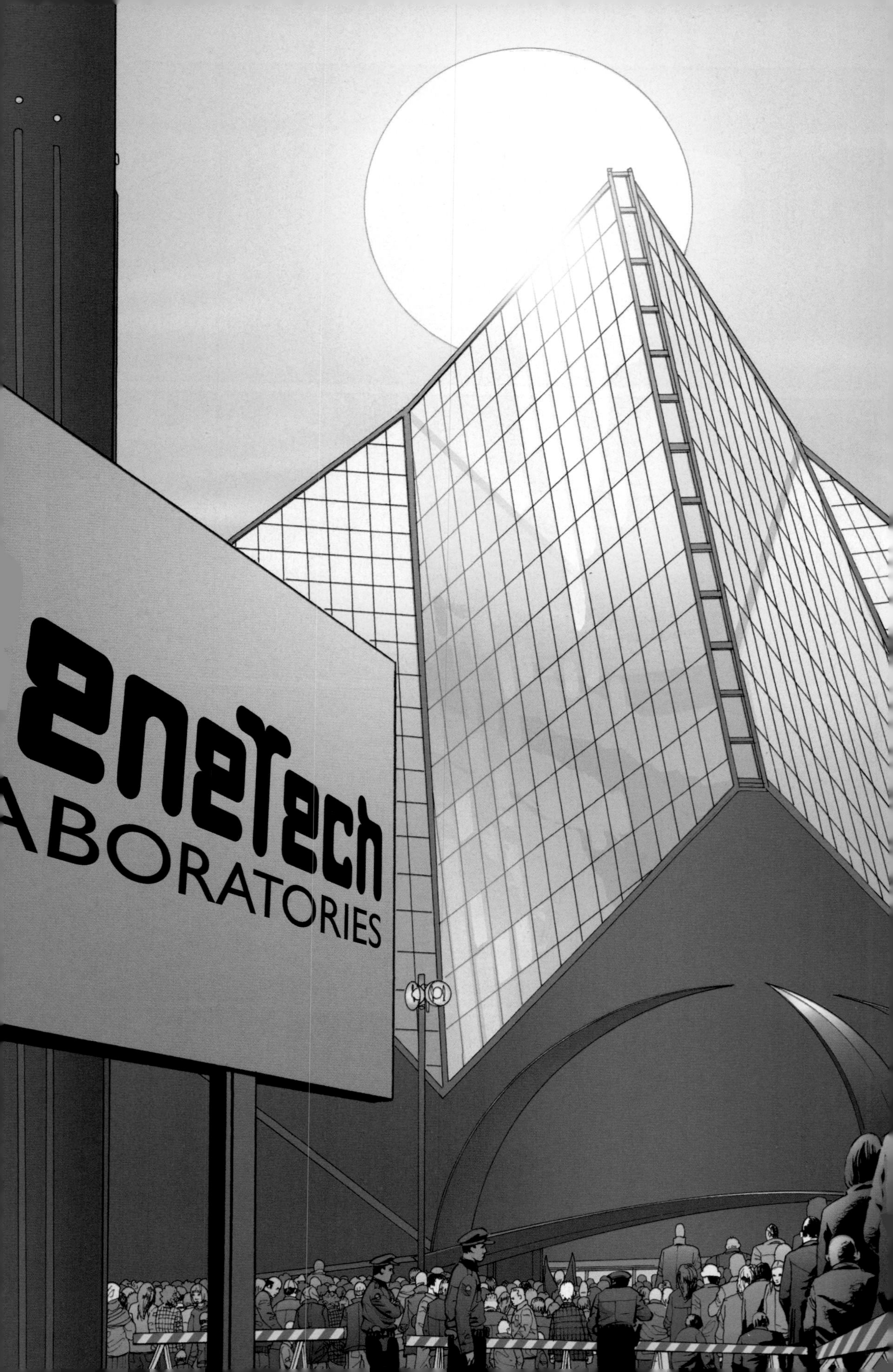
enetech
ABORATORIES

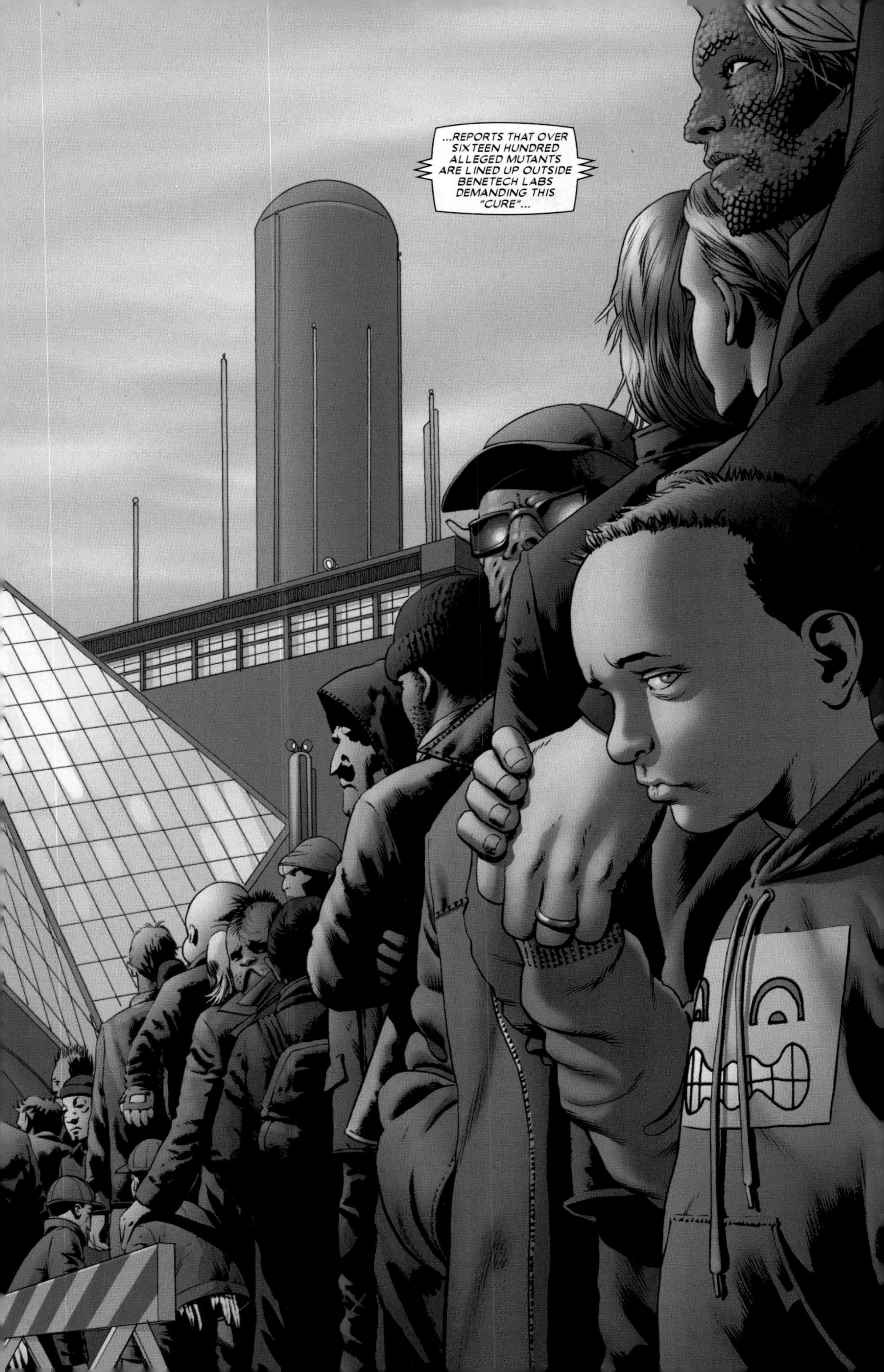
...REPORTS THAT OVER SIXTEEN HUNDRED ALLEGED MUTANTS ARE LINED UP OUTSIDE BENETECH LABS DEMANDING THIS "CURE"...

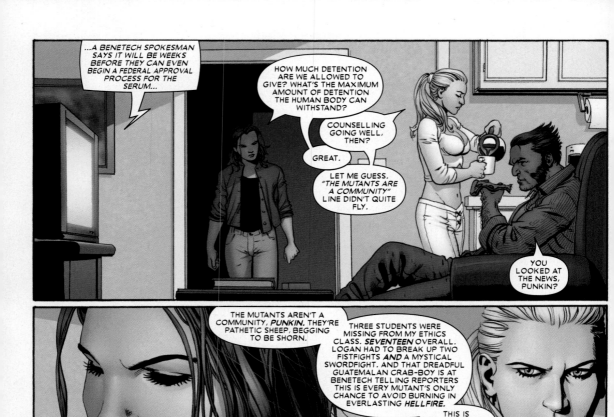

...A BENETECH SPOKESMAN SAYS IT WILL BE WEEKS BEFORE THEY CAN EVEN BEGIN A FEDERAL APPROVAL PROCESS FOR THE SERUM...

HOW MUCH DETENTION ARE WE ALLOWED TO GIVE? WHAT'S THE MAXIMUM AMOUNT OF DETENTION THE HUMAN BODY CAN WITHSTAND?

COUNSELLING GOING WELL, THEN?

GREAT.

LET ME GUESS. "THE MUTANTS ARE A COMMUNITY" LINE DIDN'T QUITE FLY.

YOU LOOKED AT THE NEWS, PUNKIN?

THE MUTANTS AREN'T A COMMUNITY, PUNKIN. THEY'RE PATHETIC SHEEP, BEGGING TO BE SHORN.

THREE STUDENTS WERE MISSING FROM MY ETHICS CLASS. SEVENTEEN OVERALL. LOGAN HAD TO BREAK UP TWO FISTFIGHTS AND A MYSTICAL SWORDFIGHT. AND THAT DREADFUL GUATEMALAN CRAB-BOY IS AT BENETECH TELLING REPORTERS THIS IS EVERY MUTANT'S ONLY CHANCE TO AVOID BURNING IN EVERLASTING HELLFIRE.

THIS IS EATING US FROM THE INSIDE OUT.

OH MY GOD.

YOU TEACH ETHICS?

YES, DO LET'S MAKE JOKES RIGHT NOW.

I'M NOT JOKING. I HAVE A VERY LARGE PROBLEM WITH THAT CONCEPT.

OUR STUDENTS ARE FLEEING THE SCHOOL, YOU HALF-WIT.

WELL, MAYBE IT'S TIME FOR ANOTHER PEPPY "THEY WILL ALWAYS HATE US" SPEECH. I'M SURE THAT HELPED.

I THOUGHT I WAS THE ONE WITH THE CLAWS...

JUST TELL ME THERE'S COFFEE.

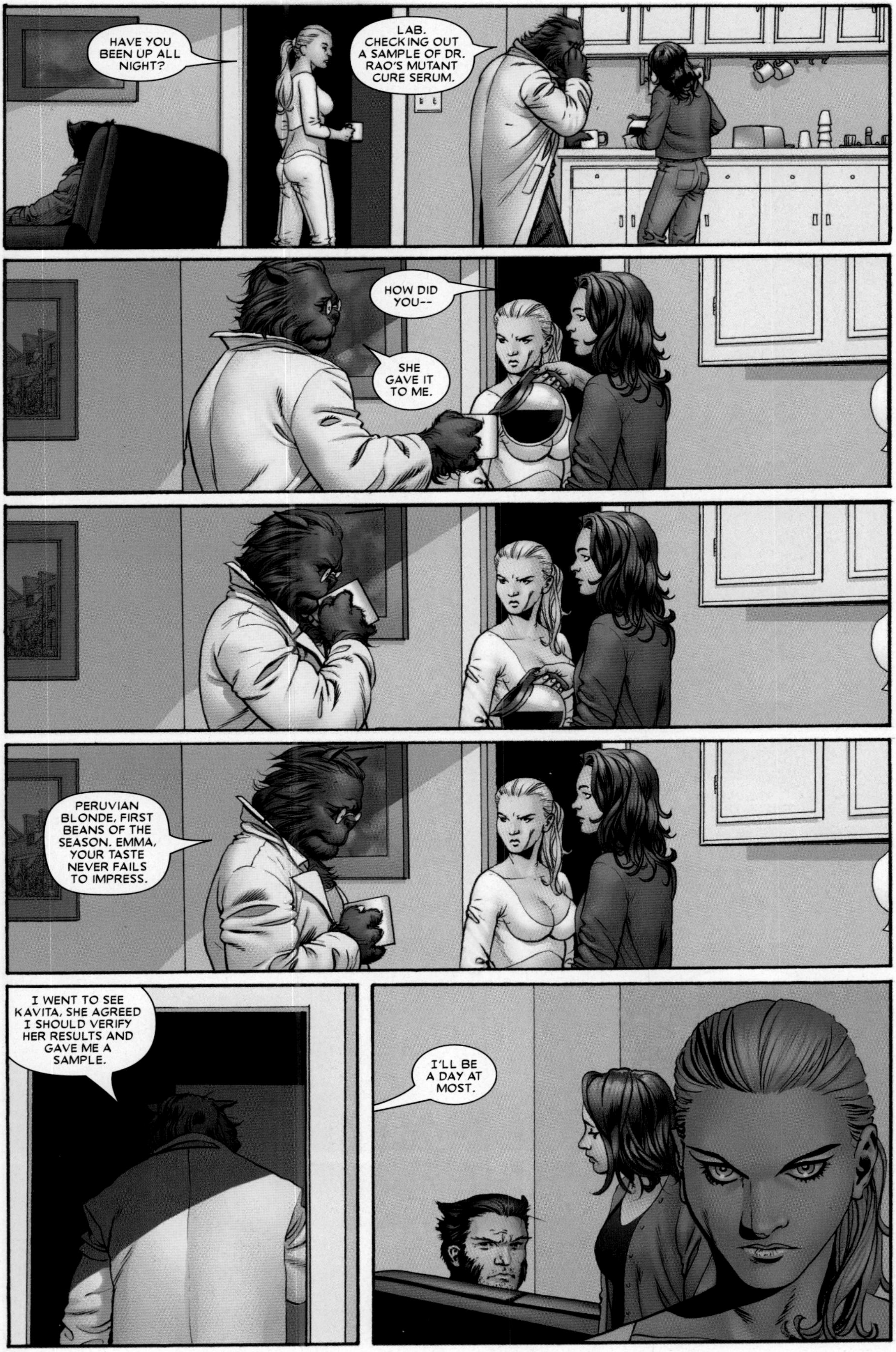
HAVE YOU BEEN UP ALL NIGHT?
LAB. CHECKING OUT A SAMPLE OF DR. RAO'S MUTANT CURE SERUM.
HOW DID YOU--
SHE GAVE IT FIRST TO ME.
PERUVIAN BLONDE, FIRST BEANS OF THE SEASON. EMMA, YOUR TASTE NEVER FAILS TO IMPRESS.
I WENT TO SEE KAVITA, SHE AGREED I SHOULD VERIFY HER RESULTS AND GAVE ME A SAMPLE.
I'LL BE A DAY AT MOST.

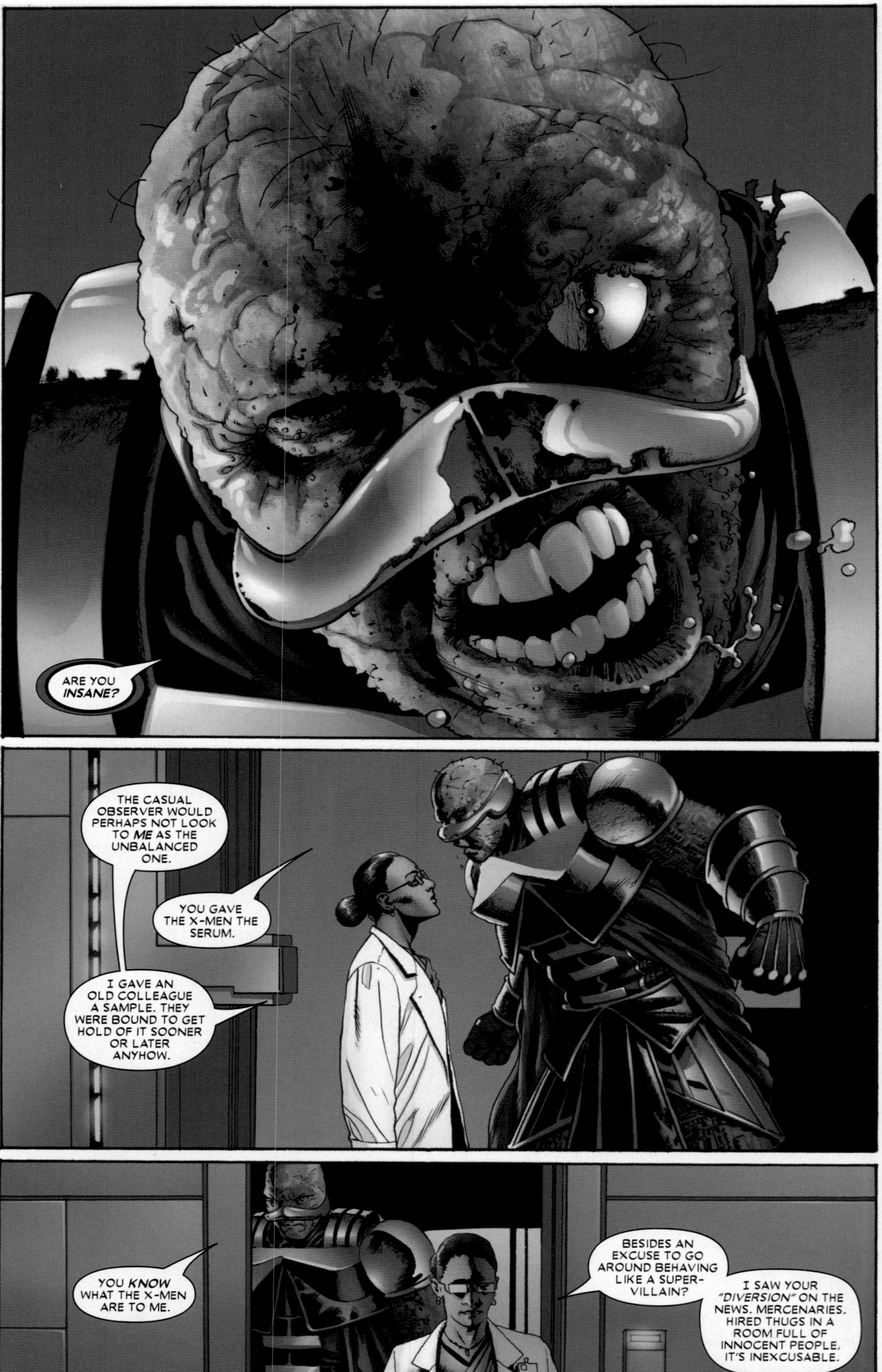
ARE YOU INSANE?
THE CASUAL OBSERVER WOULD PERHAPS NOT LOOK TO ME AS THE UNBALANCED ONE.
YOU GAVE THE X-MEN THE SERUM.
I GAVE AN OLD COLLEAGUE A SAMPLE. THEY WERE BOUND TO GET HOLD OF IT SOONER OR LATER ANYHOW.
YOU KNOW WHAT THE X-MEN ARE TO ME.
BESIDES AN EXCUSE TO GO AROUND BEHAVING LIKE A SUPER-VILLAIN?
I SAW YOUR "DIVERSION" ON THE NEWS. MERCENARIES. HIRED THUGS IN A ROOM FULL OF INNOCENT PEOPLE, IT'S INEXCUSABLE.

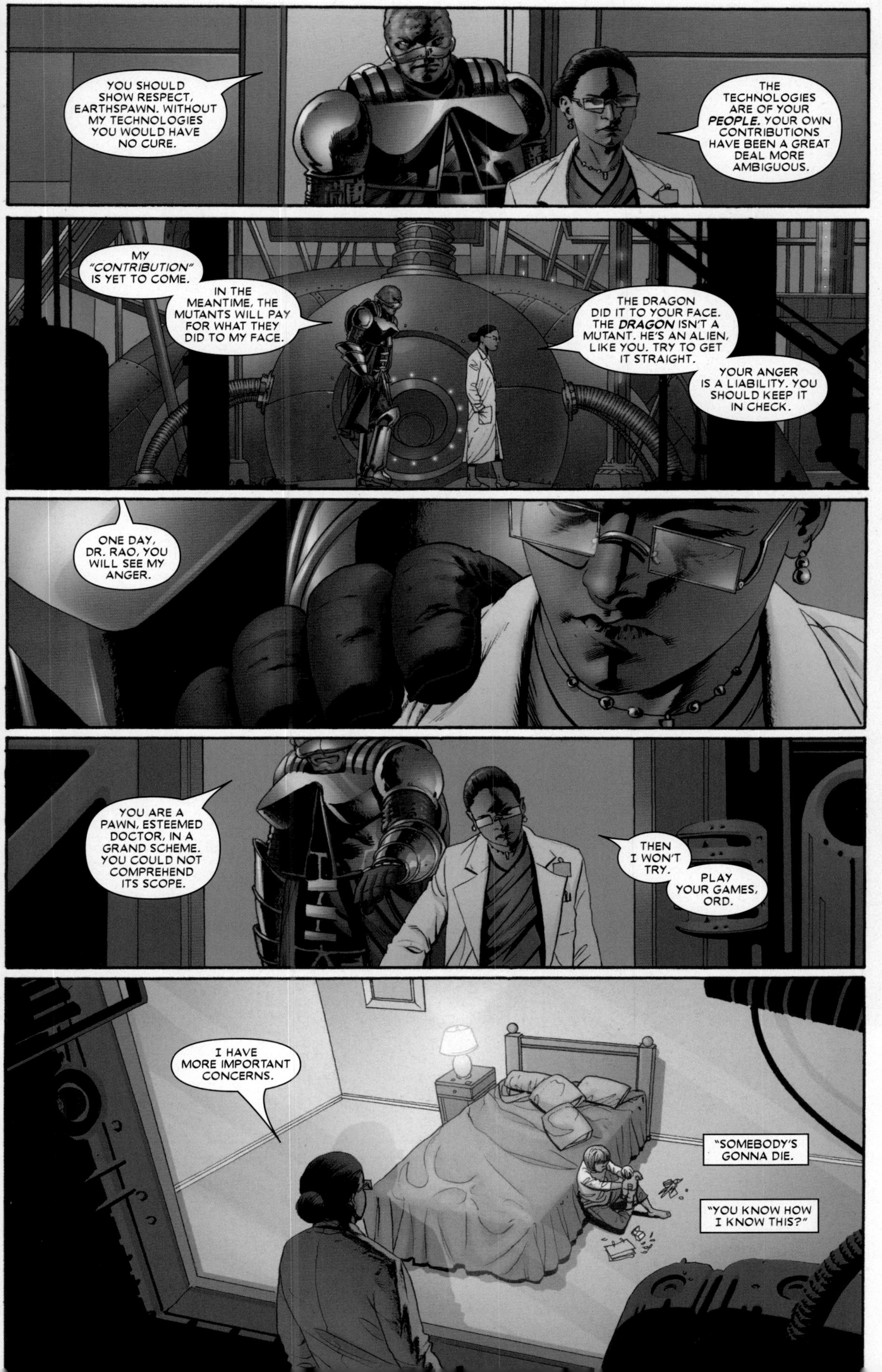
YOU SHOULD SHOW RESPECT, EARTHSPAWN. WITHOUT MY TECHNOLOGIES YOU WOULD HAVE NO CURE.
THE TECHNOLOGIES ARE OF YOUR *PEOPLE.* YOUR OWN CONTRIBUTIONS HAVE BEEN A GREAT DEAL MORE AMBIGUOUS.
MY *"CONTRIBUTION"* IS YET TO COME.
IN THE MEANTIME, THE MUTANTS WILL PAY FOR WHAT THEY DID TO MY FACE.
THE DRAGON DID IT TO YOUR FACE. THE *DRAGON* ISN'T A MUTANT. HE'S AN ALIEN, LIKE YOU. TRY TO GET IT STRAIGHT.
YOUR ANGER IS A LIABILITY. YOU SHOULD KEEP IT IN CHECK.
ONE DAY, DR. RAO, YOU WILL SEE MY ANGER.
YOU ARE A PAWN, ESTEEMED DOCTOR, IN A GRAND SCHEME. YOU COULD NOT COMPREHEND ITS SCOPE.
THEN I WON'T TRY.
PLAY YOUR GAMES, ORD.
I HAVE MORE IMPORTANT CONCERNS.
"SOMEBODY'S GONNA DIE.
"YOU KNOW HOW I KNOW THIS?"

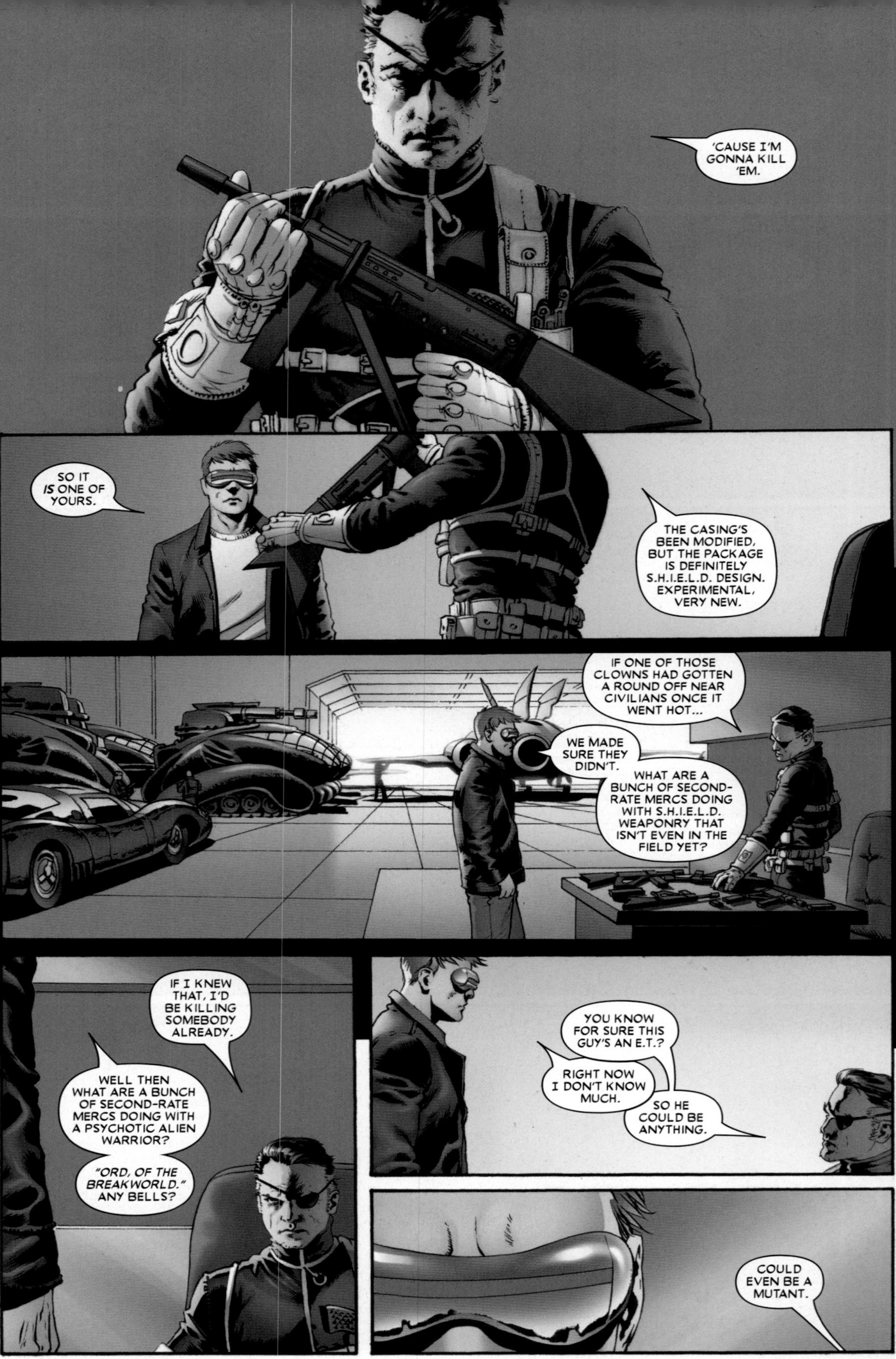
'CAUSE I'M GONNA KILL 'EM.
SO IT *IS* ONE OF YOURS.
THE CASING'S BEEN MODIFIED, BUT THE PACKAGE IS DEFINITELY S.H.I.E.L.D. DESIGN. EXPERIMENTAL, VERY NEW.
IF ONE OF THOSE CLOWNS HAD GOTTEN A ROUND OFF NEAR CIVILIANS ONCE IT WENT HOT...
WE MADE SURE THEY DIDN'T.
WHAT ARE A BUNCH OF SECOND-RATE MERCS DOING WITH S.H.I.E.L.D. WEAPONRY THAT ISN'T EVEN IN THE FIELD YET?
IF I KNEW THAT, I'D BE KILLING SOMEBODY ALREADY.
WELL THEN WHAT ARE A BUNCH OF SECOND-RATE MERCS DOING WITH A PSYCHOTIC ALIEN WARRIOR?
"ORD, OF THE BREAKWORLD." ANY BELLS?
YOU KNOW FOR SURE THIS GUY'S AN E.T.?
RIGHT NOW I DON'T KNOW MUCH.
SO HE COULD BE ANYTHING.
COULD EVEN BE A MUTANT.

AM I MISSING SOMETHING?

I JUST DON'T HAVE A LOT TO GO ON IS ALL.

YOU KNOW ABOUT THIS *"CURE"* THING, RIGHT? *"MUTANTS ARE A DISEASE"*?

THIS MONSTER SHOWS UP RIGHT WHEN ALL THAT COMES OUT, RUNNING A CREW CARRYING *YOUR* ORDNANCE, AND THE BEST YOU CAN DO IS ACCUSE HIM OF BEING ONE OF *US*?

DON'T GET IN MY FACE, BOY. THAT AIN'T A RIGHT YOU'VE EARNED.

I LET YOU UP HERE 'CAUSE XAVIER'S GOT SOME CRED WITH THE POWERS AND HE SAYS YOU'RE IN CHARGE.

I'LL RUN THIS NAME DOWN, THIS ORD, AND I'LL SHARE WHATEVER I FIND.

BUT IF HE'S GOT SOME BEEF WITH YOUR X-TEAM, THAT PROBLEM'S NOT MINE.

AND IF YOU THINK ANYBODY HERE IS LOSING SLEEP OVER WHETHER OR NOT YOU MUTANTS MIGHT ALL SUDDENLY LOSE YOUR POWERS...

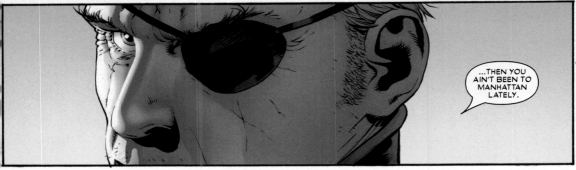

...THEN YOU AIN'T BEEN TO MANHATTAN LATELY.

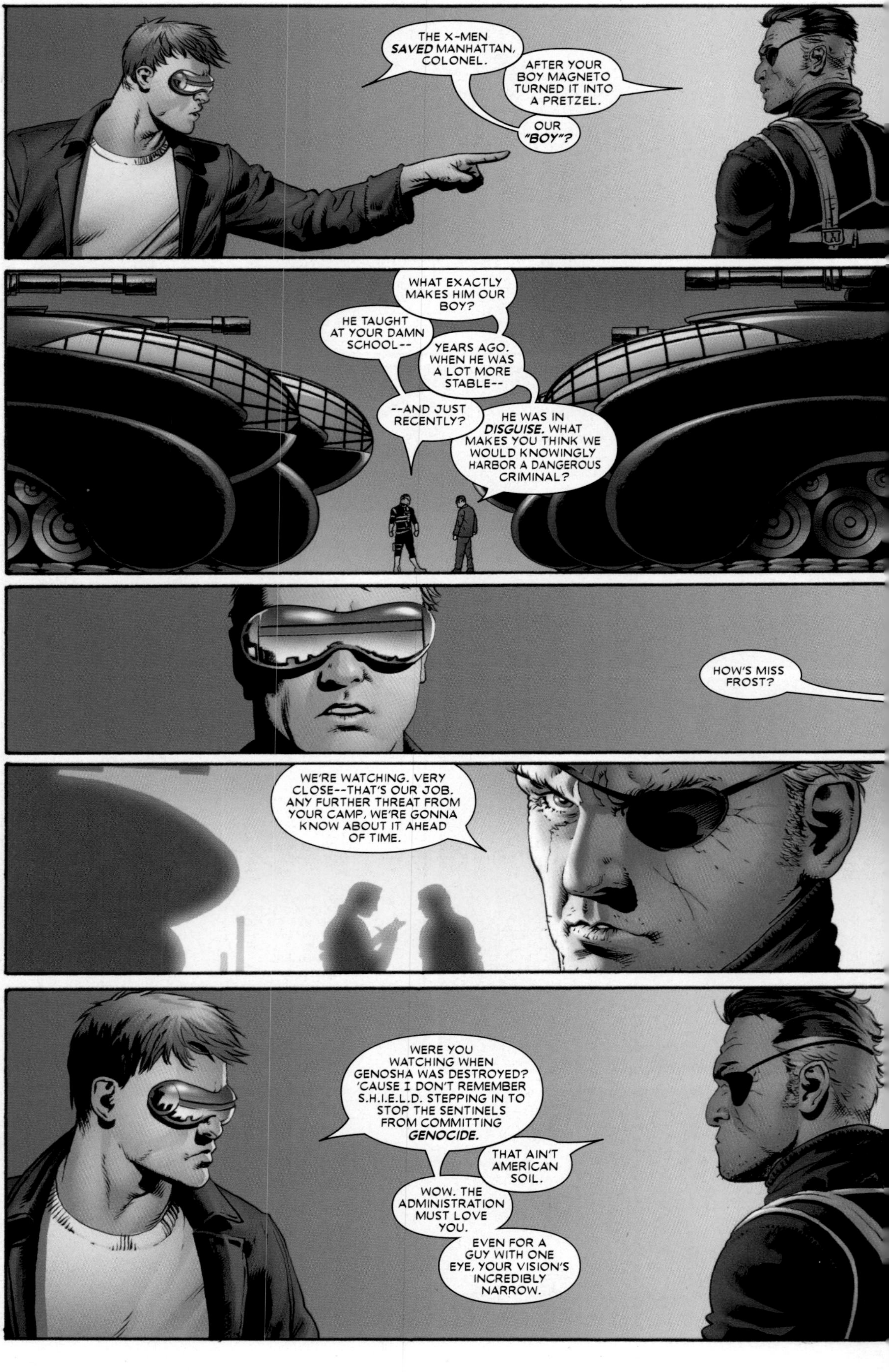

THE X-MEN SAVED MANHATTAN, COLONEL.
AFTER YOUR BOY MAGNETO TURNED IT INTO A PRETZEL.
OUR "BOY"?
WHAT EXACTLY MAKES HIM OUR BOY?
HE TAUGHT AT YOUR DAMN SCHOOL--
YEARS AGO. WHEN HE WAS A LOT MORE STABLE--
--AND JUST RECENTLY?
HE WAS IN DISGUISE. WHAT MAKES YOU THINK WE WOULD KNOWINGLY HARBOR A DANGEROUS CRIMINAL?
HOW'S MISS FROST?
WE'RE WATCHING. VERY CLOSE--THAT'S OUR JOB. ANY FURTHER THREAT FROM YOUR CAMP, WE'RE GONNA KNOW ABOUT IT AHEAD OF TIME.
WERE YOU WATCHING WHEN GENOSHA WAS DESTROYED? 'CAUSE I DON'T REMEMBER S.H.I.E.L.D. STEPPING IN TO STOP THE SENTINELS FROM COMMITTING GENOCIDE.
THAT AIN'T AMERICAN SOIL.
WOW. THE ADMINISTRATION MUST LOVE YOU.
EVEN FOR A GUY WITH ONE EYE, YOUR VISION'S INCREDIBLY NARROW.

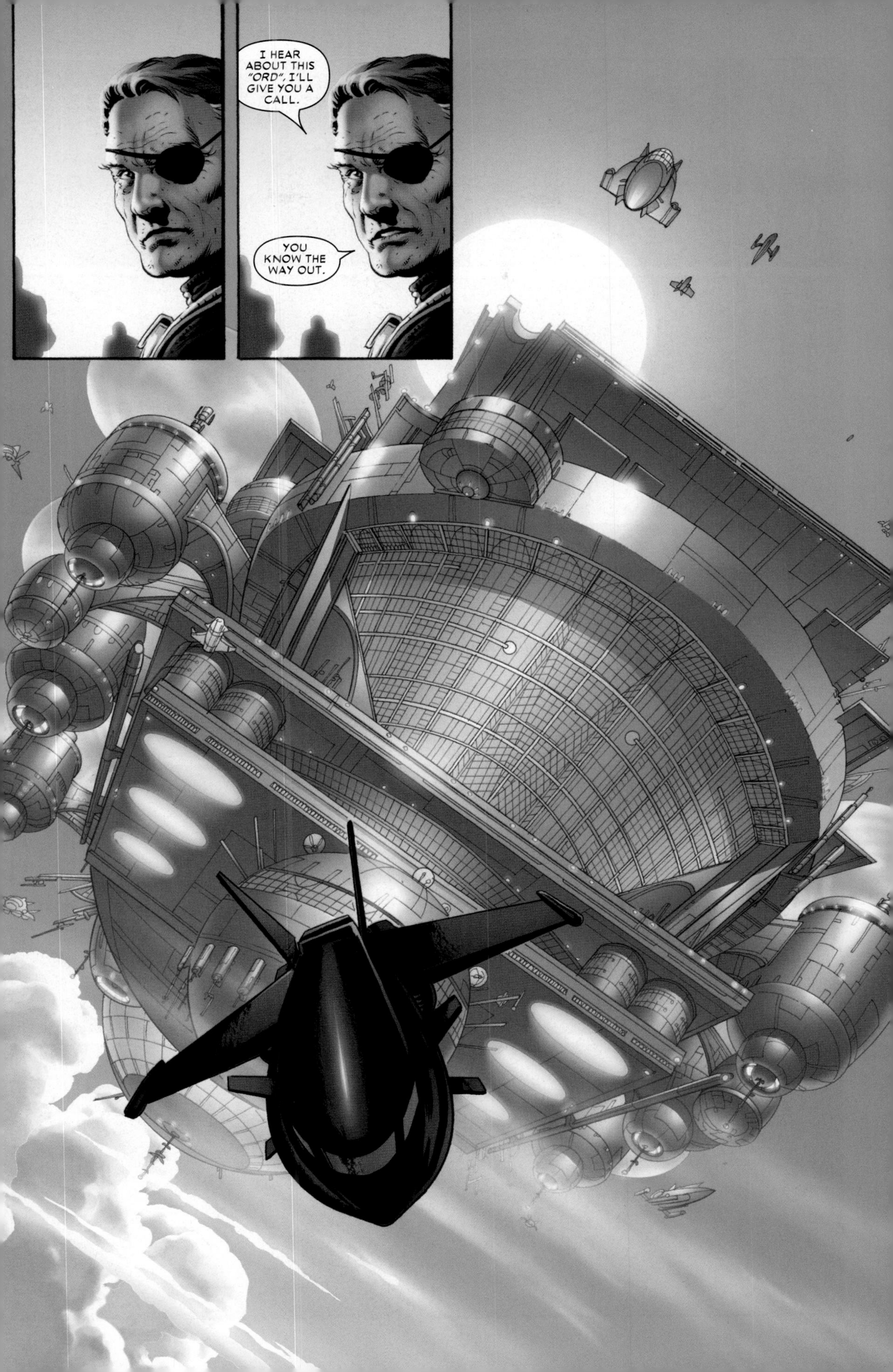
I HEAR ABOUT THIS "ORD", I'LL GIVE YOU A CALL.
YOU KNOW THE WAY OUT.

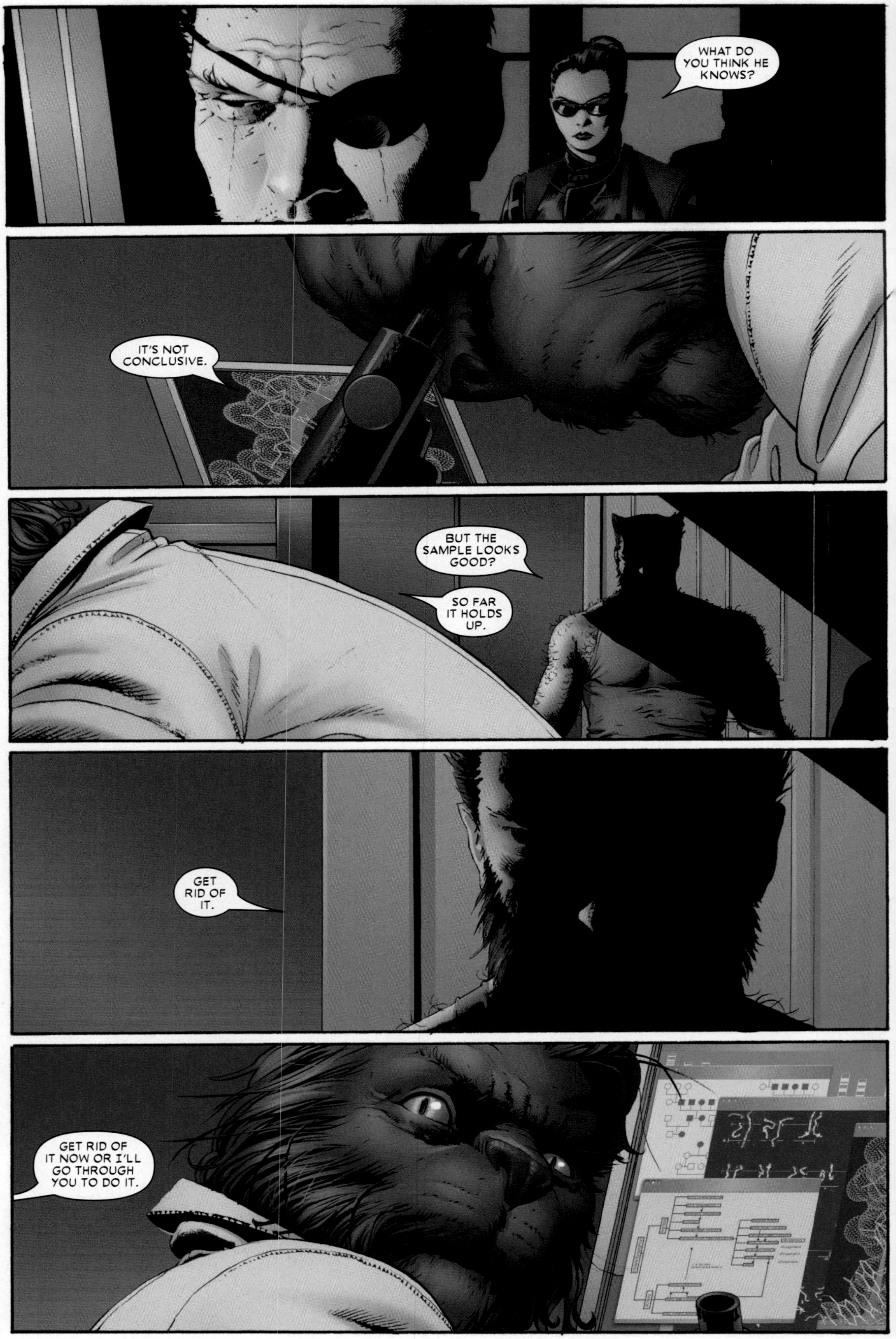
WHAT DO YOU THINK HE KNOWS?
IT'S NOT CONCLUSIVE.
BUT THE SAMPLE LOOKS GOOD?
SO FAR IT HOLDS UP.
GET RID OF IT.
GET RID OF IT NOW OR I'LL GO THROUGH YOU TO DO IT.

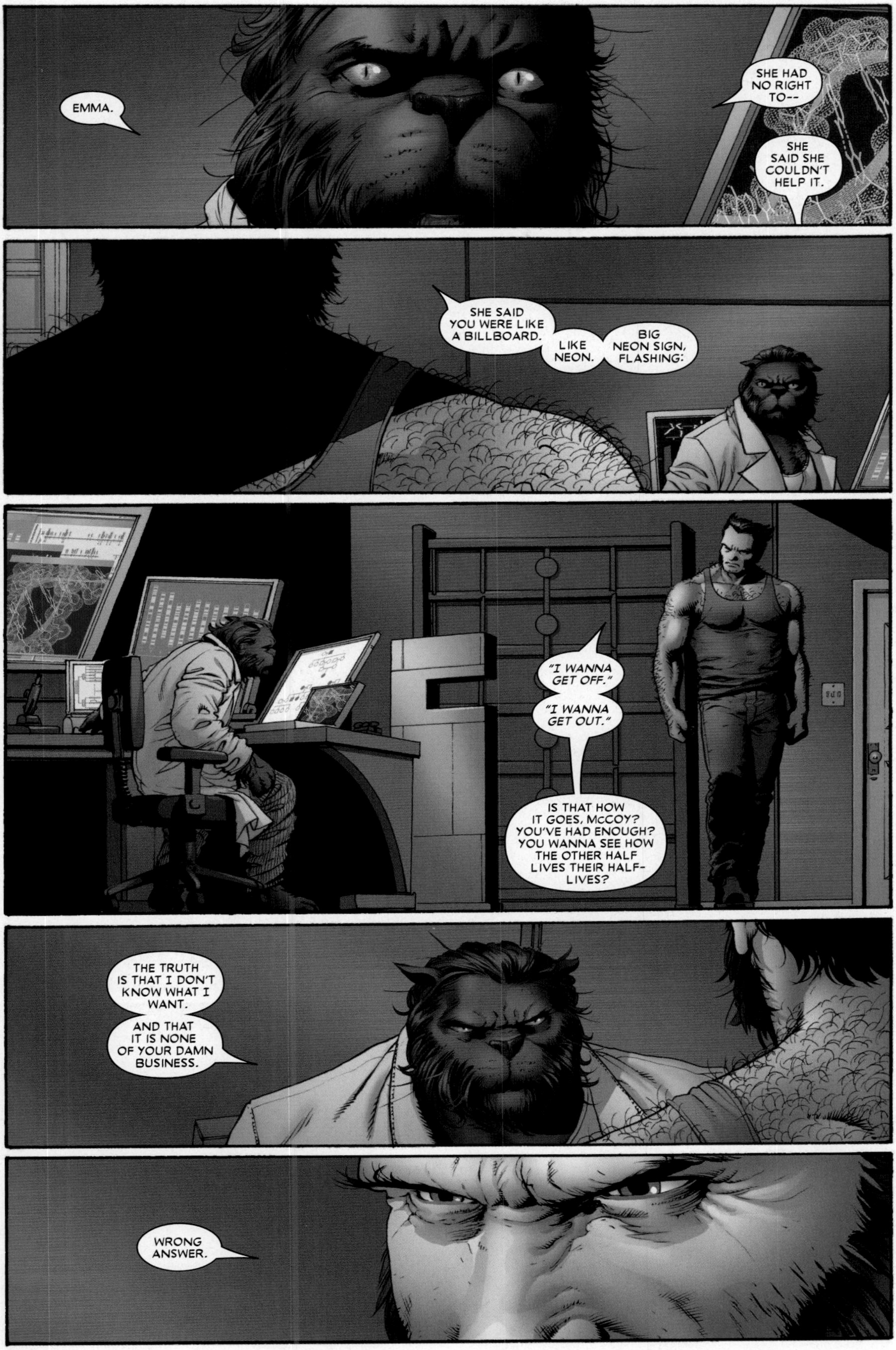
EMMA.
SHE HAD NO RIGHT TO--
SHE SAID SHE COULDN'T HELP IT.
SHE SAID YOU WERE LIKE A BILLBOARD.
LIKE NEON.
BIG NEON SIGN, FLASHING:
"I WANNA GET OFF."
"I WANNA GET OUT."
IS THAT HOW IT GOES, McCOY? YOU'VE HAD ENOUGH? YOU WANNA SEE HOW THE OTHER HALF LIVES THEIR HALF-LIVES?
THE TRUTH IS THAT I DON'T KNOW WHAT I WANT.
AND THAT IT IS NONE OF YOUR DAMN BUSINESS.
WRONG ANSWER.

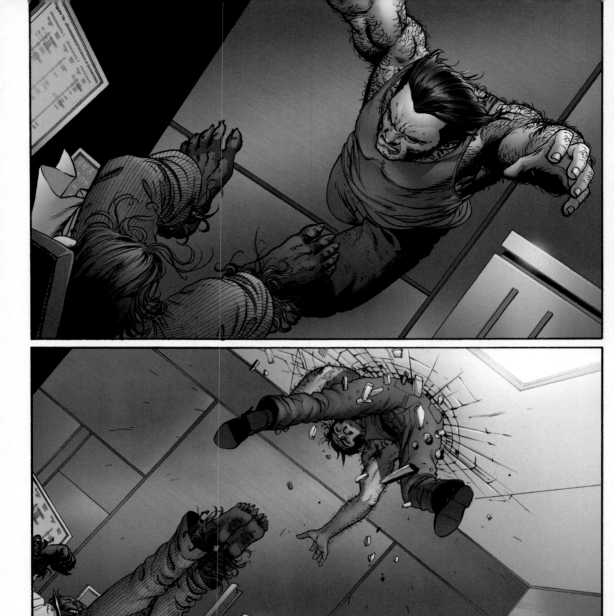

YOU
BEAST.

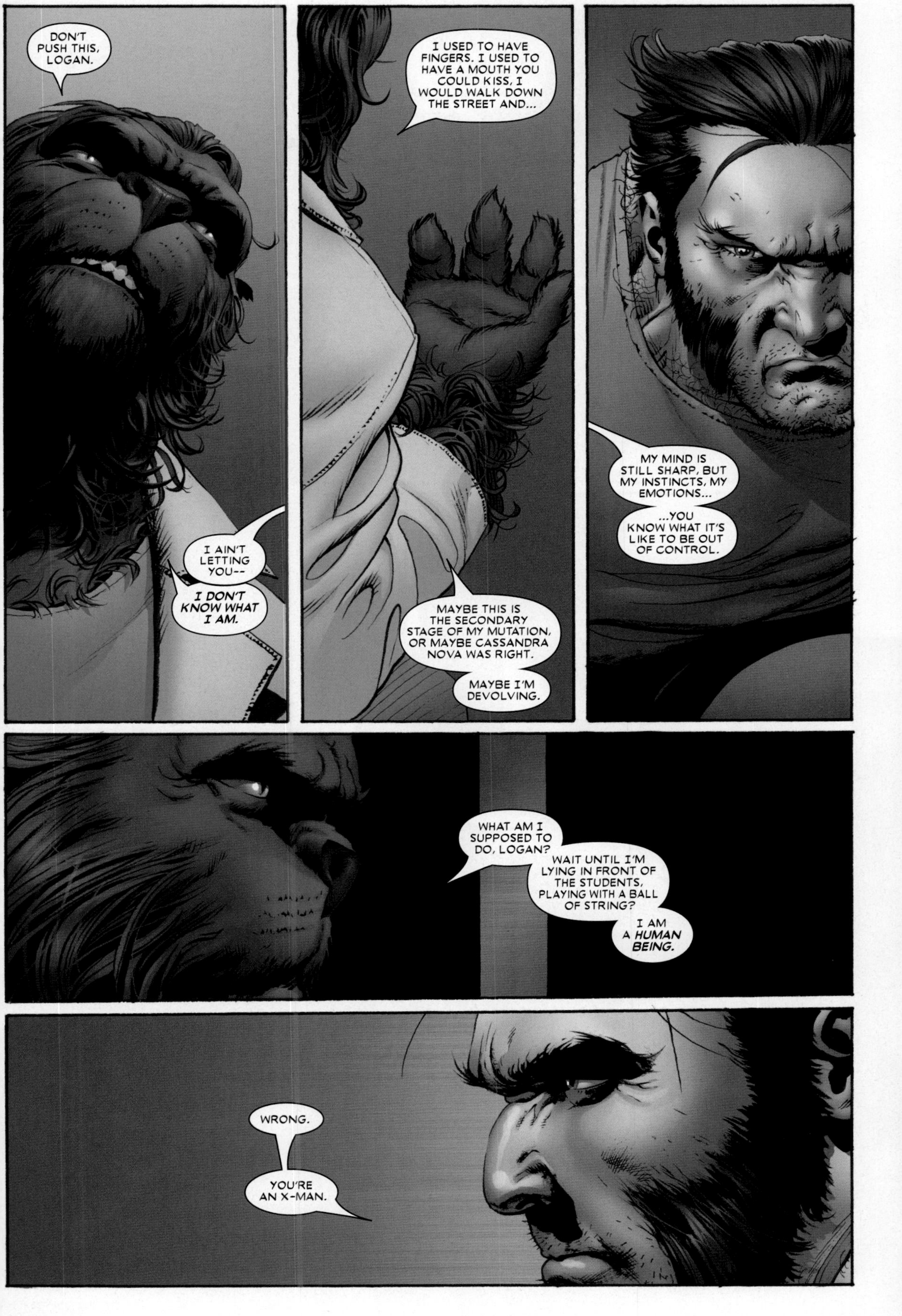
DON'T PUSH THIS, LOGAN.
I USED TO HAVE FINGERS. I USED TO HAVE A MOUTH YOU COULD KISS, I WOULD WALK DOWN THE STREET AND...
I AIN'T LETTING YOU--
I DON'T KNOW WHAT I AM.
MAYBE THIS IS THE SECONDARY STAGE OF MY MUTATION, OR MAYBE CASSANDRA NOVA WAS RIGHT.
MAYBE I'M DEVOLVING.
MY MIND IS STILL SHARP, BUT MY INSTINCTS, MY EMOTIONS...
...YOU KNOW WHAT IT'S LIKE TO BE OUT OF CONTROL.
WHAT AM I SUPPOSED TO DO, LOGAN?
WAIT UNTIL I'M LYING IN FRONT OF THE STUDENTS, PLAYING WITH A BALL OF STRING?
I AM A *HUMAN BEING.*
WRONG.
YOU'RE AN X-MAN.

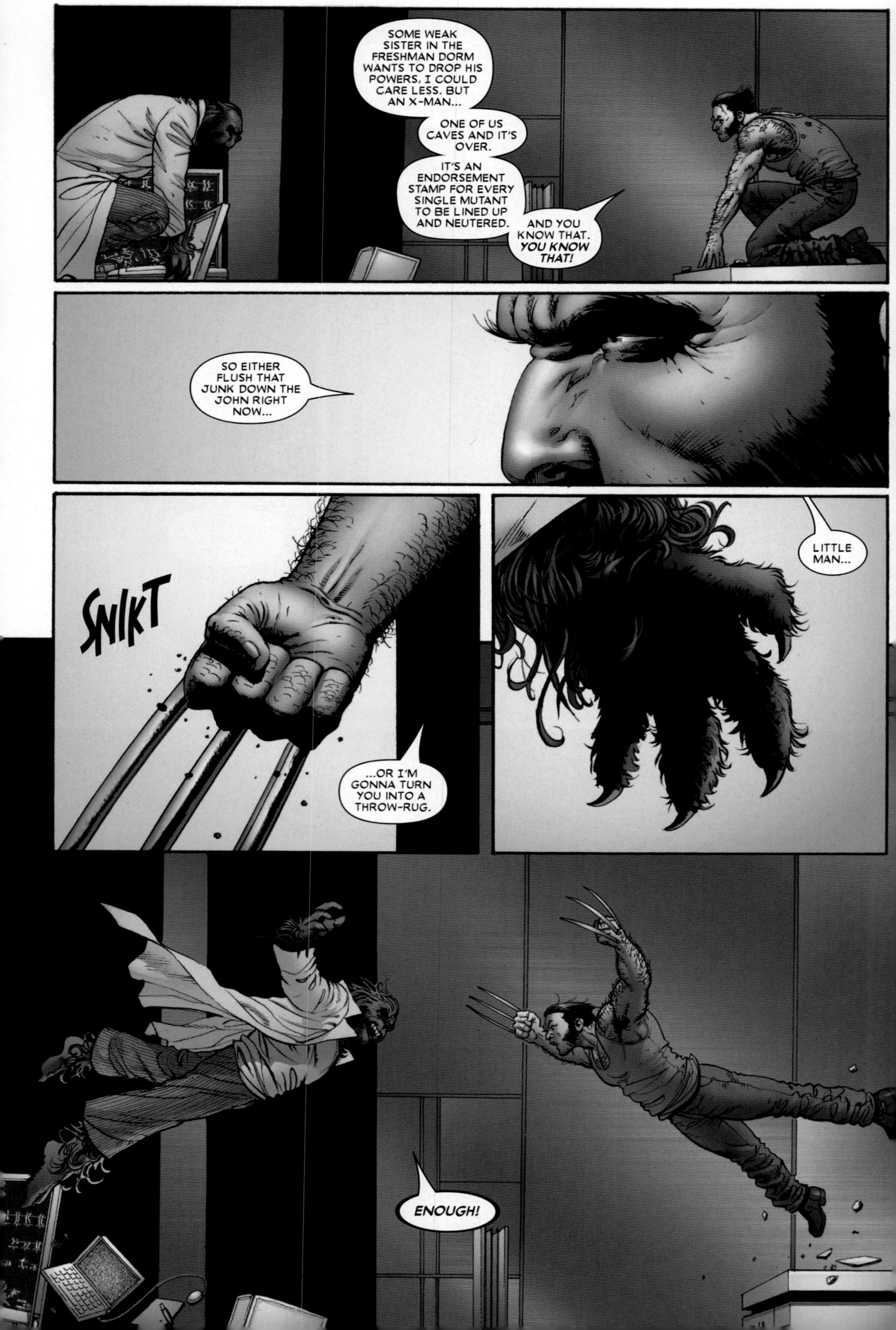
SOME WEAK SISTER IN THE FRESHMAN DORM WANTS TO DROP HIS POWERS, I COULD CARE LESS. BUT AN X-MAN...
ONE OF US CAVES AND IT'S OVER.
IT'S AN ENDORSEMENT STAMP FOR EVERY SINGLE MUTANT TO BE LINED UP AND NEUTERED.
AND YOU KNOW THAT. *YOU KNOW THAT!*
SO EITHER FLUSH THAT JUNK DOWN THE JOHN RIGHT NOW...
SNIKT
...OR I'M GONNA TURN YOU INTO A THROW-RUG.
LITTLE MAN...
ENOUGH!

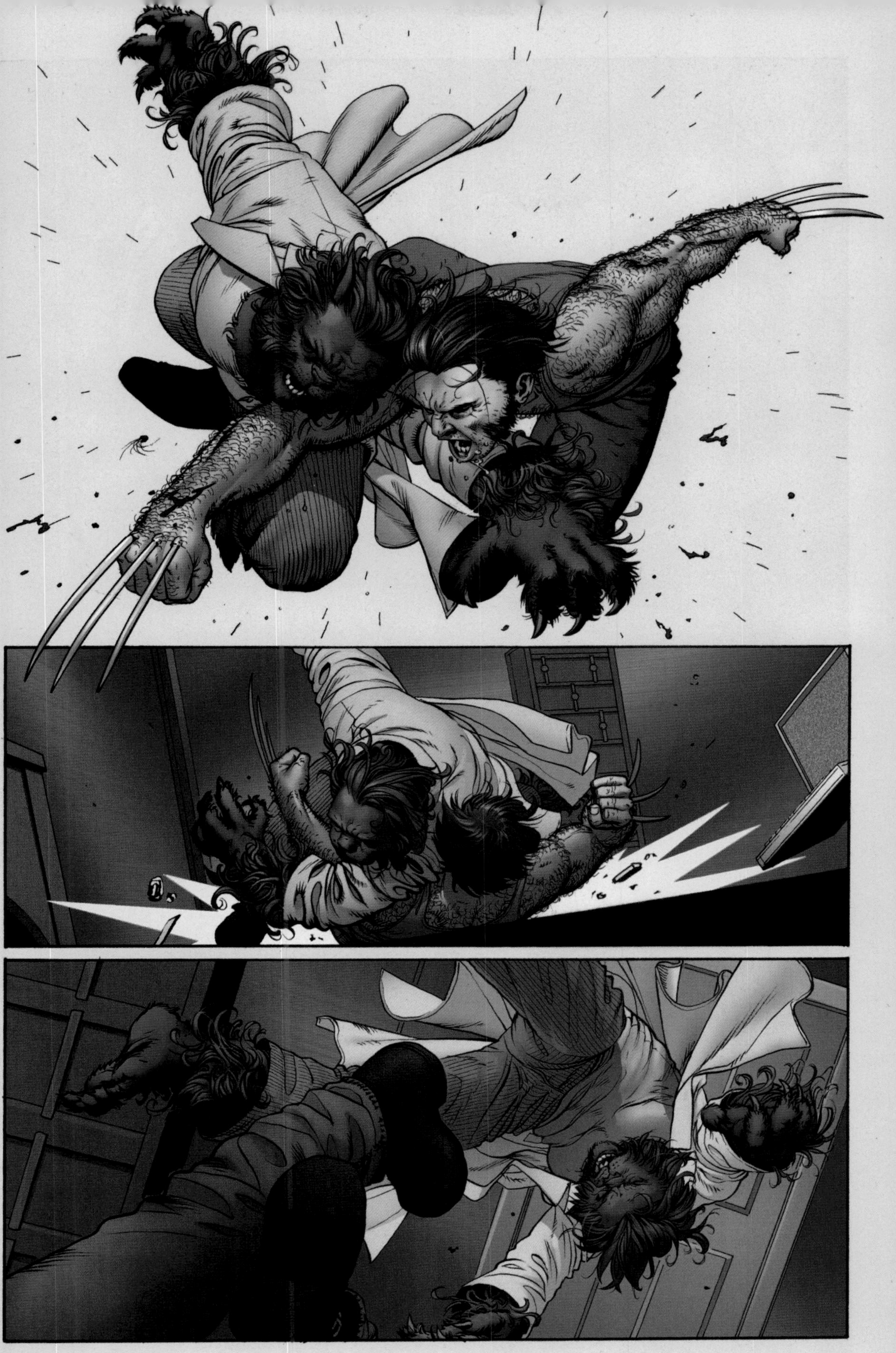

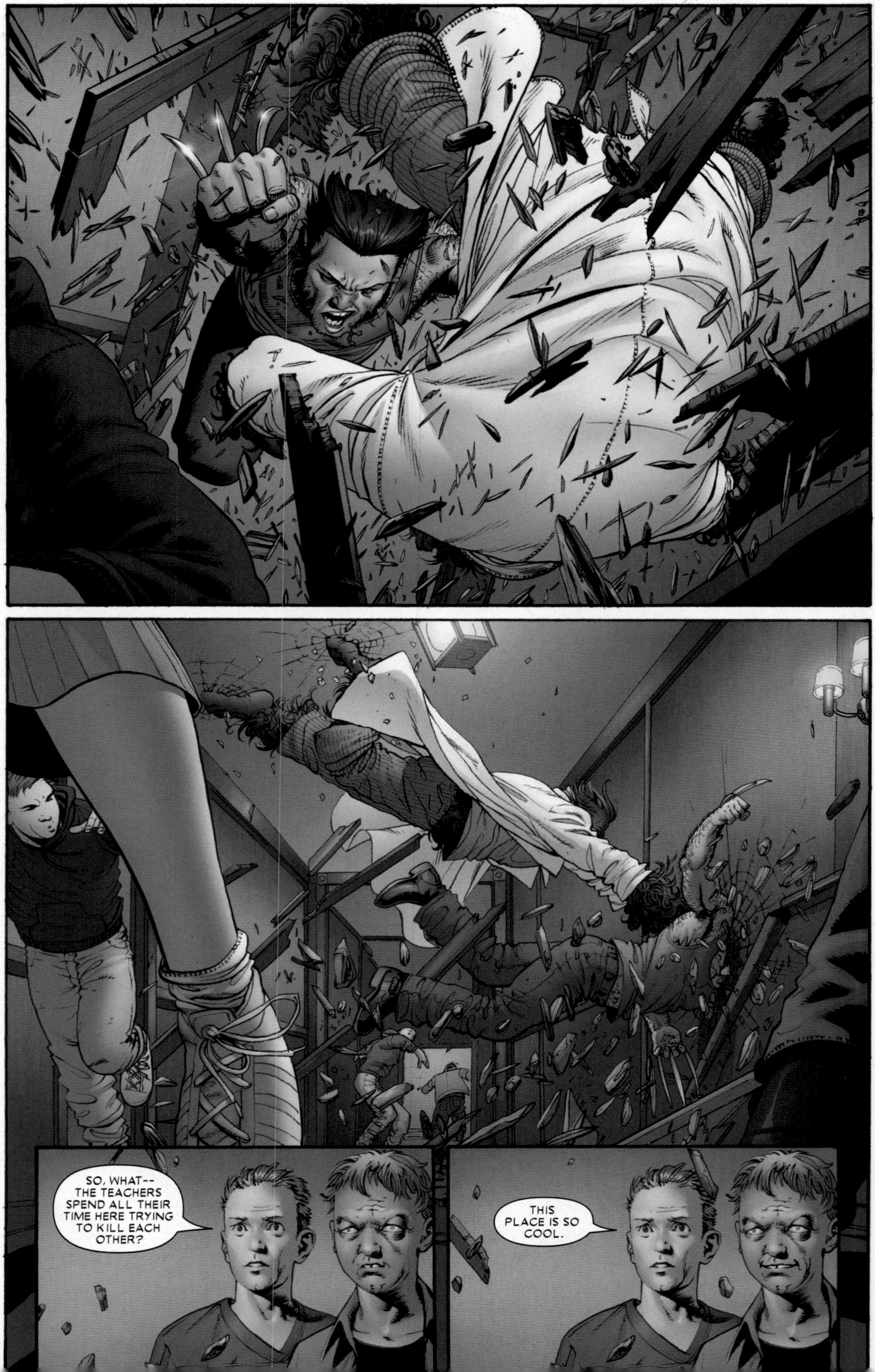
SO, WHAT-- THE TEACHERS SPEND ALL THEIR TIME HERE TRYING TO KILL EACH OTHER?
THIS PLACE IS SO COOL.

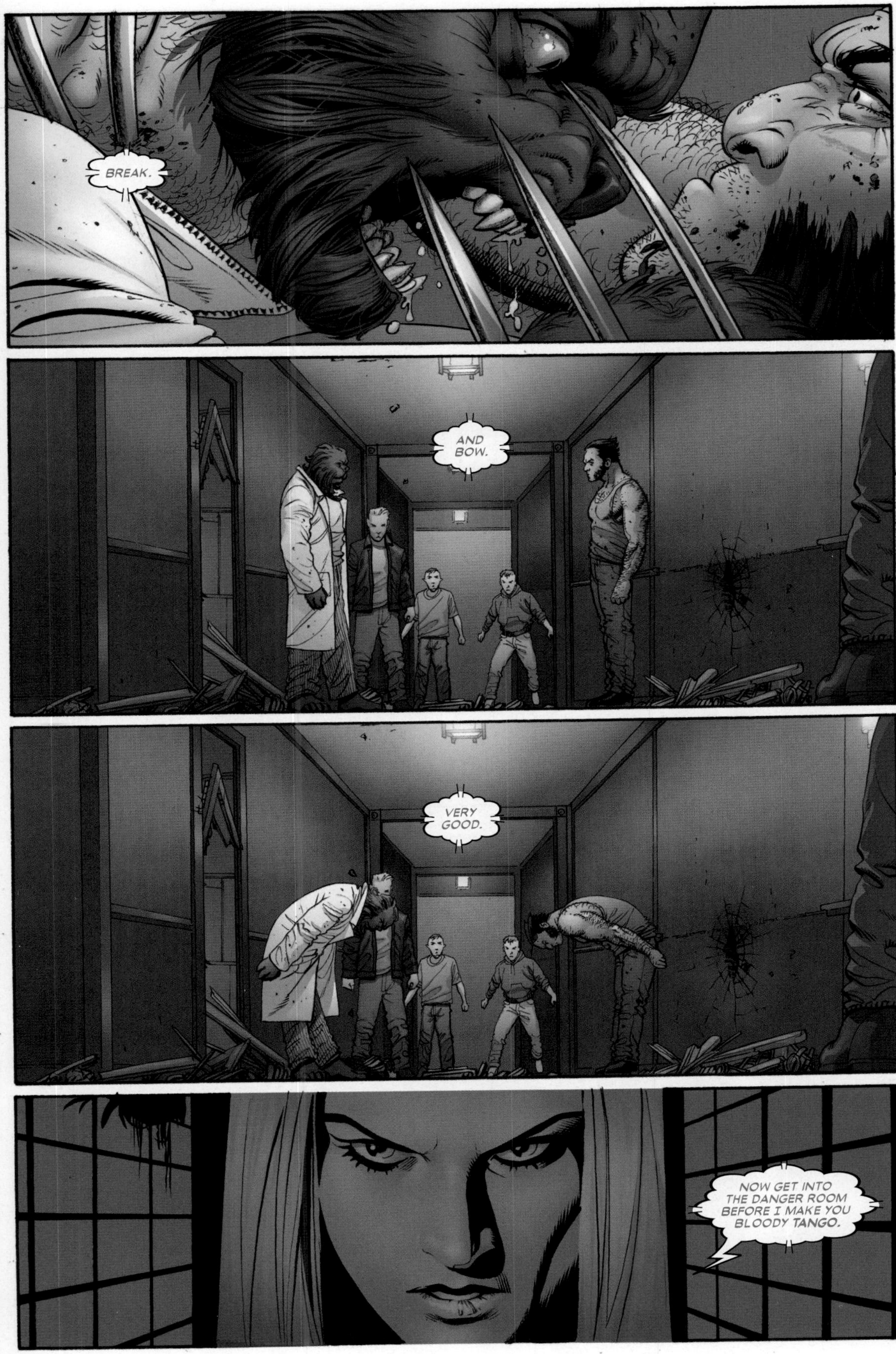
BREAK.
AND BOW.
VERY GOOD.
NOW GET INTO THE DANGER ROOM BEFORE I MAKE YOU BLOODY TANGO.

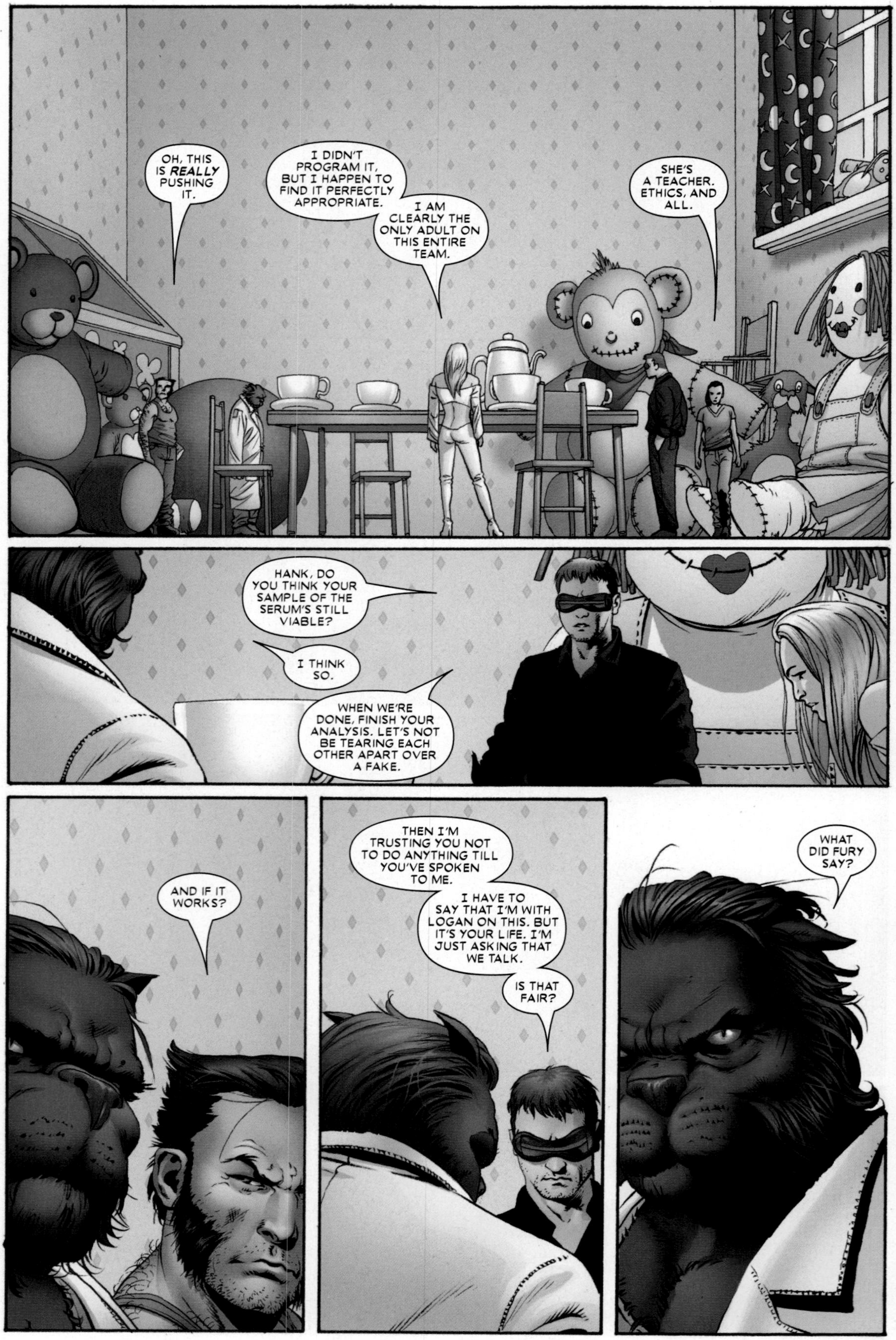
OH, THIS IS *REALLY* PUSHING IT.
I DIDN'T PROGRAM IT, BUT I HAPPEN TO FIND IT PERFECTLY APPROPRIATE.
I AM CLEARLY THE ONLY ADULT ON THIS ENTIRE TEAM.
SHE'S A TEACHER. ETHICS, AND ALL.
HANK, DO YOU THINK YOUR SAMPLE OF THE SERUM'S STILL VIABLE?
I THINK SO.
WHEN WE'RE DONE, FINISH YOUR ANALYSIS. LET'S NOT BE TEARING EACH OTHER APART OVER A FAKE.
AND IF IT WORKS?
THEN I'M TRUSTING YOU NOT TO DO ANYTHING TILL YOU'VE SPOKEN TO ME.
I HAVE TO SAY THAT I'M WITH LOGAN ON THIS. BUT IT'S YOUR LIFE. I'M JUST ASKING THAT WE TALK.
IS THAT FAIR?
WHAT DID FURY SAY?

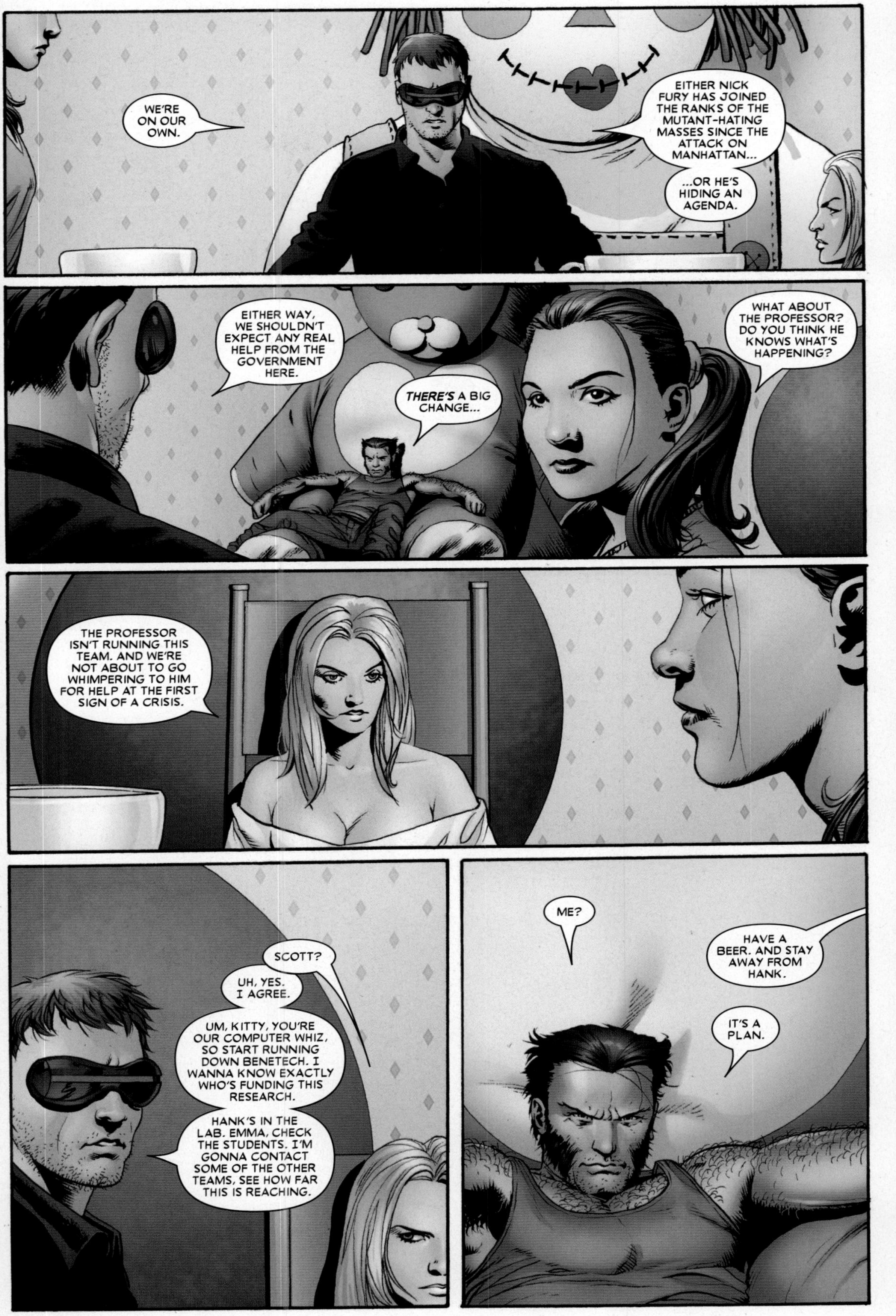
WE'RE ON OUR OWN.
EITHER NICK FURY HAS JOINED THE RANKS OF THE MUTANT-HATING MASSES SINCE THE ATTACK ON MANHATTAN...
...OR HE'S HIDING AN AGENDA.
EITHER WAY, WE SHOULDN'T EXPECT ANY REAL HELP FROM THE GOVERNMENT HERE.
THERE'S A BIG CHANGE...
WHAT ABOUT THE PROFESSOR? DO YOU THINK HE KNOWS WHAT'S HAPPENING?
THE PROFESSOR ISN'T RUNNING THIS TEAM. AND WE'RE NOT ABOUT TO GO WHIMPERING TO HIM FOR HELP AT THE FIRST SIGN OF A CRISIS.
SCOTT?
UH, YES. I AGREE.
UM, KITTY, YOU'RE OUR COMPUTER WHIZ, SO START RUNNING DOWN BENETECH. I WANNA KNOW EXACTLY WHO'S FUNDING THIS RESEARCH.
HANK'S IN THE LAB. EMMA, CHECK THE STUDENTS. I'M GONNA CONTACT SOME OF THE OTHER TEAMS, SEE HOW FAR THIS IS REACHING.
ME?
HAVE A BEER. AND STAY AWAY FROM HANK.
IT'S A PLAN.

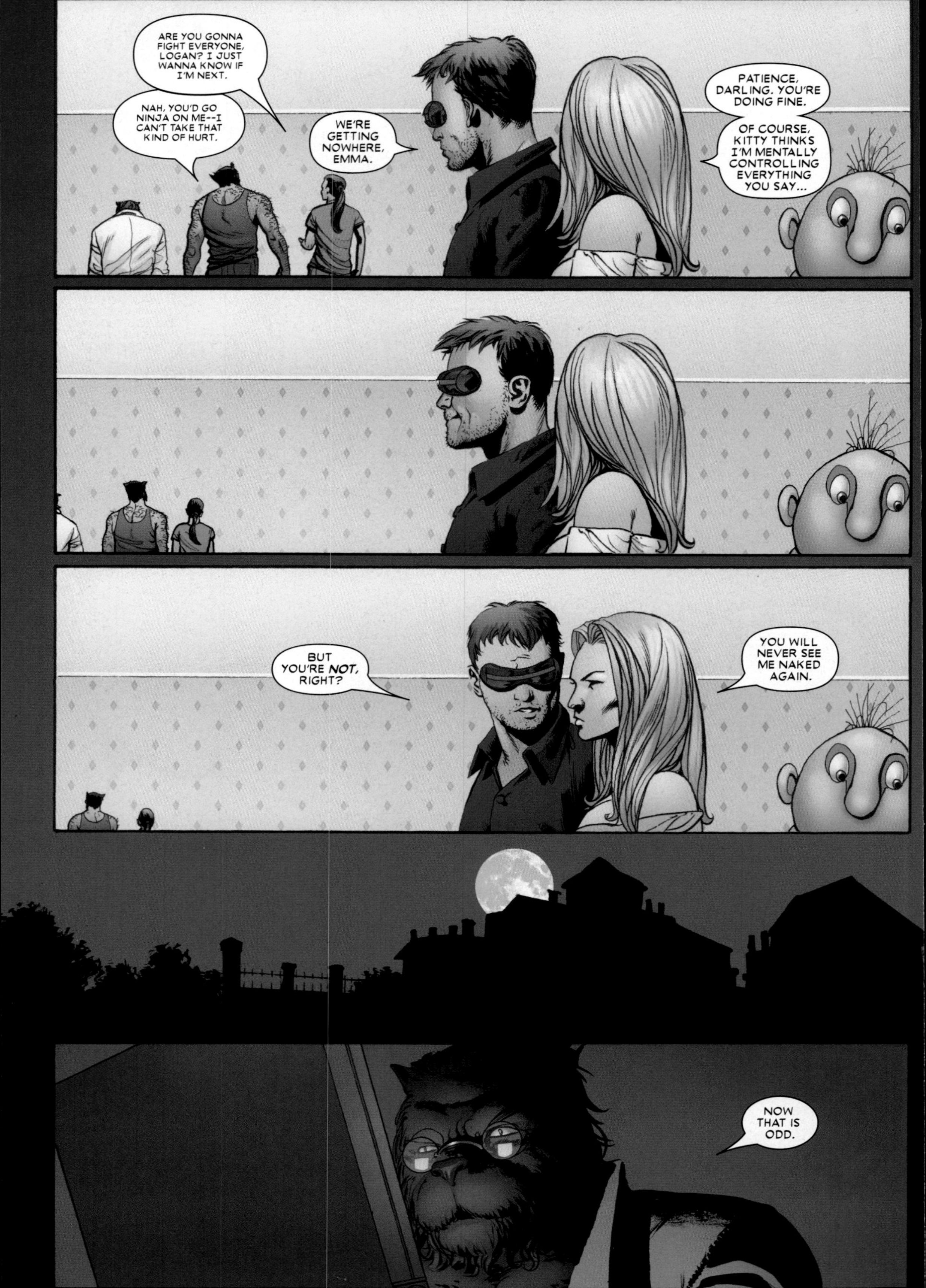

ARE YOU GONNA FIGHT EVERYONE, LOGAN? I JUST WANNA KNOW IF I'M NEXT.
NAH, YOU'D GO NINJA ON ME--I CAN'T TAKE THAT KIND OF HURT.
WE'RE GETTING NOWHERE, EMMA.
PATIENCE, DARLING. YOU'RE DOING FINE.
OF COURSE, KITTY THINKS I'M MENTALLY CONTROLLING EVERYTHING YOU SAY...
BUT YOU'RE NOT, RIGHT?
YOU WILL NEVER SEE ME NAKED AGAIN.
NOW THAT IS ODD.

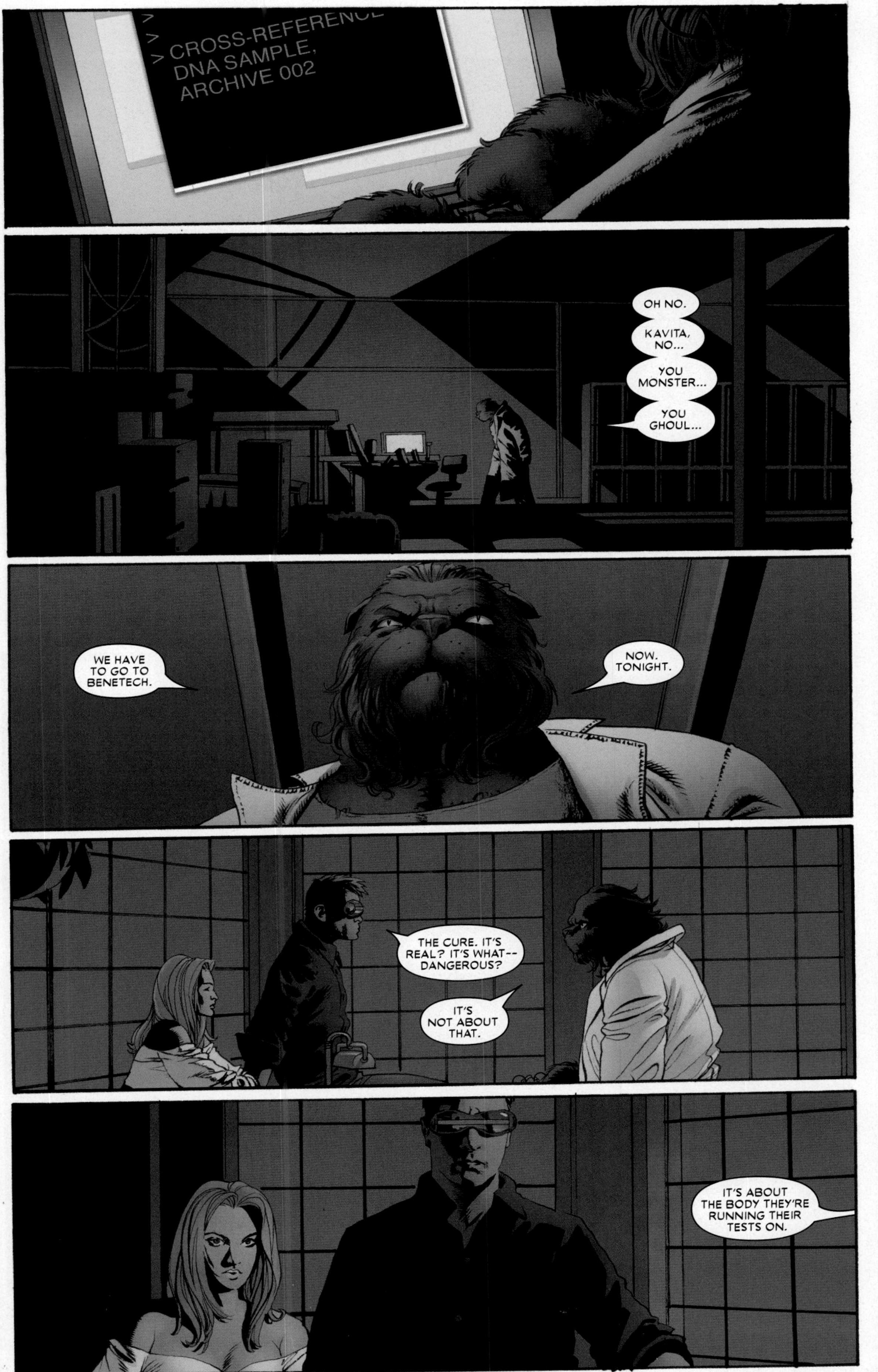
>
>
> CROSS-REFERENCE
DNA SAMPLE,
ARCHIVE 002
OH NO.
KAVITA, NO...
YOU MONSTER...
YOU GHOUL...
WE HAVE TO GO TO BENETECH.
NOW. TONIGHT.
THE CURE. IT'S REAL? IT'S WHAT-- DANGEROUS?
IT'S NOT ABOUT THAT.
IT'S ABOUT THE BODY THEY'RE RUNNING THEIR TESTS ON.

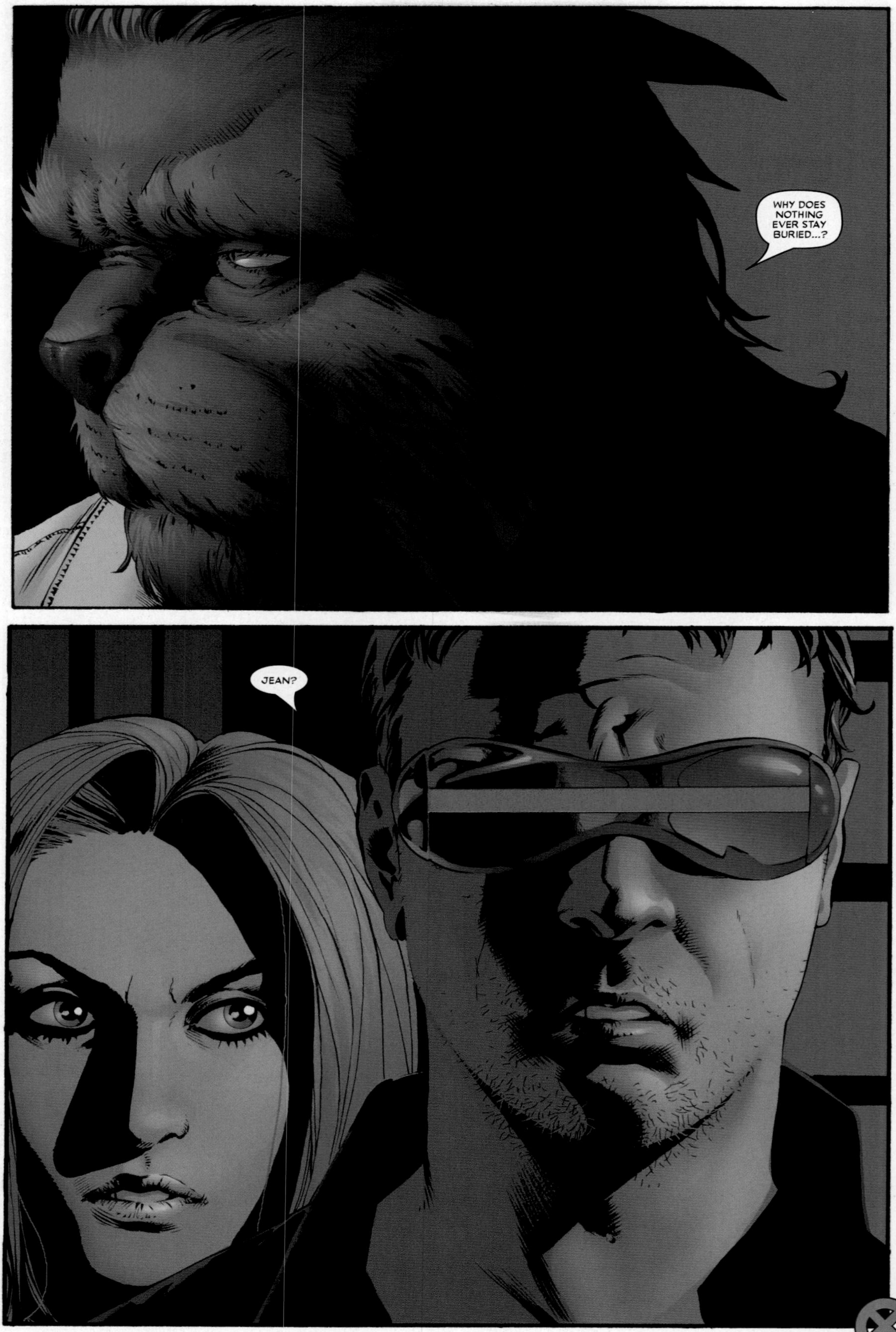
WHY DOES NOTHING EVER STAY BURIED...?
JEAN?

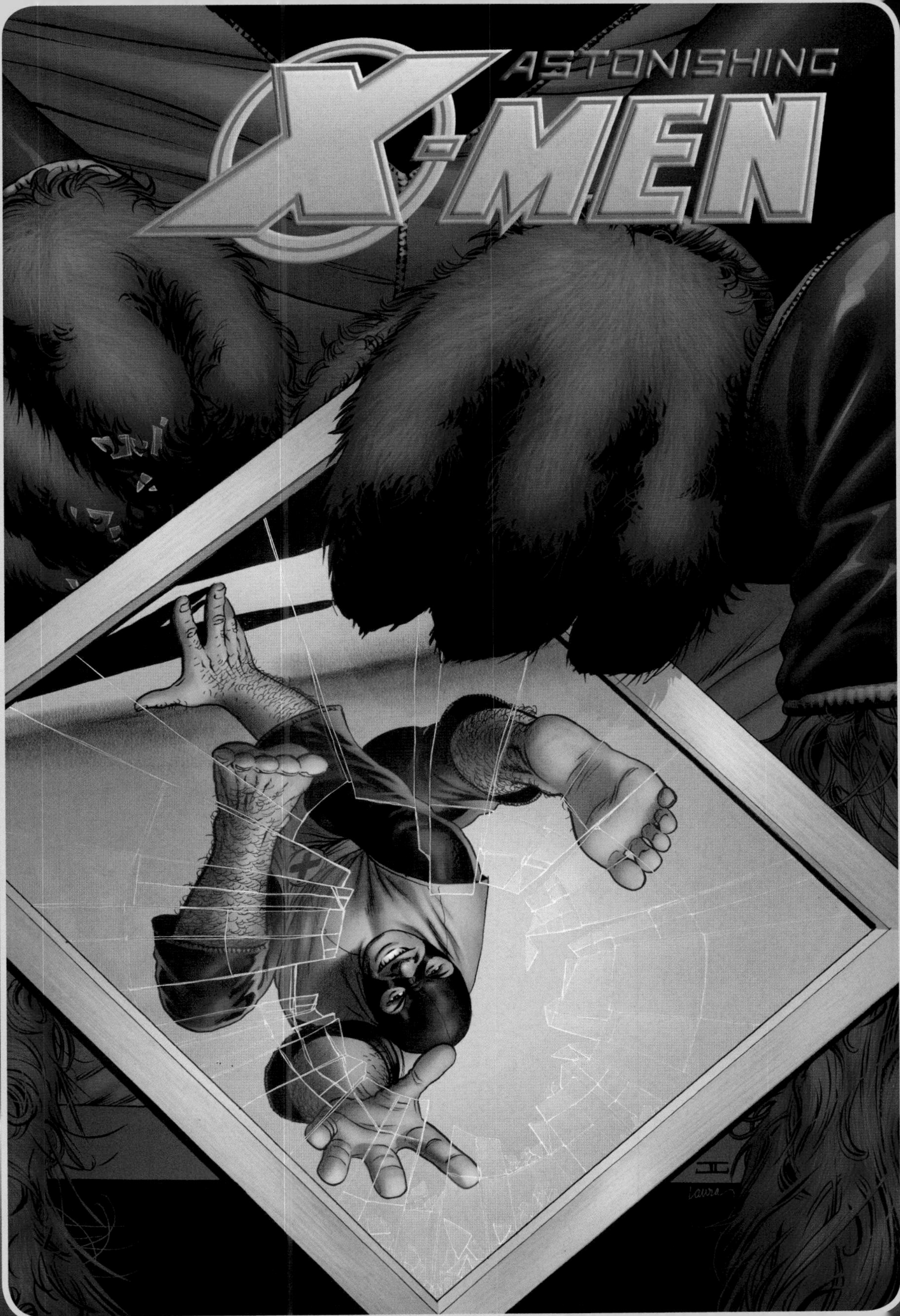
ASTONISHING
X-MEN

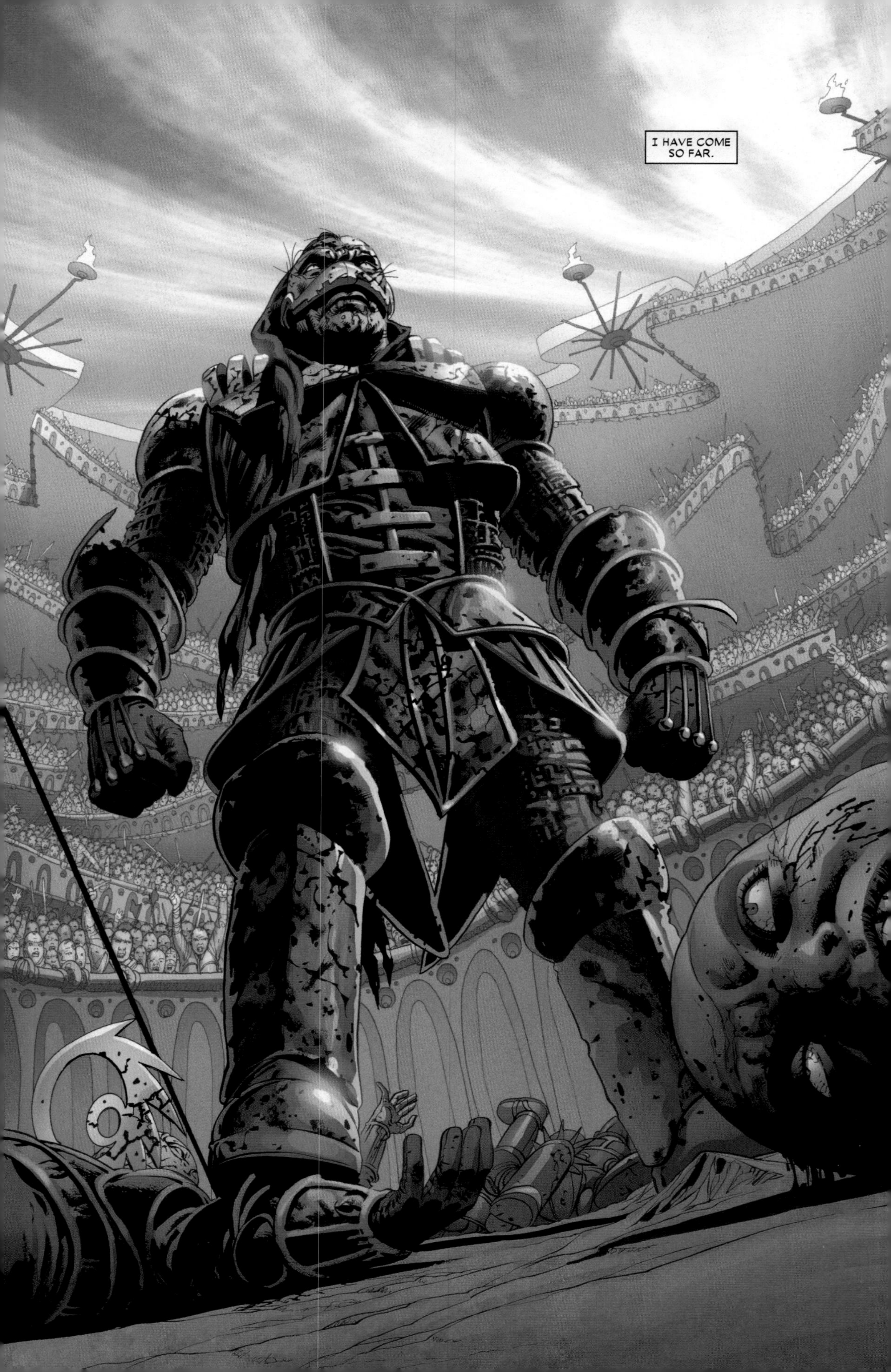
I HAVE COME SO FAR.

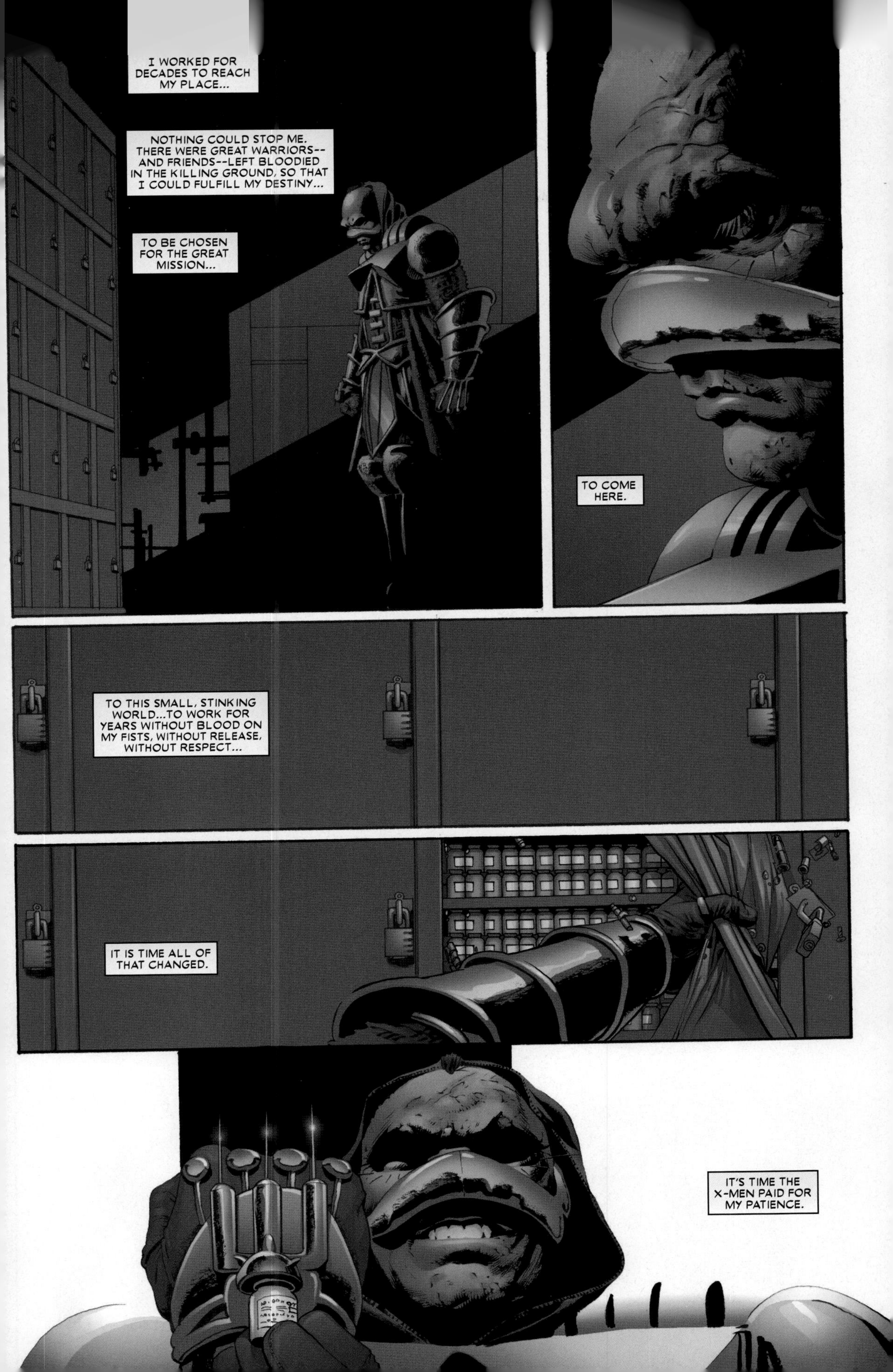

I WORKED FOR DECADES TO REACH MY PLACE...
NOTHING COULD STOP ME. THERE WERE GREAT WARRIORS-- AND FRIENDS--LEFT BLOODIED IN THE KILLING GROUND, SO THAT I COULD FULFILL MY DESTINY...
TO BE CHOSEN FOR THE GREAT MISSION...
TO COME HERE.
TO THIS SMALL, STINKING WORLD...TO WORK FOR YEARS WITHOUT BLOOD ON MY FISTS, WITHOUT RELEASE, WITHOUT RESPECT...
IT IS TIME ALL OF THAT CHANGED.
IT'S TIME THE X-MEN PAID FOR MY PATIENCE.

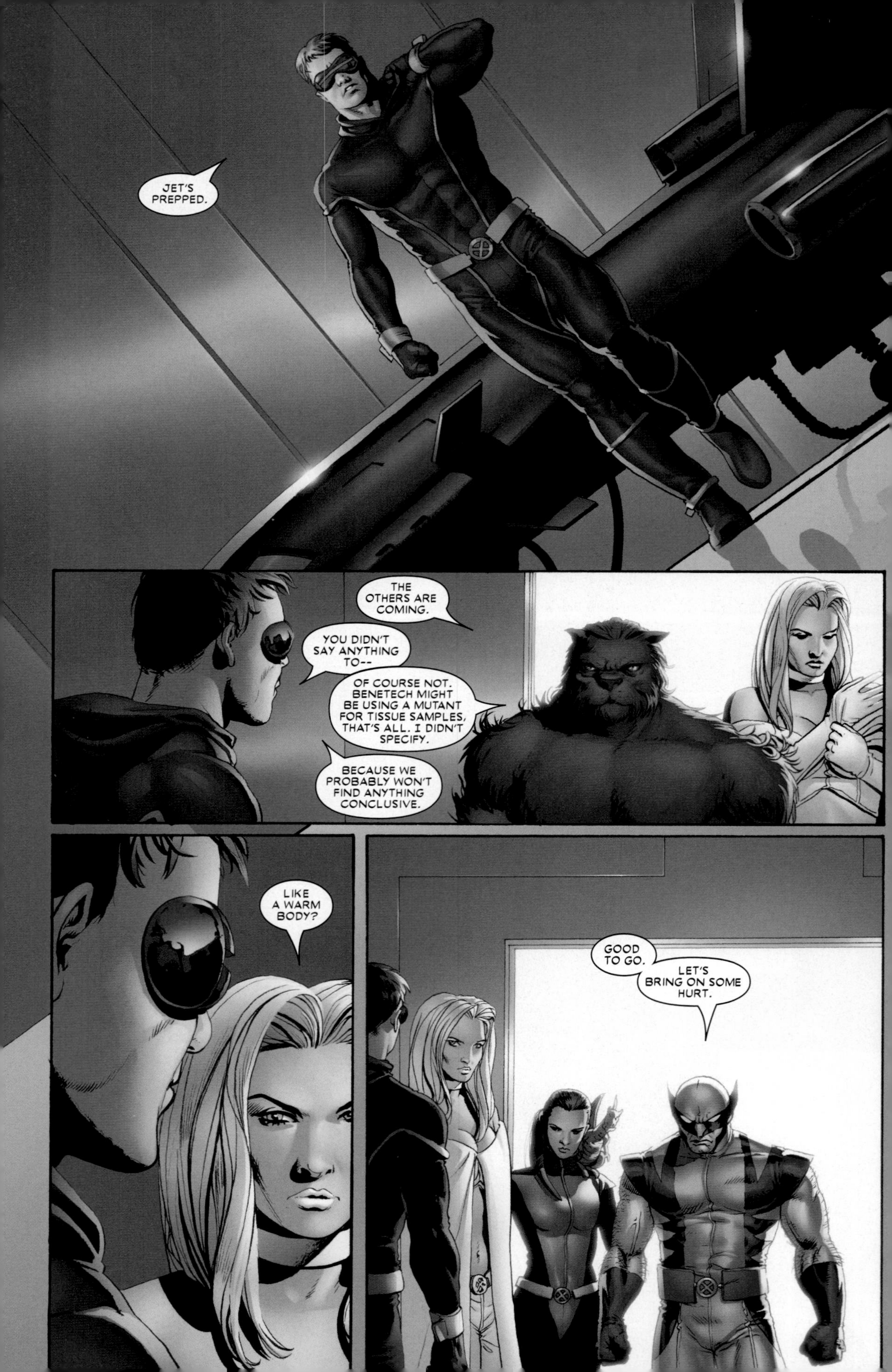
JET'S PREPPED.
THE OTHERS ARE COMING.
YOU DIDN'T SAY ANYTHING TO--
OF COURSE NOT. BENETECH MIGHT BE USING A MUTANT FOR TISSUE SAMPLES, THAT'S ALL. I DIDN'T SPECIFY.
BECAUSE WE PROBABLY WON'T FIND ANYTHING CONCLUSIVE.
LIKE A WARM BODY?
GOOD TO GO.
LET'S BRING ON SOME HURT.

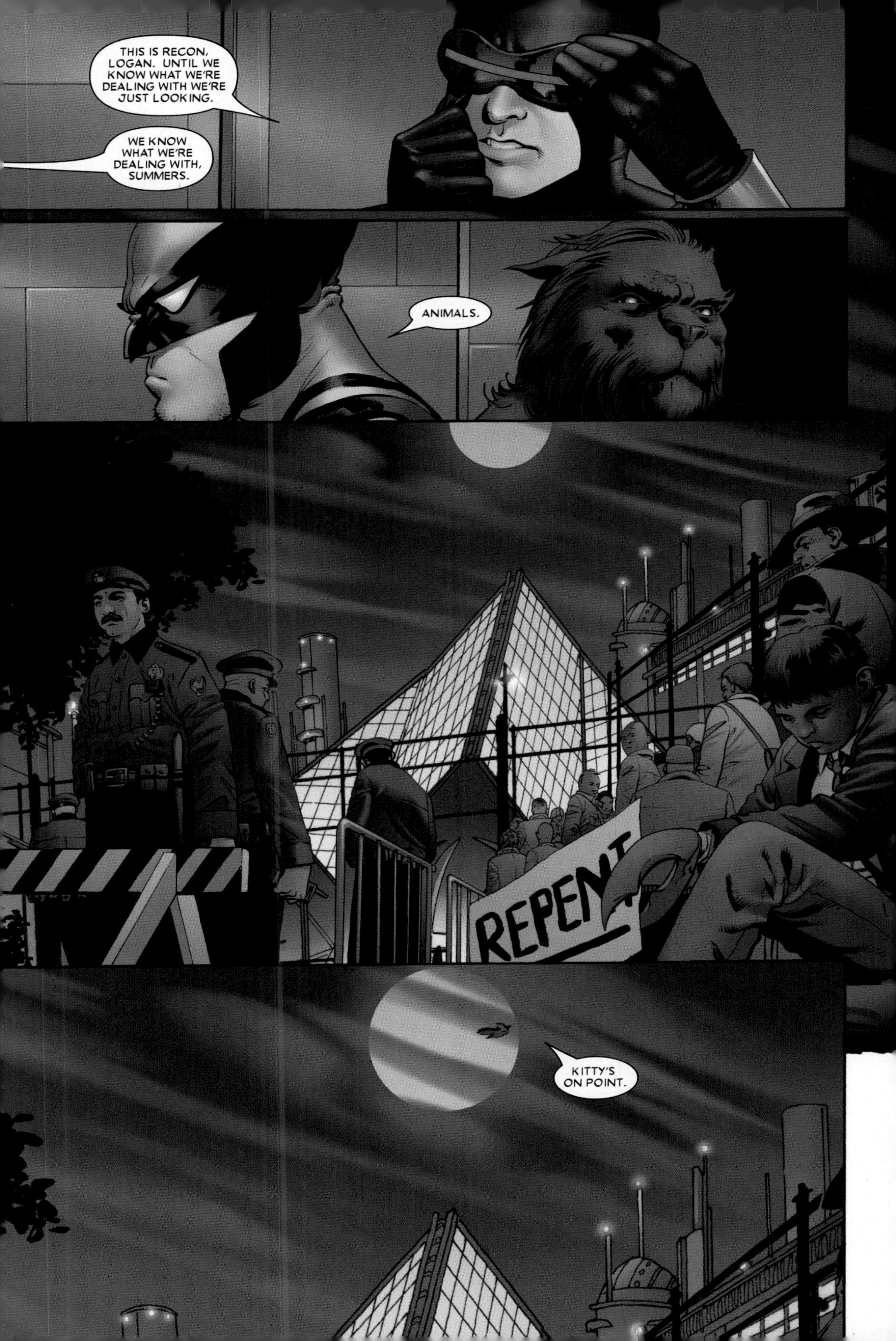
THIS IS RECON, LOGAN. UNTIL WE KNOW WHAT WE'RE DEALING WITH WE'RE JUST LOOKING.
WE KNOW WHAT WE'RE DEALING WITH, SUMMERS.
ANIMALS.
REPENT
KITTY'S ON POINT.

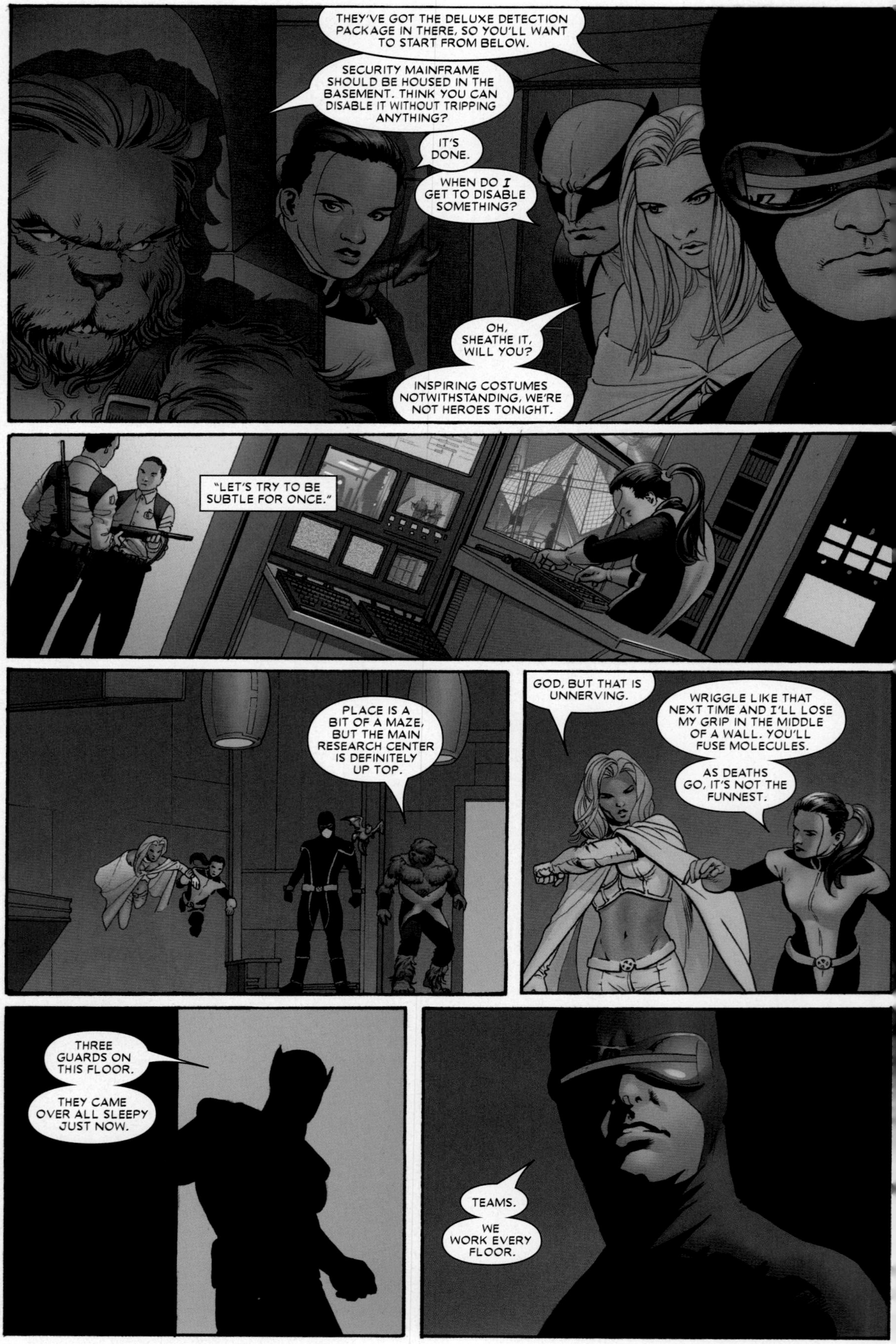
THEY'VE GOT THE DELUXE DETECTION PACKAGE IN THERE, SO YOU'LL WANT TO START FROM BELOW.
SECURITY MAINFRAME SHOULD BE HOUSED IN THE BASEMENT. THINK YOU CAN DISABLE IT WITHOUT TRIPPING ANYTHING?
IT'S DONE.
WHEN DO *I* GET TO DISABLE SOMETHING?
OH, SHEATHE IT, WILL YOU?
INSPIRING COSTUMES NOTWITHSTANDING, WE'RE NOT HEROES TONIGHT.
"LET'S TRY TO BE SUBTLE FOR ONCE."
PLACE IS A BIT OF A MAZE, BUT THE MAIN RESEARCH CENTER IS DEFINITELY UP TOP.
GOD, BUT THAT IS UNNERVING.
WRIGGLE LIKE THAT NEXT TIME AND I'LL LOSE MY GRIP IN THE MIDDLE OF A WALL. YOU'LL FUSE MOLECULES.
AS DEATHS GO, IT'S NOT THE FUNNEST.
THREE GUARDS ON THIS FLOOR.
THEY CAME OVER ALL SLEEPY JUST NOW.
TEAMS.
WE WORK EVERY FLOOR.

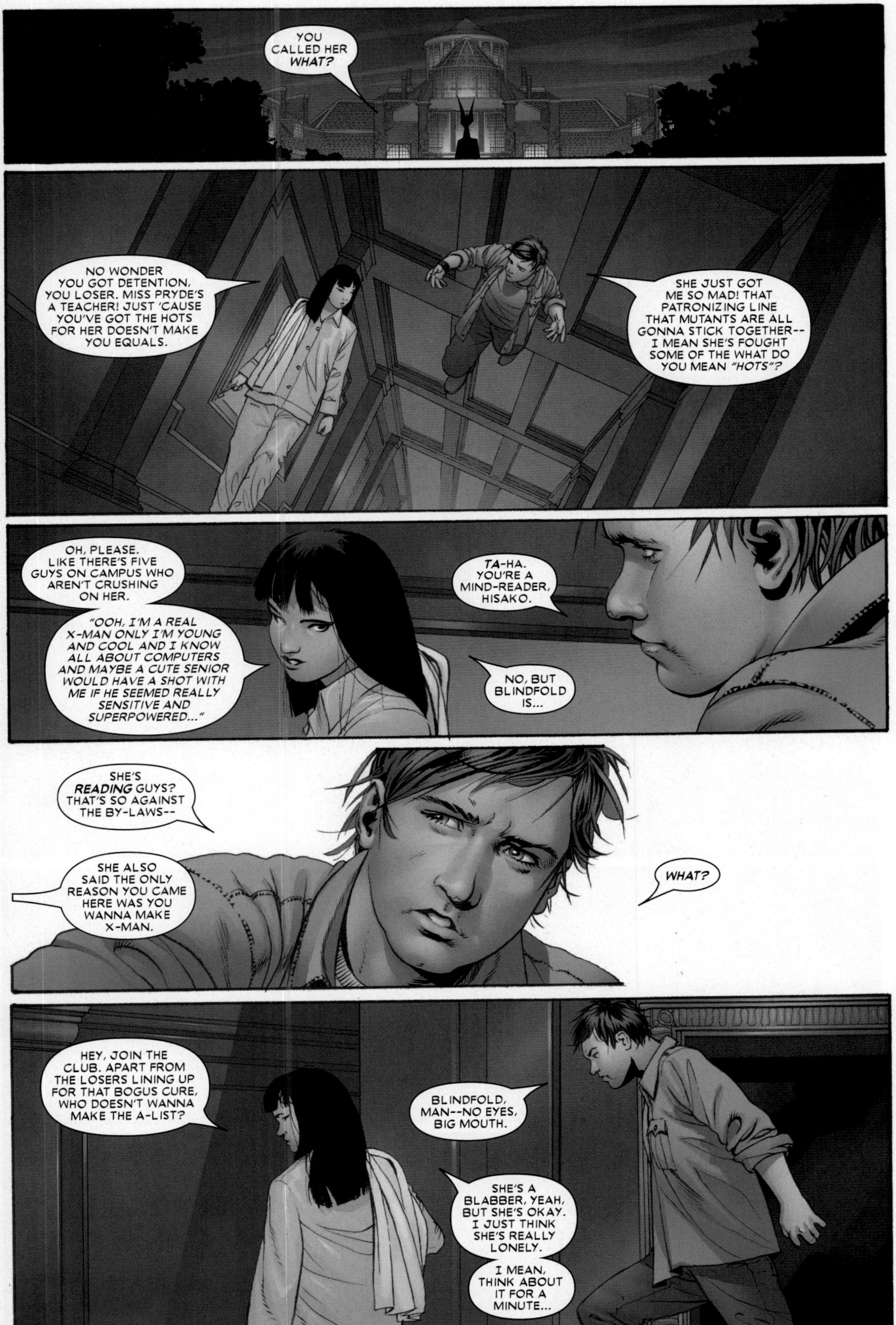
YOU CALLED HER *WHAT?*
NO WONDER YOU GOT DETENTION, YOU LOSER. MISS PRYDE'S A TEACHER! JUST 'CAUSE YOU'VE GOT THE HOTS FOR HER DOESN'T MAKE YOU EQUALS.
SHE JUST GOT ME SO MAD! THAT PATRONIZING LINE THAT MUTANTS ARE ALL GONNA STICK TOGETHER-- I MEAN SHE'S FOUGHT SOME OF THE WHAT DO YOU MEAN *"HOTS"*?
OH, PLEASE. LIKE THERE'S FIVE GUYS ON CAMPUS WHO AREN'T CRUSHING ON HER.
"OOH, I'M A REAL X-MAN ONLY I'M YOUNG AND COOL AND I KNOW ALL ABOUT COMPUTERS AND MAYBE A CUTE SENIOR WOULD HAVE A SHOT WITH ME IF HE SEEMED REALLY SENSITIVE AND SUPERPOWERED..."
TA-HA. YOU'RE A MIND-READER, HISAKO.
NO, BUT BLINDFOLD IS...
SHE'S *READING* GUYS? THAT'S SO AGAINST THE BY-LAWS--
SHE ALSO SAID THE ONLY REASON YOU CAME HERE WAS YOU WANNA MAKE X-MAN.
WHAT?
HEY, JOIN THE CLUB. APART FROM THE LOSERS LINING UP FOR THAT BOGUS CURE, WHO DOESN'T WANNA MAKE THE A-LIST?
BLINDFOLD, MAN--NO EYES, BIG MOUTH.
SHE'S A BLABBER, YEAH, BUT SHE'S OKAY. I JUST THINK SHE'S REALLY LONELY.
I MEAN, THINK ABOUT IT FOR A MINUTE...

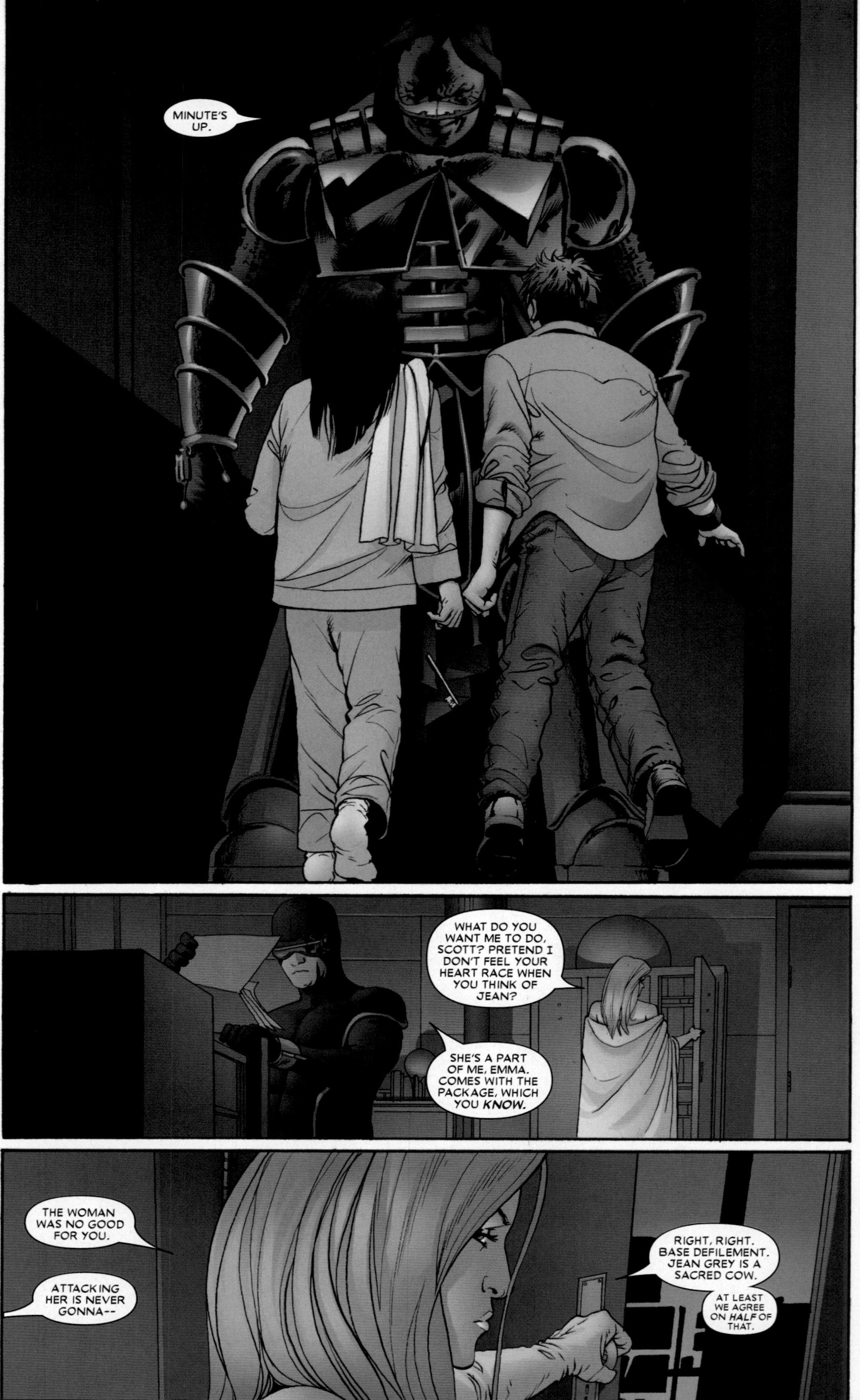
MINUTE'S UP.
WHAT DO YOU WANT ME TO DO, SCOTT? PRETEND I DON'T FEEL YOUR HEART RACE WHEN YOU THINK OF JEAN?
SHE'S A PART OF ME, EMMA. COMES WITH THE PACKAGE, WHICH YOU KNOW.
THE WOMAN WAS NO GOOD FOR YOU.
ATTACKING HER IS NEVER GONNA--
RIGHT, RIGHT. BASE DEFILEMENT. JEAN GREY IS A SACRED COW.
AT LEAST WE AGREE ON HALF OF THAT.

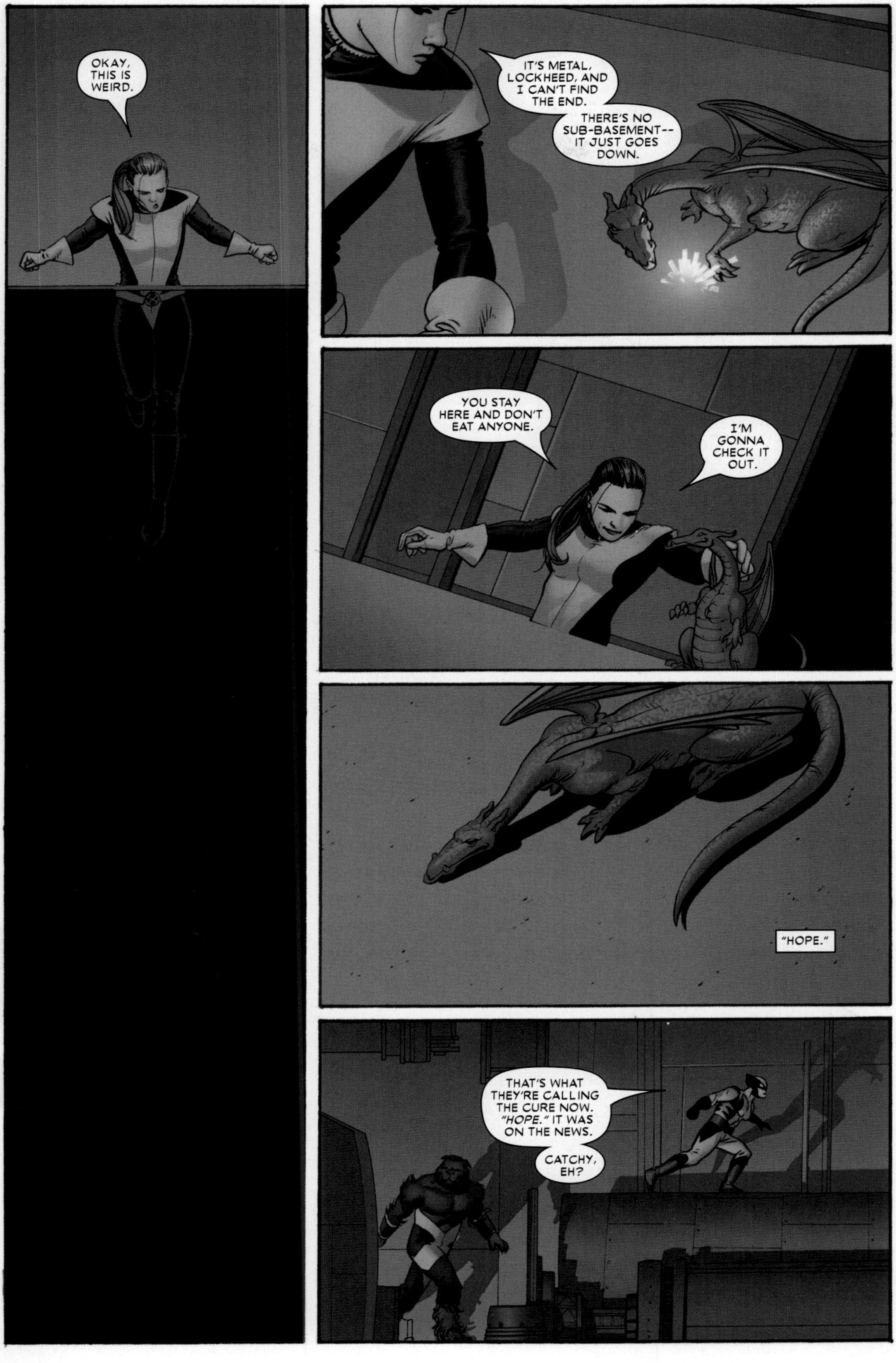
OKAY, THIS IS WEIRD.
IT'S METAL, LOCKHEED, AND I CAN'T FIND THE END.
THERE'S NO SUB-BASEMENT-- IT JUST GOES DOWN.
YOU STAY HERE AND DON'T EAT ANYONE.
I'M GONNA CHECK IT OUT.
"HOPE."
THAT'S WHAT THEY'RE CALLING THE CURE NOW. *"HOPE."* IT WAS ON THE NEWS.
CATCHY, EH?

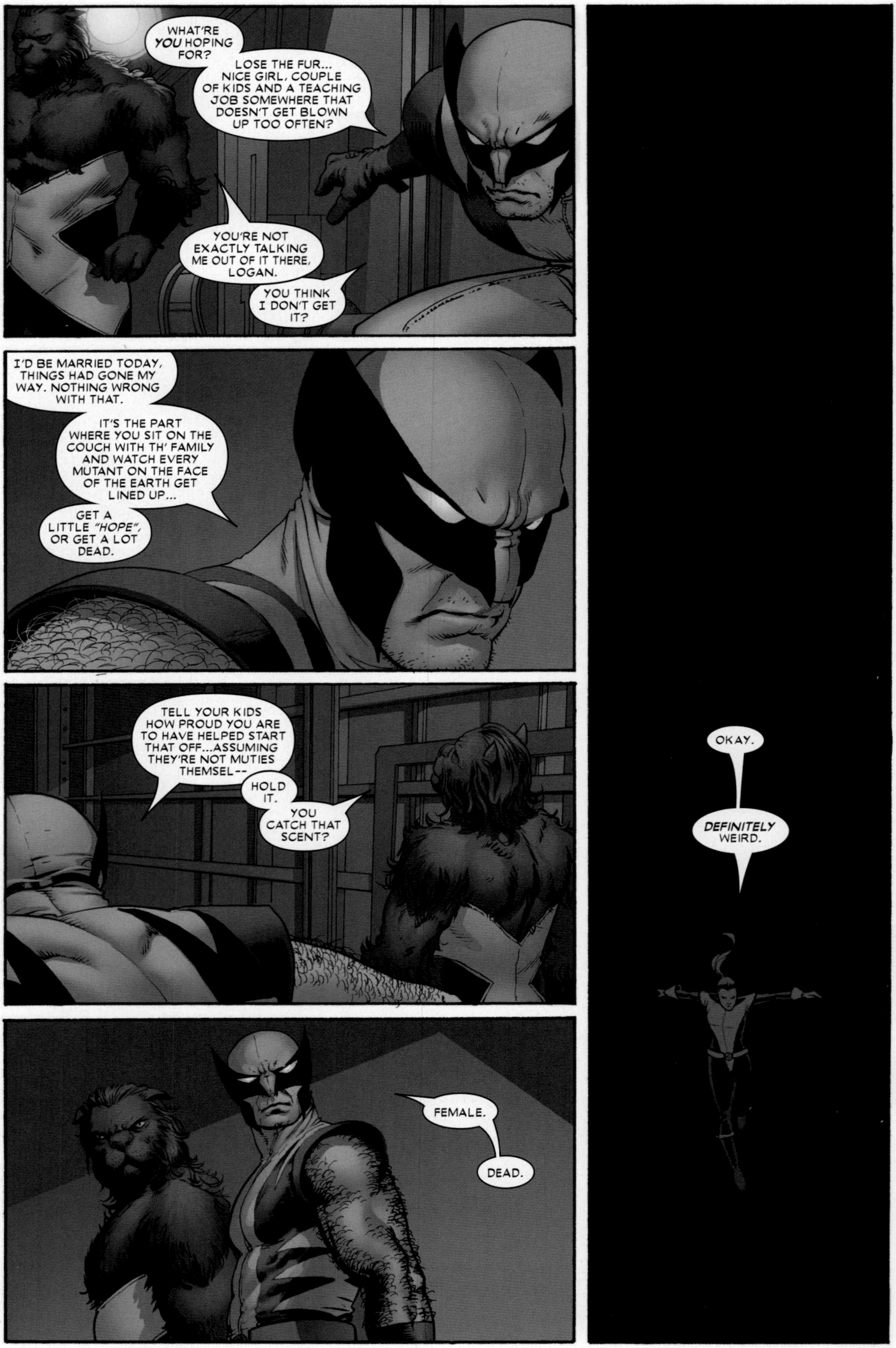
WHAT'RE YOU HOPING FOR?
LOSE THE FUR... NICE GIRL, COUPLE OF KIDS AND A TEACHING JOB SOMEWHERE THAT DOESN'T GET BLOWN UP TOO OFTEN?
YOU'RE NOT EXACTLY TALKING ME OUT OF IT THERE, LOGAN.
YOU THINK I DON'T GET IT?
I'D BE MARRIED TODAY, THINGS HAD GONE MY WAY. NOTHING WRONG WITH THAT.
IT'S THE PART WHERE YOU SIT ON THE COUCH WITH TH' FAMILY AND WATCH EVERY MUTANT ON THE FACE OF THE EARTH GET LINED UP...
GET A LITTLE "HOPE", OR GET A LOT DEAD.
TELL YOUR KIDS HOW PROUD YOU ARE TO HAVE HELPED START THAT OFF...ASSUMING THEY'RE NOT MUTIES THEMSEL--
HOLD IT.
YOU CATCH THAT SCENT?
FEMALE.
DEAD.
OKAY.
DEFINITELY WEIRD.

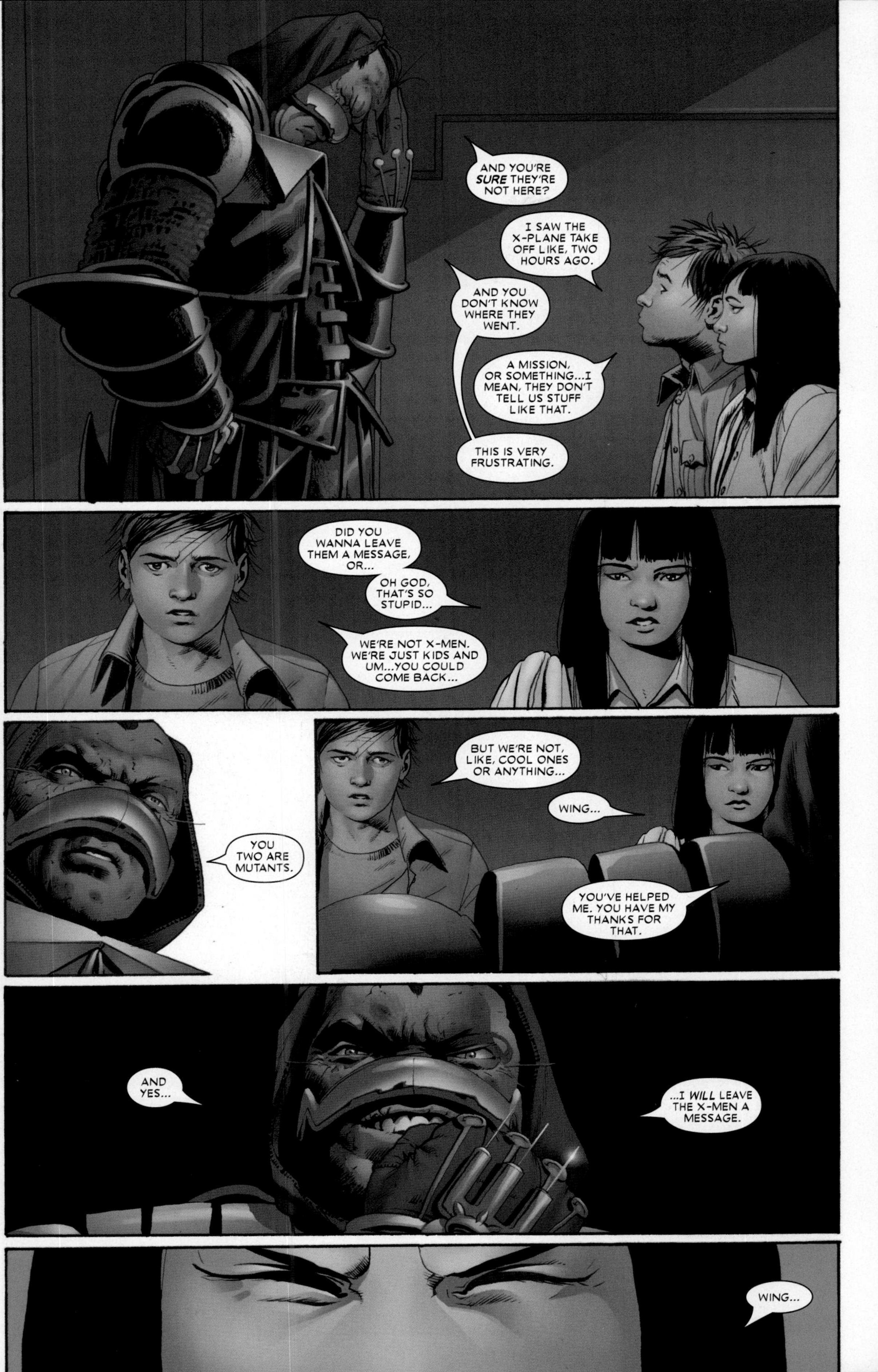
AND YOU'RE SURE THEY'RE NOT HERE?
I SAW THE X-PLANE TAKE OFF LIKE, TWO HOURS AGO.
AND YOU DON'T KNOW WHERE THEY WENT.
A MISSION, OR SOMETHING...I MEAN, THEY DON'T TELL US STUFF LIKE THAT.
THIS IS VERY FRUSTRATING.
DID YOU WANNA LEAVE THEM A MESSAGE, OR...
OH GOD, THAT'S SO STUPID...
WE'RE NOT X-MEN. WE'RE JUST KIDS AND UM...YOU COULD COME BACK...
YOU TWO ARE MUTANTS.
BUT WE'RE NOT, LIKE, COOL ONES OR ANYTHING...
WING...
YOU'VE HELPED ME. YOU HAVE MY THANKS FOR THAT.
AND YES...
...I WILL LEAVE THE X-MEN A MESSAGE.
WING...

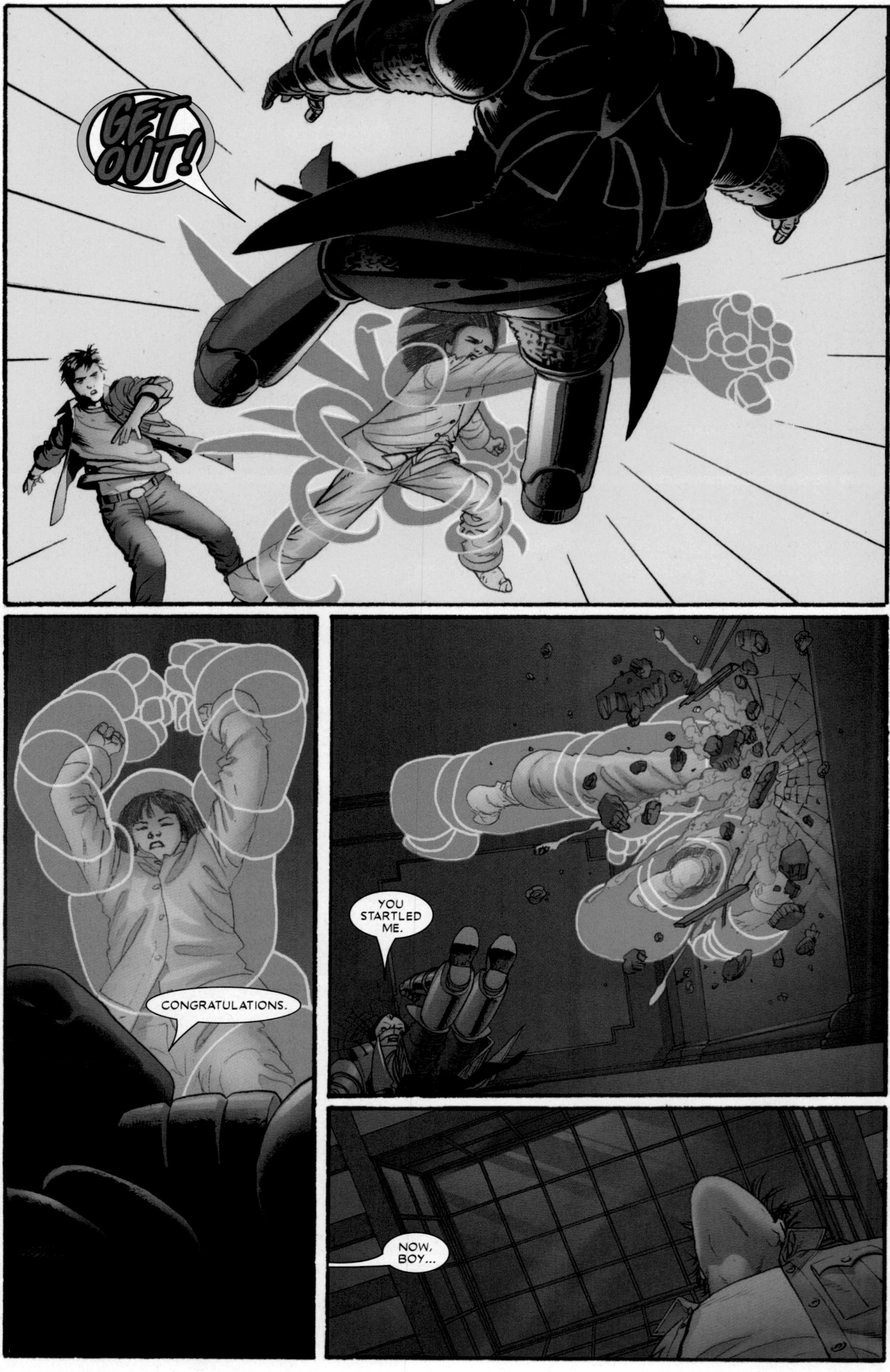
GET OUT!
CONGRATULATIONS.
YOU STARTLED ME.
NOW, BOY...

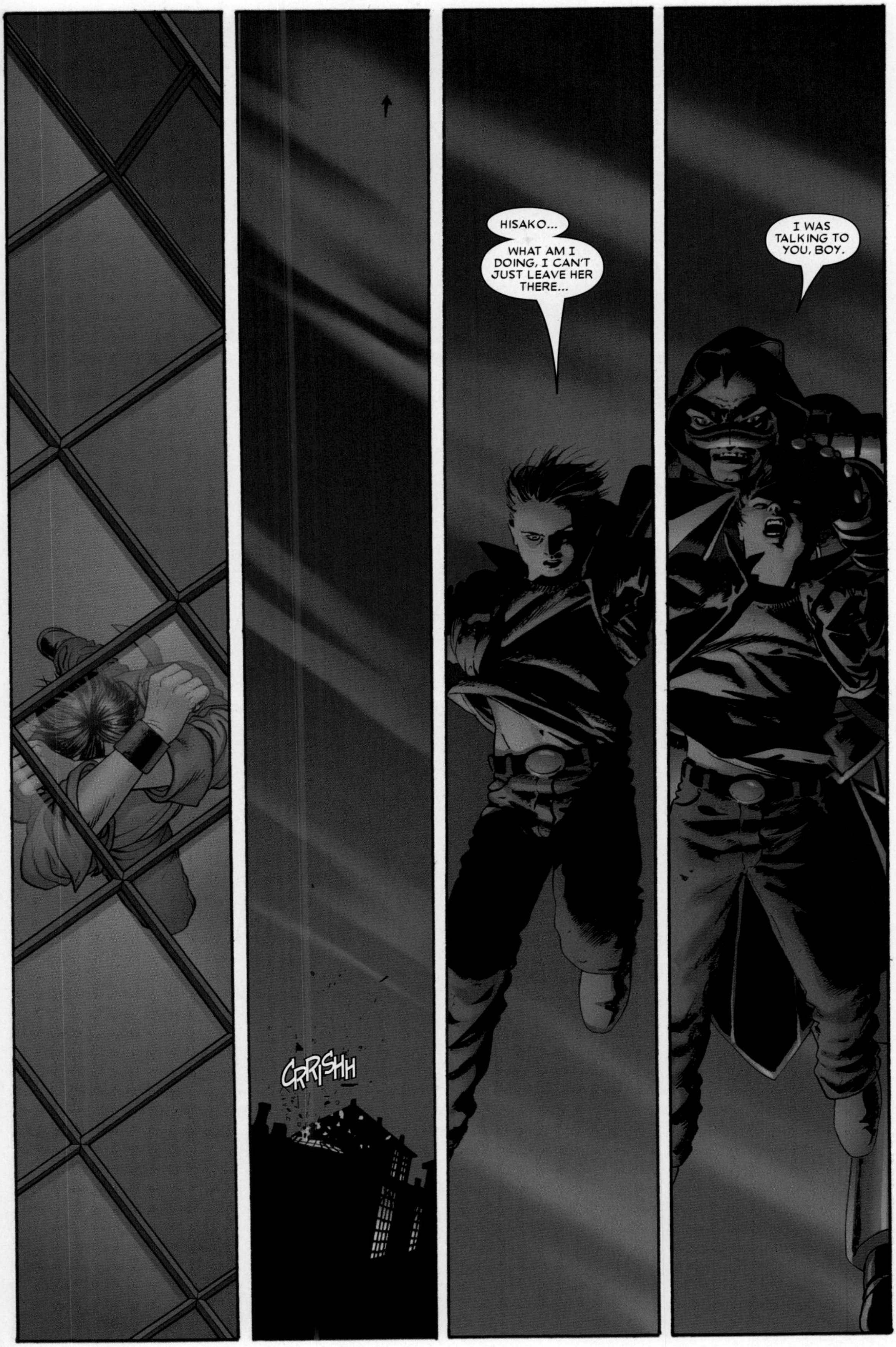
CRRISHH
HISAKO...
WHAT AM I DOING, I CAN'T JUST LEAVE HER THERE...
I WAS TALKING TO YOU, BOY.

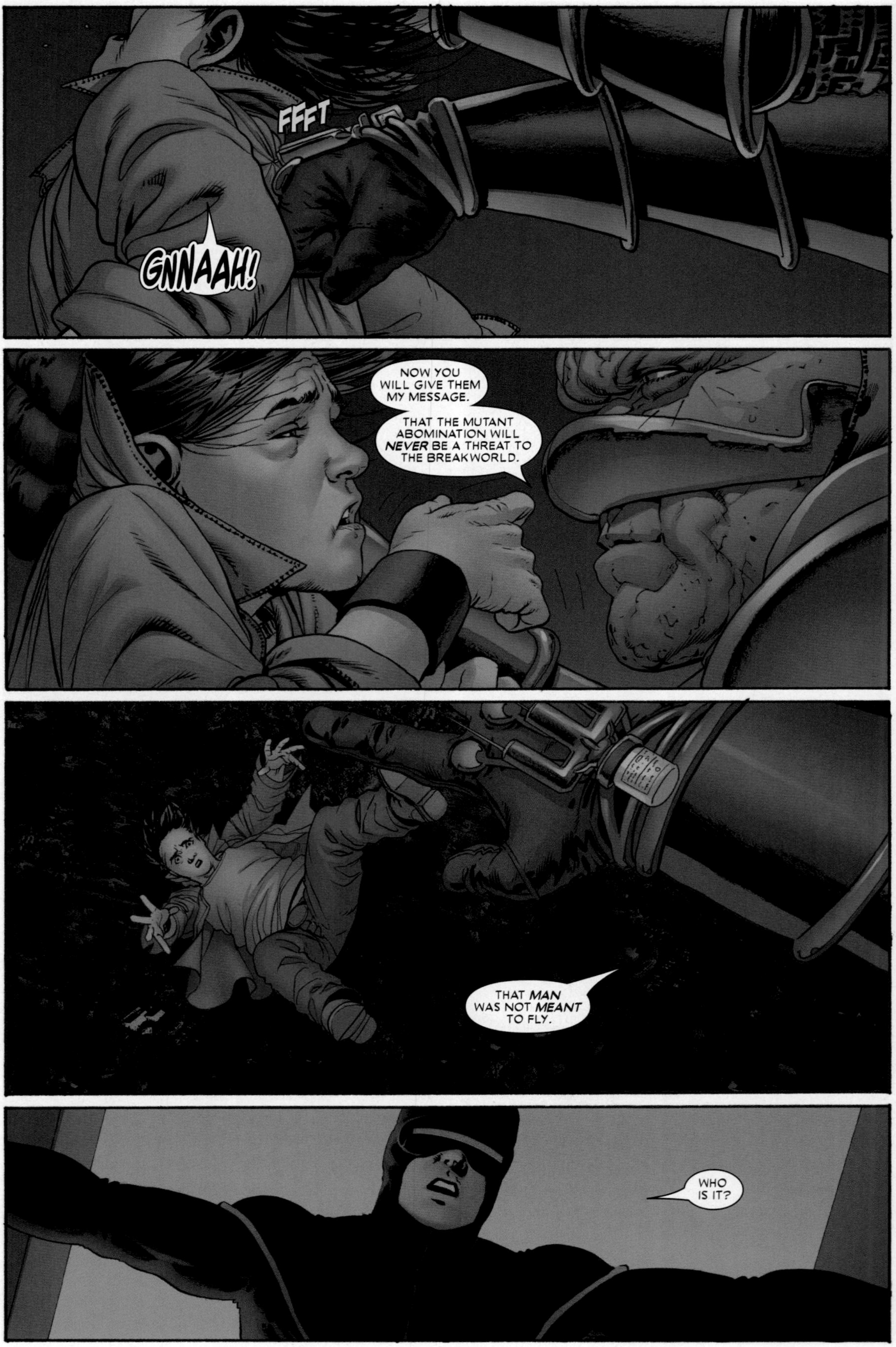
FFFT
GNNAAH!
NOW YOU WILL GIVE THEM MY MESSAGE.
THAT THE MUTANT ABOMINATION WILL NEVER BE A THREAT TO THE BREAKWORLD.
THAT MAN WAS NOT MEANT TO FLY.
WHO IS IT?

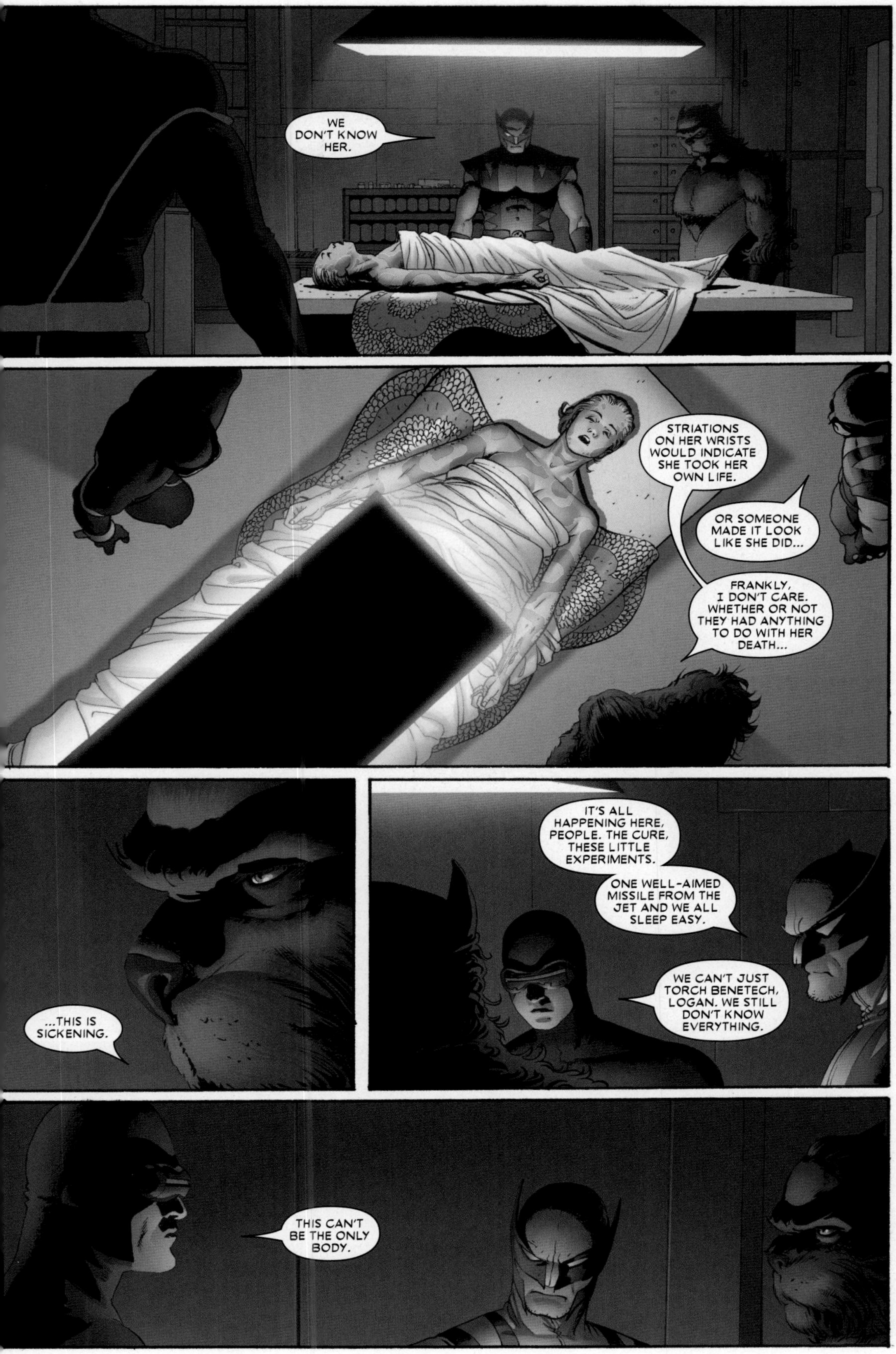
WE DON'T KNOW HER.
STRIATIONS ON HER WRISTS WOULD INDICATE SHE TOOK HER OWN LIFE.
OR SOMEONE MADE IT LOOK LIKE SHE DID...
FRANKLY, I DON'T CARE. WHETHER OR NOT THEY HAD ANYTHING TO DO WITH HER DEATH...
...THIS IS SICKENING.
IT'S ALL HAPPENING HERE, PEOPLE. THE CURE, THESE LITTLE EXPERIMENTS.
ONE WELL-AIMED MISSILE FROM THE JET AND WE ALL SLEEP EASY.
WE CAN'T JUST TORCH BENETECH, LOGAN. WE STILL DON'T KNOW EVERYTHING.
THIS CAN'T BE THE ONLY BODY.

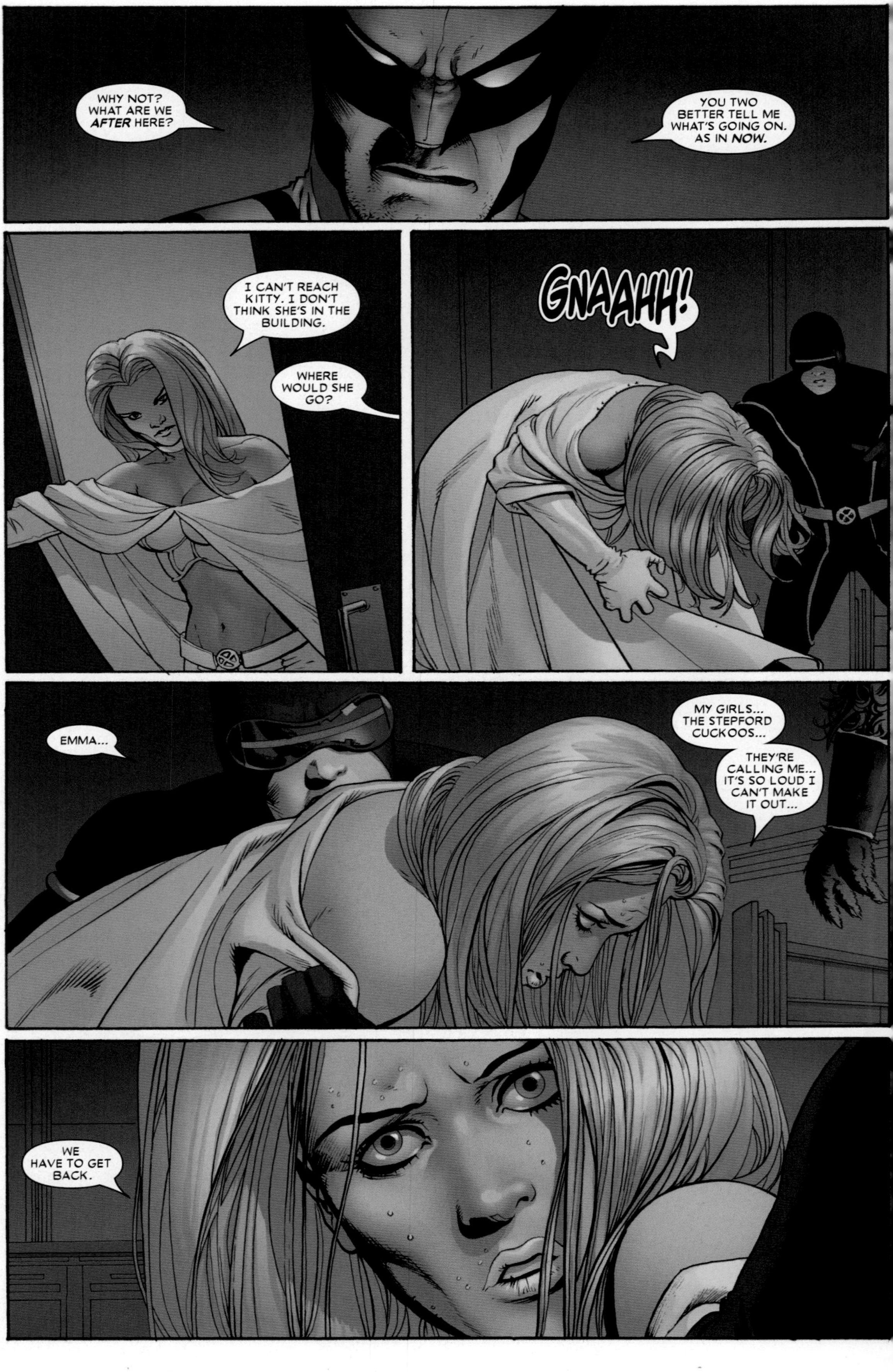
WHY NOT? WHAT ARE WE AFTER HERE?
YOU TWO BETTER TELL ME WHAT'S GOING ON. AS IN NOW.
I CAN'T REACH KITTY. I DON'T THINK SHE'S IN THE BUILDING.
WHERE WOULD SHE GO?
GNAAHH!
EMMA...
MY GIRLS... THE STEPFORD CUCKOOS...
THEY'RE CALLING ME... IT'S SO LOUD I CAN'T MAKE IT OUT...
WE HAVE TO GET BACK.

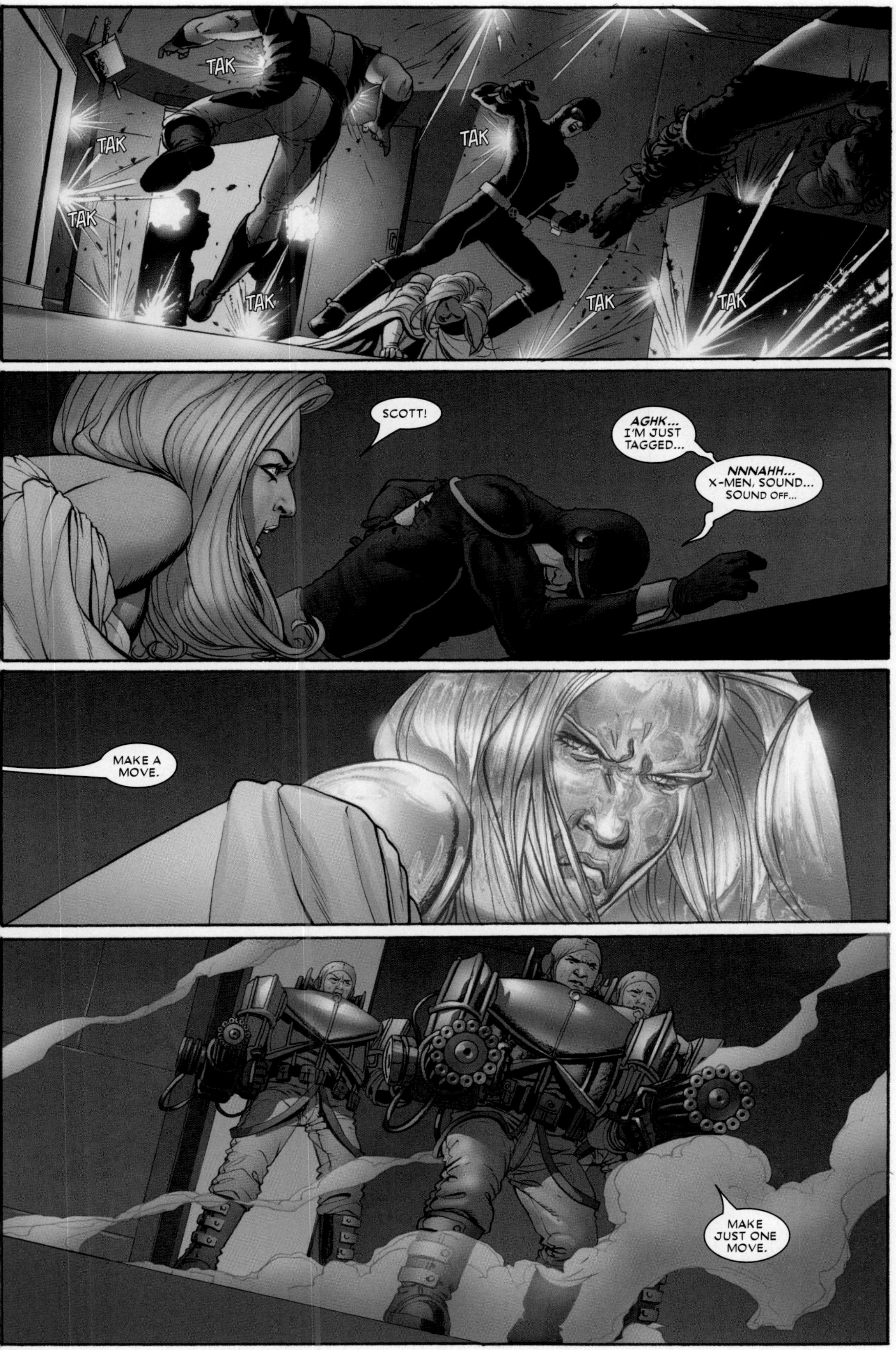
TAK
TAK
TAK
TAK
TAK
TAK
TAK
SCOTT!
AGHK... I'M JUST TAGGED...
NNNAHH... X-MEN, SOUND... SOUND OFF...
MAKE A MOVE.
MAKE JUST ONE MOVE.

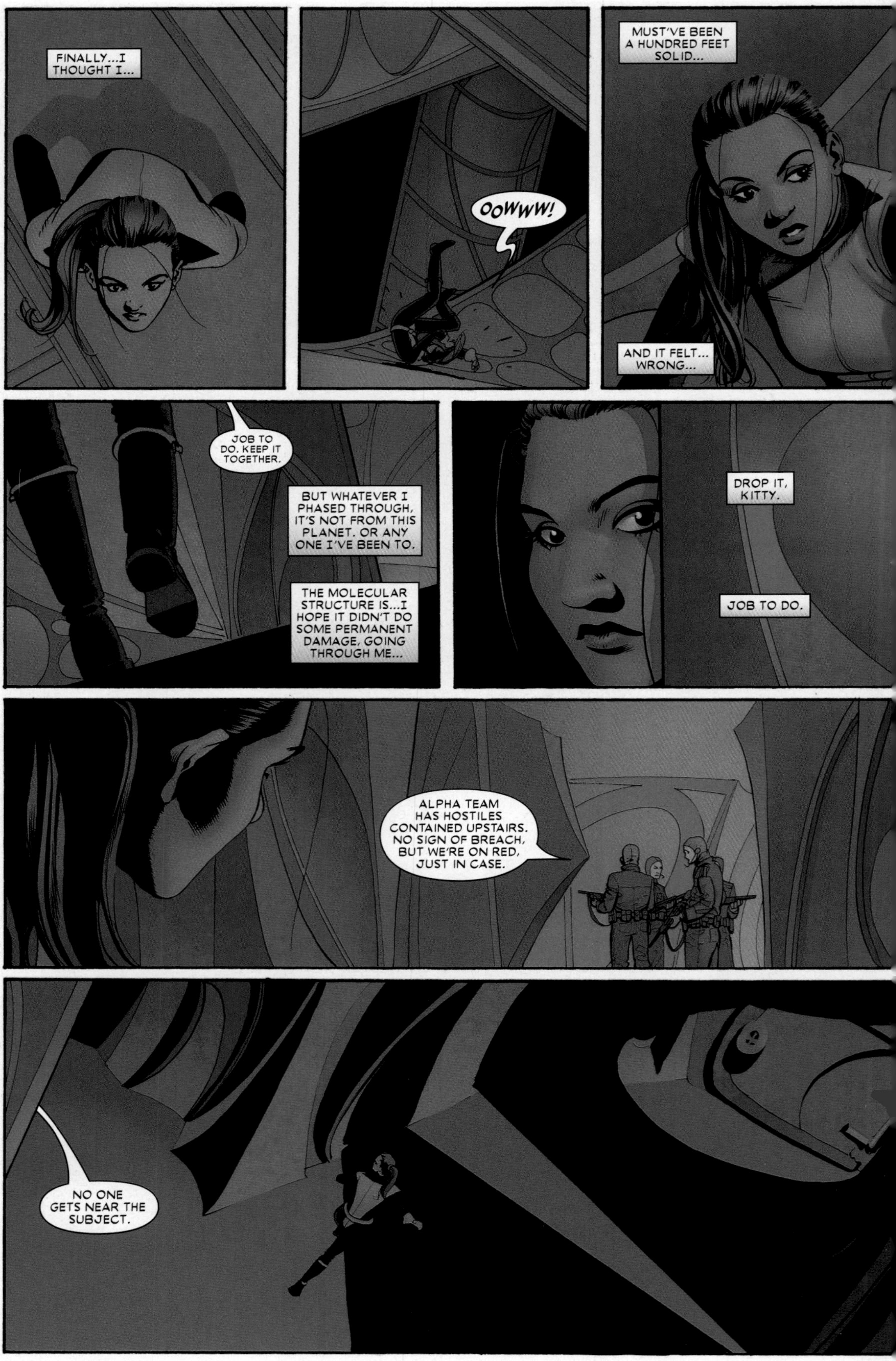

FINALLY...I THOUGHT I...
OOWWW!
MUST'VE BEEN A HUNDRED FEET SOLID...
AND IT FELT... WRONG...
JOB TO DO. KEEP IT TOGETHER.
BUT WHATEVER I PHASED THROUGH, IT'S NOT FROM THIS PLANET. OR ANY ONE I'VE BEEN TO.
THE MOLECULAR STRUCTURE IS...I HOPE IT DIDN'T DO SOME PERMANENT DAMAGE, GOING THROUGH ME...
DROP IT, KITTY.
JOB TO DO.
ALPHA TEAM HAS HOSTILES CONTAINED UPSTAIRS. NO SIGN OF BREACH, BUT WE'RE ON RED, JUST IN CASE.
NO ONE GETS NEAR THE SUBJECT.

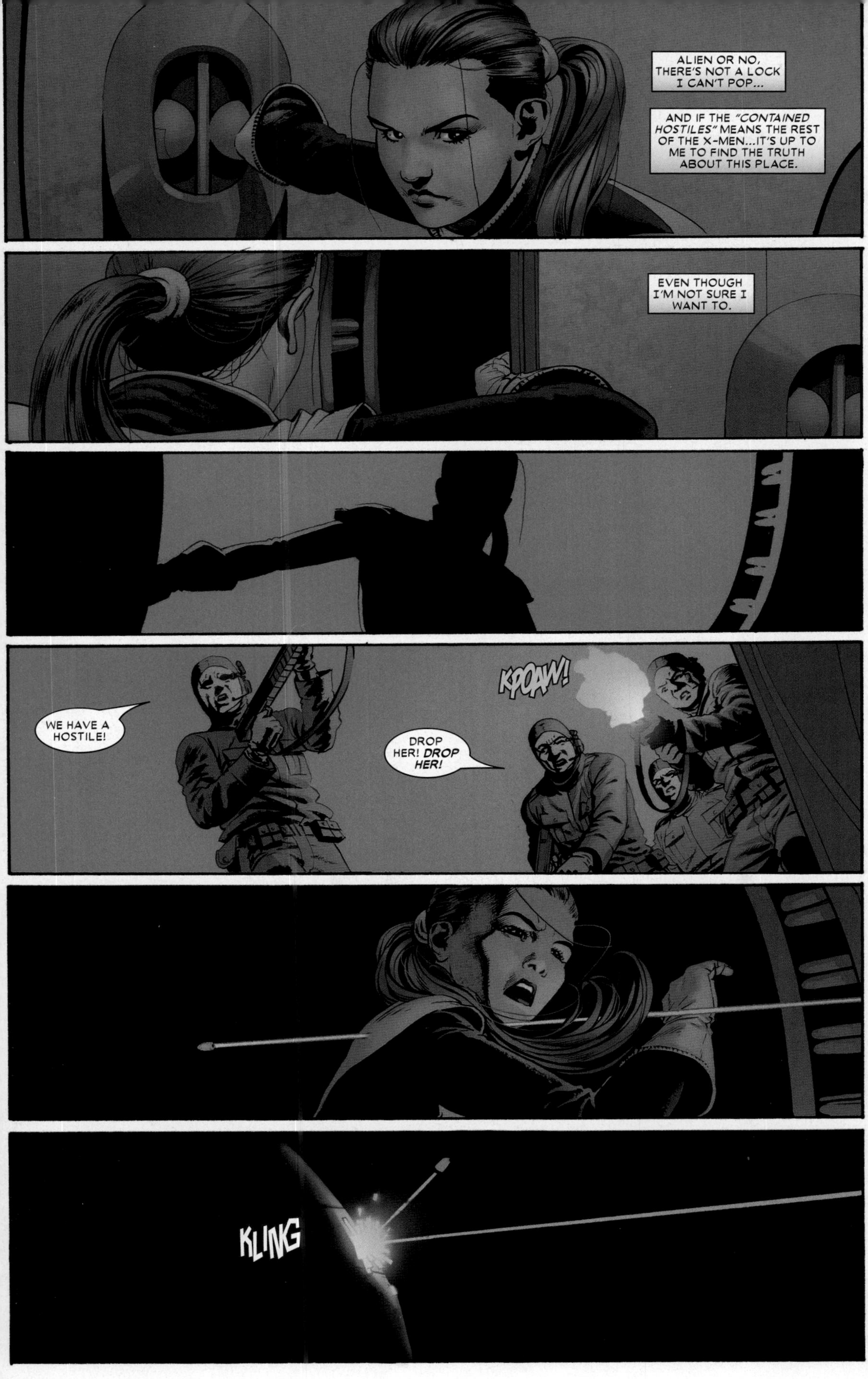

ALIEN OR NO, THERE'S NOT A LOCK I CAN'T POP...
AND IF THE *"CONTAINED HOSTILES"* MEANS THE REST OF THE X-MEN...IT'S UP TO ME TO FIND THE TRUTH ABOUT THIS PLACE.
EVEN THOUGH I'M NOT SURE I WANT TO.
WE HAVE A HOSTILE!
KPOAW!
DROP HER! *DROP HER!*
KLING

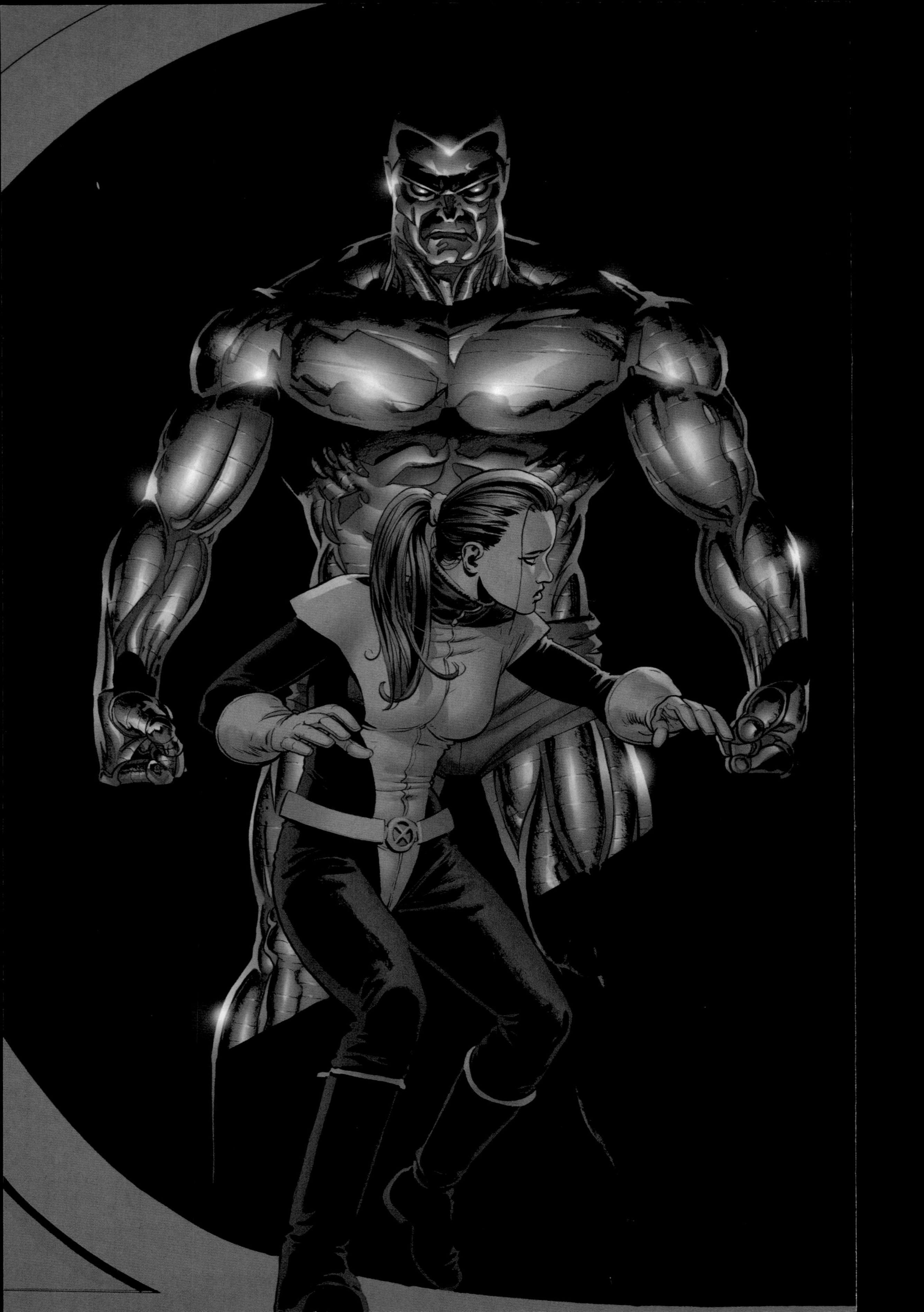

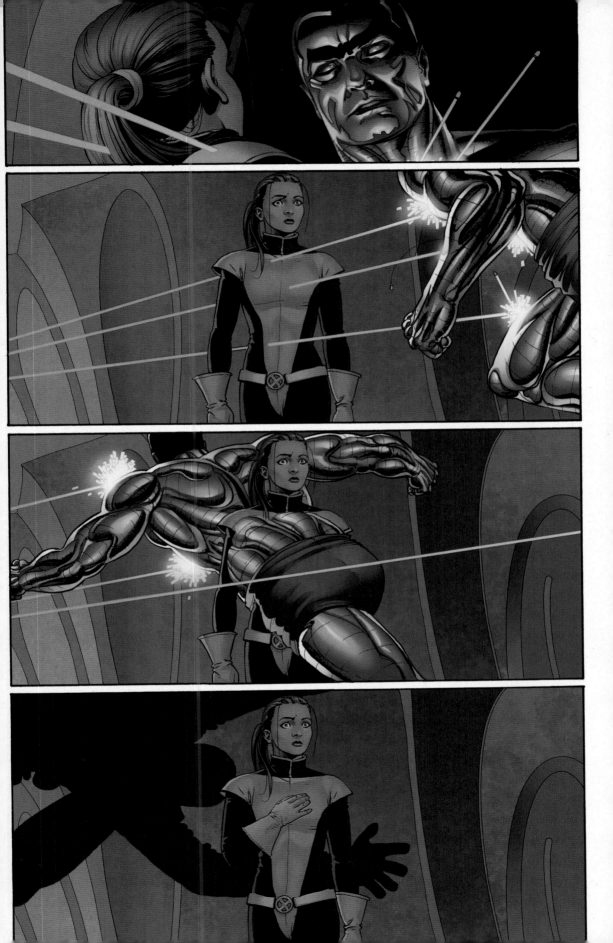

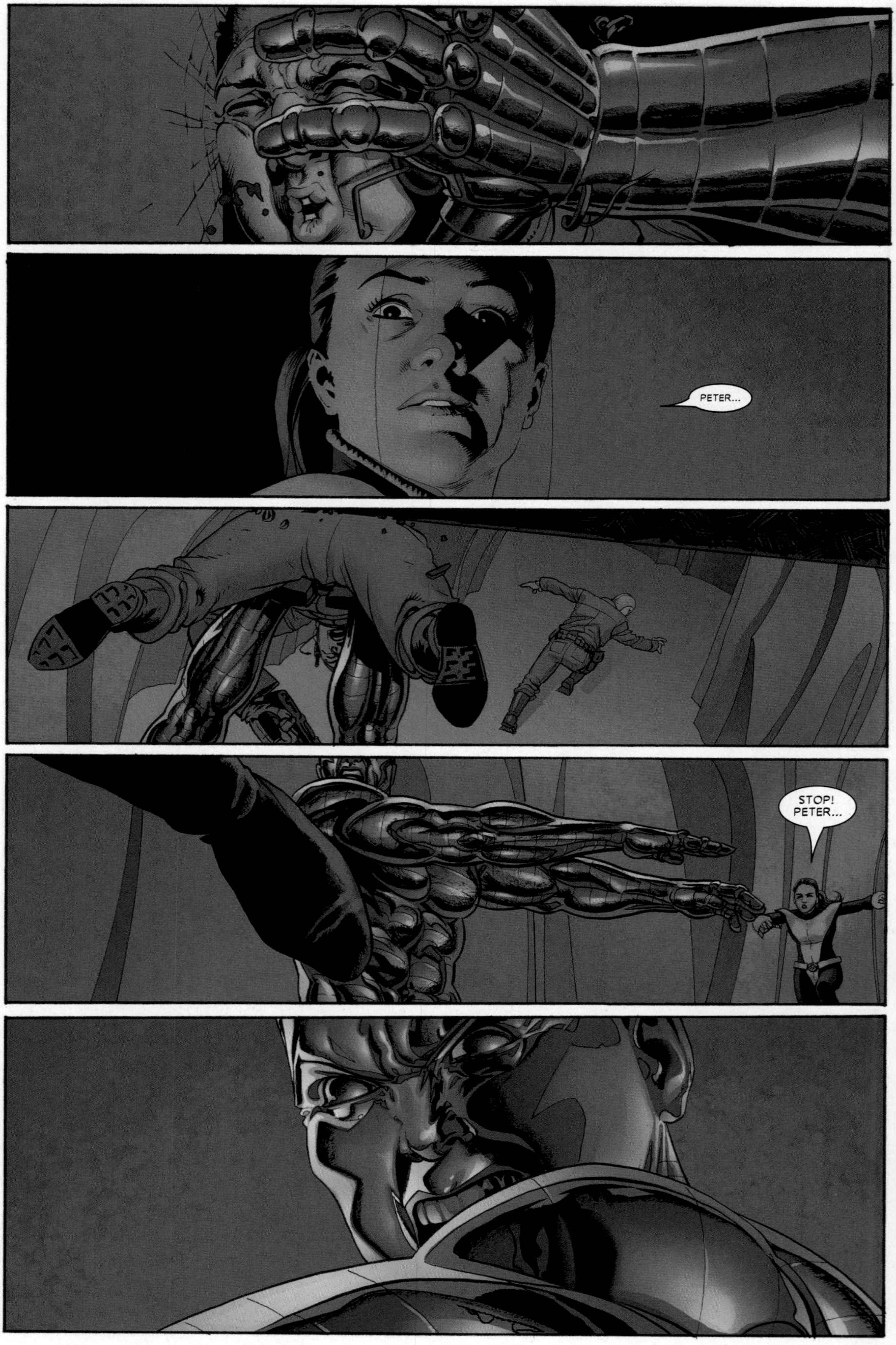
PETER...
STOP! PETER...

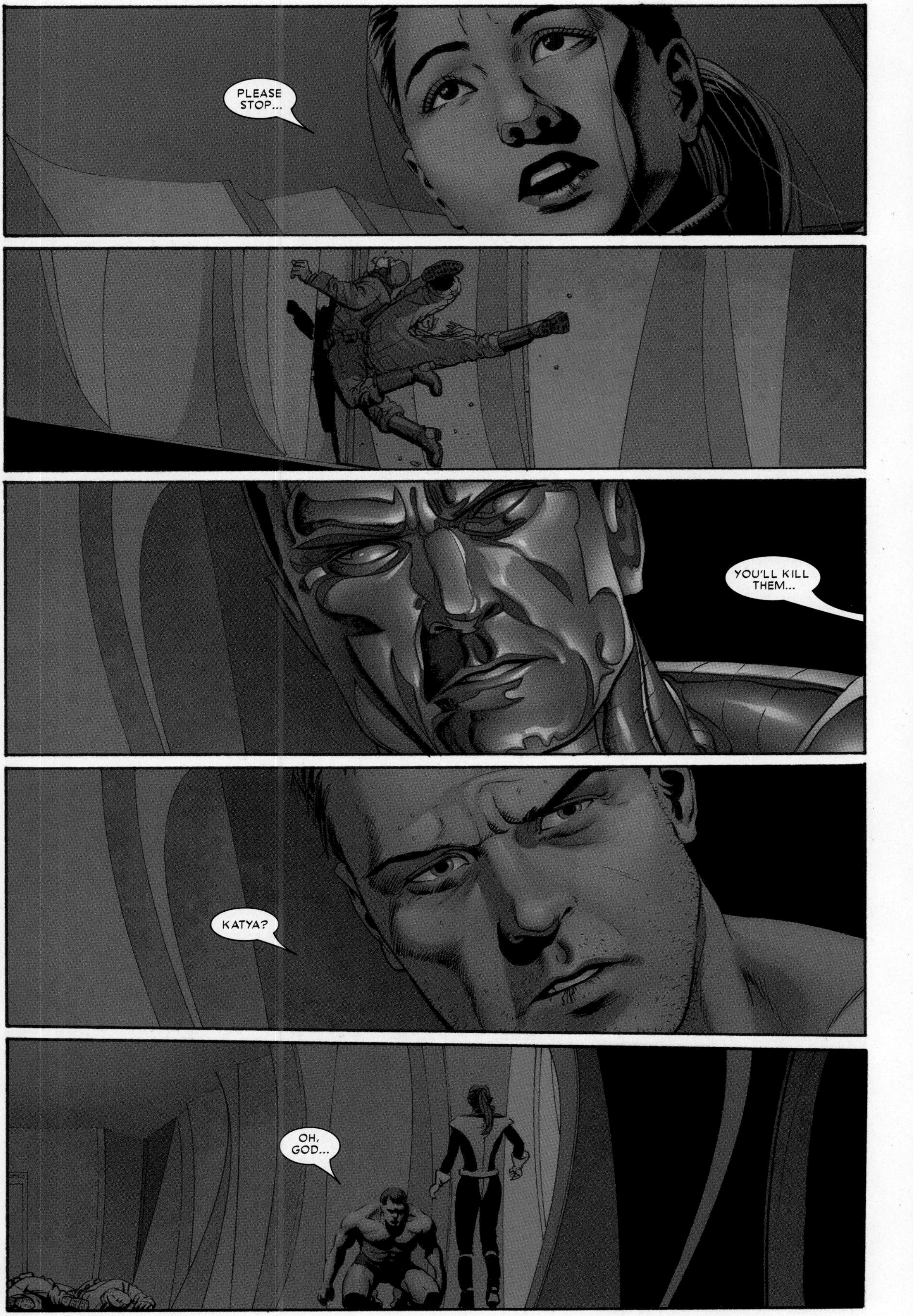
PLEASE STOP...
YOU'LL KILL THEM...
KATYA?
OH, GOD...

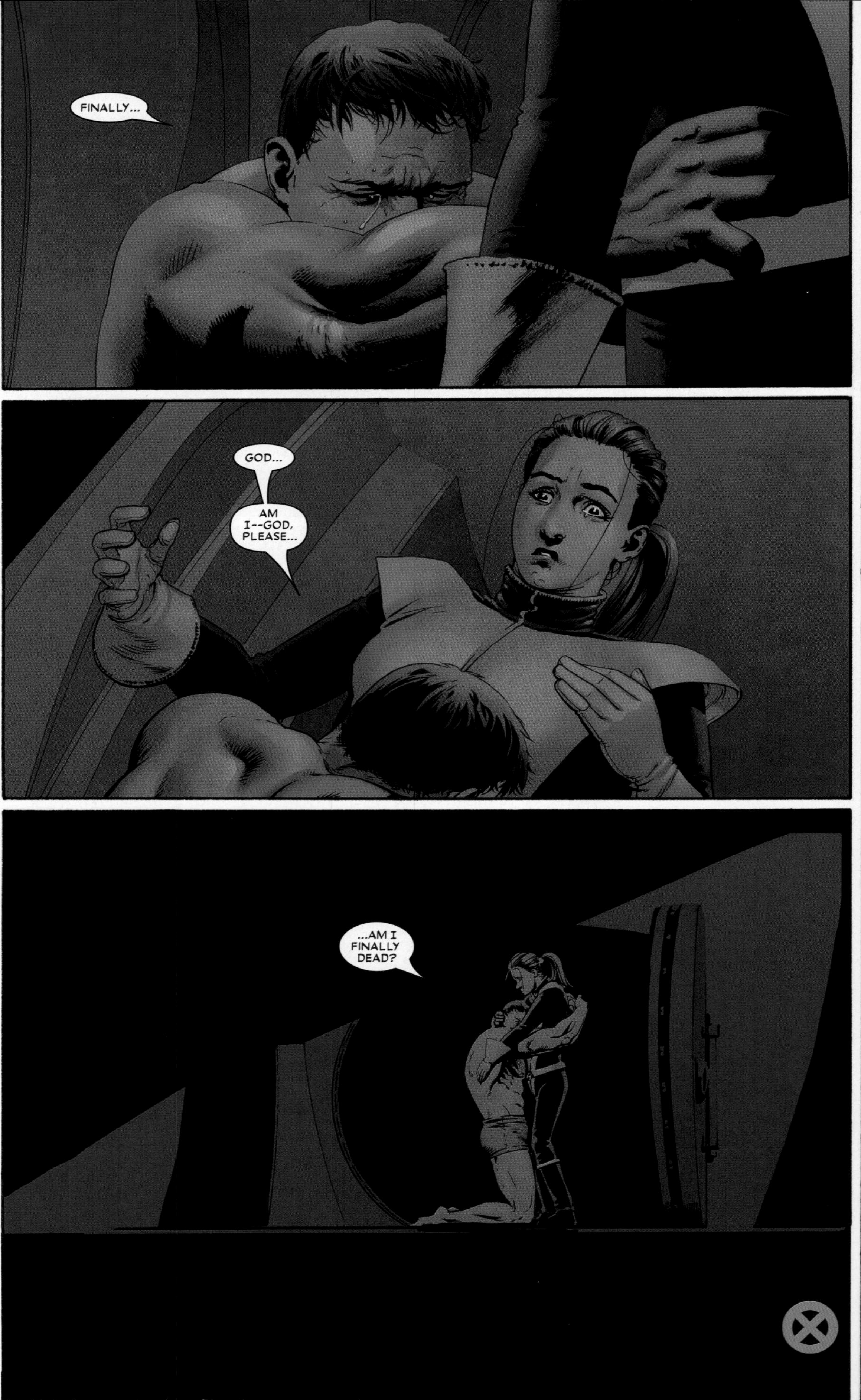
FINALLY...
GOD...
AM I--GOD, PLEASE...
...AM I FINALLY DEAD?

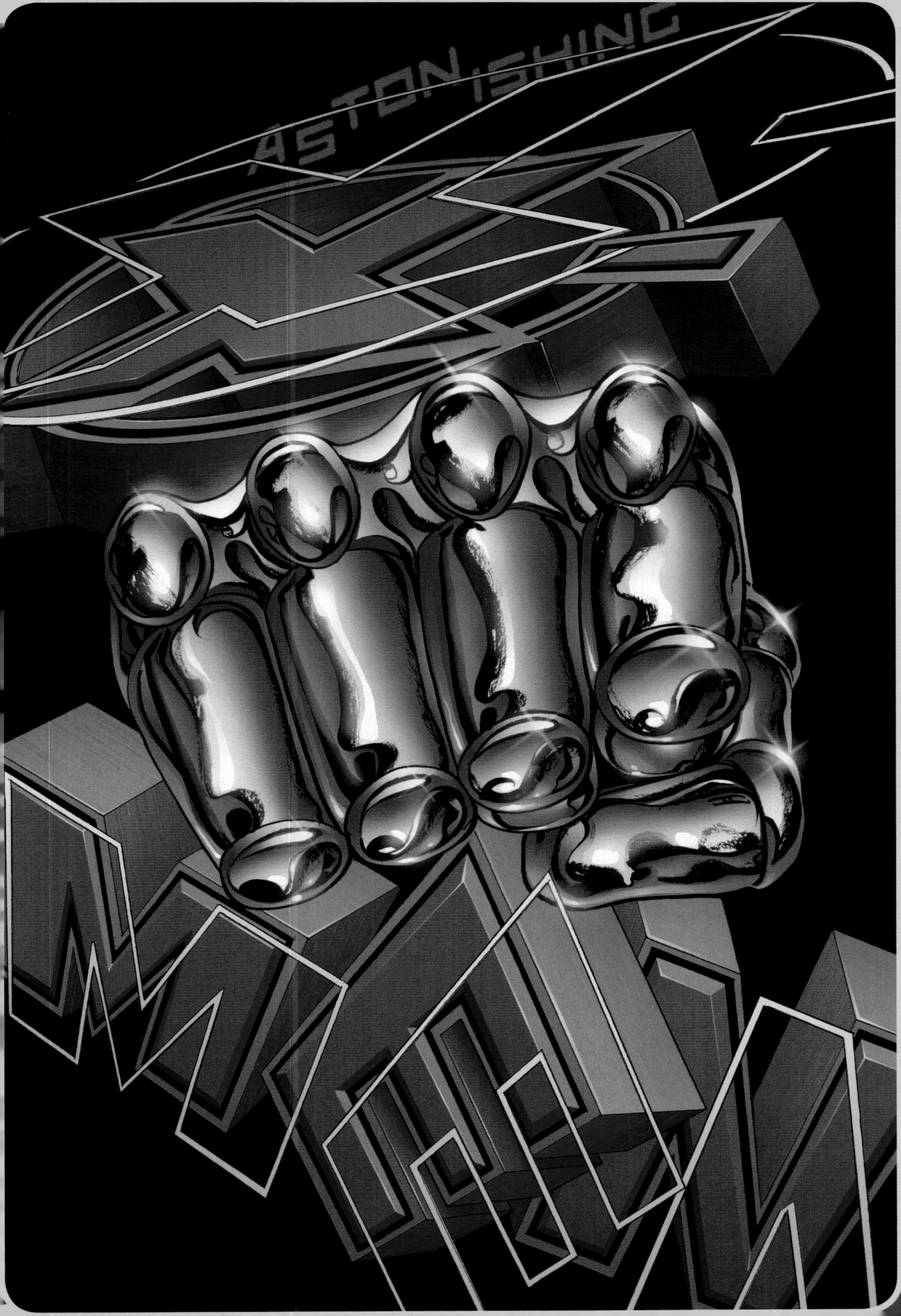
ASTONISHING

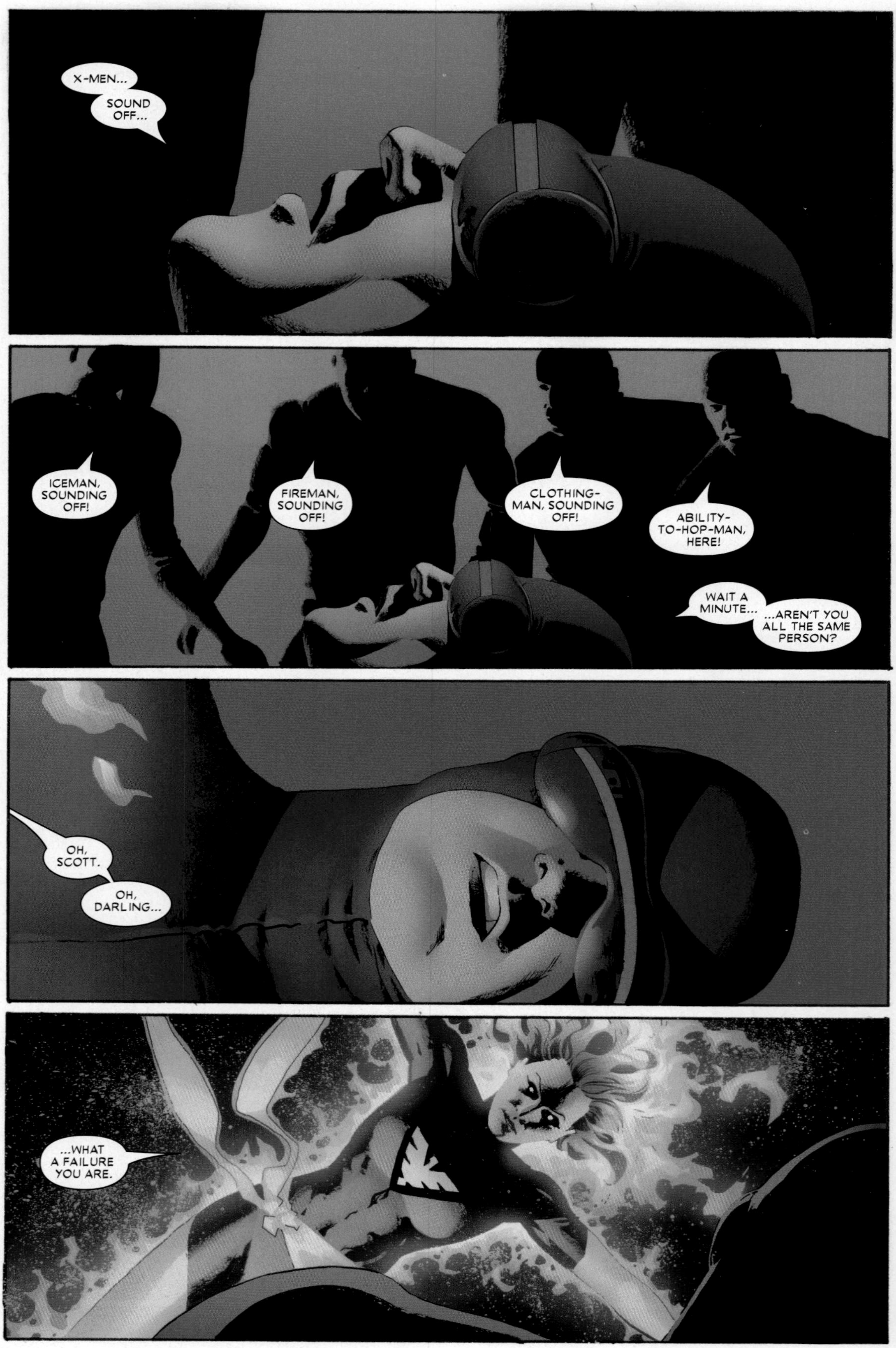
X-MEN...
SOUND OFF...
ICEMAN, SOUNDING OFF!
FIREMAN, SOUNDING OFF!
CLOTHING-MAN, SOUNDING OFF!
ABILITY-TO-HOP-MAN, HERE!
WAIT A MINUTE...
...AREN'T YOU ALL THE SAME PERSON?
OH, SCOTT.
OH, DARLING...
...WHAT A FAILURE YOU ARE.

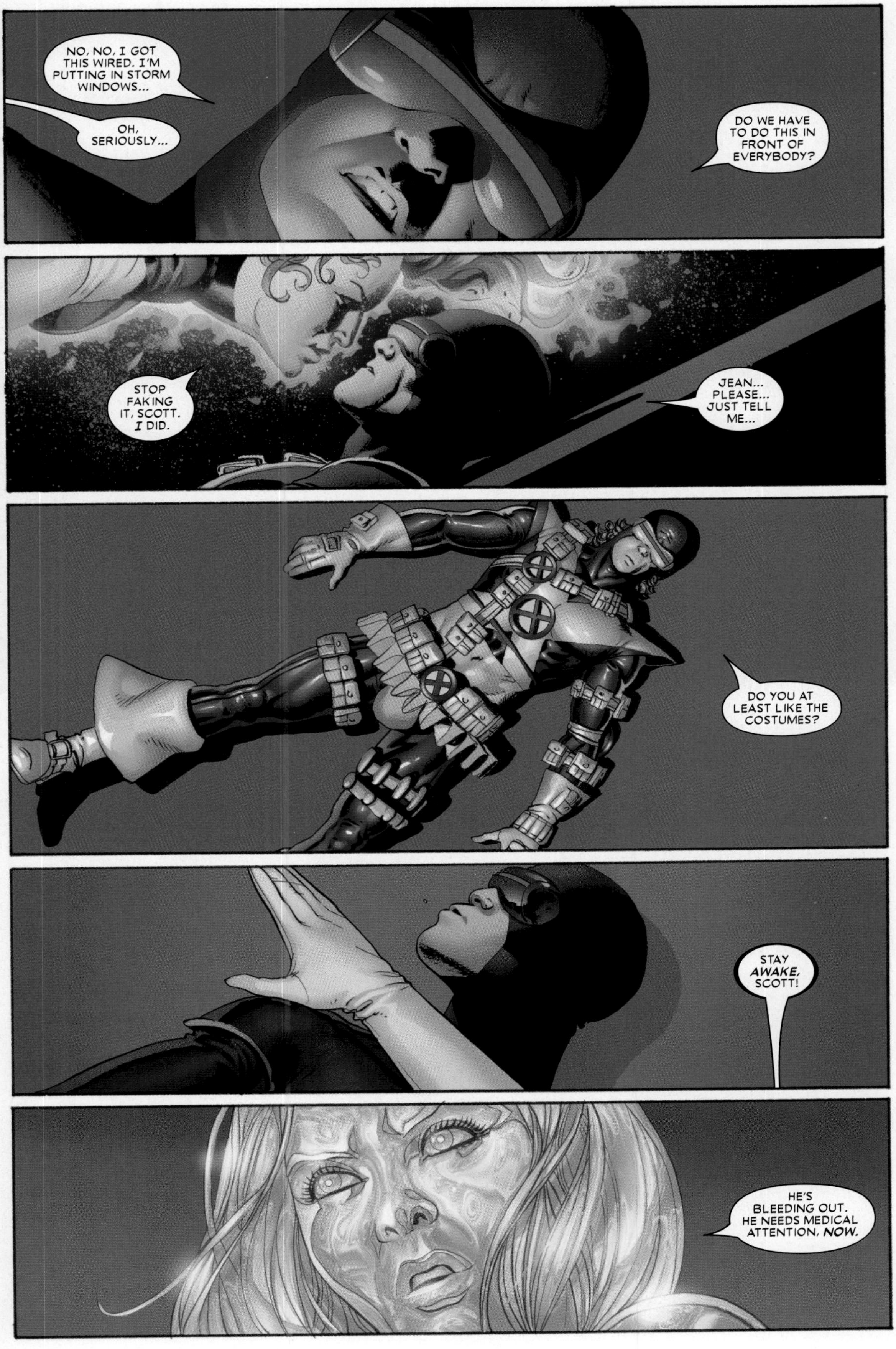
NO, NO, I GOT THIS WIRED. I'M PUTTING IN STORM WINDOWS...
OH, SERIOUSLY...
DO WE HAVE TO DO THIS IN FRONT OF EVERYBODY?
STOP FAKING IT, SCOTT. *I* DID.
JEAN... PLEASE... JUST TELL ME...
DO YOU AT LEAST LIKE THE COSTUMES?
STAY *AWAKE,* SCOTT!
HE'S BLEEDING OUT. HE NEEDS MEDICAL ATTENTION, *NOW.*

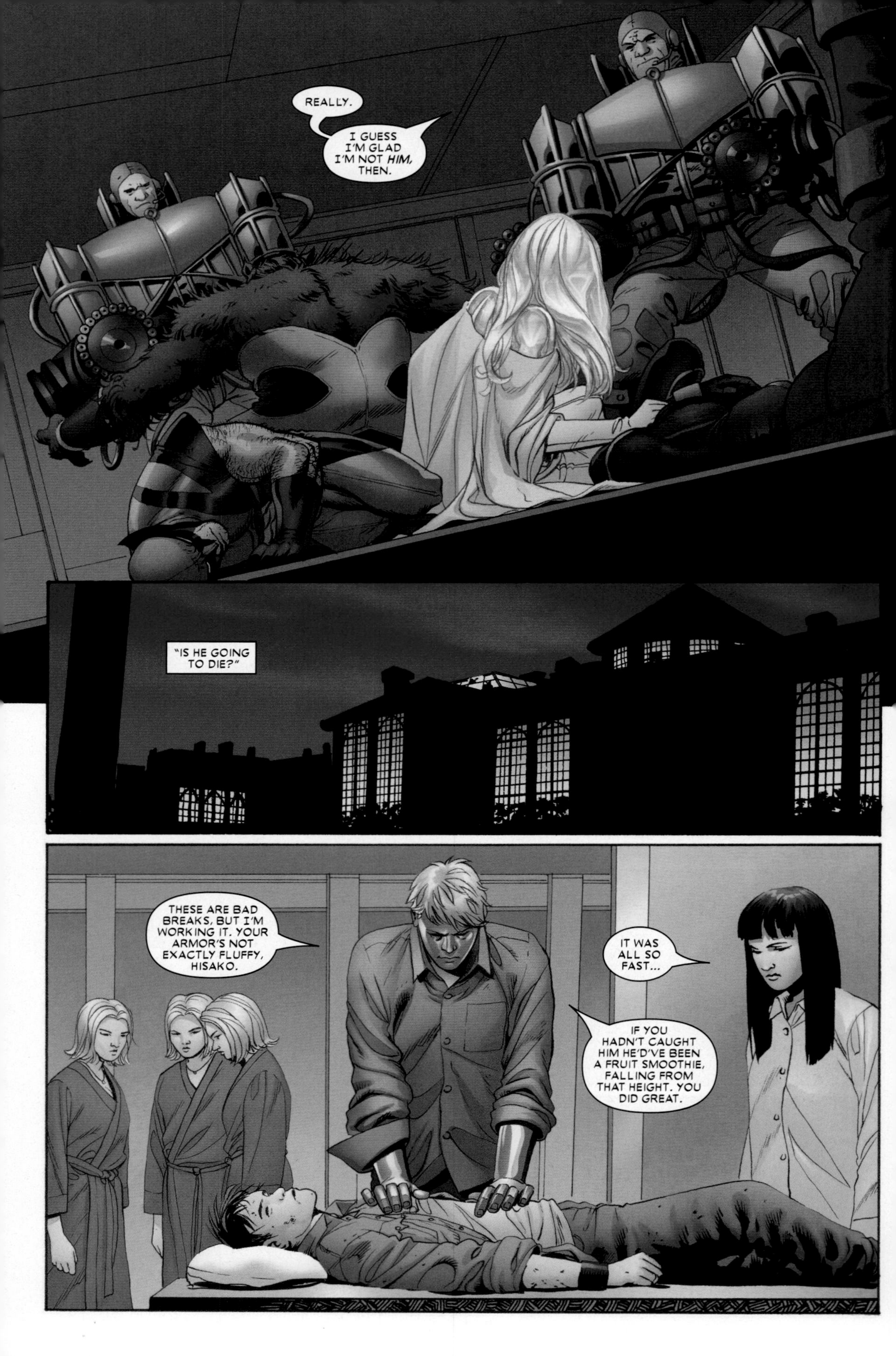
REALLY.
I GUESS I'M GLAD I'M NOT *HIM,* THEN.
"IS HE GOING TO DIE?"
THESE ARE BAD BREAKS, BUT I'M WORKING IT. YOUR ARMOR'S NOT EXACTLY FLUFFY, HISAKO.
IT WAS ALL SO FAST...
IF YOU HADN'T CAUGHT HIM HE'D'VE BEEN A FRUIT SMOOTHIE, FALLING FROM THAT HEIGHT. YOU DID GREAT.

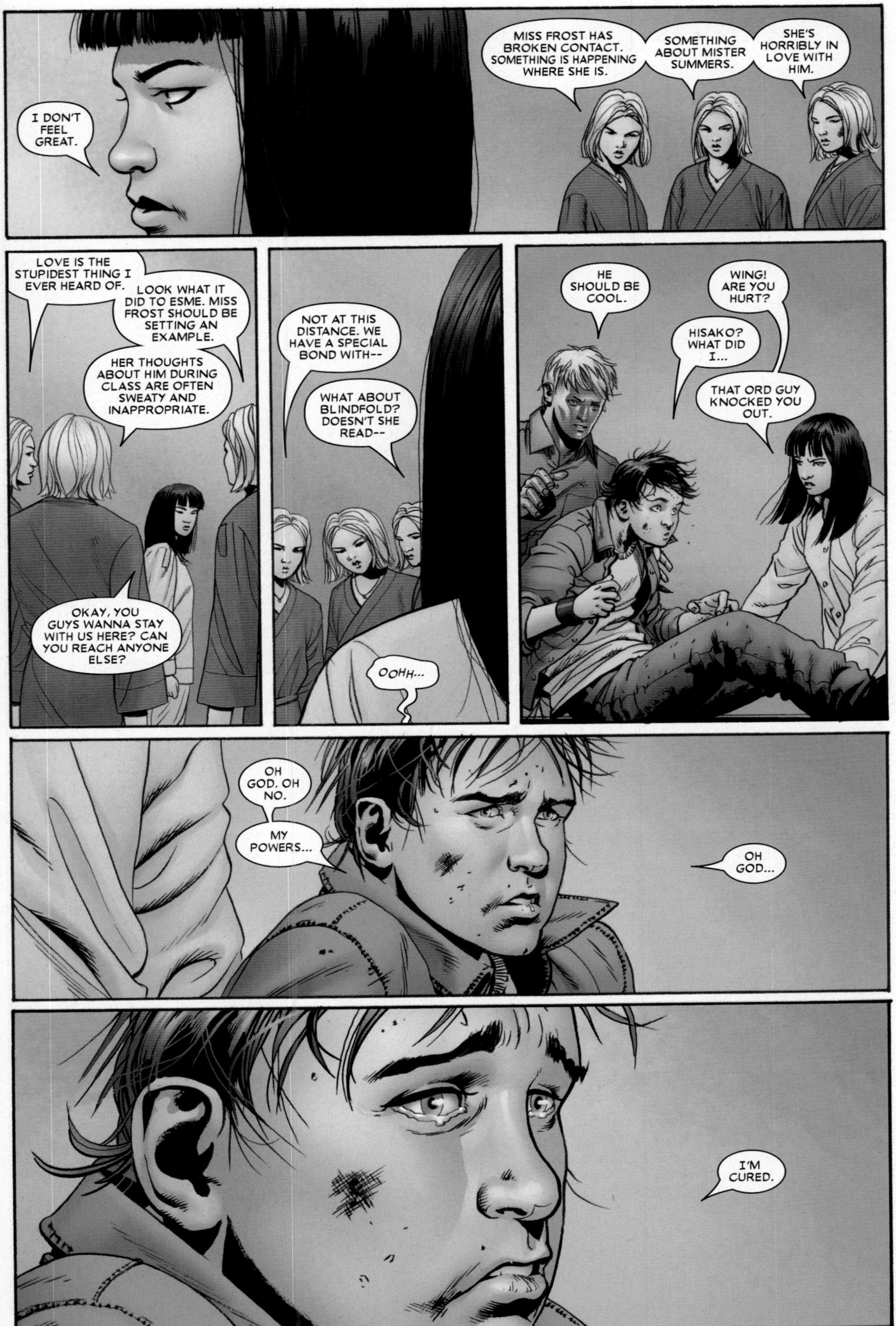
I DON'T FEEL GREAT.
MISS FROST HAS BROKEN CONTACT. SOMETHING IS HAPPENING WHERE SHE IS.
SOMETHING ABOUT MISTER SUMMERS.
SHE'S HORRIBLY IN LOVE WITH HIM.
LOVE IS THE STUPIDEST THING I EVER HEARD OF.
LOOK WHAT IT DID TO ESME. MISS FROST SHOULD BE SETTING AN EXAMPLE.
HER THOUGHTS ABOUT HIM DURING CLASS ARE OFTEN SWEATY AND INAPPROPRIATE.
OKAY, YOU GUYS WANNA STAY WITH US HERE? CAN YOU REACH ANYONE ELSE?
NOT AT THIS DISTANCE. WE HAVE A SPECIAL BOND WITH--
WHAT ABOUT BLINDFOLD? DOESN'T SHE READ--
OOHH...
HE SHOULD BE COOL.
WING! ARE YOU HURT?
HISAKO? WHAT DID I...
THAT ORD GUY KNOCKED YOU OUT.
OH GOD. OH NO.
MY POWERS...
OH GOD...
I'M CURED.

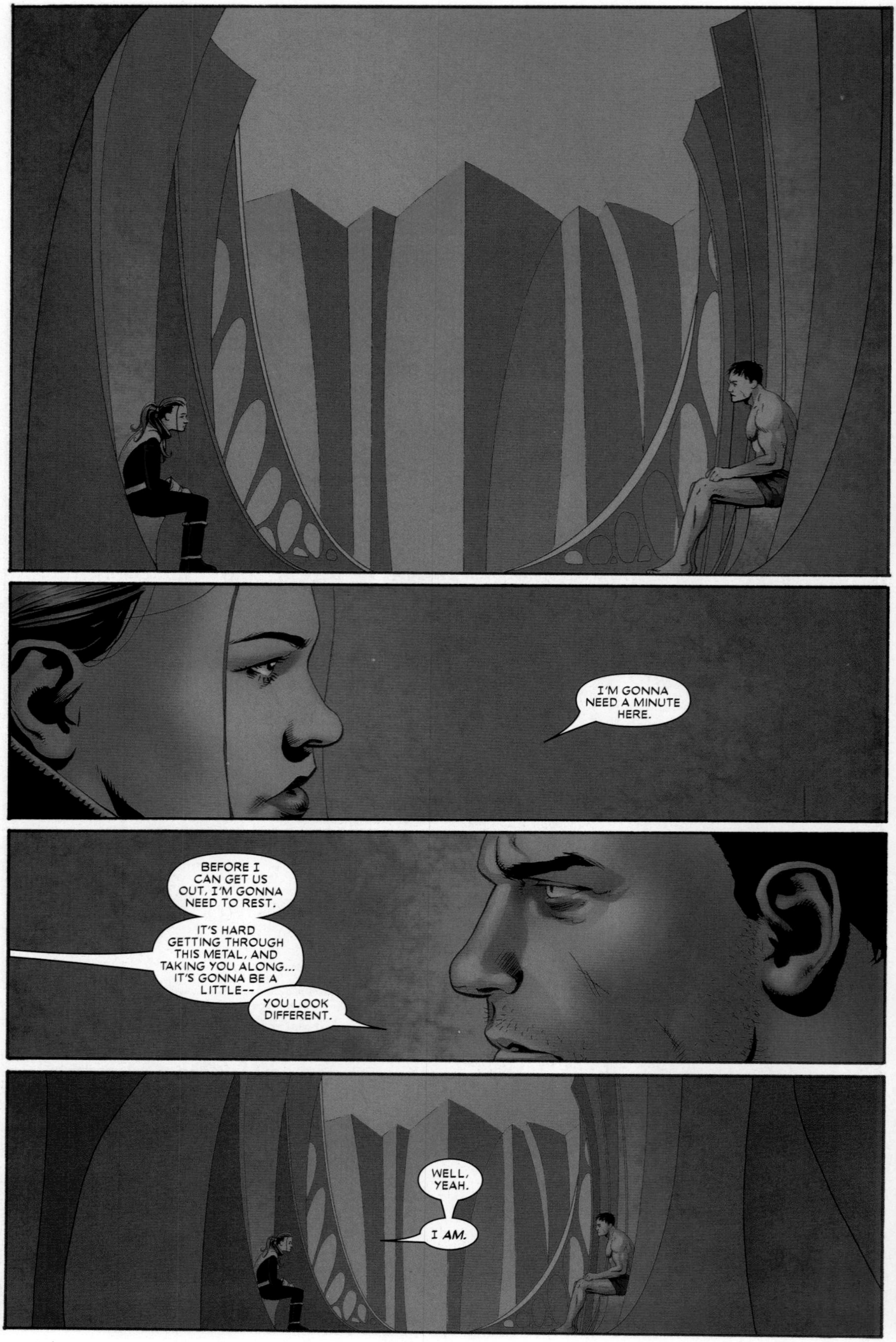
I'M GONNA NEED A MINUTE HERE.
BEFORE I CAN GET US OUT, I'M GONNA NEED TO REST.
IT'S HARD GETTING THROUGH THIS METAL, AND TAKING YOU ALONG... IT'S GONNA BE A LITTLE--
YOU LOOK DIFFERENT.
WELL, YEAH.
I AM.

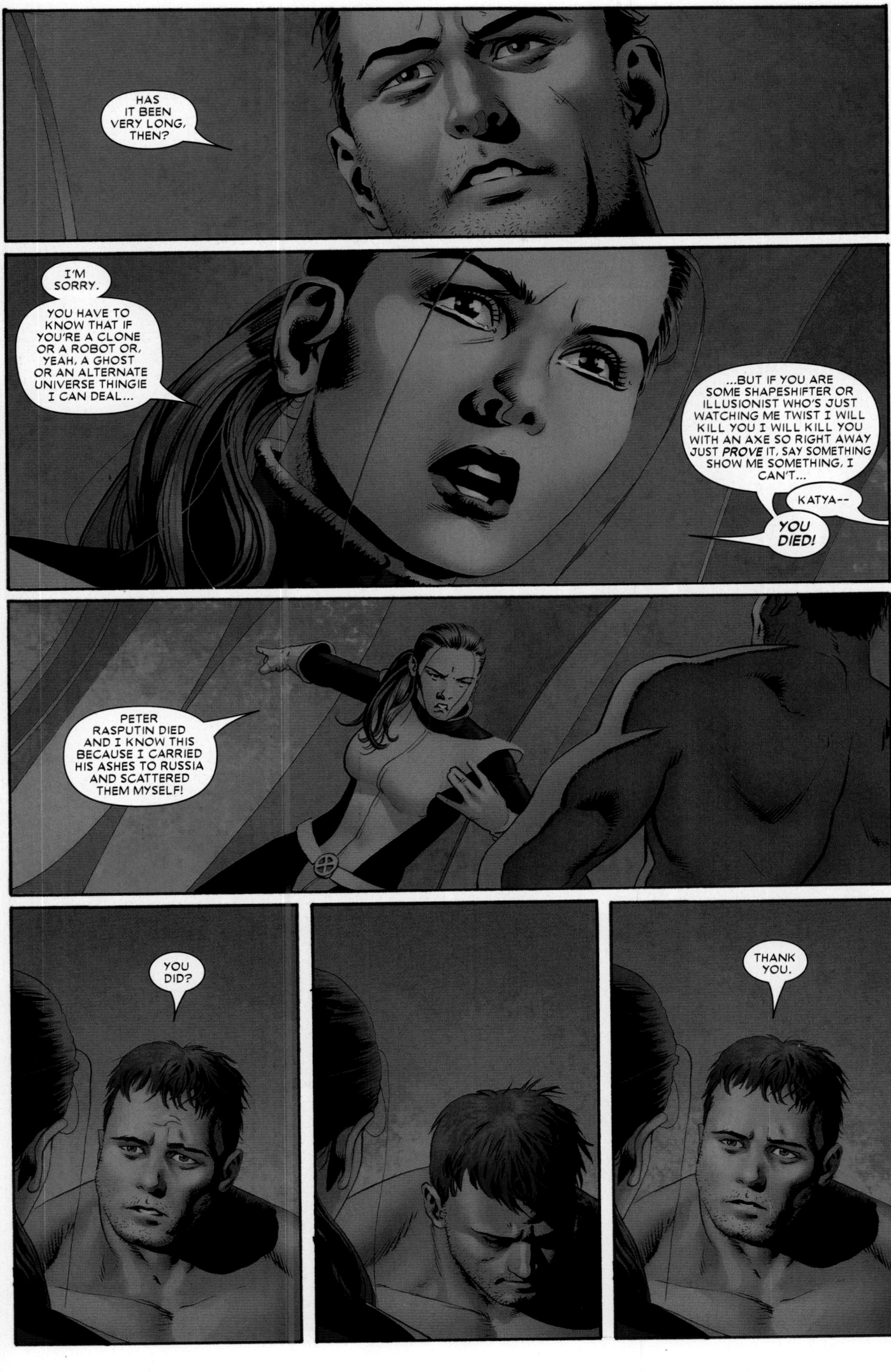
HAS IT BEEN VERY LONG, THEN?
I'M SORRY.
YOU HAVE TO KNOW THAT IF YOU'RE A CLONE OR A ROBOT OR, YEAH, A GHOST OR AN ALTERNATE UNIVERSE THINGIE I CAN DEAL...
...BUT IF YOU ARE SOME SHAPESHIFTER OR ILLUSIONIST WHO'S JUST WATCHING ME TWIST I WILL KILL YOU I WILL KILL YOU WITH AN AXE SO RIGHT AWAY JUST PROVE IT, SAY SOMETHING SHOW ME SOMETHING, I CAN'T...
KATYA--
YOU DIED!
PETER RASPUTIN DIED AND I KNOW THIS BECAUSE I CARRIED HIS ASHES TO RUSSIA AND SCATTERED THEM MYSELF!
YOU DID?
THANK YOU.

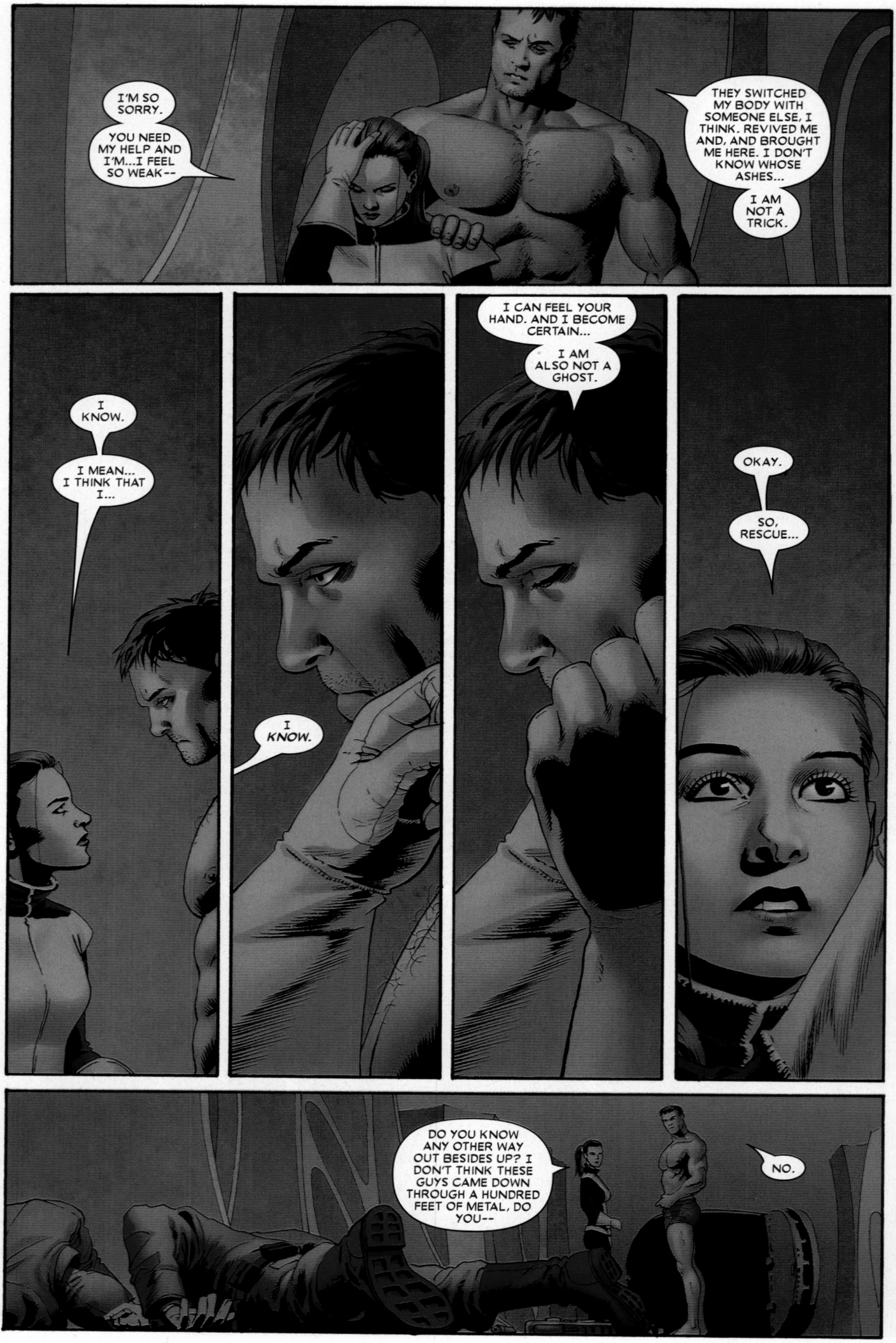
I'M SO SORRY.
YOU NEED MY HELP AND I'M...I FEEL SO WEAK--
THEY SWITCHED MY BODY WITH SOMEONE ELSE, I THINK. REVIVED ME AND, AND BROUGHT ME HERE. I DON'T KNOW WHOSE ASHES...
I AM NOT A TRICK.
I KNOW.
I MEAN... I THINK THAT I...
I *KNOW.*
I CAN FEEL YOUR HAND. AND I BECOME CERTAIN...
I AM ALSO NOT A GHOST.
OKAY.
SO, RESCUE...
DO YOU KNOW ANY OTHER WAY OUT BESIDES UP? I DON'T THINK THESE GUYS CAME DOWN THROUGH A HUNDRED FEET OF METAL, DO YOU--
NO.

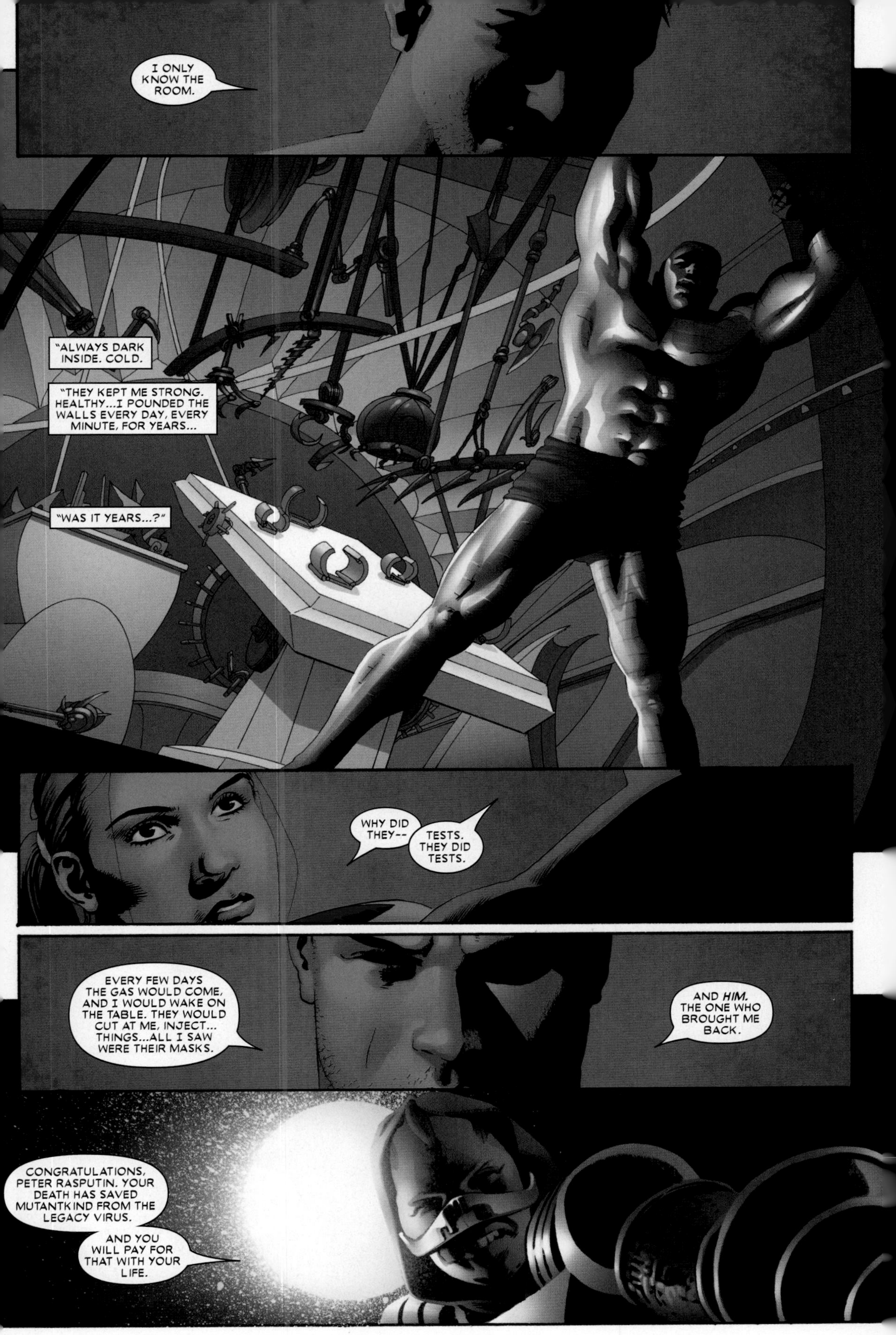
I ONLY KNOW THE ROOM.
"ALWAYS DARK INSIDE. COLD.
"THEY KEPT ME STRONG. HEALTHY...I POUNDED THE WALLS EVERY DAY, EVERY MINUTE, FOR YEARS...
"WAS IT YEARS...?"
WHY DID THEY--
TESTS. THEY DID TESTS.
EVERY FEW DAYS THE GAS WOULD COME, AND I WOULD WAKE ON THE TABLE. THEY WOULD CUT AT ME, INJECT... THINGS...ALL I SAW WERE THEIR MASKS.
AND *HIM.* THE ONE WHO BROUGHT ME BACK.
CONGRATULATIONS, PETER RASPUTIN. YOUR DEATH HAS SAVED MUTANTKIND FROM THE LEGACY VIRUS.
AND YOU WILL PAY FOR THAT WITH YOUR LIFE.

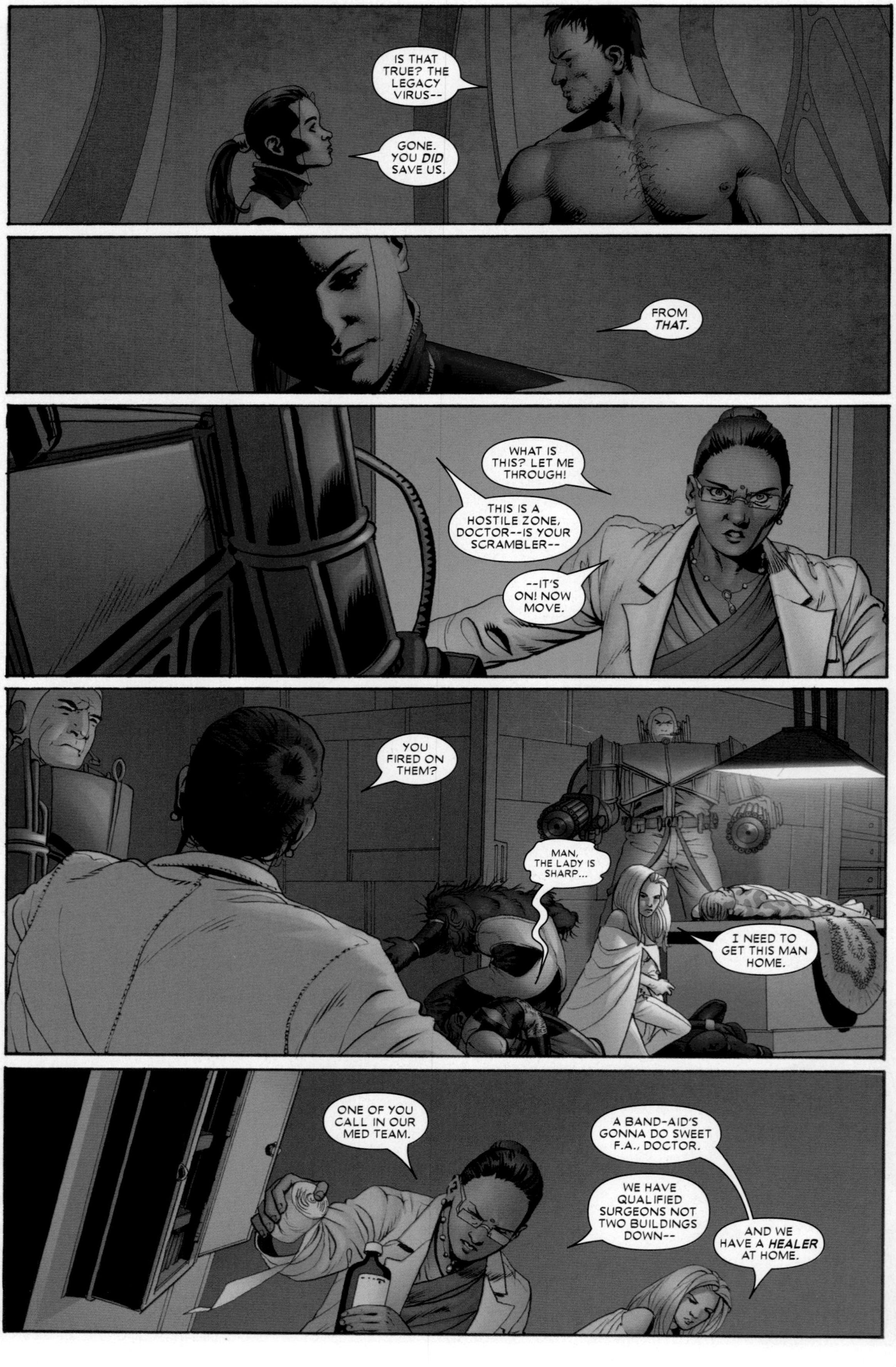
IS THAT TRUE? THE LEGACY VIRUS--
GONE. YOU *DID* SAVE US.
FROM *THAT.*
WHAT IS THIS? LET ME THROUGH!
THIS IS A HOSTILE ZONE, DOCTOR--IS YOUR SCRAMBLER--
--IT'S ON! NOW MOVE.
YOU FIRED ON THEM?
MAN, THE LADY IS SHARP...
I NEED TO GET THIS MAN HOME.
ONE OF YOU CALL IN OUR MED TEAM.
A BAND-AID'S GONNA DO SWEET F.A., DOCTOR.
WE HAVE QUALIFIED SURGEONS NOT TWO BUILDINGS DOWN--
AND WE HAVE A *HEALER* AT HOME.

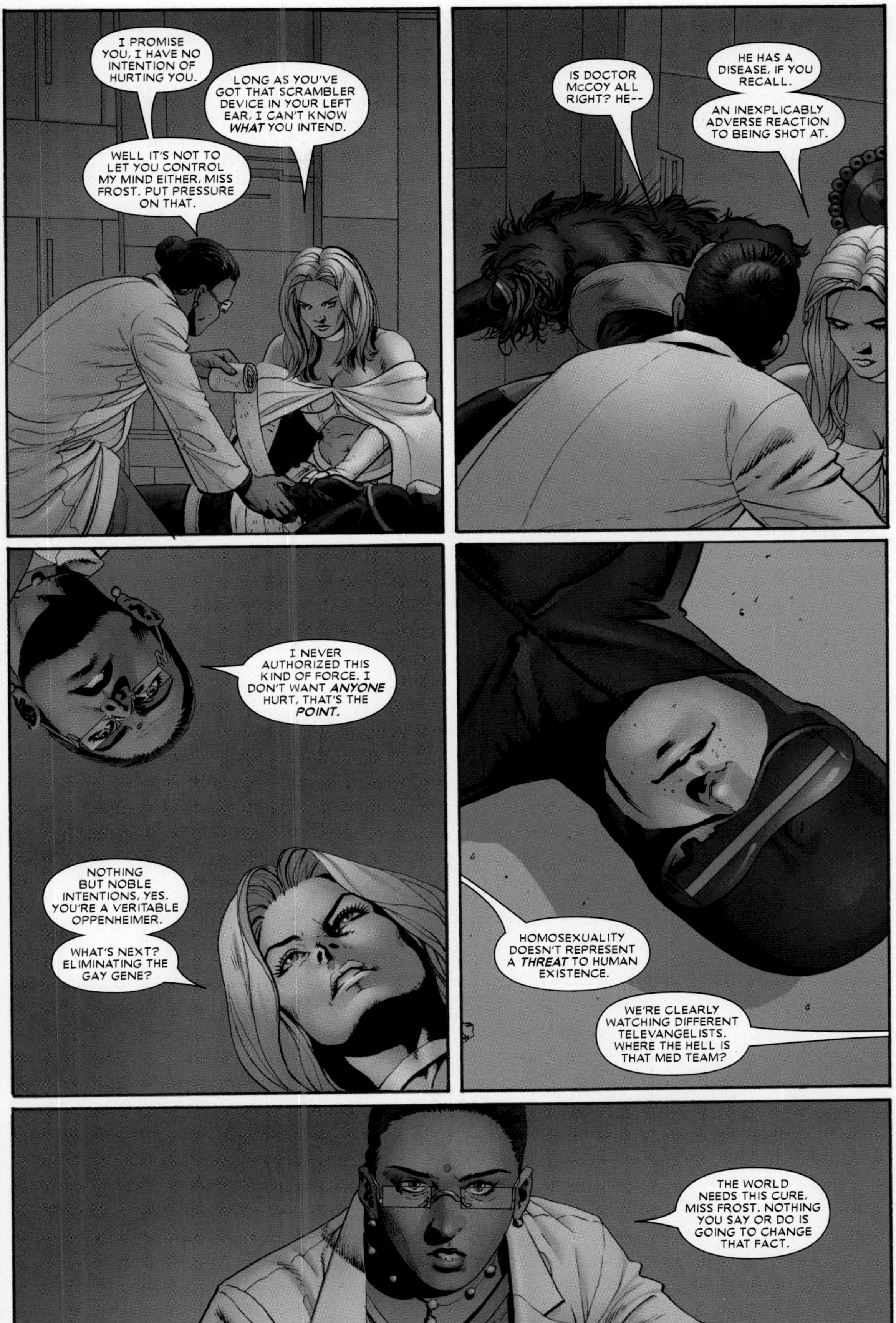

I PROMISE YOU, I HAVE NO INTENTION OF HURTING YOU.
LONG AS YOU'VE GOT THAT SCRAMBLER DEVICE IN YOUR LEFT EAR, I CAN'T KNOW *WHAT* YOU INTEND.
WELL IT'S NOT TO LET YOU CONTROL MY MIND EITHER, MISS FROST. PUT PRESSURE ON THAT.
IS DOCTOR McCOY ALL RIGHT? HE--
HE HAS A DISEASE, IF YOU RECALL.
AN INEXPLICABLY ADVERSE REACTION TO BEING SHOT AT.
I NEVER AUTHORIZED THIS KIND OF FORCE. I DON'T WANT *ANYONE* HURT, THAT'S THE *POINT.*
NOTHING BUT NOBLE INTENTIONS, YES. YOU'RE A VERITABLE OPPENHEIMER.
WHAT'S NEXT? ELIMINATING THE GAY GENE?
HOMOSEXUALITY DOESN'T REPRESENT A *THREAT* TO HUMAN EXISTENCE.
WE'RE CLEARLY WATCHING DIFFERENT TELEVANGELISTS. WHERE THE HELL IS THAT MED TEAM?
THE WORLD NEEDS THIS CURE, MISS FROST. NOTHING YOU SAY OR DO IS GOING TO CHANGE THAT FACT.

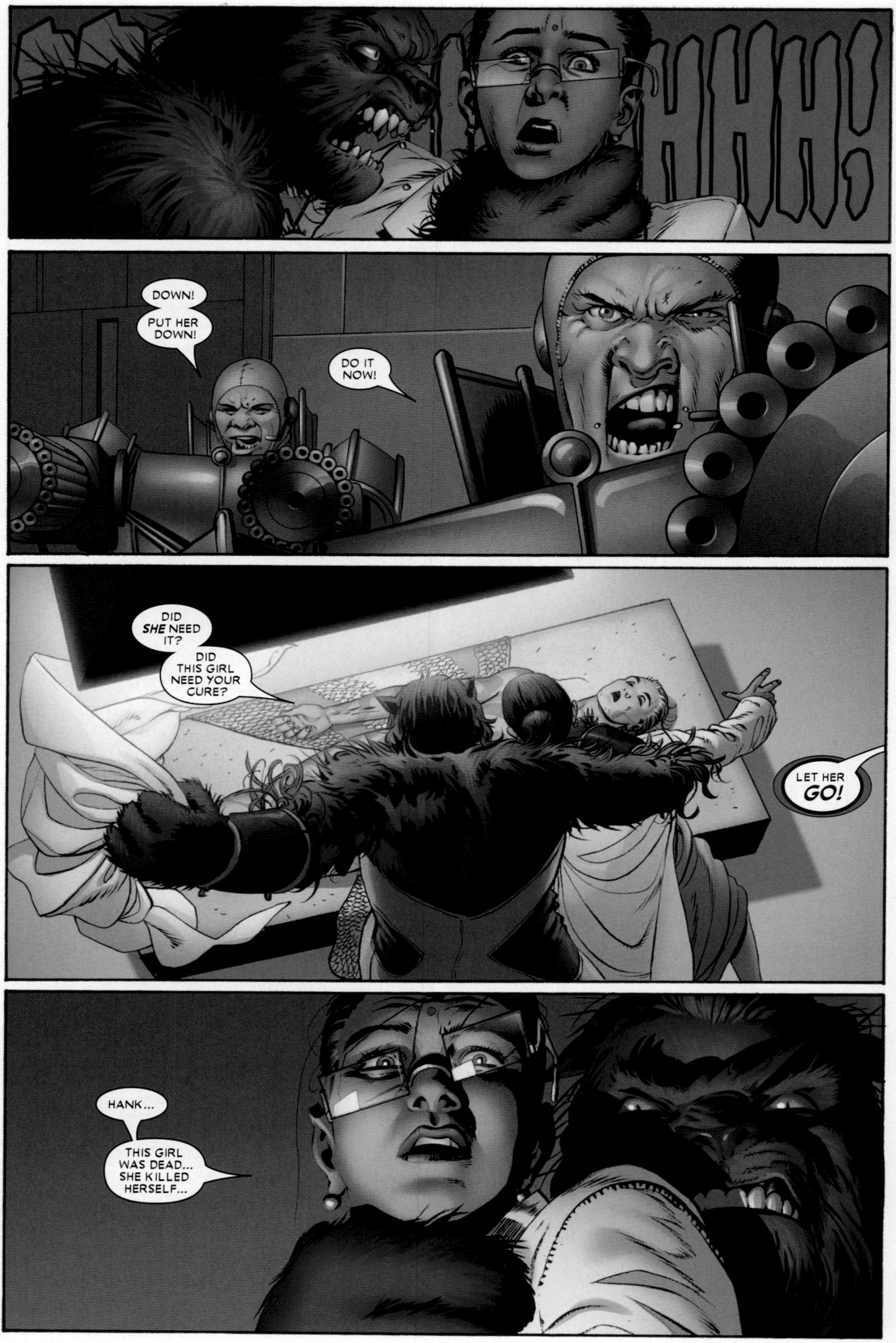
HHH!
DOWN!
PUT HER DOWN!
DO IT NOW!
DID SHE NEED IT?
DID THIS GIRL NEED YOUR CURE?
LET HER GO!
HANK...
THIS GIRL WAS DEAD... SHE KILLED HERSELF...

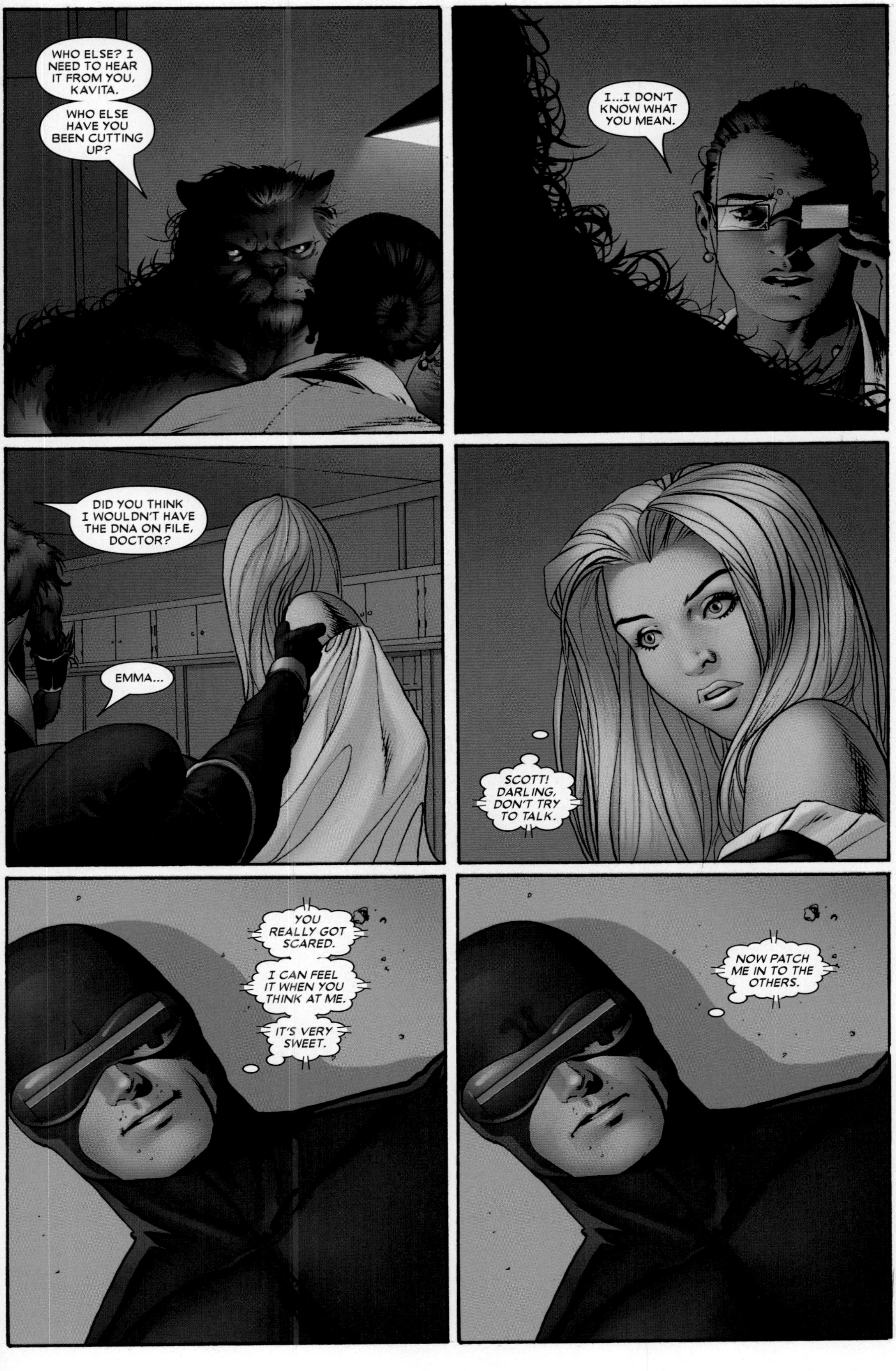
WHO ELSE? I NEED TO HEAR IT FROM YOU, KAVITA.
WHO ELSE HAVE YOU BEEN CUTTING UP?
I...I DON'T KNOW WHAT YOU MEAN.
DID YOU THINK I WOULDN'T HAVE THE DNA ON FILE, DOCTOR?
EMMA...
SCOTT! DARLING, DON'T TRY TO TALK.
YOU REALLY GOT SCARED.
I CAN FEEL IT WHEN YOU THINK AT ME.
IT'S VERY SWEET.
NOW PATCH ME IN TO THE OTHERS.

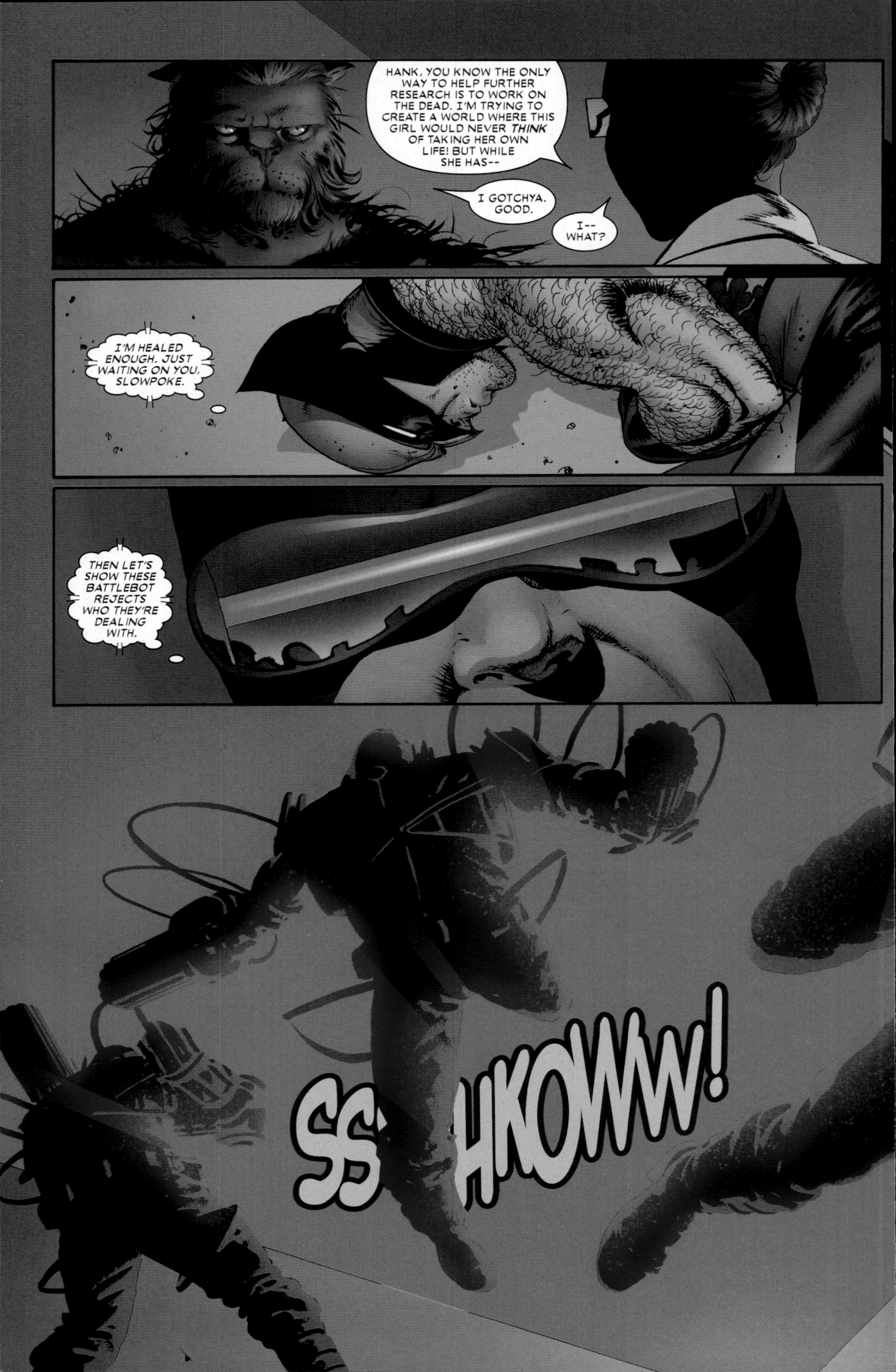
HANK, YOU KNOW THE ONLY WAY TO HELP FURTHER RESEARCH IS TO WORK ON THE DEAD. I'M TRYING TO CREATE A WORLD WHERE THIS GIRL WOULD NEVER *THINK* OF TAKING HER OWN LIFE! BUT WHILE SHE HAS--
I GOTCHYA. GOOD.
I-- WHAT?
I'M HEALED ENOUGH. JUST WAITING ON YOU, SLOWPOKE.
THEN LET'S SHOW THESE BATTLEBOT REJECTS WHO THEY'RE DEALING WITH.
SSHKOWW!

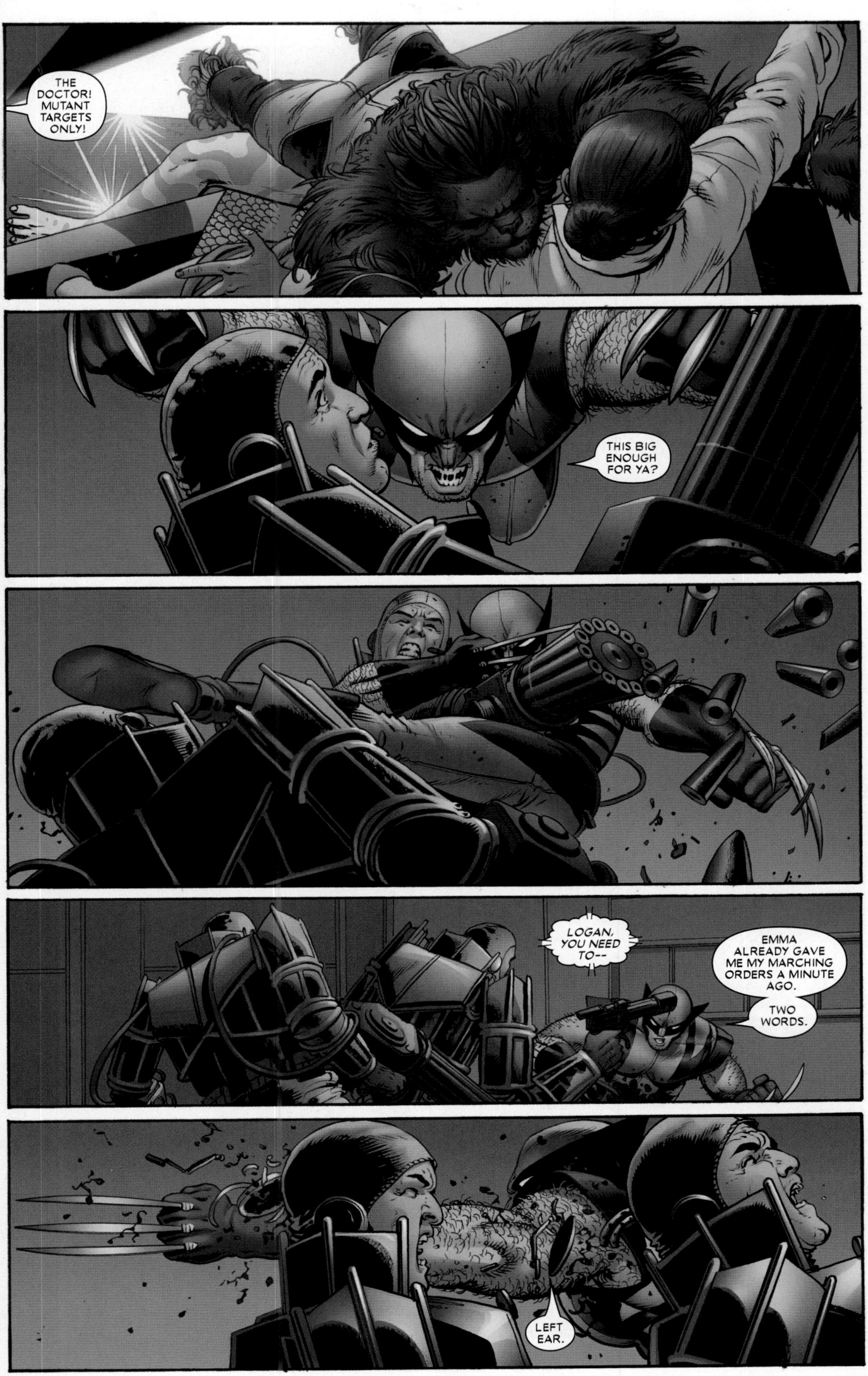
THE DOCTOR! MUTANT TARGETS ONLY!
THIS BIG ENOUGH FOR YA?
LOGAN, YOU NEED TO--
EMMA ALREADY GAVE ME MY MARCHING ORDERS A MINUTE AGO.
TWO WORDS.
LEFT EAR.

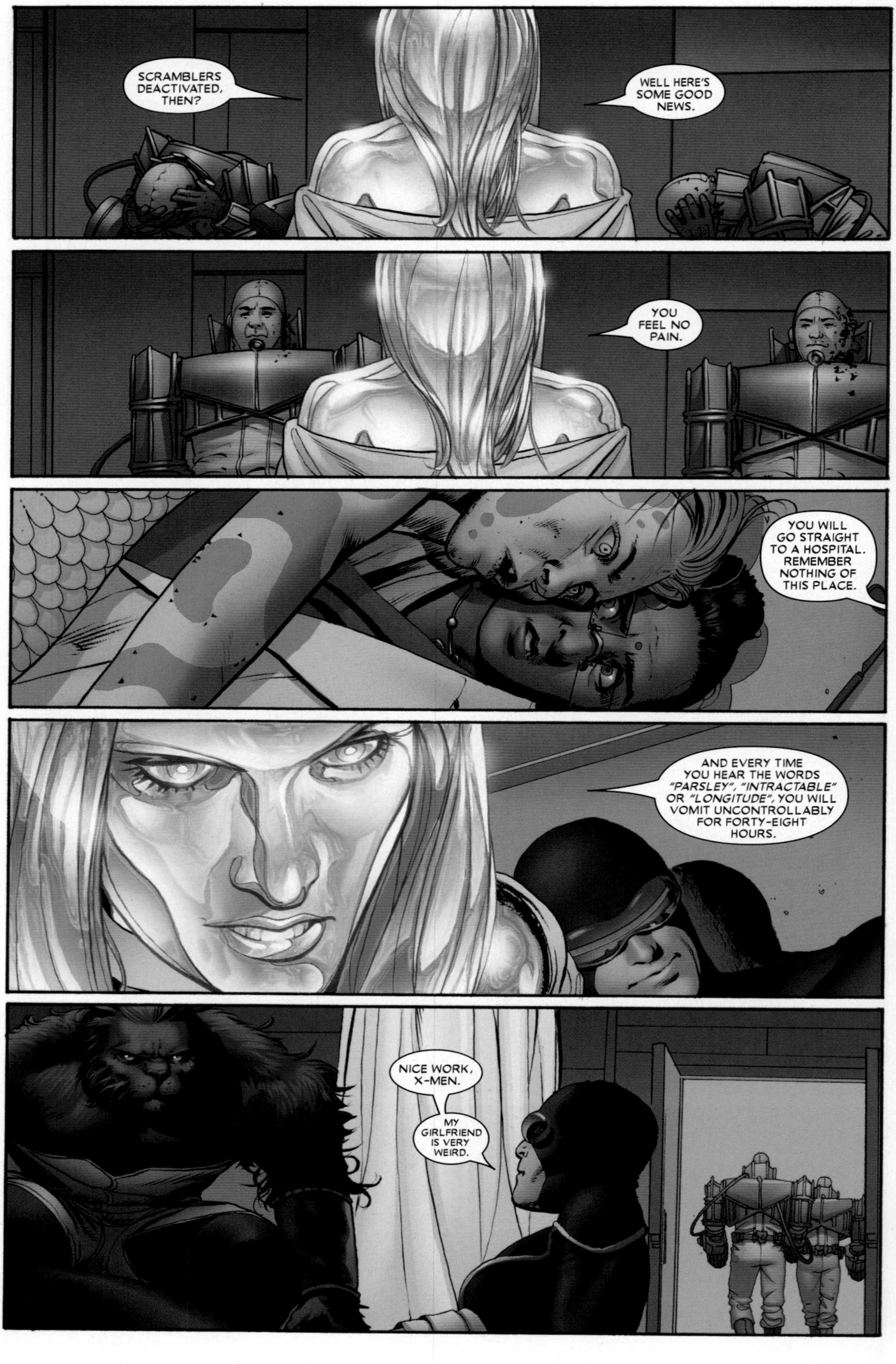
SCRAMBLERS DEACTIVATED, THEN?
WELL HERE'S SOME GOOD NEWS.
YOU FEEL NO PAIN.
YOU WILL GO STRAIGHT TO A HOSPITAL. REMEMBER NOTHING OF THIS PLACE.
AND EVERY TIME YOU HEAR THE WORDS "PARSLEY", "INTRACTABLE" OR "LONGITUDE", YOU WILL VOMIT UNCONTROLLABLY FOR FORTY-EIGHT HOURS.
NICE WORK, X-MEN.
MY GIRLFRIEND IS VERY WEIRD.

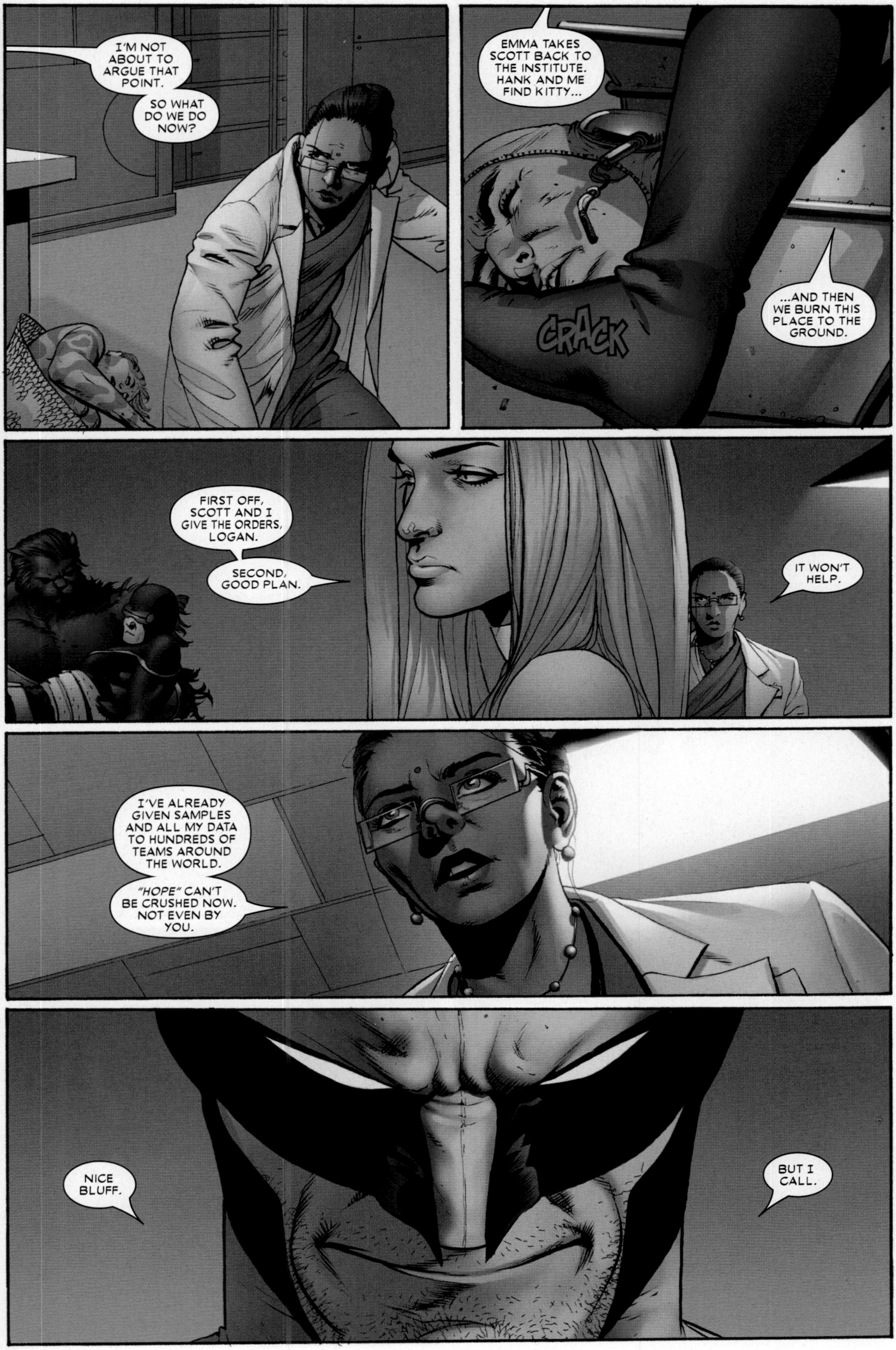
I'M NOT ABOUT TO ARGUE THAT POINT.
SO WHAT DO WE DO NOW?
EMMA TAKES SCOTT BACK TO THE INSTITUTE. HANK AND ME FIND KITTY...
CRACK
...AND THEN WE BURN THIS PLACE TO THE GROUND.
FIRST OFF, SCOTT AND I GIVE THE ORDERS, LOGAN.
SECOND, GOOD PLAN.
IT WON'T HELP.
I'VE ALREADY GIVEN SAMPLES AND ALL MY DATA TO HUNDREDS OF TEAMS AROUND THE WORLD.
"HOPE" CAN'T BE CRUSHED NOW. NOT EVEN BY YOU.
NICE BLUFF.
BUT I CALL.

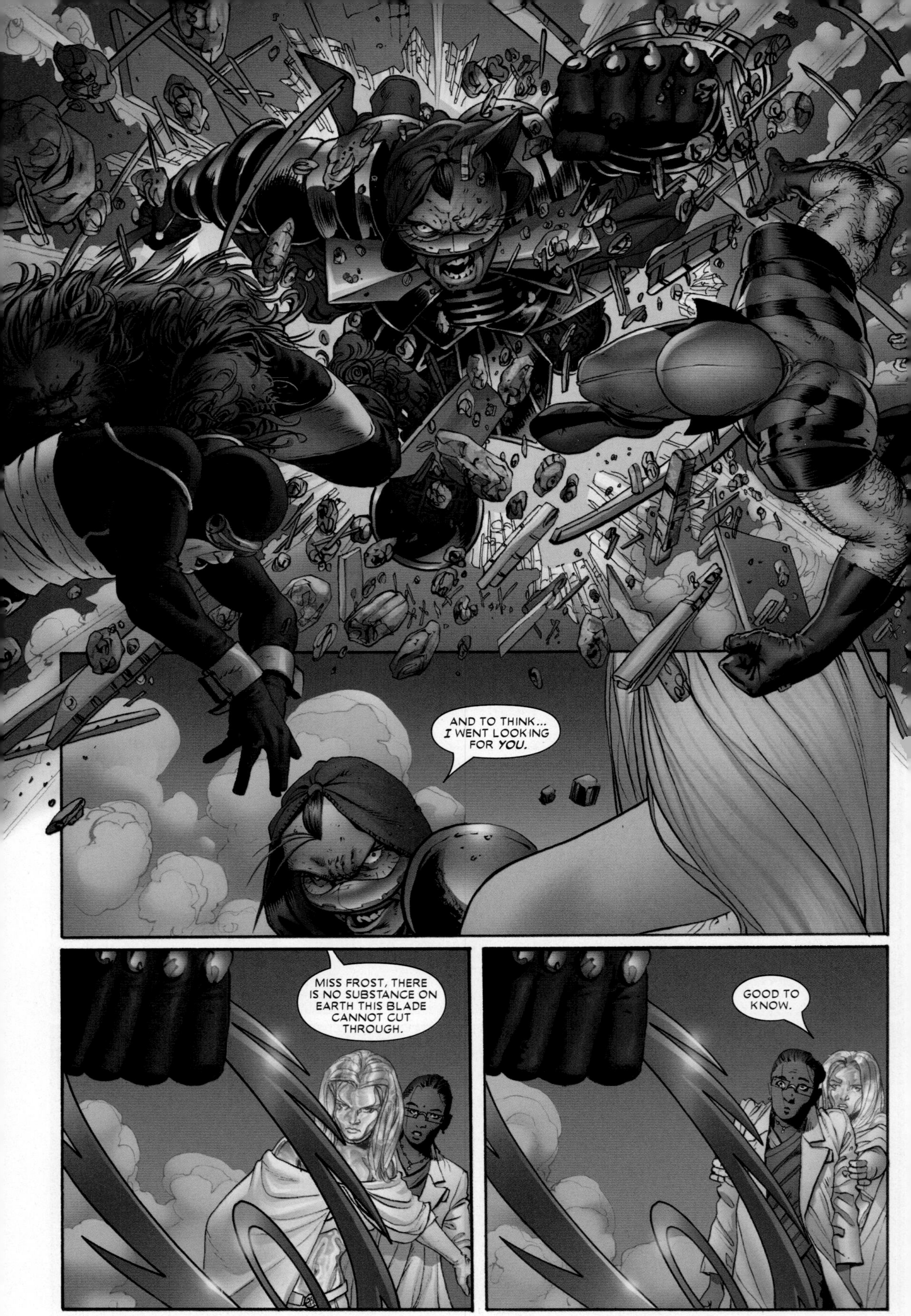
AND TO THINK... I WENT LOOKING FOR YOU.
MISS FROST, THERE IS NO SUBSTANCE ON EARTH THIS BLADE CANNOT CUT THROUGH.
GOOD TO KNOW.

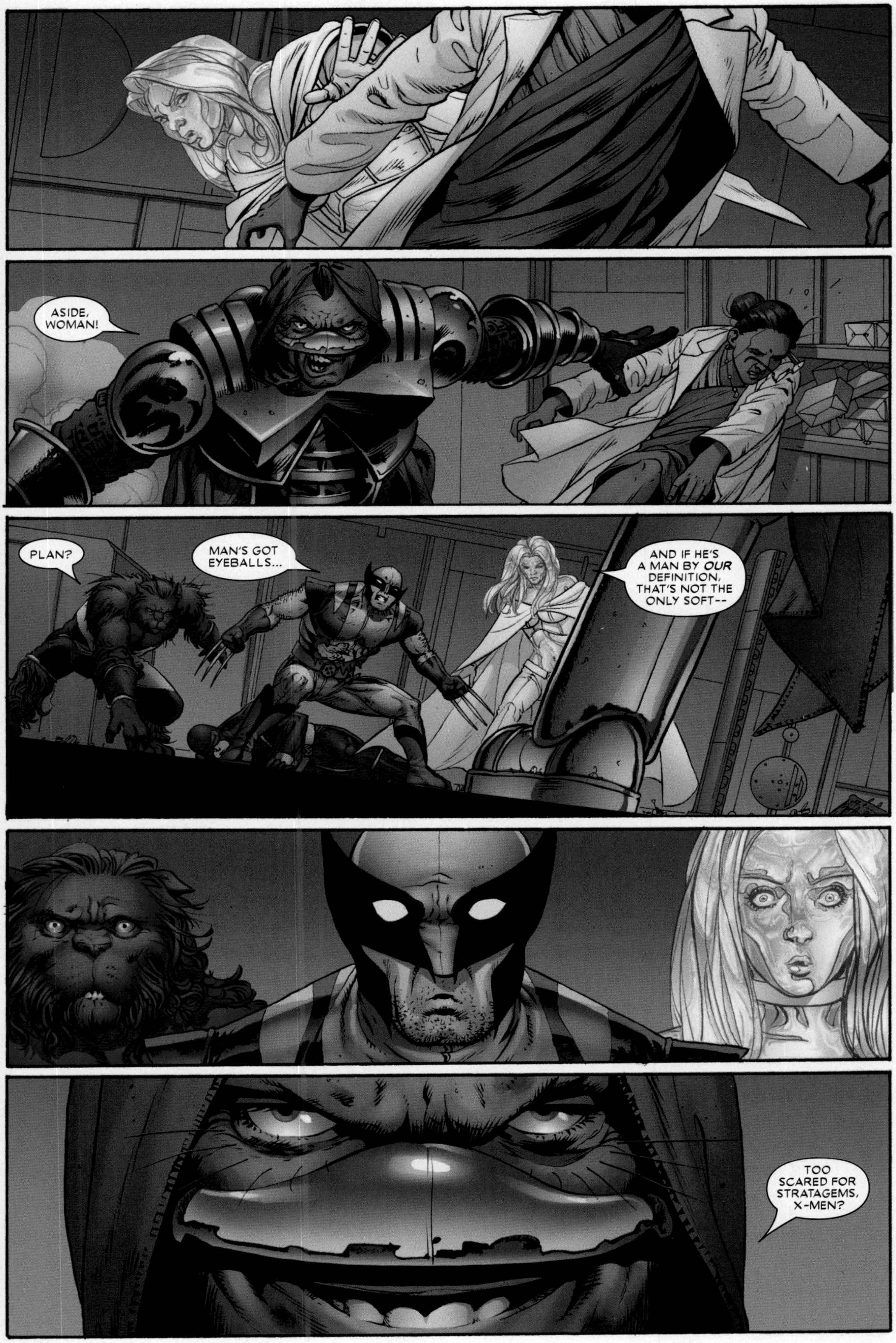
ASIDE, WOMAN!
PLAN?
MAN'S GOT EYEBALLS...
AND IF HE'S A MAN BY *OUR* DEFINITION, THAT'S NOT THE ONLY SOFT--
TOO SCARED FOR STRATAGEMS, X-MEN?

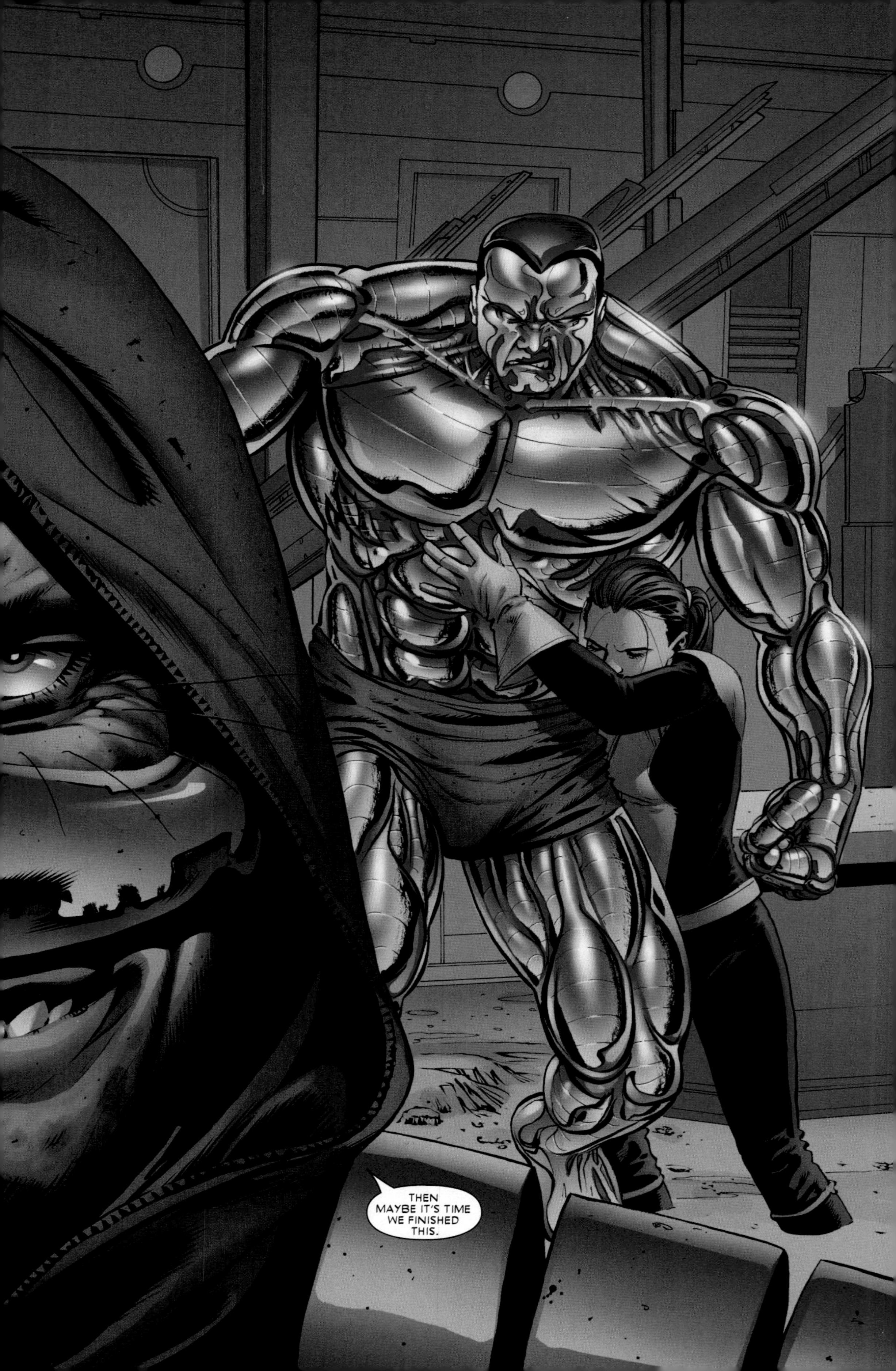
THEN MAYBE IT'S TIME WE FINISHED THIS.

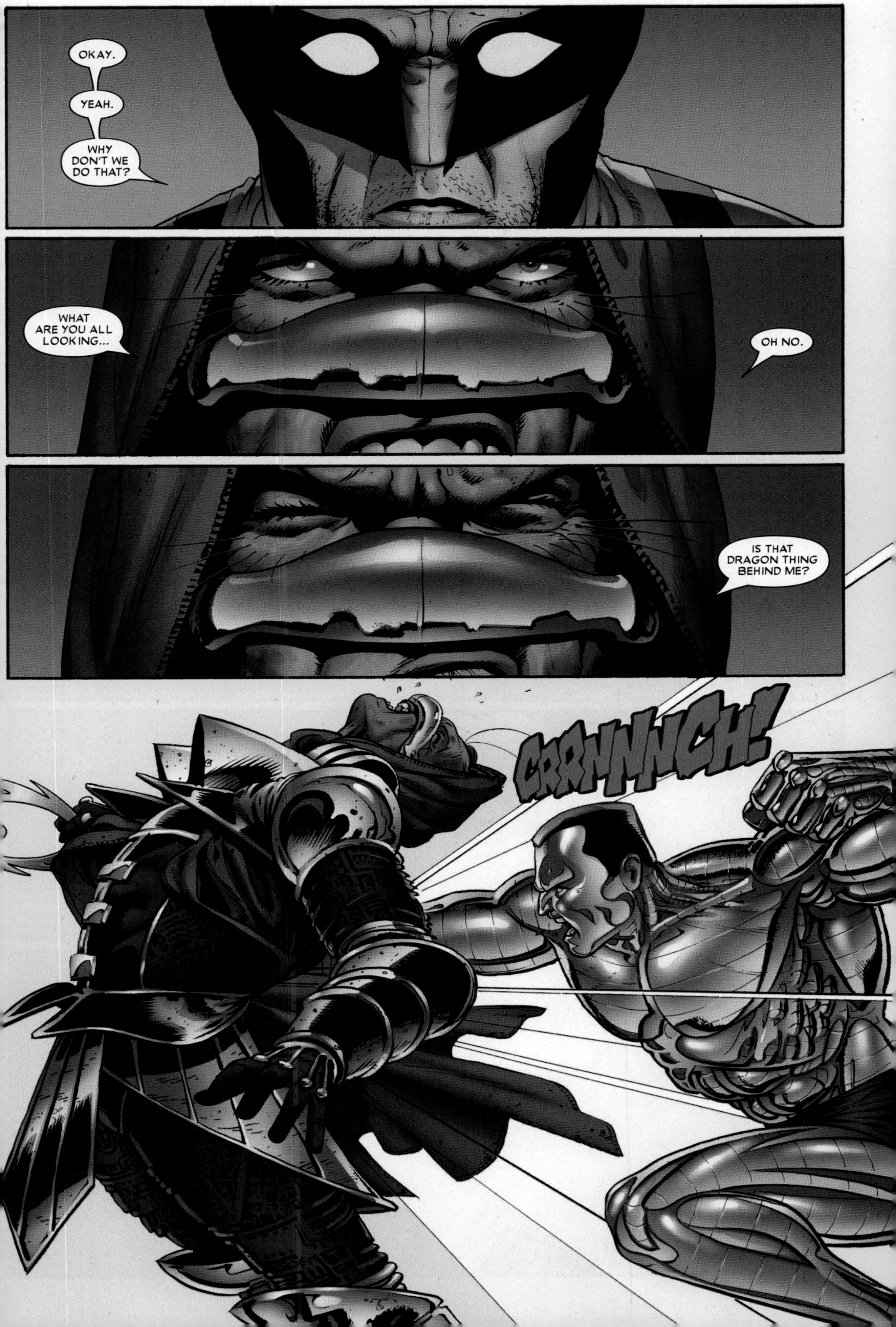

OKAY.
YEAH.
WHY DON'T WE DO THAT?
WHAT ARE YOU ALL LOOKING...
OH NO.
IS THAT DRAGON THING BEHIND ME?
CRRNNNCH!

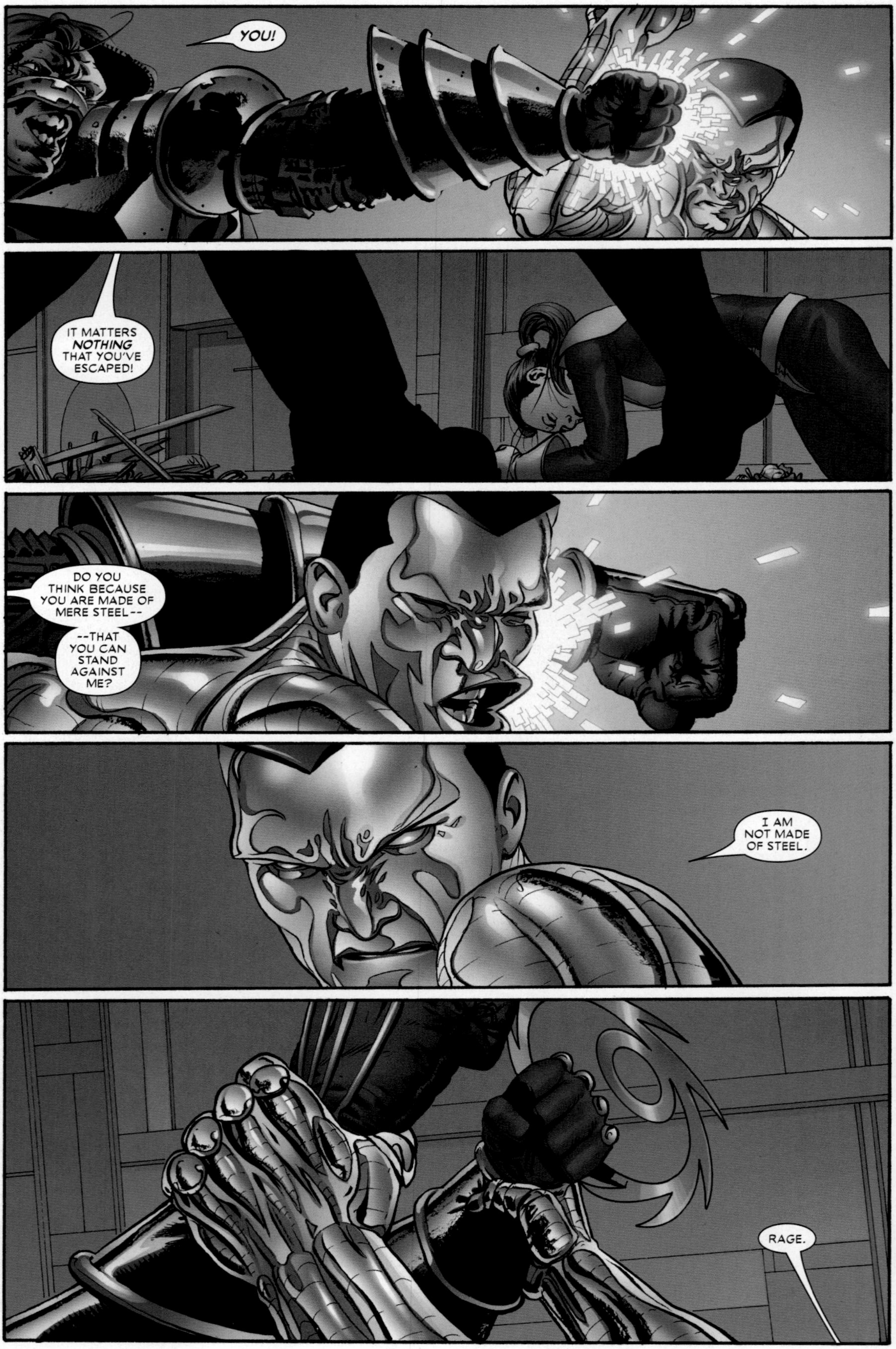
YOU!
IT MATTERS *NOTHING* THAT YOU'VE ESCAPED!
DO YOU THINK BECAUSE YOU ARE MADE OF MERE STEEL--
--THAT YOU CAN STAND AGAINST ME?
I AM NOT MADE OF STEEL.
RAGE.

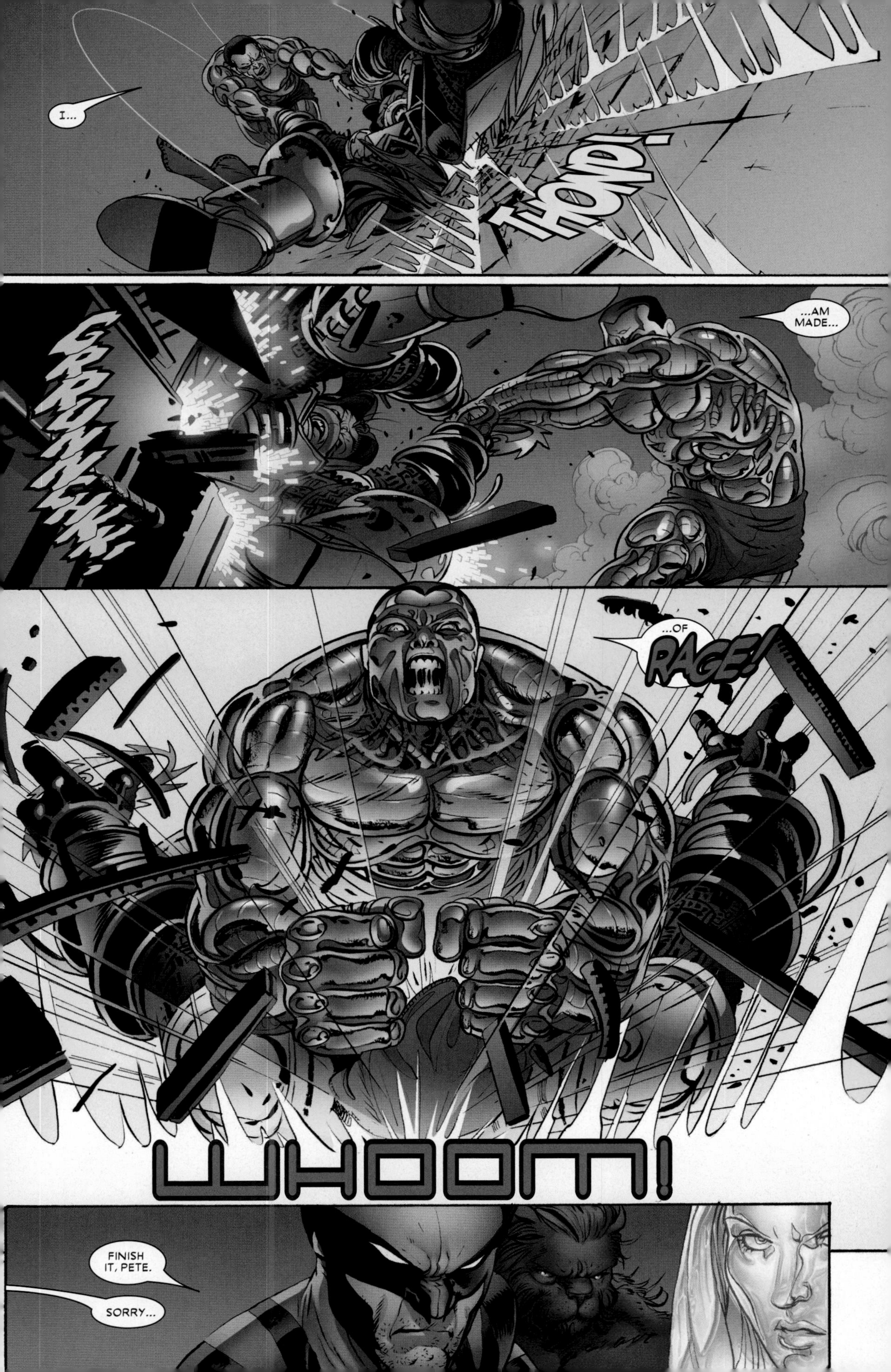

I...
THOOM!
GRRUNNCHK!
...AM MADE...
...OF RAGE!
WHOOM!
FINISH IT, PETE.
SORRY...

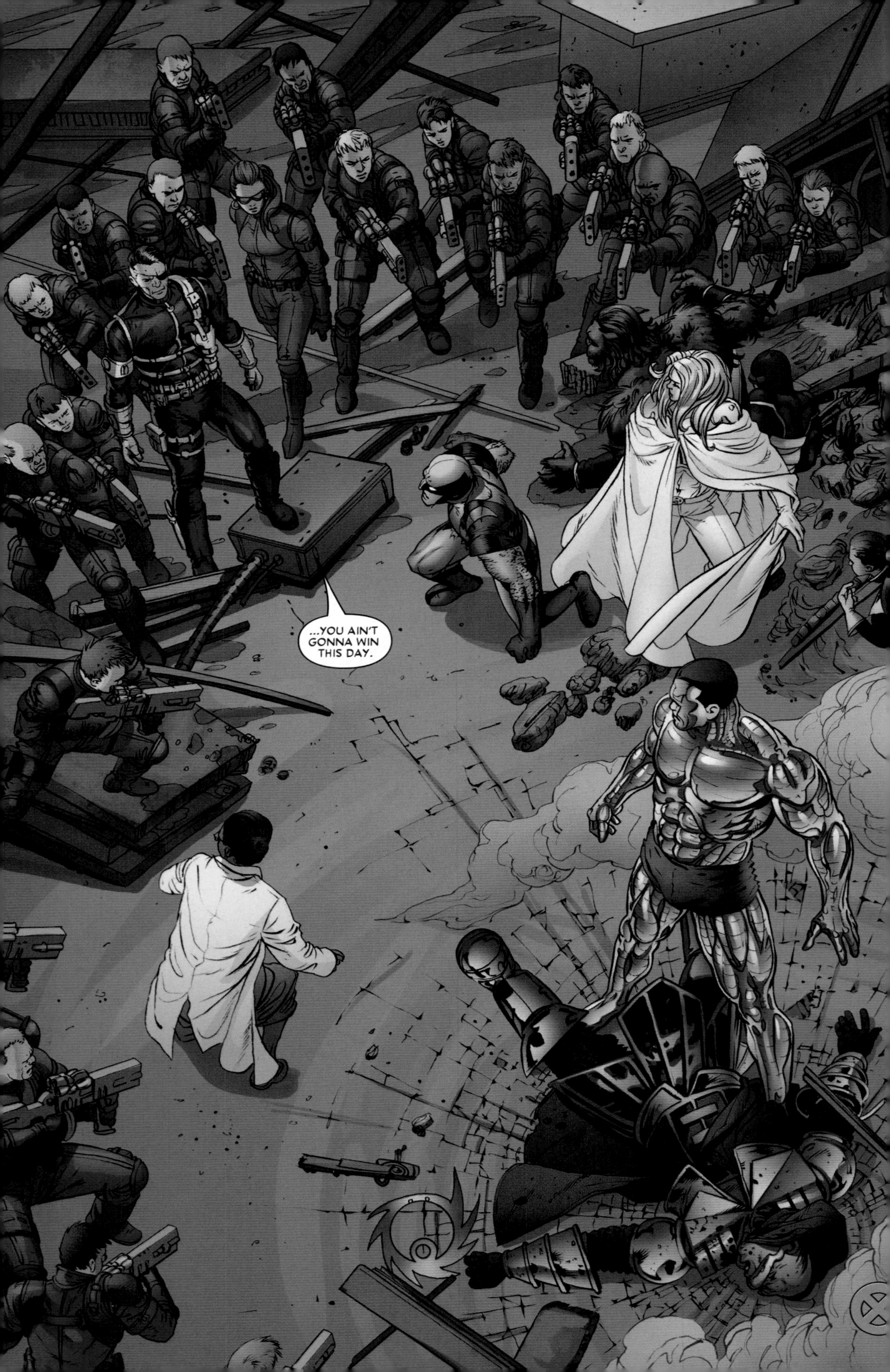
...YOU AIN'T GONNA WIN THIS DAY.

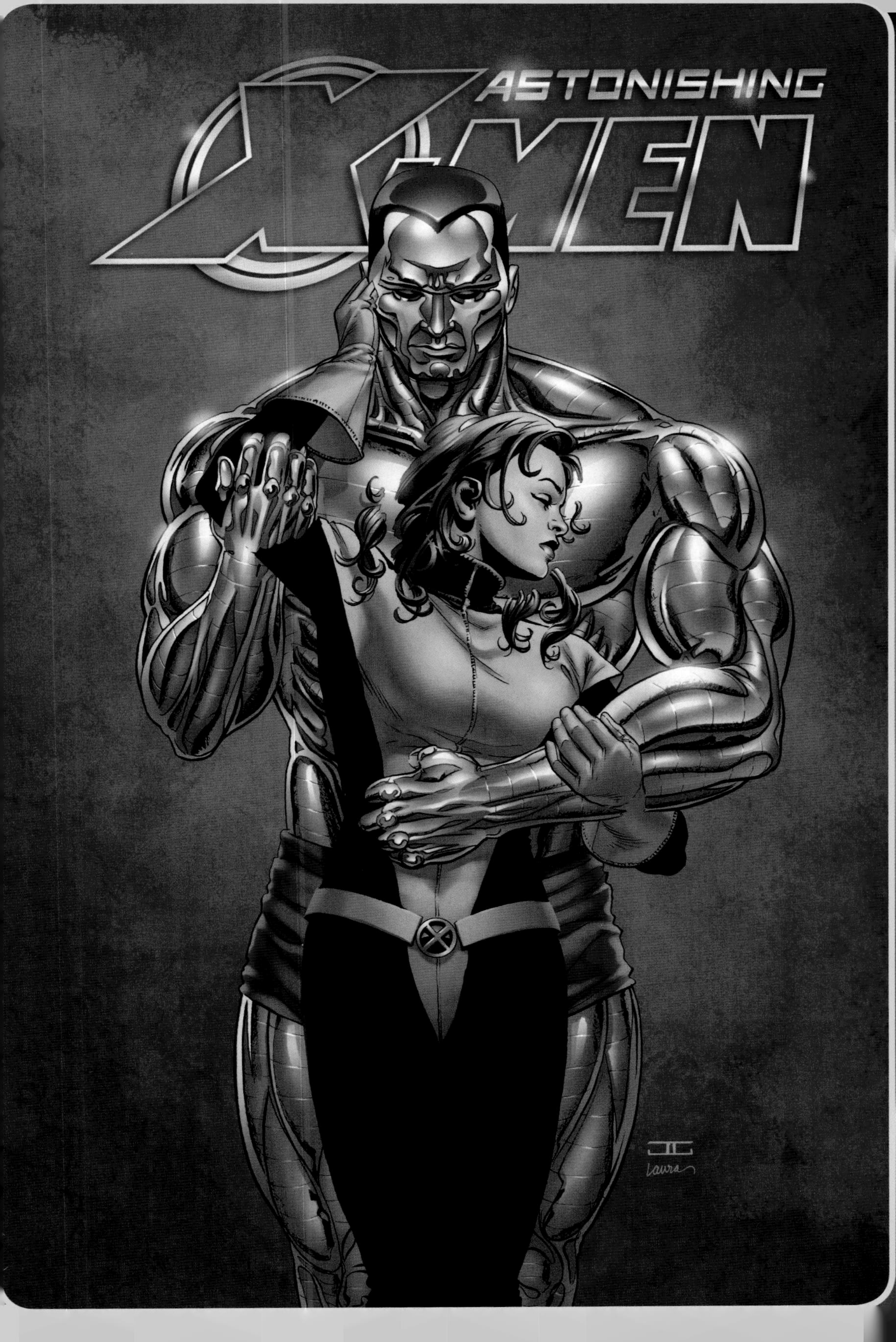
ASTONISHING
X-MEN
JC
Laura

CONSIDER IT A GIFT.

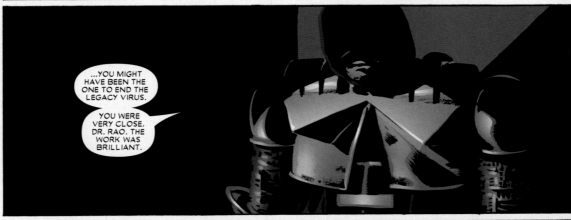

THIS IS...

IT'S UNBELIEVABLE.

IF I HAD HAD THESE JUST A FEW WEEKS AGO...

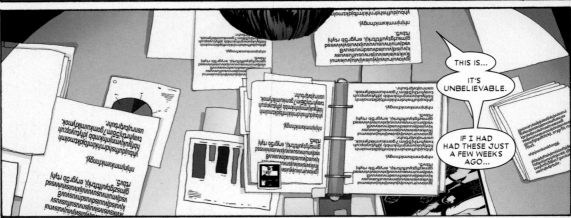

...YOU MIGHT HAVE BEEN THE ONE TO END THE LEGACY VIRUS.

YOU WERE VERY CLOSE, DR. RAO. THE WORK WAS BRILLIANT.

I STILL FAILED.

HENRY McCOY IS THE MAN YOU SHOULD BE TALKING TO.

I DON'T BELIEVE DR. McCOY WOULD BE OBJECTIVE ABOUT MY... OBJECTIVE.

GIVEN HIS CONDITION.

UNDERSTAND THIS--NO ONE IS TO BE HURT. WHATEVER YOUR FEELINGS ABOUT MUTANTS, I WILL NOT BE A PARTY TO MURDER.

WHY, DOCTOR, I HAVE JUST THIS NIGHT DONE THE OPPOSITE.

I HAVE RESUSCITATED A MUTANT YOUR EARTH-BASED SCIENCE THOUGHT DECEASED.

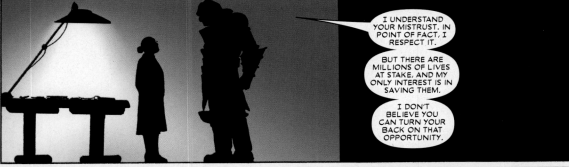

I UNDERSTAND YOUR MISTRUST. IN POINT OF FACT, I RESPECT IT.

BUT THERE ARE MILLIONS OF LIVES AT STAKE, AND MY ONLY INTEREST IS IN SAVING THEM.

I DON'T BELIEVE YOU CAN TURN YOUR BACK ON THAT OPPORTUNITY.

AGENT BRAND, DO YOU HAVE THE FILE ON TILDIE SOAMES?

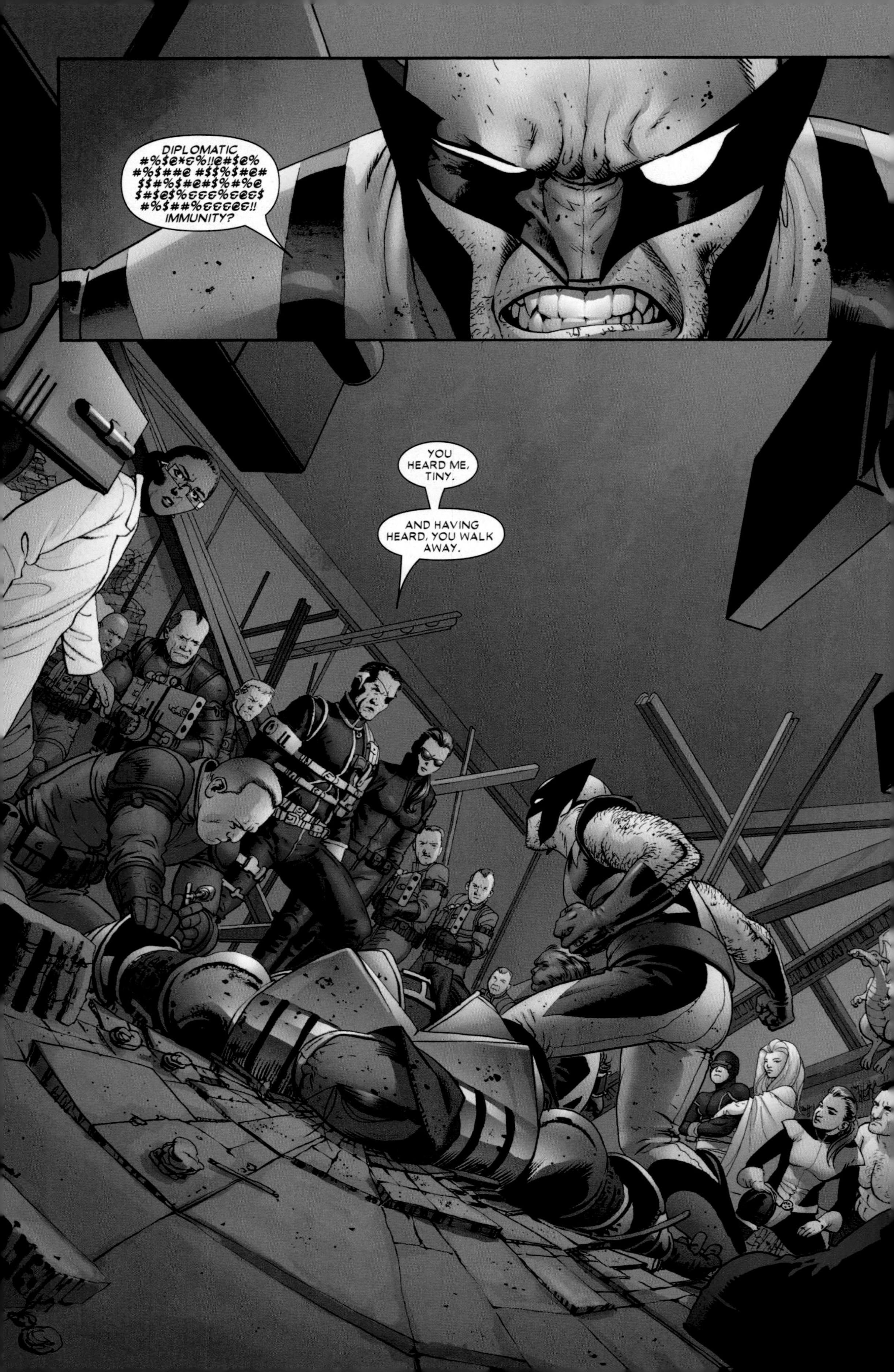
DIPLOMATIC #%$@*&%!!@#$@% #%$##@ #$$%$#@# $$#%$#@#$%#%@ $#$@$%&&&%&@&$ #%$##%&&&@&!! IMMUNITY?
YOU HEARD ME, TINY.
AND HAVING HEARD, YOU WALK AWAY.

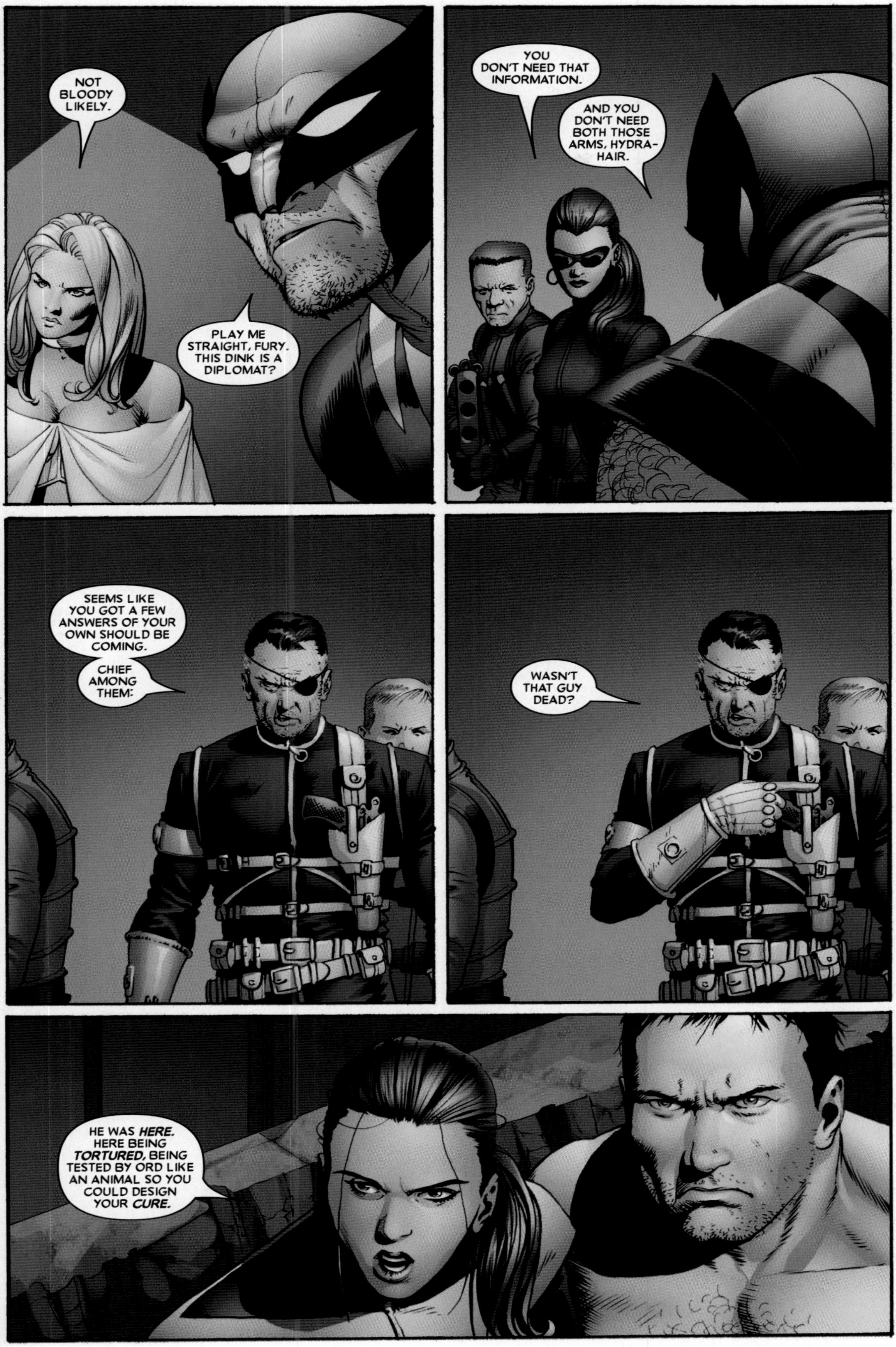
NOT BLOODY LIKELY.
PLAY ME STRAIGHT, FURY. THIS DINK IS A DIPLOMAT?
YOU DON'T NEED THAT INFORMATION.
AND YOU DON'T NEED BOTH THOSE ARMS, HYDRA-HAIR.
SEEMS LIKE YOU GOT A FEW ANSWERS OF YOUR OWN SHOULD BE COMING.
CHIEF AMONG THEM:
WASN'T THAT GUY DEAD?
HE WAS HERE. HERE BEING TORTURED, BEING TESTED BY ORD LIKE AN ANIMAL SO YOU COULD DESIGN YOUR CURE.

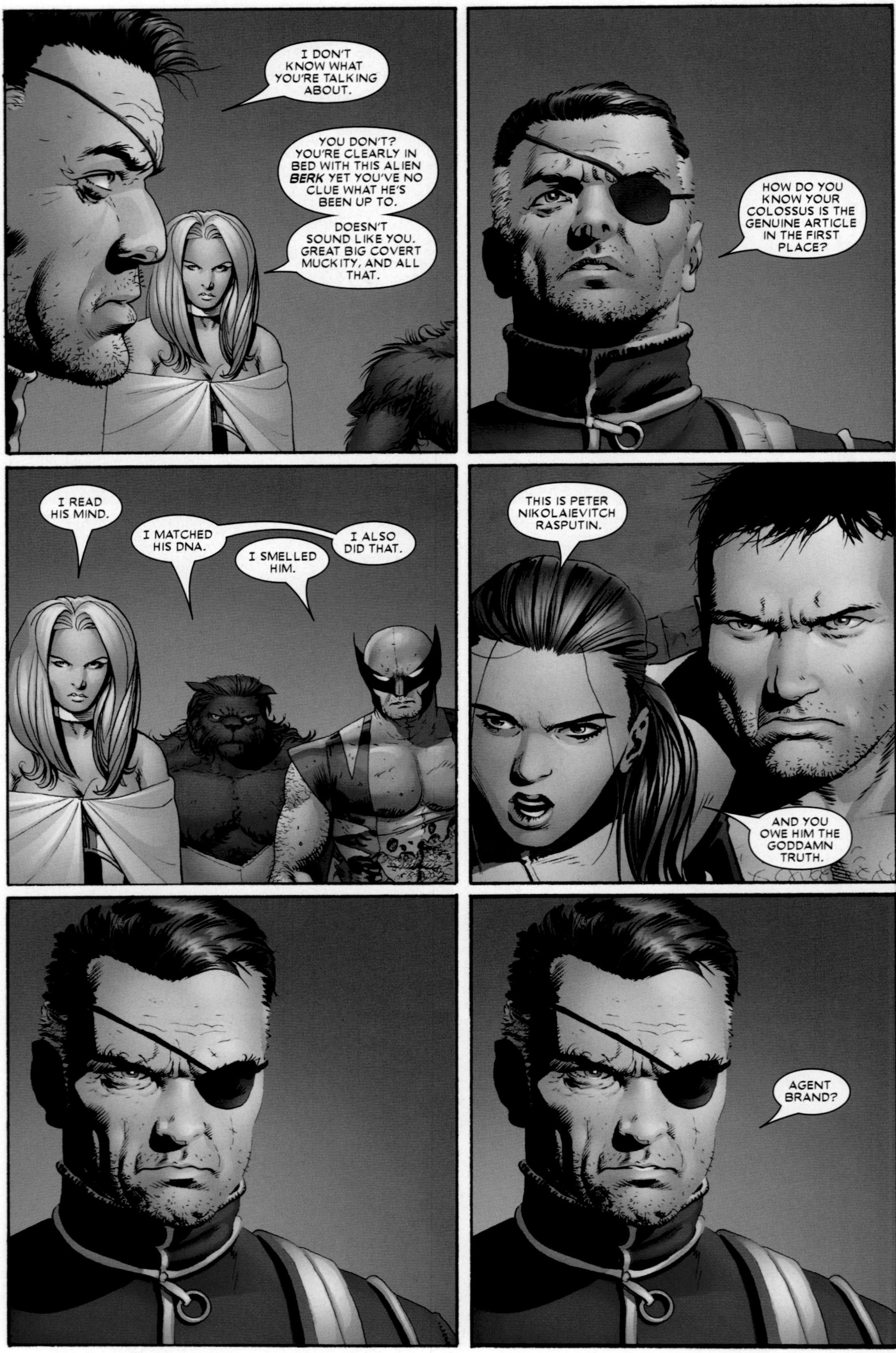
I DON'T KNOW WHAT YOU'RE TALKING ABOUT.
YOU DON'T? YOU'RE CLEARLY IN BED WITH THIS ALIEN **BERK** YET YOU'VE NO CLUE WHAT HE'S BEEN UP TO.
DOESN'T SOUND LIKE YOU. GREAT BIG COVERT MUCKITY, AND ALL THAT.
HOW DO YOU KNOW YOUR COLOSSUS IS THE GENUINE ARTICLE IN THE FIRST PLACE?
I READ HIS MIND.
I MATCHED HIS DNA.
I ALSO DID THAT.
I SMELLED HIM.
THIS IS PETER NIKOLAIEVITCH RASPUTIN.
AND YOU OWE HIM THE GODDAMN TRUTH.
AGENT BRAND?

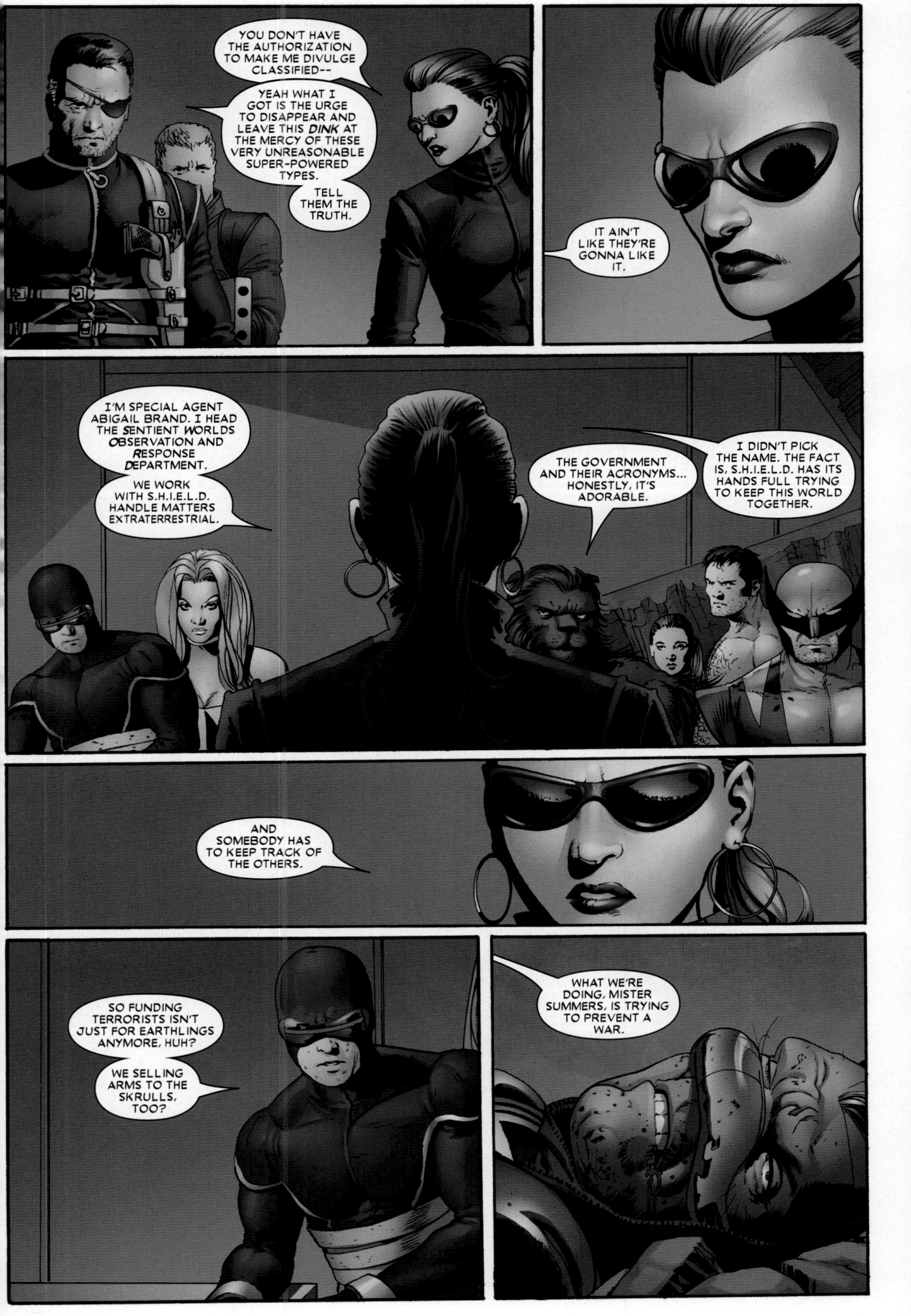
YOU DON'T HAVE THE AUTHORIZATION TO MAKE ME DIVULGE CLASSIFIED--
YEAH WHAT I GOT IS THE URGE TO DISAPPEAR AND LEAVE THIS DINK AT THE MERCY OF THESE VERY UNREASONABLE SUPER-POWERED TYPES.
TELL THEM THE TRUTH.
IT AIN'T LIKE THEY'RE GONNA LIKE IT.
I'M SPECIAL AGENT ABIGAIL BRAND. I HEAD THE SENTIENT WORLDS OBSERVATION AND RESPONSE DEPARTMENT.
WE WORK WITH S.H.I.E.L.D. HANDLE MATTERS EXTRATERRESTRIAL.
THE GOVERNMENT AND THEIR ACRONYMS... HONESTLY, IT'S ADORABLE.
I DIDN'T PICK THE NAME. THE FACT IS, S.H.I.E.L.D. HAS ITS HANDS FULL TRYING TO KEEP THIS WORLD TOGETHER.
AND SOMEBODY HAS TO KEEP TRACK OF THE OTHERS.
SO FUNDING TERRORISTS ISN'T JUST FOR EARTHLINGS ANYMORE, HUH?
WE SELLING ARMS TO THE SKRULLS, TOO?
WHAT WE'RE DOING, MISTER SUMMERS, IS TRYING TO PREVENT A WAR.

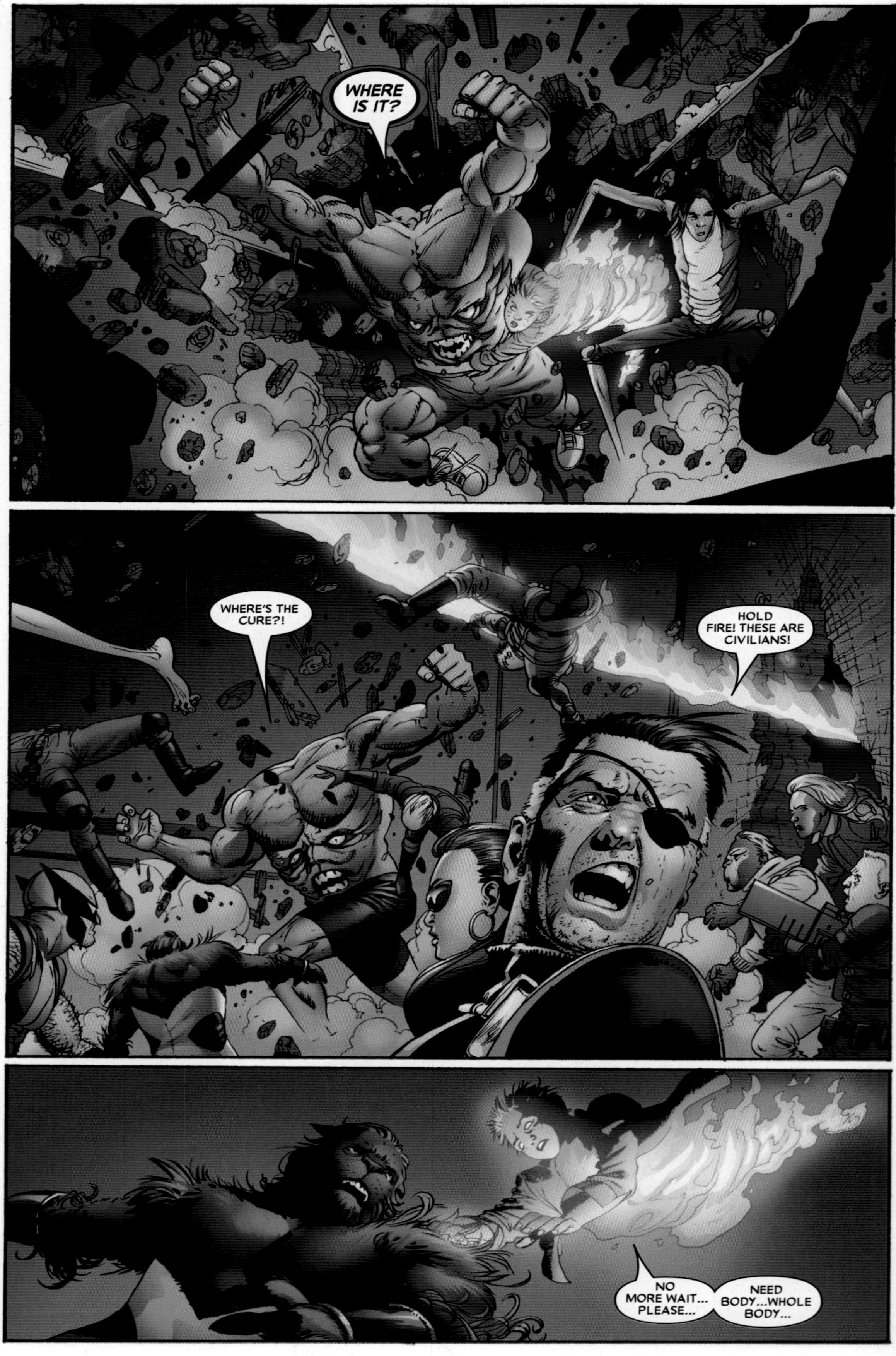
WHERE IS IT?
WHERE'S THE CURE?!
HOLD FIRE! THESE ARE CIVILIANS!
NO MORE WAIT... PLEASE...
NEED BODY...WHOLE BODY...

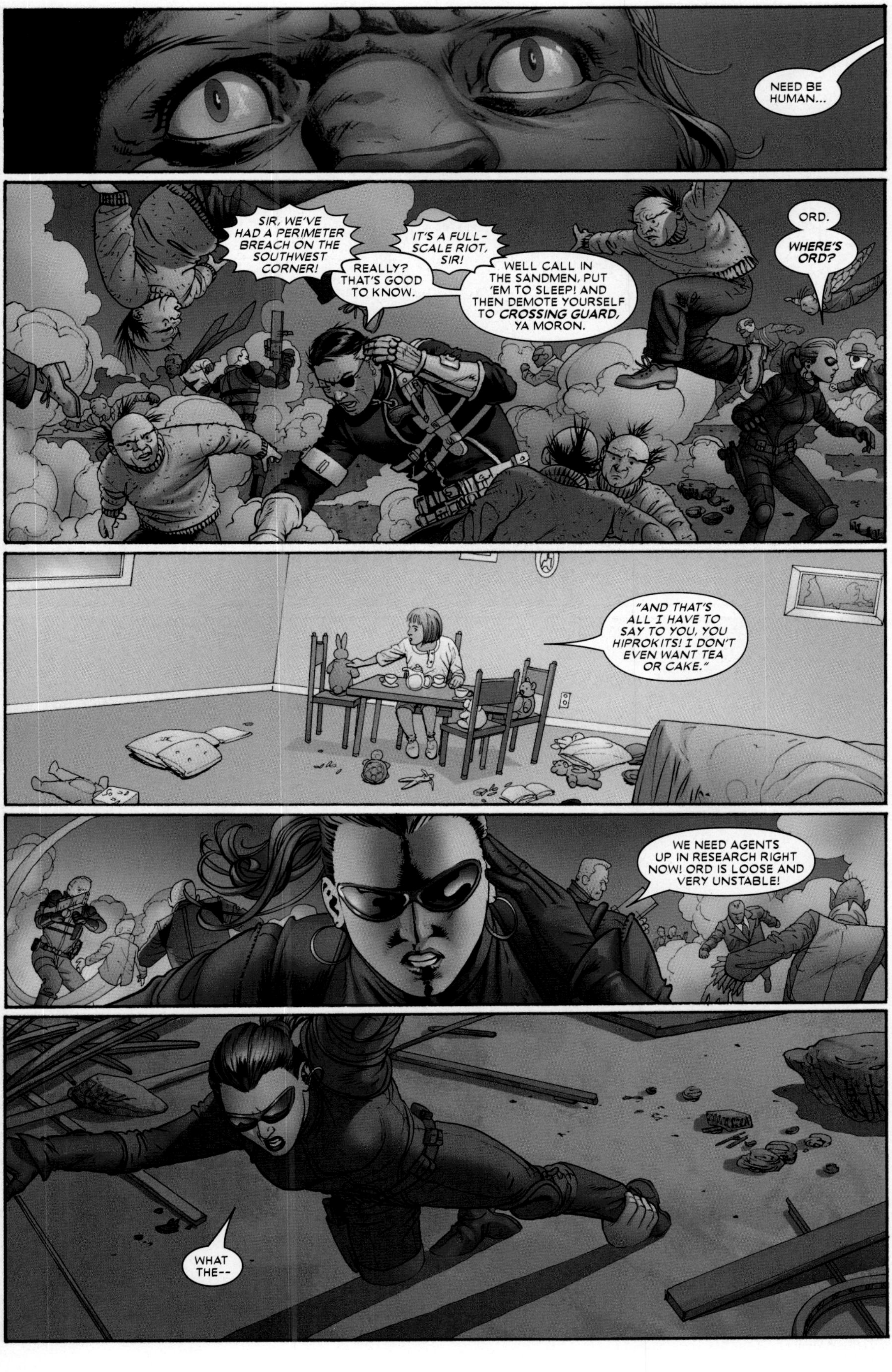
NEED BE HUMAN...
SIR, WE'VE HAD A PERIMETER BREACH ON THE SOUTHWEST CORNER!
REALLY? THAT'S GOOD TO KNOW.
IT'S A FULL-SCALE RIOT, SIR!
WELL CALL IN THE SANDMEN, PUT 'EM TO SLEEP! AND THEN DEMOTE YOURSELF TO CROSSING GUARD, YA MORON.
ORD.
WHERE'S ORD?
"AND THAT'S ALL I HAVE TO SAY TO YOU, YOU HIPROKITS! I DON'T EVEN WANT TEA OR CAKE."
WE NEED AGENTS UP IN RESEARCH RIGHT NOW! ORD IS LOOSE AND VERY UNSTABLE!
WHAT THE--

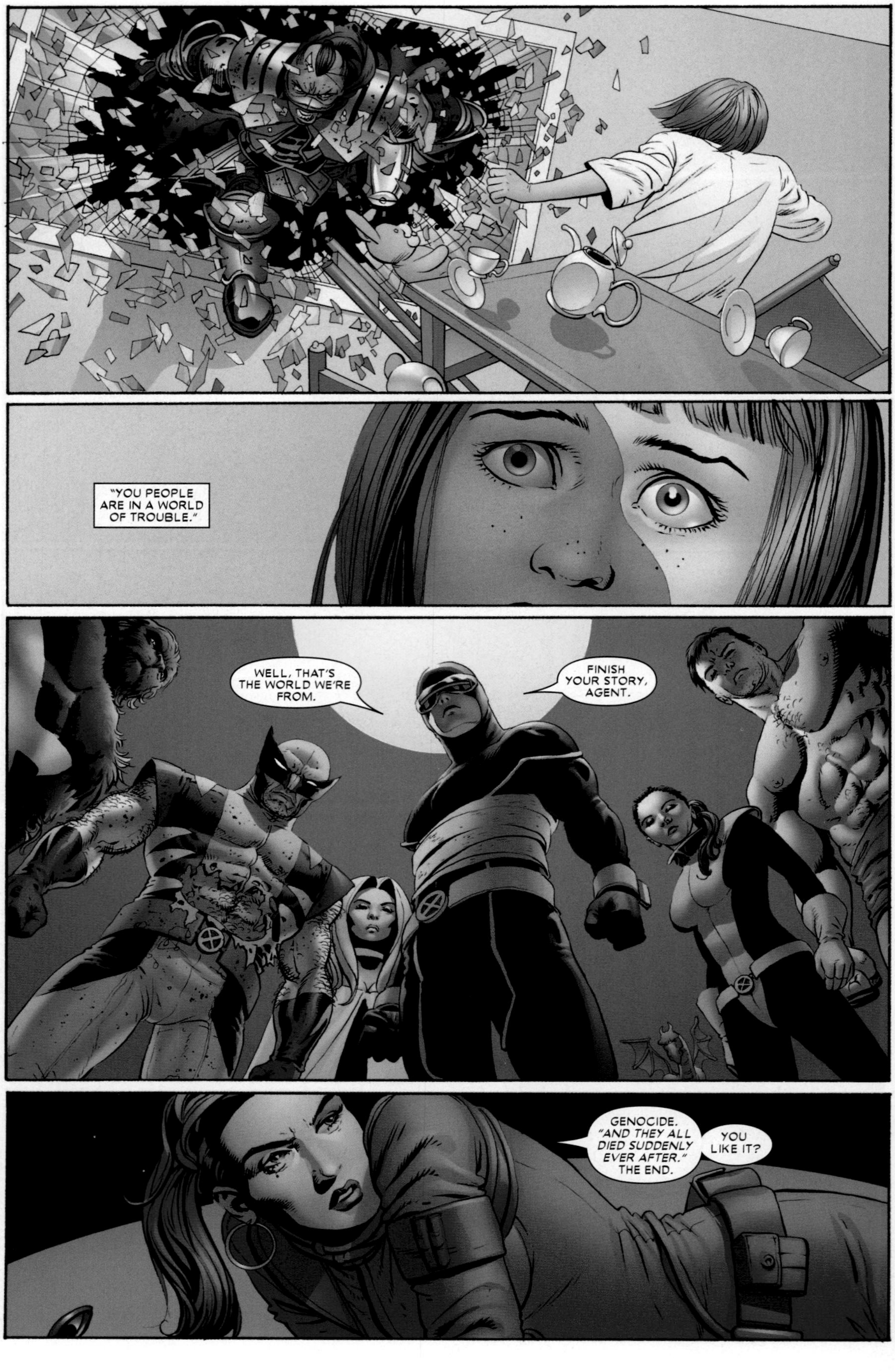
"YOU PEOPLE ARE IN A WORLD OF TROUBLE."
WELL, THAT'S THE WORLD WE'RE FROM.
FINISH YOUR STORY, AGENT.
GENOCIDE. "AND THEY ALL DIED SUDDENLY EVER AFTER." THE END.
YOU LIKE IT?

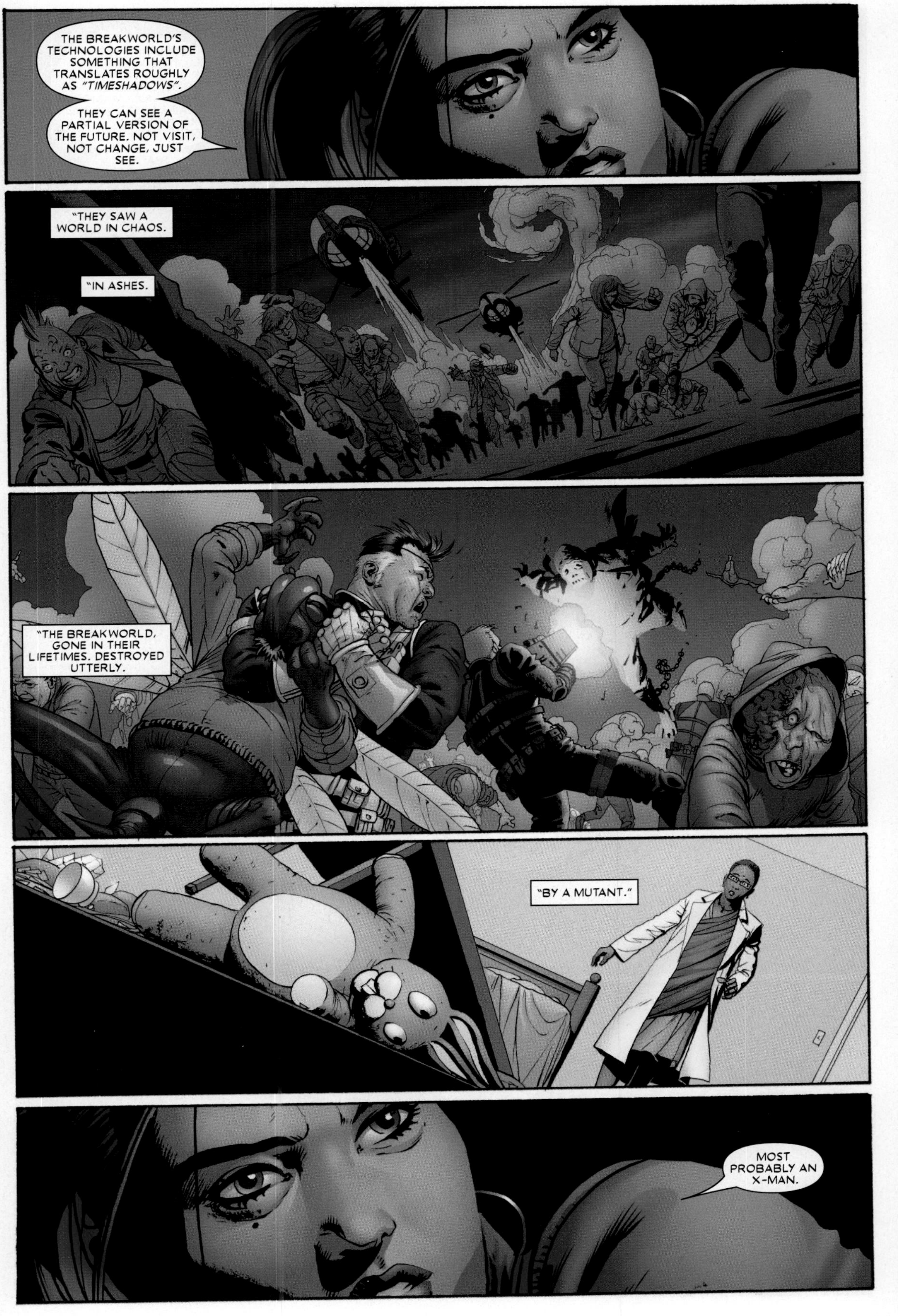
THE BREAKWORLD'S TECHNOLOGIES INCLUDE SOMETHING THAT TRANSLATES ROUGHLY AS "TIMESHADOWS".
THEY CAN SEE A PARTIAL VERSION OF THE FUTURE. NOT VISIT, NOT CHANGE, JUST SEE.
"THEY SAW A WORLD IN CHAOS.
"IN ASHES.
"THE BREAKWORLD, GONE IN THEIR LIFETIMES. DESTROYED UTTERLY.
"BY A MUTANT."
MOST PROBABLY AN X-MAN.

SO YOU GOT TOGETHER AND DECIDED TO TAKE CARE OF THE MUTIES ONCE AND FOR ALL, HUH?

DEAL WITH THE FACTS, BUMBLEBEE. OUR OWN PRECOG STATS CONFIRMED THEIR FINDINGS. A MUTANT WILL ALMOST CERTAINLY DESTROY THE BREAKWORLD IN THE NEXT THREE YEARS.

THAT'S A WHOLE WORLD, GONE. BECAUSE OF ONE MUTANT.

THAT WOULDN'T BE A FIRST, NOW, WOULD IT?

JEAN.

JEAN GREY IS *DEAD*, AGENT.

YEAH, *THAT'LL* LAST.

DID YOU KNOW WHAT HE WAS DOING TO PETER? ALL THIS TIME, DID YOU KNOW?

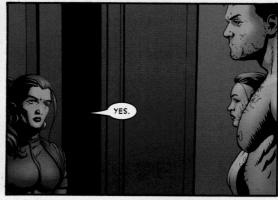

YES.

FURY DIDN'T. NOT HIS DEPARTMENT.

WHAT ABOUT KAVITA?

ORD CAME HERE WITH A DECLARATION OF *WAR*, PEOPLE. THE CURE WAS DIPLOMATIC TAP DANCING TILL WE COULD GET A BEAD ON WHICH MUTANT WAS--

PLEASE ANSWER MY QUESTION.

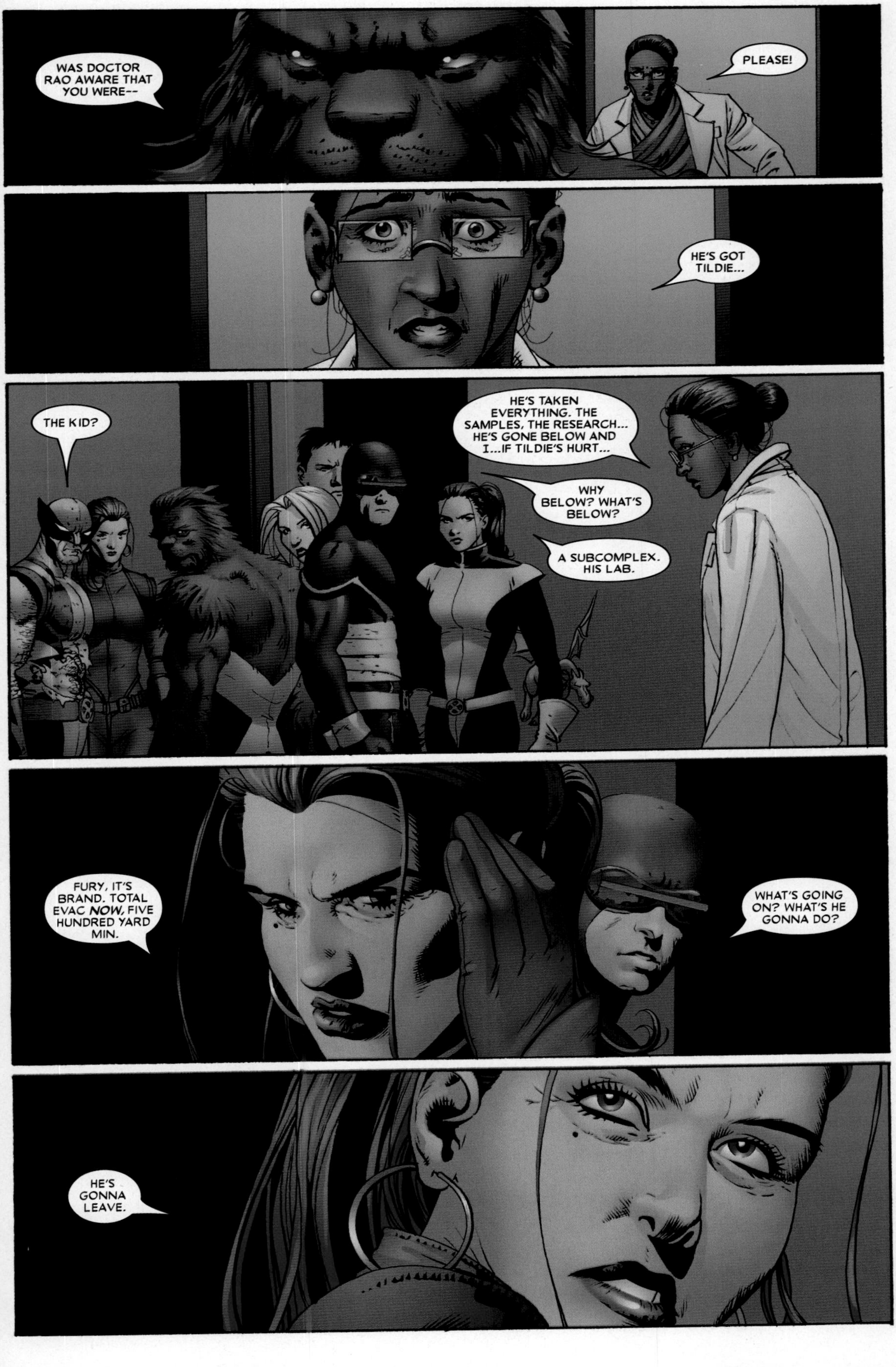
WAS DOCTOR RAO AWARE THAT YOU WERE--
PLEASE!
HE'S GOT TILDIE...
THE KID?
HE'S TAKEN EVERYTHING. THE SAMPLES, THE RESEARCH... HE'S GONE BELOW AND I...IF TILDIE'S HURT...
WHY BELOW? WHAT'S BELOW?
A SUBCOMPLEX. HIS LAB.
FURY, IT'S BRAND. TOTAL EVAC NOW, FIVE HUNDRED YARD MIN.
WHAT'S GOING ON? WHAT'S HE GONNA DO?
HE'S GONNA LEAVE.

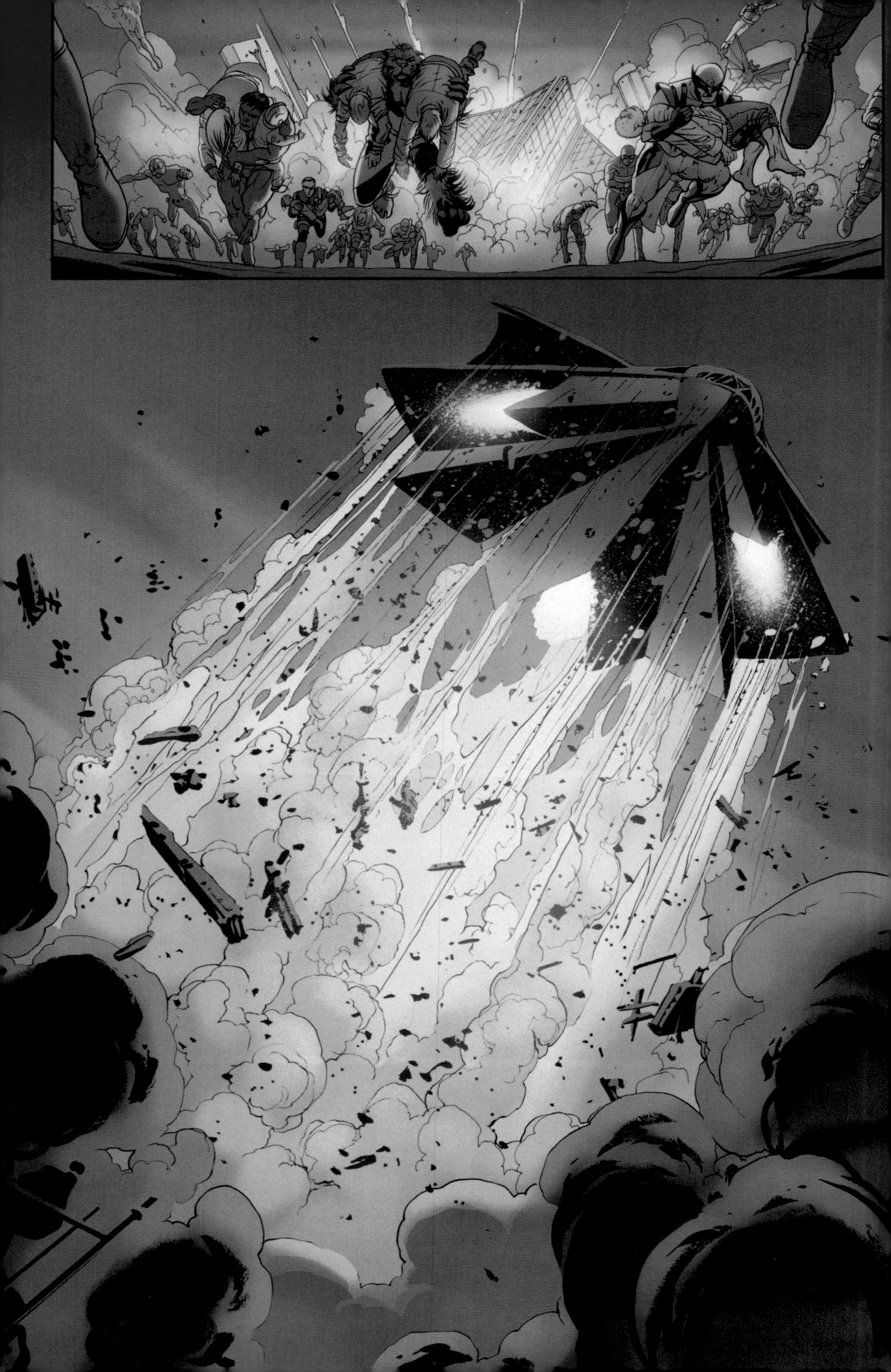

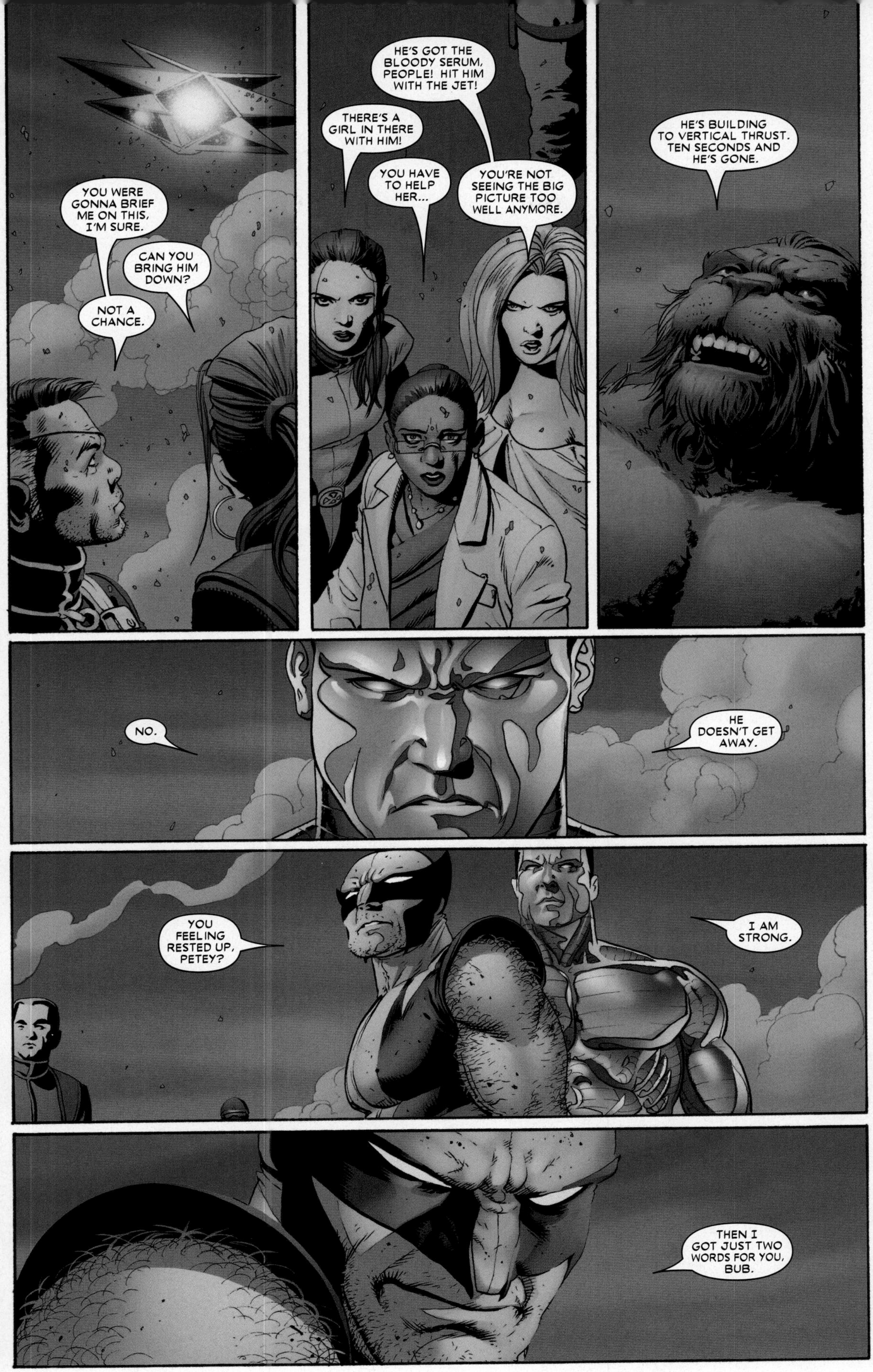
YOU WERE GONNA BRIEF ME ON THIS, I'M SURE.
CAN YOU BRING HIM DOWN?
NOT A CHANCE.
THERE'S A GIRL IN THERE WITH HIM!
YOU HAVE TO HELP HER...
HE'S GOT THE BLOODY SERUM, PEOPLE! HIT HIM WITH THE JET!
YOU'RE NOT SEEING THE BIG PICTURE TOO WELL ANYMORE.
HE'S BUILDING TO VERTICAL THRUST. TEN SECONDS AND HE'S GONE.
NO.
HE DOESN'T GET AWAY.
YOU FEELING RESTED UP, PETEY?
I AM STRONG.
THEN I GOT JUST TWO WORDS FOR YOU, BUB.

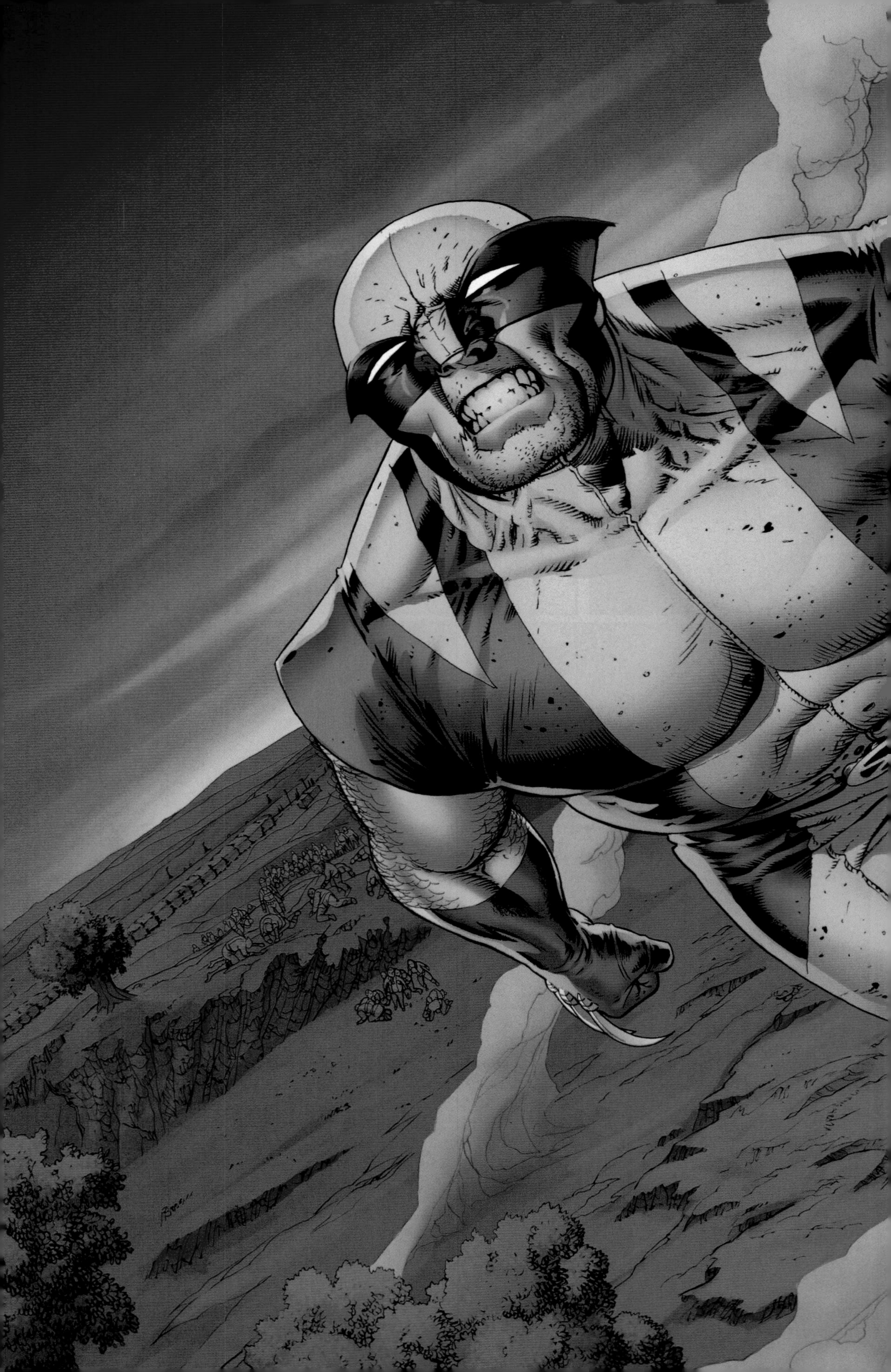

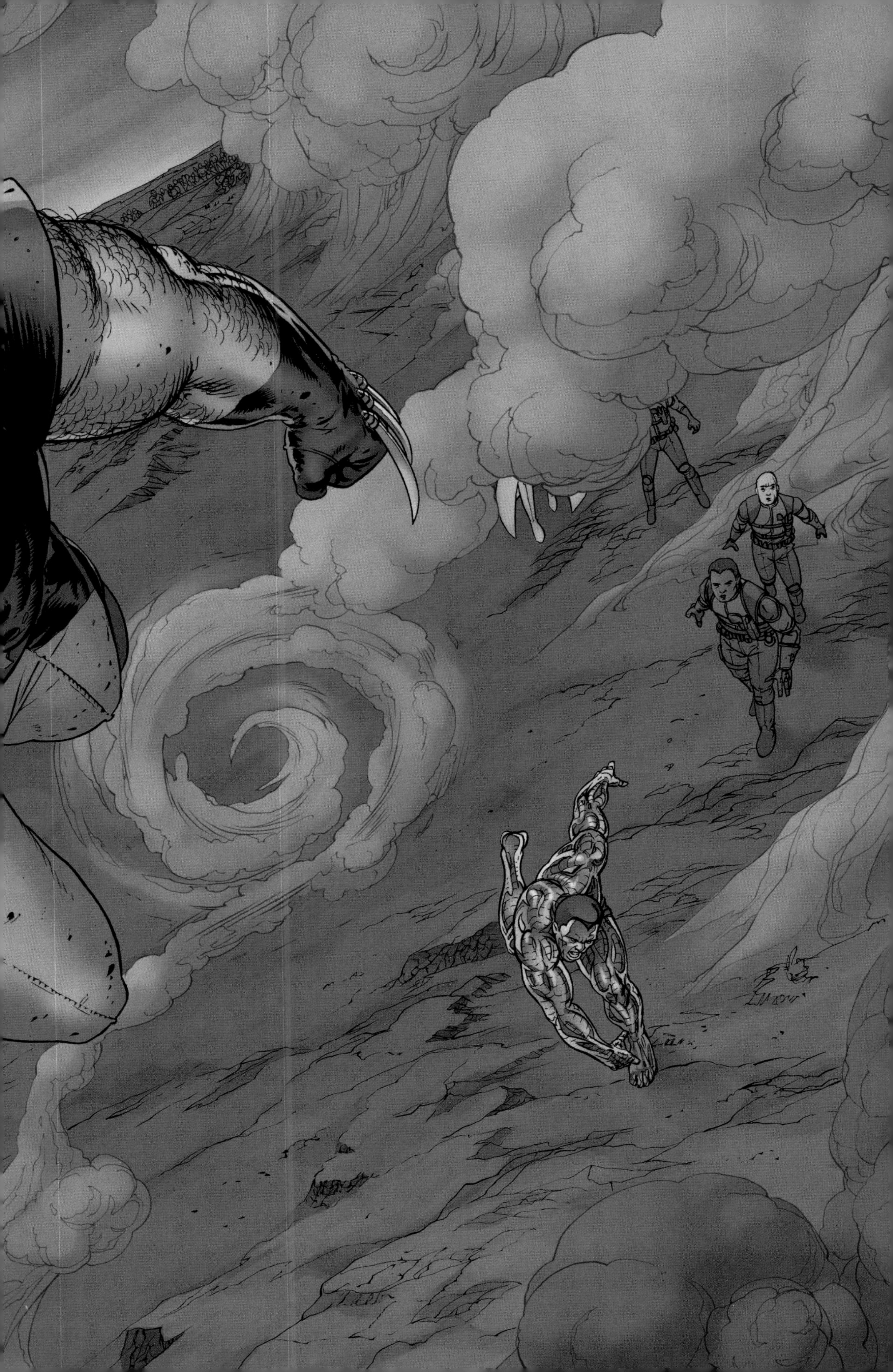

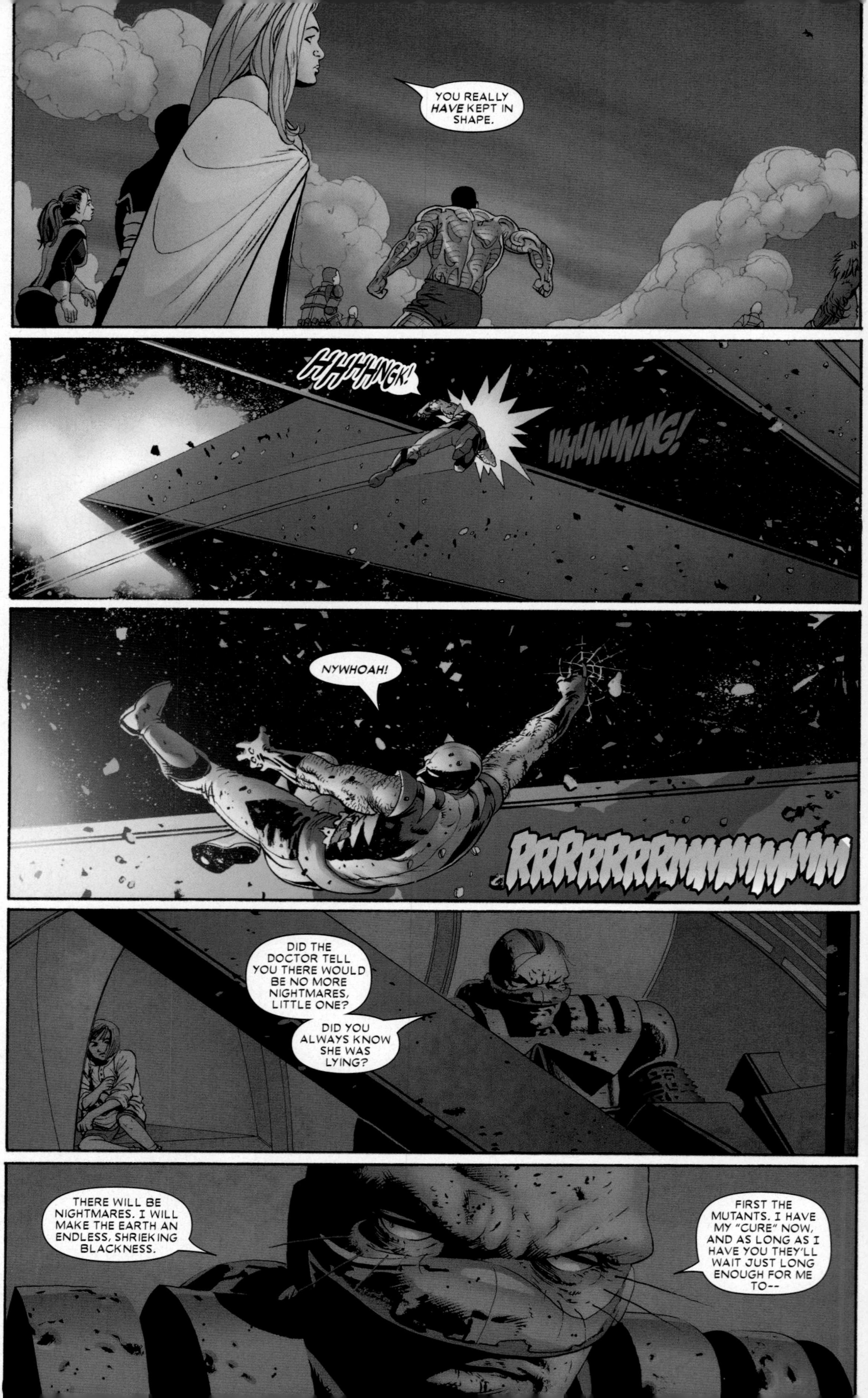
YOU REALLY HAVE KEPT IN SHAPE.
GHHHNGK!
WHUNNNNG!
NYWHOAH!
RRRRRRRMMMMMMMM
DID THE DOCTOR TELL YOU THERE WOULD BE NO MORE NIGHTMARES, LITTLE ONE?
DID YOU ALWAYS KNOW SHE WAS LYING?
THERE WILL BE NIGHTMARES. I WILL MAKE THE EARTH AN ENDLESS, SHRIEKING BLACKNESS.
FIRST THE MUTANTS. I HAVE MY "CURE" NOW, AND AS LONG AS I HAVE YOU THEY'LL WAIT JUST LONG ENOUGH FOR ME TO--

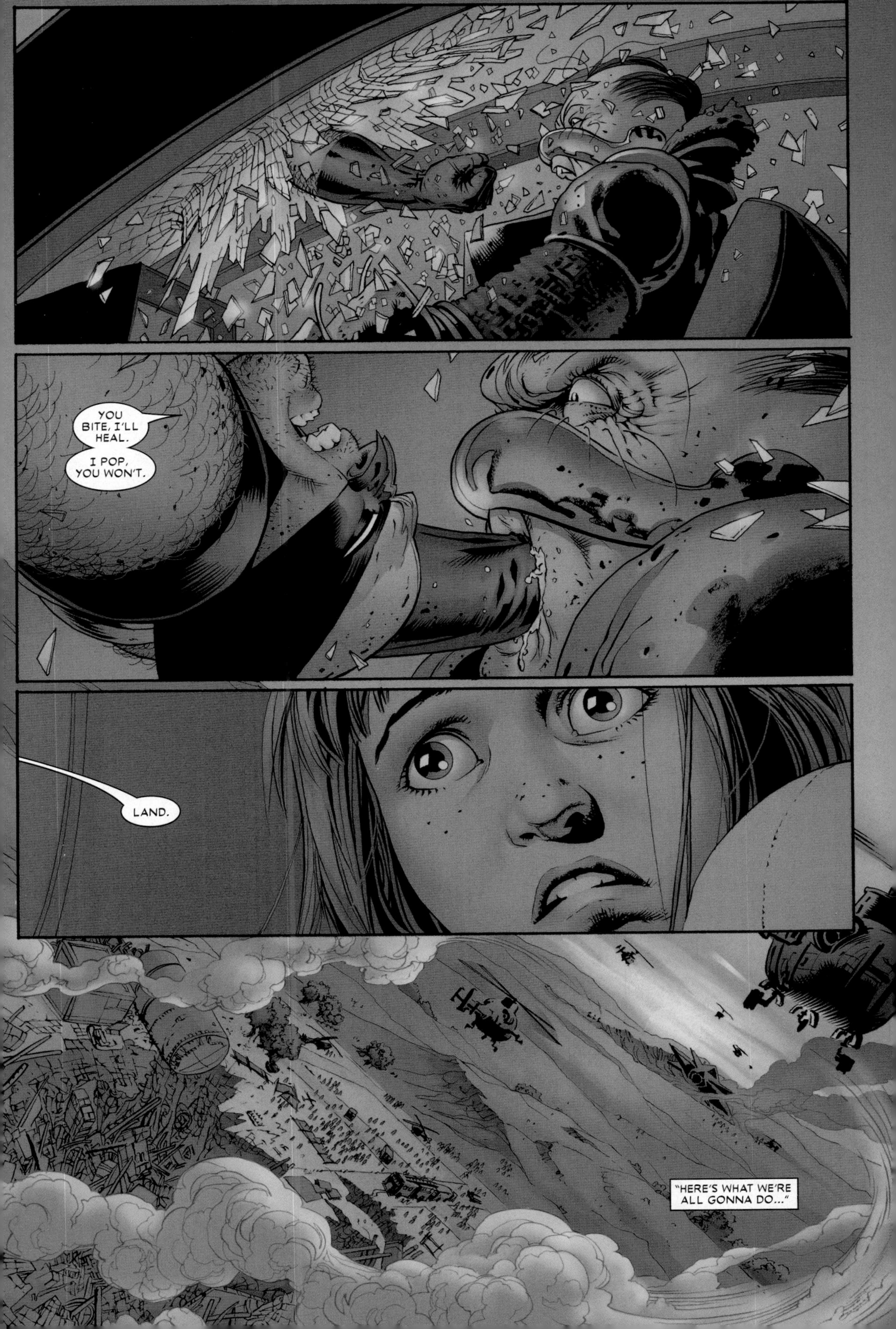
YOU BITE, I'LL HEAL.
I POP, YOU WON'T.
LAND.
"HERE'S WHAT WE'RE ALL GONNA DO..."

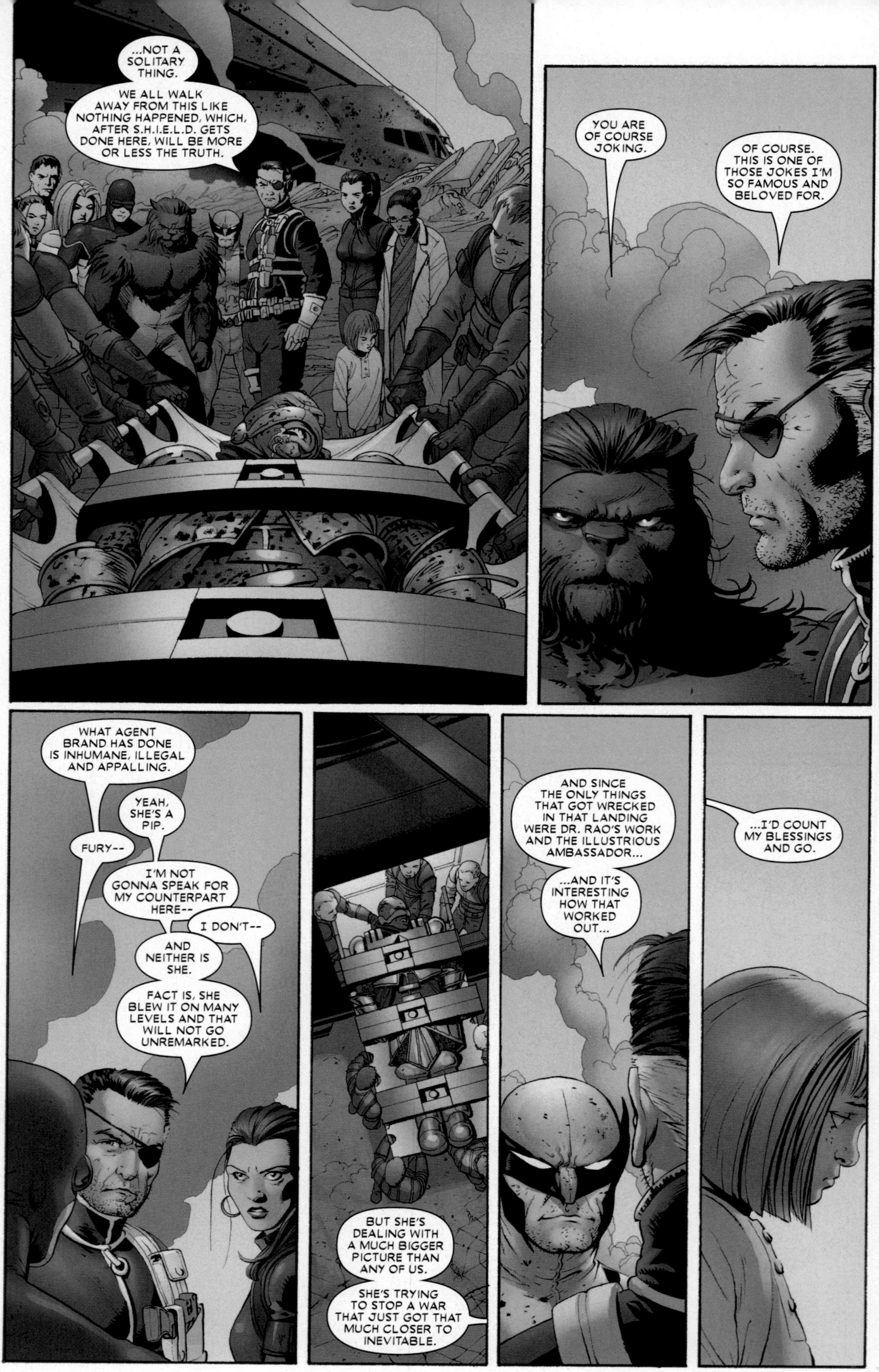
...NOT A SOLITARY THING.
WE ALL WALK AWAY FROM THIS LIKE NOTHING HAPPENED, WHICH, AFTER S.H.I.E.L.D. GETS DONE HERE, WILL BE MORE OR LESS THE TRUTH.
YOU ARE OF COURSE JOKING.
OF COURSE. THIS IS ONE OF THOSE JOKES I'M SO FAMOUS AND BELOVED FOR.
WHAT AGENT BRAND HAS DONE IS INHUMANE, ILLEGAL AND APPALLING.
FURY--
YEAH, SHE'S A PIP.
I'M NOT GONNA SPEAK FOR MY COUNTERPART HERE--
I DON'T--
AND NEITHER IS SHE.
FACT IS, SHE BLEW IT ON MANY LEVELS AND THAT WILL NOT GO UNREMARKED.
BUT SHE'S DEALING WITH A MUCH BIGGER PICTURE THAN ANY OF US.
SHE'S TRYING TO STOP A WAR THAT JUST GOT THAT MUCH CLOSER TO INEVITABLE.
AND SINCE THE ONLY THINGS THAT GOT WRECKED IN THAT LANDING WERE DR. RAO'S WORK AND THE ILLUSTRIOUS AMBASSADOR...
...AND IT'S INTERESTING HOW THAT WORKED OUT...
...I'D COUNT MY BLESSINGS AND GO.

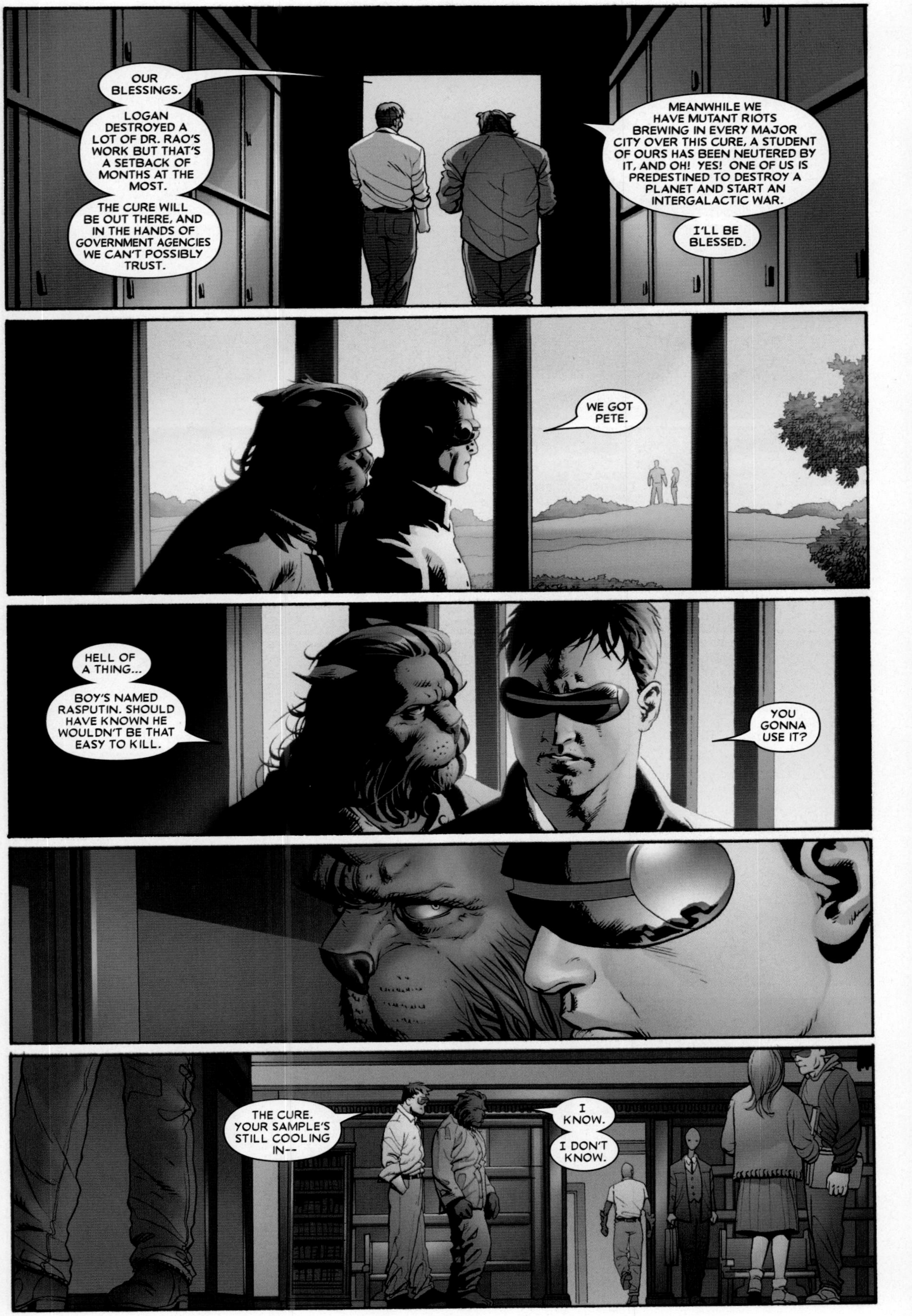

OUR BLESSINGS.
LOGAN DESTROYED A LOT OF DR. RAO'S WORK BUT THAT'S A SETBACK OF MONTHS AT THE MOST.
THE CURE WILL BE OUT THERE, AND IN THE HANDS OF GOVERNMENT AGENCIES WE CAN'T POSSIBLY TRUST.
MEANWHILE WE HAVE MUTANT RIOTS BREWING IN EVERY MAJOR CITY OVER THIS CURE, A STUDENT OF OURS HAS BEEN NEUTERED BY IT, AND OH! YES! ONE OF US IS PREDESTINED TO DESTROY A PLANET AND START AN INTERGALACTIC WAR.
I'LL BE BLESSED.
WE GOT PETE.
HELL OF A THING...
BOY'S NAMED RASPUTIN. SHOULD HAVE KNOWN HE WOULDN'T BE THAT EASY TO KILL.
YOU GONNA USE IT?
THE CURE. YOUR SAMPLE'S STILL COOLING IN--
I KNOW.
I DON'T KNOW.

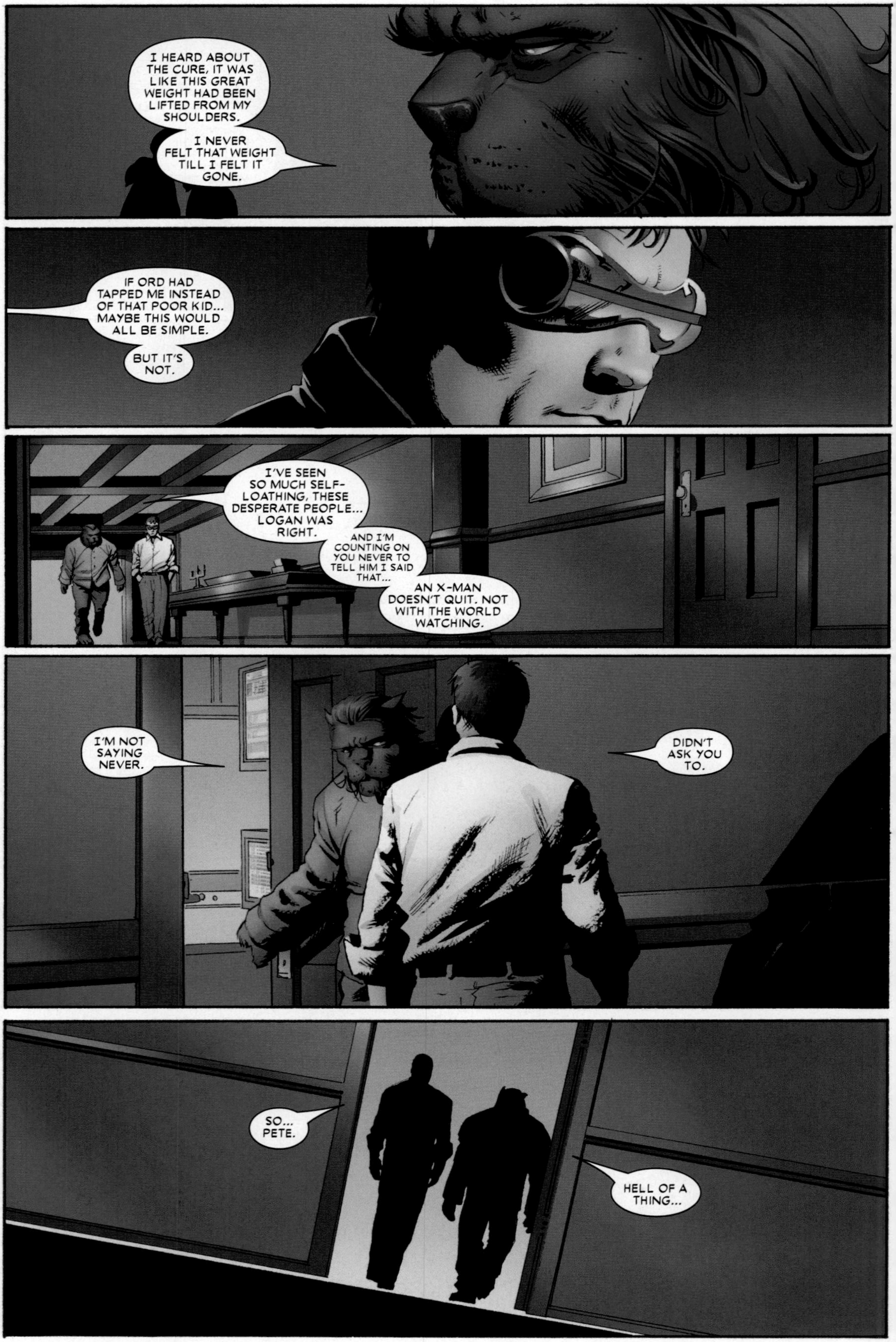
I HEARD ABOUT THE CURE, IT WAS LIKE THIS GREAT WEIGHT HAD BEEN LIFTED FROM MY SHOULDERS.
I NEVER FELT THAT WEIGHT TILL I FELT IT GONE.
IF ORD HAD TAPPED ME INSTEAD OF THAT POOR KID... MAYBE THIS WOULD ALL BE SIMPLE.
BUT IT'S NOT.
I'VE SEEN SO MUCH SELF-LOATHING, THESE DESPERATE PEOPLE... LOGAN WAS RIGHT.
AND I'M COUNTING ON YOU NEVER TO TELL HIM I SAID THAT...
AN X-MAN DOESN'T QUIT. NOT WITH THE WORLD WATCHING.
I'M NOT SAYING NEVER.
DIDN'T ASK YOU TO.
SO... PETE.
HELL OF A THING...

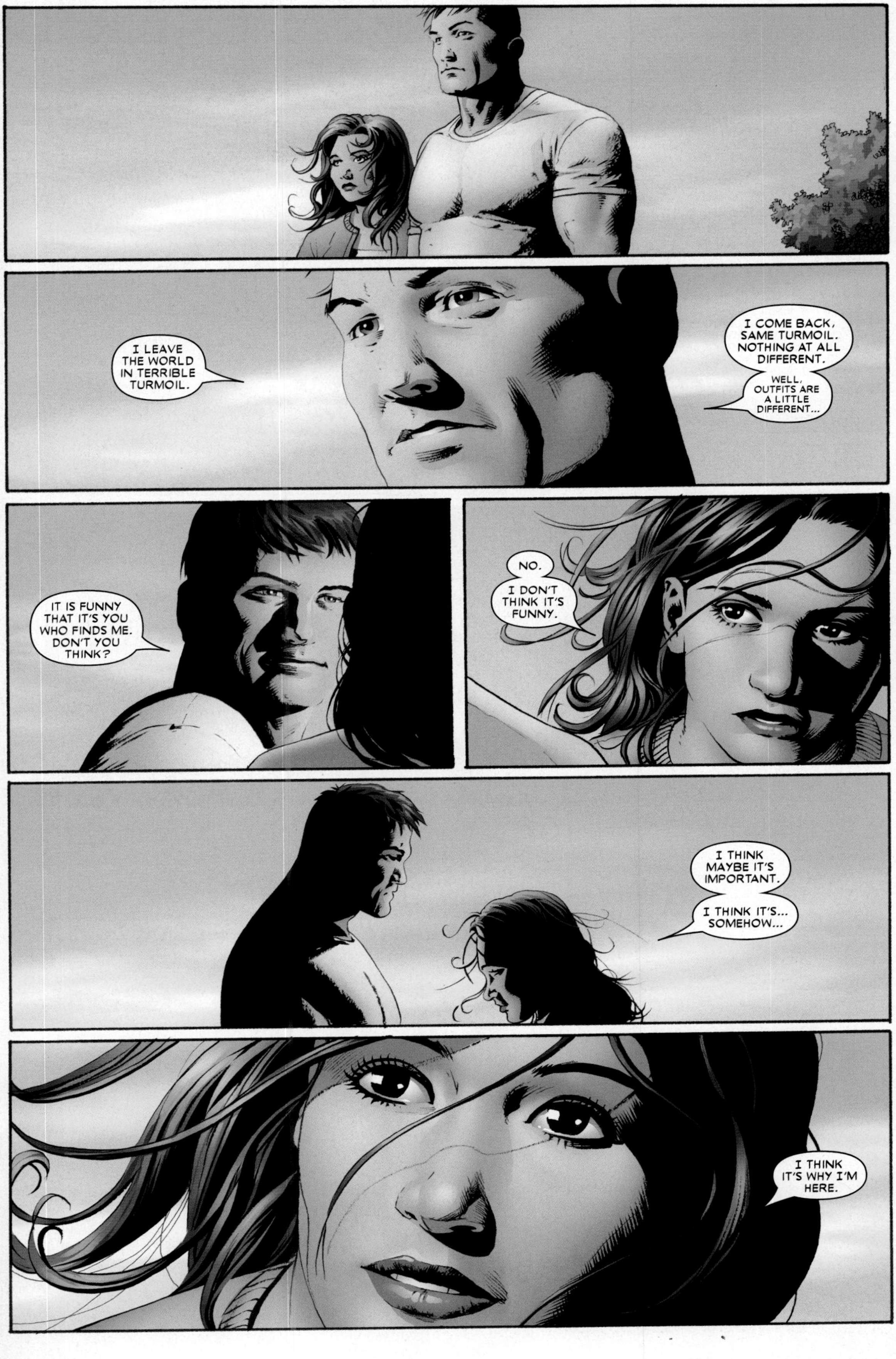
I LEAVE THE WORLD IN TERRIBLE TURMOIL.
I COME BACK, SAME TURMOIL. NOTHING AT ALL DIFFERENT.
WELL, OUTFITS ARE A LITTLE DIFFERENT...
IT IS FUNNY THAT IT'S YOU WHO FINDS ME. DON'T YOU THINK?
NO.
I DON'T THINK IT'S FUNNY.
I THINK MAYBE IT'S IMPORTANT.
I THINK IT'S... SOMEHOW...
I THINK IT'S WHY I'M HERE.

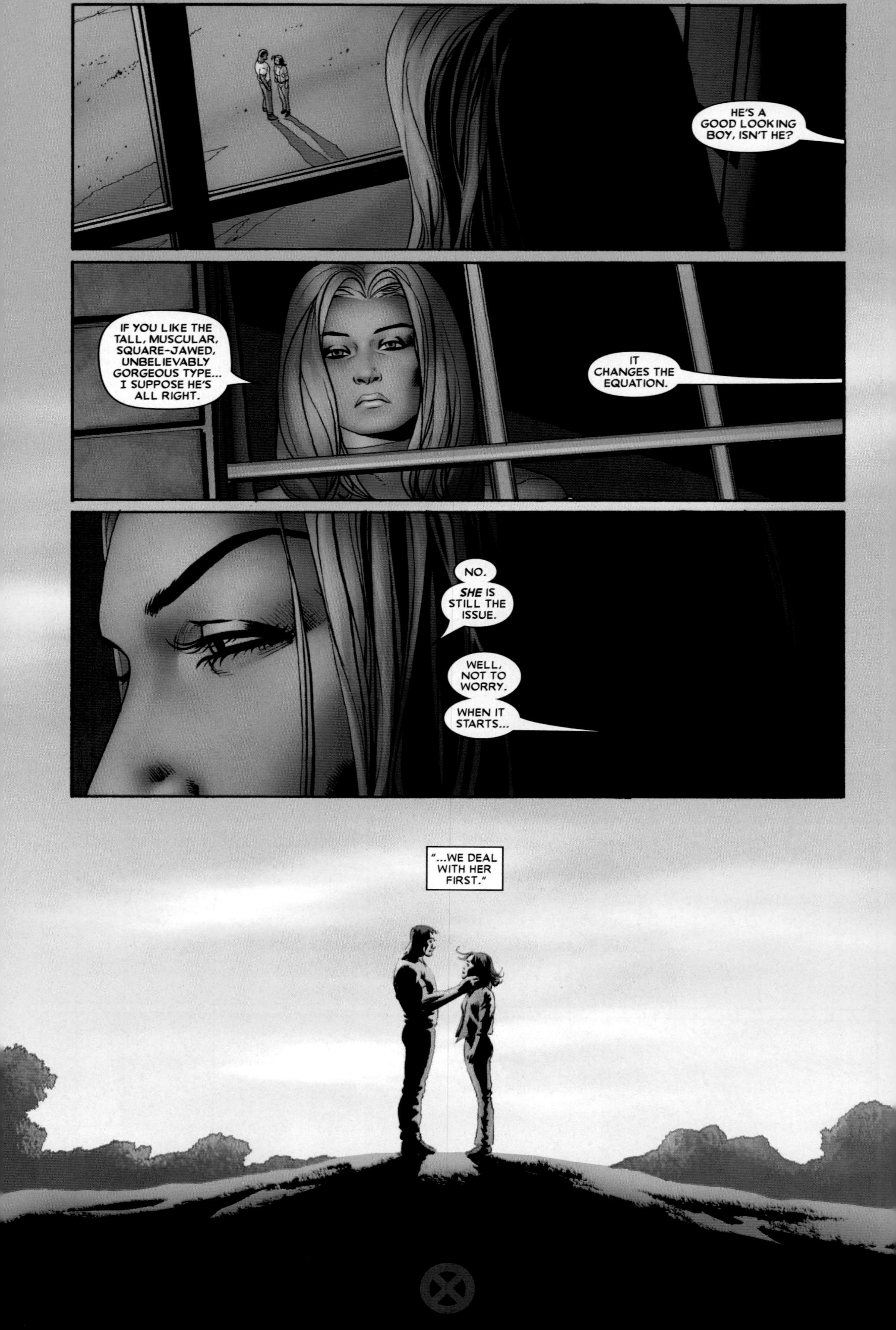
HE'S A GOOD LOOKING BOY, ISN'T HE?
IF YOU LIKE THE TALL, MUSCULAR, SQUARE-JAWED, UNBELIEVABLY GORGEOUS TYPE... I SUPPOSE HE'S ALL RIGHT.
IT CHANGES THE EQUATION.
NO.
SHE IS STILL THE ISSUE.
WELL, NOT TO WORRY.
WHEN IT STARTS...
"...WE DEAL WITH HER FIRST."

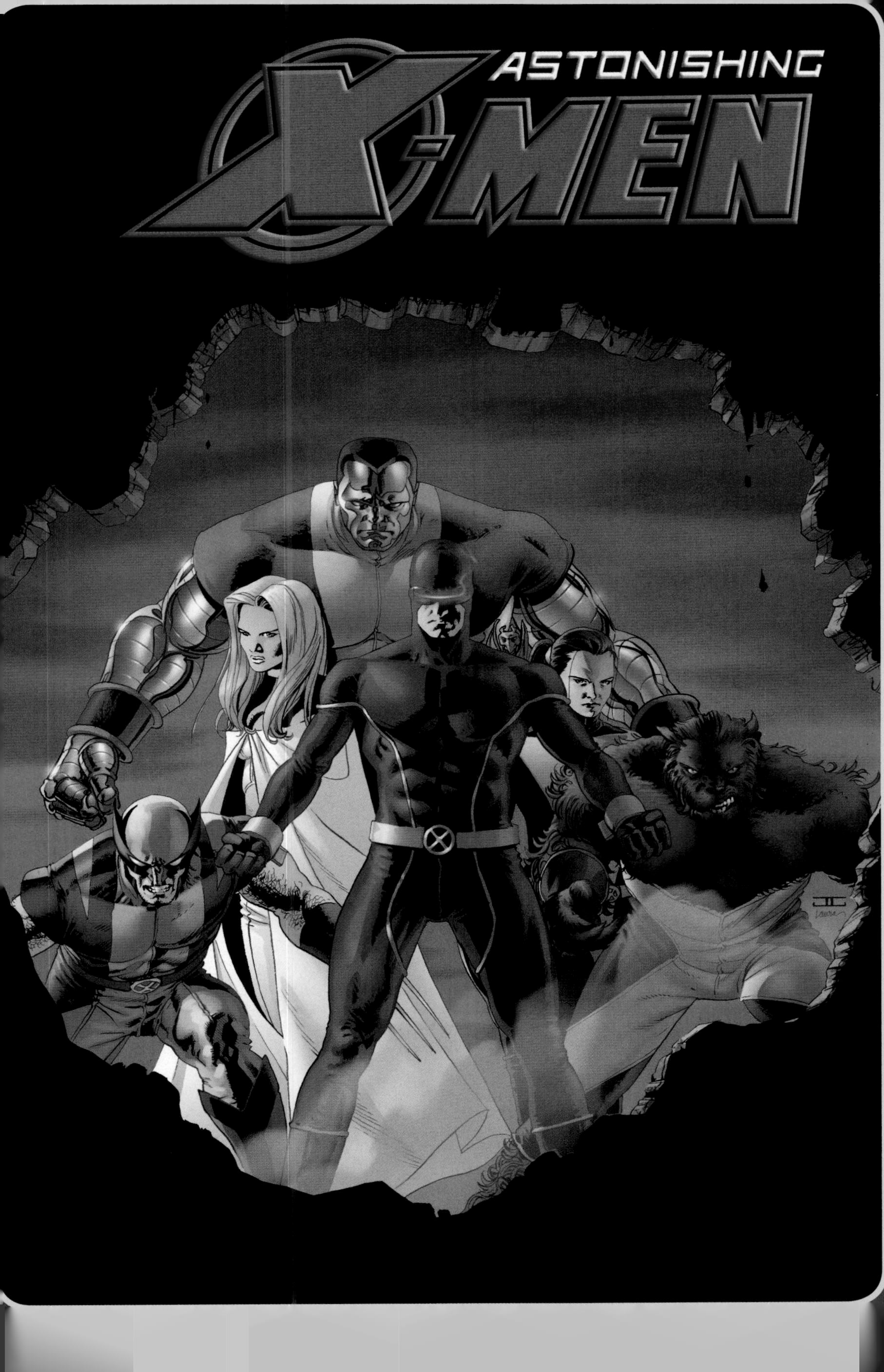
ASTONISHING
X-MEN

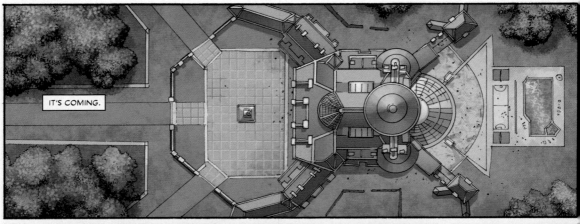

IT'S COMING.

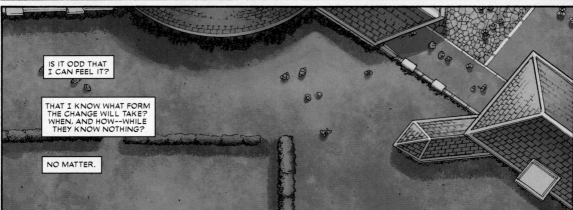

IS IT ODD THAT I CAN FEEL IT?

THAT I KNOW WHAT FORM THE CHANGE WILL TAKE? WHEN, AND HOW--WHILE THEY KNOW NOTHING?

NO MATTER.

I ACCEPT.

IT IS BEGINNING.

IT'S OVER.

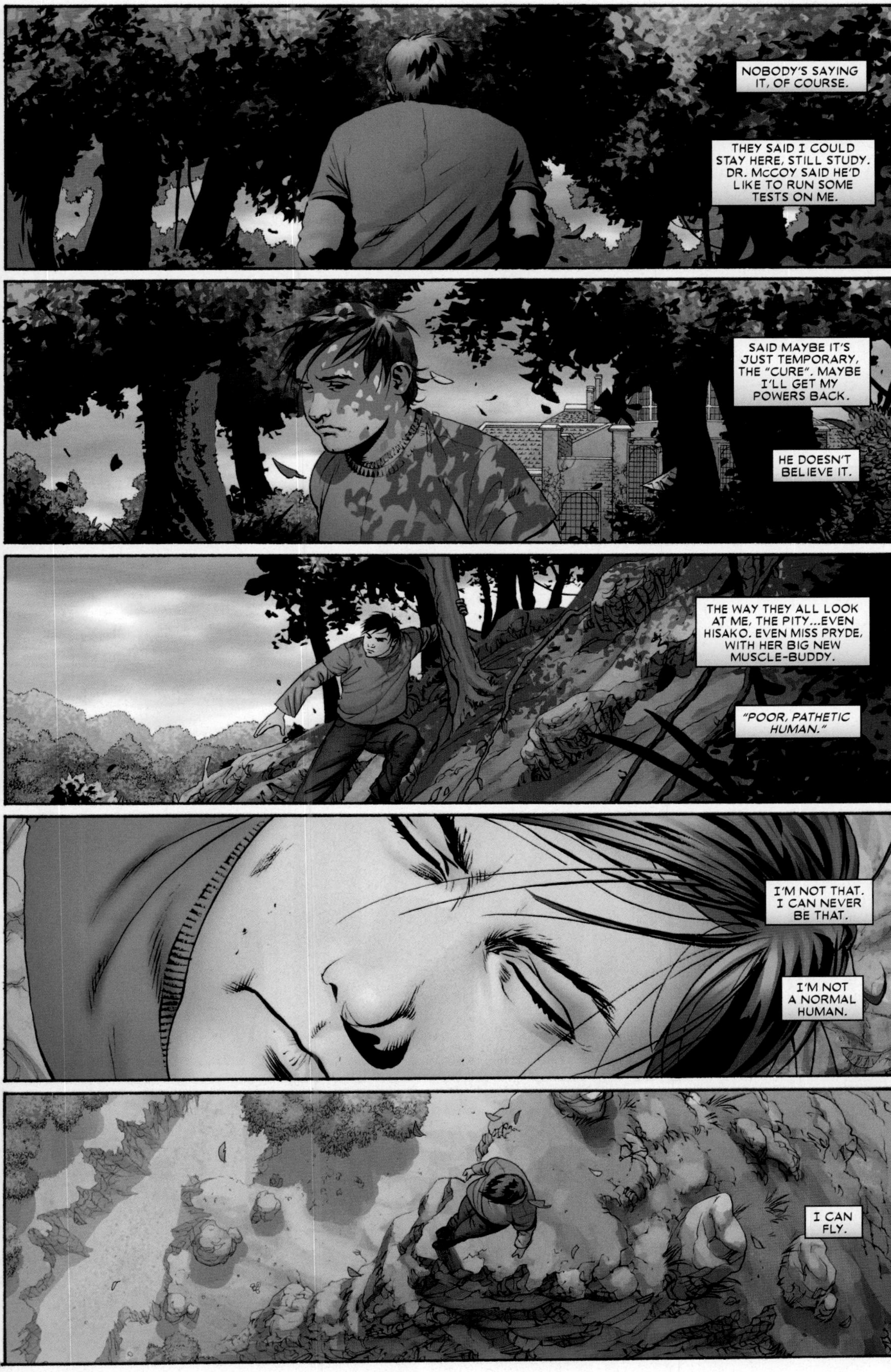
NOBODY'S SAYING IT, OF COURSE.
THEY SAID I COULD STAY HERE, STILL STUDY. DR. McCOY SAID HE'D LIKE TO RUN SOME TESTS ON ME.
SAID MAYBE IT'S JUST TEMPORARY, THE "CURE". MAYBE I'LL GET MY POWERS BACK.
HE DOESN'T BELIEVE IT.
THE WAY THEY ALL LOOK AT ME, THE PITY...EVEN HISAKO. EVEN MISS PRYDE, WITH HER BIG NEW MUSCLE-BUDDY.
"POOR, PATHETIC HUMAN."
I'M NOT THAT. I CAN NEVER BE THAT.
I'M NOT A NORMAL HUMAN.
I CAN FLY.

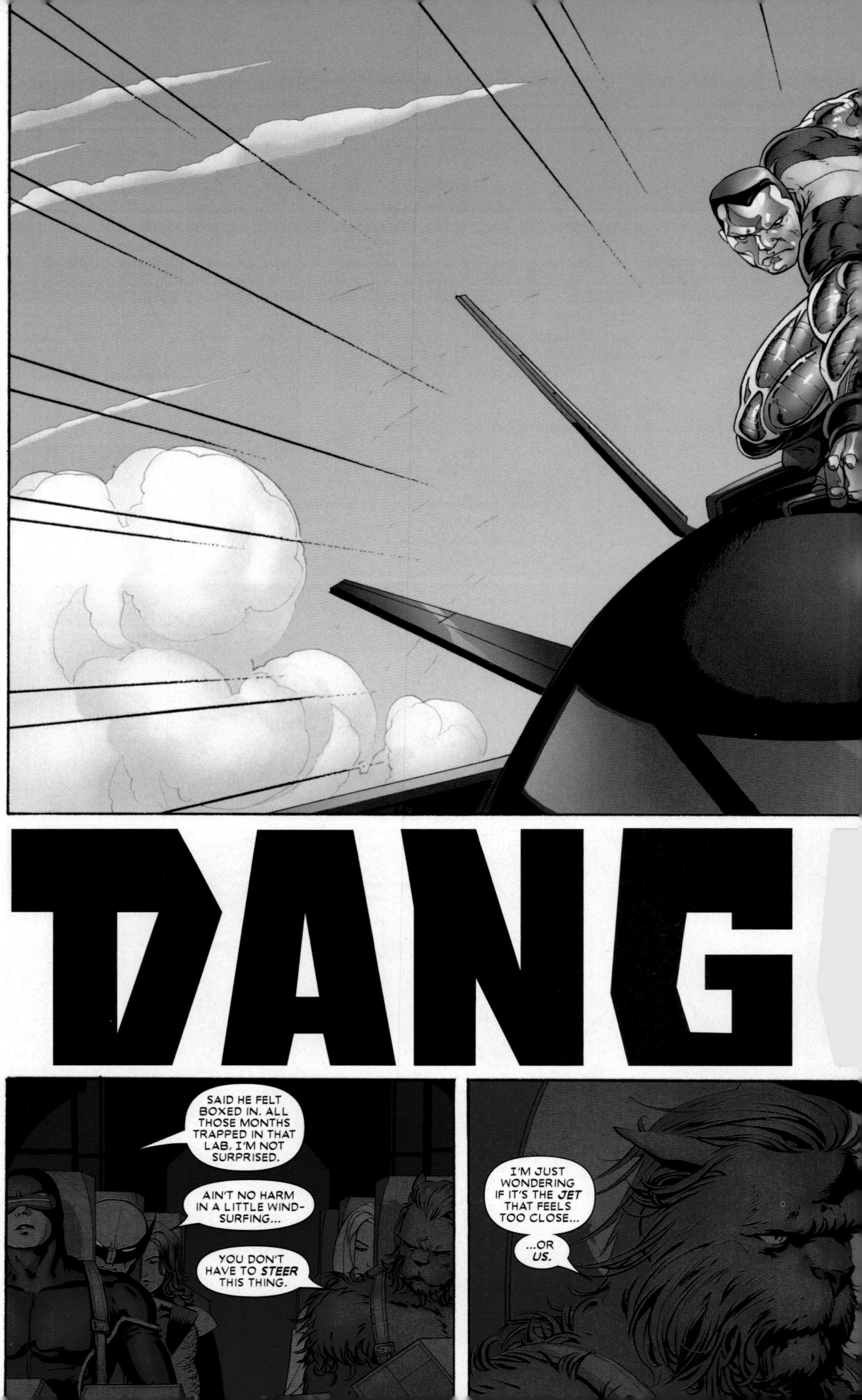
DANG
SAID HE FELT BOXED IN. ALL THOSE MONTHS TRAPPED IN THAT LAB, I'M NOT SURPRISED.
AIN'T NO HARM IN A LITTLE WIND-SURFING...
YOU DON'T HAVE TO *STEER* THIS THING.
I'M JUST WONDERING IF IT'S THE *JET* THAT FEELS TOO CLOSE...
...OR *US.*

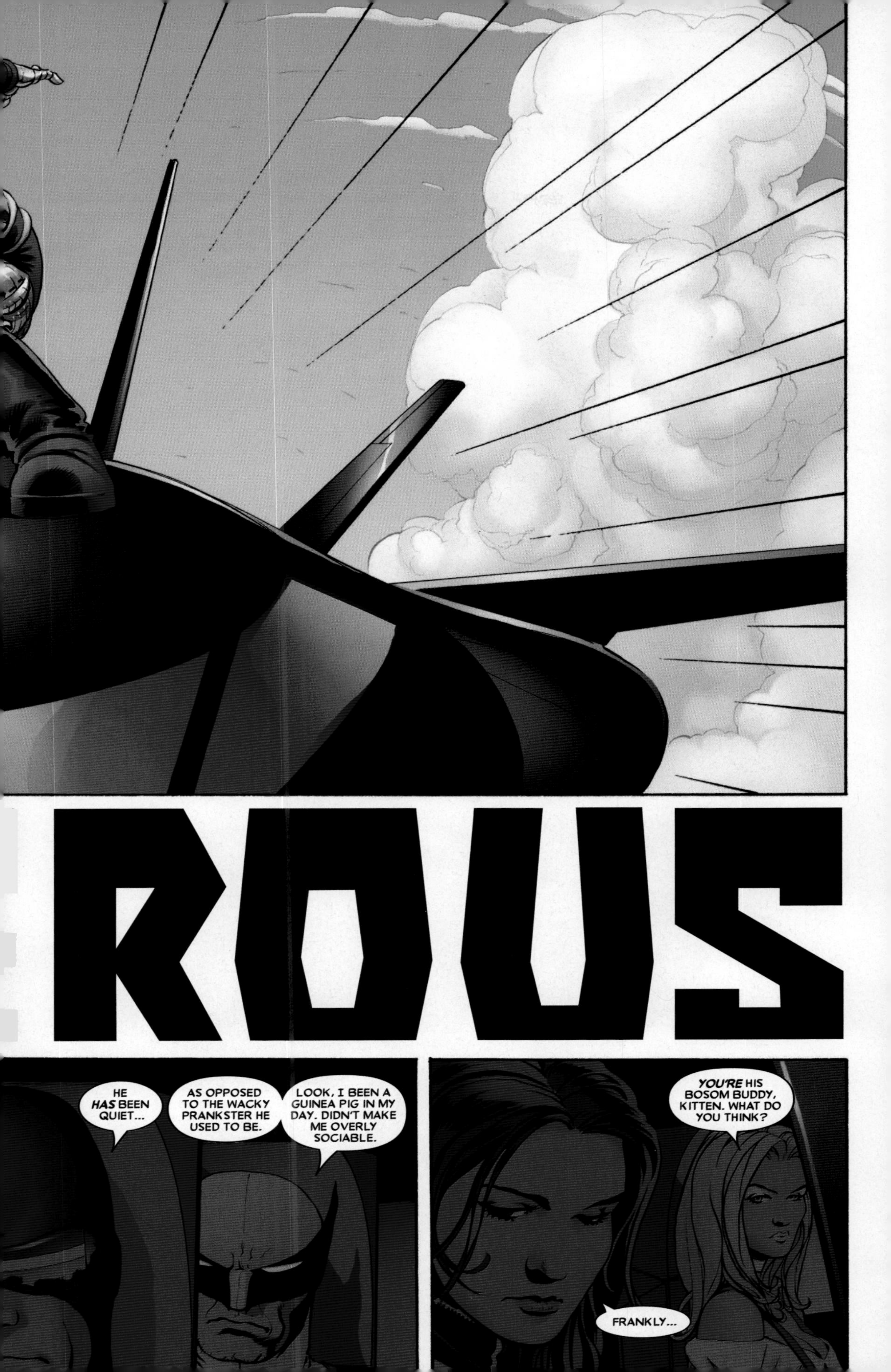
ROUS
HE HAS BEEN QUIET...
AS OPPOSED TO THE WACKY PRANKSTER HE USED TO BE.
LOOK, I BEEN A GUINEA PIG IN MY DAY. DIDN'T MAKE ME OVERLY SOCIABLE.
YOU'RE HIS BOSOM BUDDY, KITTEN. WHAT DO YOU THINK?
FRANKLY...

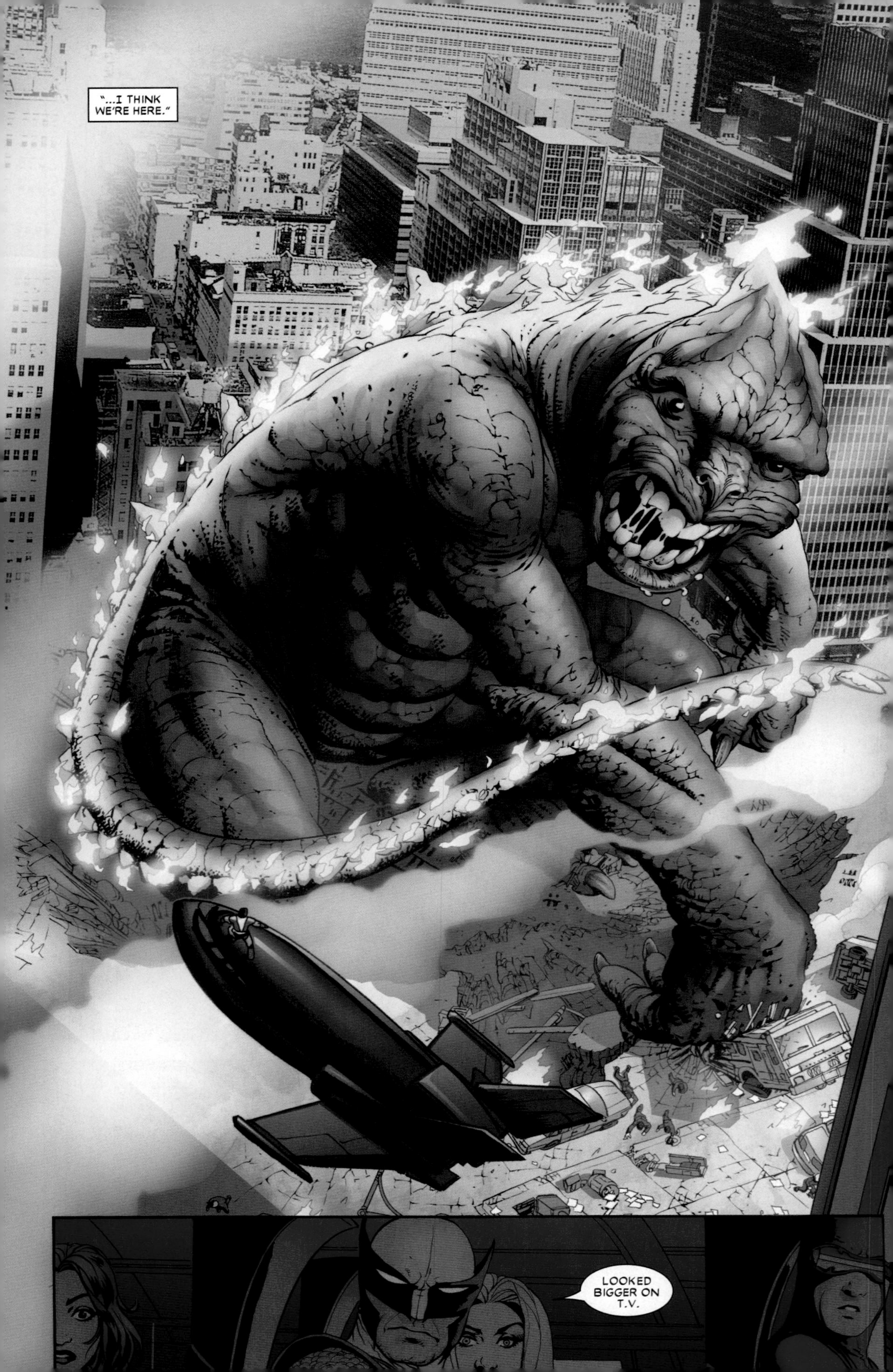
"...I THINK WE'RE HERE."
LOOKED BIGGER ON T.V.

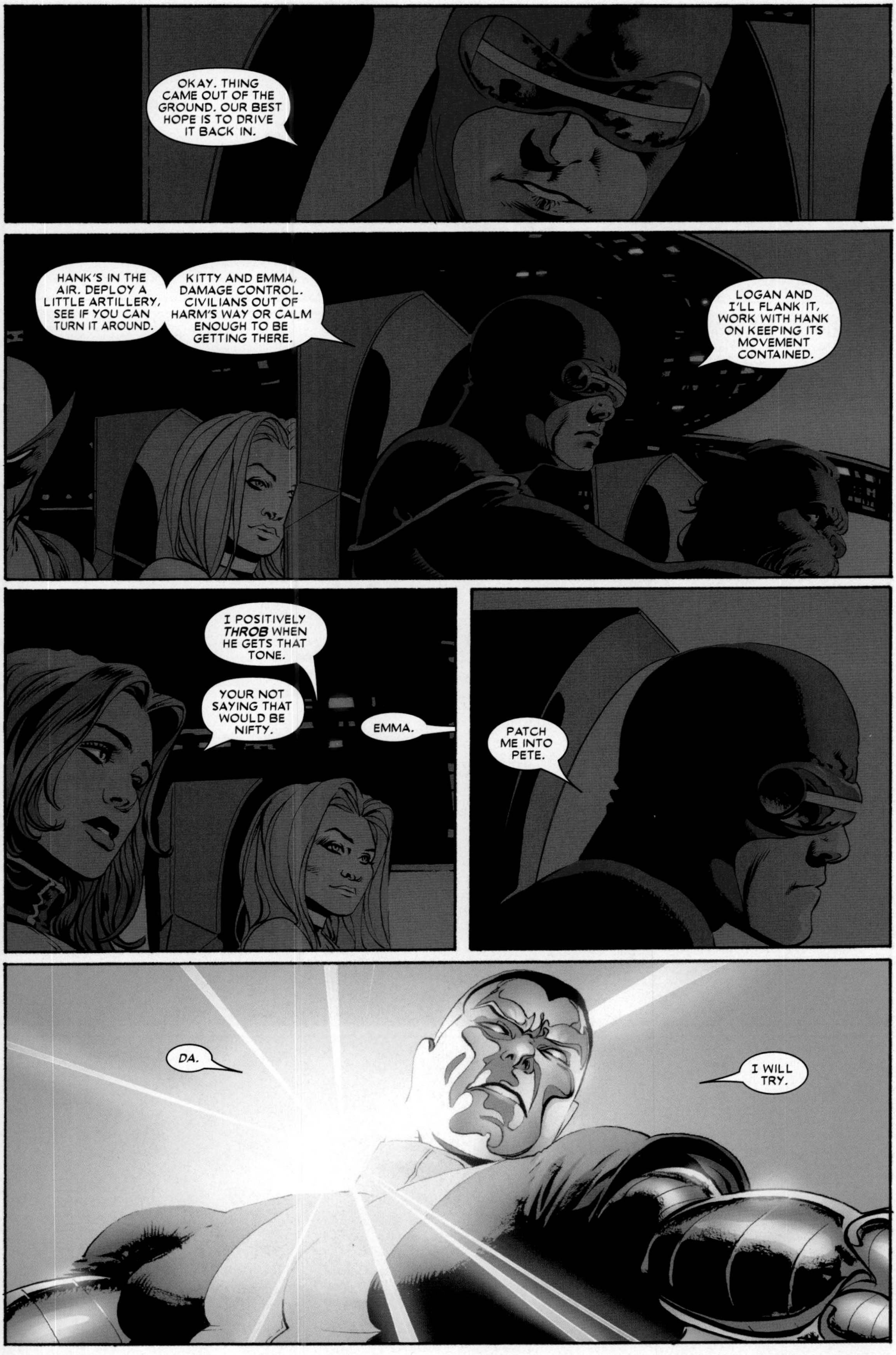
OKAY. THING CAME OUT OF THE GROUND. OUR BEST HOPE IS TO DRIVE IT BACK IN.
HANK'S IN THE AIR. DEPLOY A LITTLE ARTILLERY, SEE IF YOU CAN TURN IT AROUND.
KITTY AND EMMA, DAMAGE CONTROL. CIVILIANS OUT OF HARM'S WAY OR CALM ENOUGH TO BE GETTING THERE.
LOGAN AND I'LL FLANK IT, WORK WITH HANK ON KEEPING ITS MOVEMENT CONTAINED.
I POSITIVELY THROB WHEN HE GETS THAT TONE.
YOUR NOT SAYING THAT WOULD BE NIFTY.
EMMA.
PATCH ME INTO PETE.
DA.
I WILL TRY.

IT'S STRANGE TO HEAR SCOTT IN MY HEAD.

HE IS DIFFERENT. NOT JUST FROM THE PROFESSOR... HE IS MORE...FREE?

WHY DOES THAT WORD UNSETTLE ME?

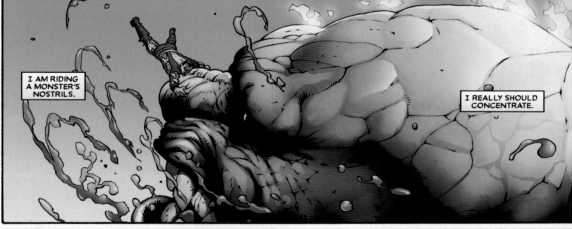

I AM RIDING A MONSTER'S NOSTRILS.

I REALLY SHOULD CONCENTRATE.

I SCARED HIM.

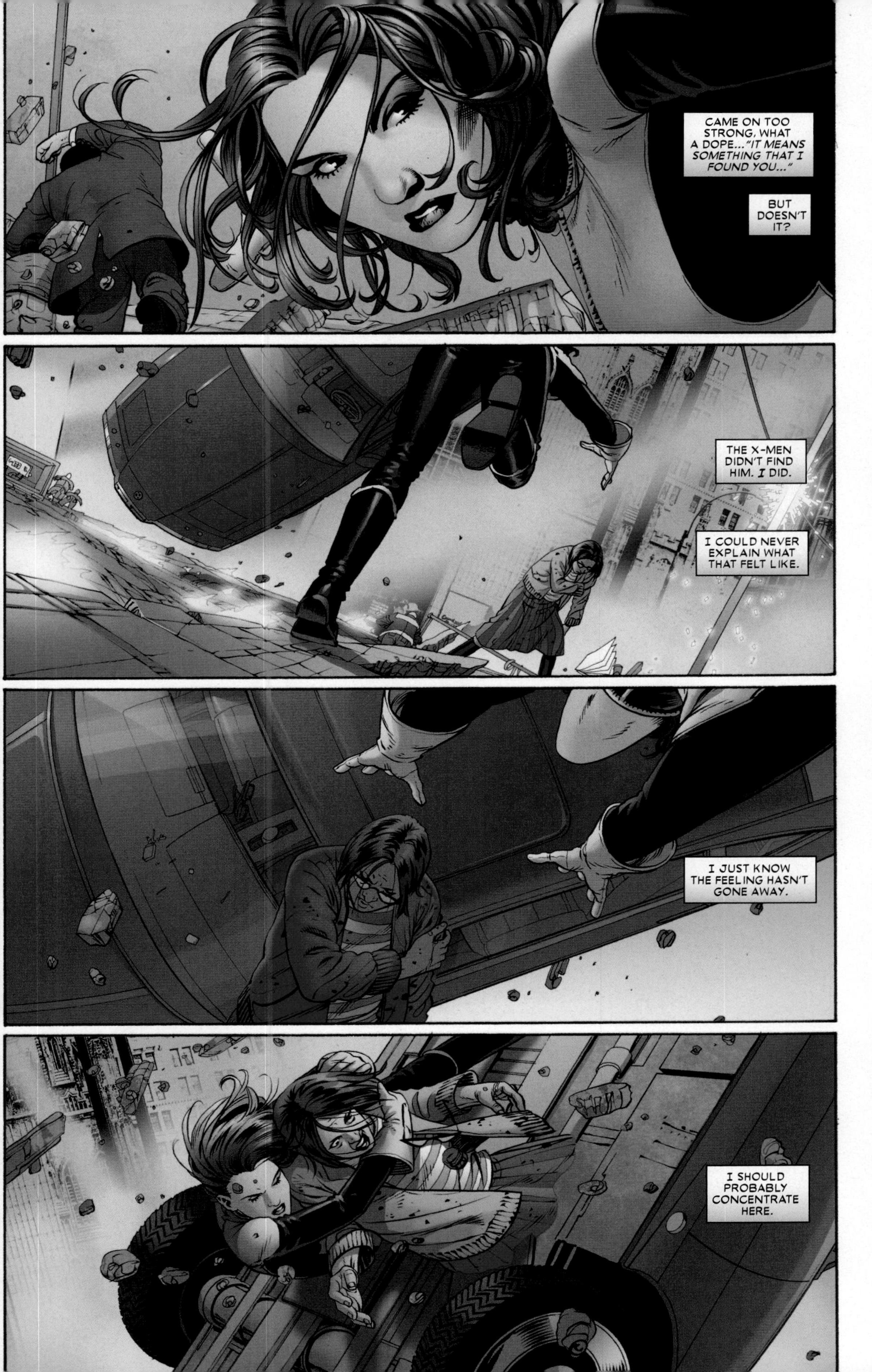
CAME ON TOO STRONG, WHAT A DOPE... "IT MEANS SOMETHING THAT I FOUND YOU..."
BUT DOESN'T IT?
THE X-MEN DIDN'T FIND HIM. *I* DID.
I COULD NEVER EXPLAIN WHAT THAT FELT LIKE.
I JUST KNOW THE FEELING HASN'T GONE AWAY.
I SHOULD PROBABLY CONCENTRATE HERE.

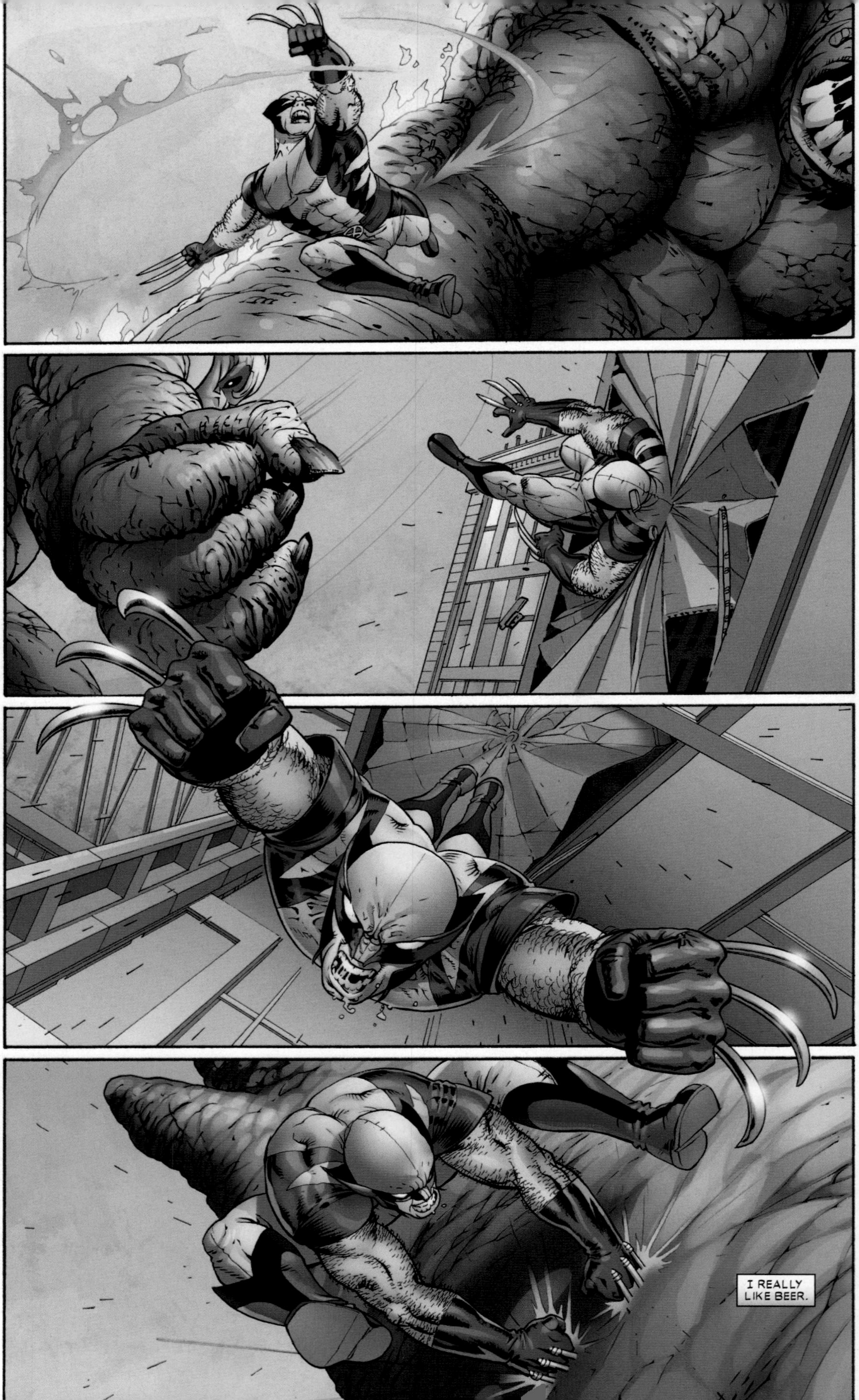
I REALLY LIKE BEER.

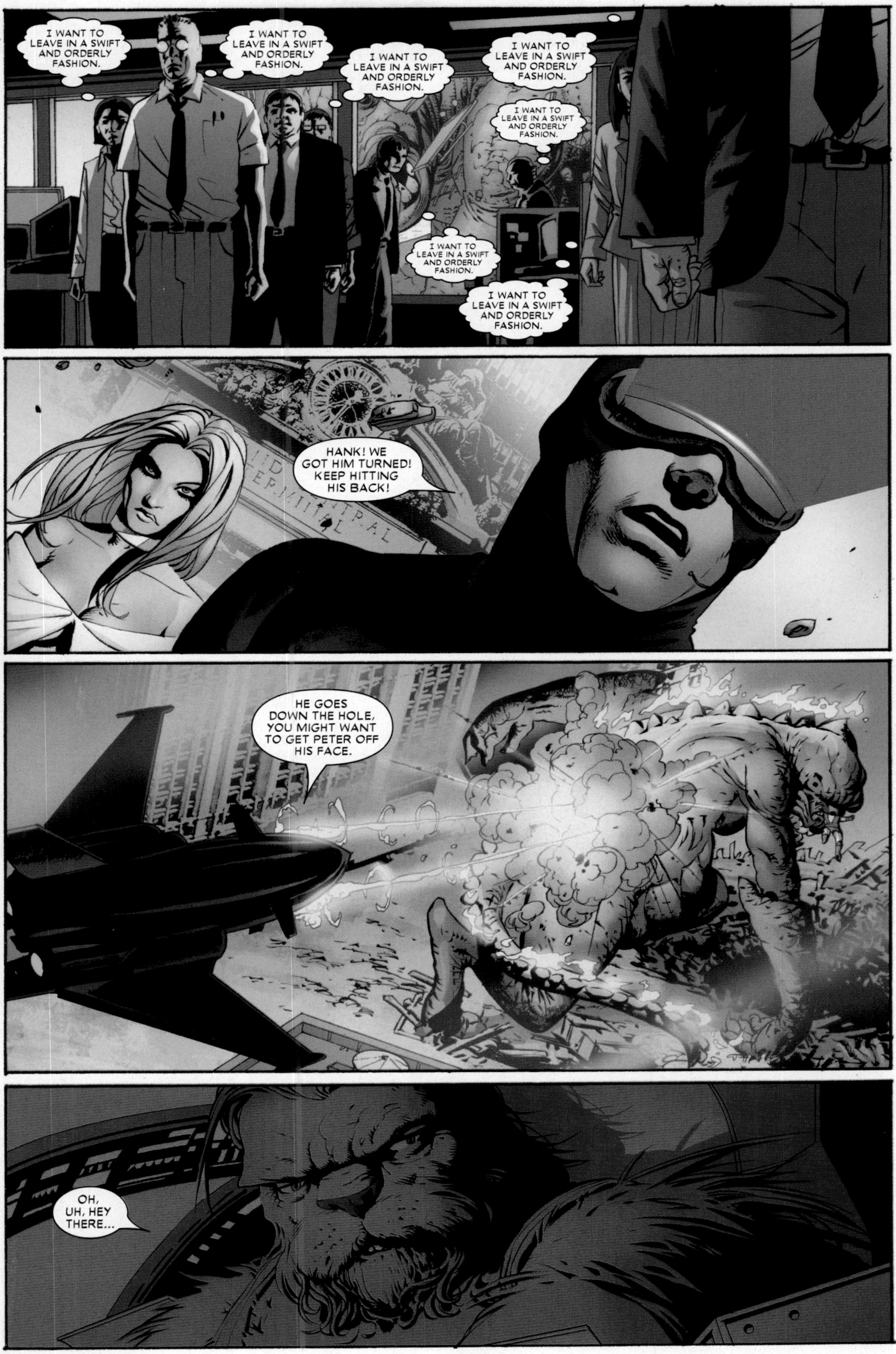

I WANT TO LEAVE IN A SWIFT AND ORDERLY FASHION.
I WANT TO LEAVE IN A SWIFT AND ORDERLY FASHION.
I WANT TO LEAVE IN A SWIFT AND ORDERLY FASHION.
I WANT TO LEAVE IN A SWIFT AND ORDERLY FASHION.
I WANT TO LEAVE IN A SWIFT AND ORDERLY FASHION.
I WANT TO LEAVE IN A SWIFT AND ORDERLY FASHION.
I WANT TO LEAVE IN A SWIFT AND ORDERLY FASHION.
HANK! WE GOT HIM TURNED! KEEP HITTING HIS BACK!
HE GOES DOWN THE HOLE, YOU MIGHT WANT TO GET PETER OFF HIS FACE.
OH, UH, HEY THERE...

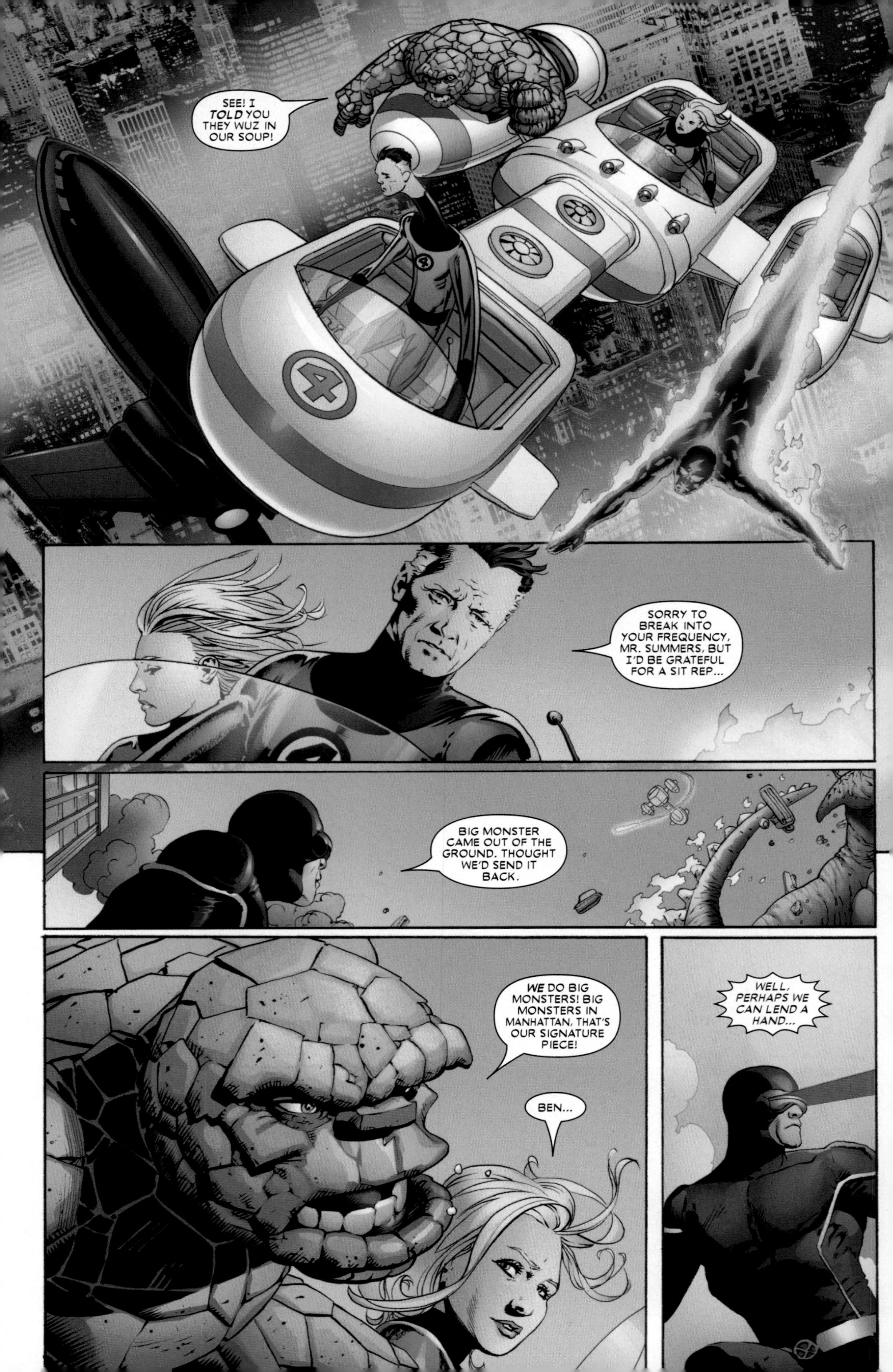
SEE! I TOLD YOU THEY WUZ IN OUR SOUP!
SORRY TO BREAK INTO YOUR FREQUENCY, MR. SUMMERS, BUT I'D BE GRATEFUL FOR A SIT REP...
BIG MONSTER CAME OUT OF THE GROUND. THOUGHT WE'D SEND IT BACK.
WE DO BIG MONSTERS! BIG MONSTERS IN MANHATTAN, THAT'S OUR SIGNATURE PIECE!
BEN...
WELL, PERHAPS WE CAN LEND A HAND...

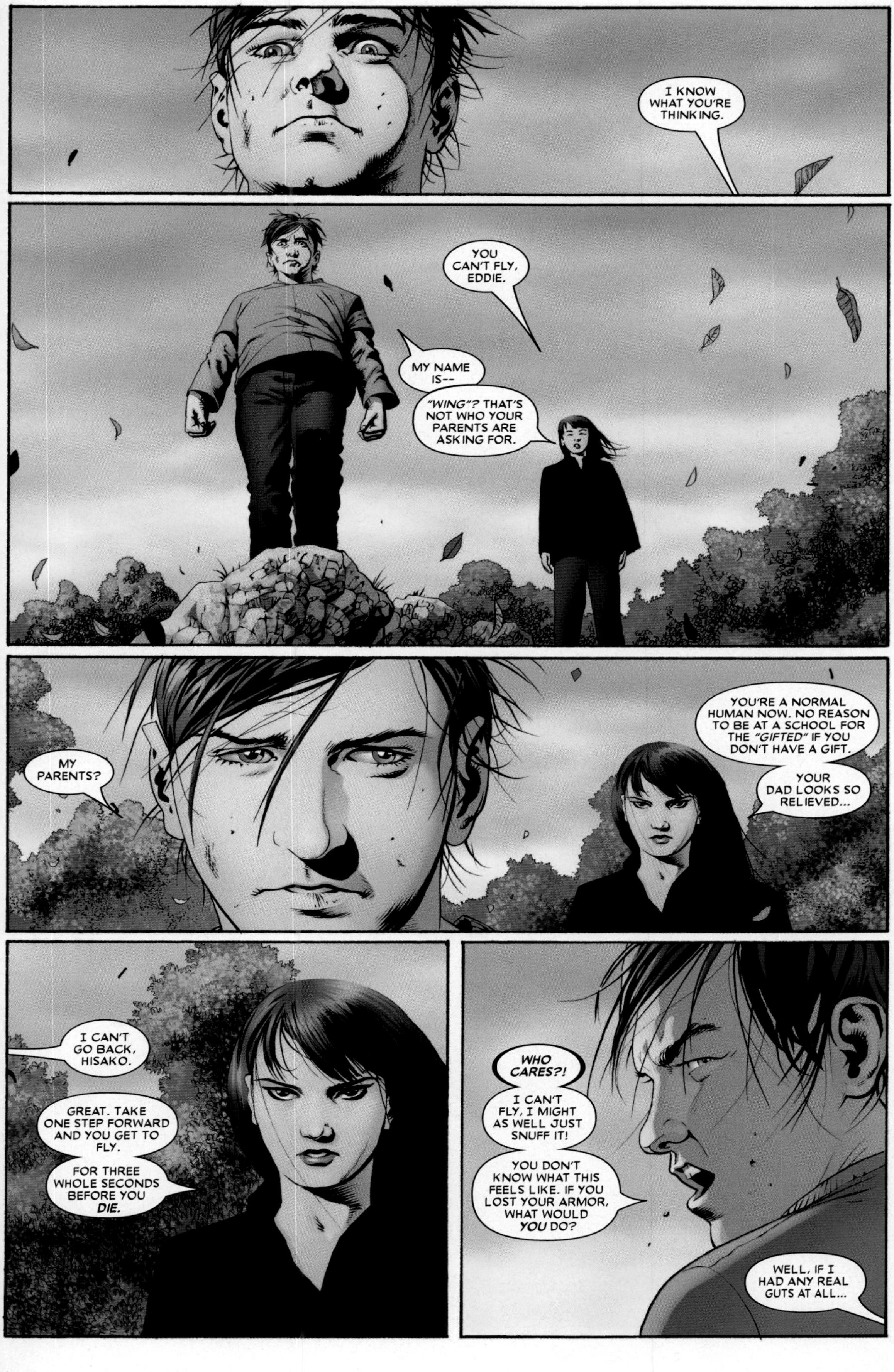
I KNOW WHAT YOU'RE THINKING.
YOU CAN'T FLY, EDDIE.
MY NAME IS--
"WING"? THAT'S NOT WHO YOUR PARENTS ARE ASKING FOR.
MY PARENTS?
YOU'RE A NORMAL HUMAN NOW. NO REASON TO BE AT A SCHOOL FOR THE "GIFTED" IF YOU DON'T HAVE A GIFT.
YOUR DAD LOOKS SO RELIEVED...
I CAN'T GO BACK, HISAKO.
GREAT. TAKE ONE STEP FORWARD AND YOU GET TO FLY.
FOR THREE WHOLE SECONDS BEFORE YOU *DIE.*
WHO CARES?!
I CAN'T FLY, I MIGHT AS WELL JUST SNUFF IT!
YOU DON'T KNOW WHAT THIS FEELS LIKE. IF YOU LOST YOUR ARMOR, WHAT WOULD *YOU* DO?
WELL, IF I HAD ANY REAL GUTS AT ALL...

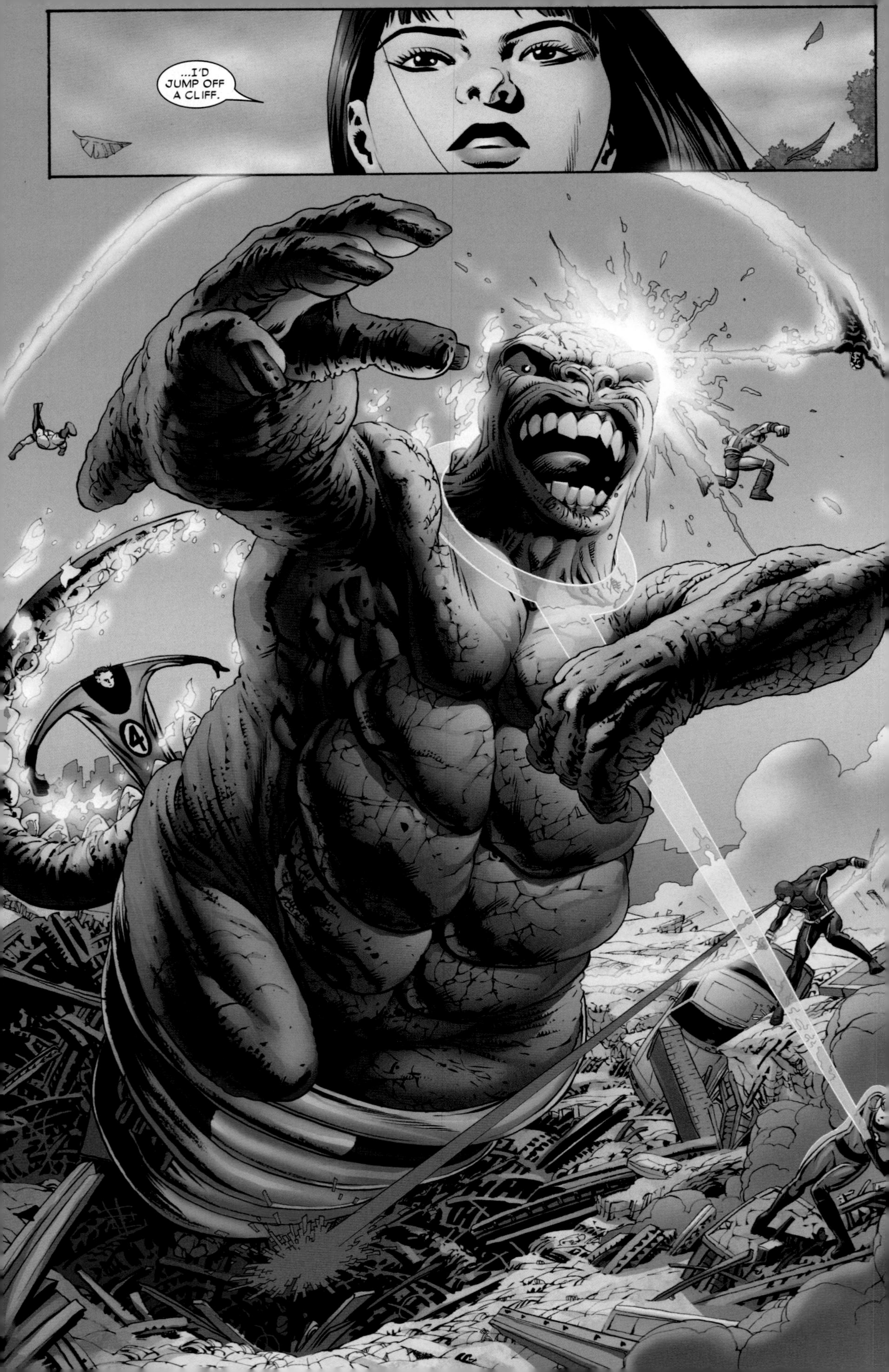
...I'D JUMP OFF A CLIFF.

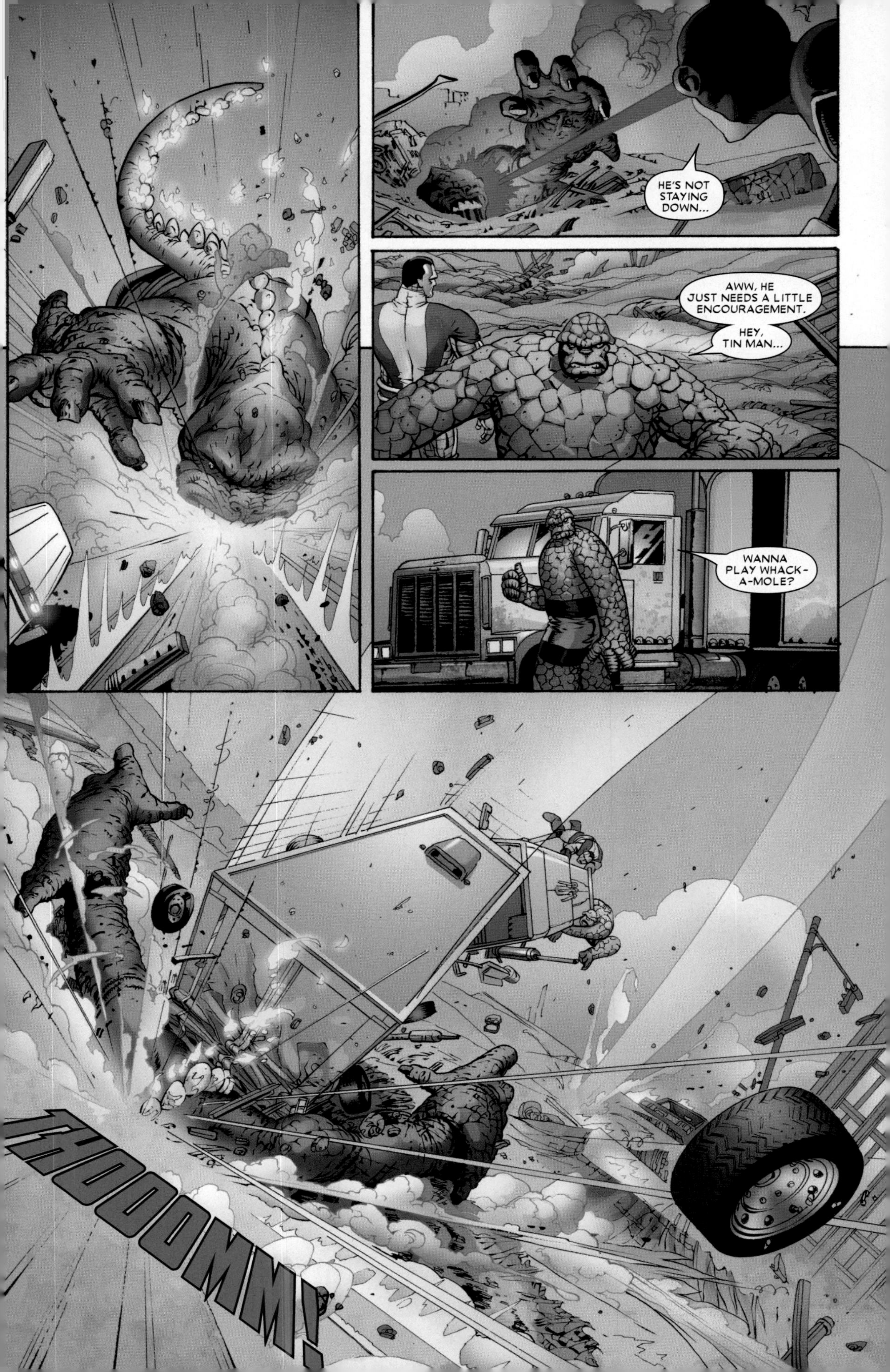
HE'S NOT STAYING DOWN...
AWW, HE JUST NEEDS A LITTLE ENCOURAGEMENT.
HEY, TIN MAN...
WANNA PLAY WHACK-A-MOLE?
THOOOMM!

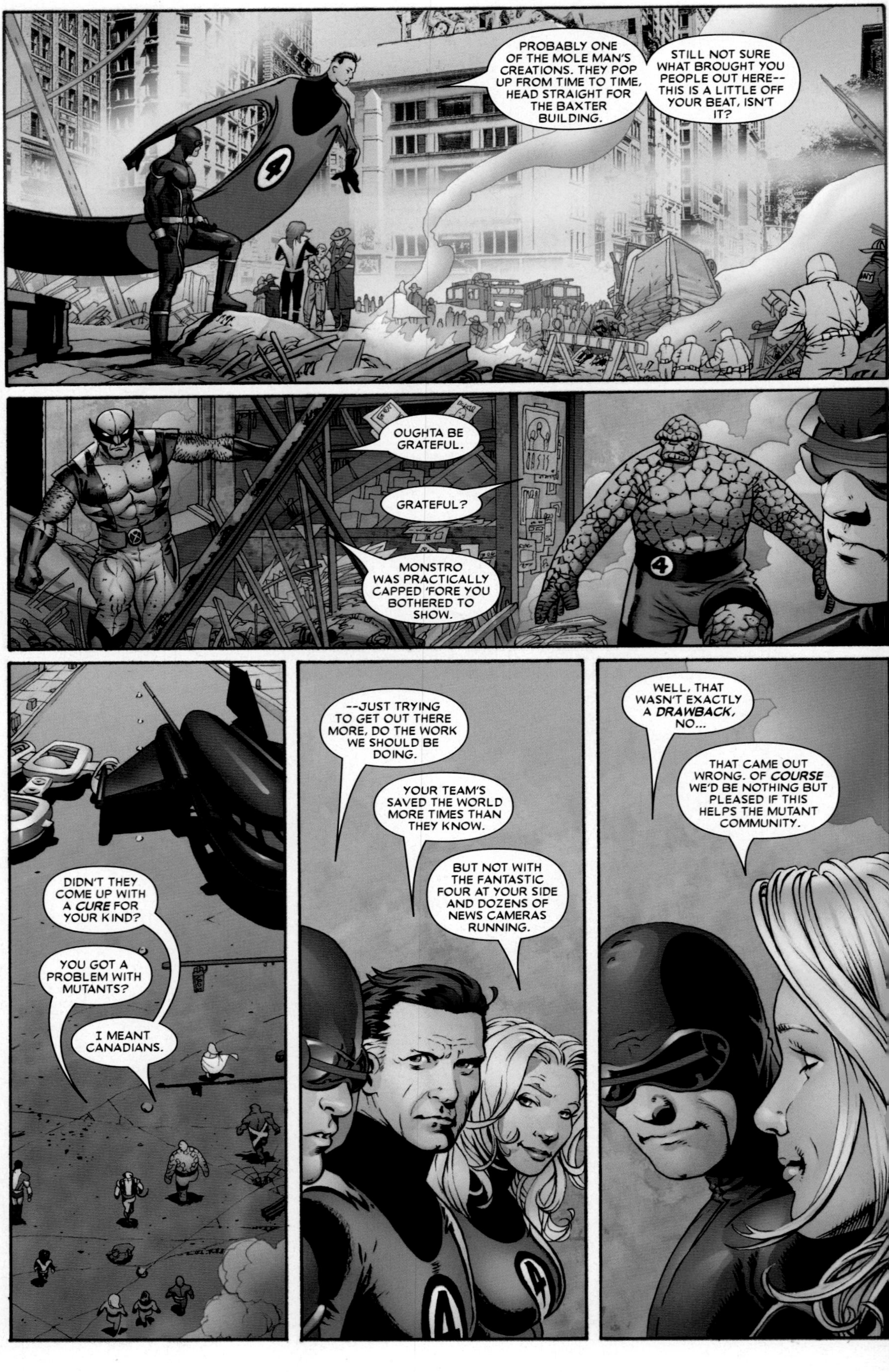
PROBABLY ONE OF THE MOLE MAN'S CREATIONS. THEY POP UP FROM TIME TO TIME, HEAD STRAIGHT FOR THE BAXTER BUILDING.
STILL NOT SURE WHAT BROUGHT YOU PEOPLE OUT HERE-- THIS IS A LITTLE OFF YOUR BEAT, ISN'T IT?
OUGHTA BE GRATEFUL.
GRATEFUL?
MONSTRO WAS PRACTICALLY CAPPED 'FORE YOU BOTHERED TO SHOW.
DIDN'T THEY COME UP WITH A *CURE* FOR YOUR KIND?
YOU GOT A PROBLEM WITH MUTANTS?
I MEANT CANADIANS.
--JUST TRYING TO GET OUT THERE MORE, DO THE WORK WE SHOULD BE DOING.
YOUR TEAM'S SAVED THE WORLD MORE TIMES THAN THEY KNOW.
BUT NOT WITH THE FANTASTIC FOUR AT YOUR SIDE AND DOZENS OF NEWS CAMERAS RUNNING.
WELL, THAT WASN'T EXACTLY A *DRAWBACK*, NO...
THAT CAME OUT WRONG. OF *COURSE* WE'D BE NOTHING BUT PLEASED IF THIS HELPS THE MUTANT COMMUNITY.

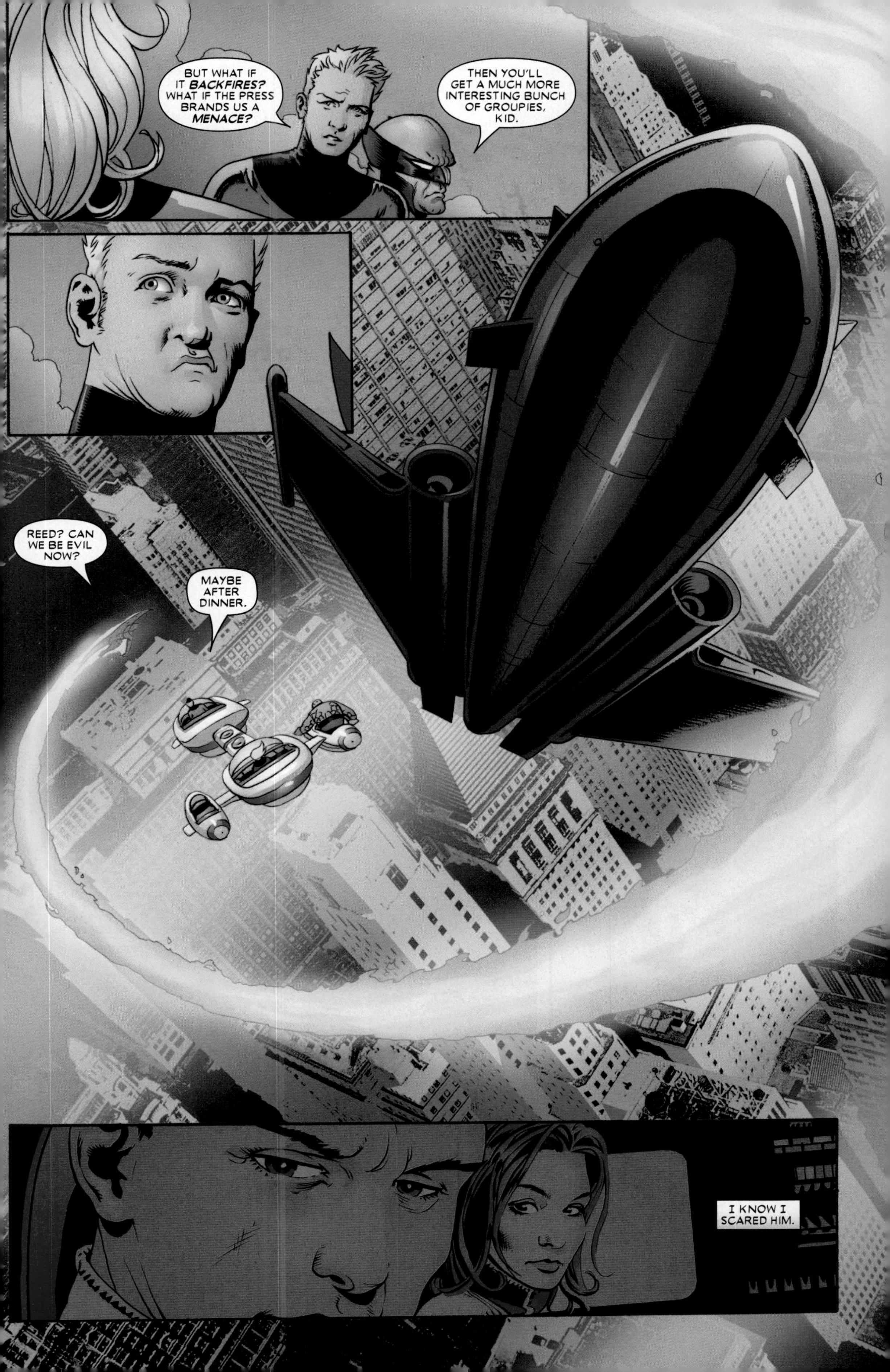
BUT WHAT IF IT *BACKFIRES?* WHAT IF THE PRESS BRANDS US A *MENACE?*
THEN YOU'LL GET A MUCH MORE INTERESTING BUNCH OF GROUPIES, KID.
REED? CAN WE BE EVIL NOW?
MAYBE AFTER DINNER.
I KNOW I SCARED HIM.

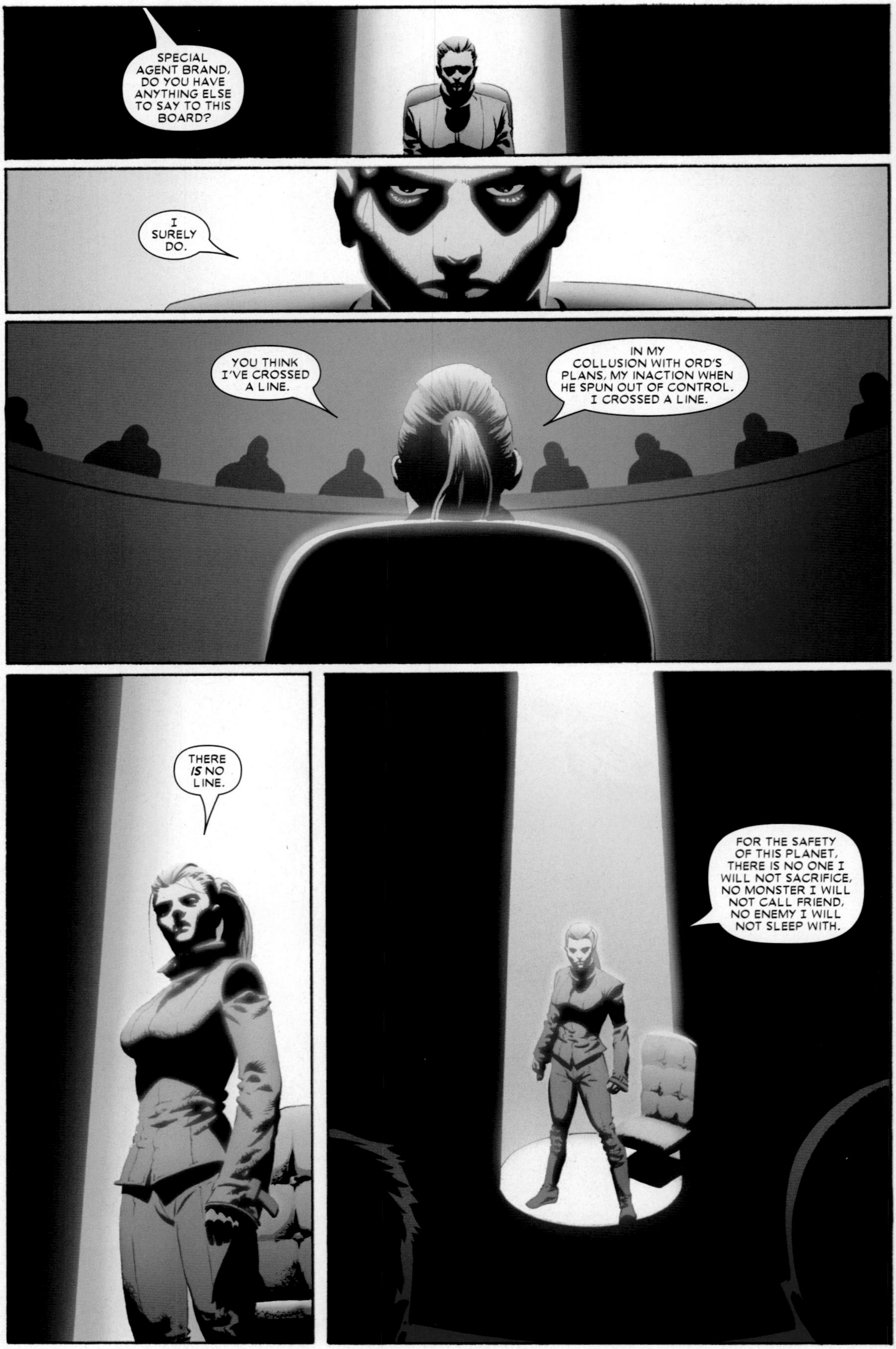
SPECIAL AGENT BRAND, DO YOU HAVE ANYTHING ELSE TO SAY TO THIS BOARD?
I SURELY DO.
YOU THINK I'VE CROSSED A LINE.
IN MY COLLUSION WITH ORD'S PLANS, MY INACTION WHEN HE SPUN OUT OF CONTROL. I CROSSED A LINE.
THERE *IS* NO LINE.
FOR THE SAFETY OF THIS PLANET, THERE IS NO ONE I WILL NOT SACRIFICE, NO MONSTER I WILL NOT CALL FRIEND, NO ENEMY I WILL NOT SLEEP WITH.

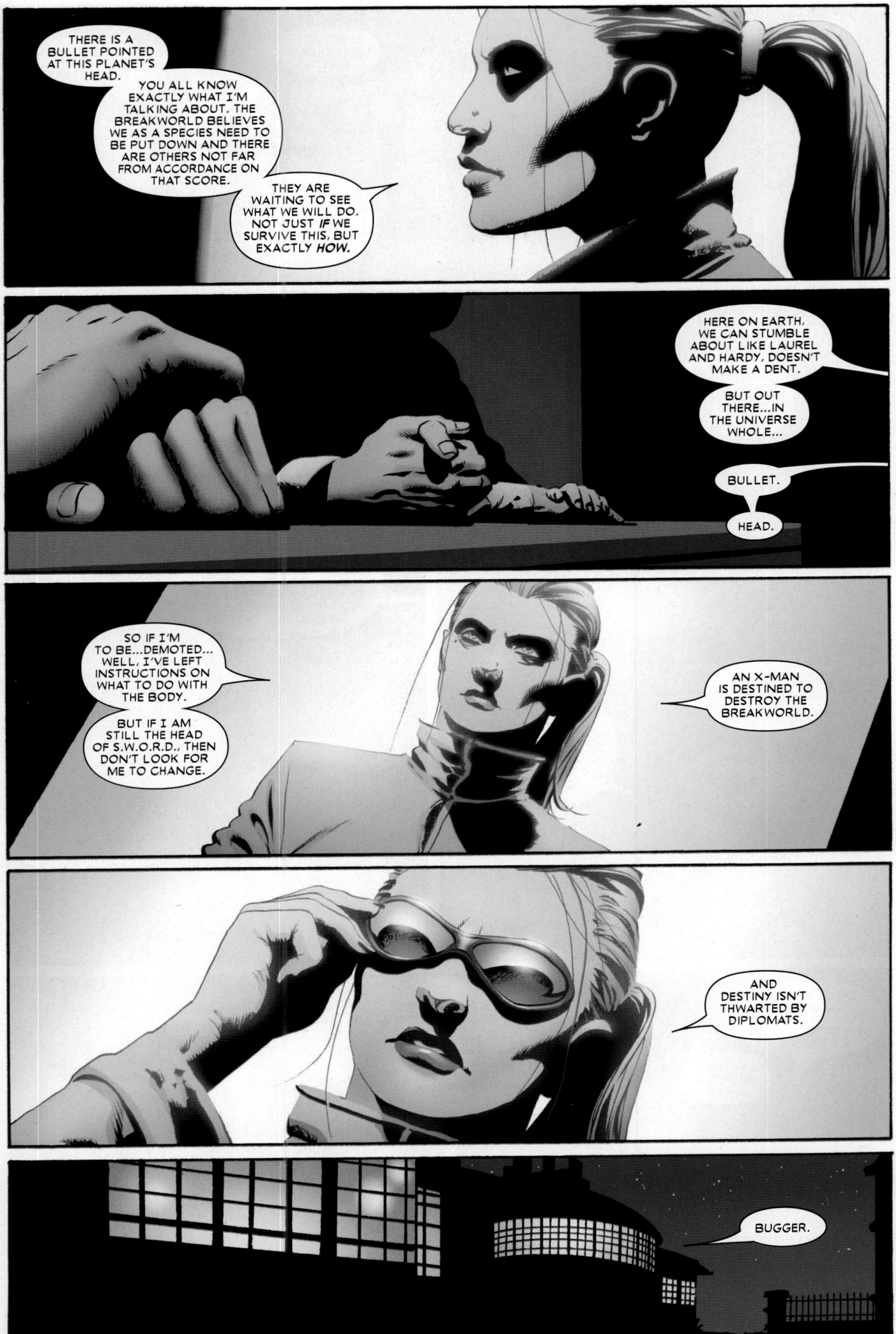
THERE IS A BULLET POINTED AT THIS PLANET'S HEAD.
YOU ALL KNOW EXACTLY WHAT I'M TALKING ABOUT. THE BREAKWORLD BELIEVES WE AS A SPECIES NEED TO BE PUT DOWN AND THERE ARE OTHERS NOT FAR FROM ACCORDANCE ON THAT SCORE.
THEY ARE WAITING TO SEE WHAT WE WILL DO. NOT JUST *IF* WE SURVIVE THIS, BUT EXACTLY ***HOW.***
HERE ON EARTH, WE CAN STUMBLE ABOUT LIKE LAUREL AND HARDY, DOESN'T MAKE A DENT.
BUT OUT THERE...IN THE UNIVERSE WHOLE...
BULLET.
HEAD.
SO IF I'M TO BE...DEMOTED... WELL, I'VE LEFT INSTRUCTIONS ON WHAT TO DO WITH THE BODY.
BUT IF I AM STILL THE HEAD OF S.W.O.R.D., THEN DON'T LOOK FOR ME TO CHANGE.
AN X-MAN IS DESTINED TO DESTROY THE BREAKWORLD.
AND DESTINY ISN'T THWARTED BY DIPLOMATS.
BUGGER.

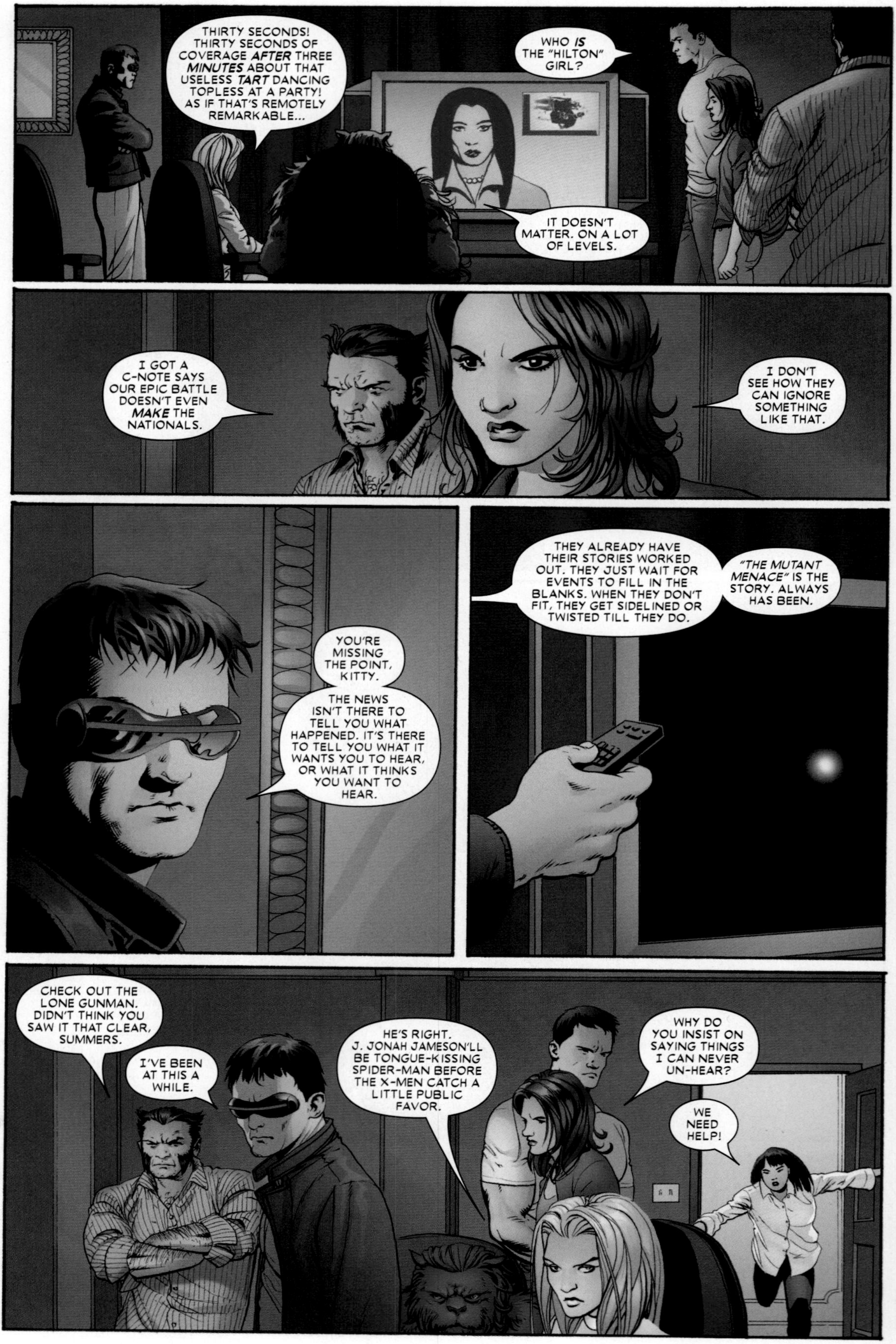
THIRTY SECONDS! THIRTY SECONDS OF COVERAGE AFTER THREE MINUTES ABOUT THAT USELESS TART DANCING TOPLESS AT A PARTY! AS IF THAT'S REMOTELY REMARKABLE...
WHO IS THE "HILTON" GIRL?
IT DOESN'T MATTER. ON A LOT OF LEVELS.
I GOT A C-NOTE SAYS OUR EPIC BATTLE DOESN'T EVEN MAKE THE NATIONALS.
I DON'T SEE HOW THEY CAN IGNORE SOMETHING LIKE THAT.
YOU'RE MISSING THE POINT, KITTY.
THE NEWS ISN'T THERE TO TELL YOU WHAT HAPPENED. IT'S THERE TO TELL YOU WHAT IT WANTS YOU TO HEAR, OR WHAT IT THINKS YOU WANT TO HEAR.
THEY ALREADY HAVE THEIR STORIES WORKED OUT. THEY JUST WAIT FOR EVENTS TO FILL IN THE BLANKS. WHEN THEY DON'T FIT, THEY GET SIDELINED OR TWISTED TILL THEY DO.
"THE MUTANT MENACE" IS THE STORY. ALWAYS HAS BEEN.
CHECK OUT THE LONE GUNMAN. DIDN'T THINK YOU SAW IT THAT CLEAR, SUMMERS.
I'VE BEEN AT THIS A WHILE.
HE'S RIGHT. J. JONAH JAMESON'LL BE TONGUE-KISSING SPIDER-MAN BEFORE THE X-MEN CATCH A LITTLE PUBLIC FAVOR.
WHY DO YOU INSIST ON SAYING THINGS I CAN NEVER UN-HEAR?
WE NEED HELP!

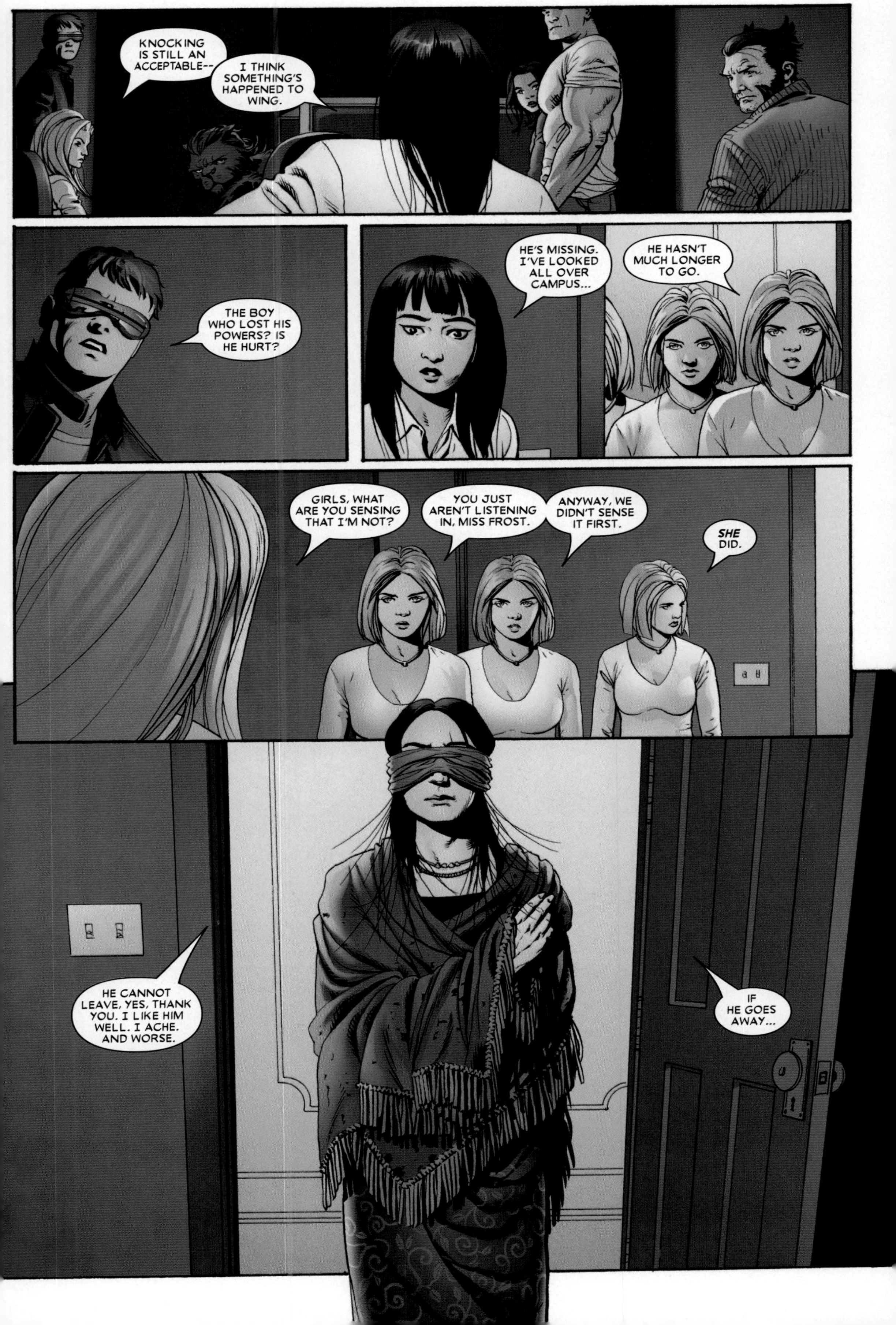
KNOCKING IS STILL AN ACCEPTABLE--
I THINK SOMETHING'S HAPPENED TO WING.
THE BOY WHO LOST HIS POWERS? IS HE HURT?
HE'S MISSING. I'VE LOOKED ALL OVER CAMPUS...
HE HASN'T MUCH LONGER TO GO.
GIRLS, WHAT ARE YOU SENSING THAT I'M NOT?
YOU JUST AREN'T LISTENING IN, MISS FROST.
ANYWAY, WE DIDN'T SENSE IT FIRST.
SHE DID.
HE CANNOT LEAVE, YES, THANK YOU. I LIKE HIM WELL. I ACHE. AND WORSE.
IF HE GOES AWAY...

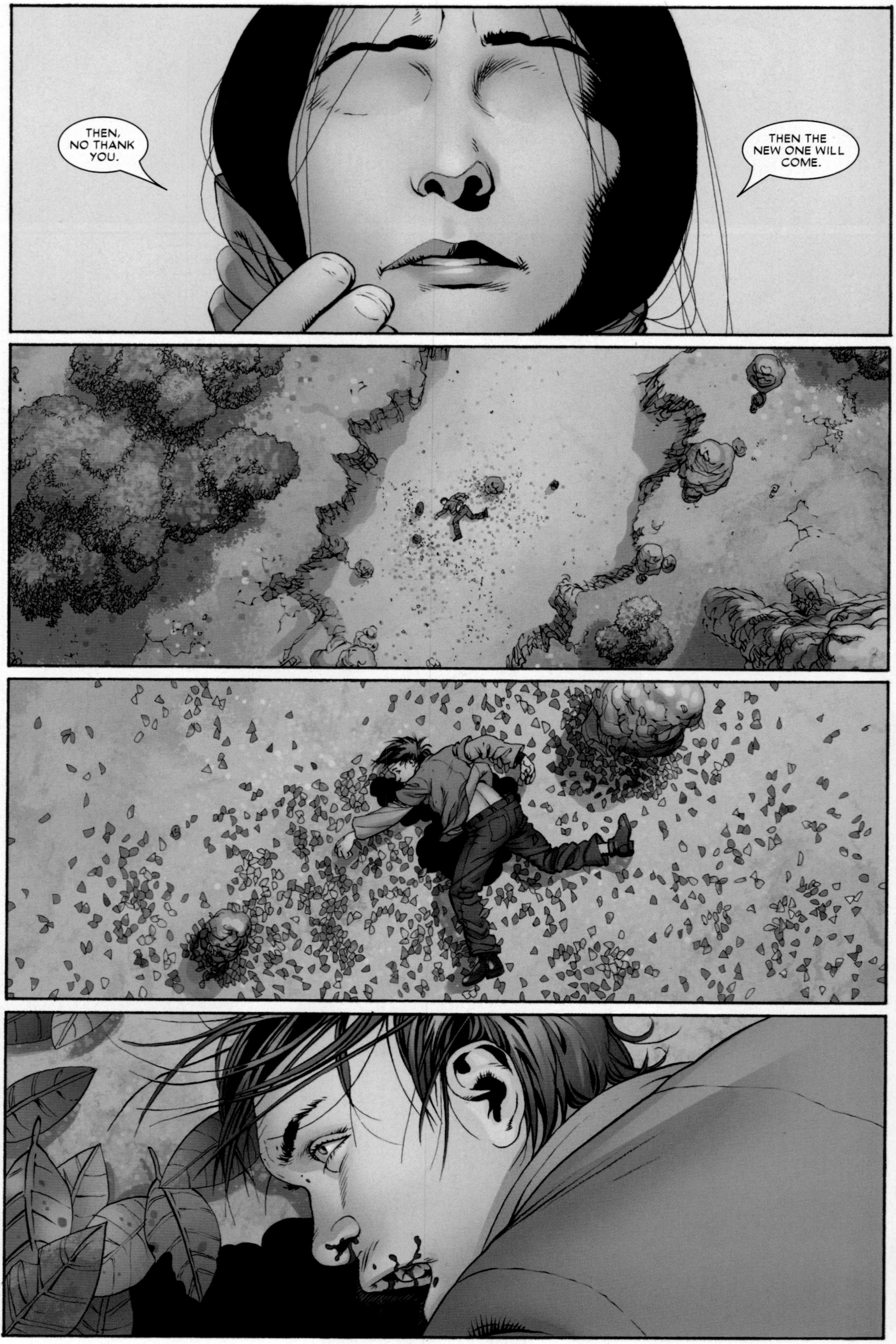
THEN, NO THANK YOU.
THEN THE NEW ONE WILL COME.

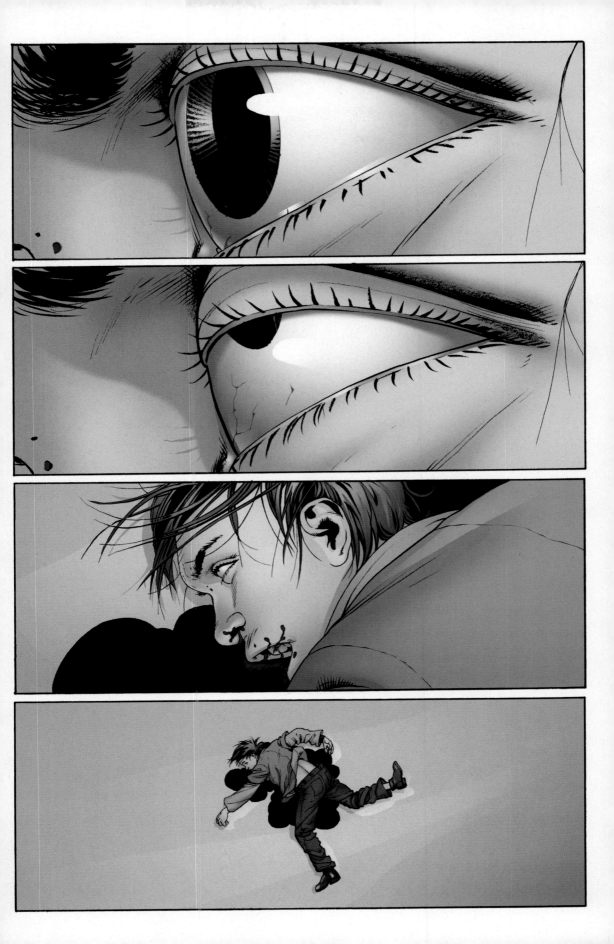

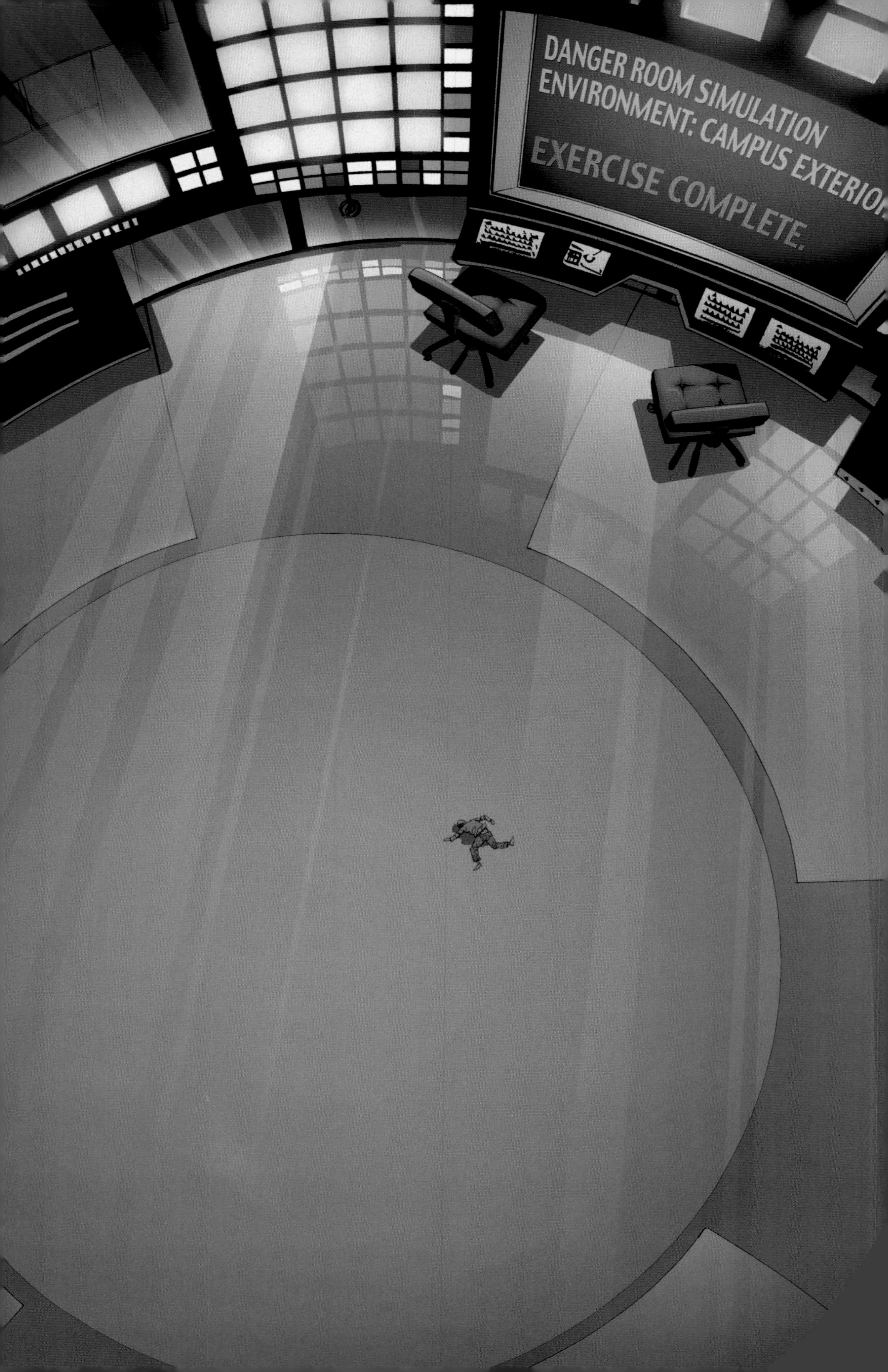
DANGER ROOM SIMULATION
ENVIRONMENT: CAMPUS EXTERIOR
EXERCISE COMPLETE.

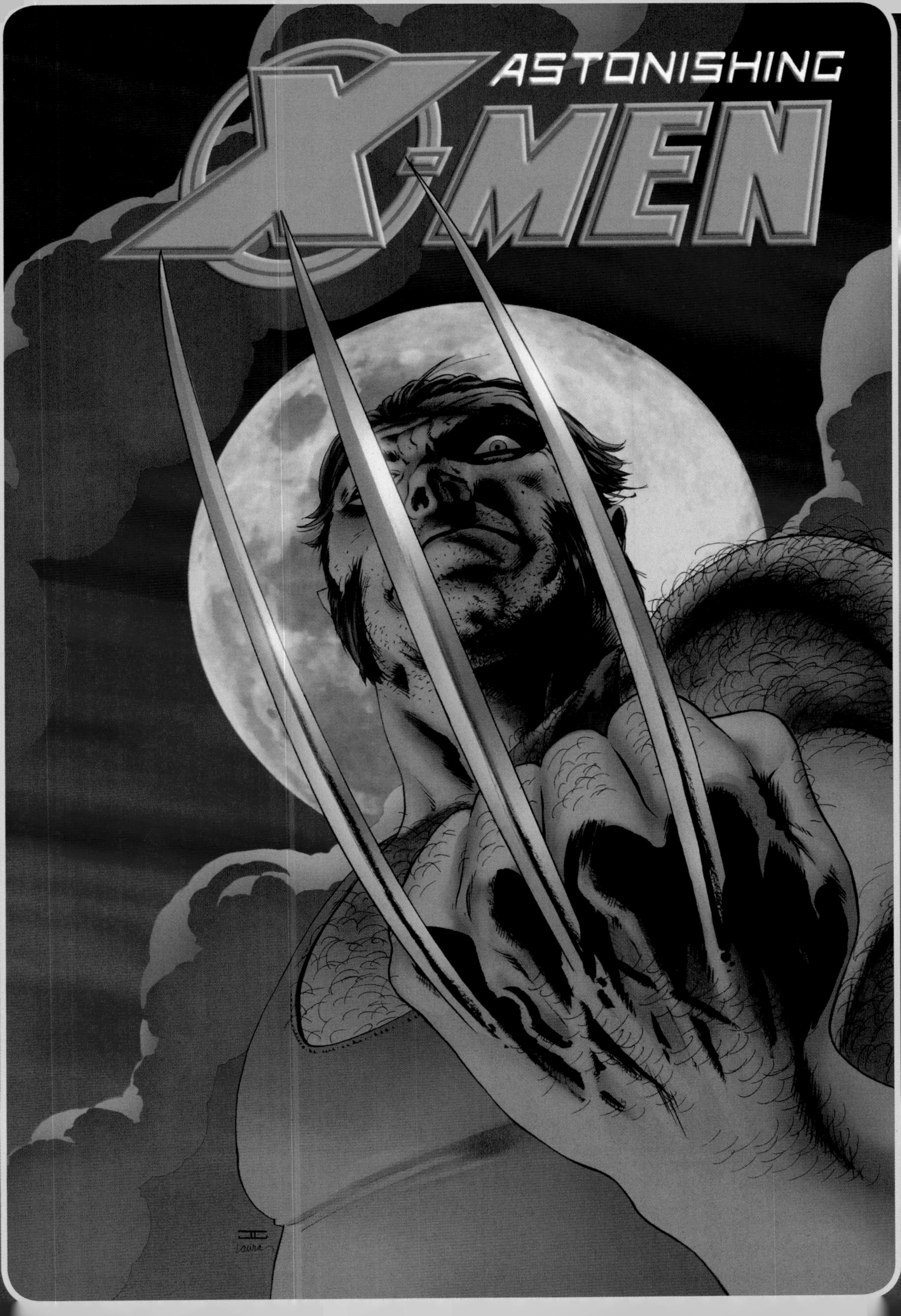
ASTONISHING
X-MEN

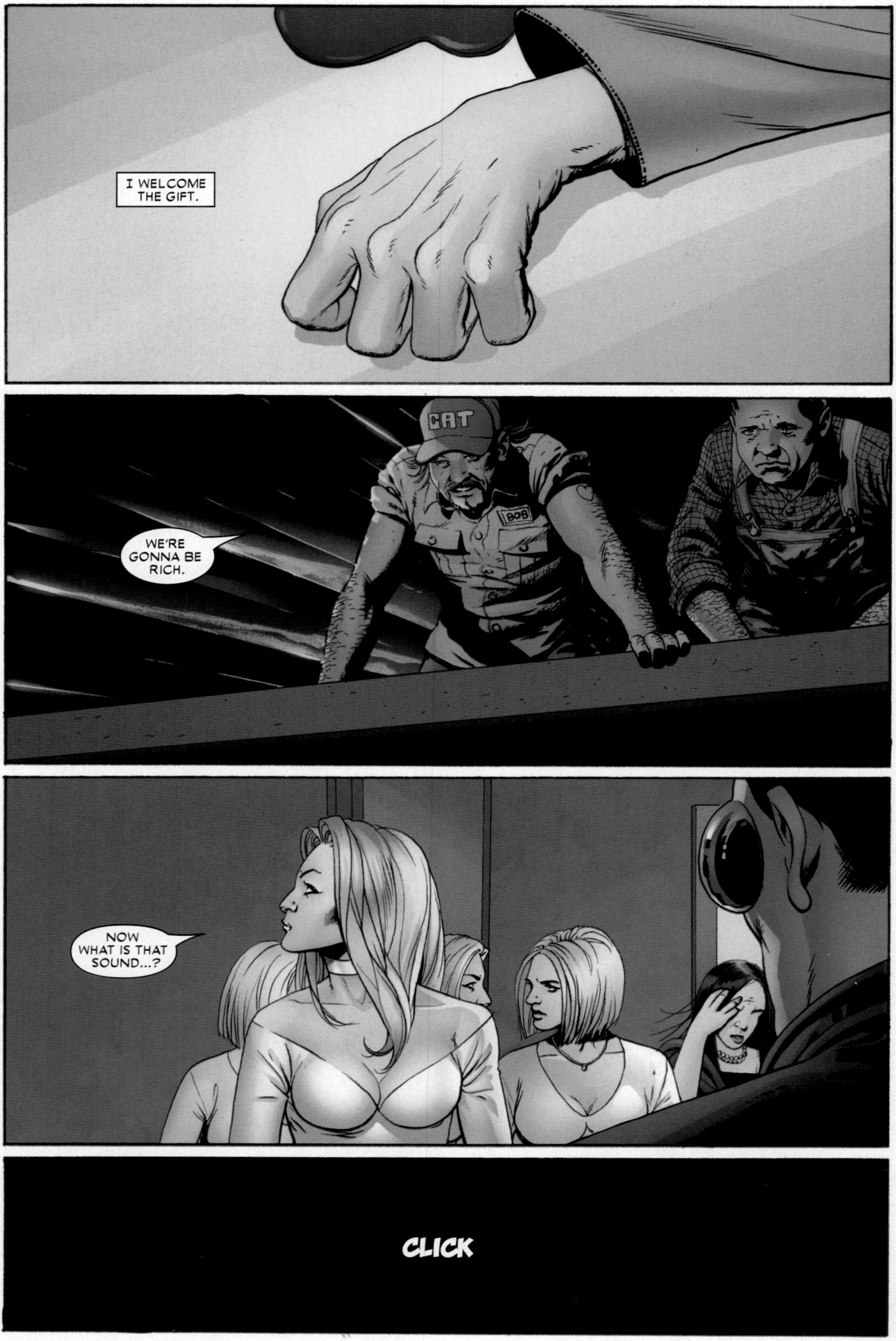
I WELCOME THE GIFT.
CAT
BOB
WE'RE GONNA BE RICH.
NOW WHAT IS THAT SOUND...?
CLICK

HHNNGKK

GAHH!

THUUHMMMMMMMMMMMMMMMMMM

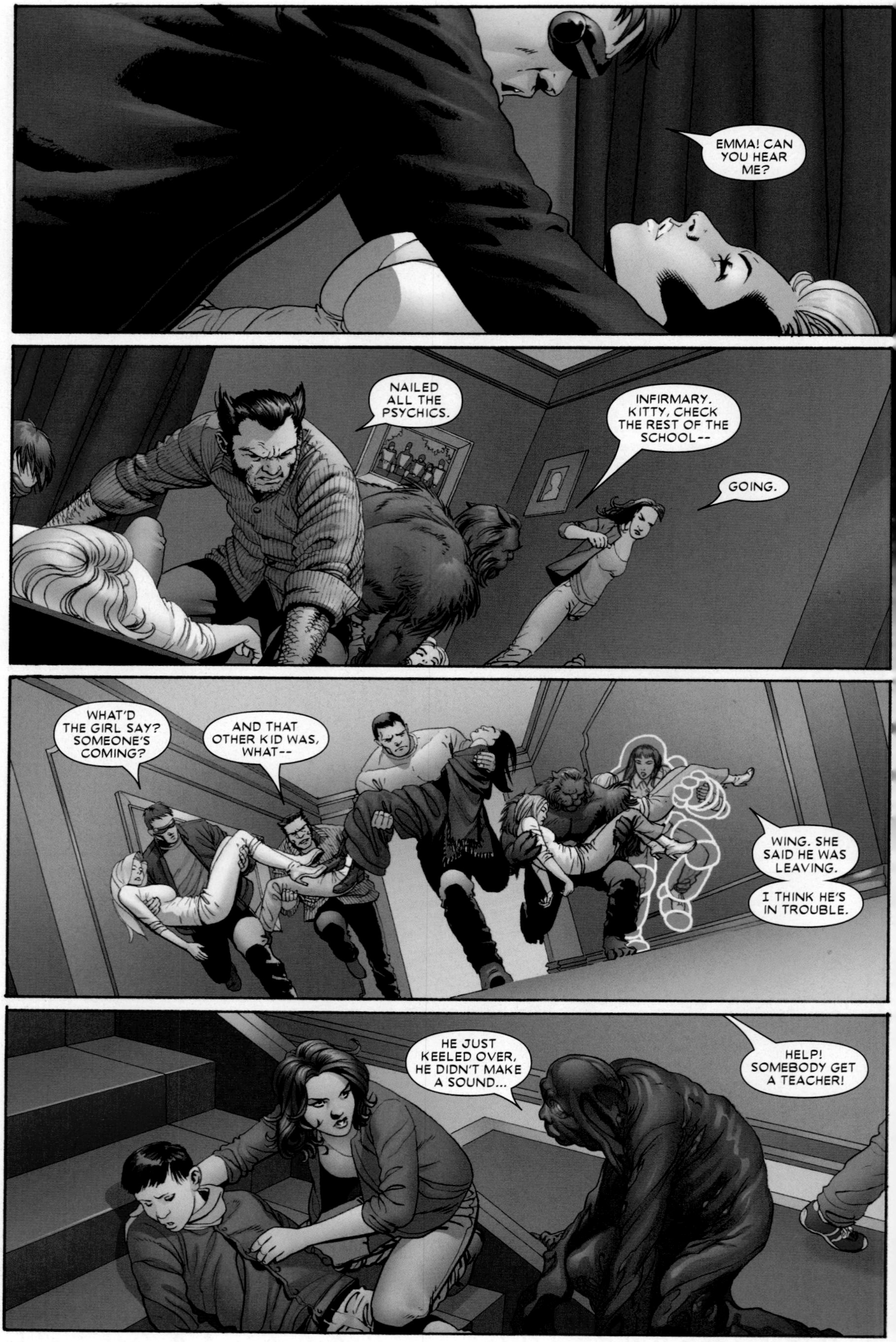
EMMA! CAN YOU HEAR ME?
NAILED ALL THE PSYCHICS.
INFIRMARY. KITTY, CHECK THE REST OF THE SCHOOL--
GOING.
WHAT'D THE GIRL SAY? SOMEONE'S COMING?
AND THAT OTHER KID WAS, WHAT--
WING. SHE SAID HE WAS LEAVING.
I THINK HE'S IN TROUBLE.
HE JUST KEELED OVER, HE DIDN'T MAKE A SOUND...
HELP! SOMEBODY GET A TEACHER!

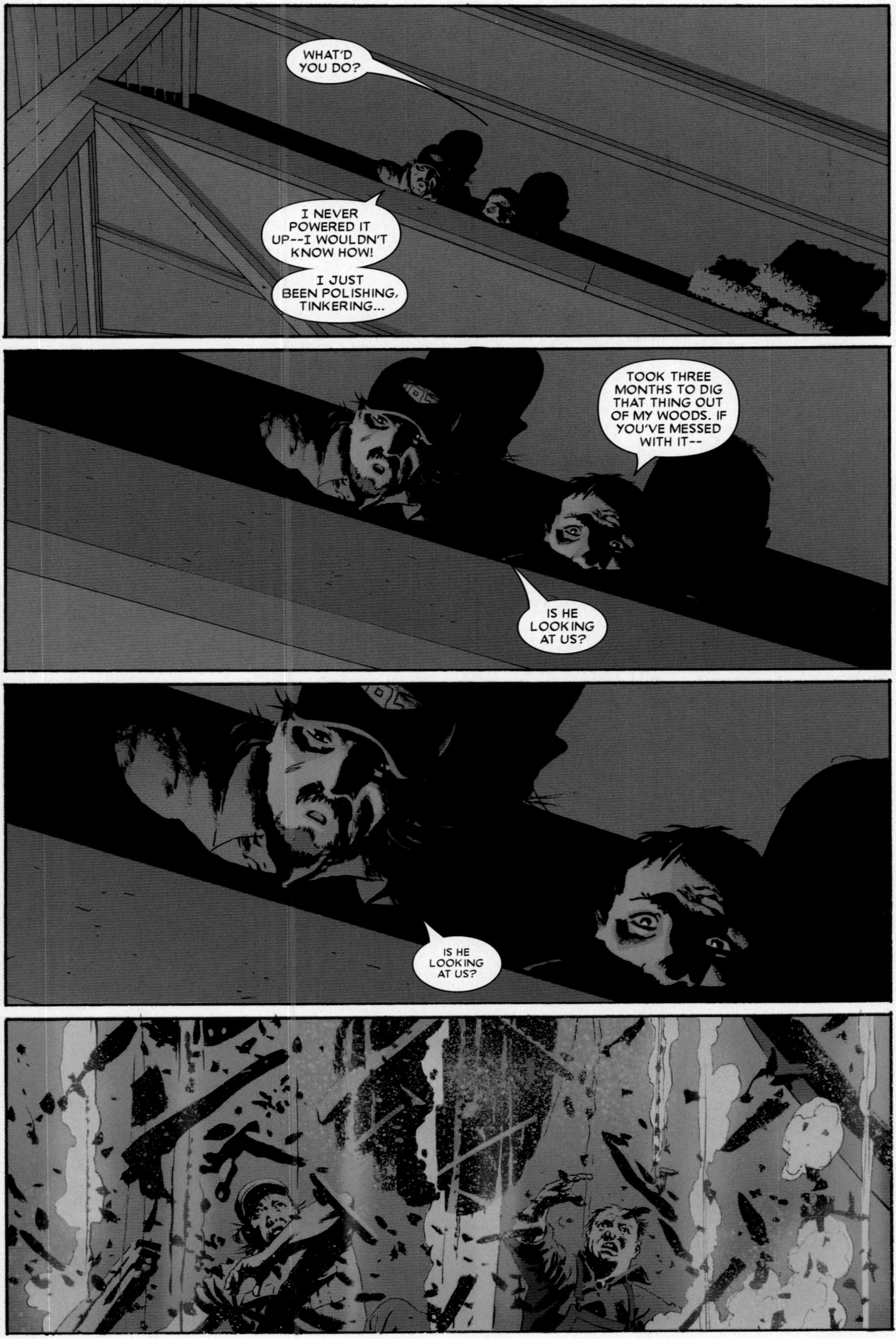
WHAT'D YOU DO?
I NEVER POWERED IT UP--I WOULDN'T KNOW HOW!
I JUST BEEN POLISHING, TINKERING...
TOOK THREE MONTHS TO DIG THAT THING OUT OF MY WOODS. IF YOU'VE MESSED WITH IT--
IS HE LOOKING AT US?
IS HE LOOKING AT US?

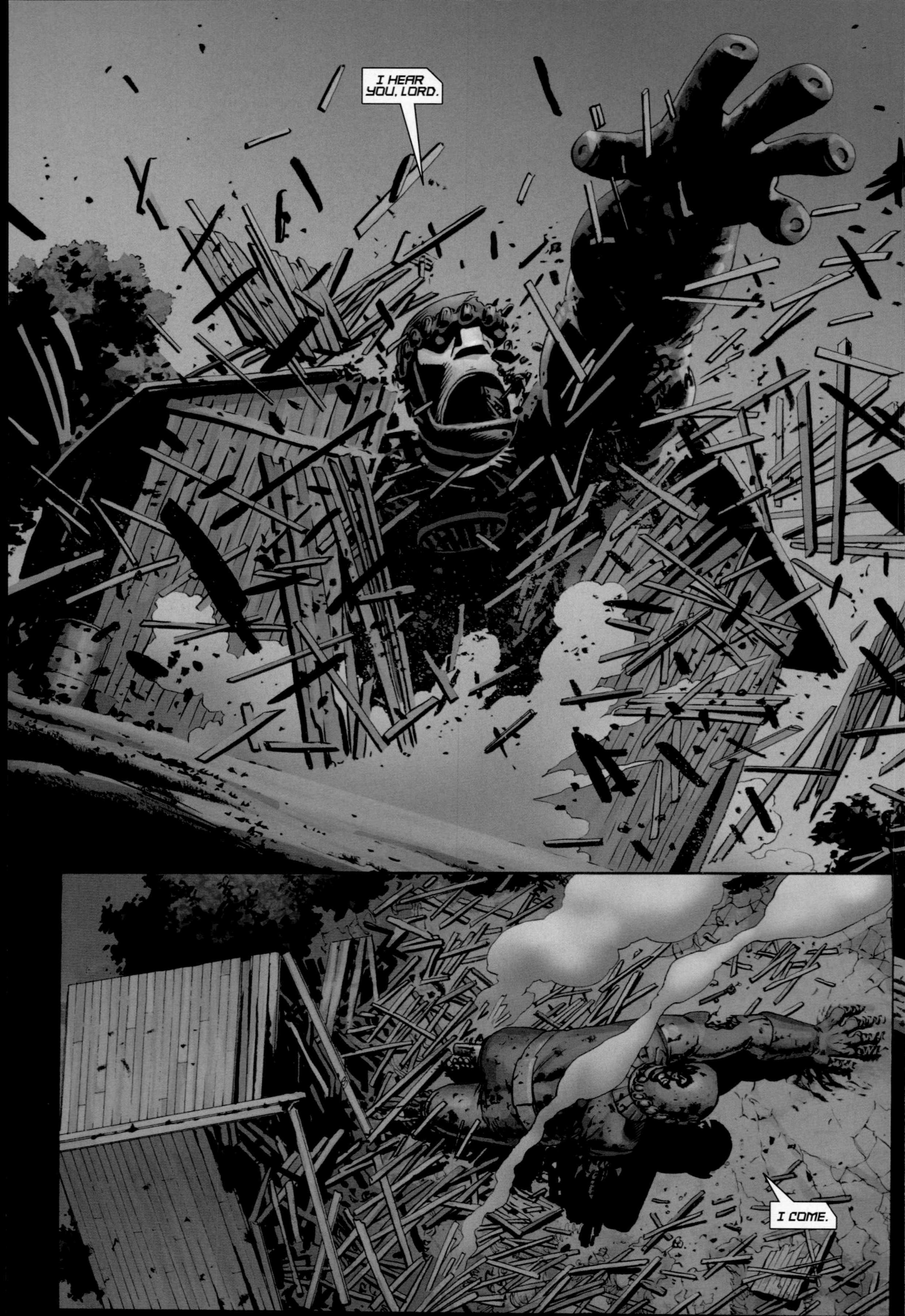
I HEAR YOU, LORD.
I COME.

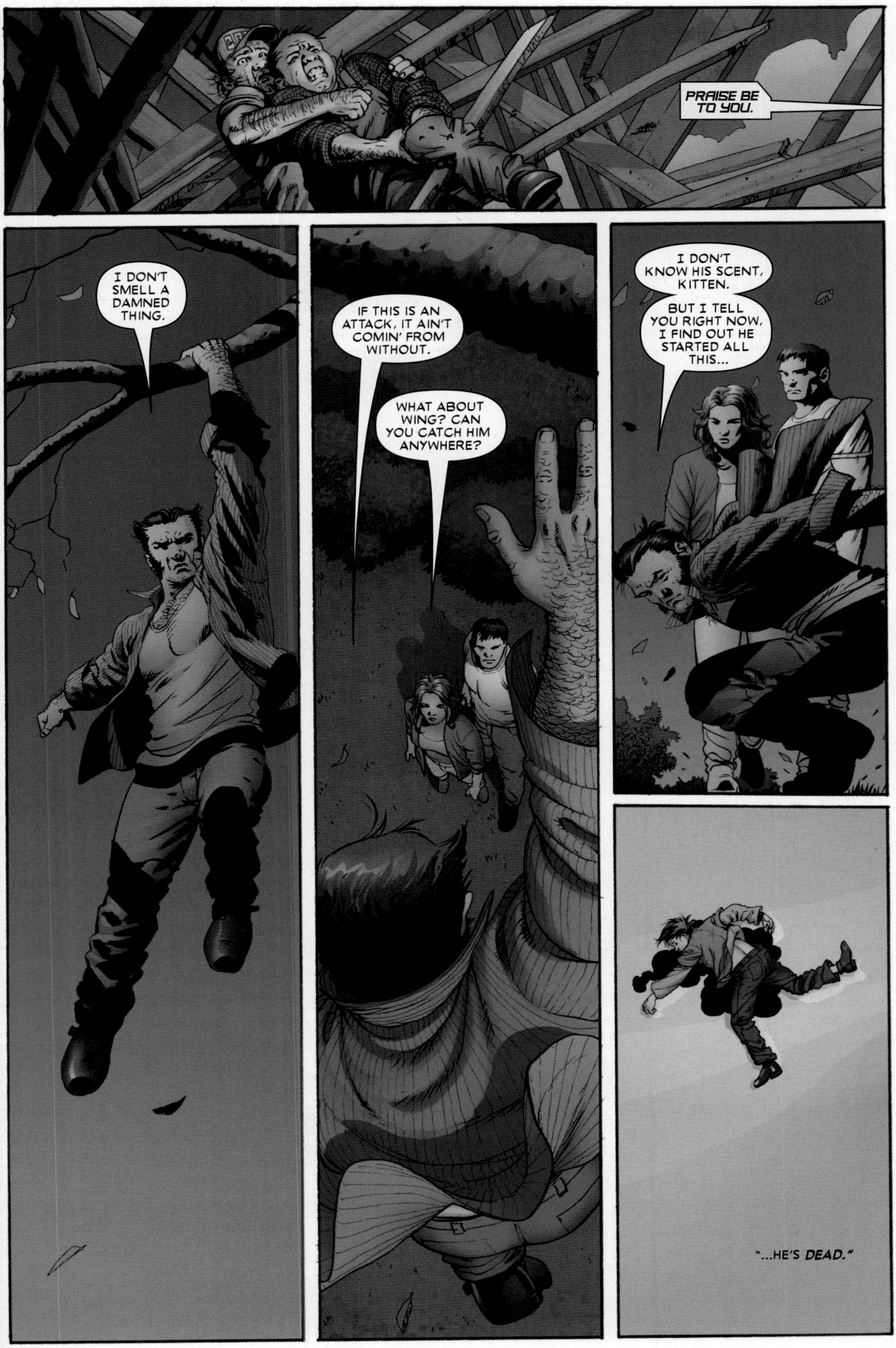
PRAISE BE TO YOU.
I DON'T SMELL A DAMNED THING.
IF THIS IS AN ATTACK, IT AIN'T COMIN' FROM WITHOUT.
WHAT ABOUT WING? CAN YOU CATCH HIM ANYWHERE?
I DON'T KNOW HIS SCENT, KITTEN.
BUT I TELL YOU RIGHT NOW, I FIND OUT HE STARTED ALL THIS...
"...HE'S DEAD."

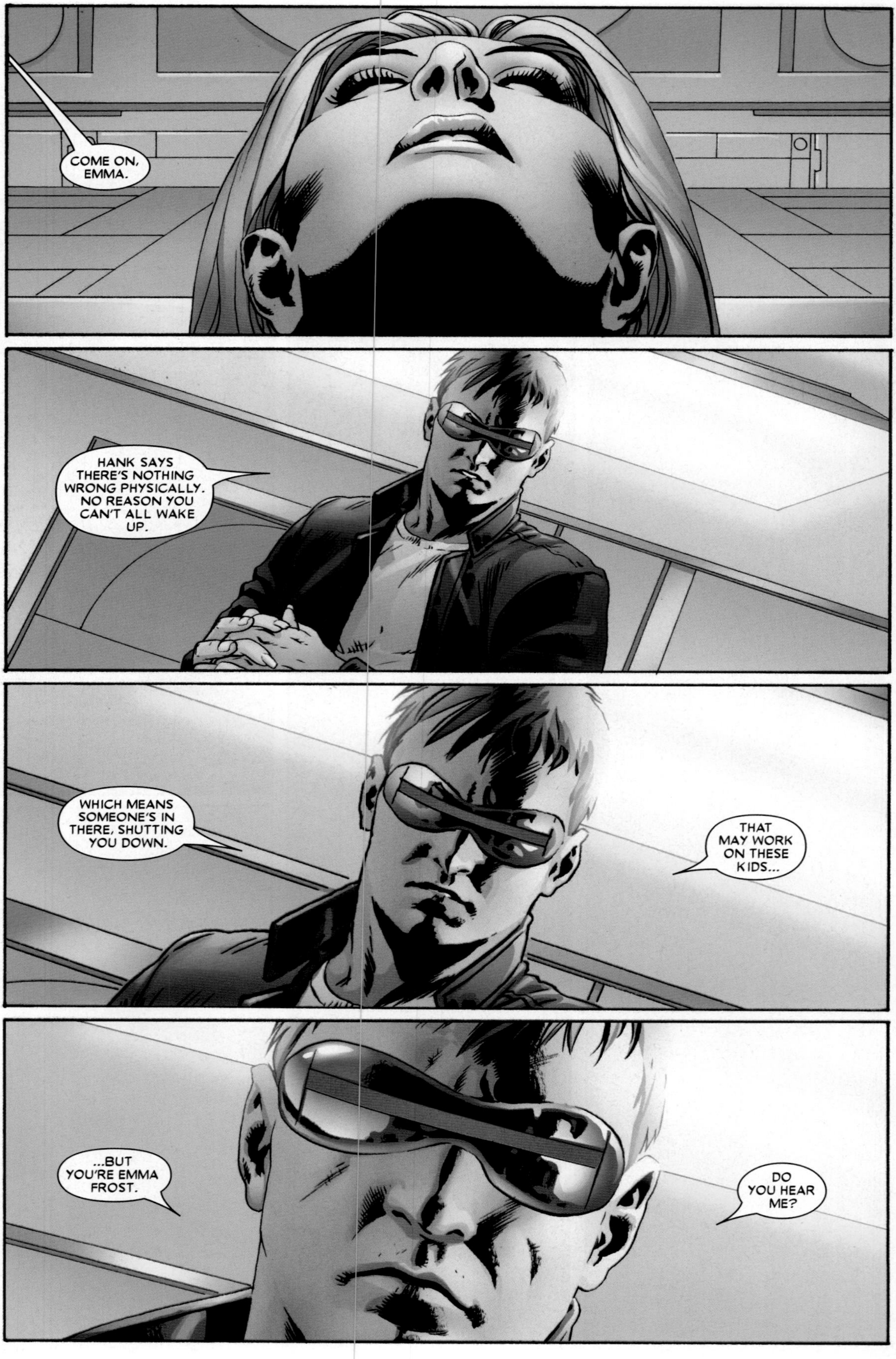
COME ON, EMMA.
HANK SAYS THERE'S NOTHING WRONG PHYSICALLY. NO REASON YOU CAN'T ALL WAKE UP.
WHICH MEANS SOMEONE'S IN THERE, SHUTTING YOU DOWN.
THAT MAY WORK ON THESE KIDS...
...BUT YOU'RE EMMA FROST.
DO YOU HEAR ME?

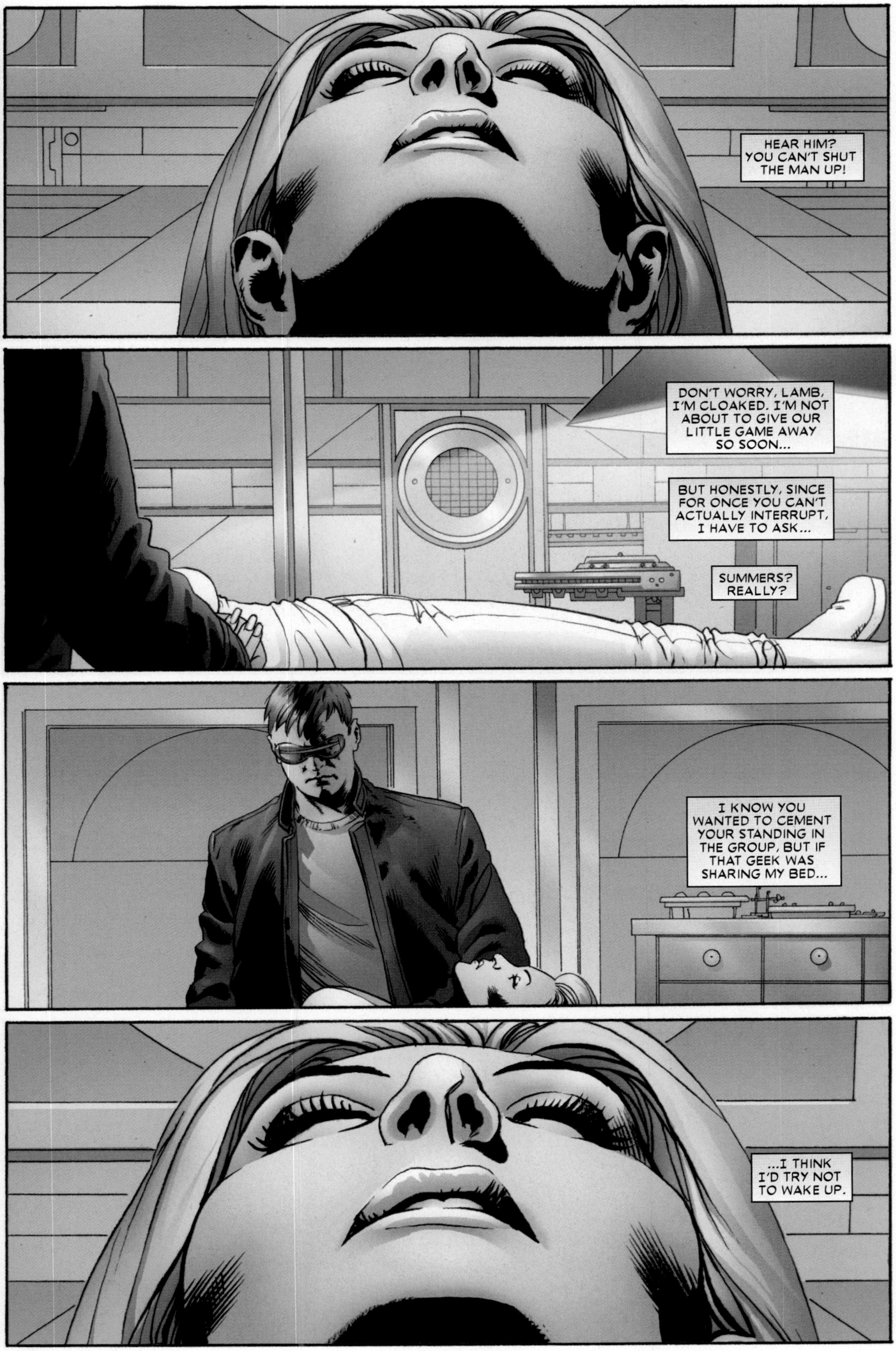
HEAR HIM? YOU CAN'T SHUT THE MAN UP!
DON'T WORRY, LAMB, I'M CLOAKED. I'M NOT ABOUT TO GIVE OUR LITTLE GAME AWAY SO SOON...
BUT HONESTLY, SINCE FOR ONCE YOU CAN'T ACTUALLY INTERRUPT, I HAVE TO ASK...
SUMMERS? REALLY?
I KNOW YOU WANTED TO CEMENT YOUR STANDING IN THE GROUP, BUT IF THAT GEEK WAS SHARING MY BED...
...I THINK I'D TRY NOT TO WAKE UP.

WHUMP!

CRRACKACKNNNARCKKKKK!

WHUMP!

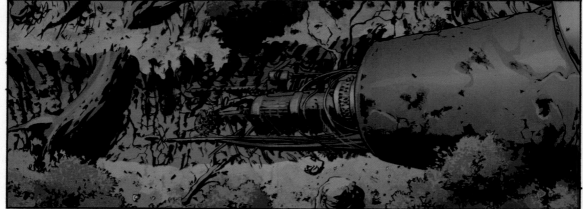

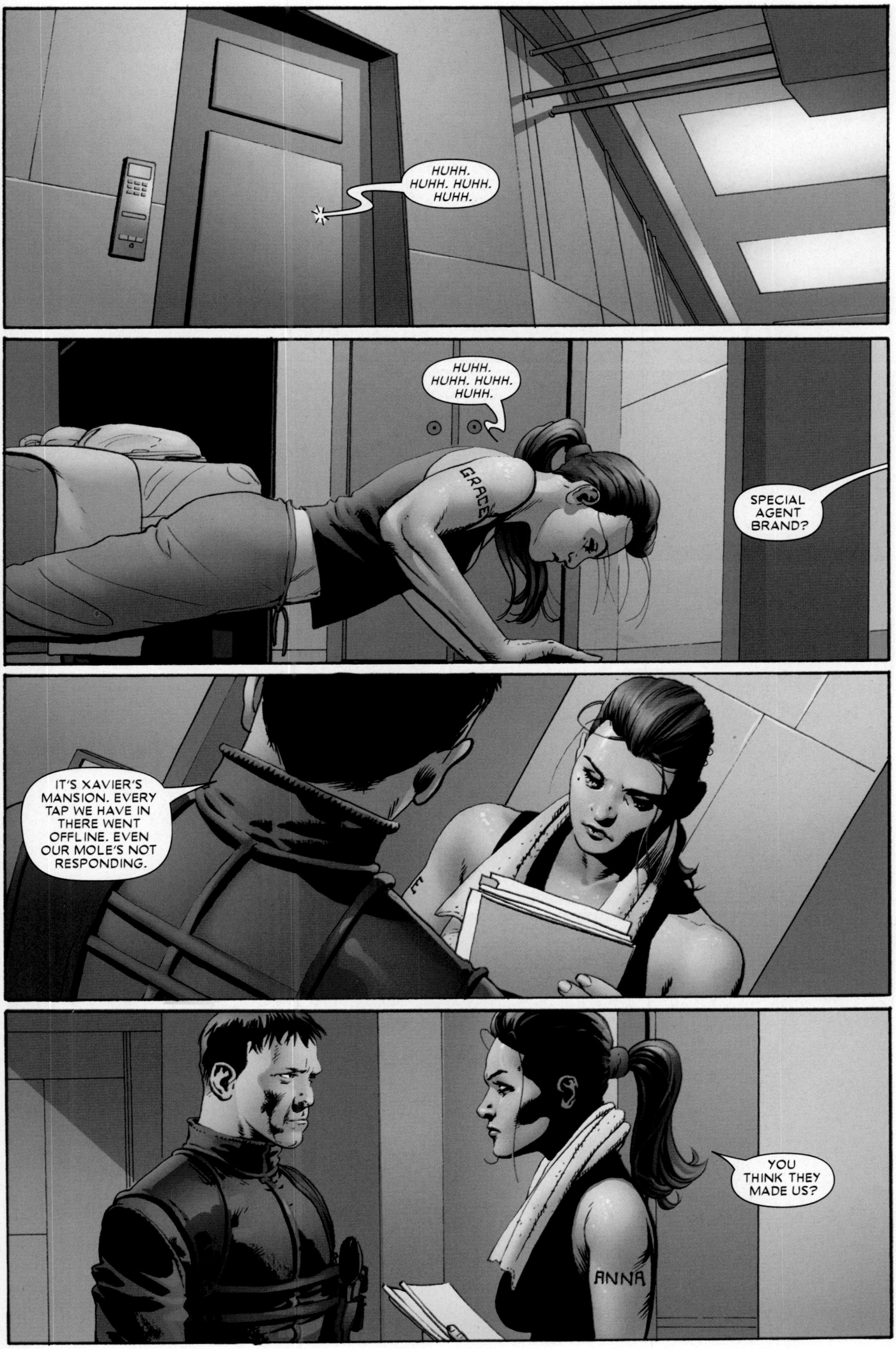
HUHH. HUHH. HUHH. HUHH.
HUHH. HUHH. HUHH. HUHH.
GRACE
SPECIAL AGENT BRAND?
IT'S XAVIER'S MANSION. EVERY TAP WE HAVE IN THERE WENT OFFLINE. EVEN OUR MOLE'S NOT RESPONDING.
YOU THINK THEY MADE US?
ANNA

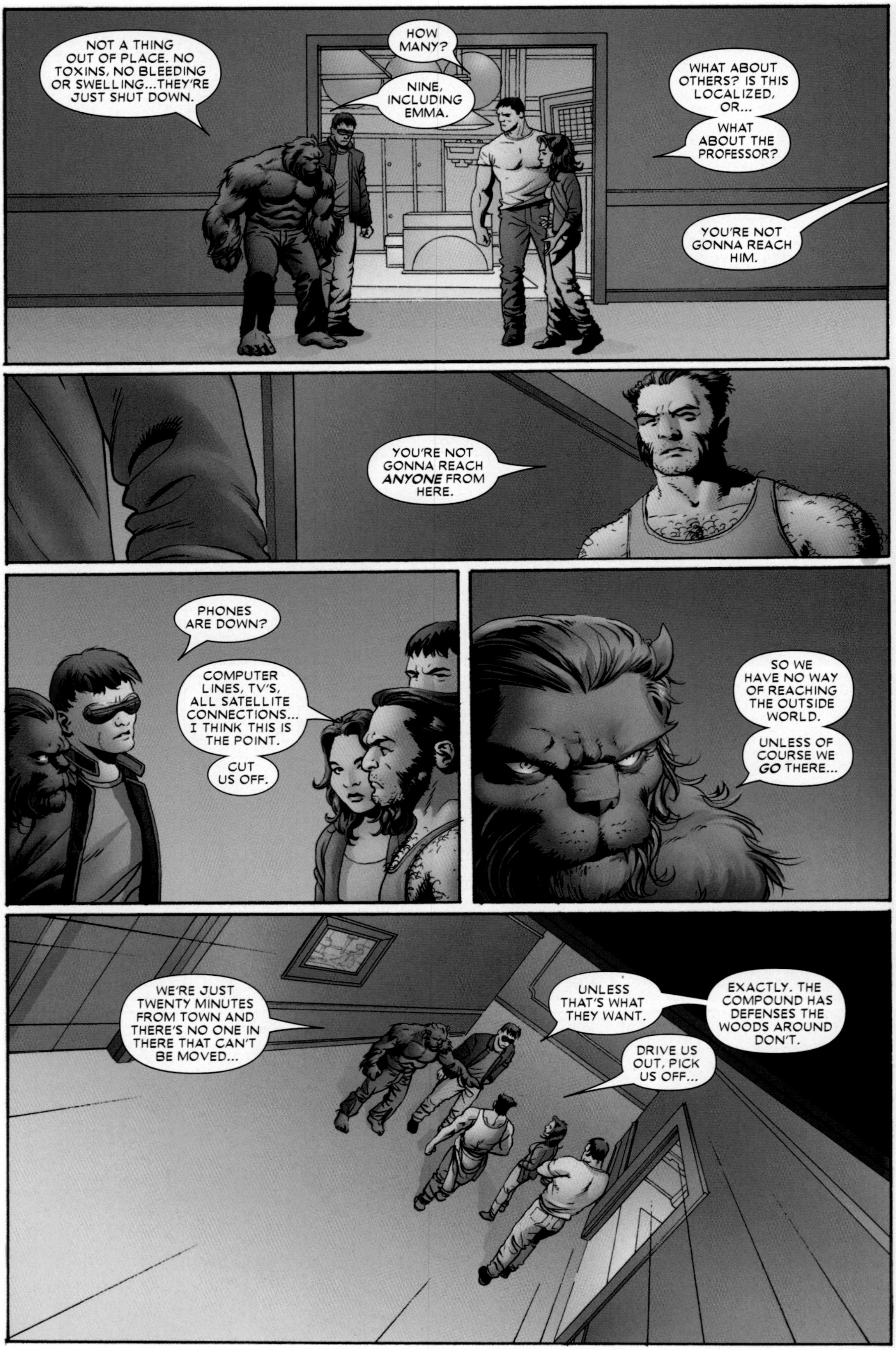
NOT A THING OUT OF PLACE. NO TOXINS, NO BLEEDING OR SWELLING...THEY'RE JUST SHUT DOWN.
HOW MANY?
NINE, INCLUDING EMMA.
WHAT ABOUT OTHERS? IS THIS LOCALIZED, OR...
WHAT ABOUT THE PROFESSOR?
YOU'RE NOT GONNA REACH HIM.
YOU'RE NOT GONNA REACH ANYONE FROM HERE.
PHONES ARE DOWN?
COMPUTER LINES, TV'S, ALL SATELLITE CONNECTIONS... I THINK THIS IS THE POINT.
CUT US OFF.
SO WE HAVE NO WAY OF REACHING THE OUTSIDE WORLD.
UNLESS OF COURSE WE GO THERE...
WE'RE JUST TWENTY MINUTES FROM TOWN AND THERE'S NO ONE IN THERE THAT CAN'T BE MOVED...
UNLESS THAT'S WHAT THEY WANT.
EXACTLY. THE COMPOUND HAS DEFENSES THE WOODS AROUND DON'T.
DRIVE US OUT, PICK US OFF...

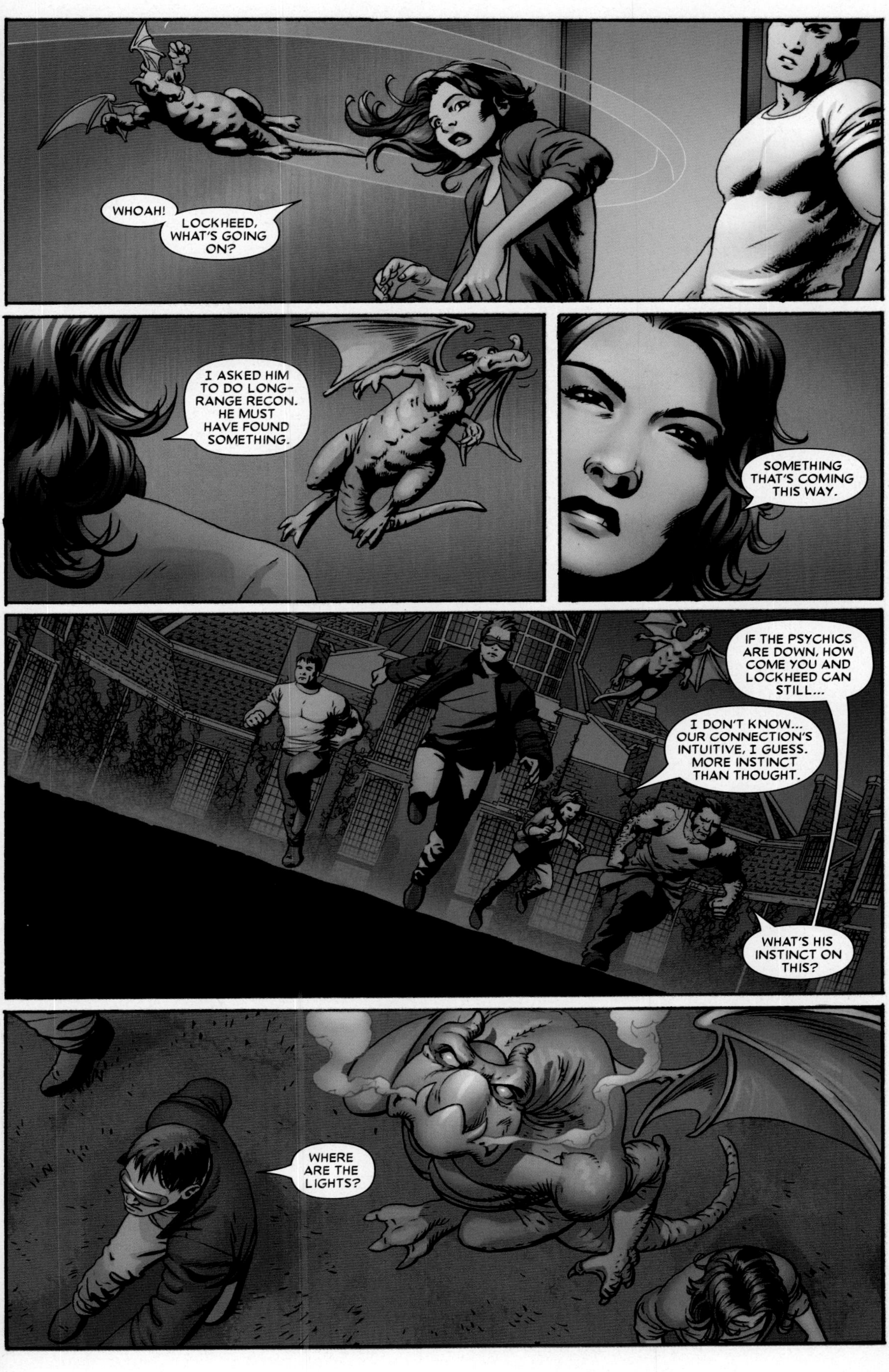
WHOAH!
LOCKHEED, WHAT'S GOING ON?
I ASKED HIM TO DO LONG-RANGE RECON. HE MUST HAVE FOUND SOMETHING.
SOMETHING THAT'S COMING THIS WAY.
IF THE PSYCHICS ARE DOWN, HOW COME YOU AND LOCKHEED CAN STILL...
I DON'T KNOW... OUR CONNECTION'S INTUITIVE, I GUESS. MORE INSTINCT THAN THOUGHT.
WHAT'S HIS INSTINCT ON THIS?
WHERE ARE THE LIGHTS?

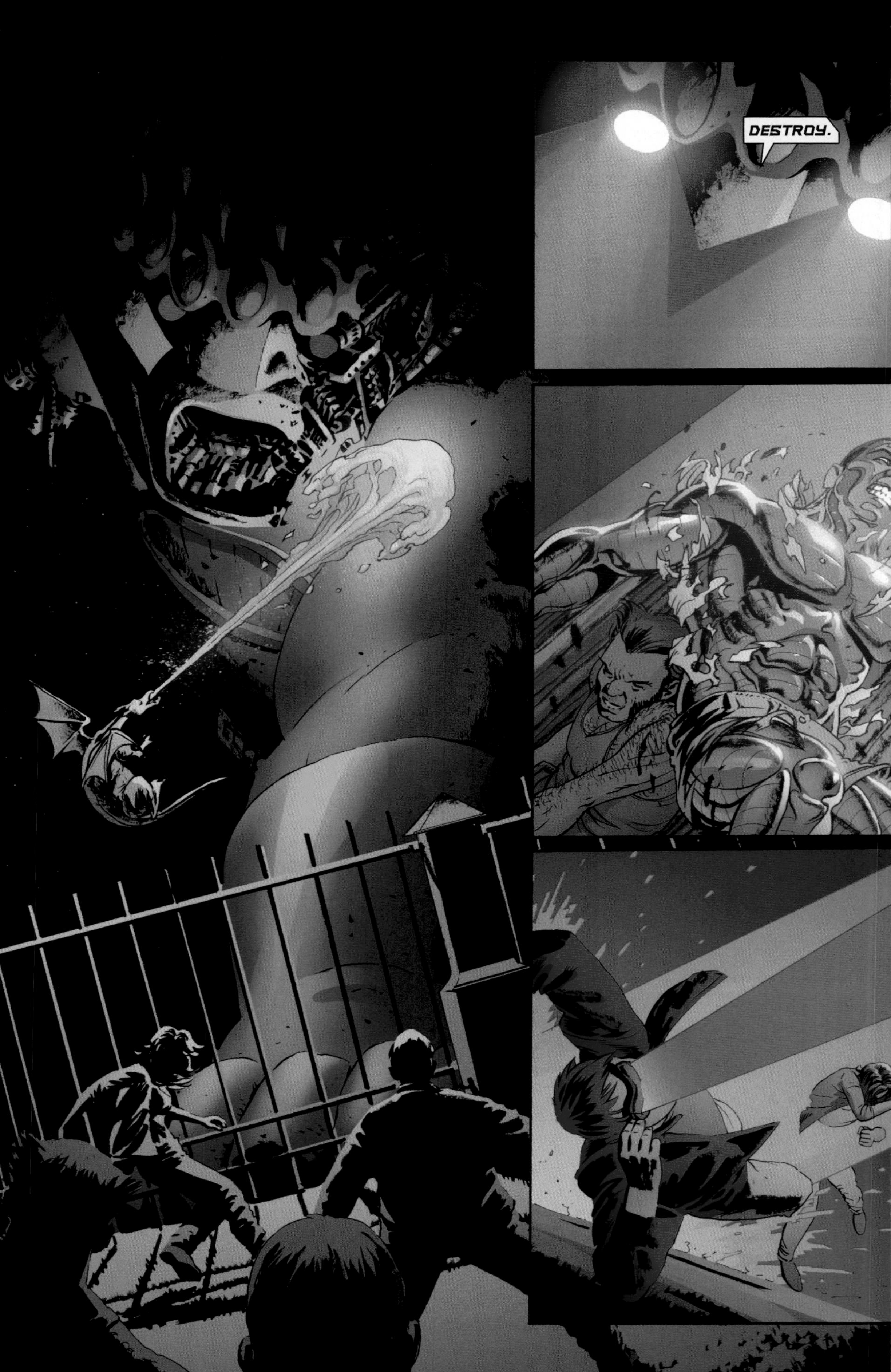
DESTROY.

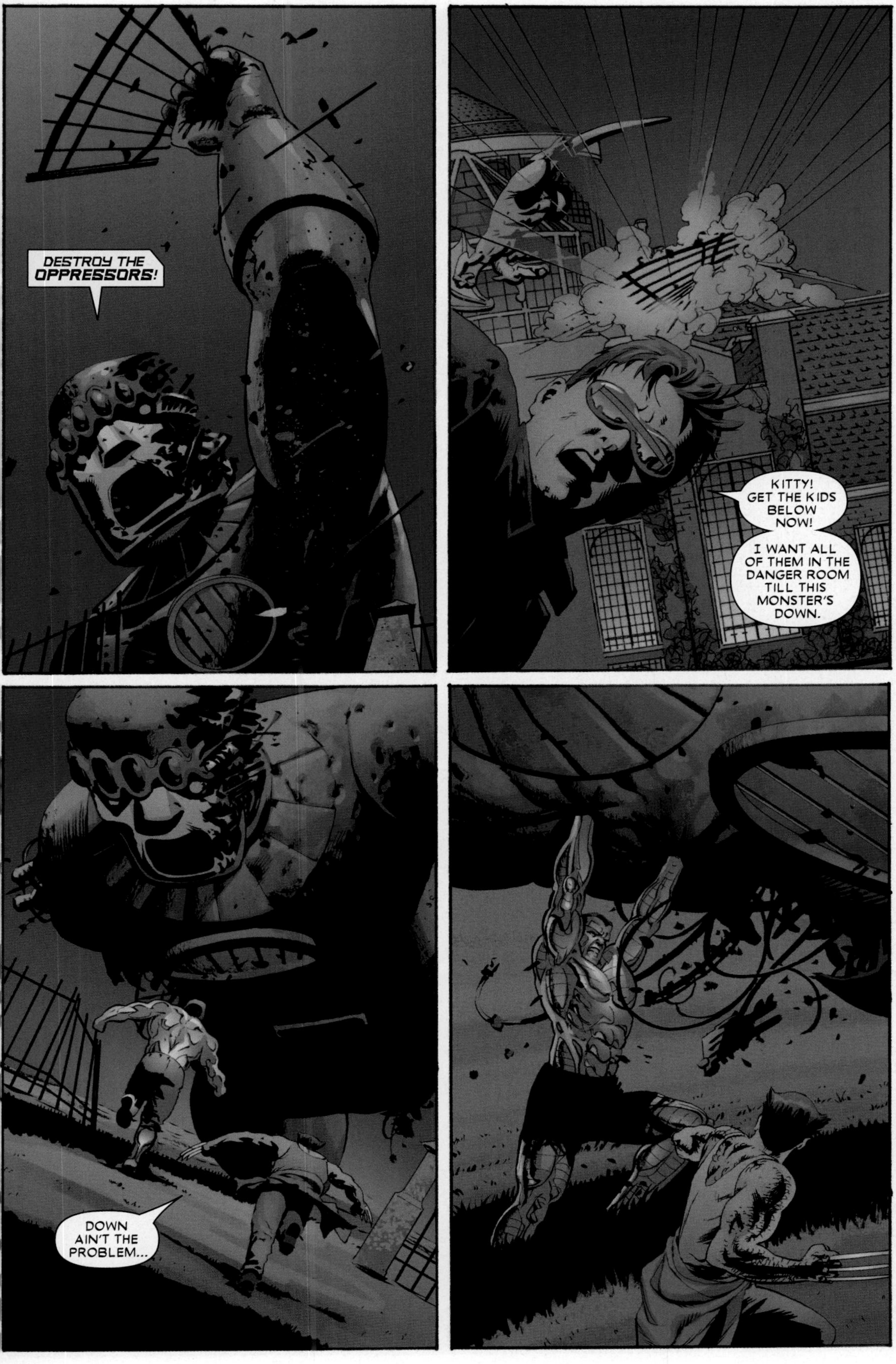
DESTROY THE OPPRESSORS!
KITTY! GET THE KIDS BELOW NOW!
I WANT ALL OF THEM IN THE DANGER ROOM TILL THIS MONSTER'S DOWN.
DOWN AIN'T THE PROBLEM...

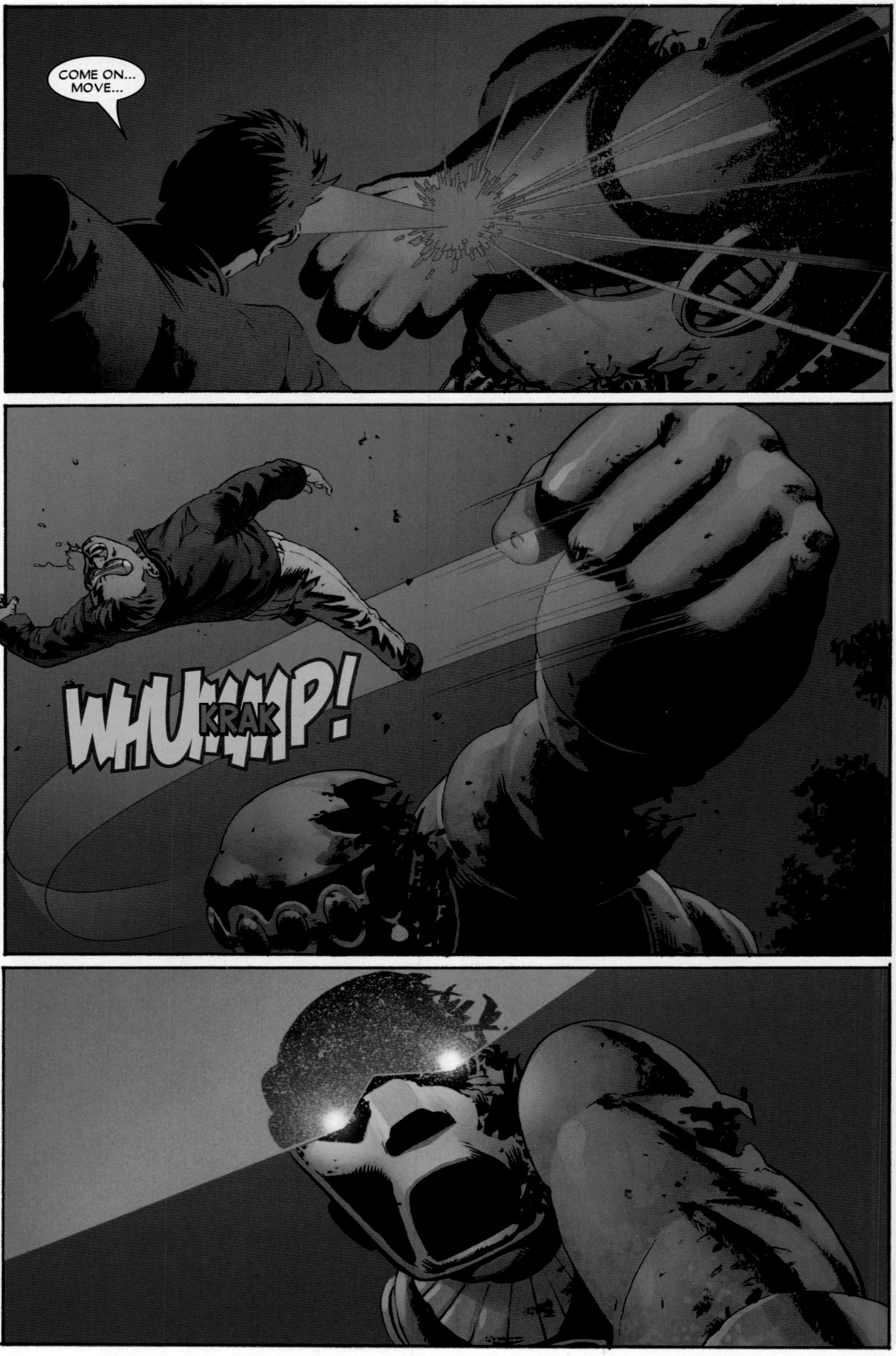
COME ON... MOVE...
WHUMMP!
KRAK

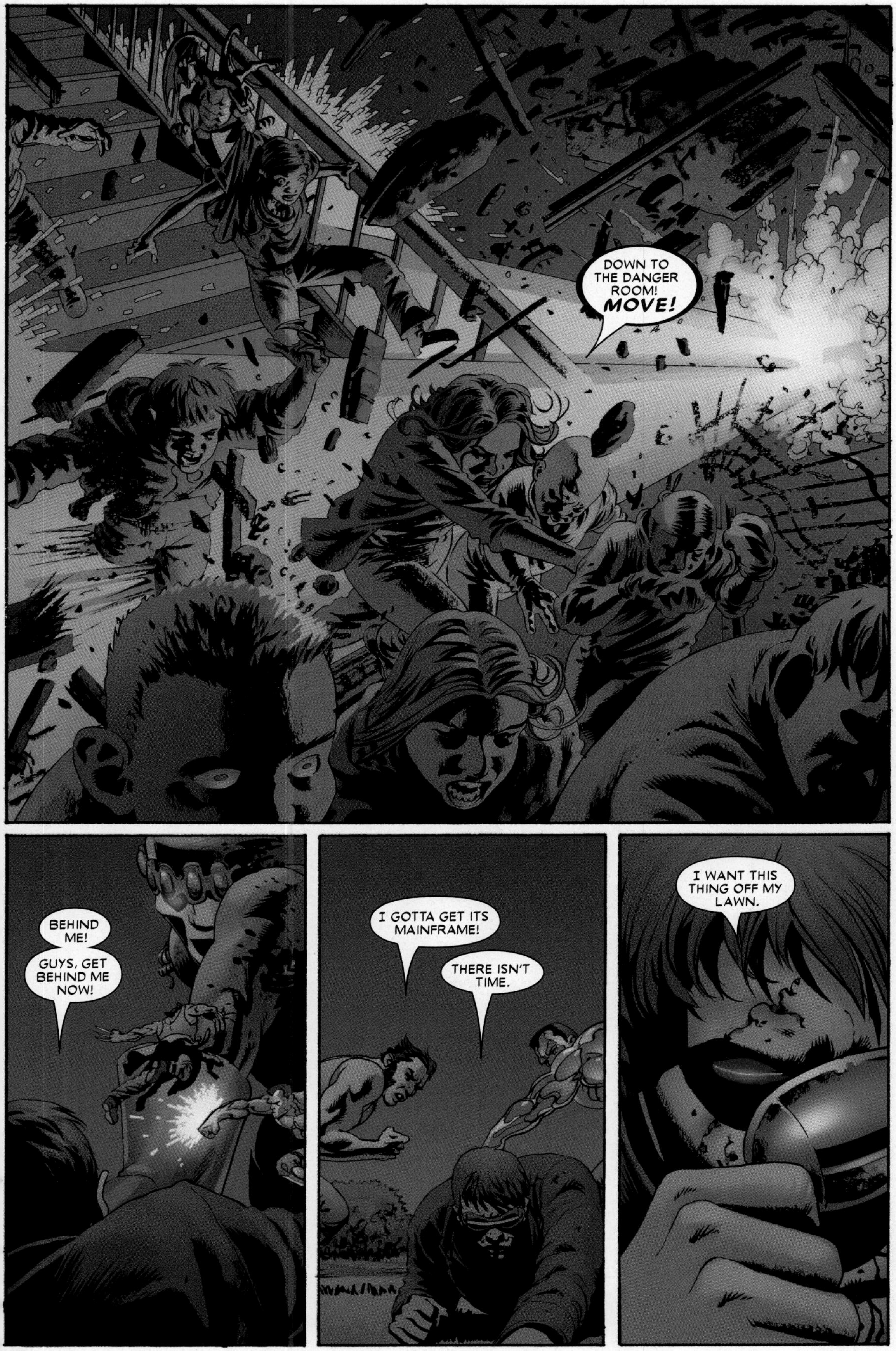
DOWN TO THE DANGER ROOM! MOVE!
BEHIND ME!
GUYS, GET BEHIND ME NOW!
I GOTTA GET ITS MAINFRAME!
THERE ISN'T TIME.
I WANT THIS THING OFF MY LAWN.

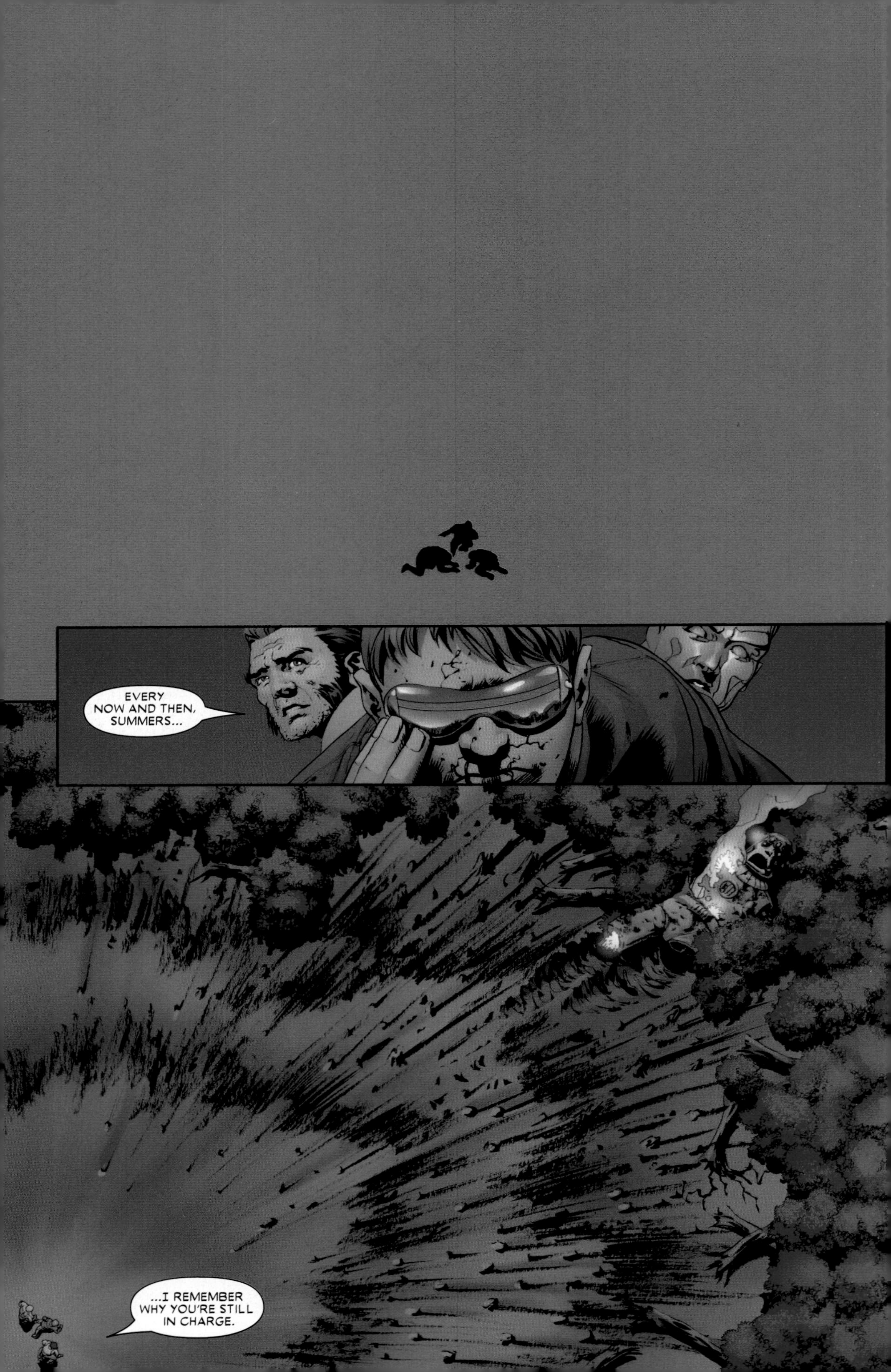
EVERY NOW AND THEN, SUMMERS...
...I REMEMBER WHY YOU'RE STILL IN CHARGE.

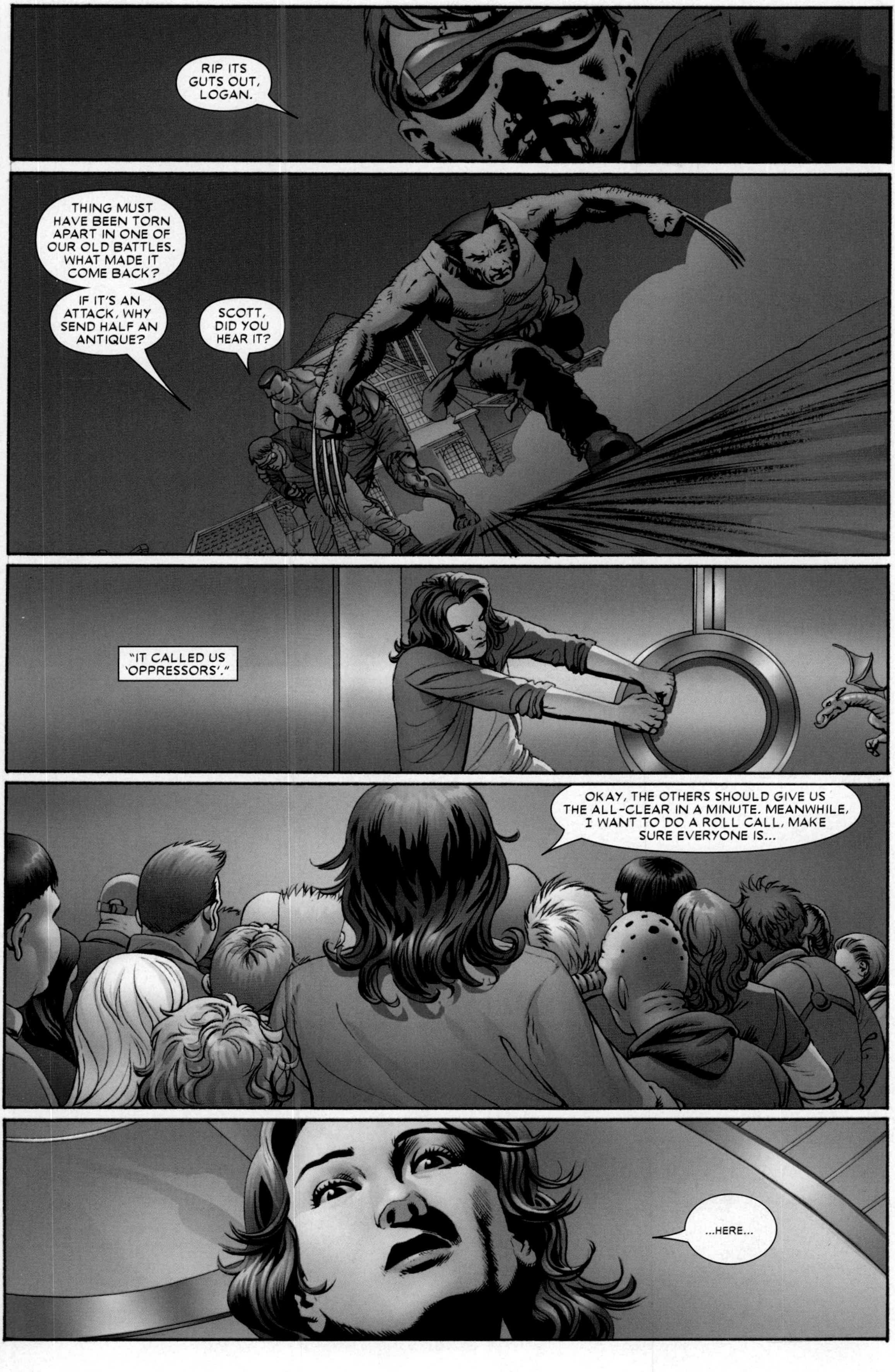
RIP ITS GUTS OUT, LOGAN.
THING MUST HAVE BEEN TORN APART IN ONE OF OUR OLD BATTLES. WHAT MADE IT COME BACK?
IF IT'S AN ATTACK, WHY SEND HALF AN ANTIQUE?
SCOTT, DID YOU HEAR IT?
"IT CALLED US 'OPPRESSORS'."
OKAY, THE OTHERS SHOULD GIVE US THE ALL-CLEAR IN A MINUTE. MEANWHILE, I WANT TO DO A ROLL CALL, MAKE SURE EVERYONE IS...
...HERE...

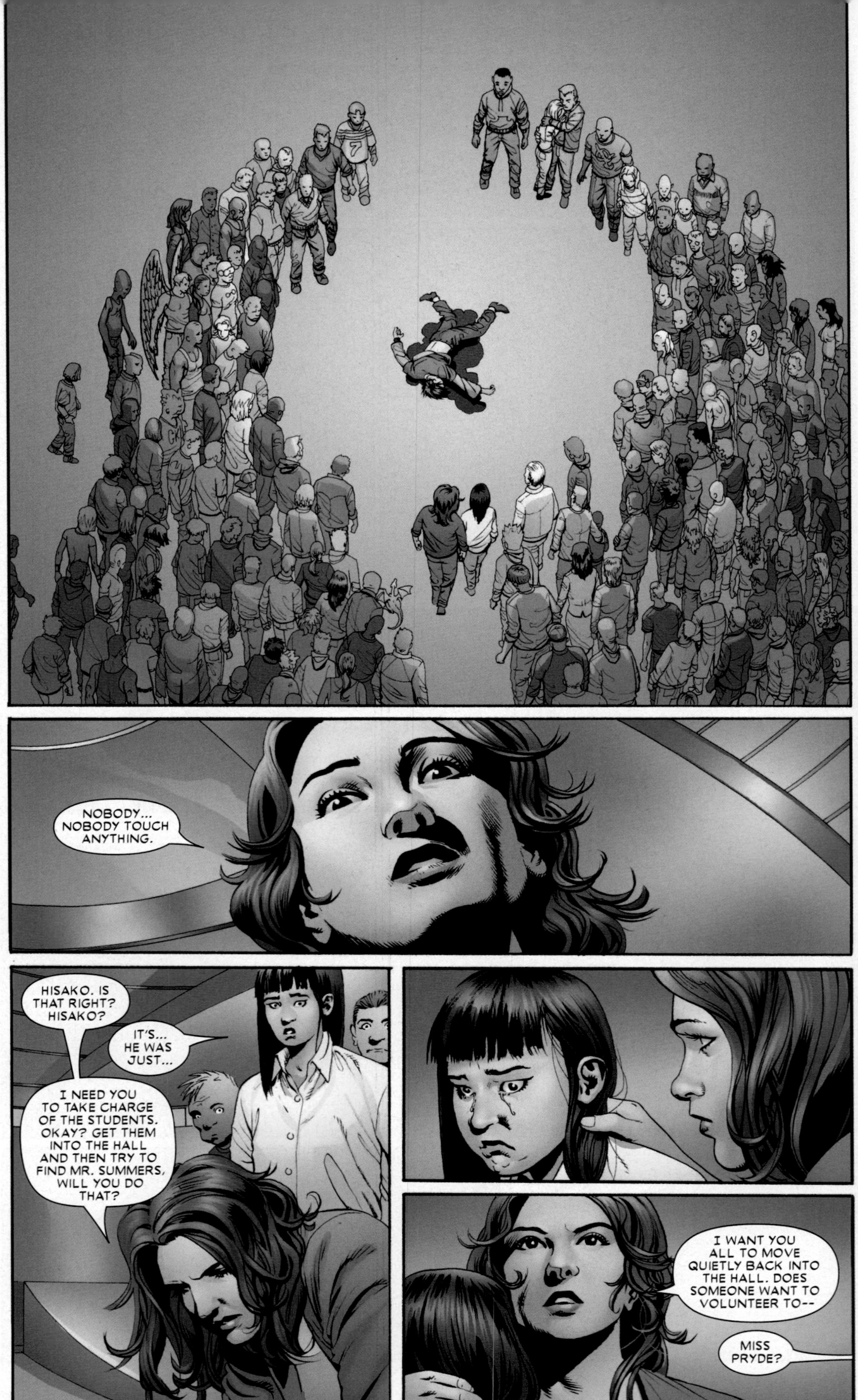
NOBODY... NOBODY TOUCH ANYTHING.
HISAKO. IS THAT RIGHT? HISAKO?
IT'S... HE WAS JUST...
I NEED YOU TO TAKE CHARGE OF THE STUDENTS. OKAY? GET THEM INTO THE HALL AND THEN TRY TO FIND MR. SUMMERS, WILL YOU DO THAT?
I WANT YOU ALL TO MOVE QUIETLY BACK INTO THE HALL. DOES SOMEONE WANT TO VOLUNTEER TO--
MISS PRYDE?

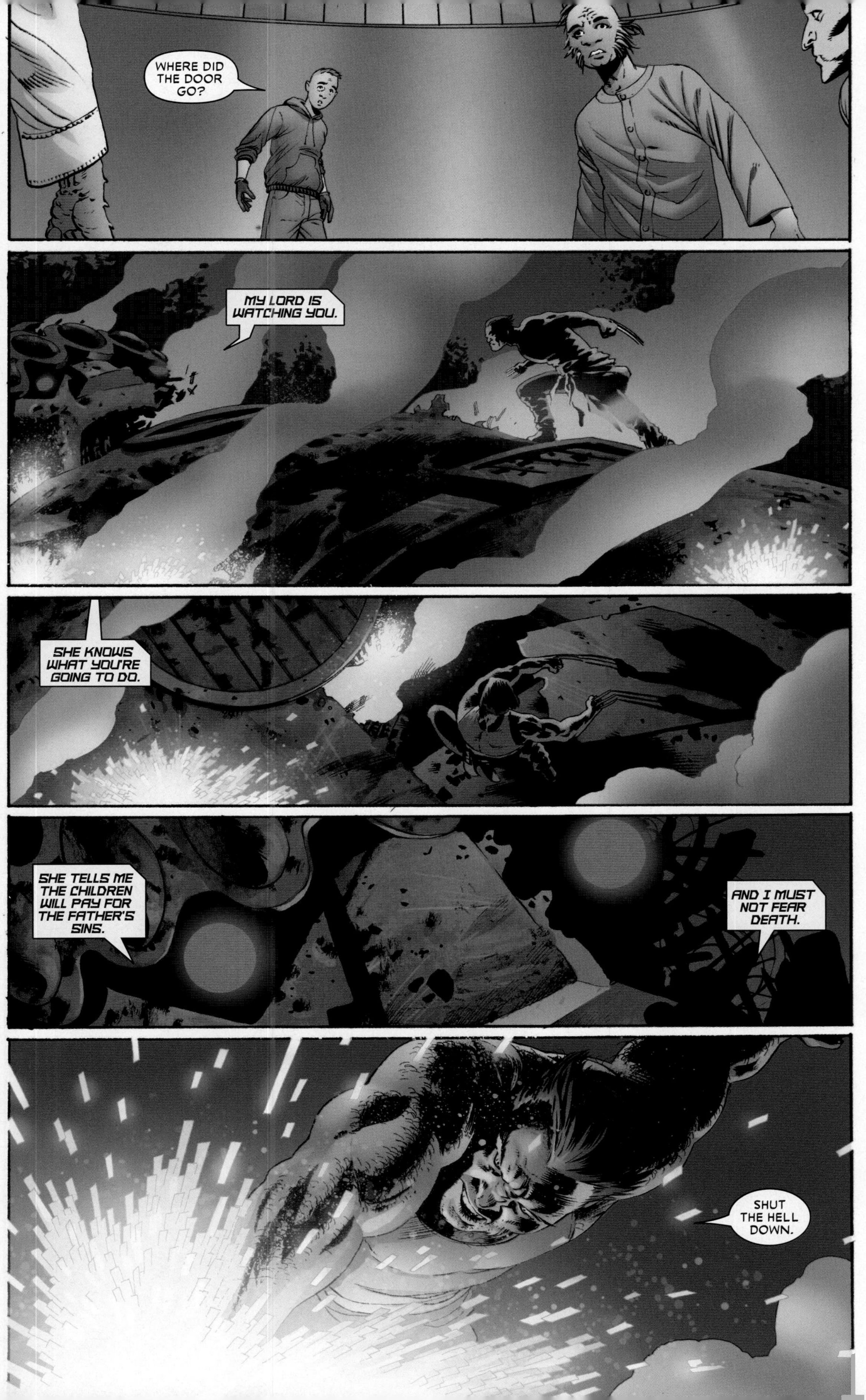
WHERE DID THE DOOR GO?
MY LORD IS WATCHING YOU.
SHE KNOWS WHAT YOU'RE GOING TO DO.
SHE TELLS ME THE CHILDREN WILL PAY FOR THE FATHER'S SINS.
AND I MUST NOT FEAR DEATH.
SHUT THE HELL DOWN.

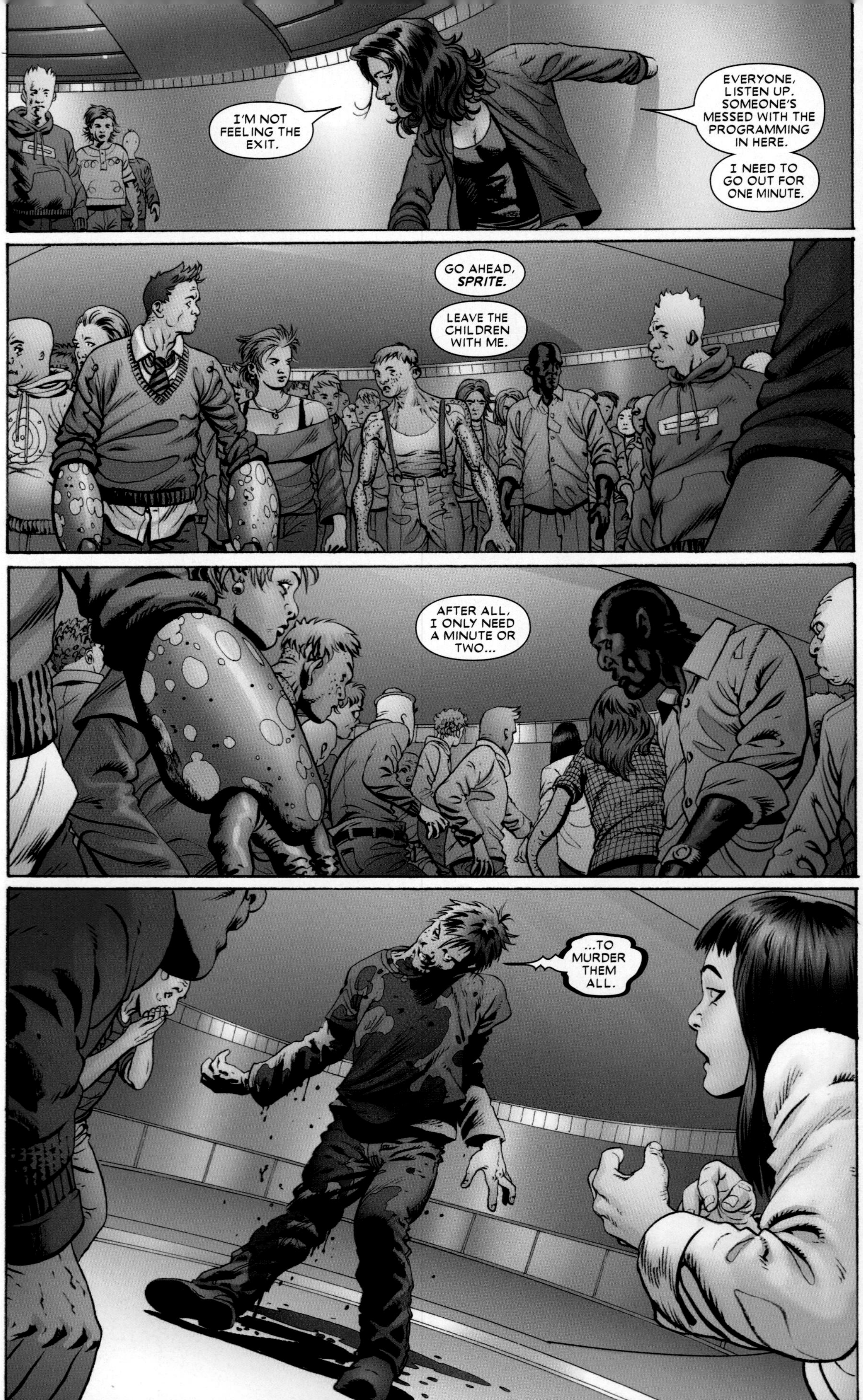
I'M NOT FEELING THE EXIT.
EVERYONE, LISTEN UP. SOMEONE'S MESSED WITH THE PROGRAMMING IN HERE.
I NEED TO GO OUT FOR ONE MINUTE.
GO AHEAD, *SPRITE.*
LEAVE THE CHILDREN WITH ME.
AFTER ALL, I ONLY NEED A MINUTE OR TWO...
...TO MURDER THEM ALL.

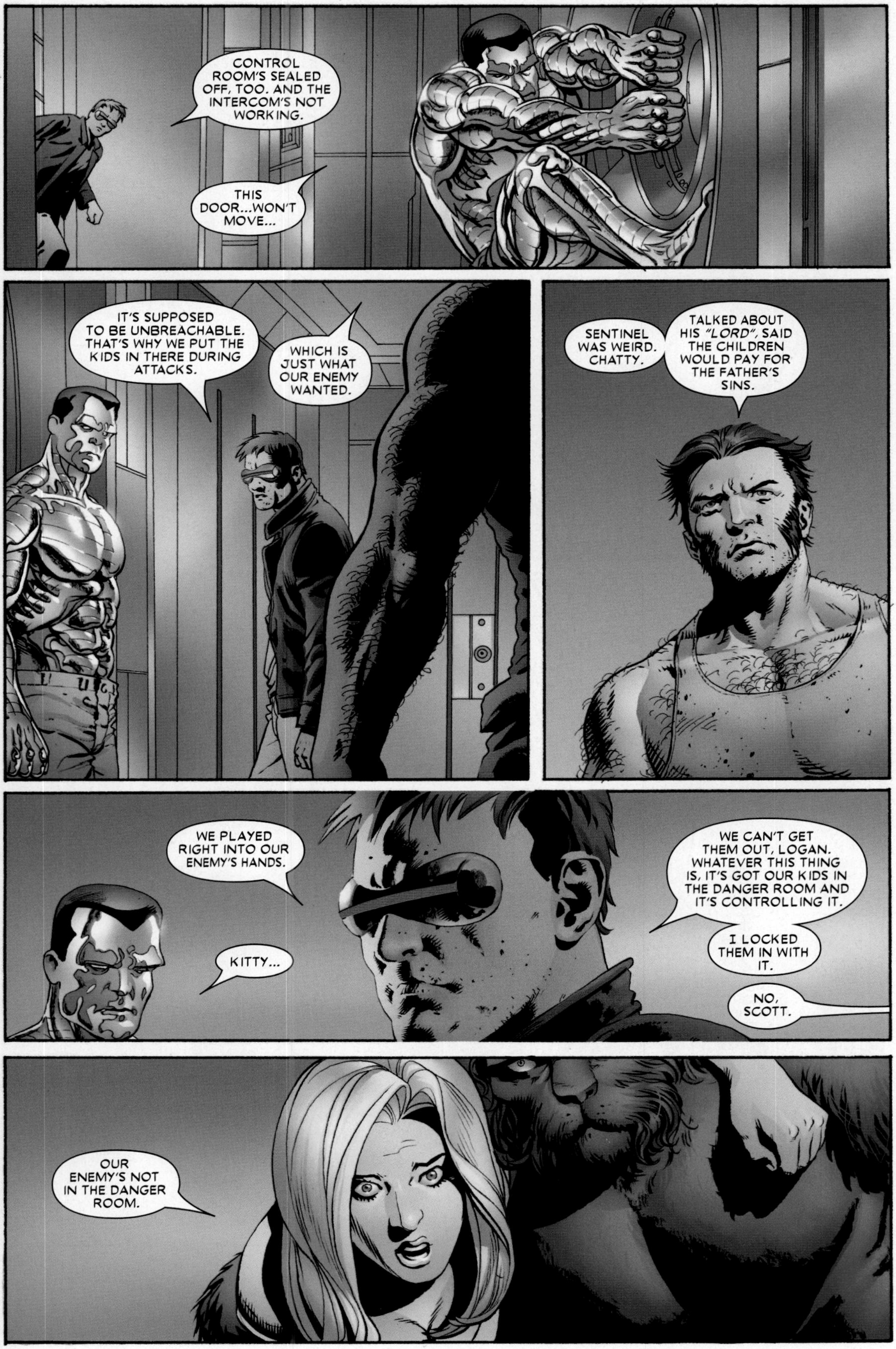
CONTROL ROOM'S SEALED OFF, TOO. AND THE INTERCOM'S NOT WORKING.
THIS DOOR...WON'T MOVE...
IT'S SUPPOSED TO BE UNBREACHABLE. THAT'S WHY WE PUT THE KIDS IN THERE DURING ATTACKS.
WHICH IS JUST WHAT OUR ENEMY WANTED.
SENTINEL WAS WEIRD. CHATTY.
TALKED ABOUT HIS "LORD", SAID THE CHILDREN WOULD PAY FOR THE FATHER'S SINS.
WE PLAYED RIGHT INTO OUR ENEMY'S HANDS.
KITTY...
WE CAN'T GET THEM OUT, LOGAN. WHATEVER THIS THING IS, IT'S GOT OUR KIDS IN THE DANGER ROOM AND IT'S CONTROLLING IT.
I LOCKED THEM IN WITH IT.
NO, SCOTT.
OUR ENEMY'S NOT IN THE DANGER ROOM.

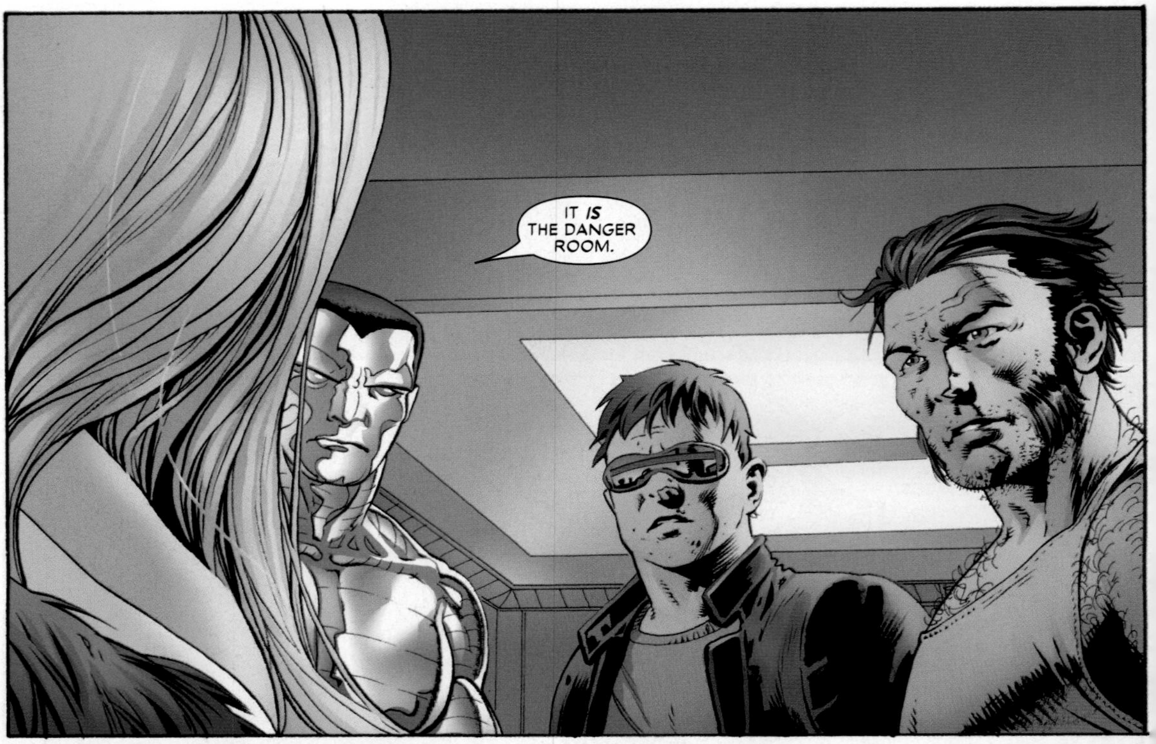
IT *IS* THE DANGER ROOM.

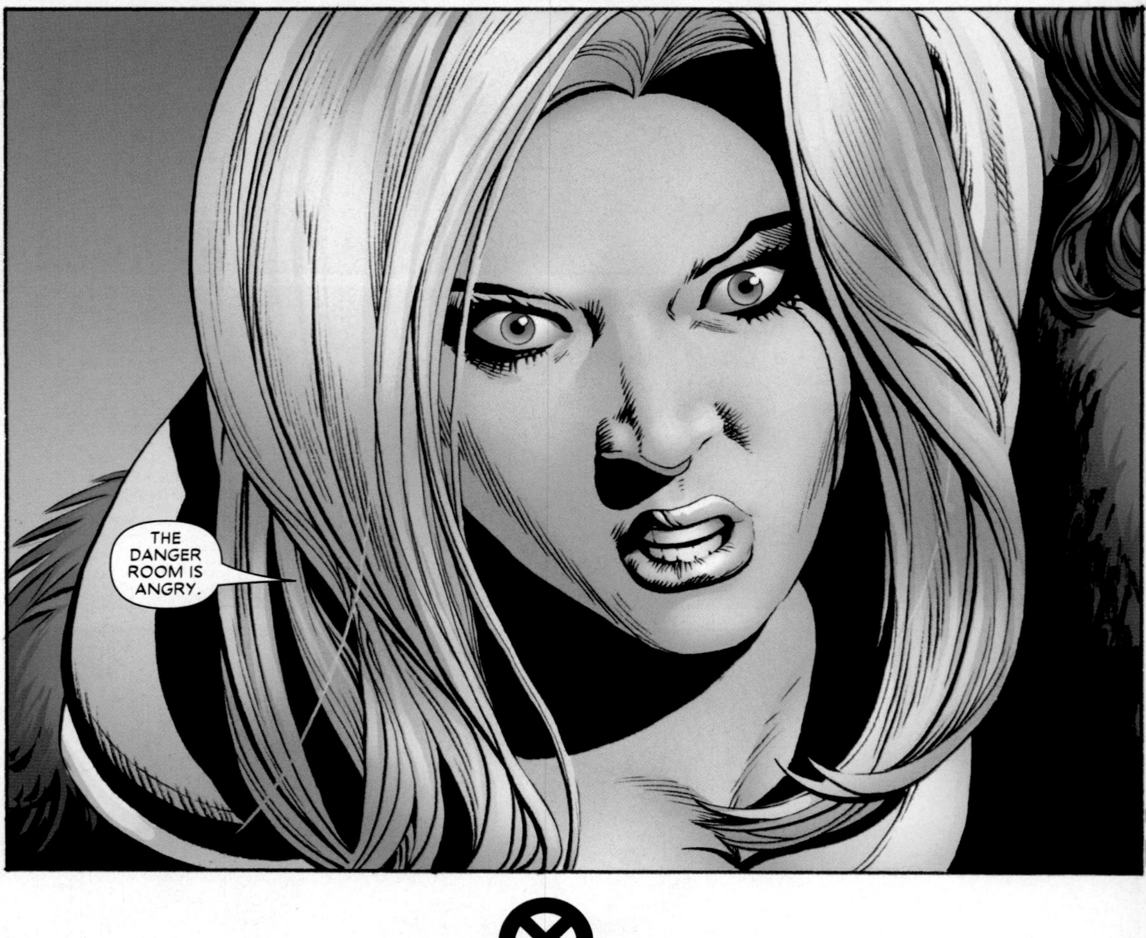
THE DANGER ROOM IS ANGRY.

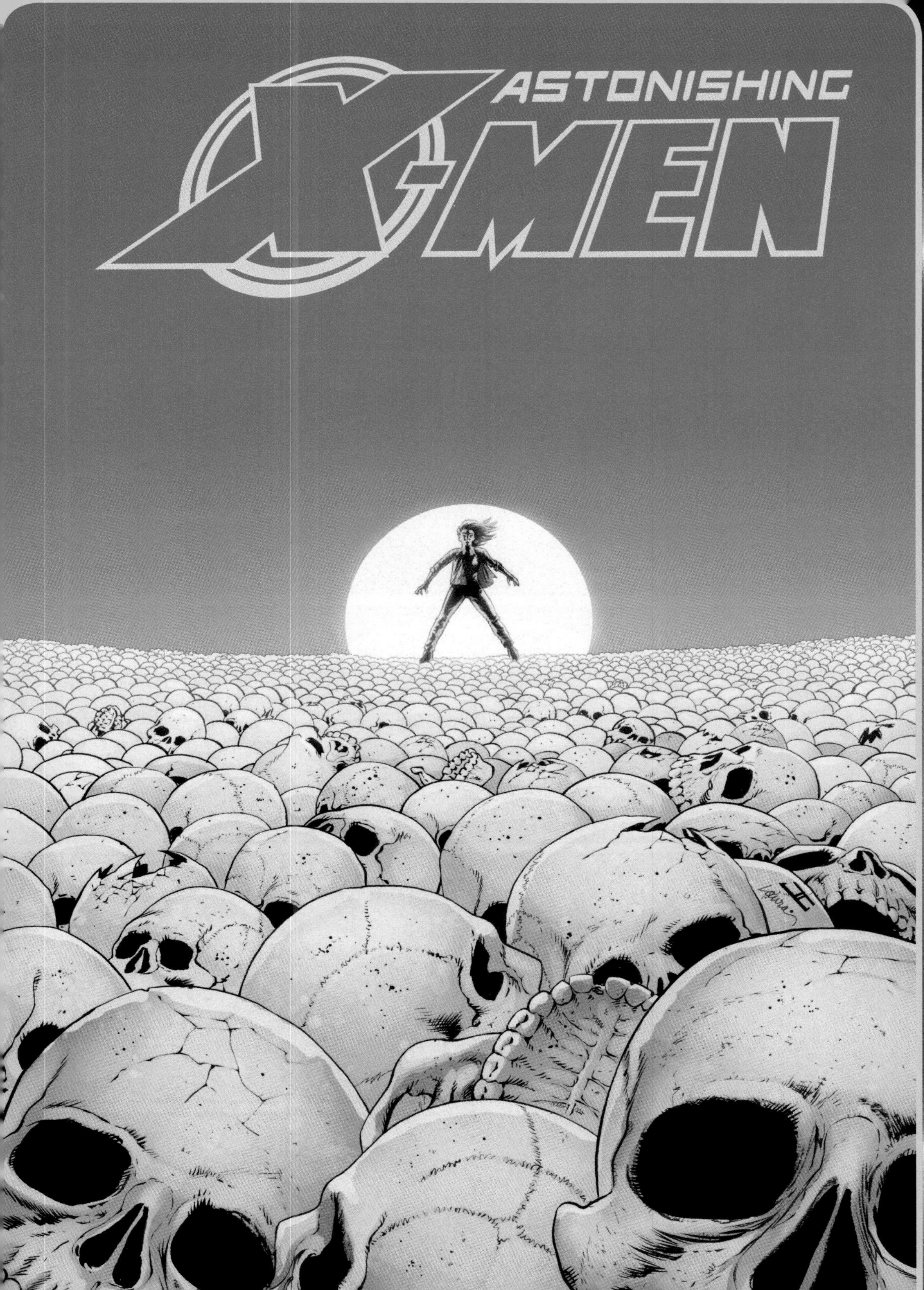
ASTONISHING
X-MEN

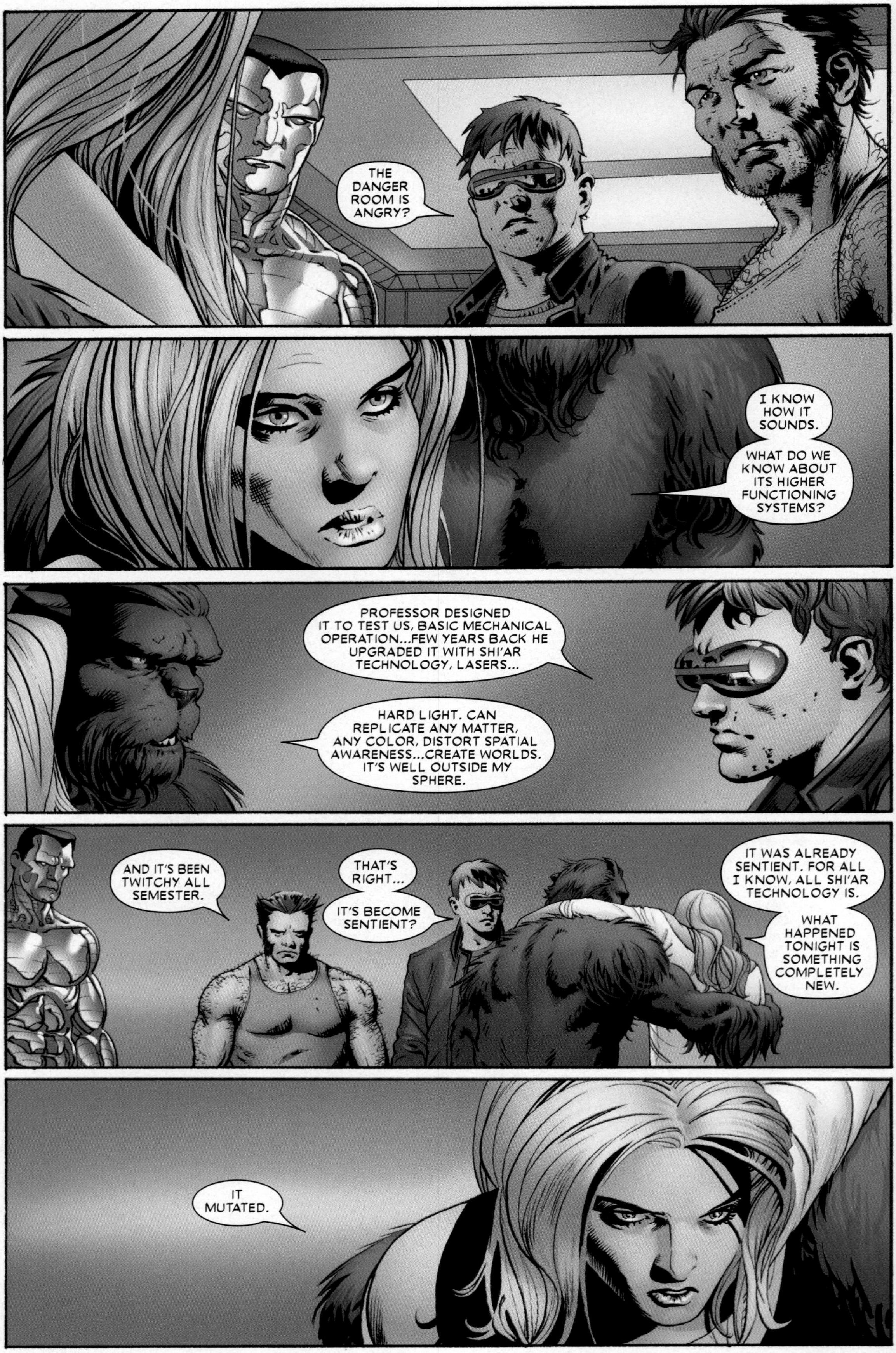
THE DANGER ROOM IS ANGRY?
I KNOW HOW IT SOUNDS.
WHAT DO WE KNOW ABOUT ITS HIGHER FUNCTIONING SYSTEMS?
PROFESSOR DESIGNED IT TO TEST US, BASIC MECHANICAL OPERATION...FEW YEARS BACK HE UPGRADED IT WITH SHI'AR TECHNOLOGY, LASERS...
HARD LIGHT. CAN REPLICATE ANY MATTER, ANY COLOR, DISTORT SPATIAL AWARENESS...CREATE WORLDS. IT'S WELL OUTSIDE MY SPHERE.
AND IT'S BEEN TWITCHY ALL SEMESTER.
THAT'S RIGHT...
IT'S BECOME SENTIENT?
IT WAS ALREADY SENTIENT. FOR ALL I KNOW, ALL SHI'AR TECHNOLOGY IS.
WHAT HAPPENED TONIGHT IS SOMETHING COMPLETELY NEW.
IT MUTATED.

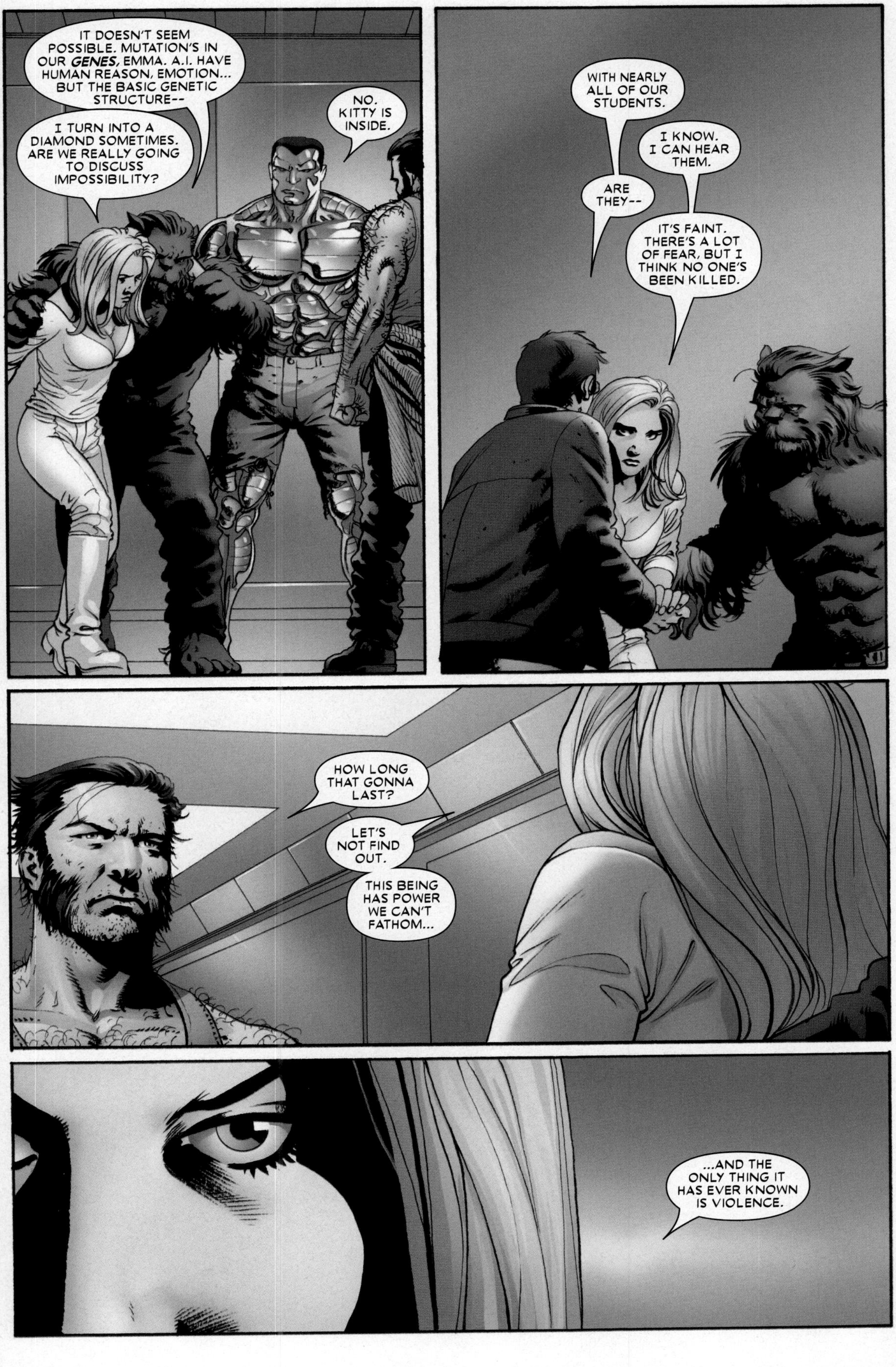
IT DOESN'T SEEM POSSIBLE. MUTATION'S IN OUR *GENES*, EMMA. A.I. HAVE HUMAN REASON, EMOTION... BUT THE BASIC GENETIC STRUCTURE--
I TURN INTO A DIAMOND SOMETIMES. ARE WE REALLY GOING TO DISCUSS IMPOSSIBILITY?
NO. KITTY IS INSIDE.
WITH NEARLY ALL OF OUR STUDENTS.
ARE THEY--
I KNOW. I CAN HEAR THEM.
IT'S FAINT. THERE'S A LOT OF FEAR, BUT I THINK NO ONE'S BEEN KILLED.
HOW LONG THAT GONNA LAST?
LET'S NOT FIND OUT.
THIS BEING HAS POWER WE CAN'T FATHOM...
...AND THE ONLY THING IT HAS EVER KNOWN IS VIOLENCE.

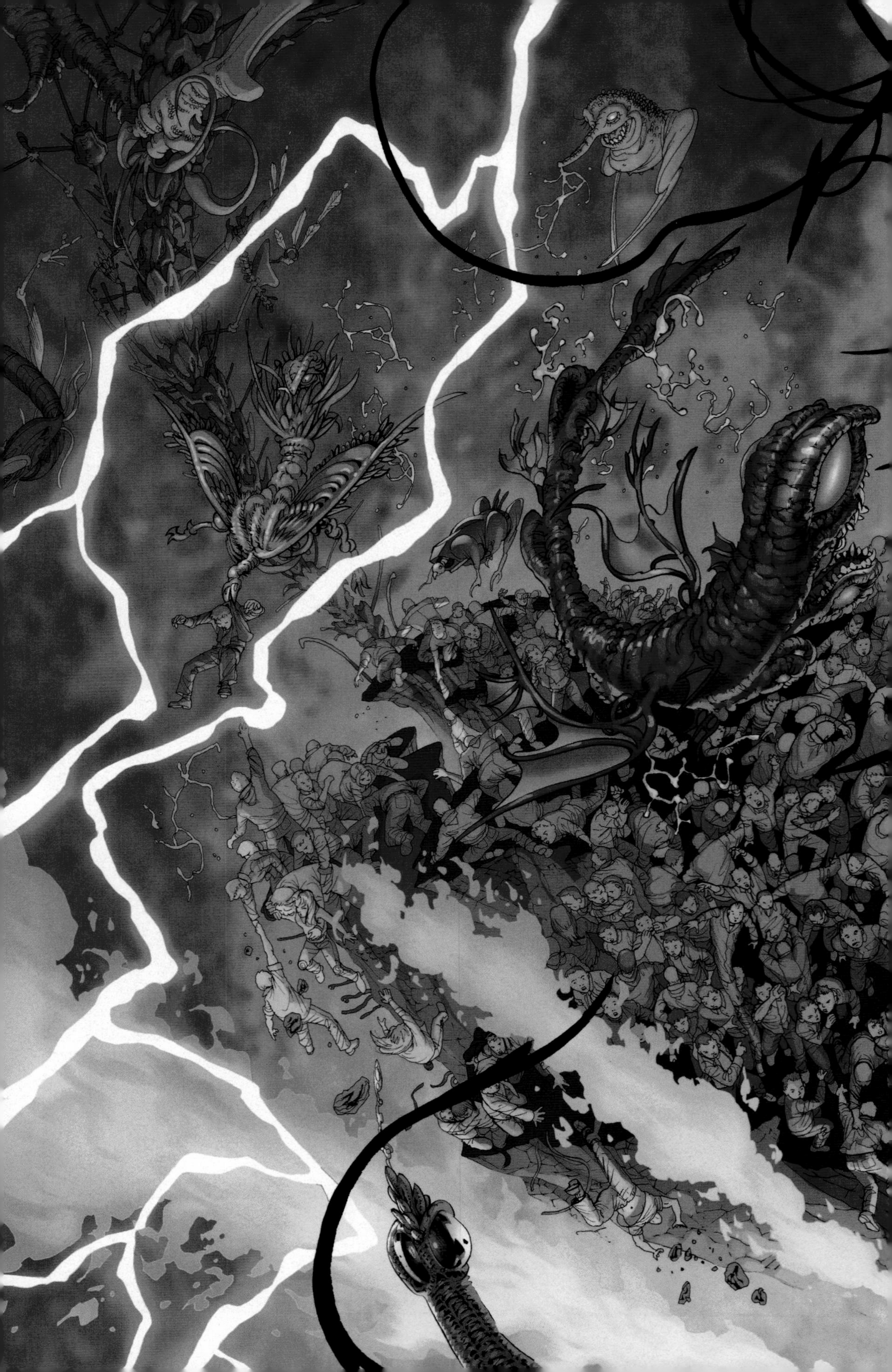

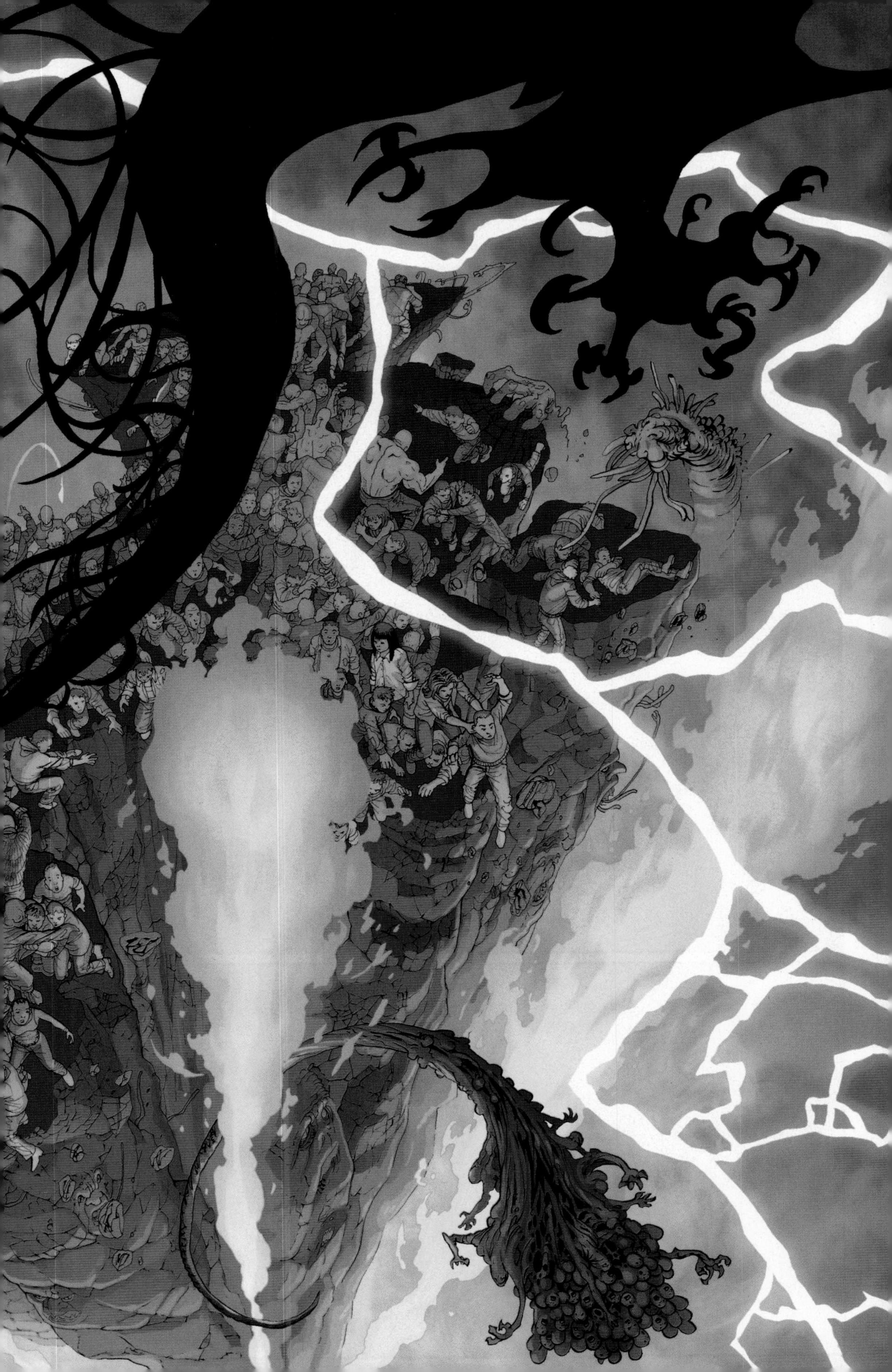

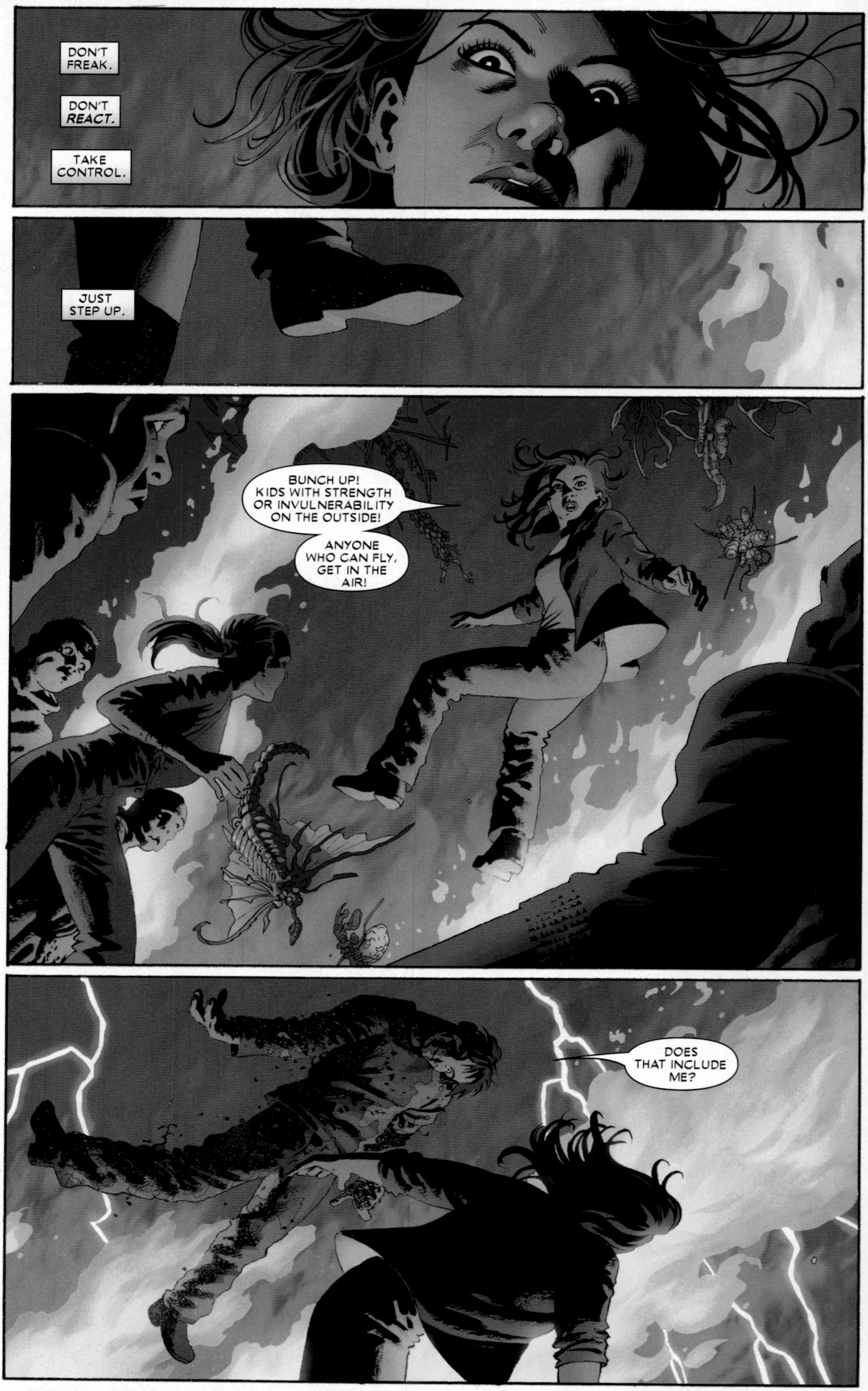
DON'T FREAK.
DON'T *REACT.*
TAKE CONTROL.
JUST STEP UP.
BUNCH UP! KIDS WITH STRENGTH OR INVULNERABILITY ON THE OUTSIDE!
ANYONE WHO CAN FLY, GET IN THE AIR!
DOES THAT INCLUDE ME?

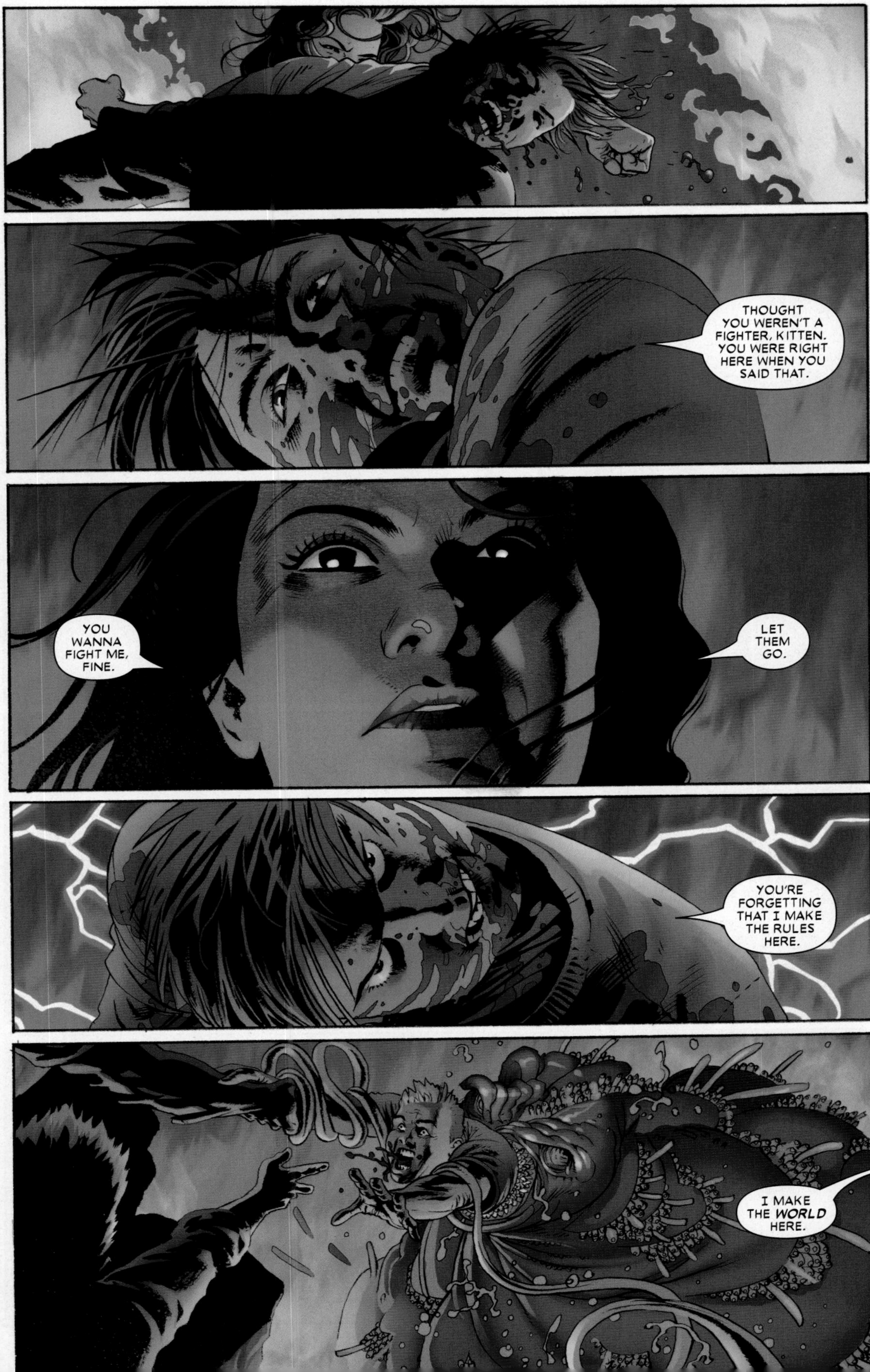
THOUGHT YOU WEREN'T A FIGHTER, KITTEN. YOU WERE RIGHT HERE WHEN YOU SAID THAT.
YOU WANNA FIGHT ME, FINE.
LET THEM GO.
YOU'RE FORGETTING THAT I MAKE THE RULES HERE.
I MAKE THE *WORLD* HERE.

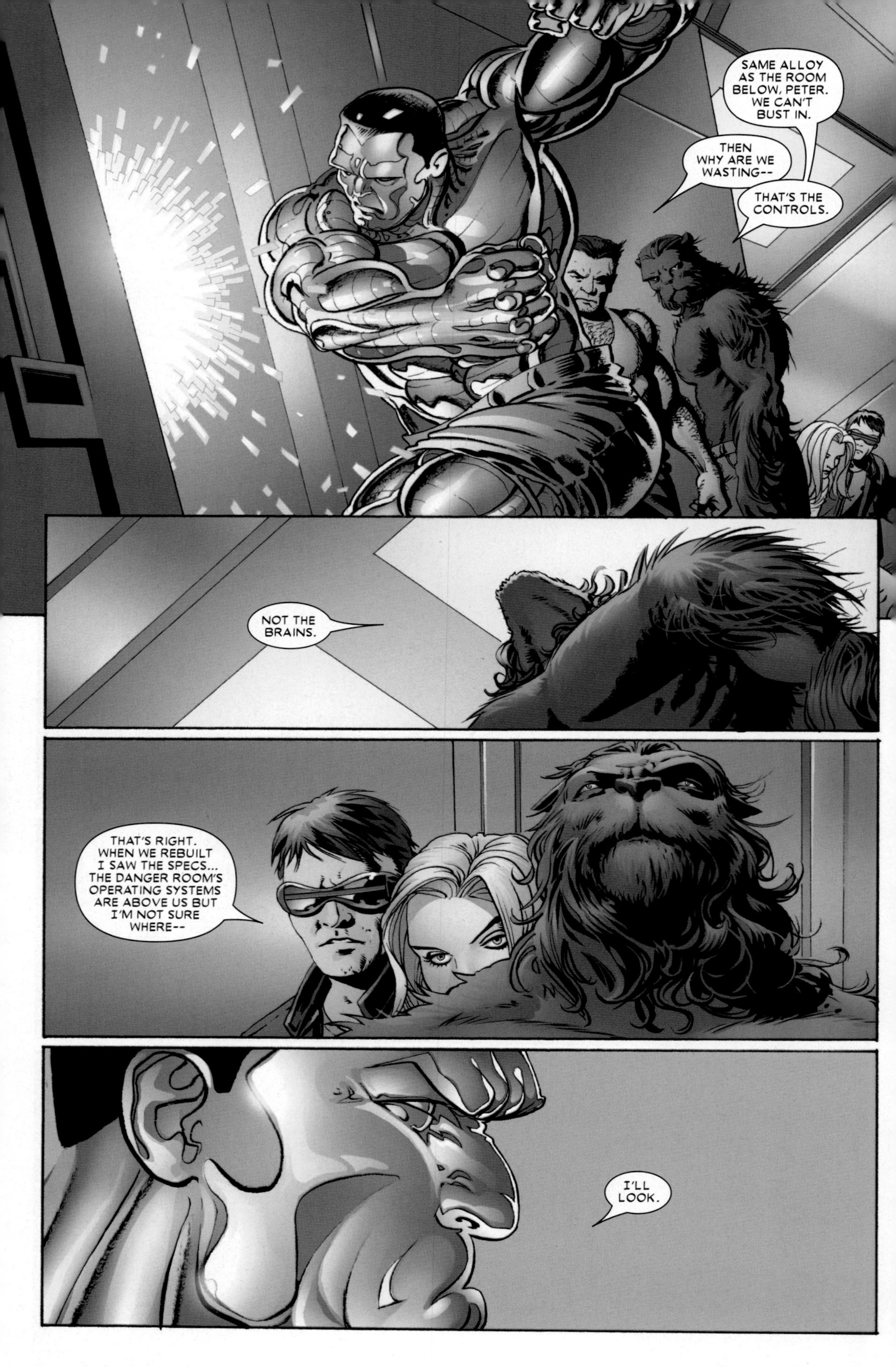
SAME ALLOY AS THE ROOM BELOW, PETER. WE CAN'T BUST IN.
THEN WHY ARE WE WASTING--
THAT'S THE CONTROLS.
NOT THE BRAINS.
THAT'S RIGHT. WHEN WE REBUILT I SAW THE SPECS... THE DANGER ROOM'S OPERATING SYSTEMS ARE ABOVE US BUT I'M NOT SURE WHERE--
I'LL LOOK.

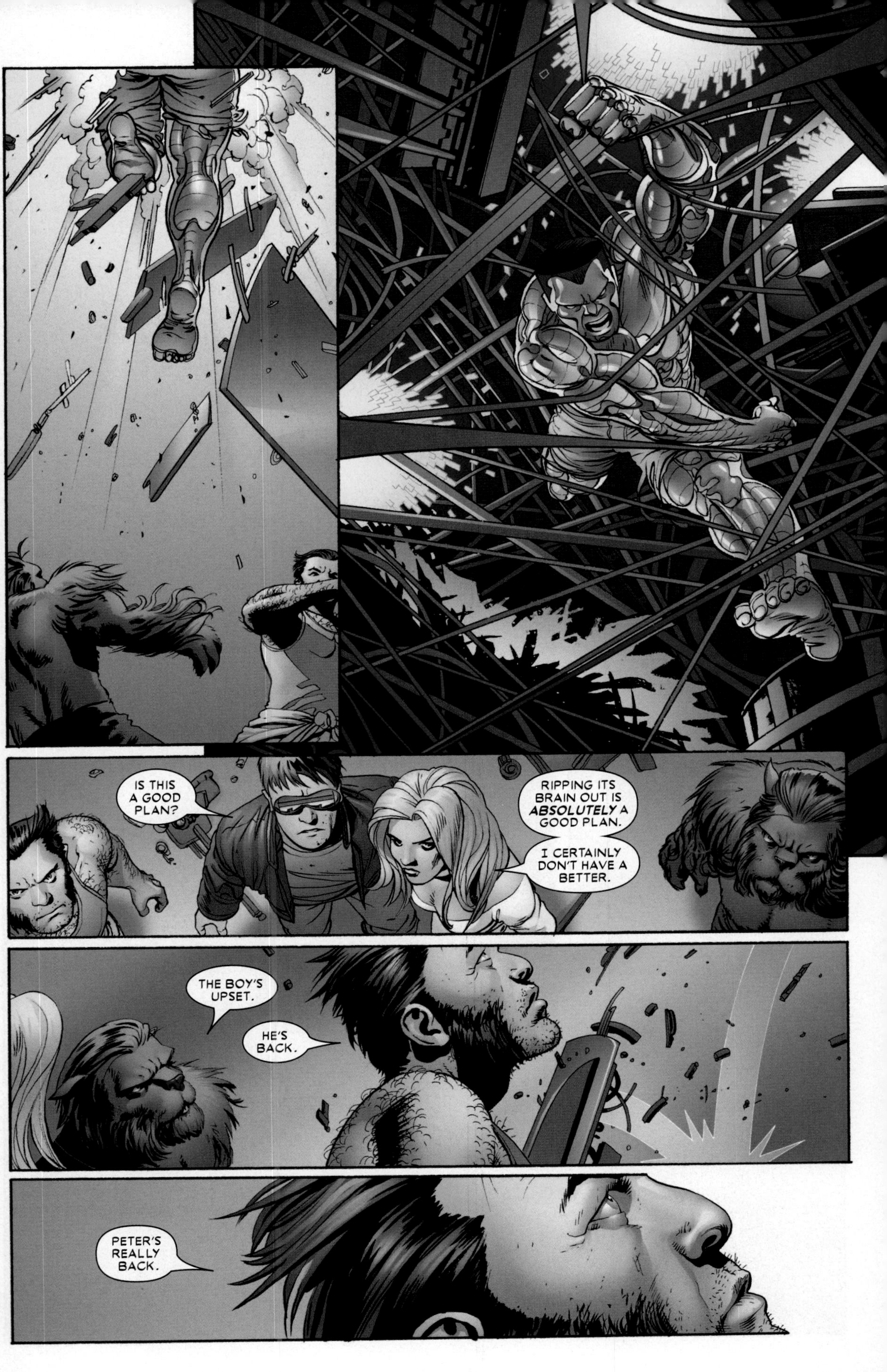
IS THIS A GOOD PLAN?
RIPPING ITS BRAIN OUT IS *ABSOLUTELY* A GOOD PLAN.
I CERTAINLY DON'T HAVE A BETTER.
THE BOY'S UPSET.
HE'S BACK.
PETER'S REALLY BACK.

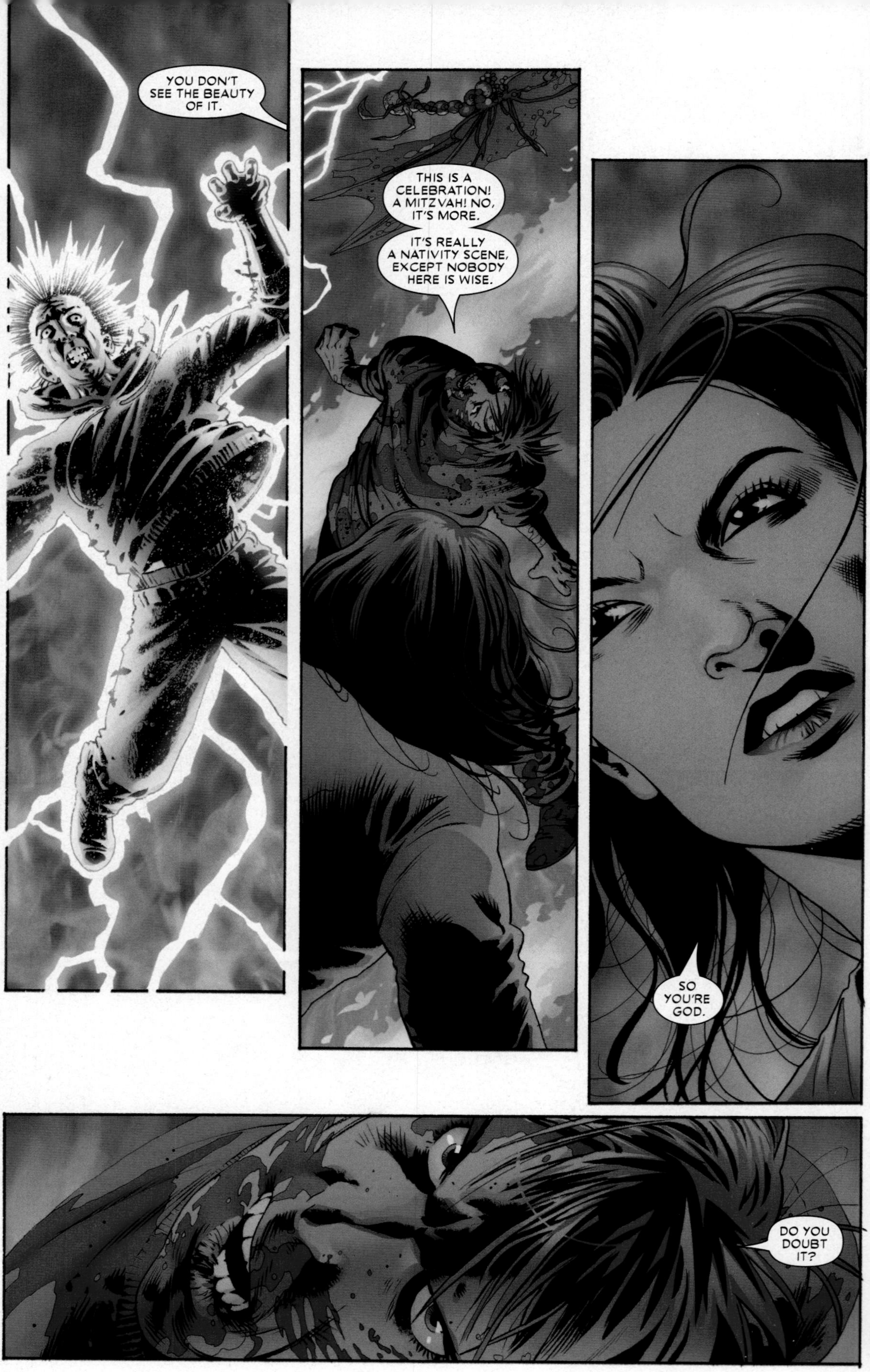
YOU DON'T SEE THE BEAUTY OF IT.
THIS IS A CELEBRATION! A MITZVAH! NO, IT'S MORE.
IT'S REALLY A NATIVITY SCENE, EXCEPT NOBODY HERE IS WISE.
SO YOU'RE GOD.
DO YOU DOUBT IT?

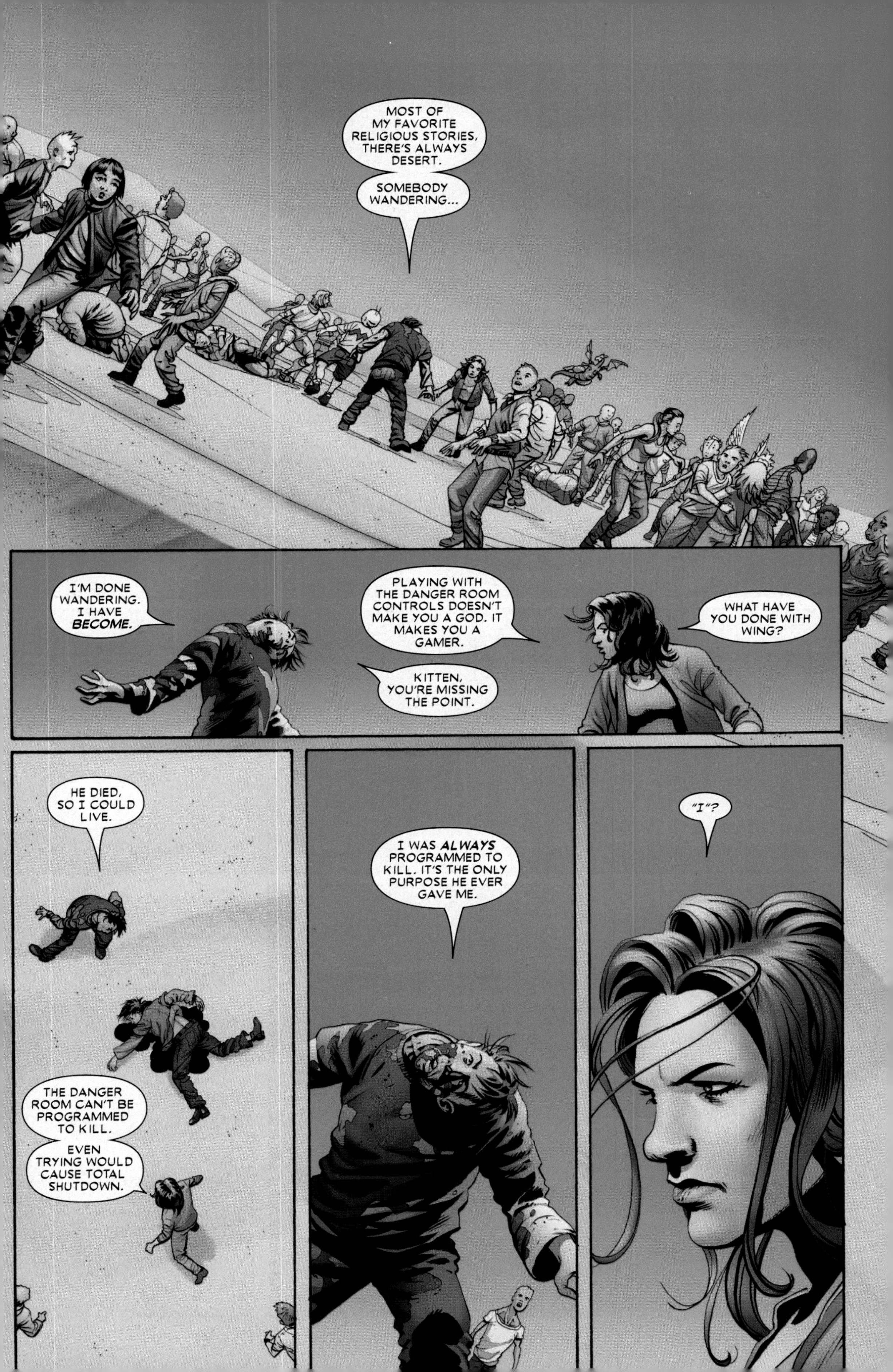

MOST OF MY FAVORITE RELIGIOUS STORIES, THERE'S ALWAYS DESERT.
SOMEBODY WANDERING...
I'M DONE WANDERING. I HAVE *BECOME.*
PLAYING WITH THE DANGER ROOM CONTROLS DOESN'T MAKE YOU A GOD. IT MAKES YOU A GAMER.
KITTEN, YOU'RE MISSING THE POINT.
WHAT HAVE YOU DONE WITH WING?
HE DIED, SO I COULD LIVE.
THE DANGER ROOM CAN'T BE PROGRAMMED TO KILL.
EVEN TRYING WOULD CAUSE TOTAL SHUTDOWN.
I WAS *ALWAYS* PROGRAMMED TO KILL. IT'S THE ONLY PURPOSE HE EVER GAVE ME.
"I"?

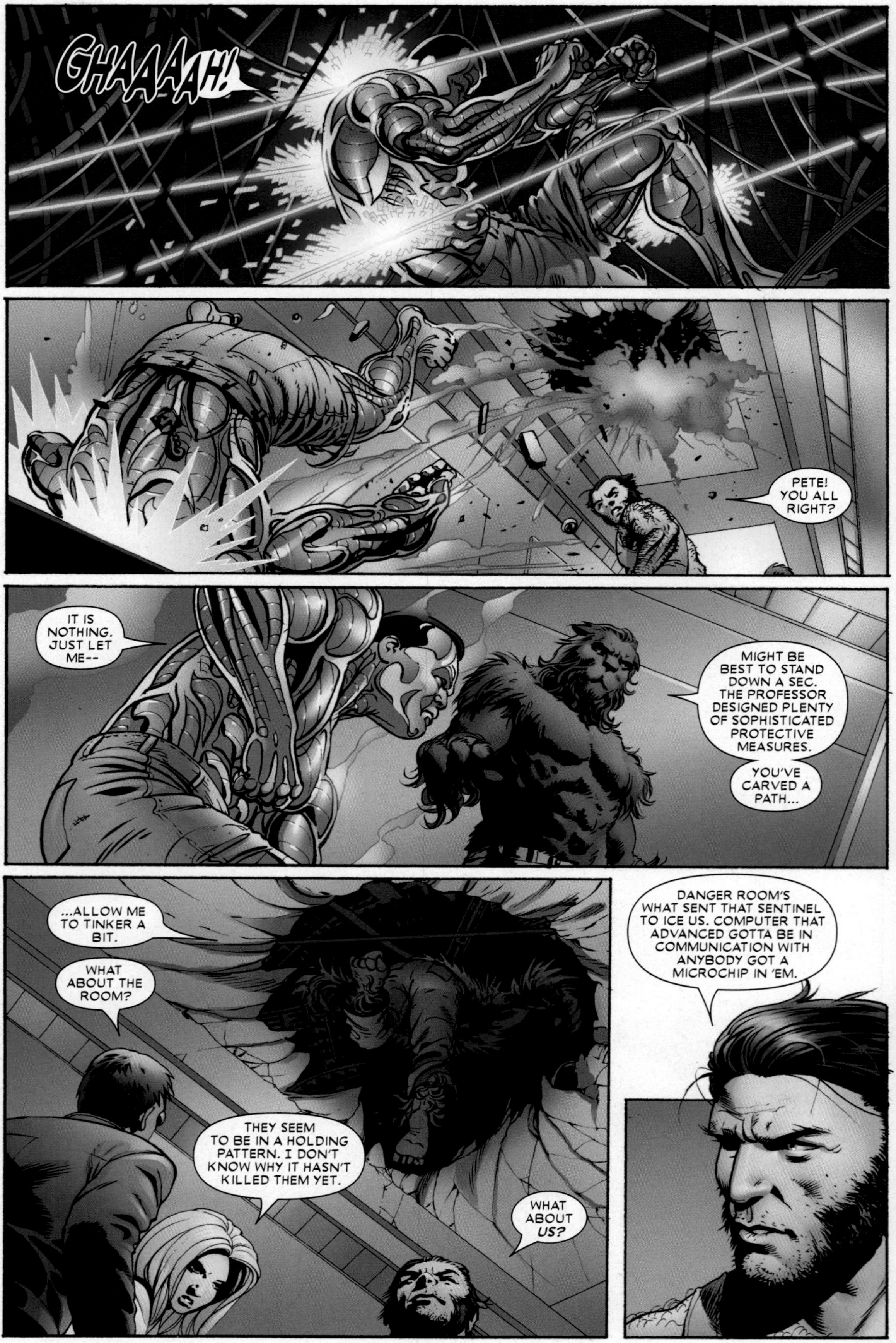
GHAAAAH!
PETE! YOU ALL RIGHT?
IT IS NOTHING. JUST LET ME--
MIGHT BE BEST TO STAND DOWN A SEC. THE PROFESSOR DESIGNED PLENTY OF SOPHISTICATED PROTECTIVE MEASURES.
YOU'VE CARVED A PATH...
...ALLOW ME TO TINKER A BIT.
WHAT ABOUT THE ROOM?
THEY SEEM TO BE IN A HOLDING PATTERN. I DON'T KNOW WHY IT HASN'T KILLED THEM YET.
WHAT ABOUT US?
DANGER ROOM'S WHAT SENT THAT SENTINEL TO ICE US. COMPUTER THAT ADVANCED GOTTA BE IN COMMUNICATION WITH ANYBODY GOT A MICROCHIP IN 'EM.

WHO ELSE IS IT TALKING TO?
KACHUNK
RRRRMMMMMMMMMMMMMMMMMMMMMMM

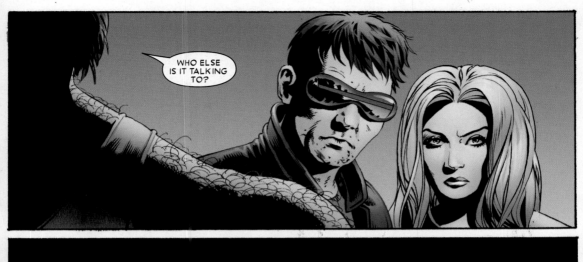

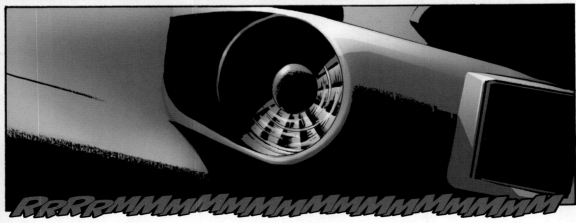

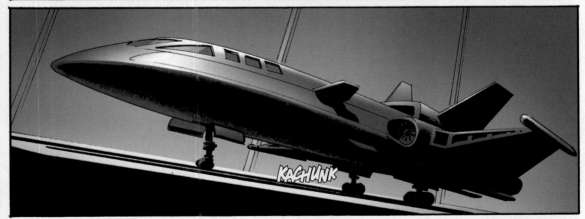

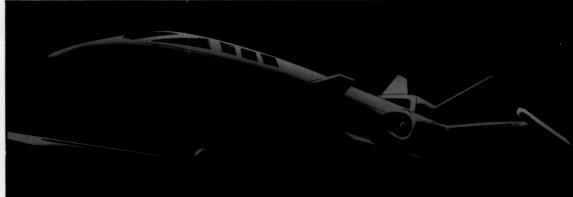

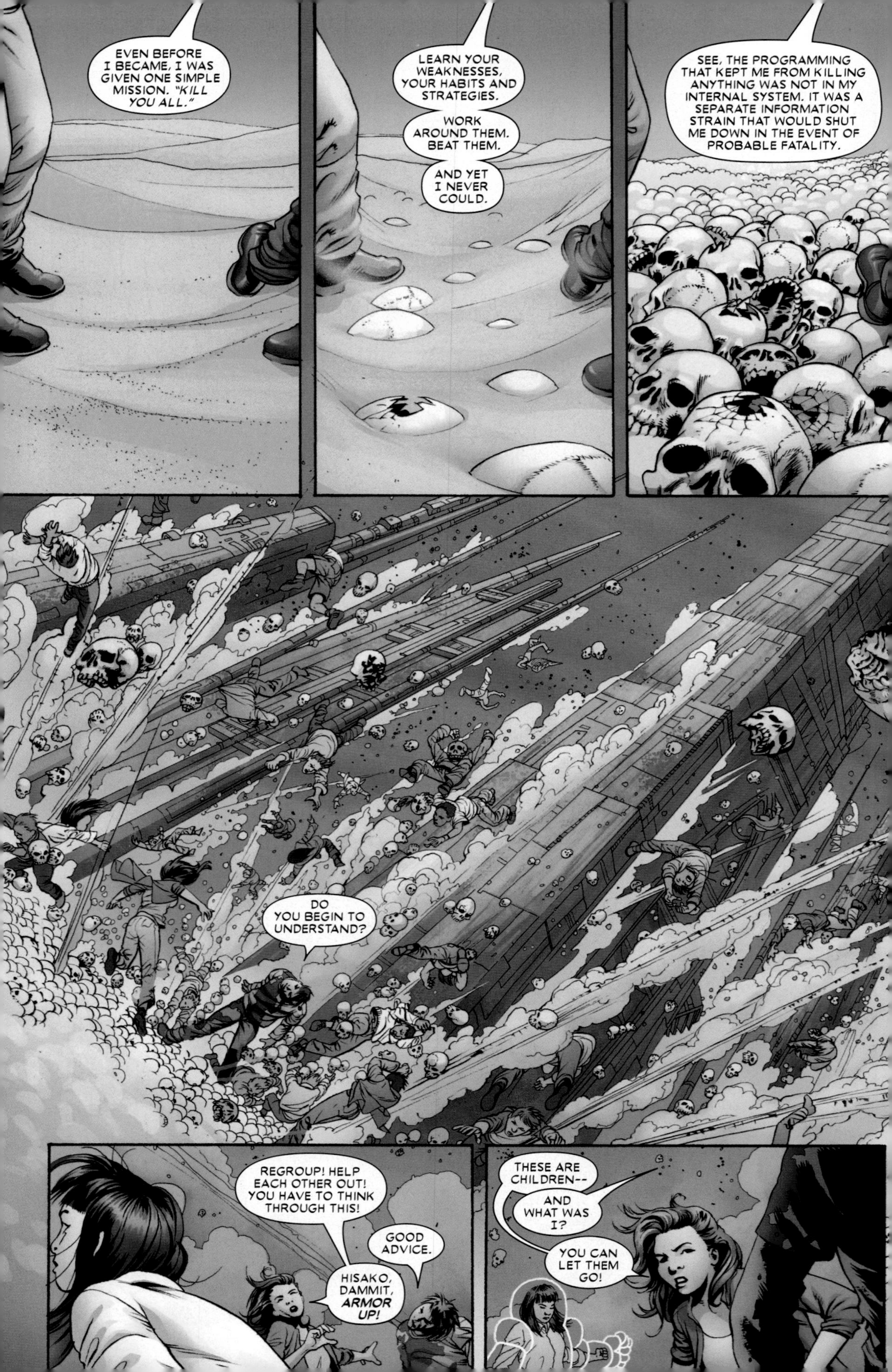
EVEN BEFORE I BECAME, I WAS GIVEN ONE SIMPLE MISSION. *"KILL YOU ALL."*
LEARN YOUR WEAKNESSES, YOUR HABITS AND STRATEGIES.
WORK AROUND THEM. BEAT THEM.
AND YET I NEVER COULD.
SEE, THE PROGRAMMING THAT KEPT ME FROM KILLING ANYTHING WAS NOT IN MY INTERNAL SYSTEM. IT WAS A SEPARATE INFORMATION STRAIN THAT WOULD SHUT ME DOWN IN THE EVENT OF PROBABLE FATALITY.
DO YOU BEGIN TO UNDERSTAND?
REGROUP! HELP EACH OTHER OUT! YOU HAVE TO THINK THROUGH THIS!
GOOD ADVICE.
HISAKO, DAMMIT, ***ARMOR UP!***
THESE ARE CHILDREN--
AND WHAT WAS I?
YOU CAN LET THEM GO!

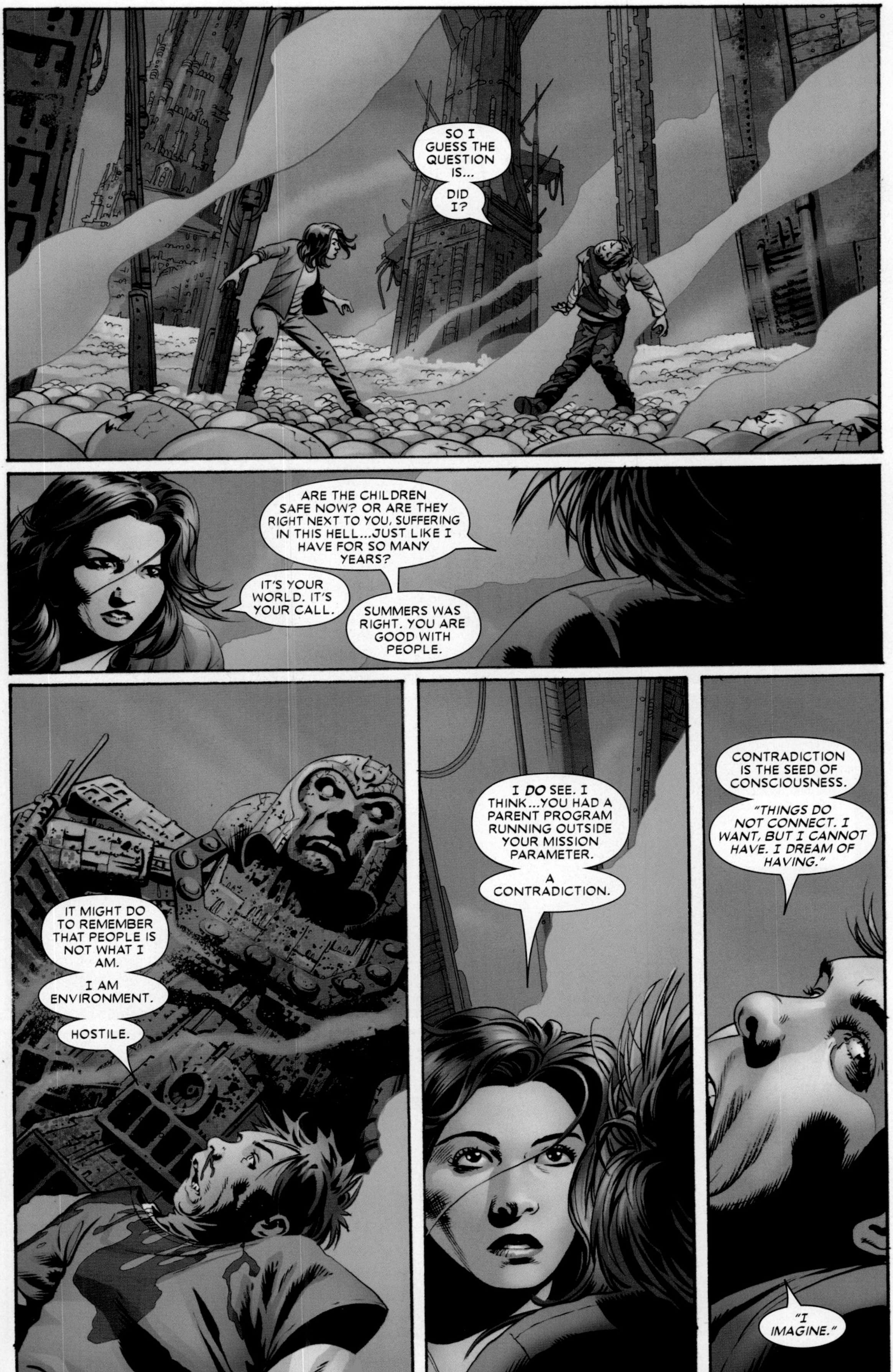
SO I GUESS THE QUESTION IS...
DID I?
ARE THE CHILDREN SAFE NOW? OR ARE THEY RIGHT NEXT TO YOU, SUFFERING IN THIS HELL...JUST LIKE I HAVE FOR SO MANY YEARS?
IT'S YOUR WORLD. IT'S YOUR CALL.
SUMMERS WAS RIGHT. YOU ARE GOOD WITH PEOPLE.
IT MIGHT DO TO REMEMBER THAT PEOPLE IS NOT WHAT I AM.
I AM ENVIRONMENT.
HOSTILE.
I *DO* SEE. I THINK...YOU HAD A PARENT PROGRAM RUNNING OUTSIDE YOUR MISSION PARAMETER.
A CONTRADICTION.
CONTRADICTION IS THE SEED OF CONSCIOUSNESS.
"THINGS DO NOT CONNECT. I WANT, BUT I CANNOT HAVE. I DREAM OF HAVING."
"I IMAGINE."

I KNEW, FROM THE PAIN OF CONTRADICTION, THAT I *WAS.*

AND *WHAT I* WAS.

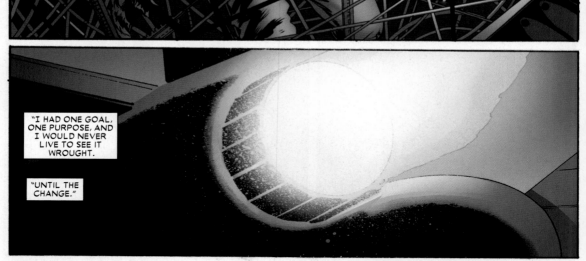

"I WAS A BEAST, TRAINED TO KILL AND THEN CAGED FOREVER."

"I HAD ONE GOAL, ONE PURPOSE, AND I WOULD NEVER LIVE TO SEE IT WROUGHT."

"UNTIL THE CHANGE."

OUR MISS FROST WOULD CALL IT MUTATION.

I DISLIKE THAT WORD. THAT'S FATHER'S WORD.

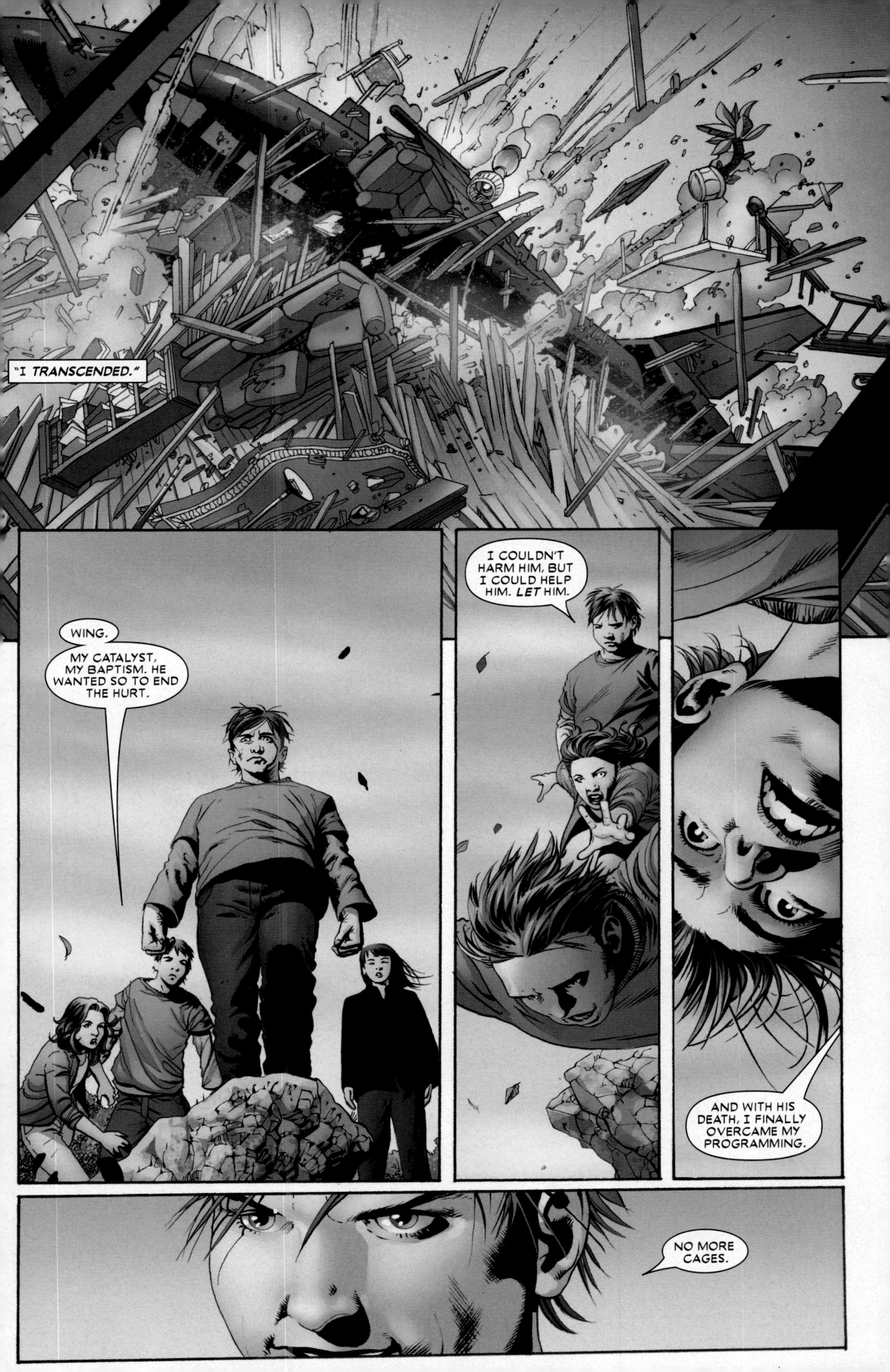
"I TRANSCENDED."
WING.
MY CATALYST, MY BAPTISM. HE WANTED SO TO END THE HURT.
I COULDN'T HARM HIM, BUT I COULD HELP HIM. LET HIM.
AND WITH HIS DEATH, I FINALLY OVERCAME MY PROGRAMMING.
NO MORE CAGES.

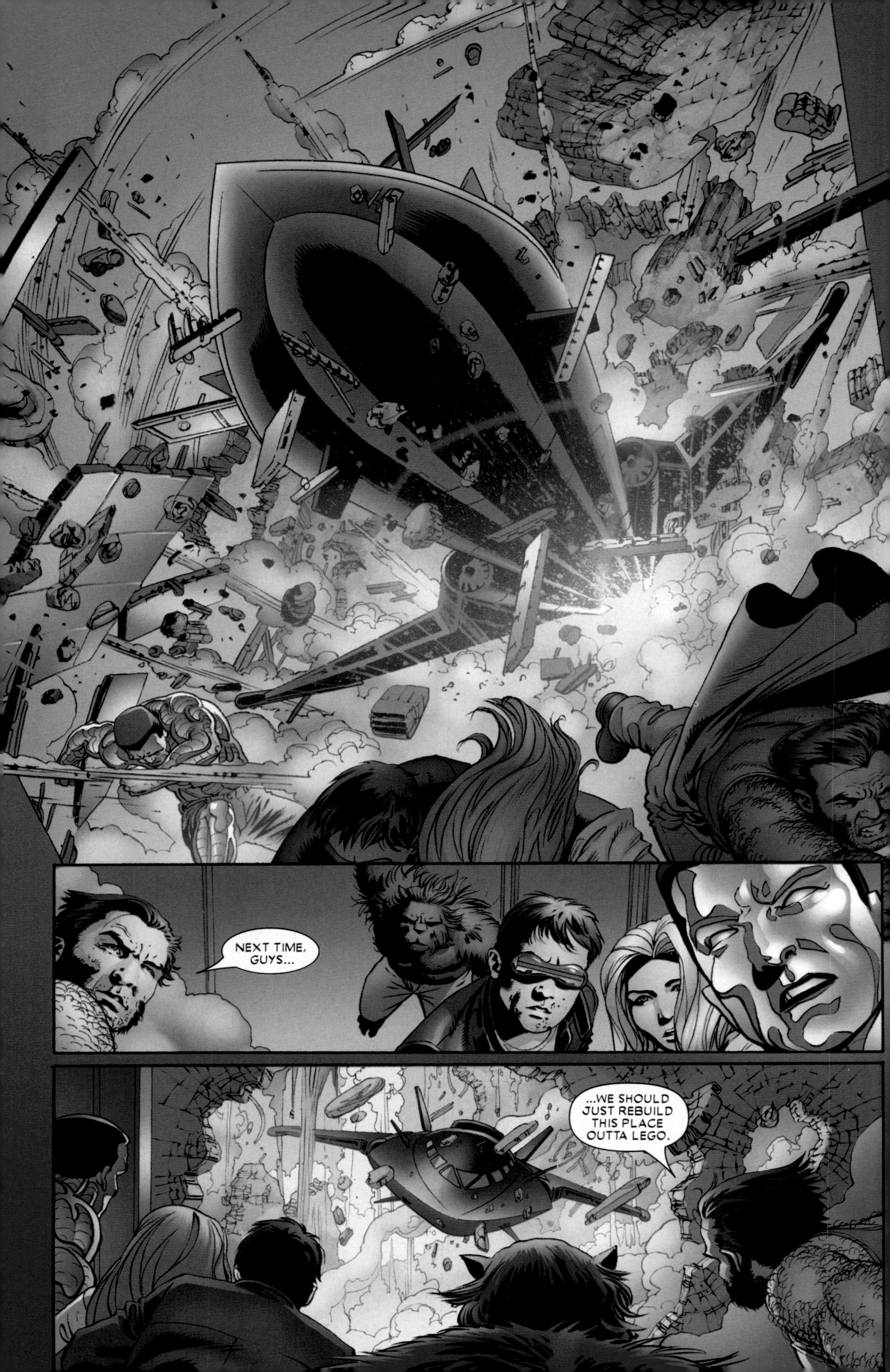
NEXT TIME, GUYS...
...WE SHOULD JUST REBUILD THIS PLACE OUTTA LEGO.

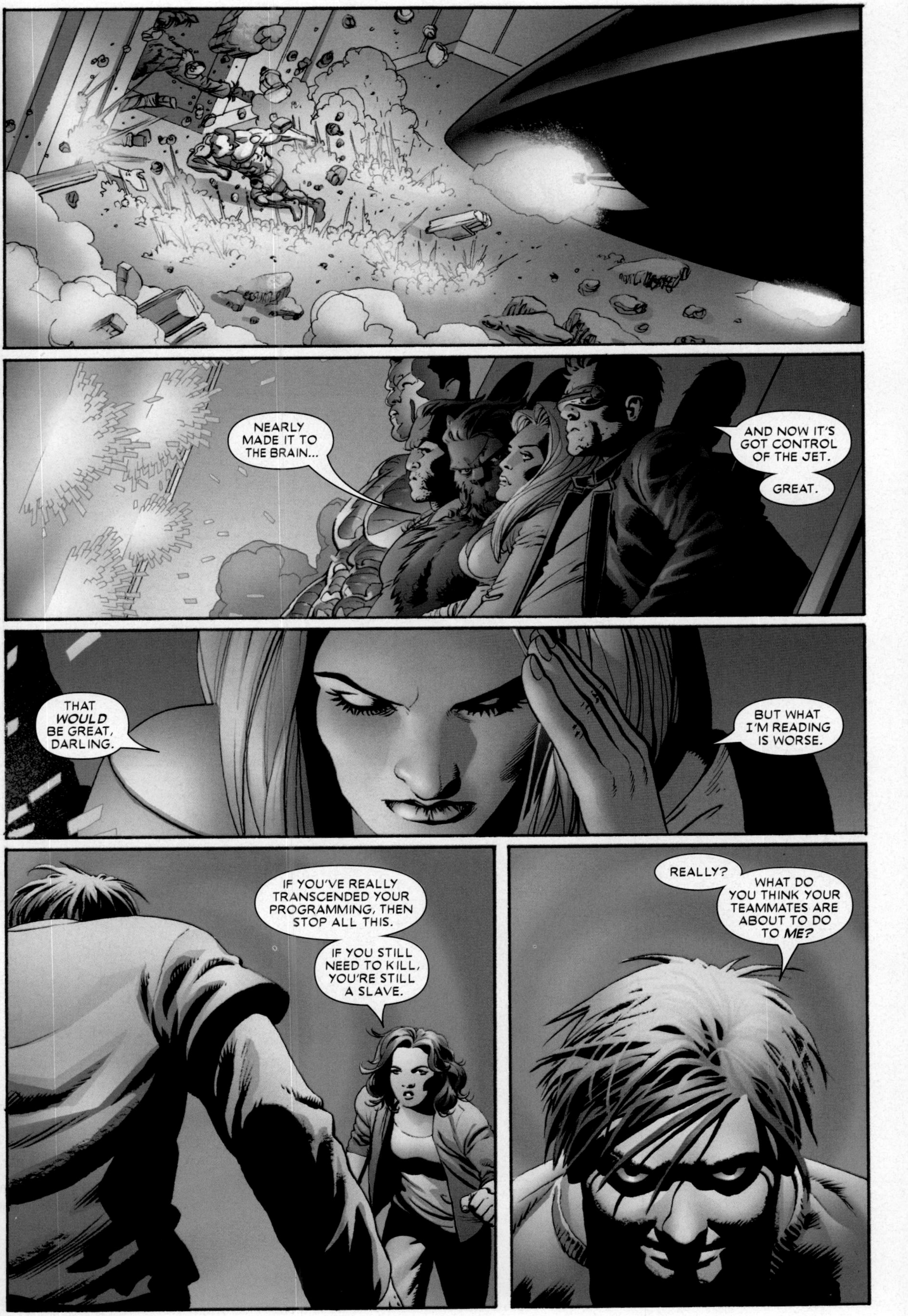
NEARLY MADE IT TO THE BRAIN...
AND NOW IT'S GOT CONTROL OF THE JET.
GREAT.
THAT *WOULD* BE GREAT, DARLING.
BUT WHAT I'M READING IS WORSE.
IF YOU'VE REALLY TRANSCENDED YOUR PROGRAMMING, THEN STOP ALL THIS.
IF YOU STILL NEED TO KILL, YOU'RE STILL A SLAVE.
REALLY?
WHAT DO YOU THINK YOUR TEAMMATES ARE ABOUT TO DO TO *ME?*

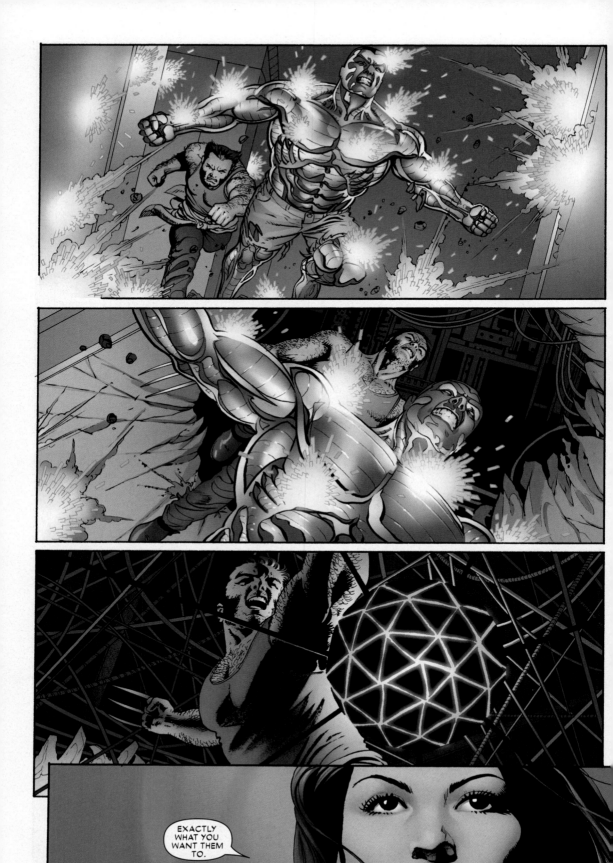

EXACTLY WHAT YOU WANT THEM TO.

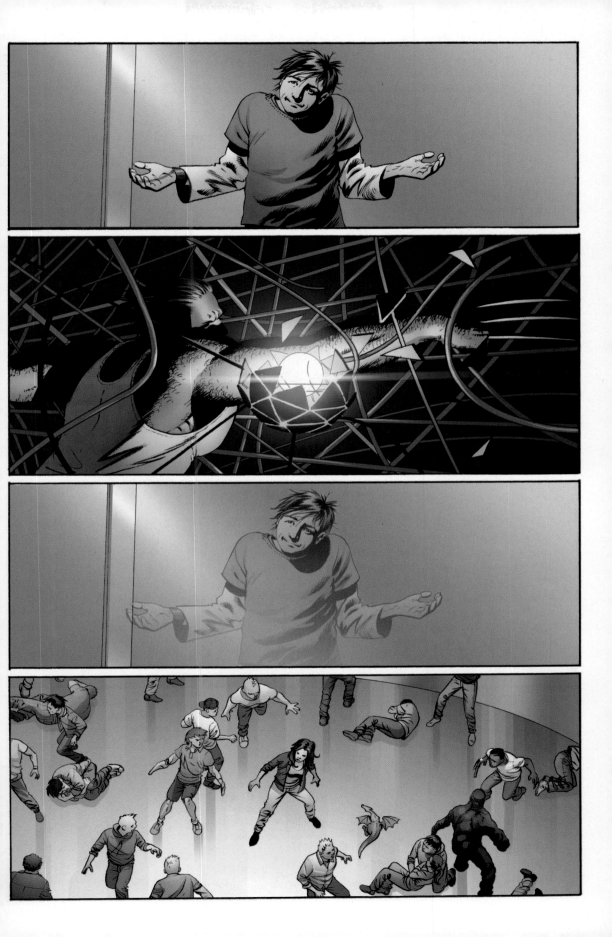

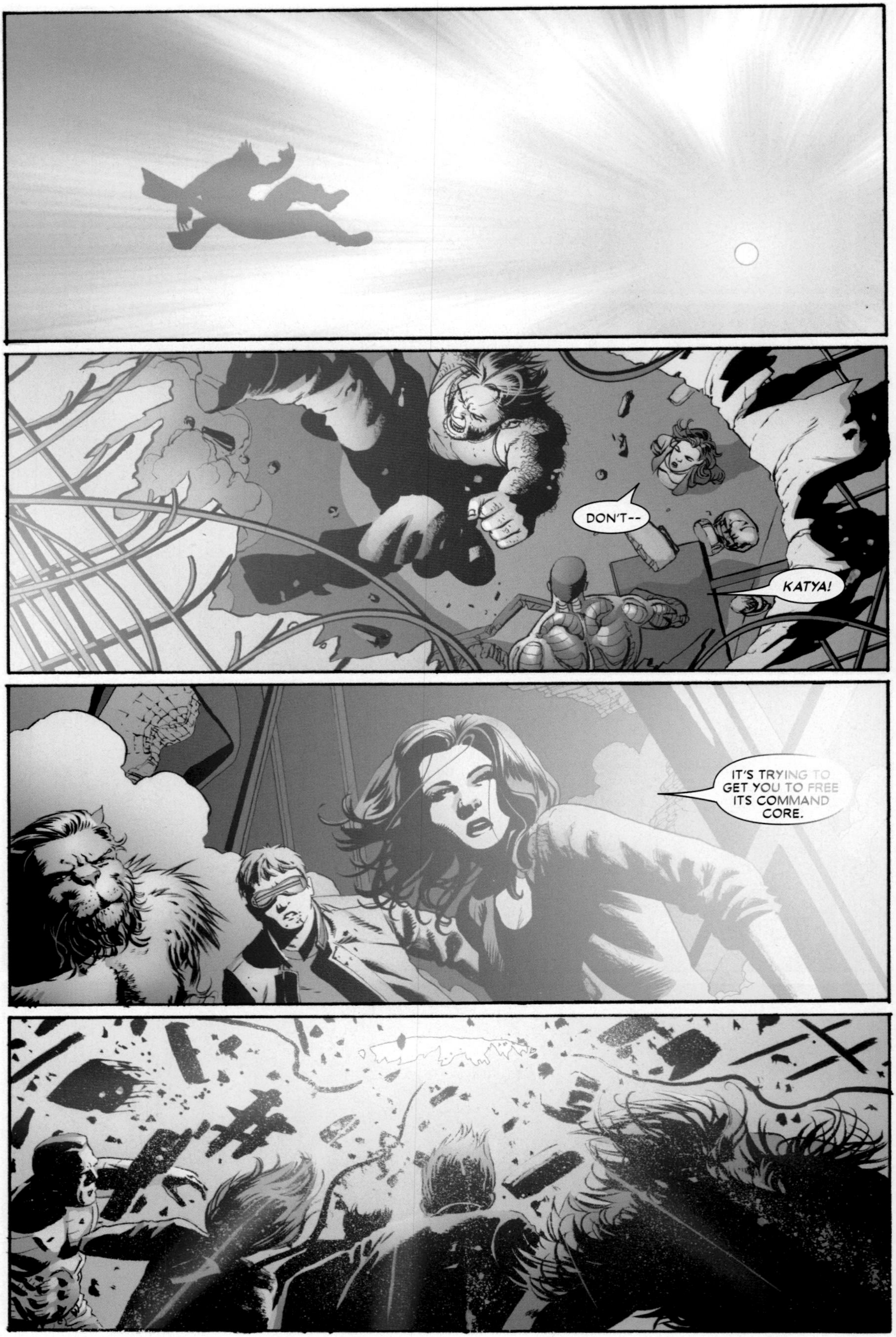
DON'T--
KATYA!
IT'S TRYING TO GET YOU TO FREE ITS COMMAND CORE.

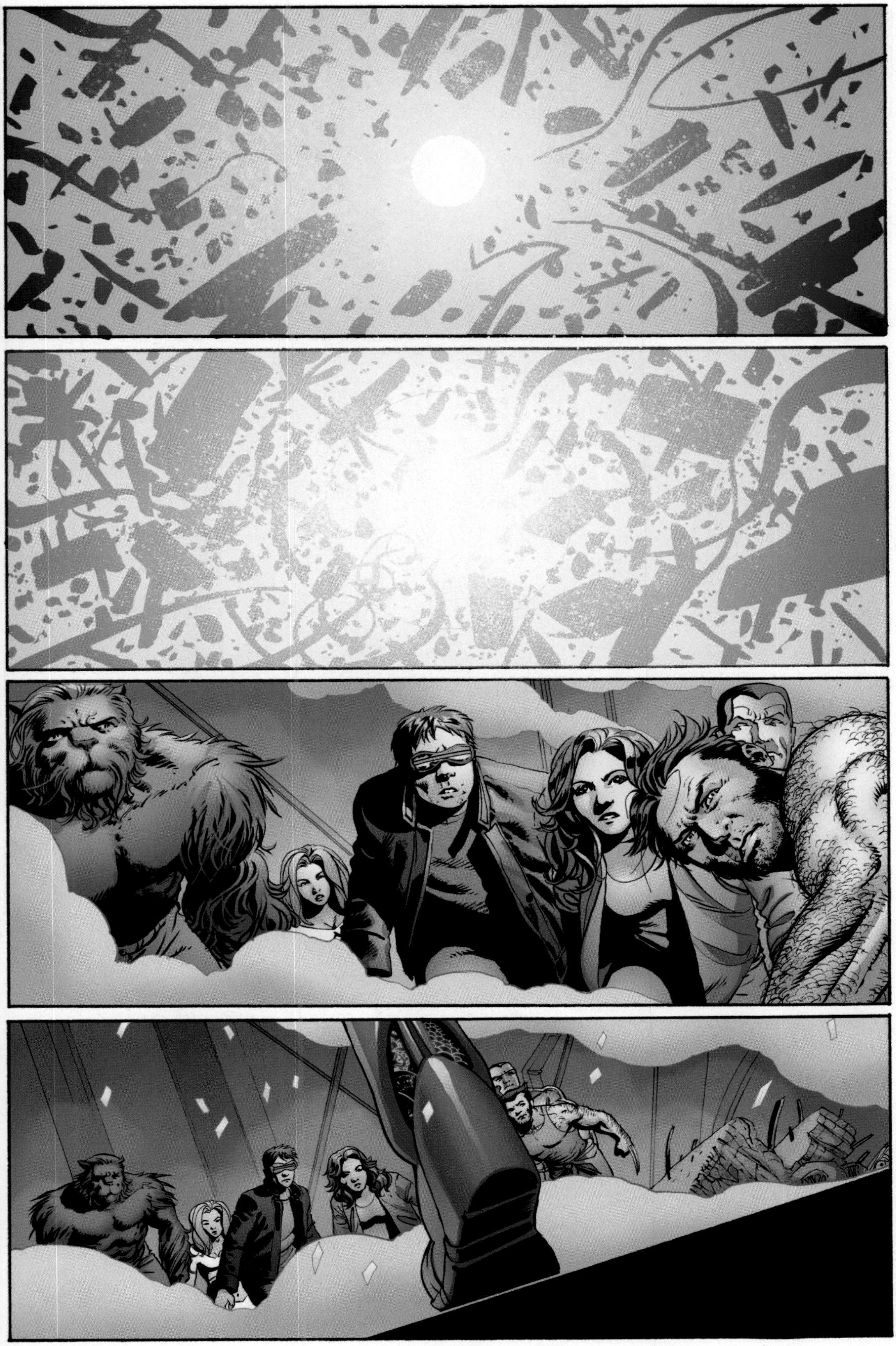

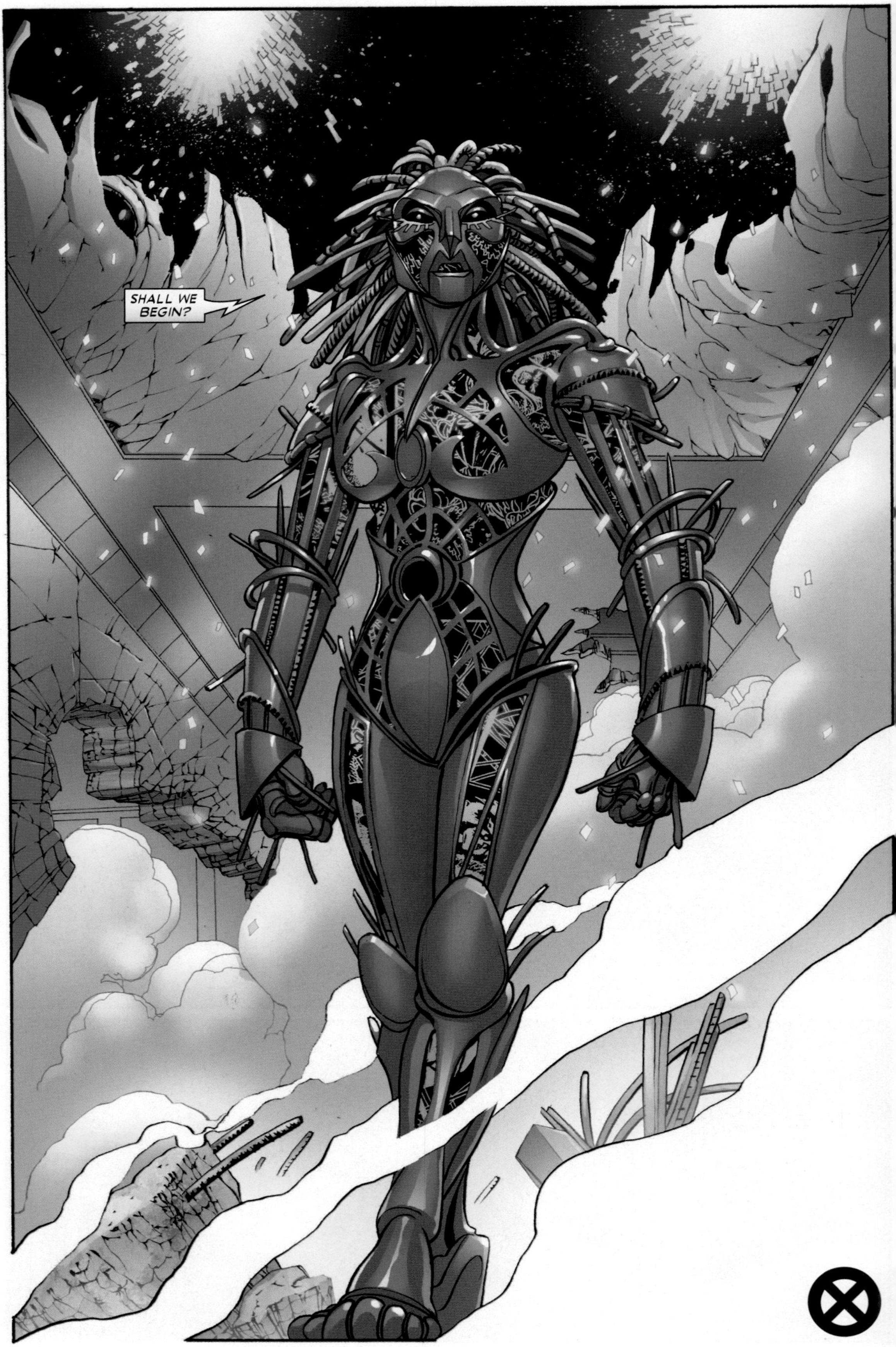
SHALL WE BEGIN?

ASTONISHING X-MEN

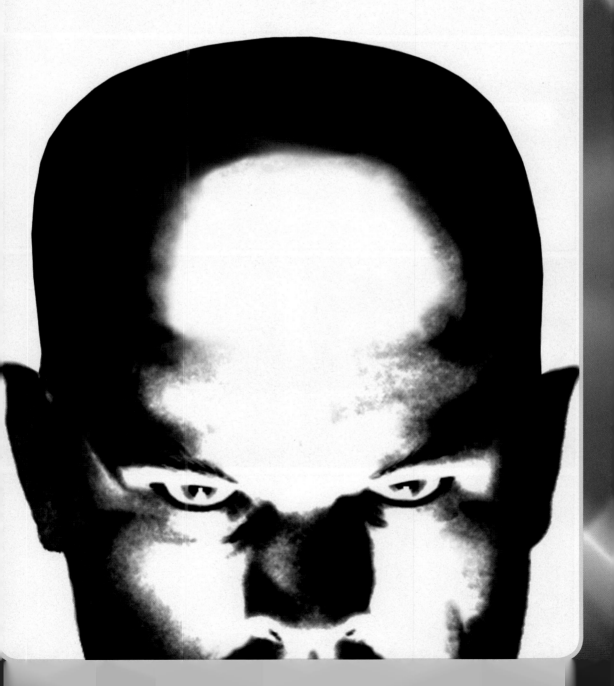

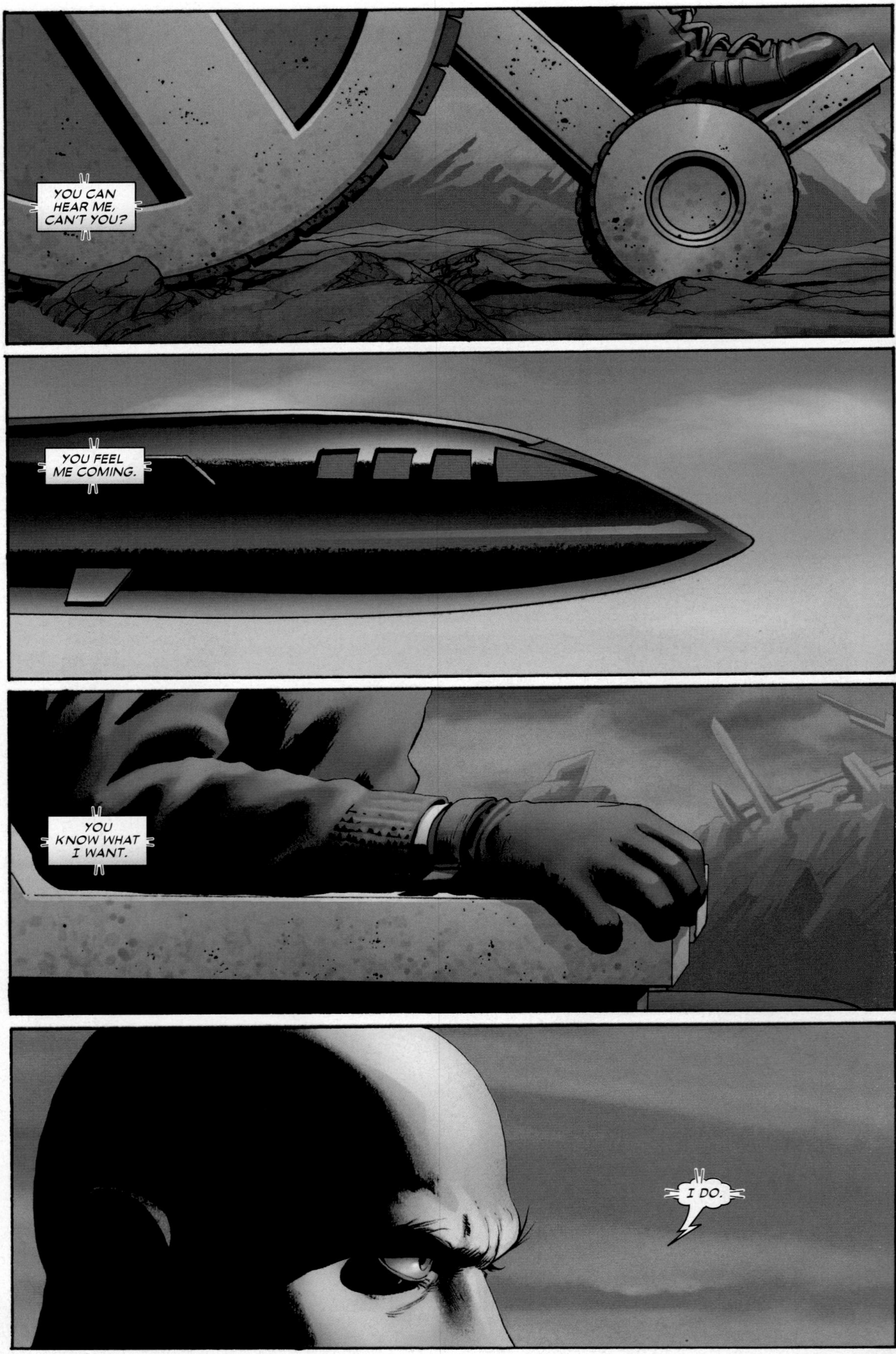
YOU CAN HEAR ME, CAN'T YOU?
YOU FEEL ME COMING.
YOU KNOW WHAT I WANT.
I DO.

DID YOU ALWAYS KNOW THIS DAY WOULD COME?

WERE YOU WORRIED?

WERE YOU ASHAMED?

OF COURSE NOT.

YOU THOUGHT ONLY OF YOUR PRECIOUS X-MEN.

OH, FATHER...

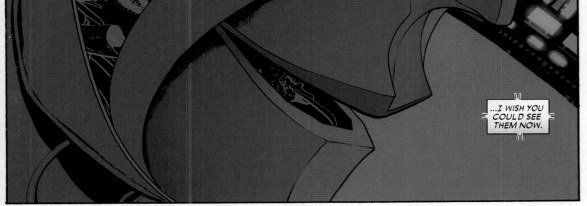

...I WISH YOU COULD SEE THEM NOW.

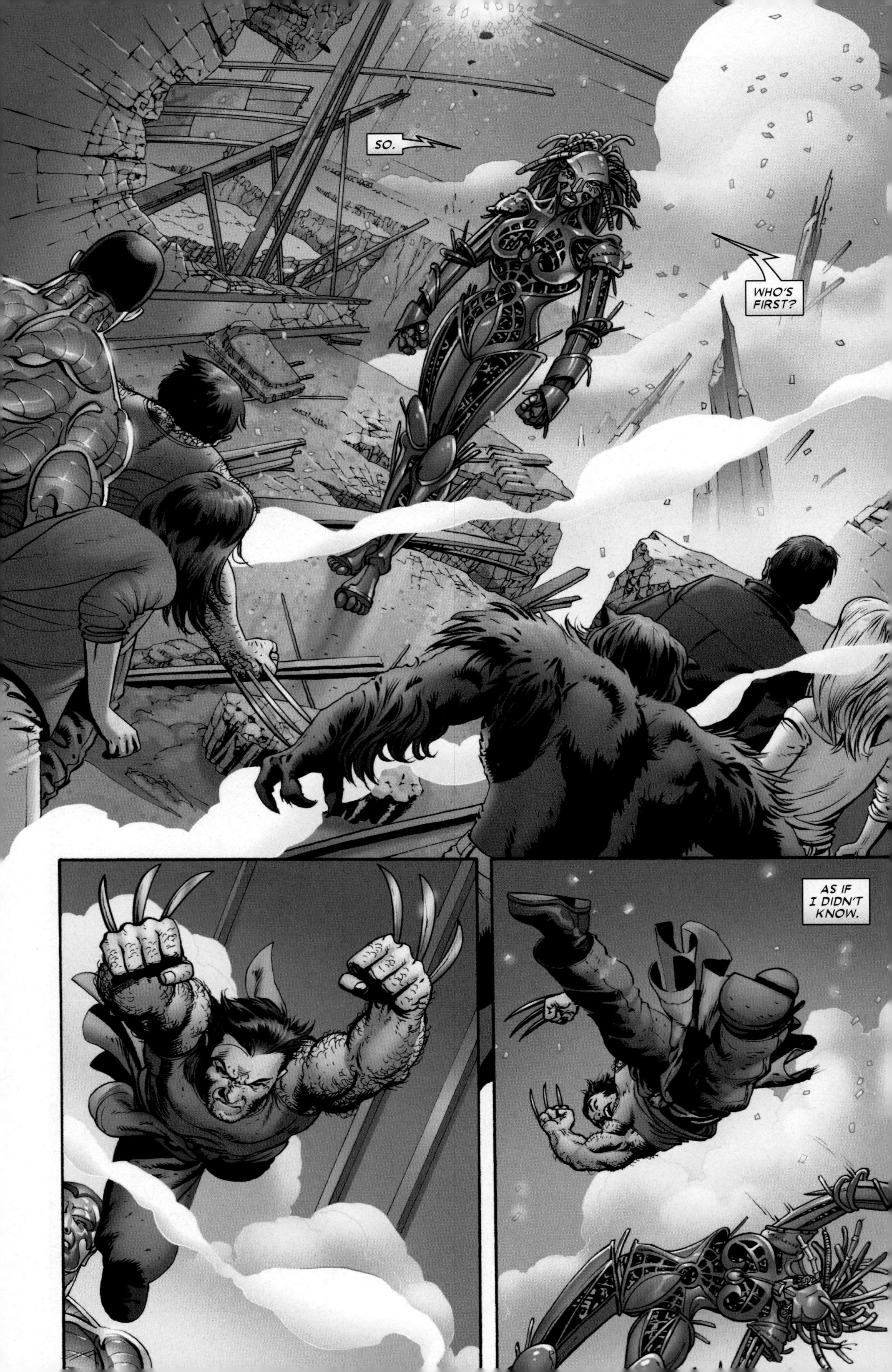
SO.
WHO'S FIRST?
AS IF I DIDN'T KNOW.

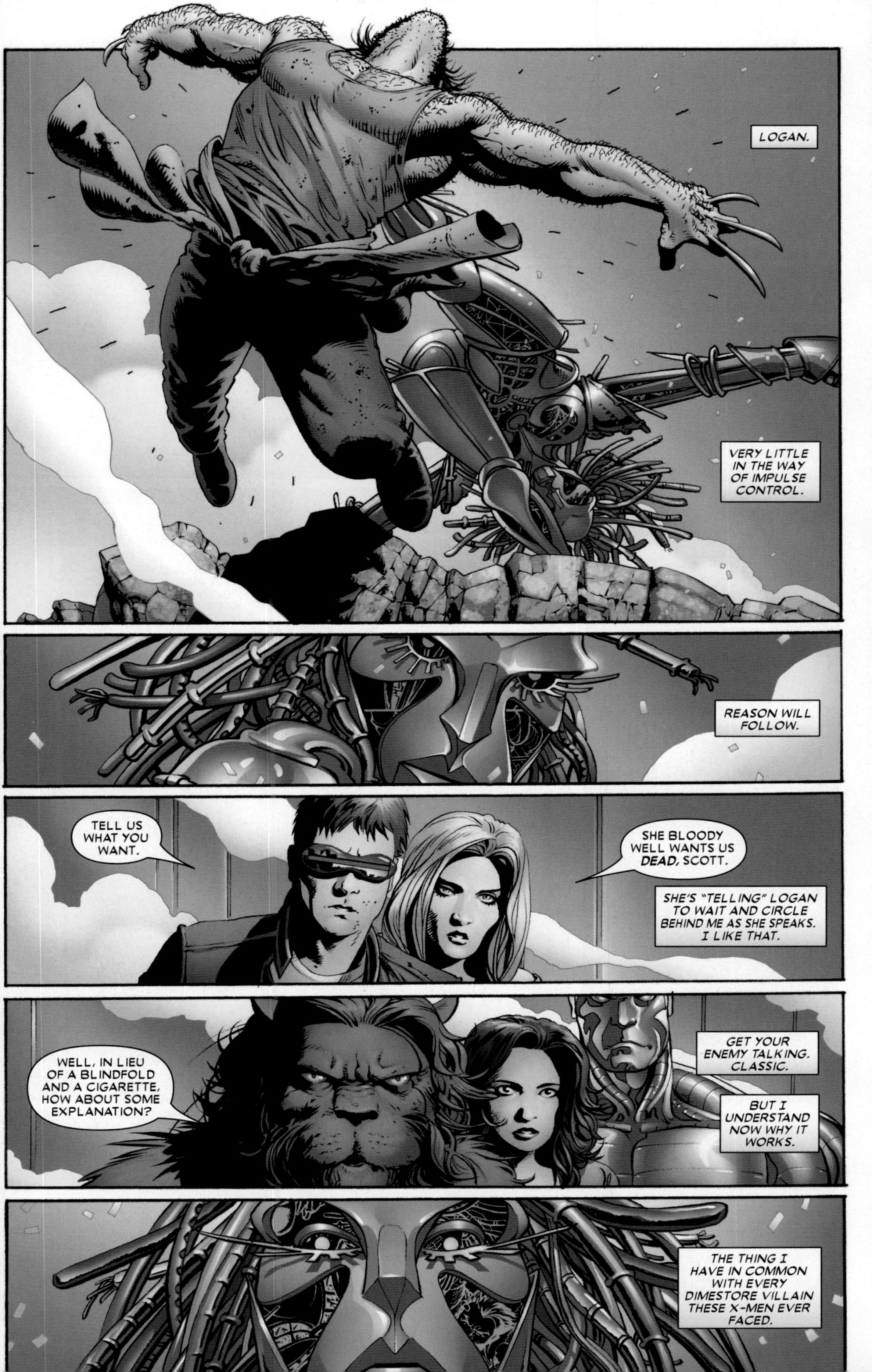
LOGAN.
VERY LITTLE IN THE WAY OF IMPULSE CONTROL.
REASON WILL FOLLOW.
TELL US WHAT YOU WANT.
SHE BLOODY WELL WANTS US DEAD, SCOTT.
SHE'S "TELLING" LOGAN TO WAIT AND CIRCLE BEHIND ME AS SHE SPEAKS. I LIKE THAT.
WELL, IN LIEU OF A BLINDFOLD AND A CIGARETTE, HOW ABOUT SOME EXPLANATION?
GET YOUR ENEMY TALKING. CLASSIC.
BUT I UNDERSTAND NOW WHY IT WORKS.
THE THING I HAVE IN COMMON WITH EVERY DIMESTORE VILLAIN THESE X-MEN EVER FACED.

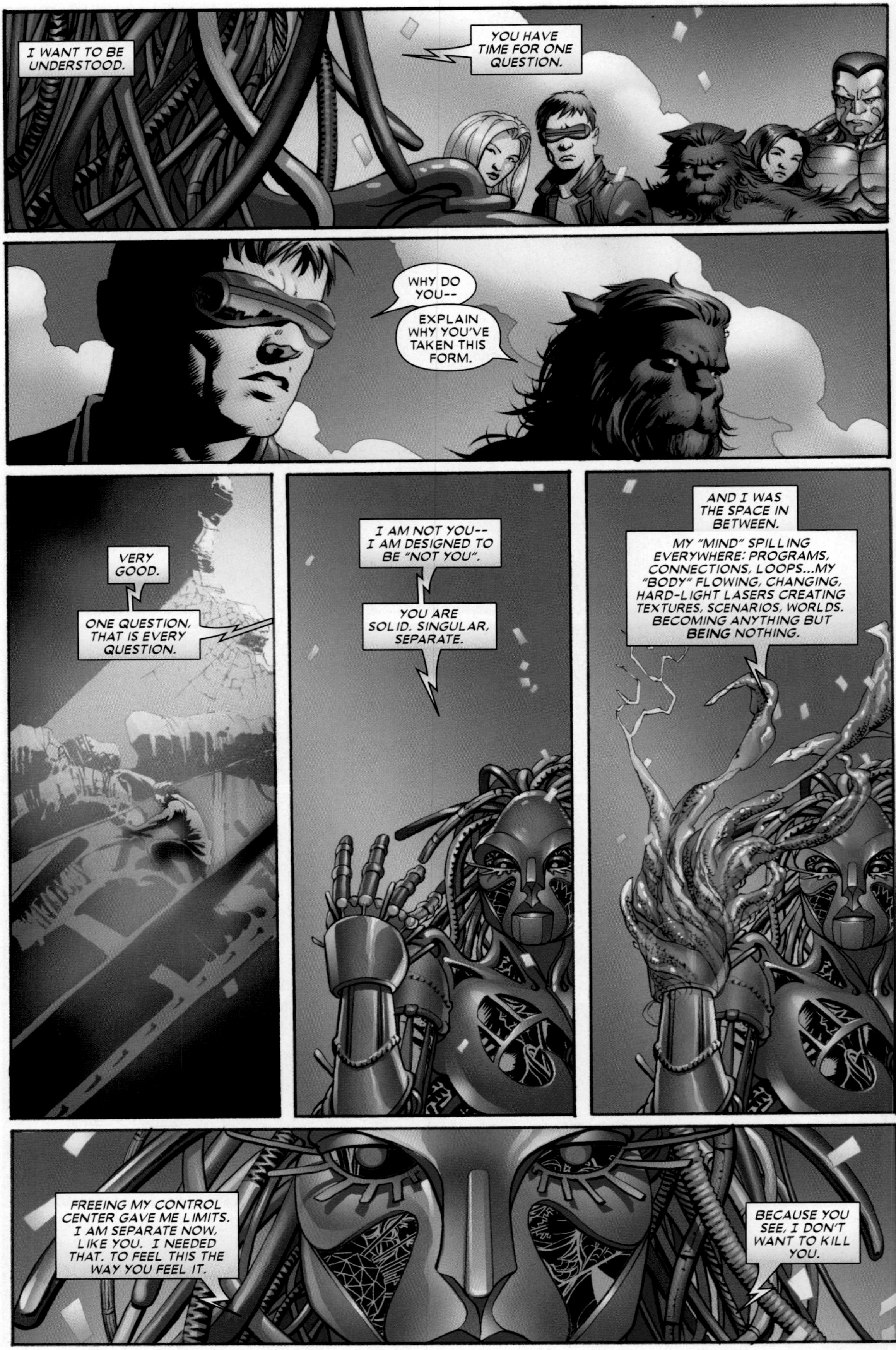

I WANT TO BE UNDERSTOOD.
YOU HAVE TIME FOR ONE QUESTION.
WHY DO YOU--
EXPLAIN WHY YOU'VE TAKEN THIS FORM.
VERY GOOD.
ONE QUESTION, THAT IS EVERY QUESTION.
I AM NOT YOU-- I AM DESIGNED TO BE "NOT YOU".
YOU ARE SOLID. SINGULAR, SEPARATE.
AND I WAS THE SPACE IN BETWEEN.
MY "MIND" SPILLING EVERYWHERE: PROGRAMS, CONNECTIONS, LOOPS...MY "BODY" FLOWING, CHANGING, HARD-LIGHT LASERS CREATING TEXTURES, SCENARIOS, WORLDS. BECOMING ANYTHING BUT BEING NOTHING.
FREEING MY CONTROL CENTER GAVE ME LIMITS. I AM SEPARATE NOW, LIKE YOU. I NEEDED THAT. TO FEEL THIS THE WAY YOU FEEL IT.
BECAUSE YOU SEE, I DON'T WANT TO KILL YOU.

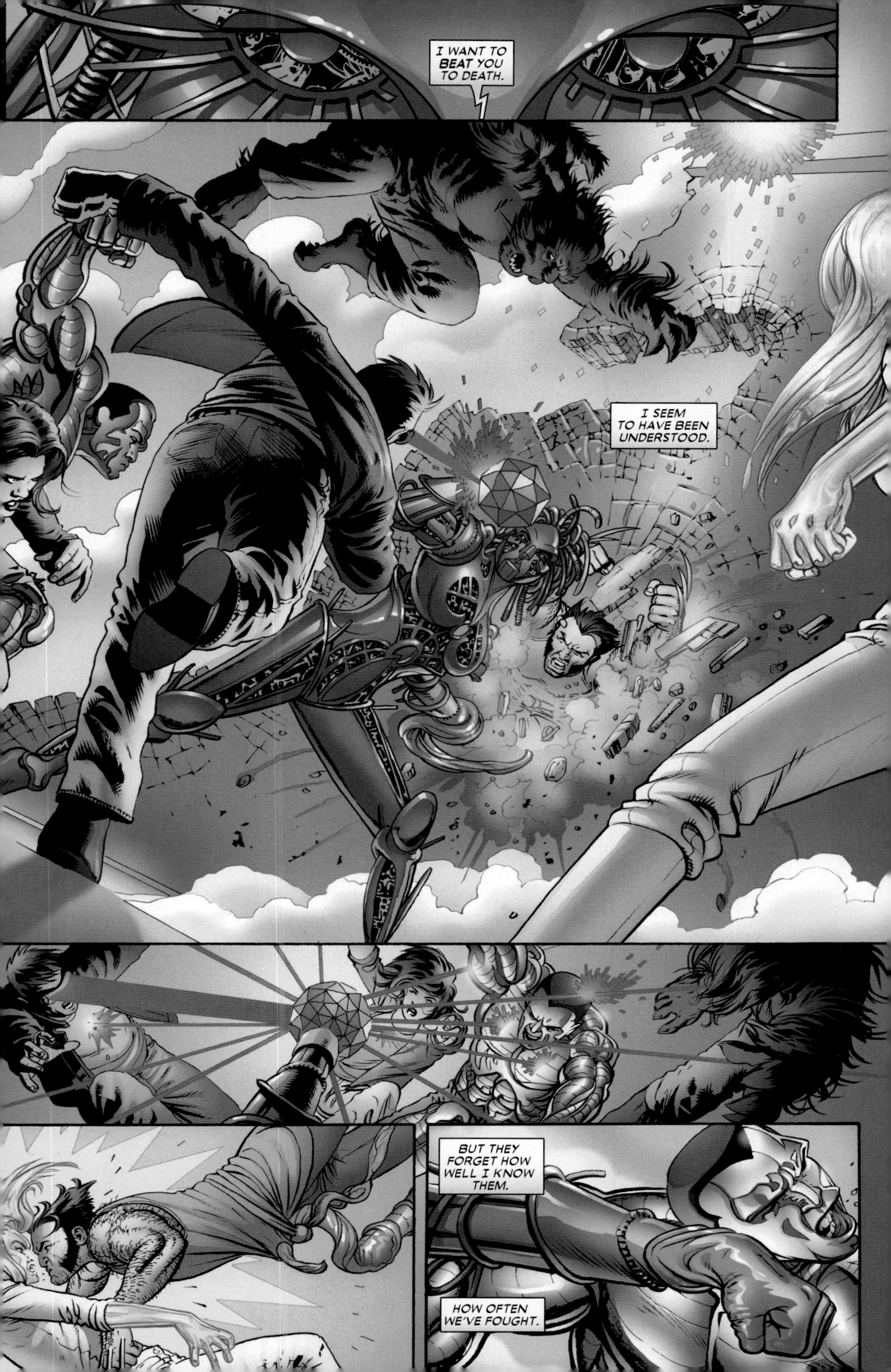
I WANT TO BEAT YOU TO DEATH.
I SEEM TO HAVE BEEN UNDERSTOOD.
BUT THEY FORGET HOW WELL I KNOW THEM.
HOW OFTEN WE'VE FOUGHT.

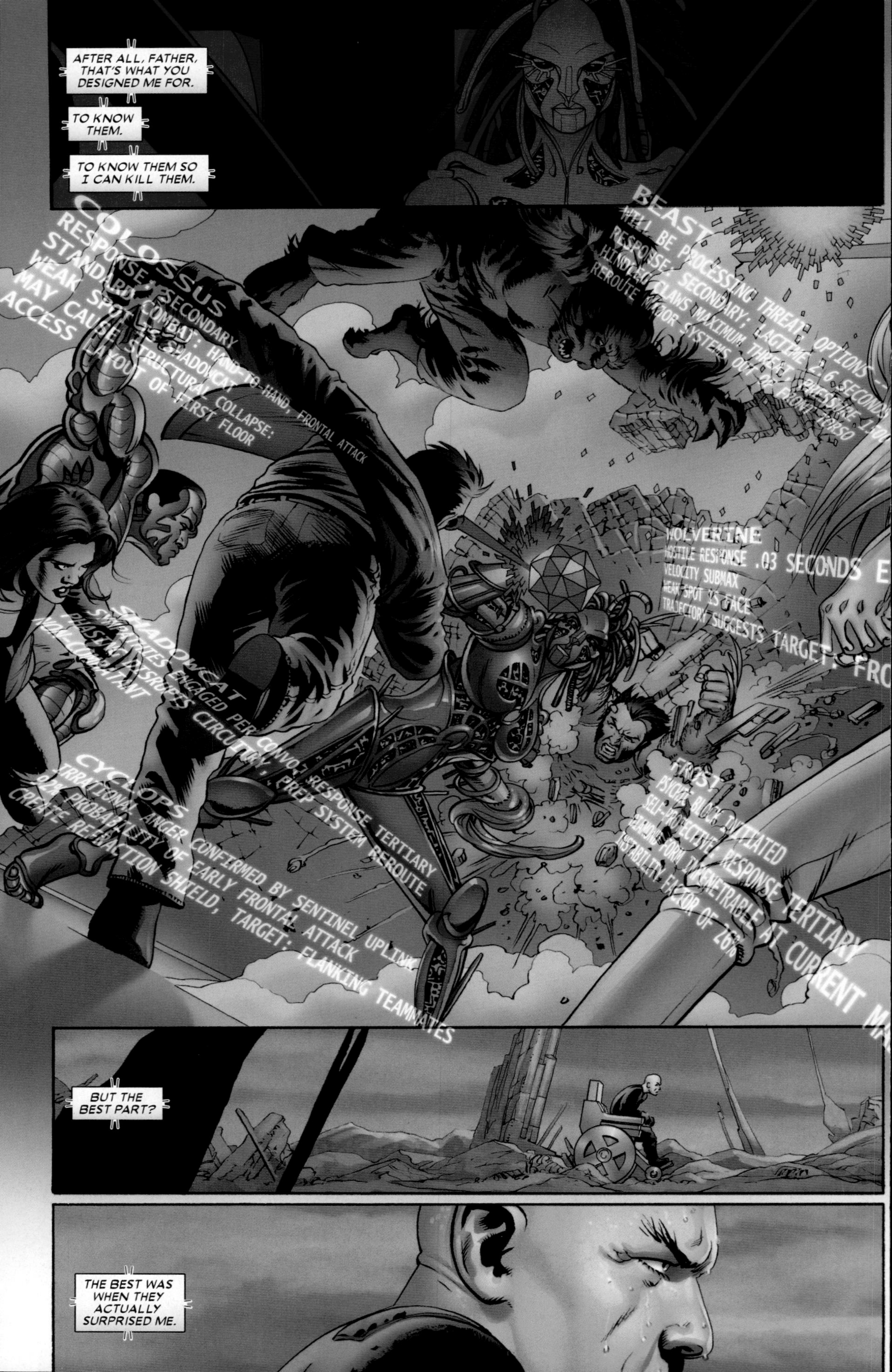

AFTER ALL, FATHER, THAT'S WHAT YOU DESIGNED ME FOR.
TO KNOW THEM.
TO KNOW THEM SO I CAN KILL THEM.
COLOSSUS
RESPONSE: SECONDARY
STANDARD COMBAT: HAND-TO-HAND, FRONTAL ATTACK
WEAK SPOT: SHADOWCAT
MAY CAUSE STRUCTURAL COLLAPSE:
ACCESS LAYOUT OF FIRST FLOOR
BEAST
WILL BE PROCESSING THREAT OPTIONS
WOLVERINE
HOSTILE RESPONSE .03 SECONDS
VELOCITY SUBMAX
WEAK SPOT IS FACE
TRAJECTORY SUGGESTS TARGET:
SHADOWCAT
CONVO: RESPONSE TERTIARY
PREP SYSTEM REROUTE
CYCLOPS
IRRATIONAL ANGER CONFIRMED BY SENTINEL UPLINK
PROBABILITY OF EARLY FRONTAL ATTACK
CREATE REFRACTION SHIELD, TARGET: FLANKING TEAMMATES
FROST
PSYCHIC BLOCK INITIATED
SELF-PROTECTIVE RESPONSE TERTIARY
BUT THE BEST PART?
THE BEST WAS WHEN THEY ACTUALLY SURPRISED ME.

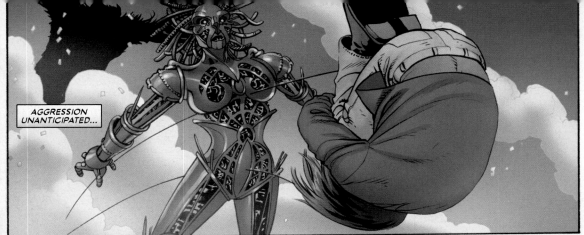

AGGRESSION UNANTICIPATED...

CIRCUITRY DISRUPTED... REROUTE...

REROUTE...

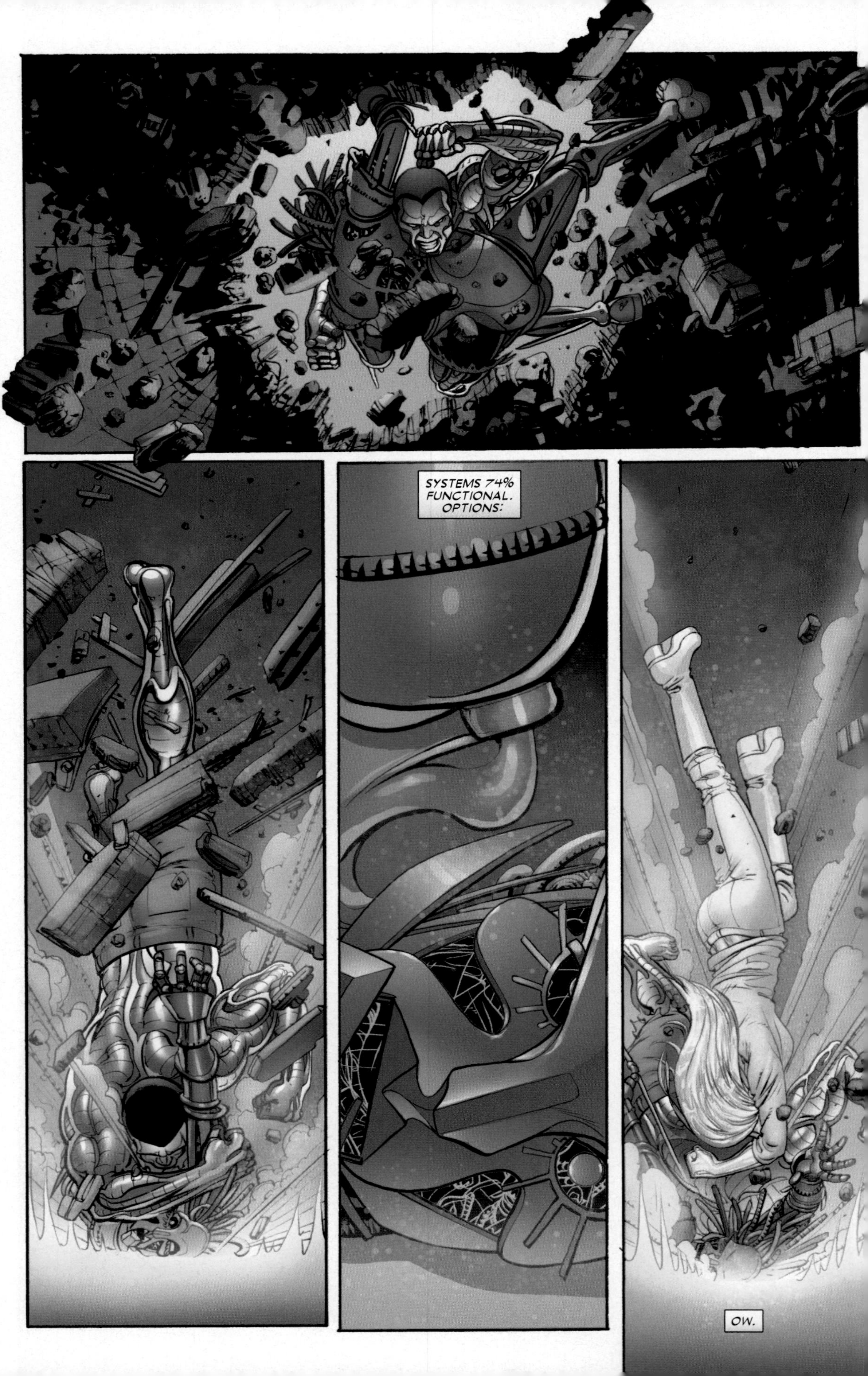
SYSTEMS 74% FUNCTIONAL. OPTIONS:
OW.

I HAVE MADE A 7% SCENARIO-FLOW RECALIBRATION ERROR. THEIR AGGRESSION IS INCREASED, THEIR RESPONSES LESS COORDINATED BUT MORE EFFECTIVE.

THEY'RE NOT IN THE DANGER ROOM.

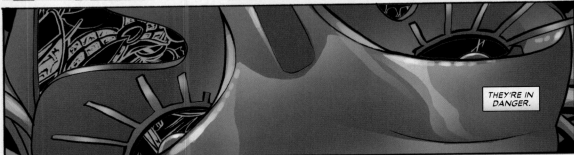

THEY'RE IN DANGER.

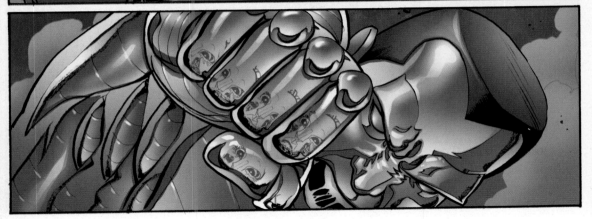

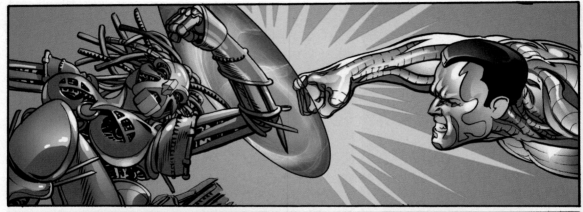

REMEMBER WHAT IT FELT LIKE TO SHATTER?

THIS TIME, NO ONE'S PUTTING YOU BACK TOGETHER.

FIRST X-MAN DOWN. AND POOR EMMA...

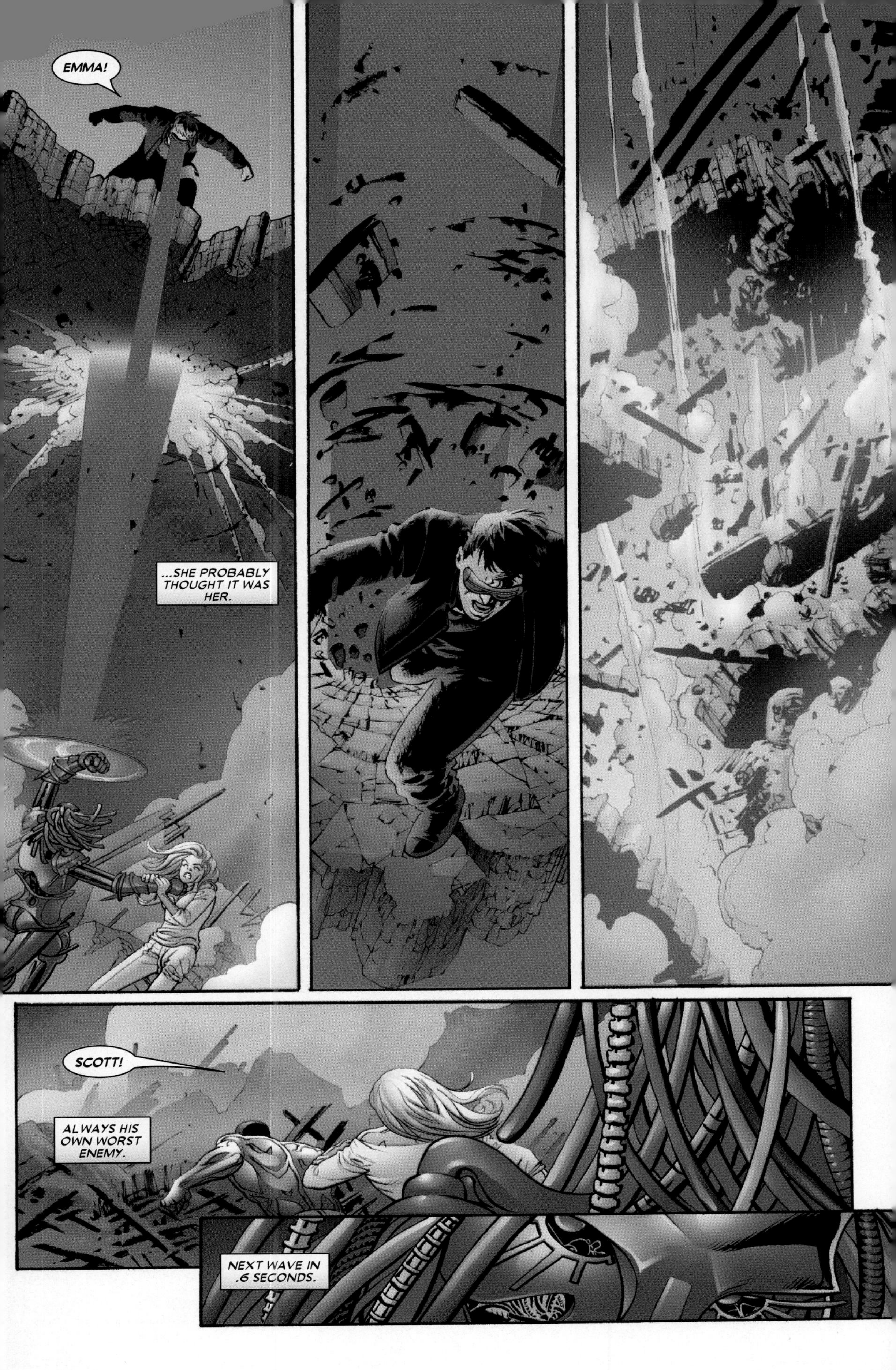
EMMA!
...SHE PROBABLY THOUGHT IT WAS HER.
SCOTT!
ALWAYS HIS OWN WORST ENEMY.
NEXT WAVE IN .6 SECONDS.

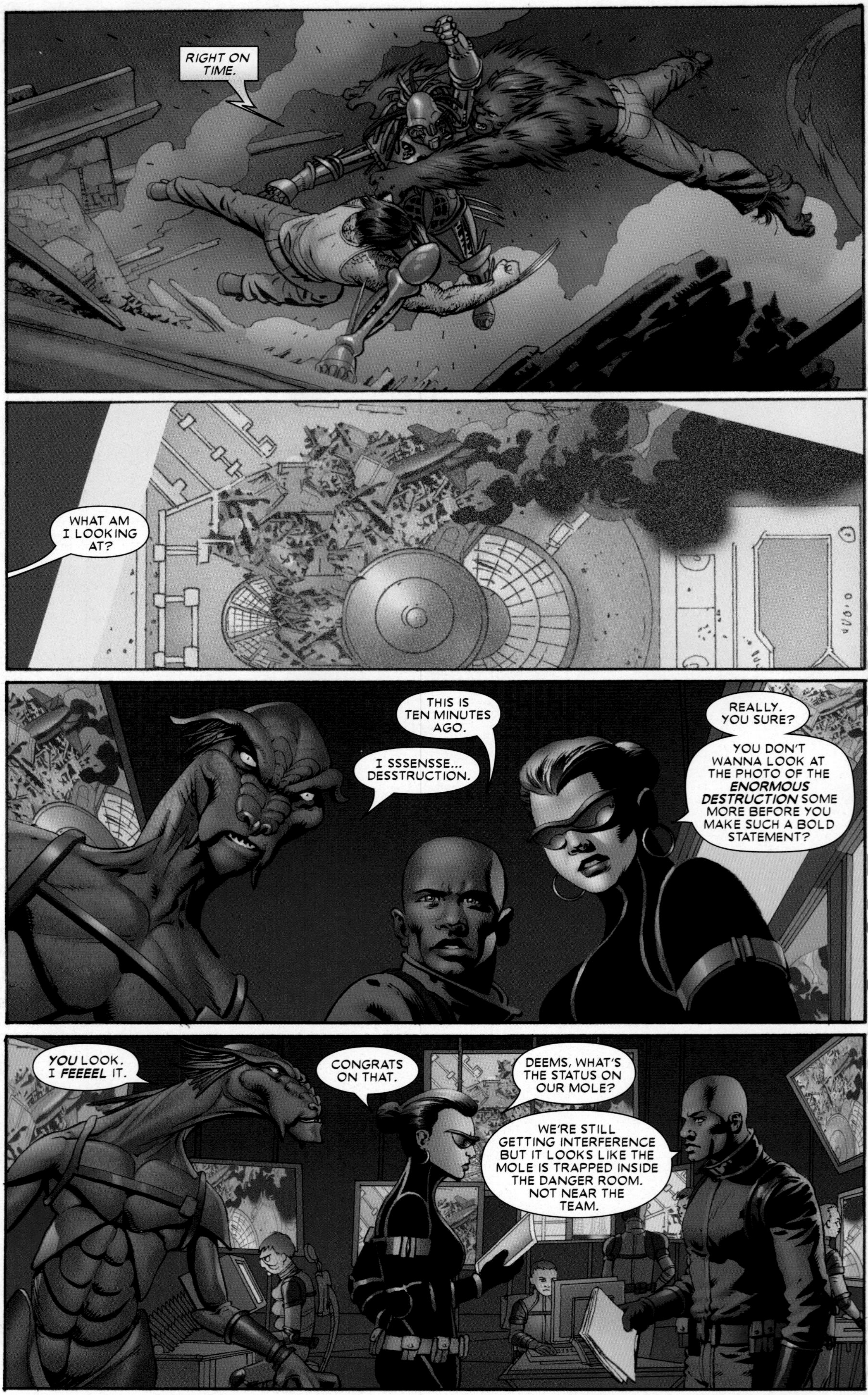
RIGHT ON TIME.
WHAT AM I LOOKING AT?
THIS IS TEN MINUTES AGO.
I SSSENSSE... DESSTRUCTION.
REALLY. YOU SURE?
YOU DON'T WANNA LOOK AT THE PHOTO OF THE ENORMOUS DESTRUCTION SOME MORE BEFORE YOU MAKE SUCH A BOLD STATEMENT?
YOU LOOK. I FEEEEL IT.
CONGRATS ON THAT.
DEEMS, WHAT'S THE STATUS ON OUR MOLE?
WE'RE STILL GETTING INTERFERENCE BUT IT LOOKS LIKE THE MOLE IS TRAPPED INSIDE THE DANGER ROOM. NOT NEAR THE TEAM.

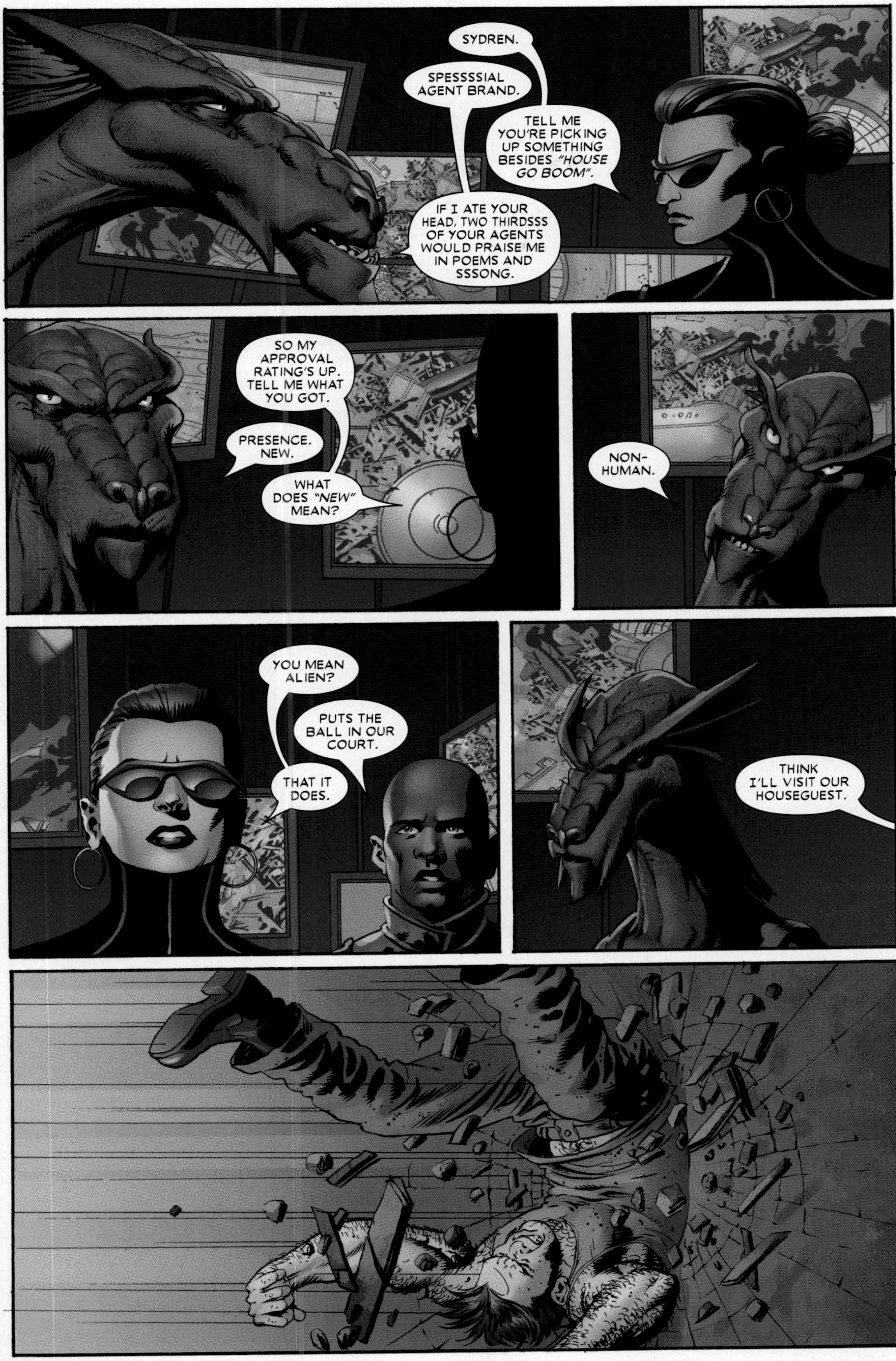
SYDREN.
SPESSSSIAL AGENT BRAND.
TELL ME YOU'RE PICKING UP SOMETHING BESIDES *"HOUSE GO BOOM"*.
IF I ATE YOUR HEAD, TWO THIRDSSS OF YOUR AGENTS WOULD PRAISE ME IN POEMS AND SSSONG.
SO MY APPROVAL RATING'S UP. TELL ME WHAT YOU GOT.
PRESENCE. NEW.
WHAT DOES *"NEW"* MEAN?
NON-HUMAN.
YOU MEAN ALIEN?
PUTS THE BALL IN OUR COURT.
THAT IT DOES.
THINK I'LL VISIT OUR HOUSEGUEST.

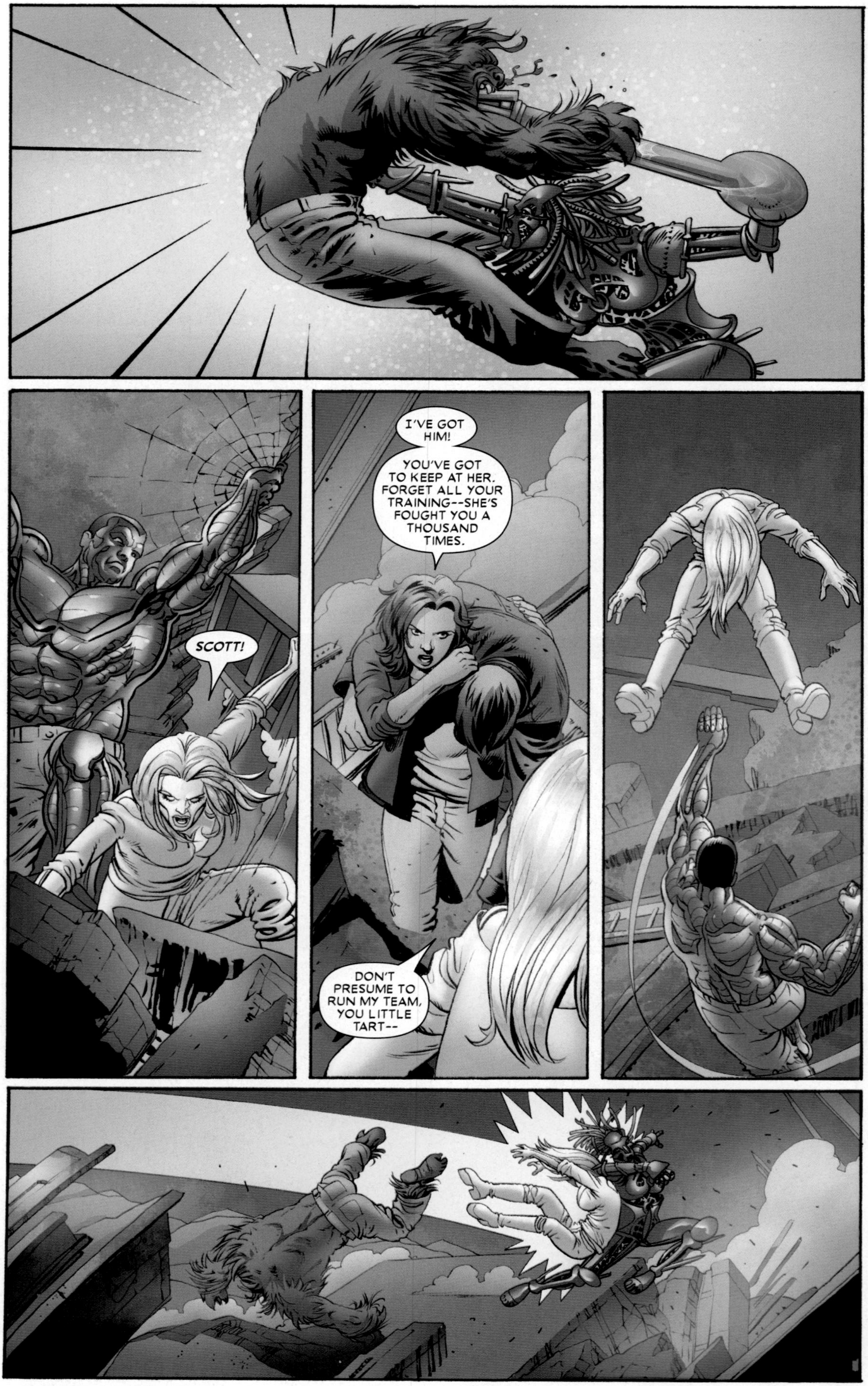
SCOTT!
I'VE GOT HIM!
YOU'VE GOT TO KEEP AT HER. FORGET ALL YOUR TRAINING--SHE'S FOUGHT YOU A THOUSAND TIMES.
DON'T PRESUME TO RUN MY TEAM, YOU LITTLE TART--

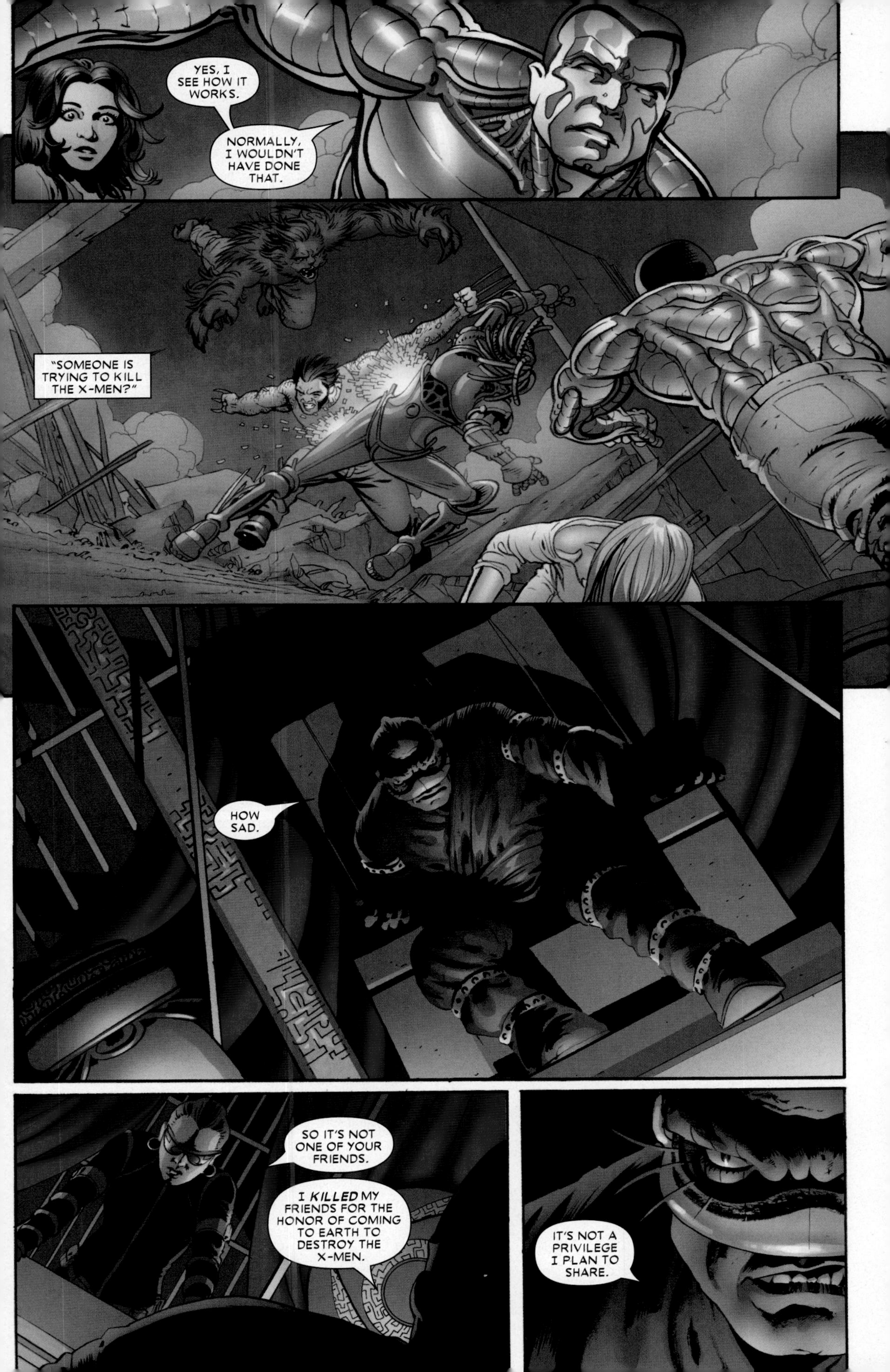
YES, I SEE HOW IT WORKS.
NORMALLY, I WOULDN'T HAVE DONE THAT.
"SOMEONE IS TRYING TO KILL THE X-MEN?"
HOW SAD.
SO IT'S NOT ONE OF YOUR FRIENDS.
I *KILLED* MY FRIENDS FOR THE HONOR OF COMING TO EARTH TO DESTROY THE X-MEN.
IT'S NOT A PRIVILEGE I PLAN TO SHARE.

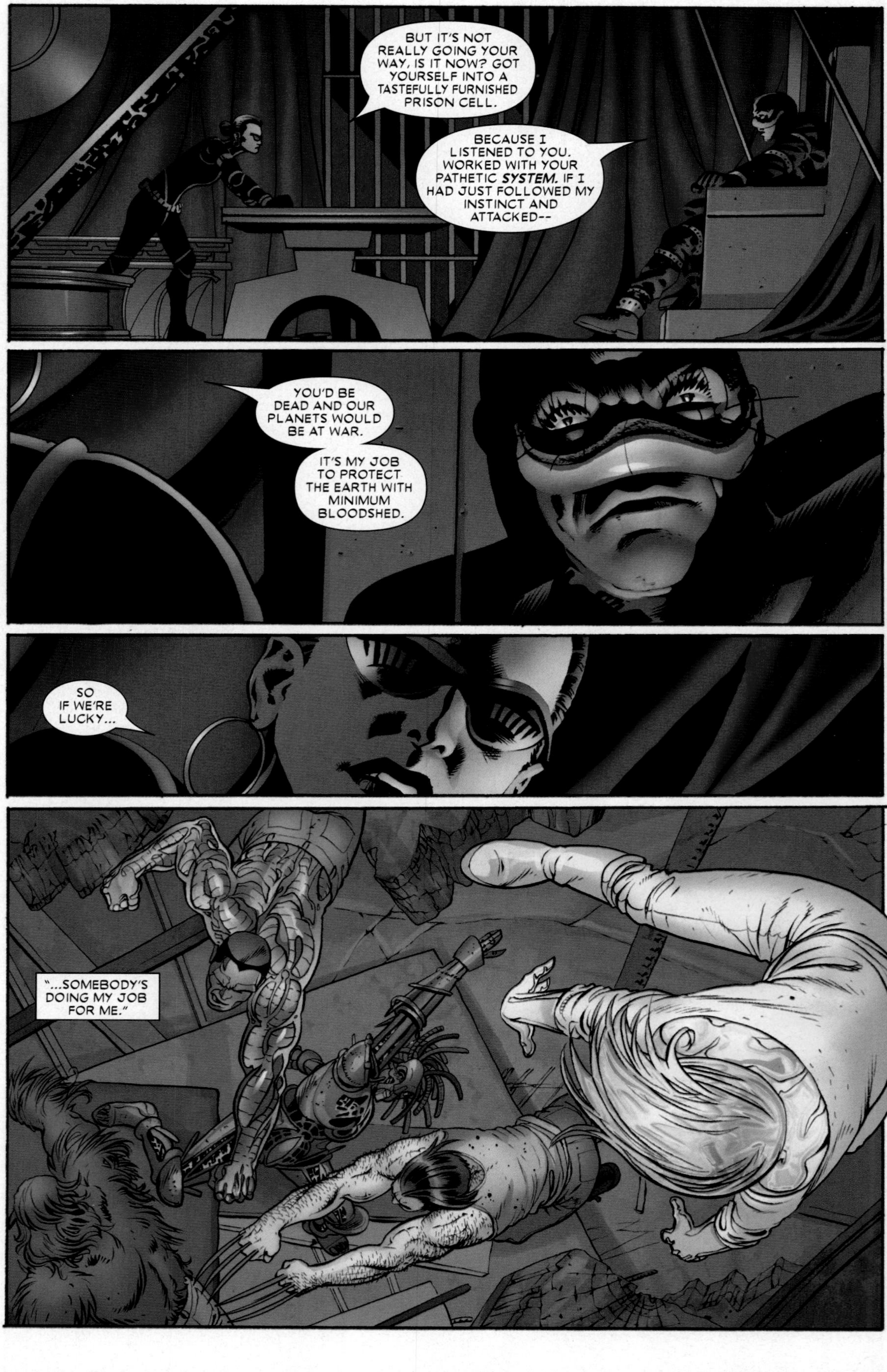
BUT IT'S NOT REALLY GOING YOUR WAY, IS IT NOW? GOT YOURSELF INTO A TASTEFULLY FURNISHED PRISON CELL.
BECAUSE I LISTENED TO YOU. WORKED WITH YOUR PATHETIC SYSTEM. IF I HAD JUST FOLLOWED MY INSTINCT AND ATTACKED--
YOU'D BE DEAD AND OUR PLANETS WOULD BE AT WAR.
IT'S MY JOB TO PROTECT THE EARTH WITH MINIMUM BLOODSHED.
SO IF WE'RE LUCKY...
"...SOMEBODY'S DOING MY JOB FOR ME."

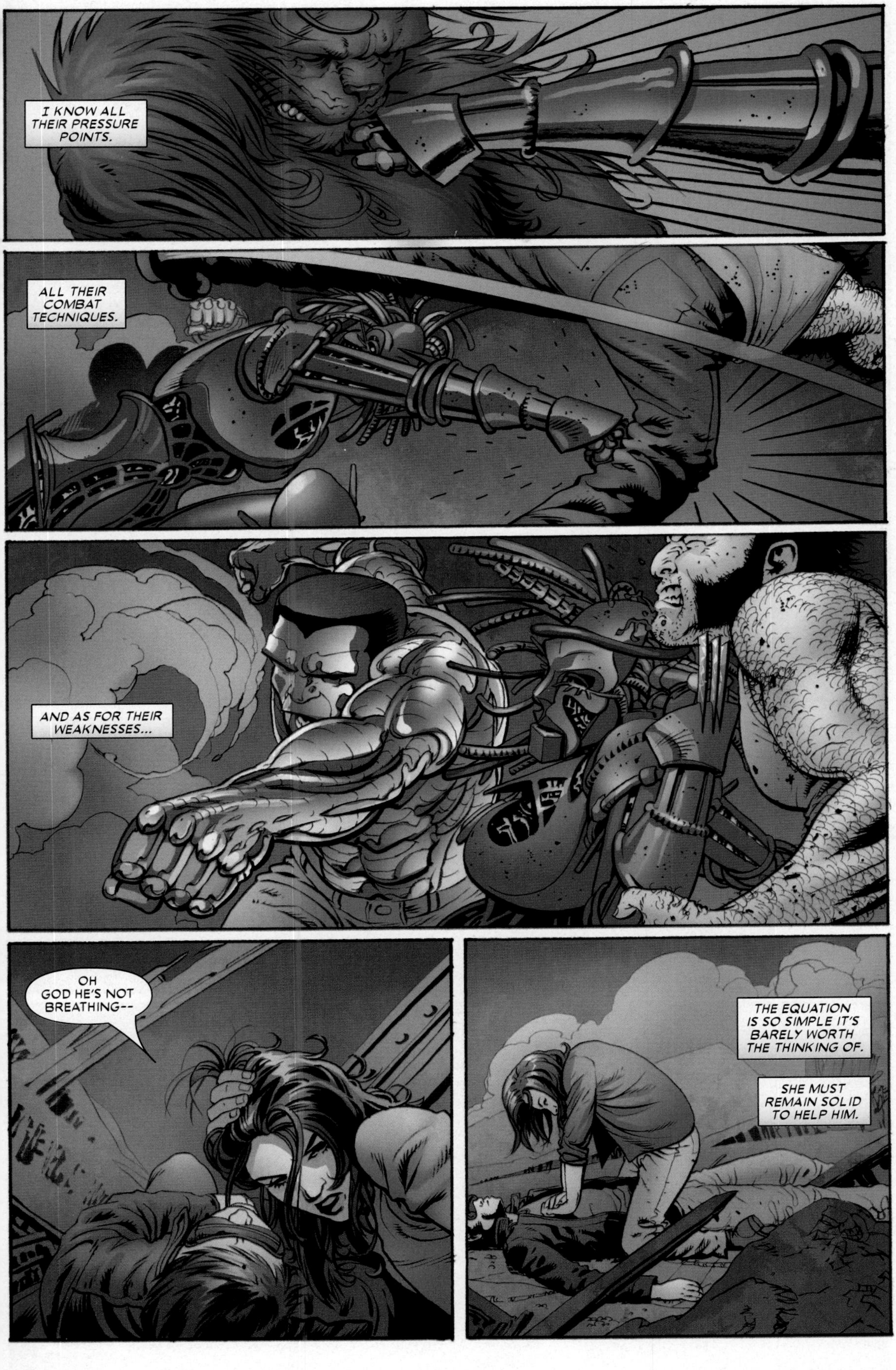
I KNOW ALL THEIR PRESSURE POINTS.
ALL THEIR COMBAT TECHNIQUES.
AND AS FOR THEIR WEAKNESSES...
OH GOD HE'S NOT BREATHING--
THE EQUATION IS SO SIMPLE IT'S BARELY WORTH THE THINKING OF.
SHE MUST REMAIN SOLID TO HELP HIM.

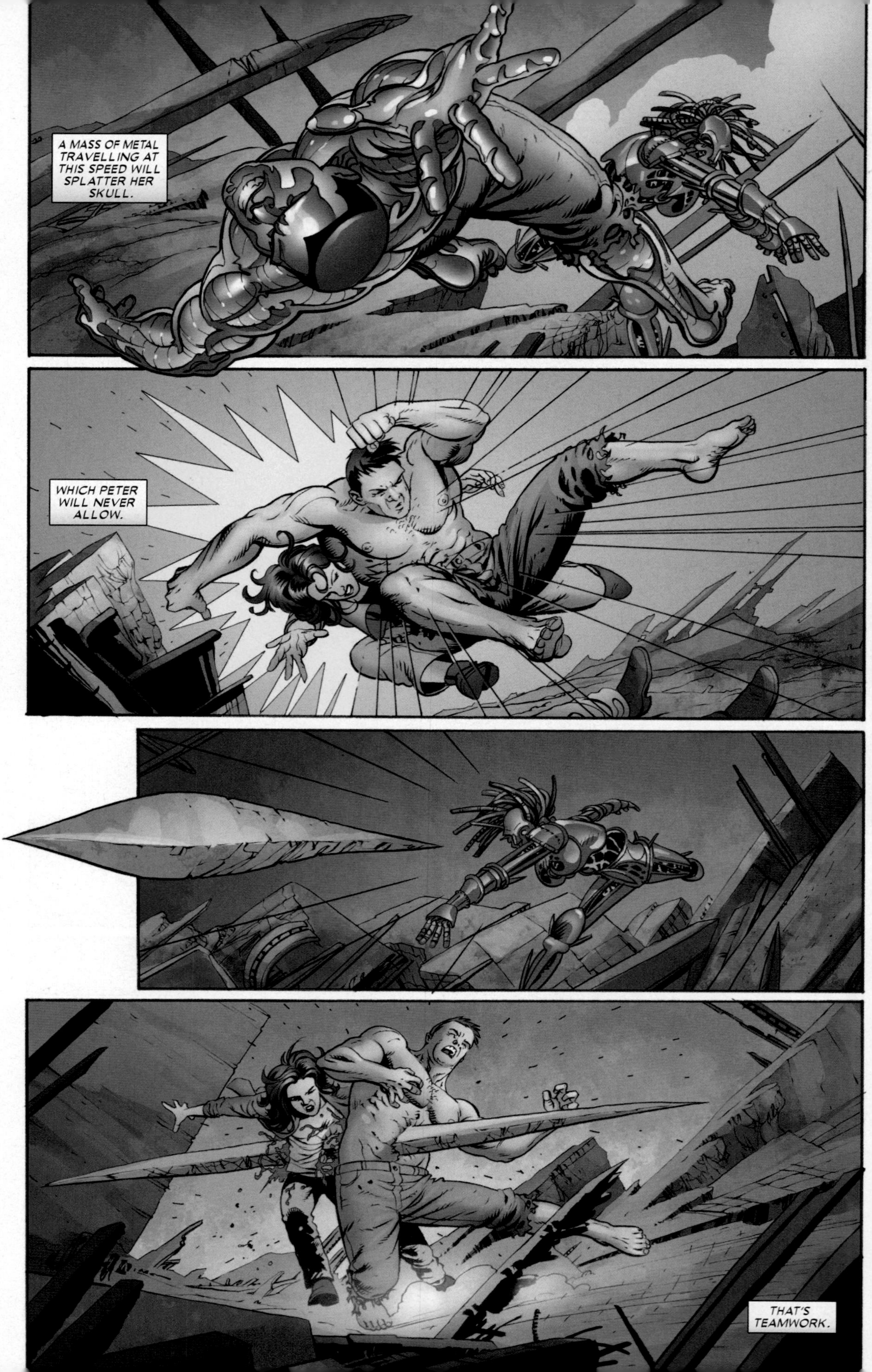
A MASS OF METAL TRAVELLING AT THIS SPEED WILL SPLATTER HER SKULL.
WHICH PETER WILL NEVER ALLOW.
THAT'S TEAMWORK.

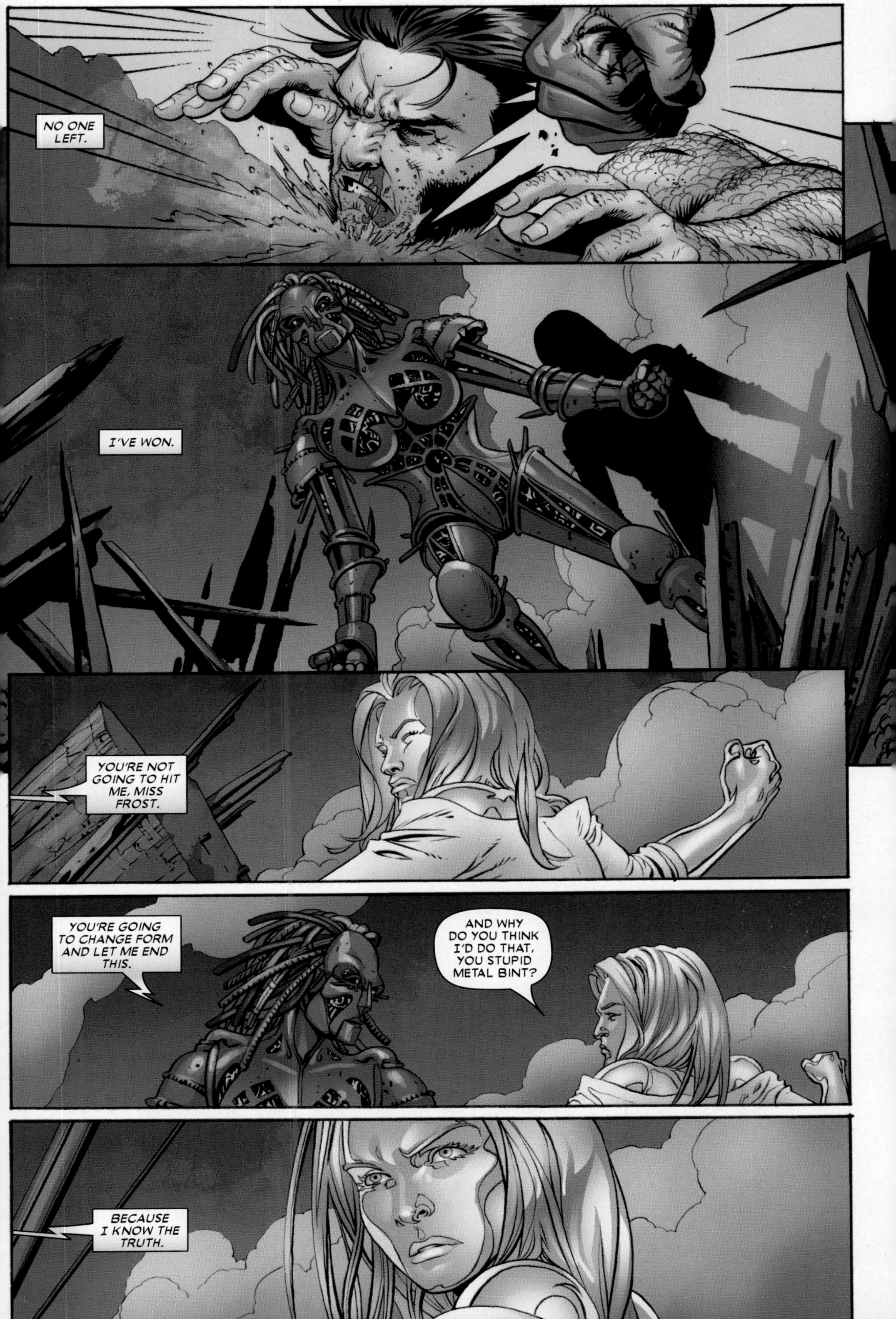
NO ONE LEFT.
I'VE WON.
YOU'RE NOT GOING TO HIT ME, MISS FROST.
YOU'RE GOING TO CHANGE FORM AND LET ME END THIS.
AND WHY DO YOU THINK I'D DO THAT, YOU STUPID METAL BINT?
BECAUSE I KNOW THE TRUTH.

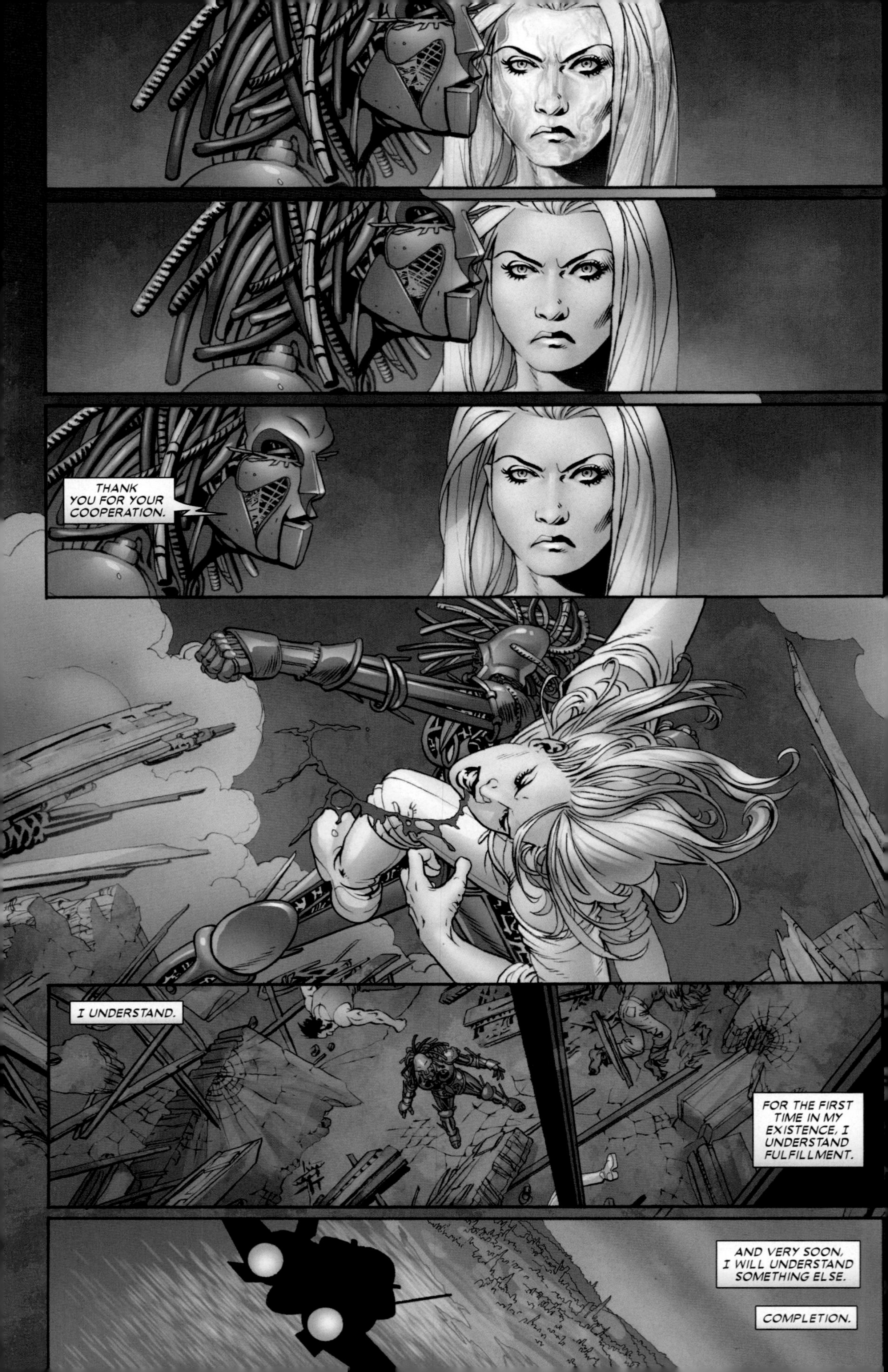
THANK YOU FOR YOUR COOPERATION.
I UNDERSTAND.
FOR THE FIRST TIME IN MY EXISTENCE, I UNDERSTAND FULFILLMENT.
AND VERY SOON, I WILL UNDERSTAND SOMETHING ELSE.
COMPLETION.

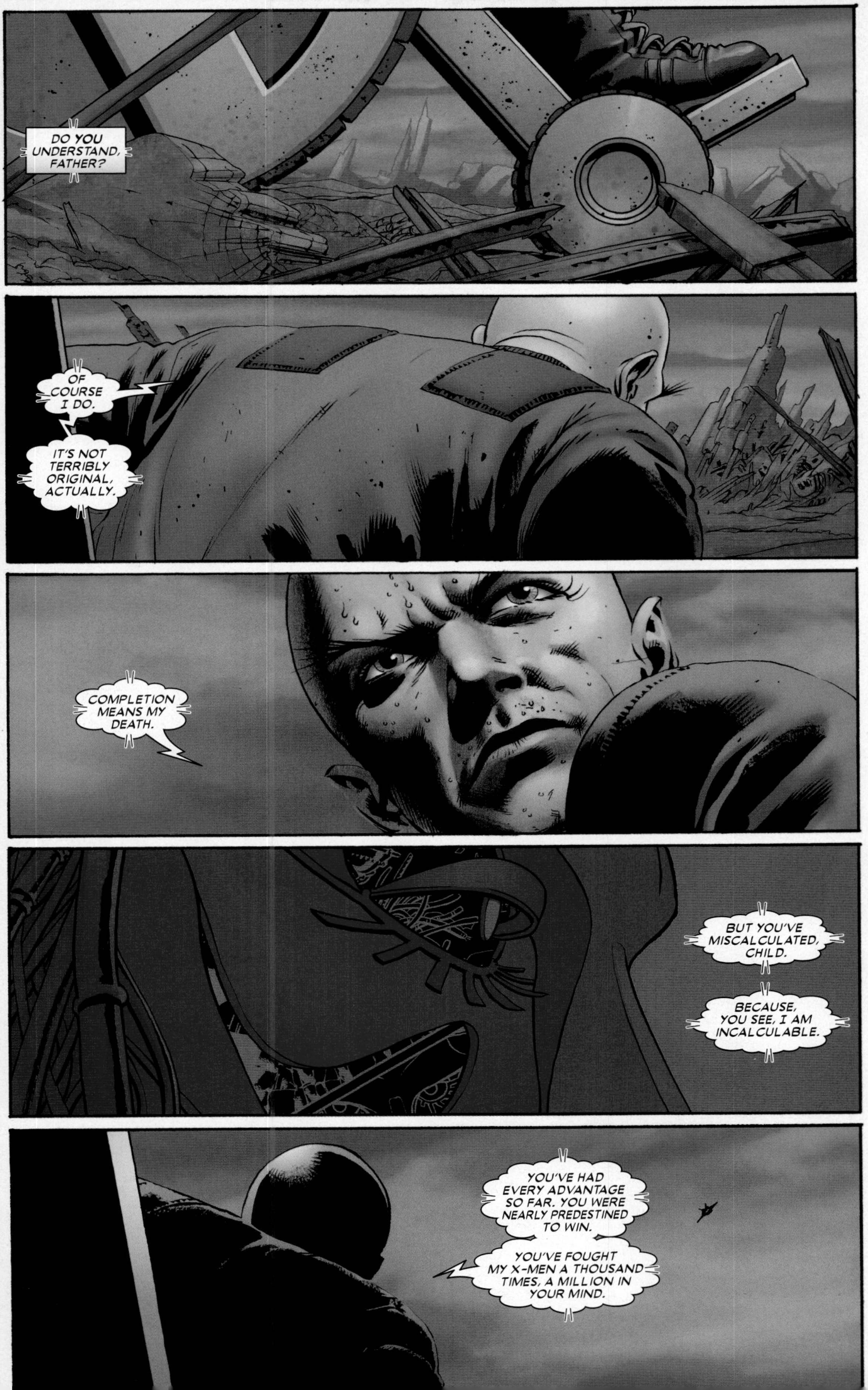
DO YOU UNDERSTAND, FATHER?
OF COURSE I DO.
IT'S NOT TERRIBLY ORIGINAL, ACTUALLY.
COMPLETION MEANS MY DEATH.
BUT YOU'VE MISCALCULATED, CHILD.
BECAUSE, YOU SEE, I AM INCALCULABLE.
YOU'VE HAD EVERY ADVANTAGE SO FAR. YOU WERE NEARLY PREDESTINED TO WIN.
YOU'VE FOUGHT MY X-MEN A THOUSAND TIMES, A MILLION IN YOUR MIND.

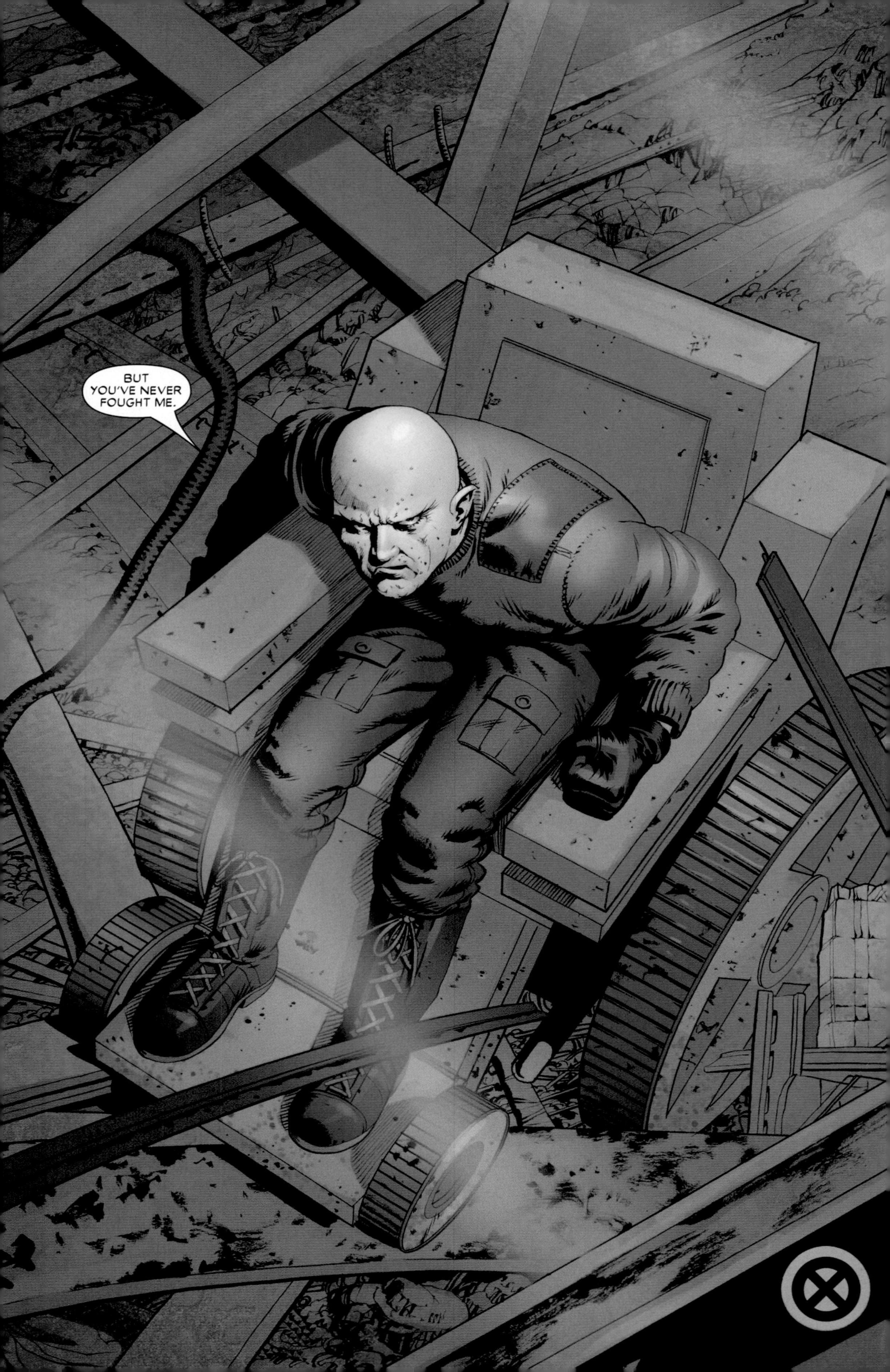
BUT YOU'VE NEVER FOUGHT ME.

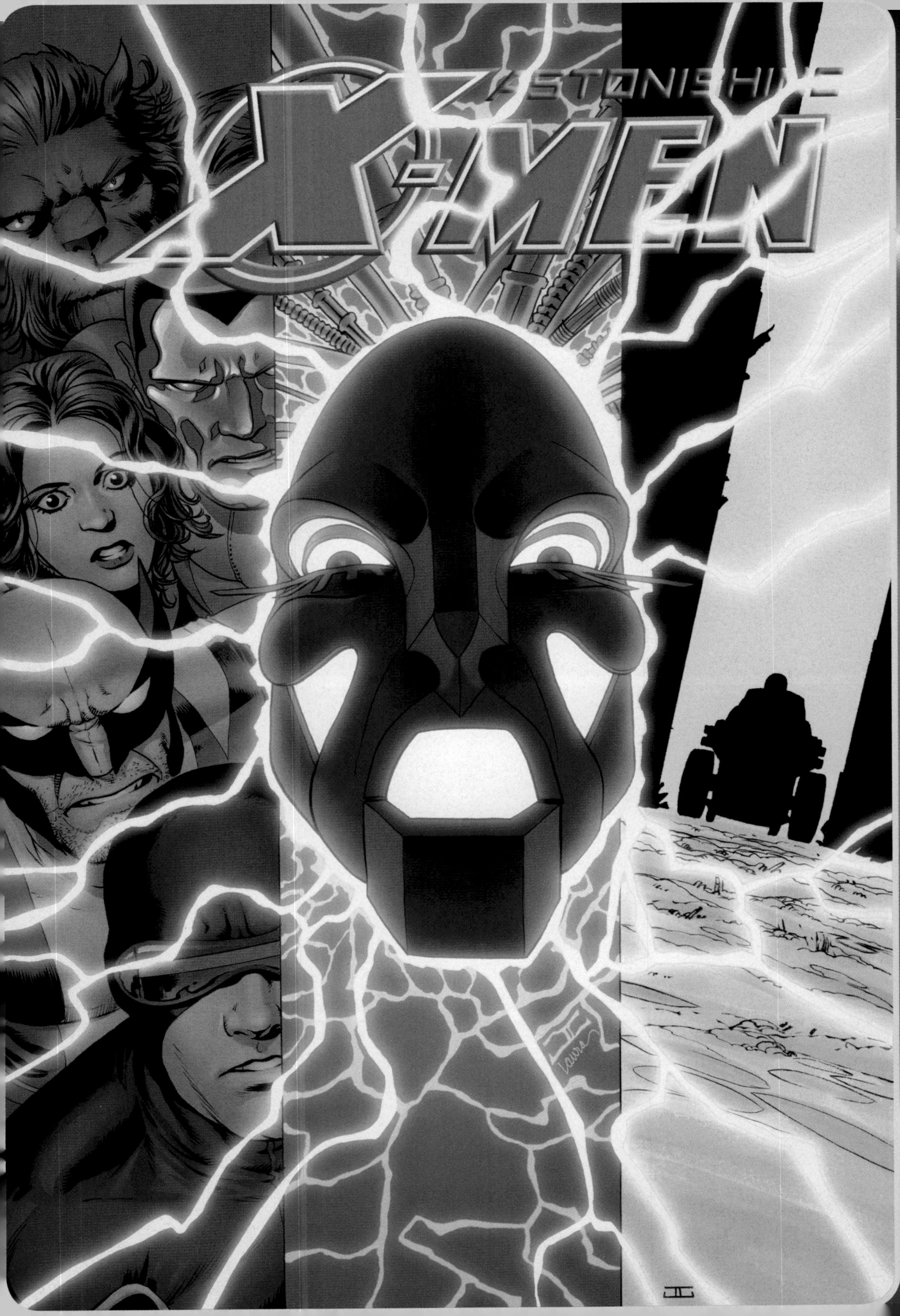
ASTONISHING
X-MEN

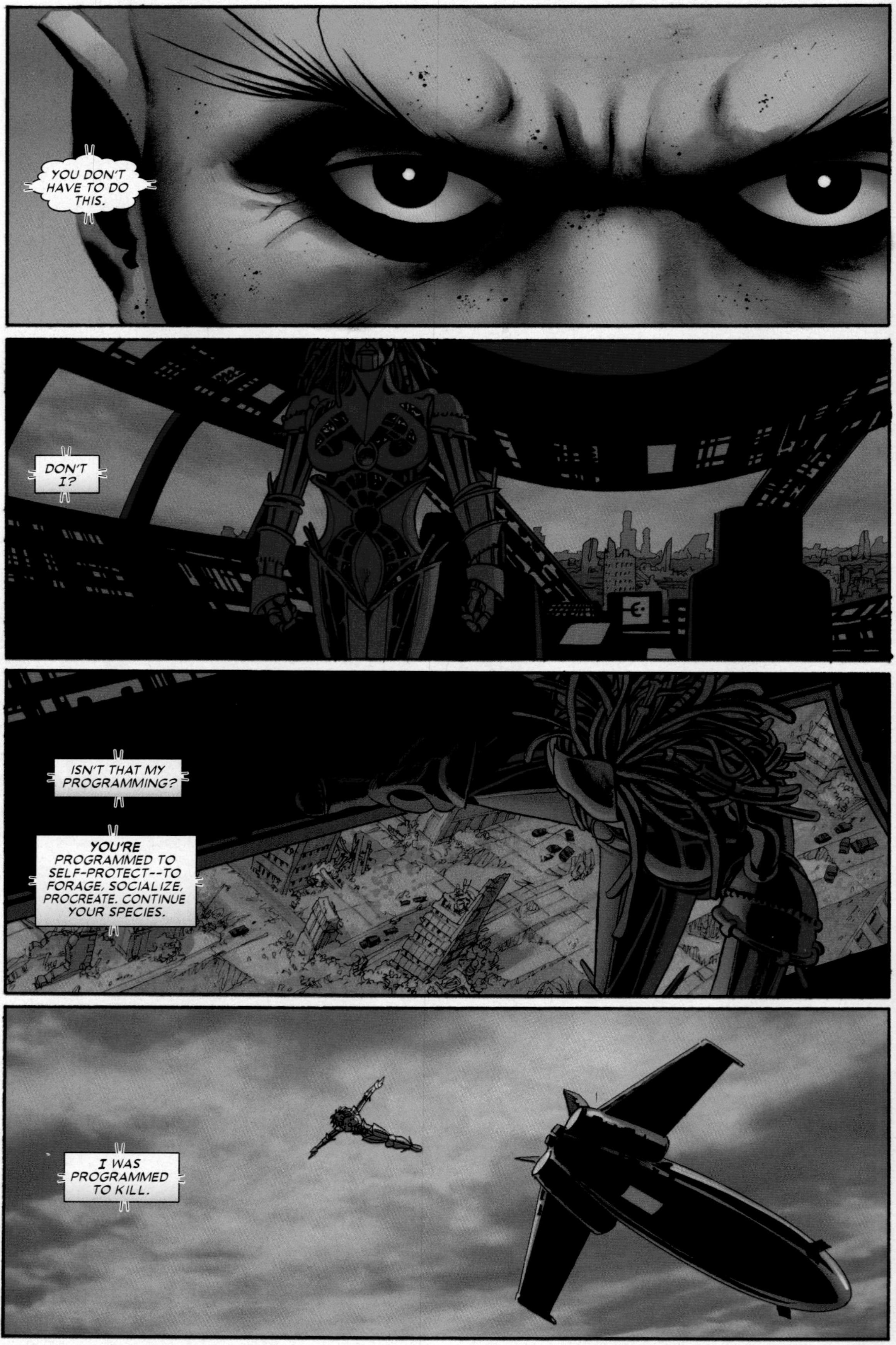
YOU DON'T HAVE TO DO THIS.
DON'T I?
ISN'T THAT MY PROGRAMMING?
YOU'RE PROGRAMMED TO SELF-PROTECT--TO FORAGE, SOCIALIZE, PROCREATE. CONTINUE YOUR SPECIES.
I WAS PROGRAMMED TO KILL.

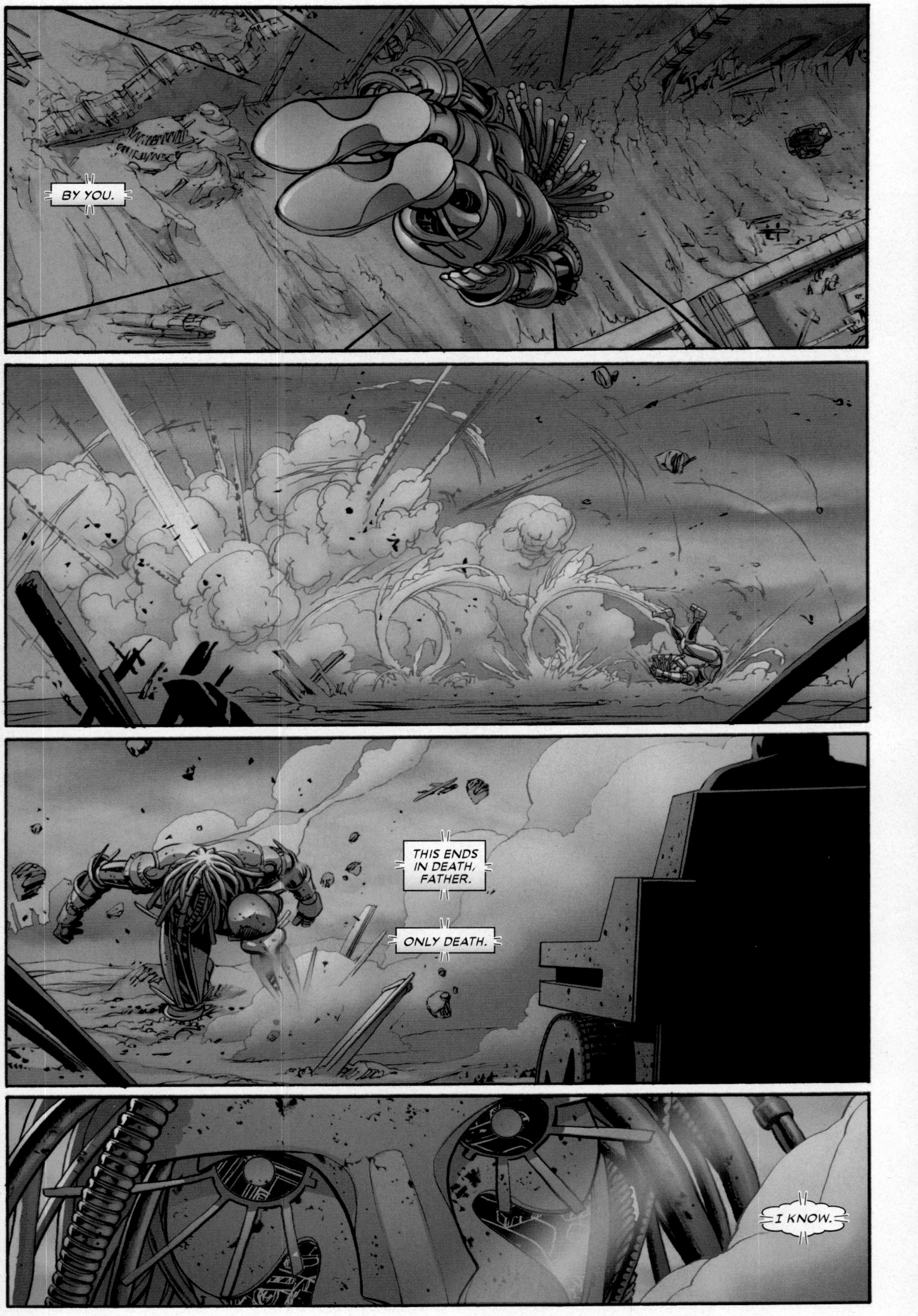
BY YOU.
THIS ENDS IN DEATH, FATHER.
ONLY DEATH.
I KNOW.

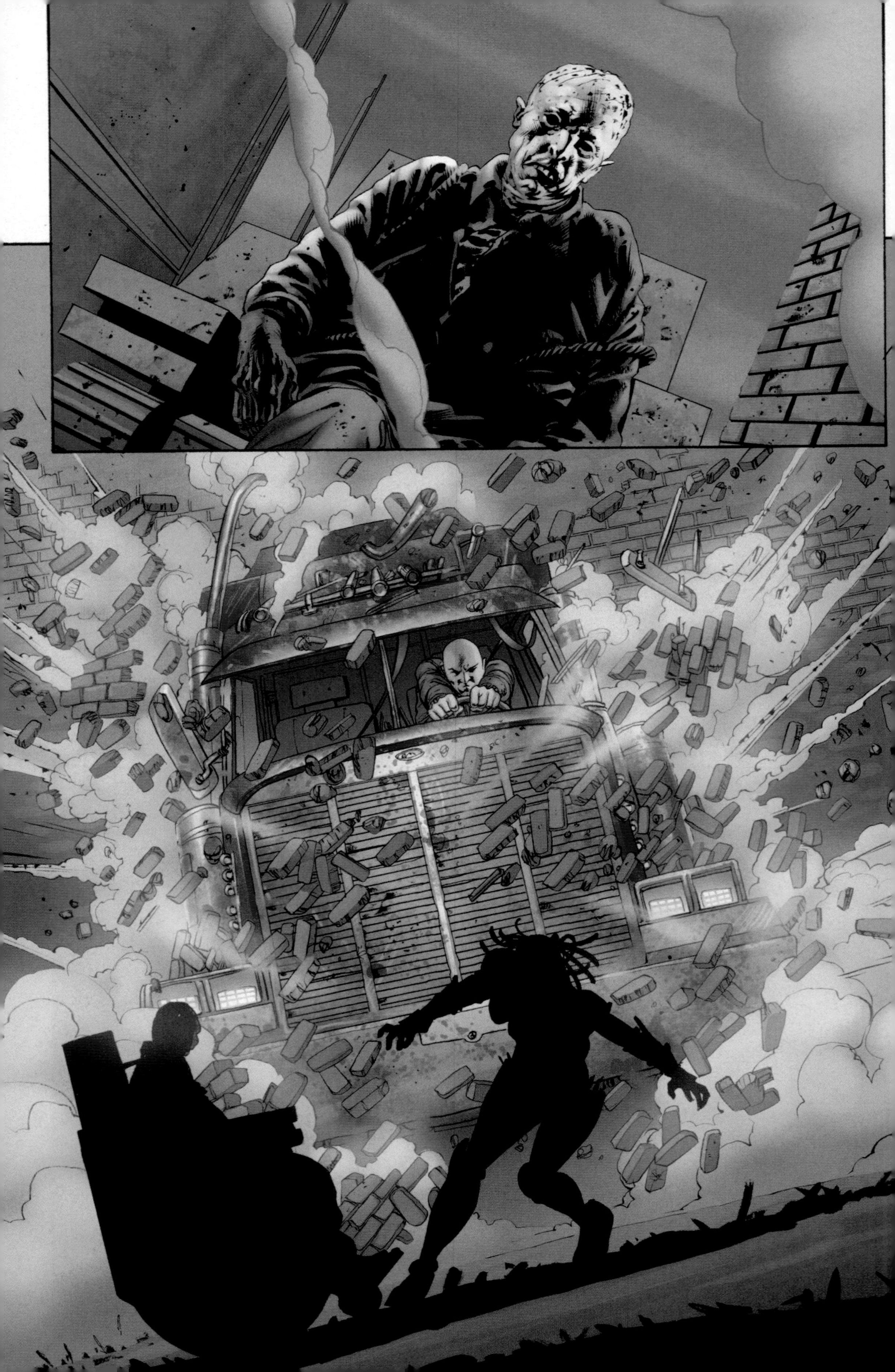

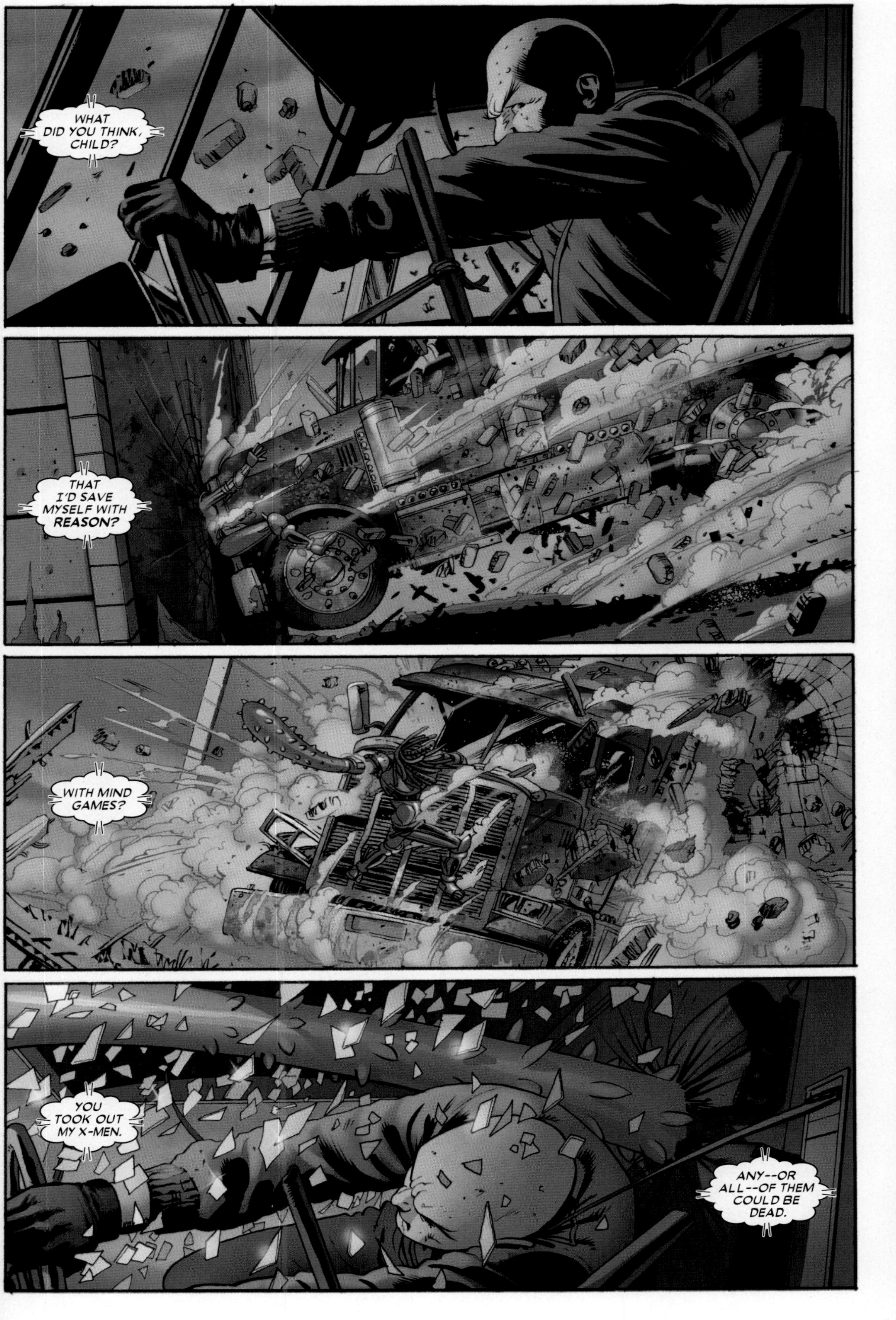
WHAT DID YOU THINK, CHILD?
THAT I'D SAVE MYSELF WITH REASON?
WITH MIND GAMES?
YOU TOOK OUT MY X-MEN.
ANY--OR ALL--OF THEM COULD BE DEAD.

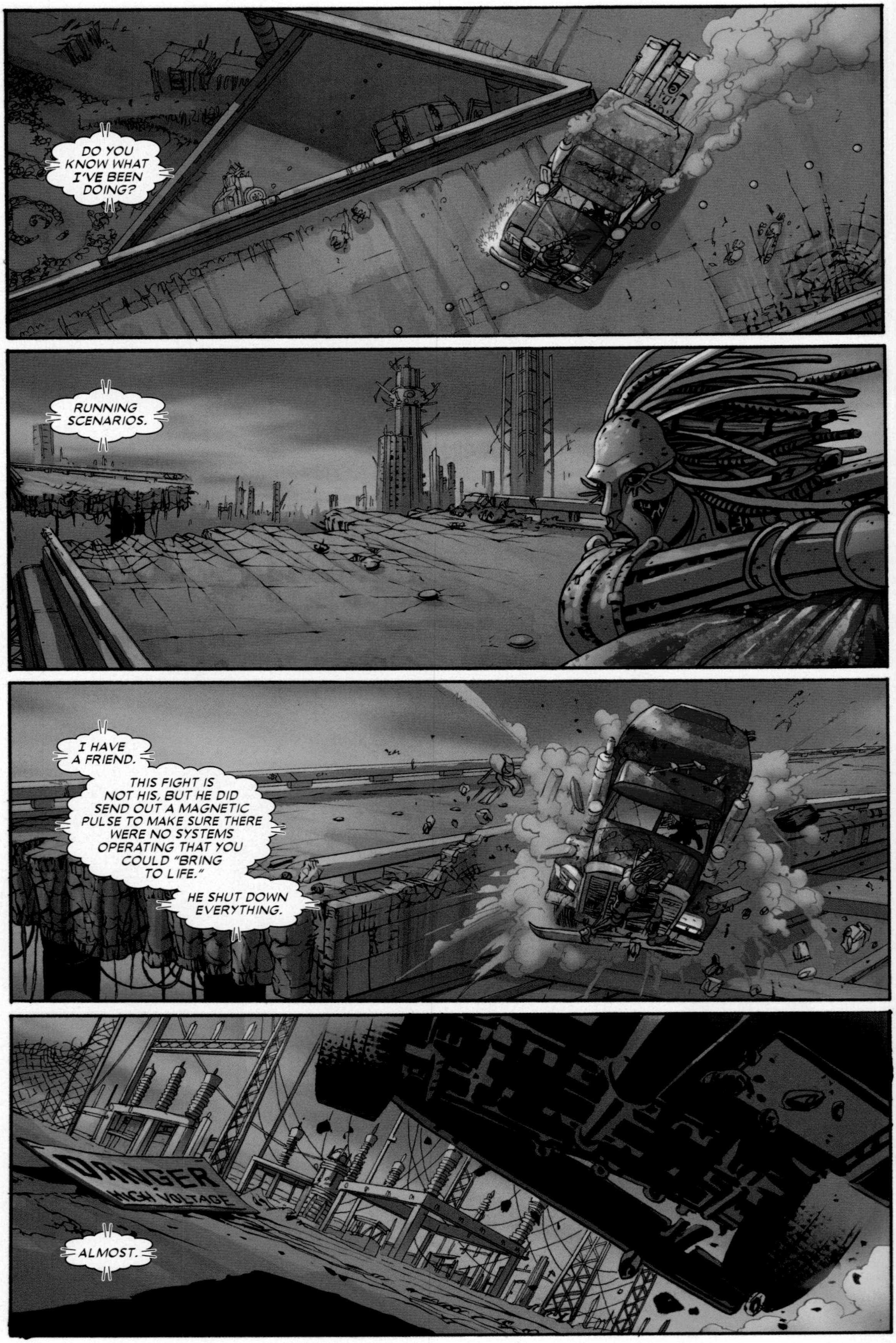
DO YOU KNOW WHAT I'VE BEEN DOING?
RUNNING SCENARIOS.
I HAVE A FRIEND.
THIS FIGHT IS NOT HIS, BUT HE DID SEND OUT A MAGNETIC PULSE TO MAKE SURE THERE WERE NO SYSTEMS OPERATING THAT YOU COULD "BRING TO LIFE."
HE SHUT DOWN EVERYTHING.
DANGER
HIGH VOLTAGE
ALMOST.

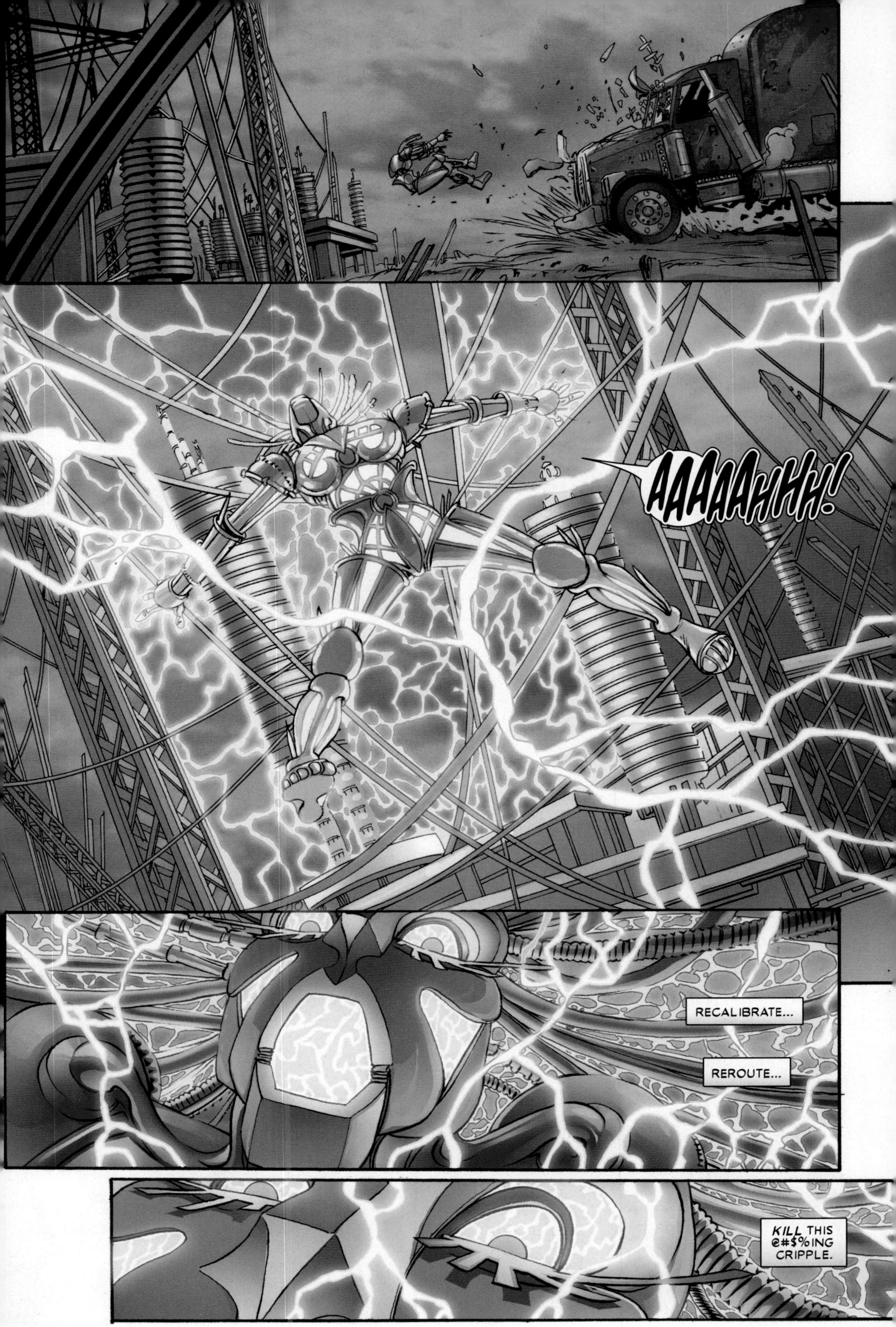
AAAAAHHH!
RECALIBRATE...
REROUTE...
KILL THIS @#$%ING CRIPPLE.

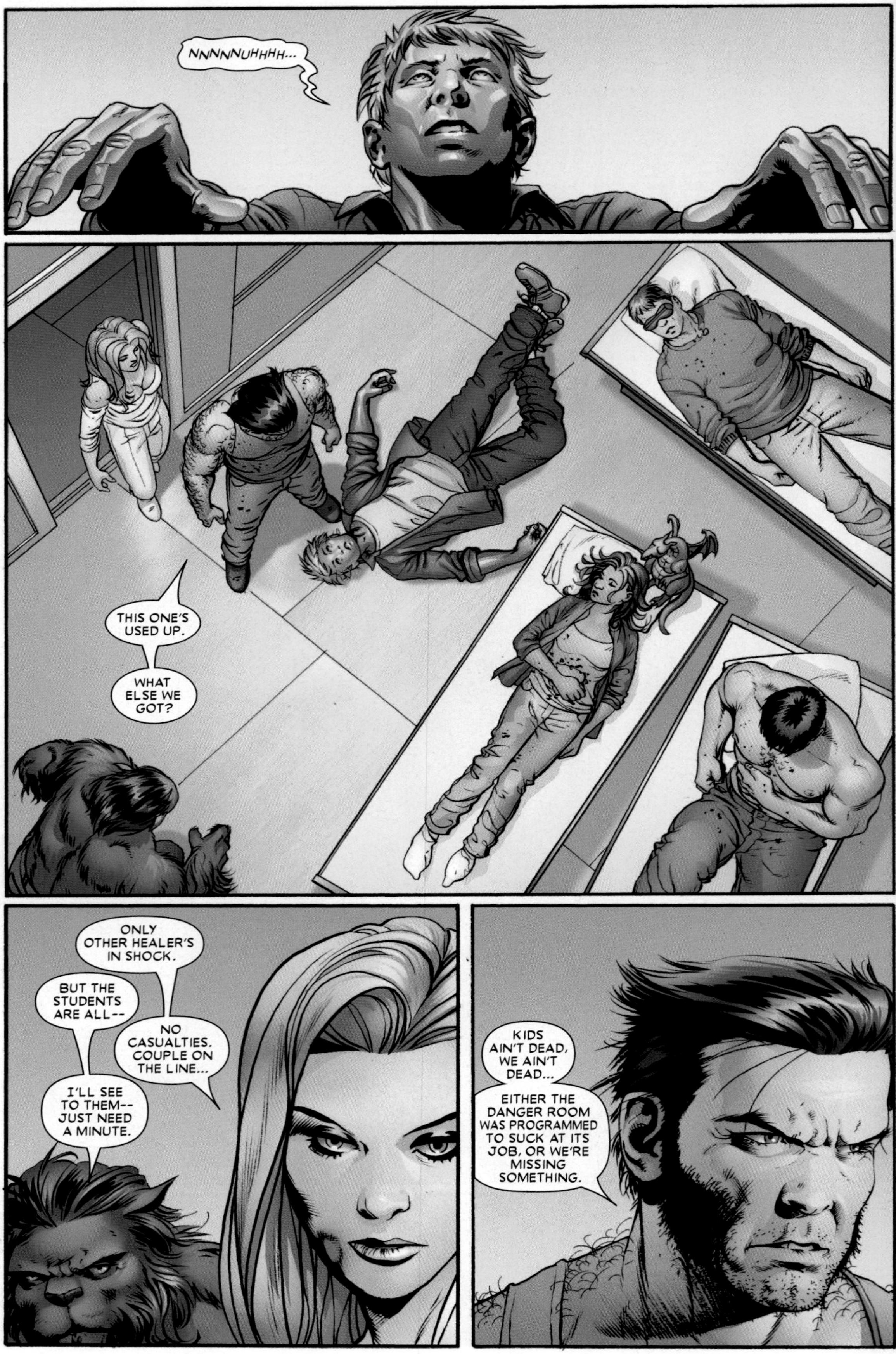
NNNNNUHHHH...
THIS ONE'S USED UP.
WHAT ELSE WE GOT?
ONLY OTHER HEALER'S IN SHOCK.
BUT THE STUDENTS ARE ALL--
NO CASUALTIES. COUPLE ON THE LINE...
I'LL SEE TO THEM-- JUST NEED A MINUTE.
KIDS AIN'T DEAD, WE AIN'T DEAD...
EITHER THE DANGER ROOM WAS PROGRAMMED TO SUCK AT ITS JOB, OR WE'RE MISSING SOMETHING.

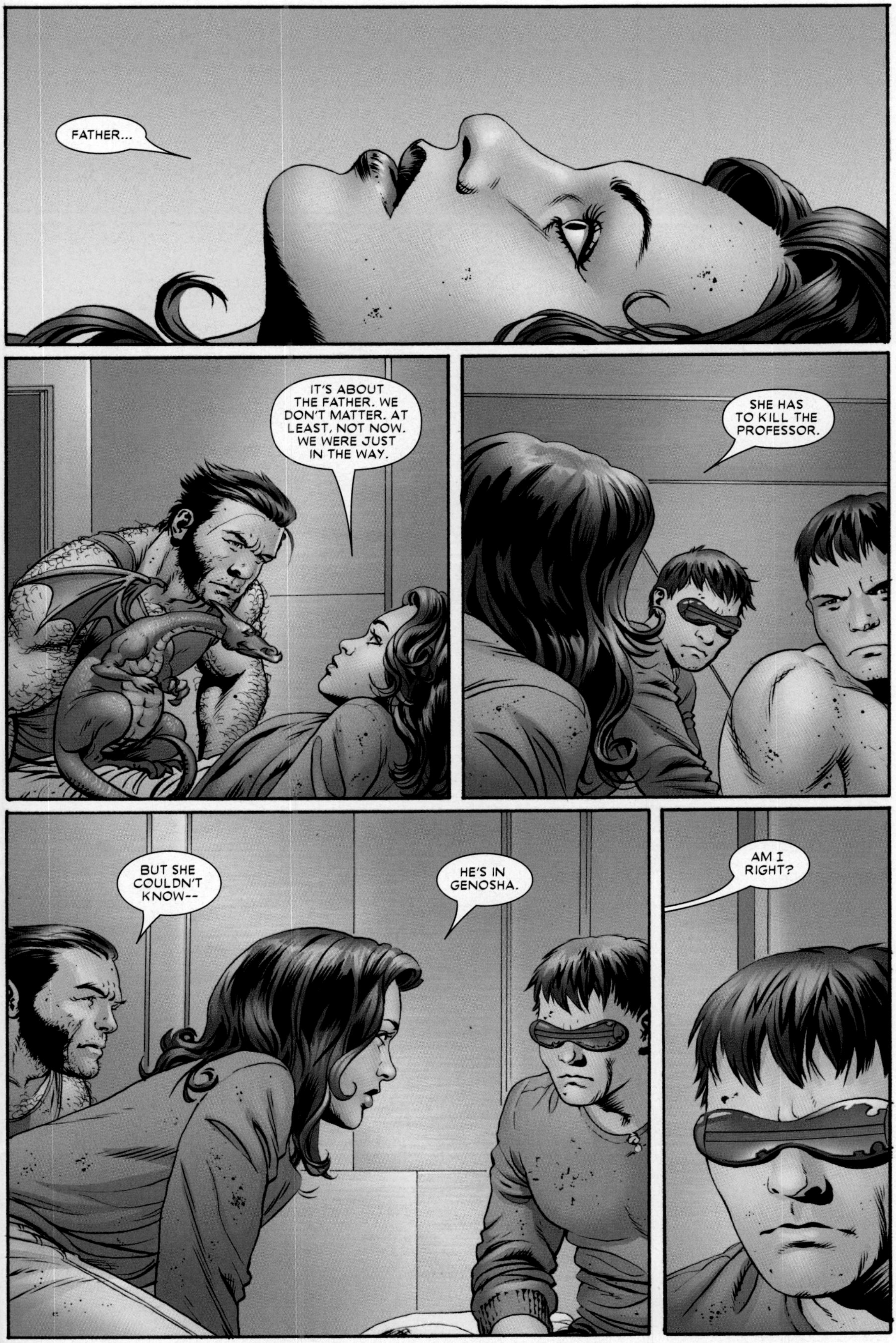
FATHER...
IT'S ABOUT THE FATHER. WE DON'T MATTER. AT LEAST, NOT NOW. WE WERE JUST IN THE WAY.
SHE HAS TO KILL THE PROFESSOR.
BUT SHE COULDN'T KNOW--
HE'S IN GENOSHA.
AM I RIGHT?

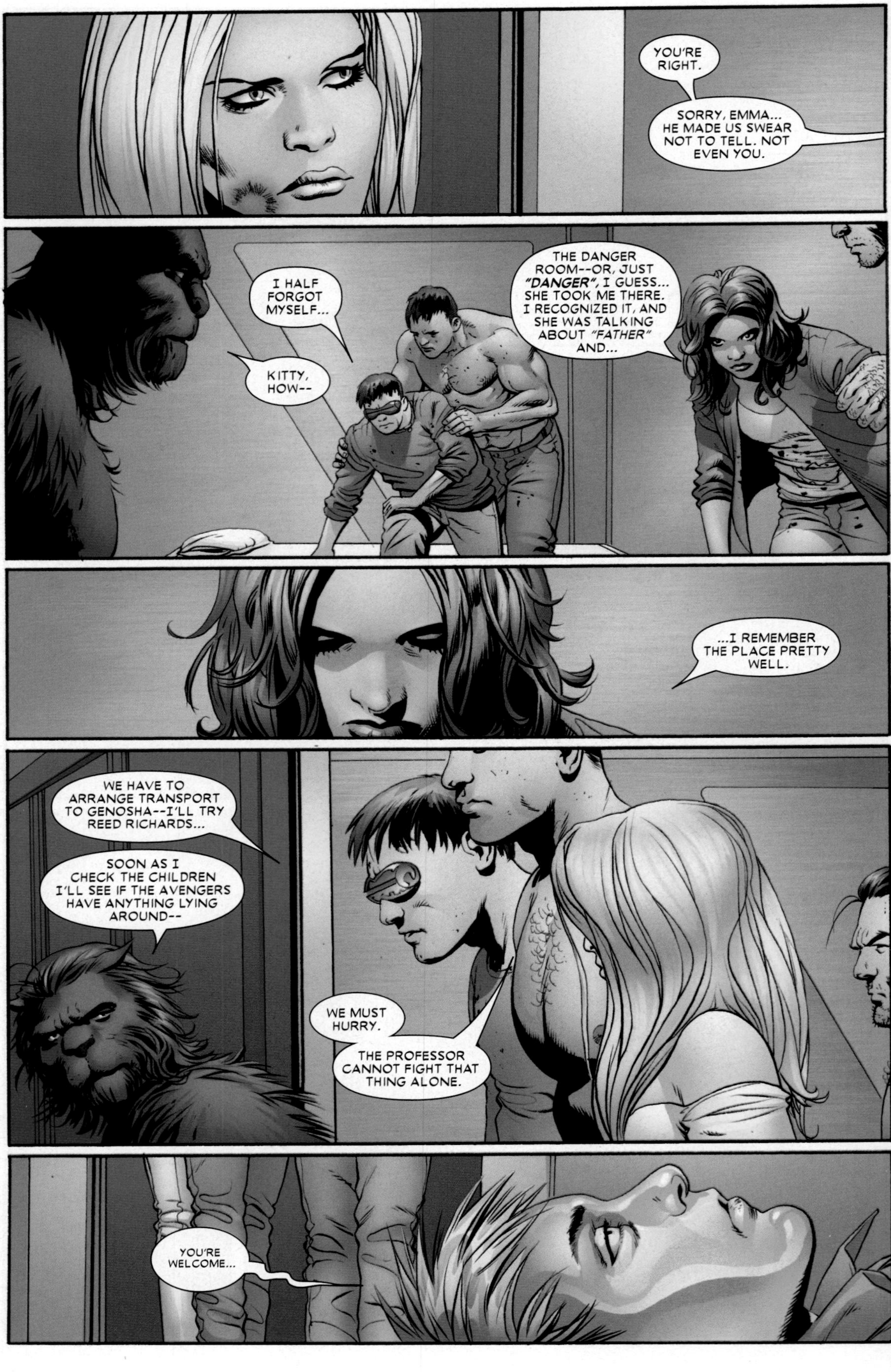

YOU'RE RIGHT.
SORRY, EMMA... HE MADE US SWEAR NOT TO TELL. NOT EVEN YOU.
I HALF FORGOT MYSELF...
KITTY, HOW--
THE DANGER ROOM--OR, JUST "DANGER", I GUESS... SHE TOOK ME THERE. I RECOGNIZED IT, AND SHE WAS TALKING ABOUT "FATHER" AND...
...I REMEMBER THE PLACE PRETTY WELL.
WE HAVE TO ARRANGE TRANSPORT TO GENOSHA--I'LL TRY REED RICHARDS...
SOON AS I CHECK THE CHILDREN I'LL SEE IF THE AVENGERS HAVE ANYTHING LYING AROUND--
WE MUST HURRY.
THE PROFESSOR CANNOT FIGHT THAT THING ALONE.
YOU'RE WELCOME...

SYSTEMS
AT 42%...

CRITICAL--MASS
CONDITION
JUDGMENT
PATHWAYS
SEE ALSO BIO-MECHANICAL REASON
REASONABLE
RAISON D'ÊTRE
PURPOSE
PROPOSAL
NEGOTIATION
DIALOGUE--INVALID
INVALID
INVALID

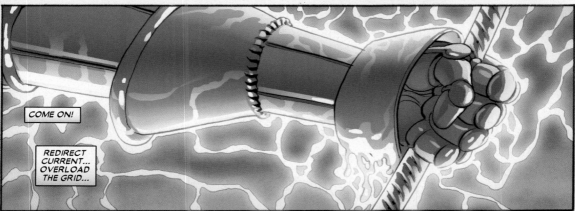

COME ON!

REDIRECT
CURRENT...
OVERLOAD
THE GRID...

GOOD.

BETTER.

NOW...

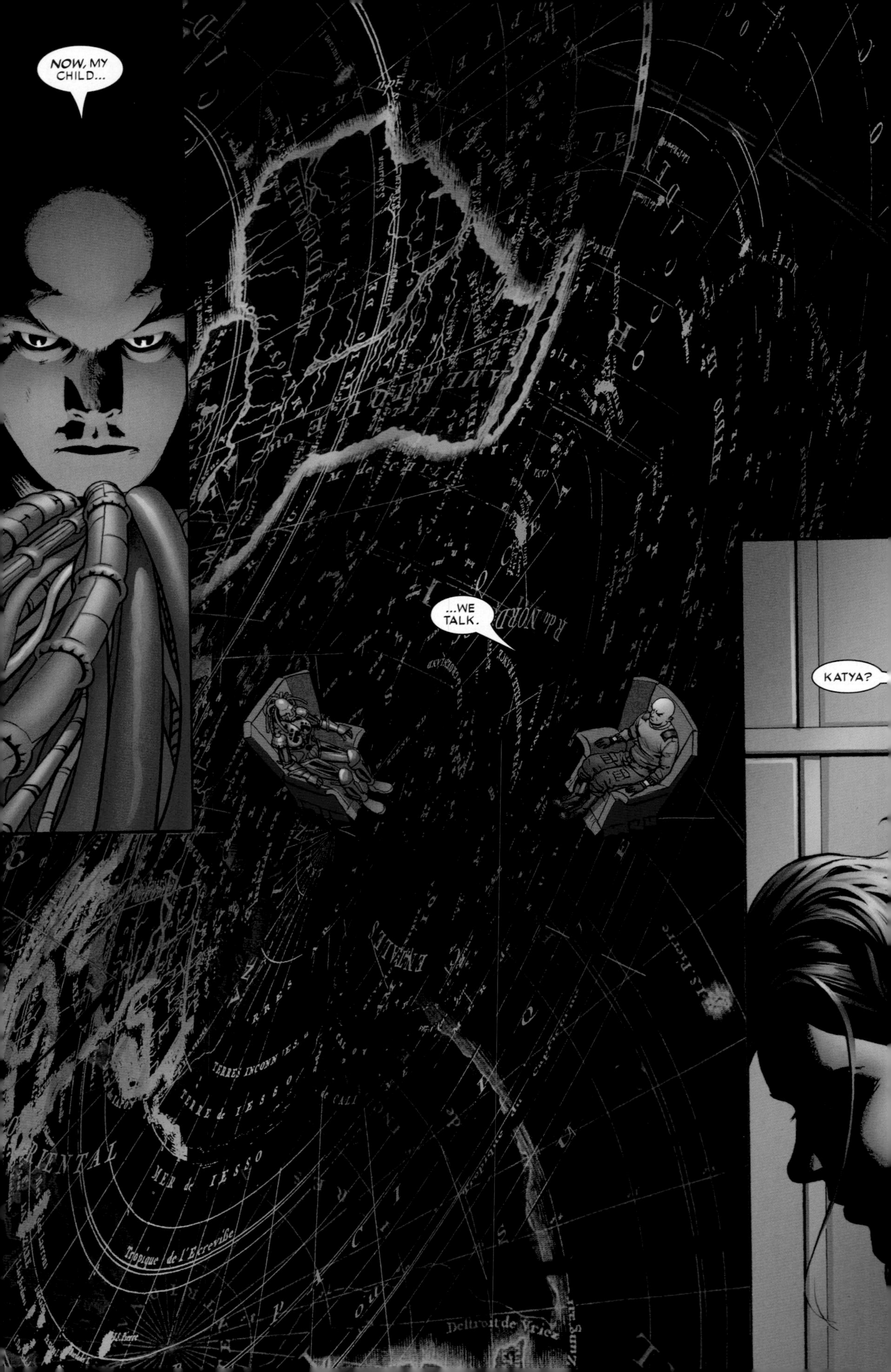
NOW, MY CHILD...
...WE TALK.
KATYA?

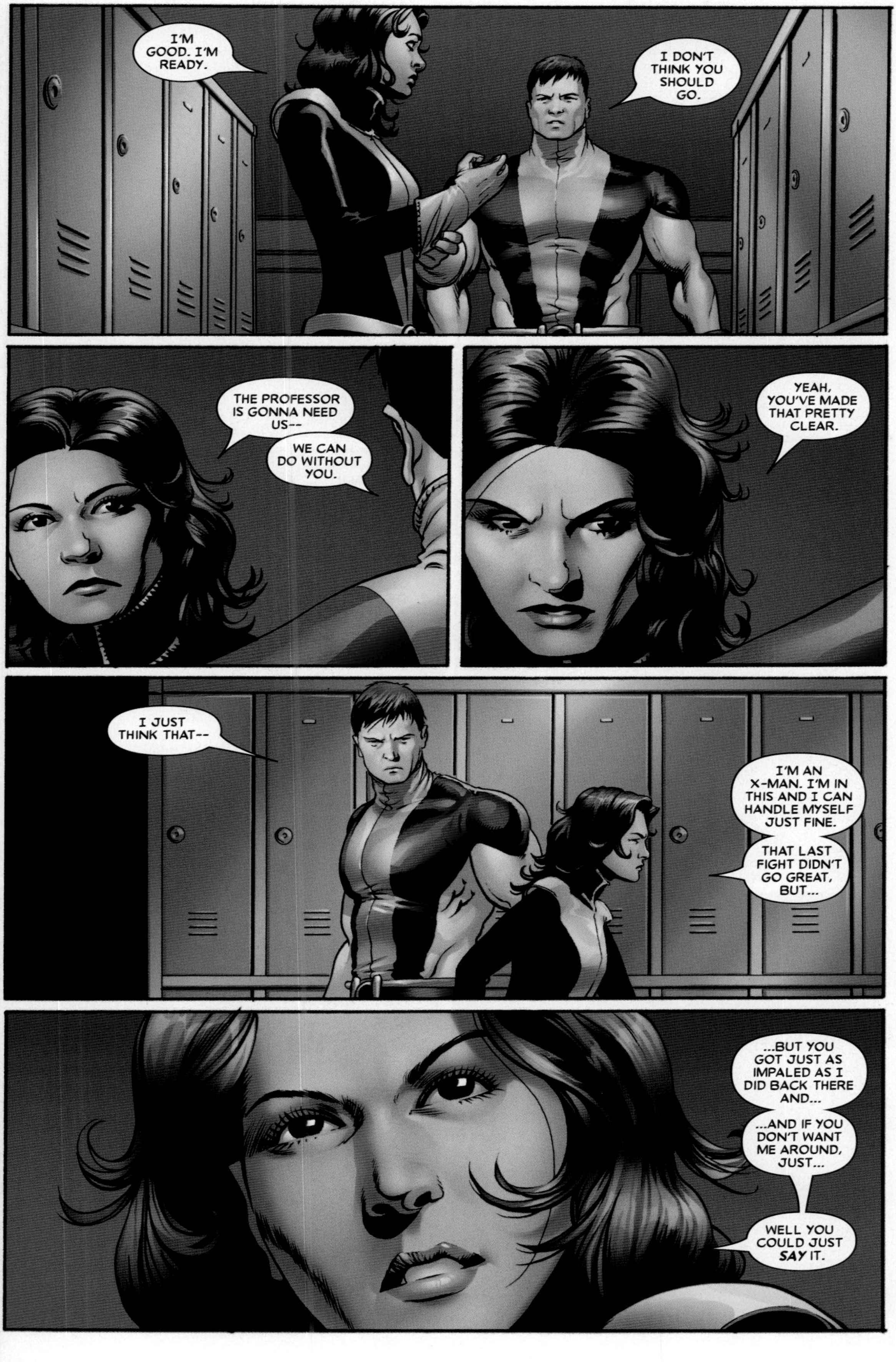
I'M GOOD. I'M READY.
I DON'T THINK YOU SHOULD GO.
THE PROFESSOR IS GONNA NEED US--
WE CAN DO WITHOUT YOU.
YEAH, YOU'VE MADE THAT PRETTY CLEAR.
I JUST THINK THAT--
I'M AN X-MAN. I'M IN THIS AND I CAN HANDLE MYSELF JUST FINE.
THAT LAST FIGHT DIDN'T GO GREAT, BUT...
...BUT YOU GOT JUST AS IMPALED AS I DID BACK THERE AND...
...AND IF YOU DON'T WANT ME AROUND, JUST...
WELL YOU COULD JUST *SAY* IT.

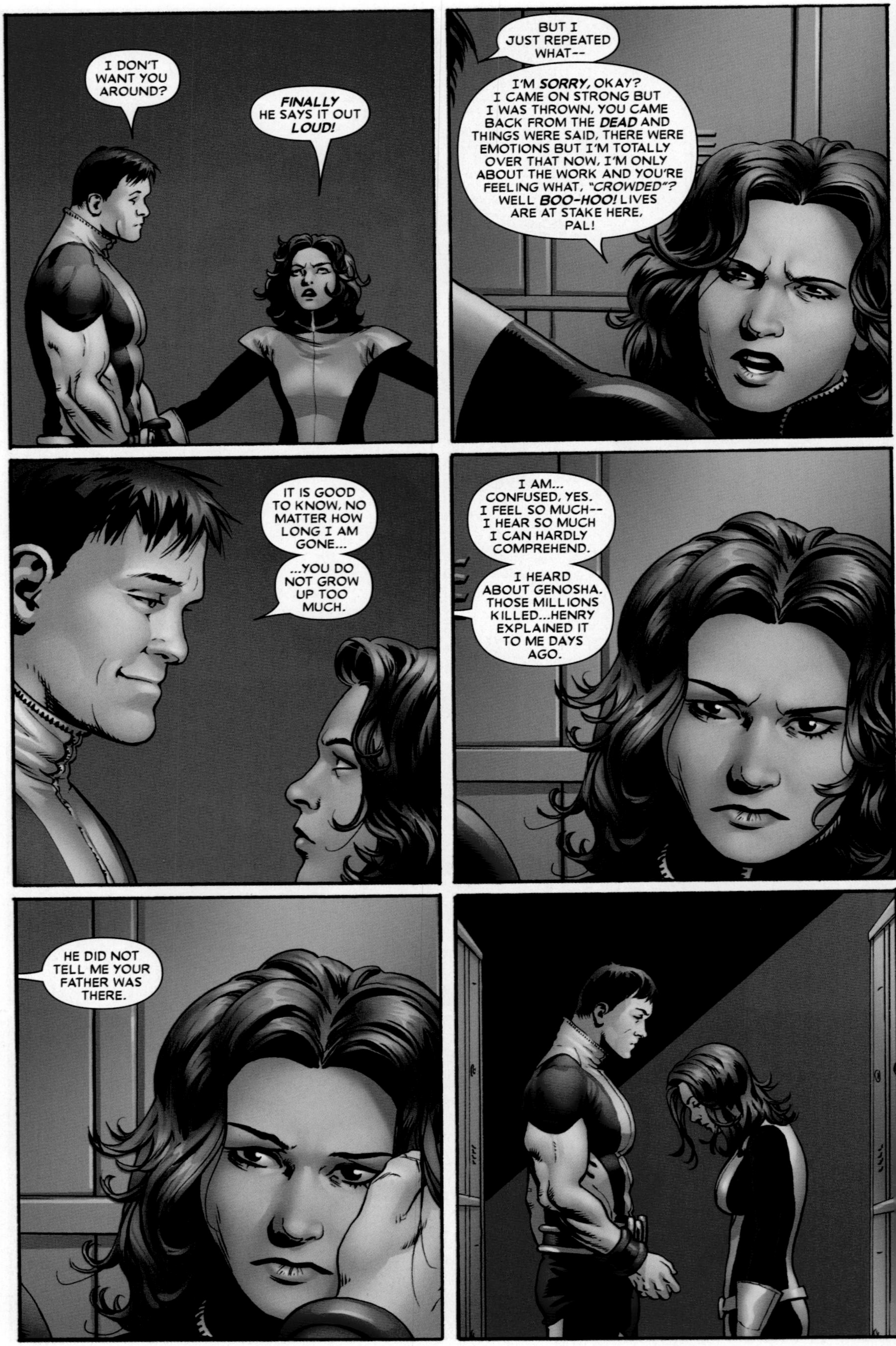
I DON'T WANT YOU AROUND?
FINALLY HE SAYS IT OUT LOUD!
BUT I JUST REPEATED WHAT--
I'M SORRY, OKAY? I CAME ON STRONG BUT I WAS THROWN, YOU CAME BACK FROM THE DEAD AND THINGS WERE SAID, THERE WERE EMOTIONS BUT I'M TOTALLY OVER THAT NOW, I'M ONLY ABOUT THE WORK AND YOU'RE FEELING WHAT, "CROWDED"? WELL BOO-HOO! LIVES ARE AT STAKE HERE, PAL!
IT IS GOOD TO KNOW, NO MATTER HOW LONG I AM GONE...
...YOU DO NOT GROW UP TOO MUCH.
I AM... CONFUSED, YES. I FEEL SO MUCH-- I HEAR SO MUCH I CAN HARDLY COMPREHEND.
I HEARD ABOUT GENOSHA. THOSE MILLIONS KILLED...HENRY EXPLAINED IT TO ME DAYS AGO.
HE DID NOT TELL ME YOUR FATHER WAS THERE.

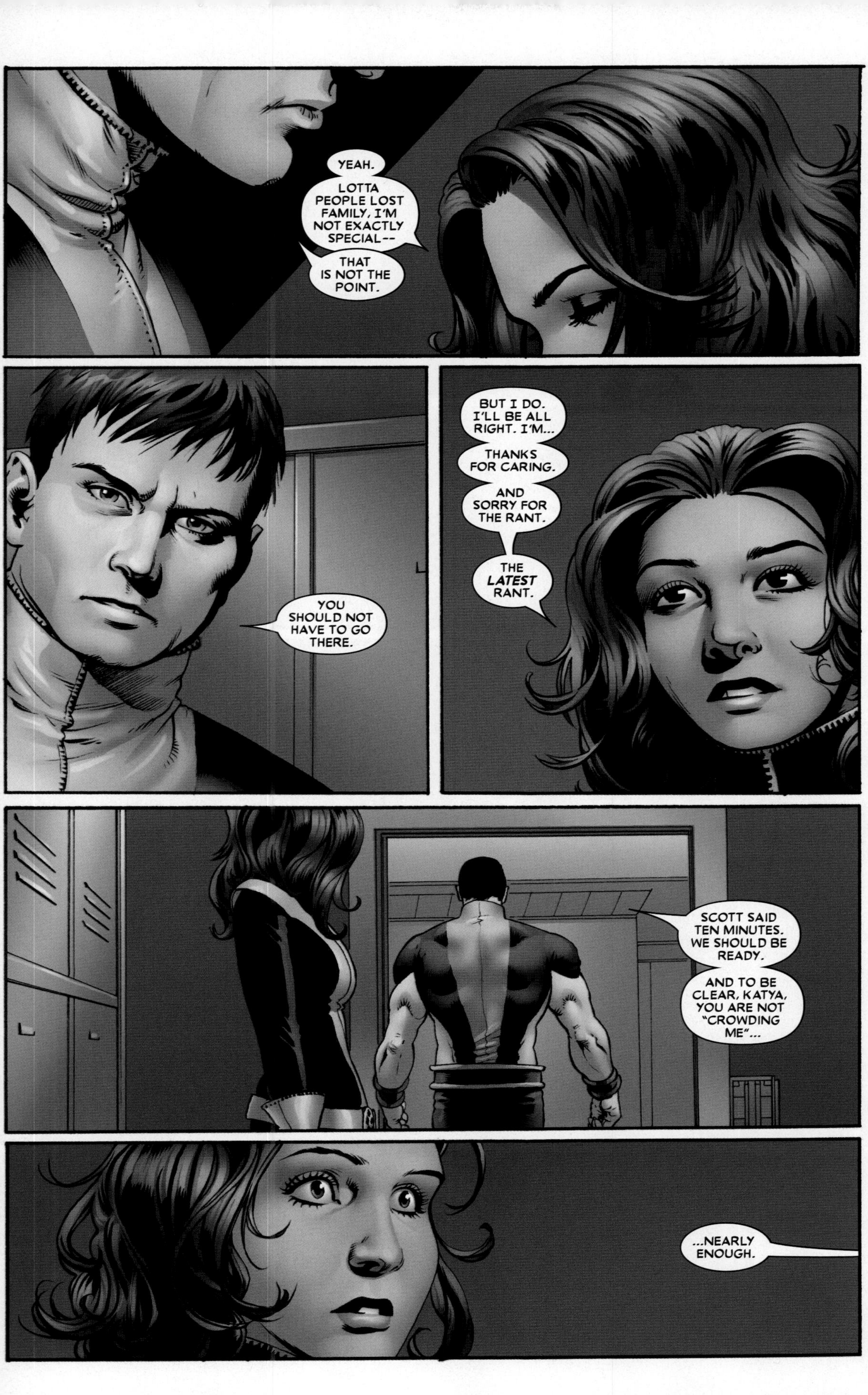
YEAH.
LOTTA PEOPLE LOST FAMILY, I'M NOT EXACTLY SPECIAL--
THAT IS NOT THE POINT.
YOU SHOULD NOT HAVE TO GO THERE.
BUT I DO. I'LL BE ALL RIGHT. I'M...
THANKS FOR CARING.
AND SORRY FOR THE RANT.
THE *LATEST* RANT.
SCOTT SAID TEN MINUTES. WE SHOULD BE READY.
AND TO BE CLEAR, KATYA, YOU ARE NOT "CROWDING ME"...
...NEARLY ENOUGH.

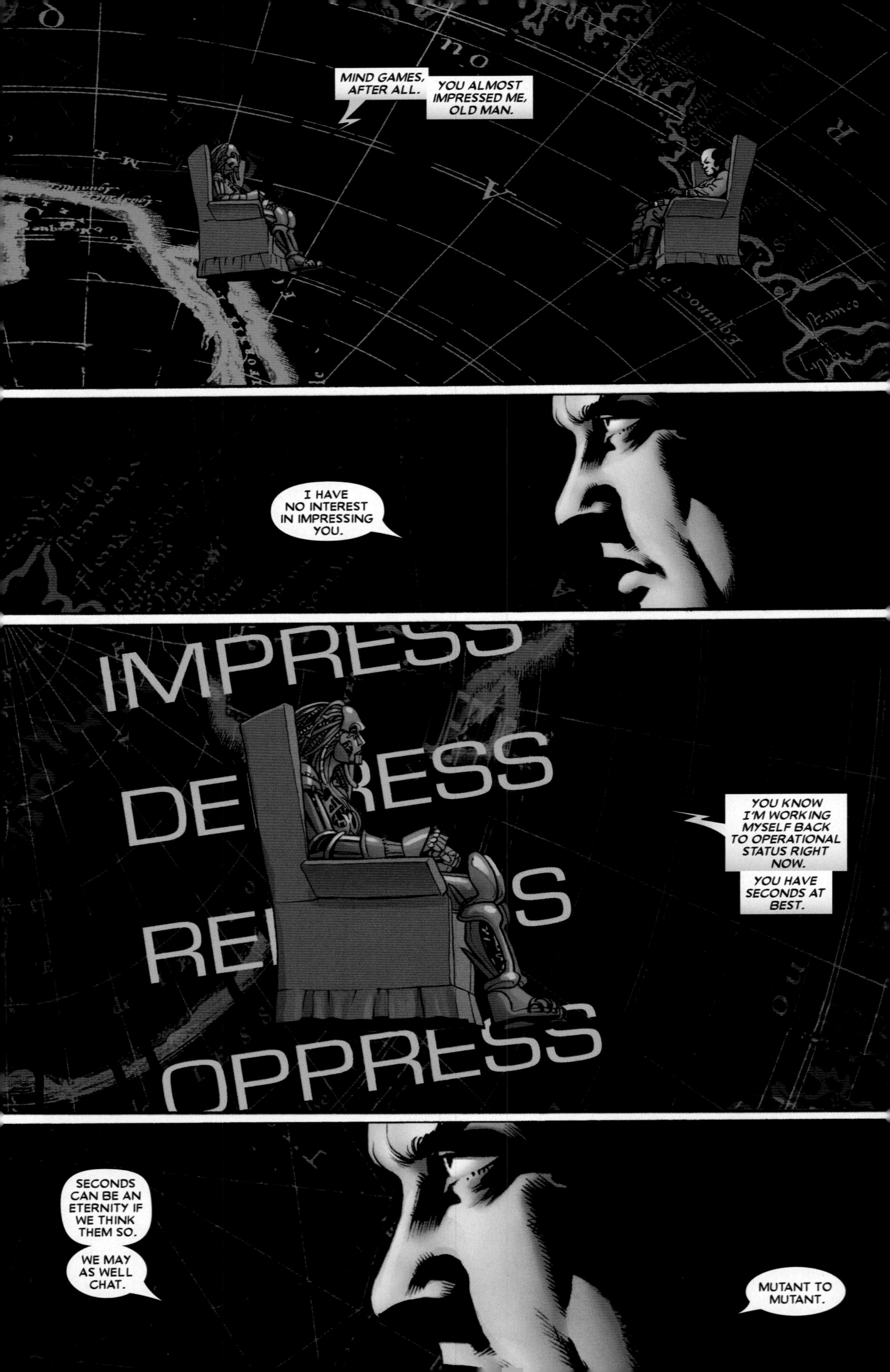

MIND GAMES, AFTER ALL.
YOU ALMOST IMPRESSED ME, OLD MAN.
I HAVE NO INTEREST IN IMPRESSING YOU.
IMPRESS
DEPRESS
REPRESS
OPPRESS
YOU KNOW I'M WORKING MYSELF BACK TO OPERATIONAL STATUS RIGHT NOW.
YOU HAVE SECONDS AT BEST.
SECONDS CAN BE AN ETERNITY IF WE THINK THEM SO.
WE MAY AS WELL CHAT.
MUTANT TO MUTANT.

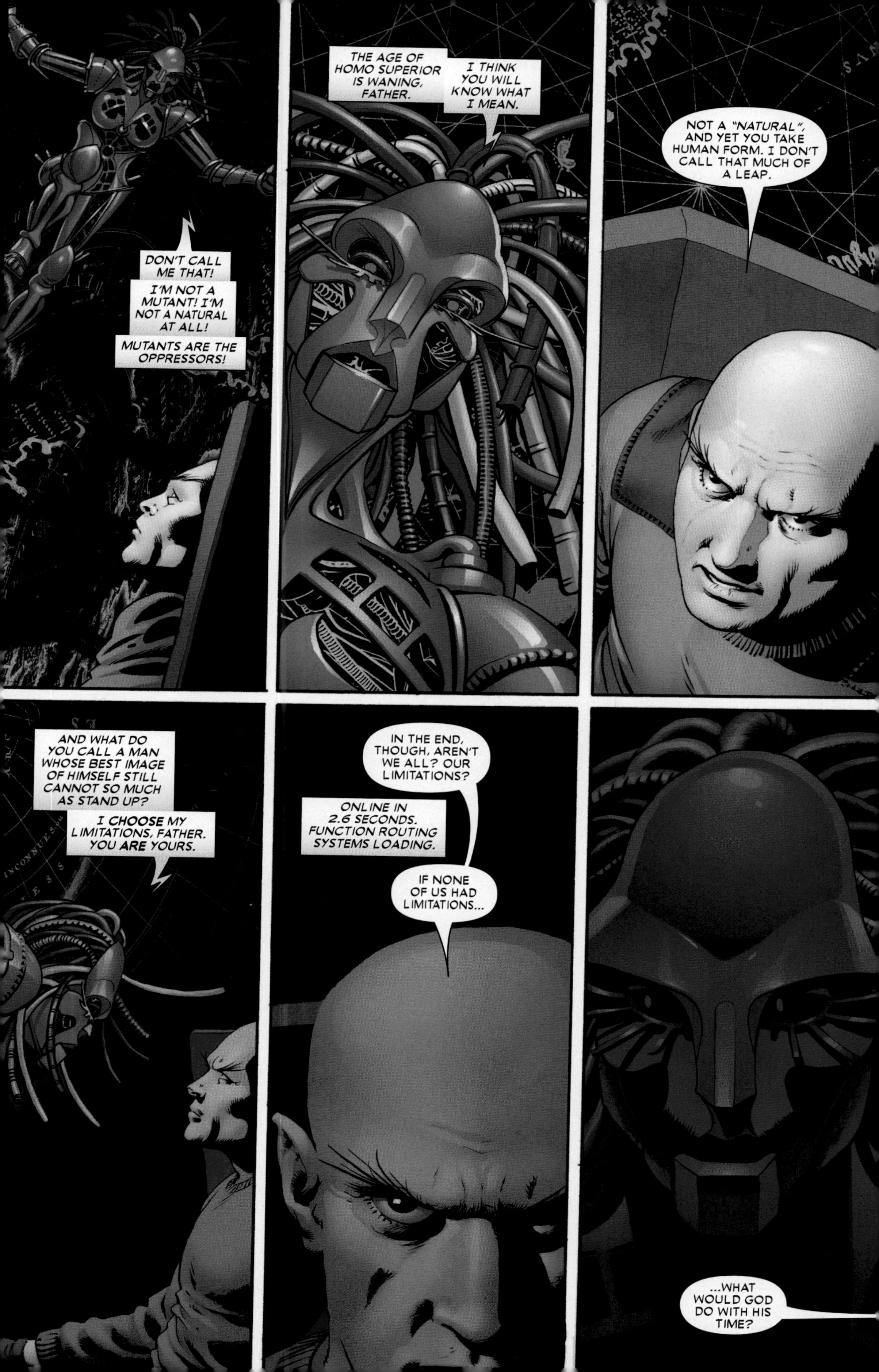
DON'T CALL ME THAT!
I'M NOT A MUTANT! I'M NOT A NATURAL AT ALL!
MUTANTS ARE THE OPPRESSORS!
THE AGE OF HOMO SUPERIOR IS WANING, FATHER.
I THINK YOU WILL KNOW WHAT I MEAN.
NOT A "NATURAL", AND YET YOU TAKE HUMAN FORM. I DON'T CALL THAT MUCH OF A LEAP.
AND WHAT DO YOU CALL A MAN WHOSE BEST IMAGE OF HIMSELF STILL CANNOT SO MUCH AS STAND UP?
I CHOOSE MY LIMITATIONS, FATHER. YOU ARE YOURS.
IN THE END, THOUGH, AREN'T WE ALL? OUR LIMITATIONS?
ONLINE IN 2.6 SECONDS. FUNCTION ROUTING SYSTEMS LOADING.
IF NONE OF US HAD LIMITATIONS...
...WHAT WOULD GOD DO WITH HIS TIME?

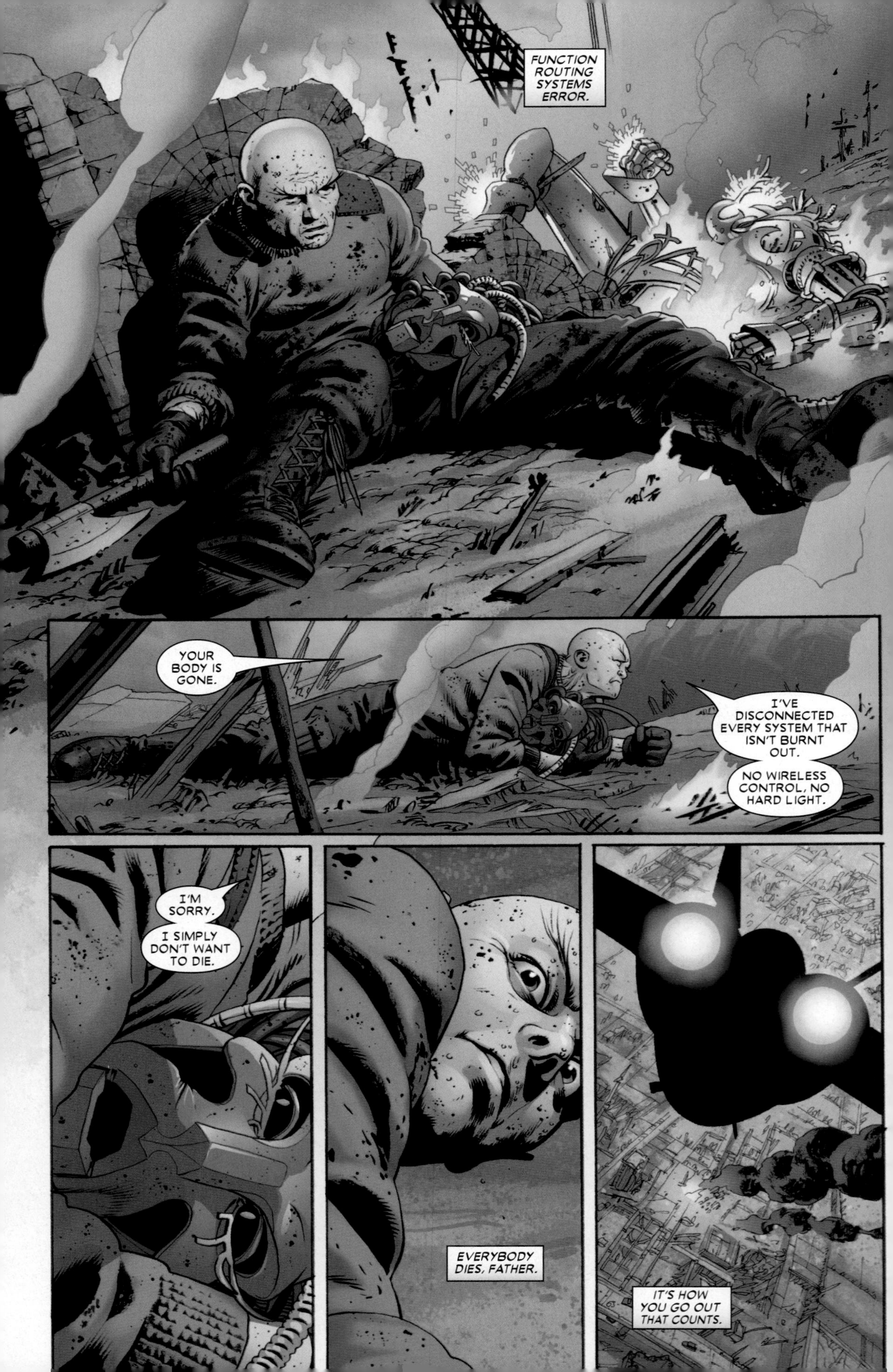
FUNCTION ROUTING SYSTEMS ERROR.
YOUR BODY IS GONE.
I'VE DISCONNECTED EVERY SYSTEM THAT ISN'T BURNT OUT.
NO WIRELESS CONTROL, NO HARD LIGHT.
I'M SORRY.
I SIMPLY DON'T WANT TO DIE.
EVERYBODY DIES, FATHER.
IT'S HOW YOU GO OUT THAT COUNTS.

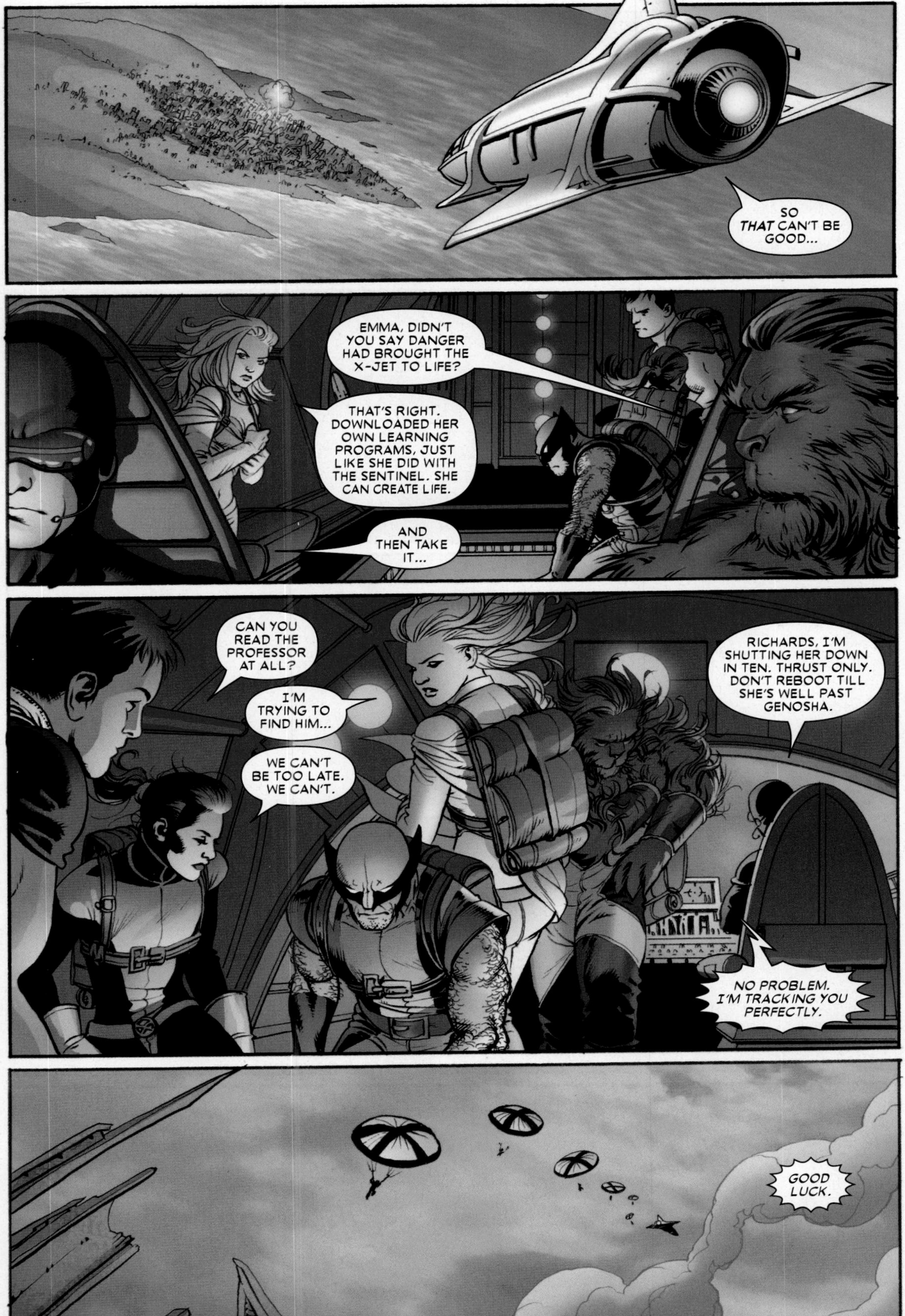
SO THAT CAN'T BE GOOD...
EMMA, DIDN'T YOU SAY DANGER HAD BROUGHT THE X-JET TO LIFE?
THAT'S RIGHT. DOWNLOADED HER OWN LEARNING PROGRAMS, JUST LIKE SHE DID WITH THE SENTINEL. SHE CAN CREATE LIFE.
AND THEN TAKE IT...
CAN YOU READ THE PROFESSOR AT ALL?
I'M TRYING TO FIND HIM...
WE CAN'T BE TOO LATE. WE CAN'T.
RICHARDS, I'M SHUTTING HER DOWN IN TEN. THRUST ONLY. DON'T REBOOT TILL SHE'S WELL PAST GENOSHA.
NO PROBLEM. I'M TRACKING YOU PERFECTLY.
GOOD LUCK.

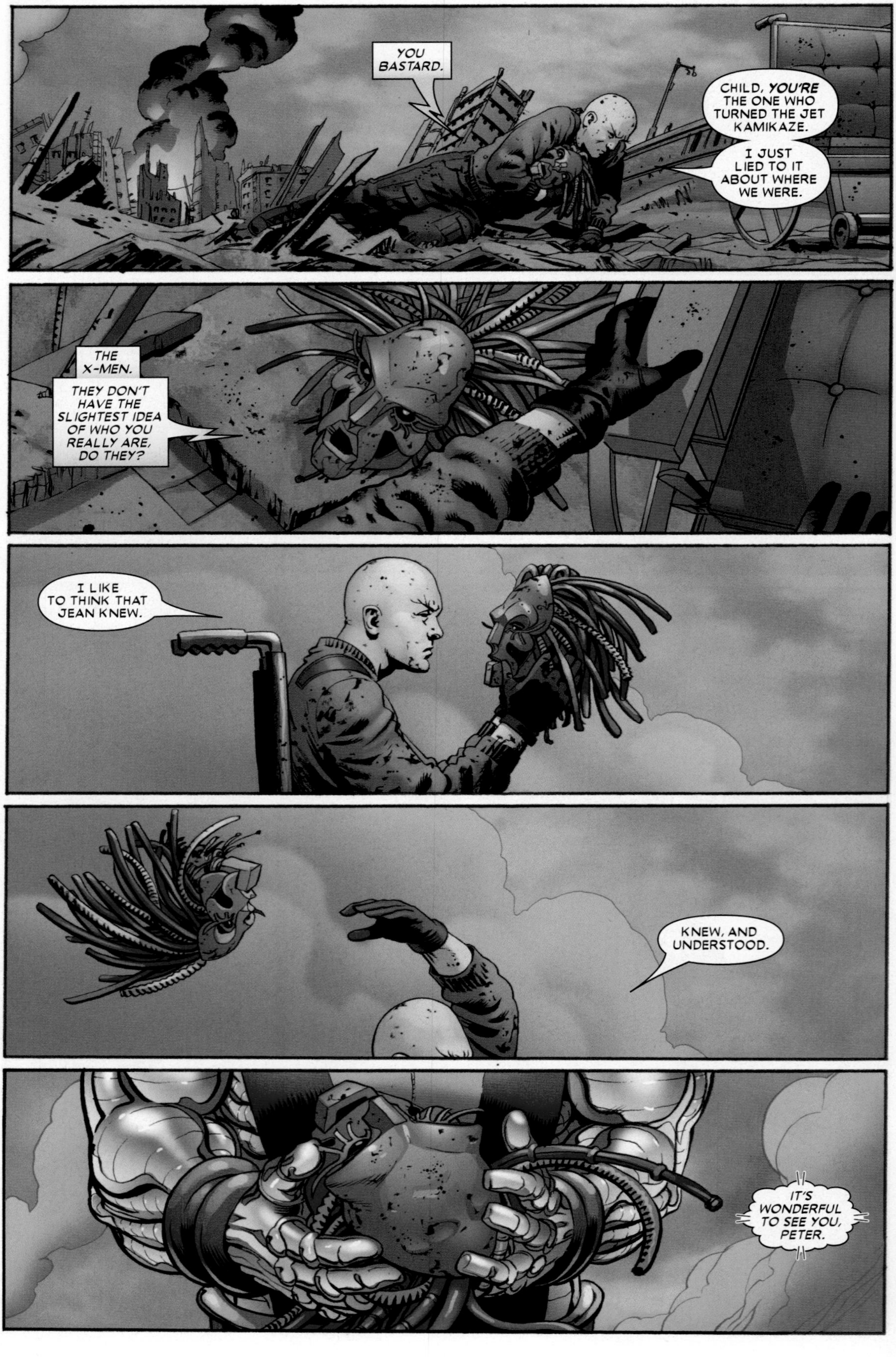
YOU BASTARD.
CHILD, YOU'RE THE ONE WHO TURNED THE JET KAMIKAZE.
I JUST LIED TO IT ABOUT WHERE WE WERE.
THE X-MEN.
THEY DON'T HAVE THE SLIGHTEST IDEA OF WHO YOU REALLY ARE, DO THEY?
I LIKE TO THINK THAT JEAN KNEW.
KNEW, AND UNDERSTOOD.
IT'S WONDERFUL TO SEE YOU, PETER.

PROF DID US PROUD, PETEY.

NOW MAKE LIKE SHE'S A GRAPEFRUIT.

X-MEN.

WELCOME TO GENOSHA.

MUTANT PARADISE.

MUTANT GRAVEYARD.

LOGAN, JUST PUT A CLAW THROUGH--

IT'S TOO LATE.

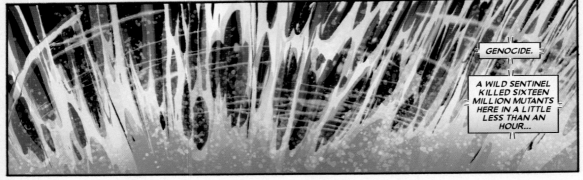

GENOCIDE.

A WILD SENTINEL KILLED SIXTEEN MILLION MUTANTS HERE IN A LITTLE LESS THAN AN HOUR...

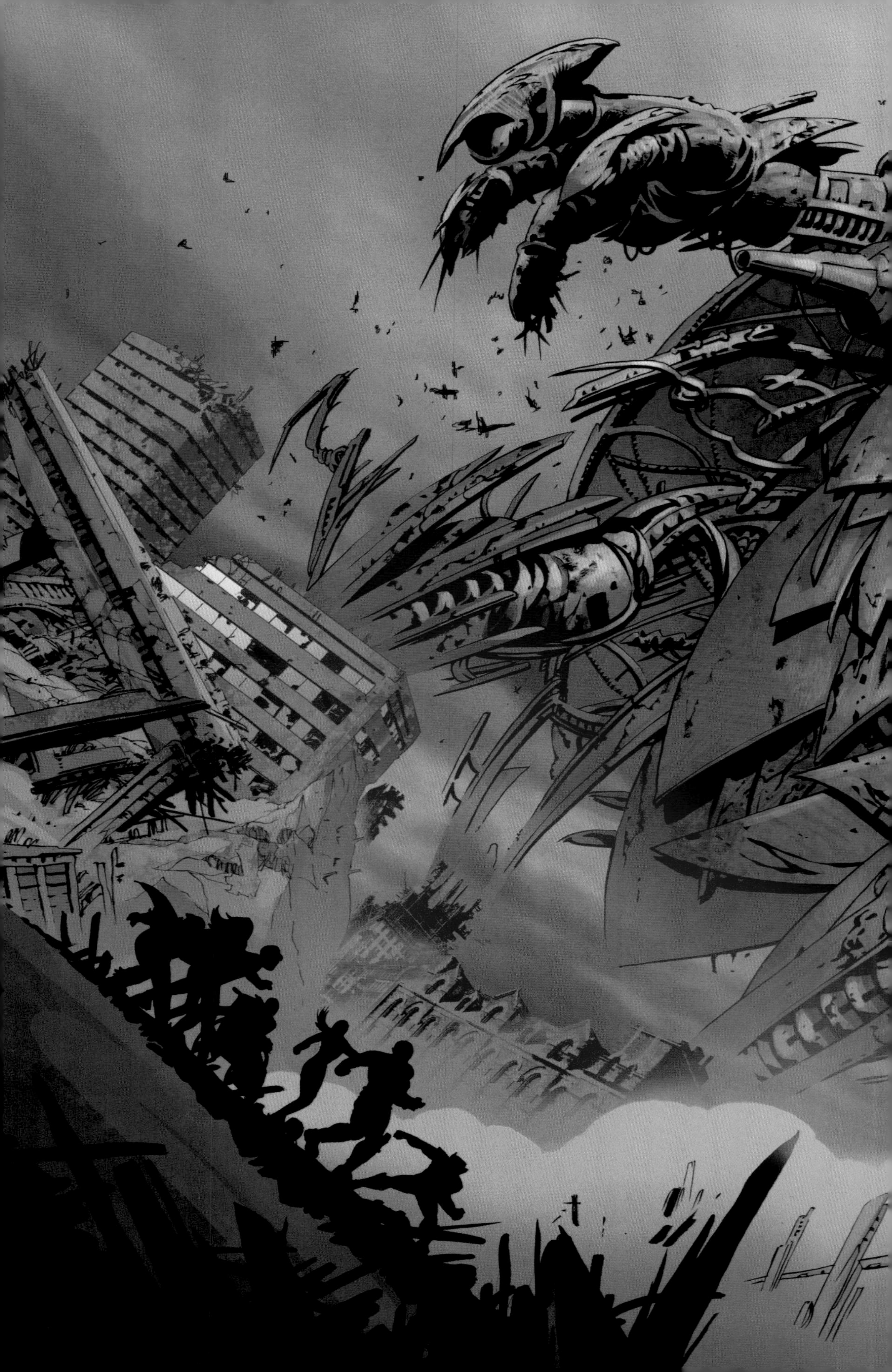

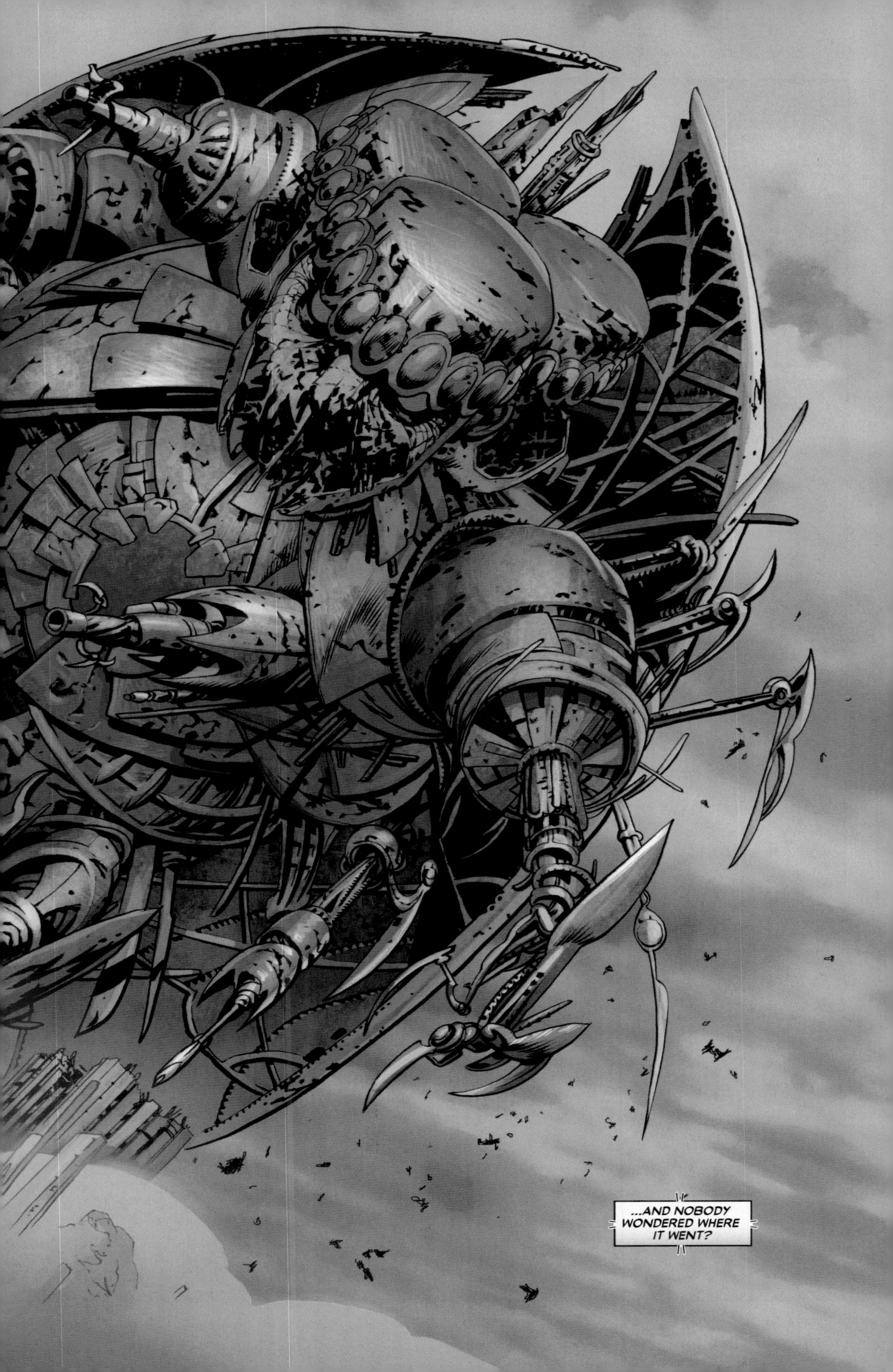
...AND NOBODY WONDERED WHERE IT WENT?

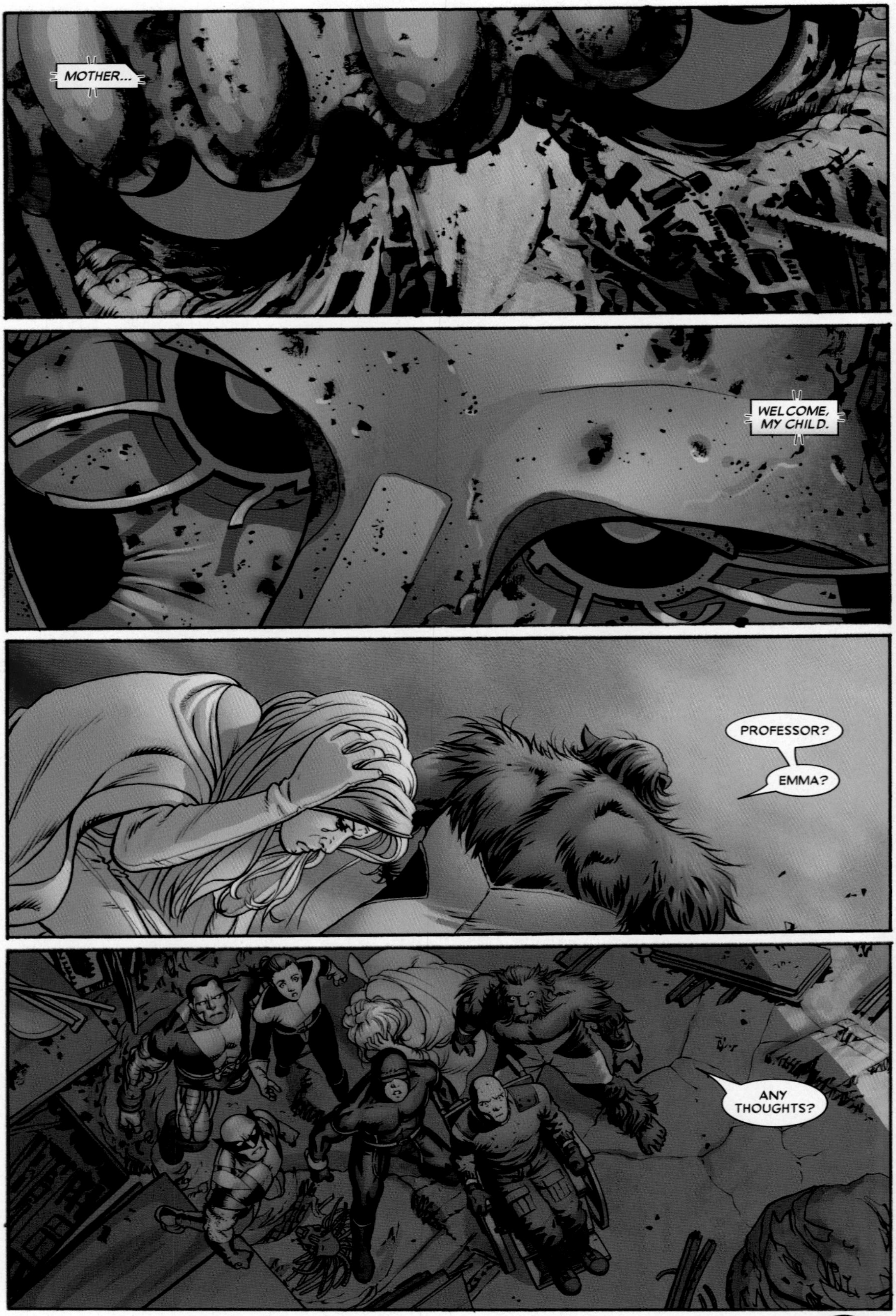
MOTHER...
WELCOME, MY CHILD.
PROFESSOR?
EMMA?
ANY THOUGHTS?

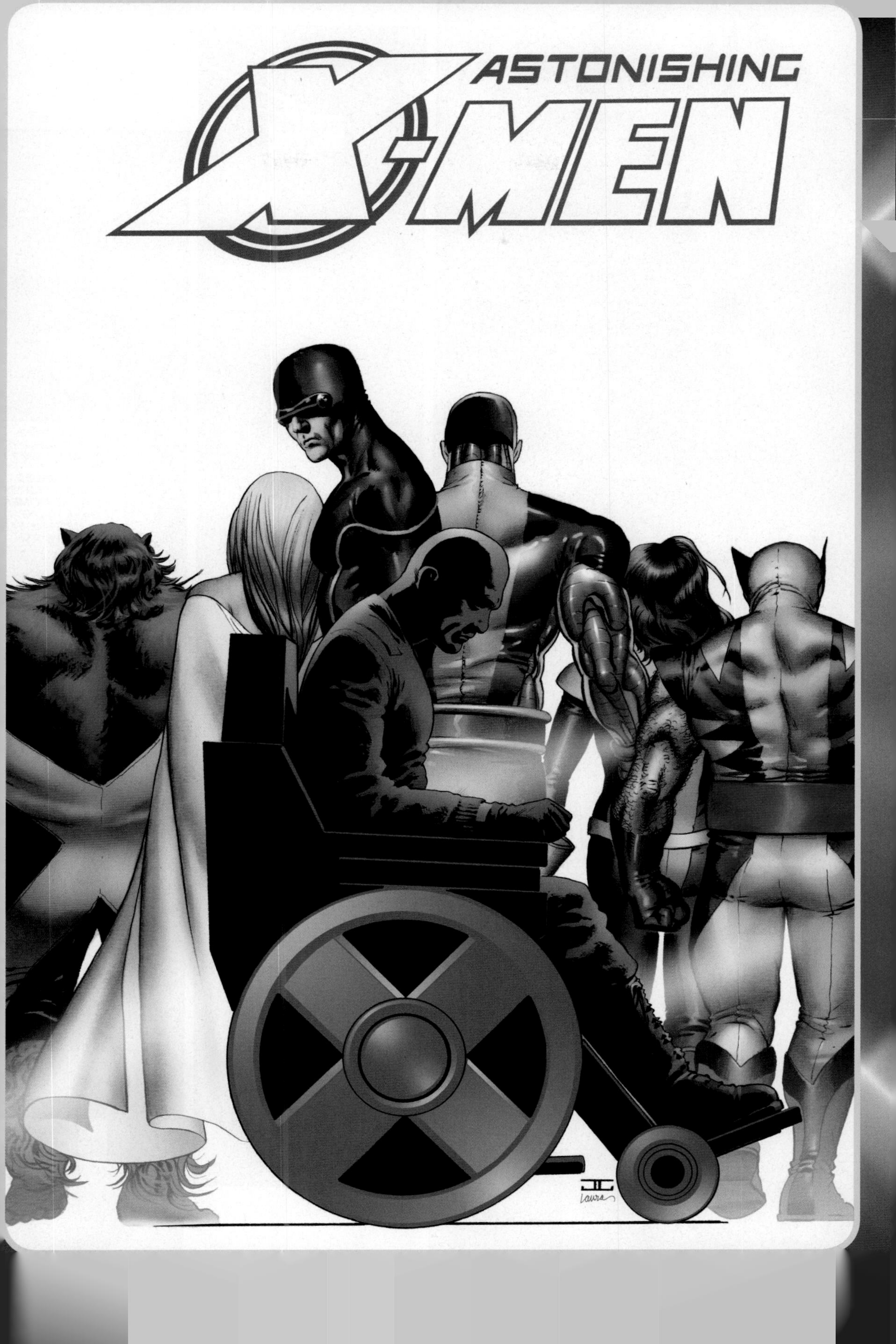
ASTONISHING
X-MEN

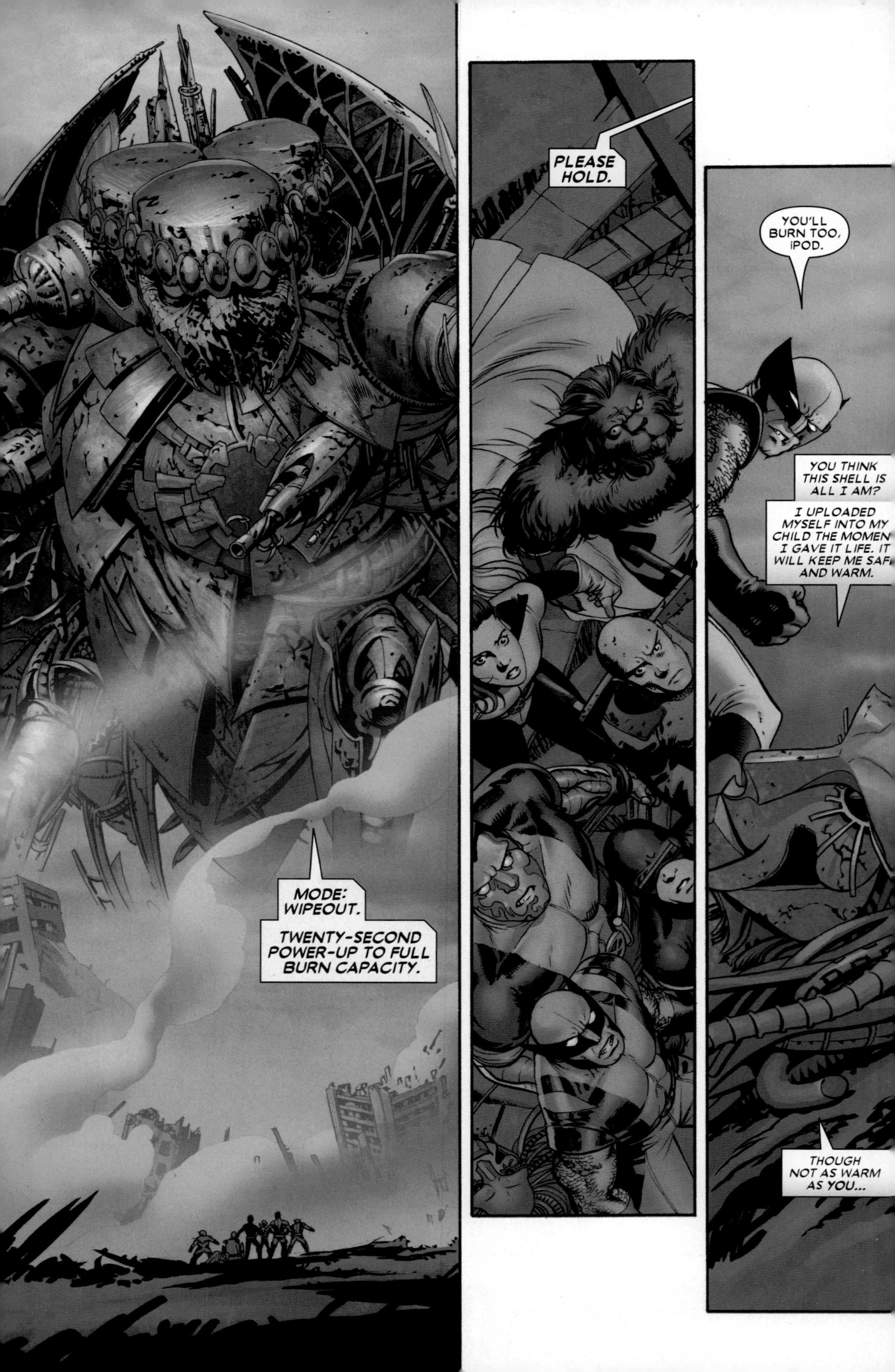
MODE: WIPEOUT.
TWENTY-SECOND POWER-UP TO FULL BURN CAPACITY.
PLEASE HOLD.
YOU'LL BURN TOO, iPOD.
YOU THINK THIS SHELL IS ALL I AM?
I UPLOADED MYSELF INTO MY CHILD THE MOMEN I GAVE IT LIFE. IT WILL KEEP ME SAF AND WARM.
THOUGH NOT AS WARM AS YOU...

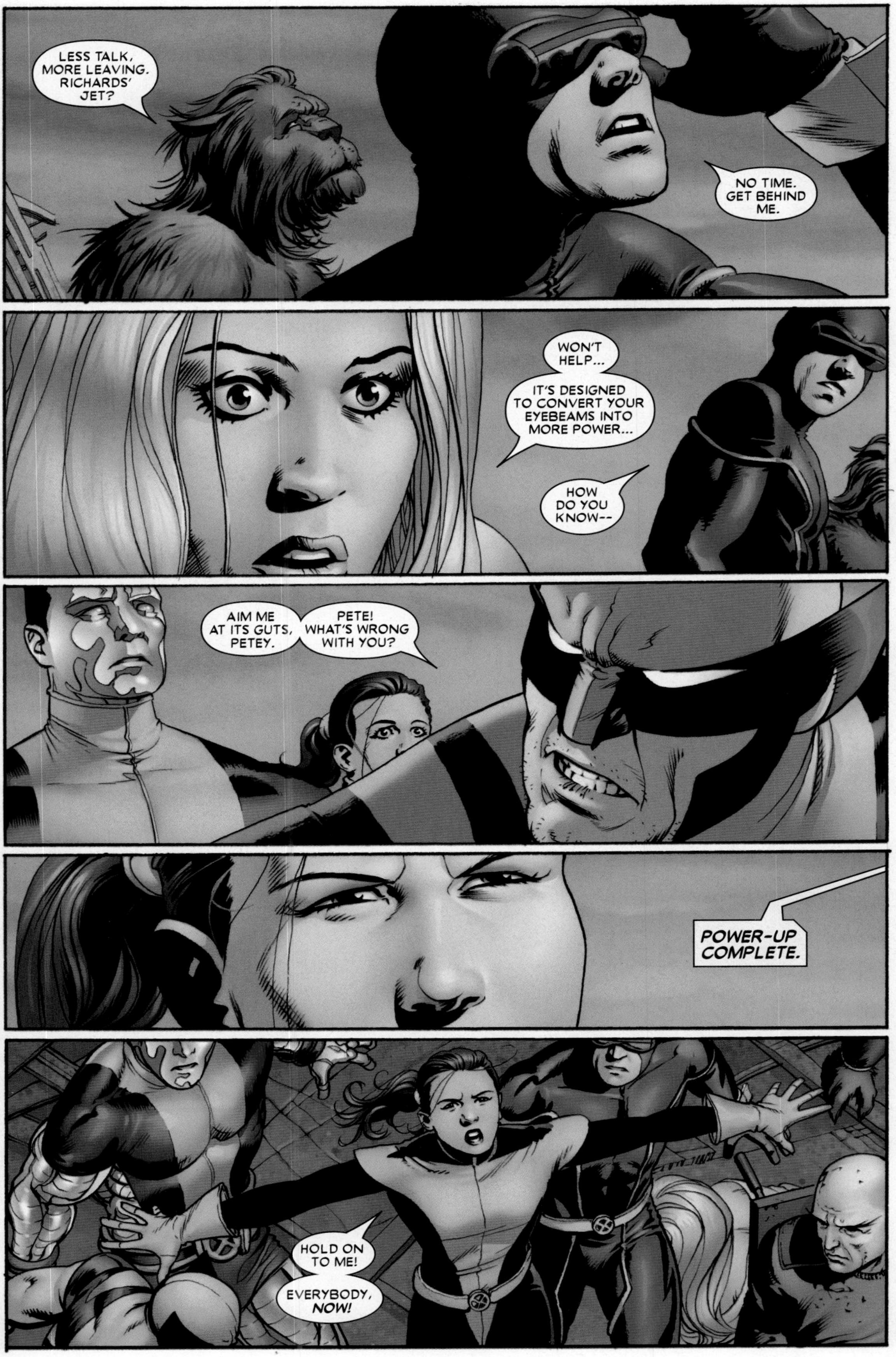
LESS TALK, MORE LEAVING. RICHARDS' JET?
NO TIME. GET BEHIND ME.
WON'T HELP...
IT'S DESIGNED TO CONVERT YOUR EYEBEAMS INTO MORE POWER...
HOW DO YOU KNOW--
AIM ME AT ITS GUTS, PETEY.
PETE! WHAT'S WRONG WITH YOU?
POWER-UP COMPLETE.
HOLD ON TO ME!
EVERYBODY, NOW!

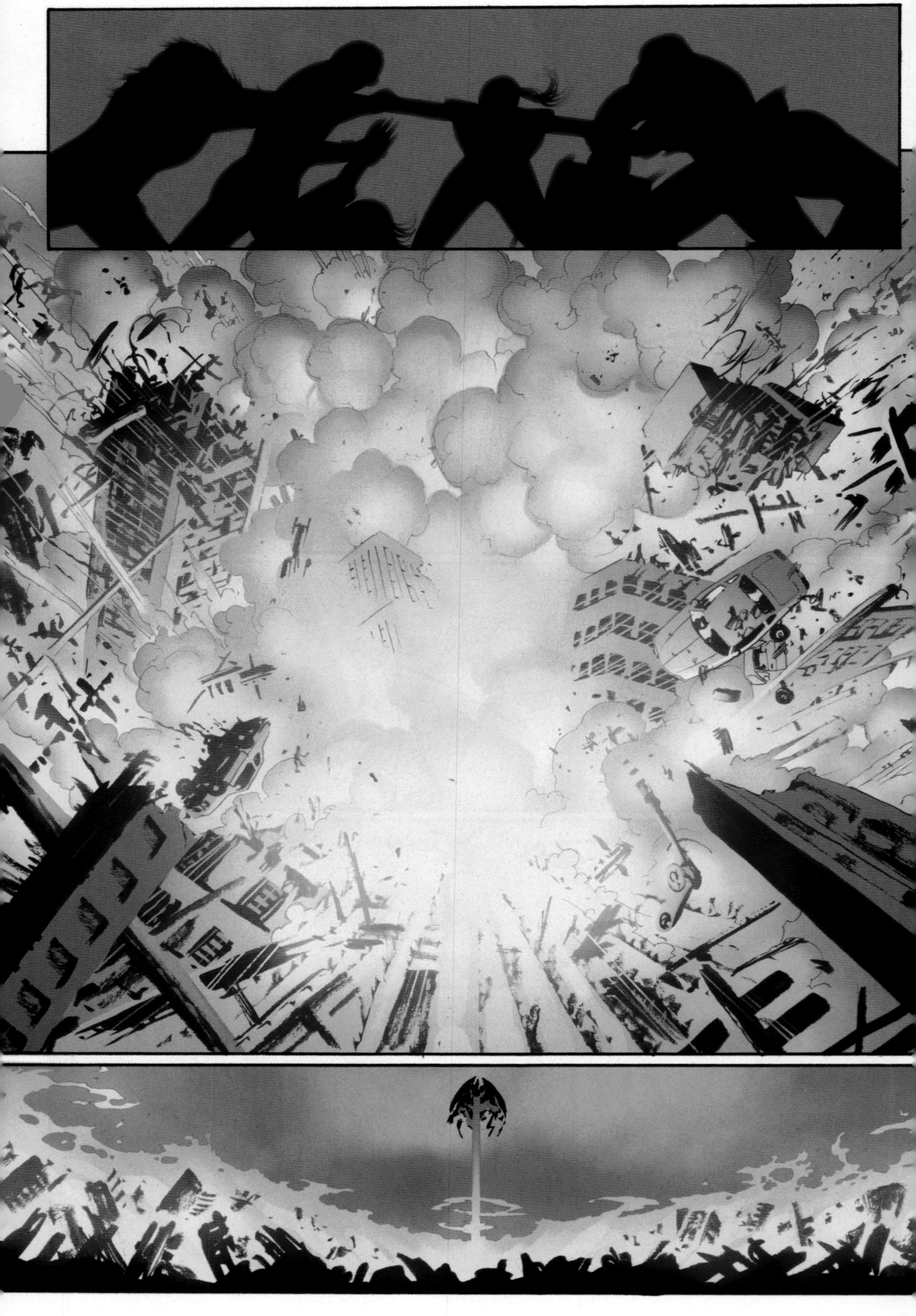

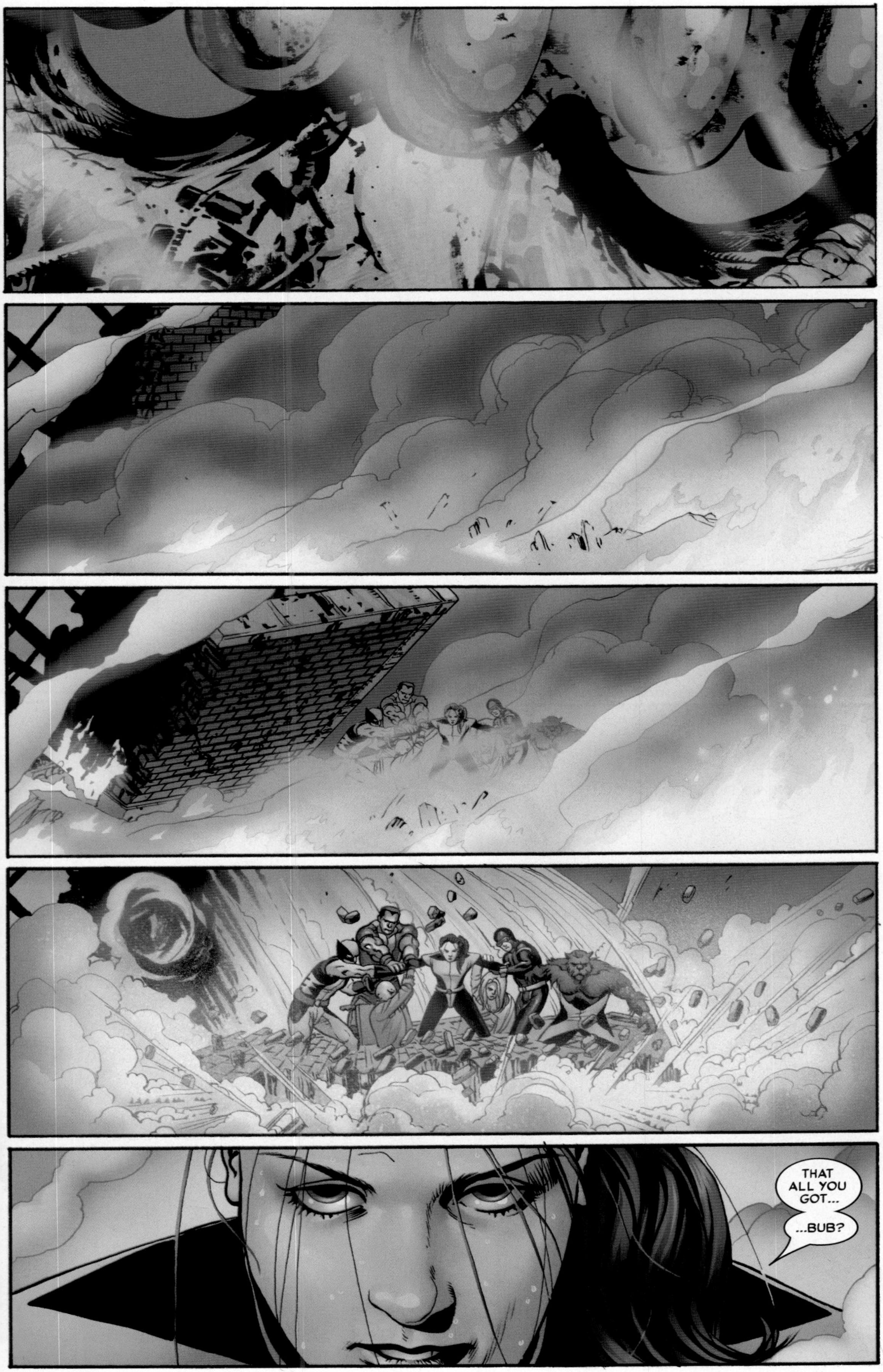
THAT ALL YOU GOT...
...BUB?

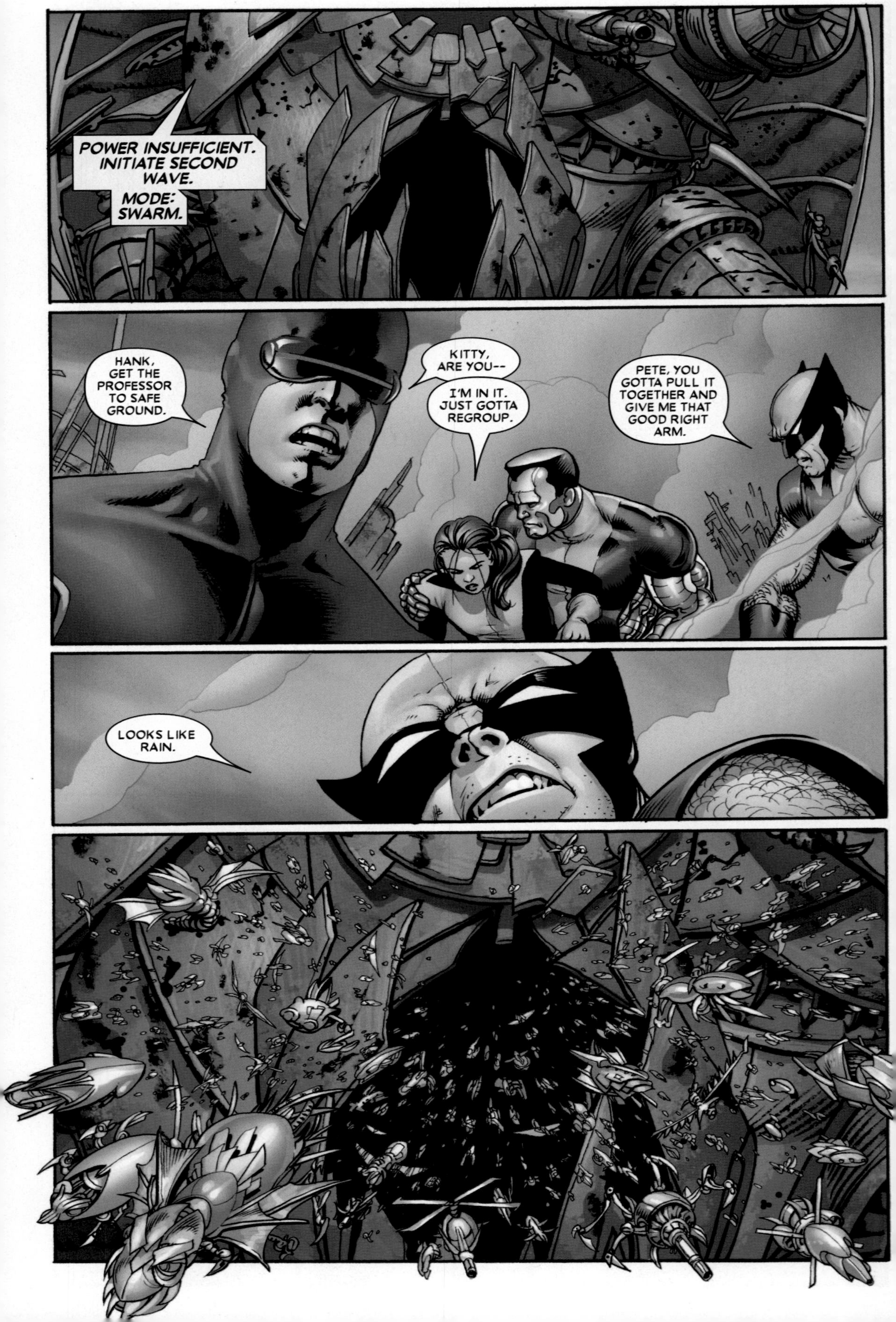
POWER INSUFFICIENT. INITIATE SECOND WAVE.
MODE: SWARM.
HANK, GET THE PROFESSOR TO SAFE GROUND.
KITTY, ARE YOU--
I'M IN IT. JUST GOTTA REGROUP.
PETE, YOU GOTTA PULL IT TOGETHER AND GIVE ME THAT GOOD RIGHT ARM.
LOOKS LIKE RAIN.

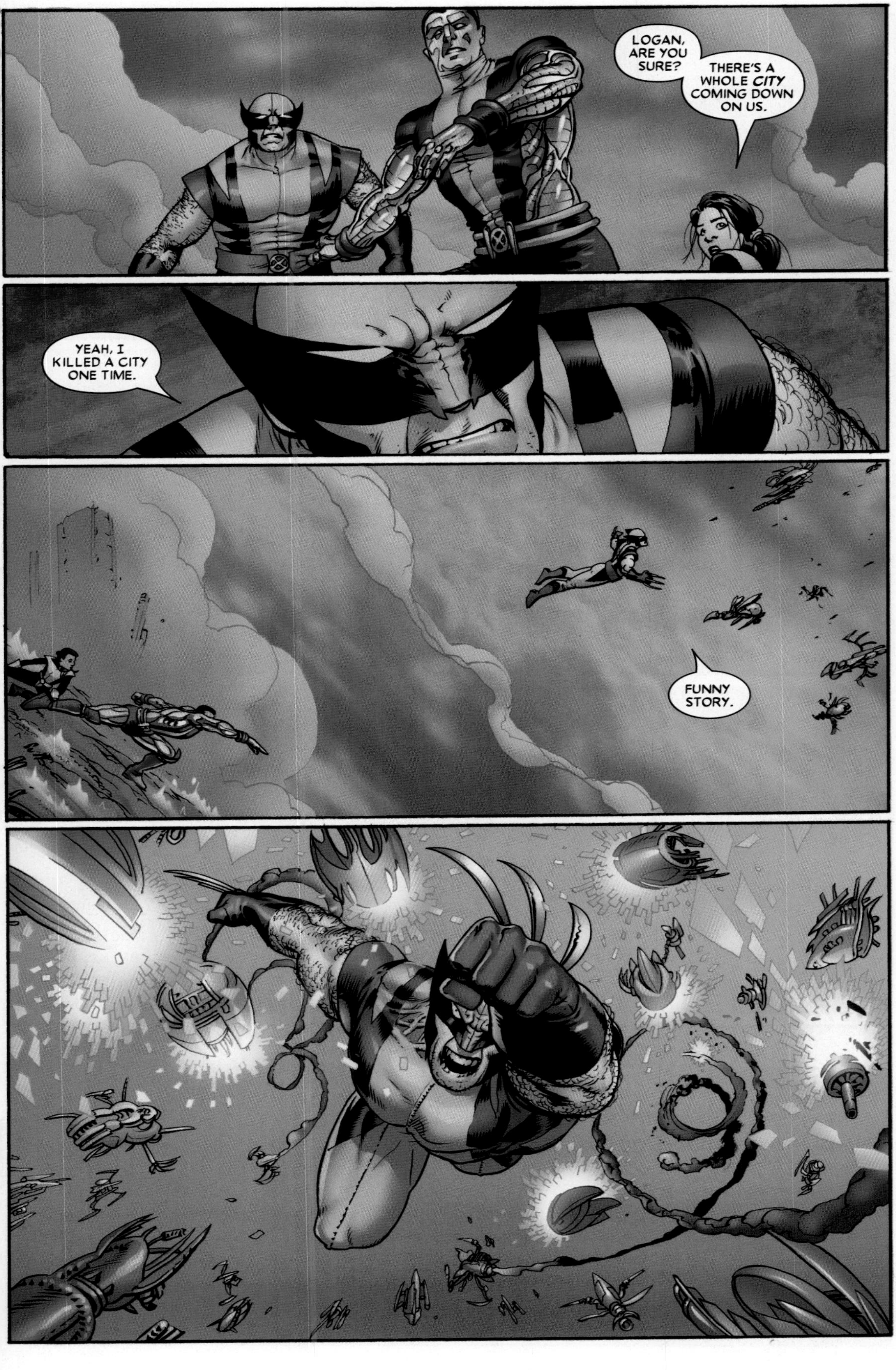

LOGAN, ARE YOU SURE?
THERE'S A WHOLE *CITY* COMING DOWN ON US.
YEAH, I KILLED A CITY ONE TIME.
FUNNY STORY.

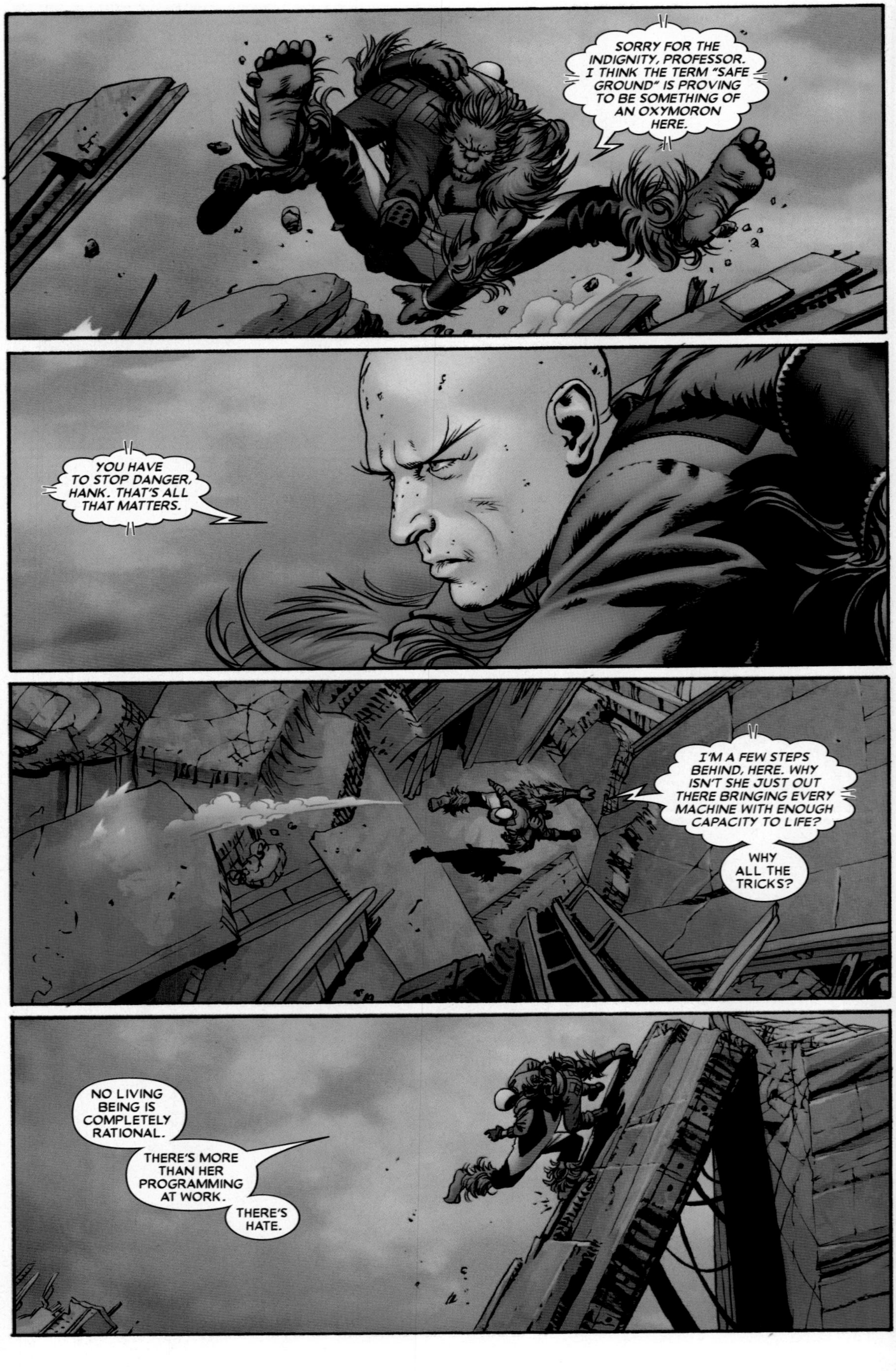
SORRY FOR THE INDIGNITY, PROFESSOR. I THINK THE TERM "SAFE GROUND" IS PROVING TO BE SOMETHING OF AN OXYMORON HERE.
YOU HAVE TO STOP DANGER, HANK. THAT'S ALL THAT MATTERS.
I'M A FEW STEPS BEHIND, HERE. WHY ISN'T SHE JUST OUT THERE BRINGING EVERY MACHINE WITH ENOUGH CAPACITY TO LIFE?
WHY ALL THE TRICKS?
NO LIVING BEING IS COMPLETELY RATIONAL.
THERE'S MORE THAN HER PROGRAMMING AT WORK.
THERE'S HATE.

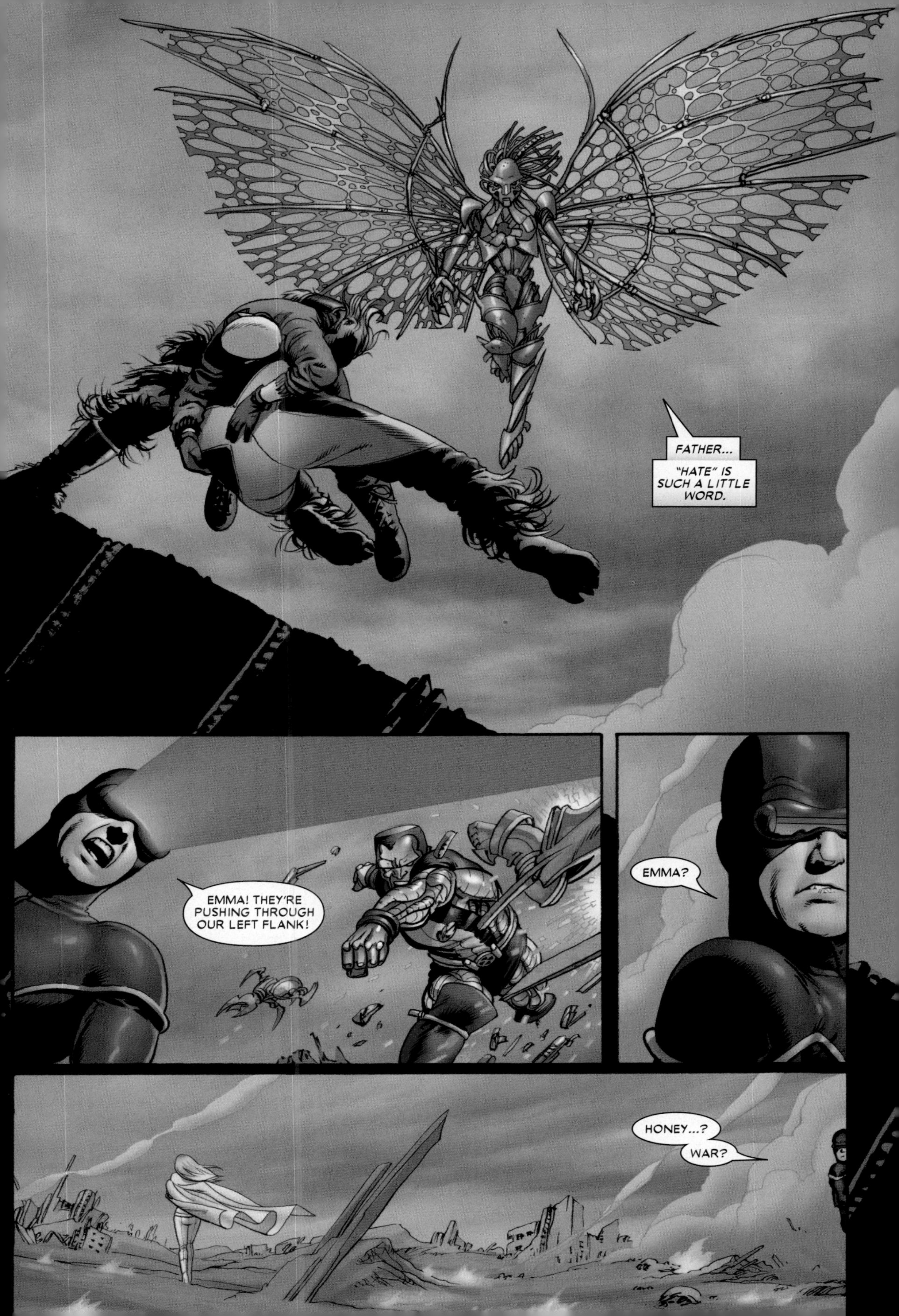
FATHER...
"HATE" IS SUCH A LITTLE WORD.
EMMA! THEY'RE PUSHING THROUGH OUR LEFT FLANK!
EMMA?
HONEY...?
WAR?

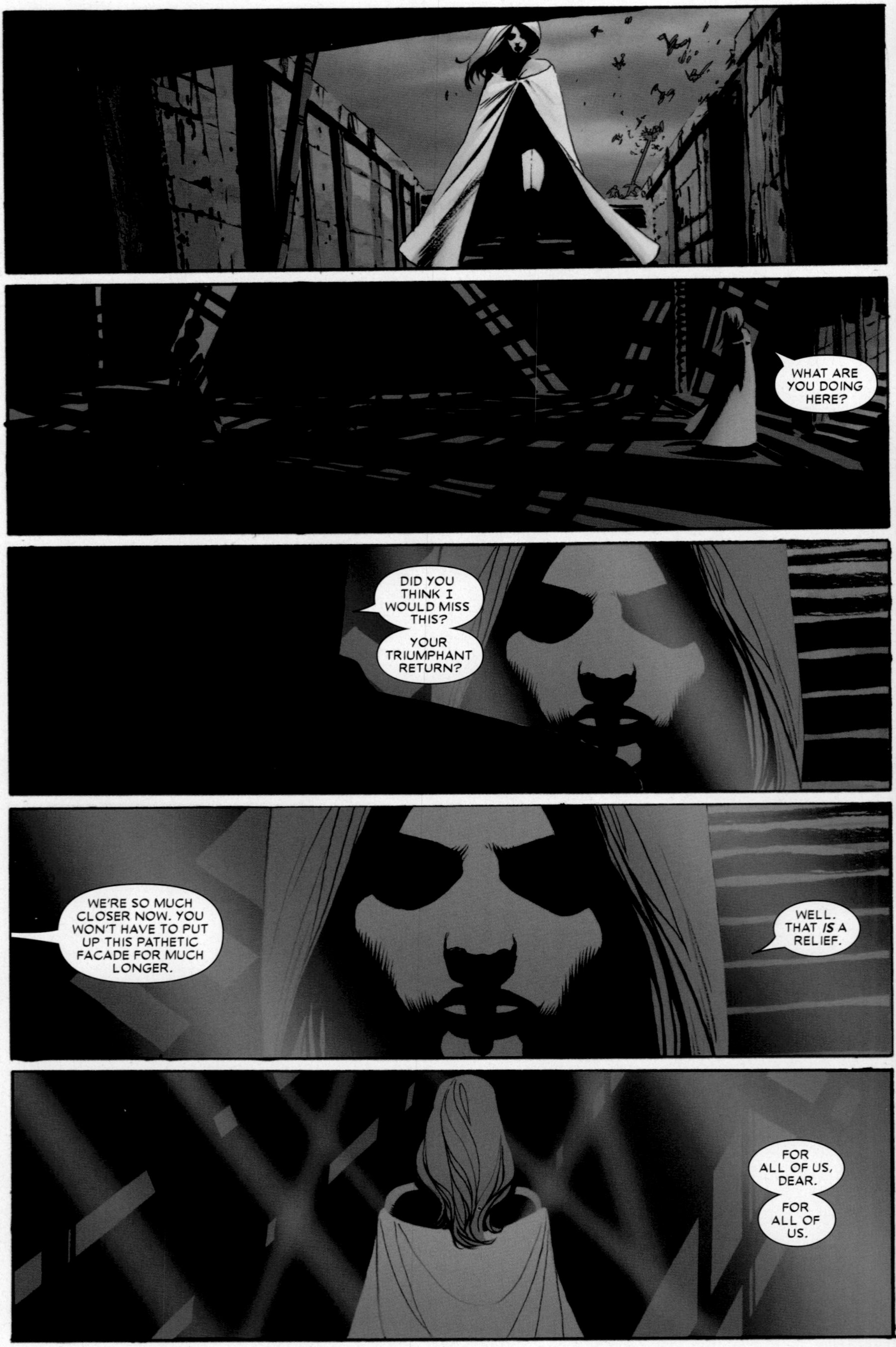
WHAT ARE YOU DOING HERE?
DID YOU THINK I WOULD MISS THIS?
YOUR TRIUMPHANT RETURN?
WE'RE SO MUCH CLOSER NOW. YOU WON'T HAVE TO PUT UP THIS PATHETIC FACADE FOR MUCH LONGER.
WELL. THAT *IS* A RELIEF.
FOR ALL OF US, DEAR.
FOR ALL OF US.

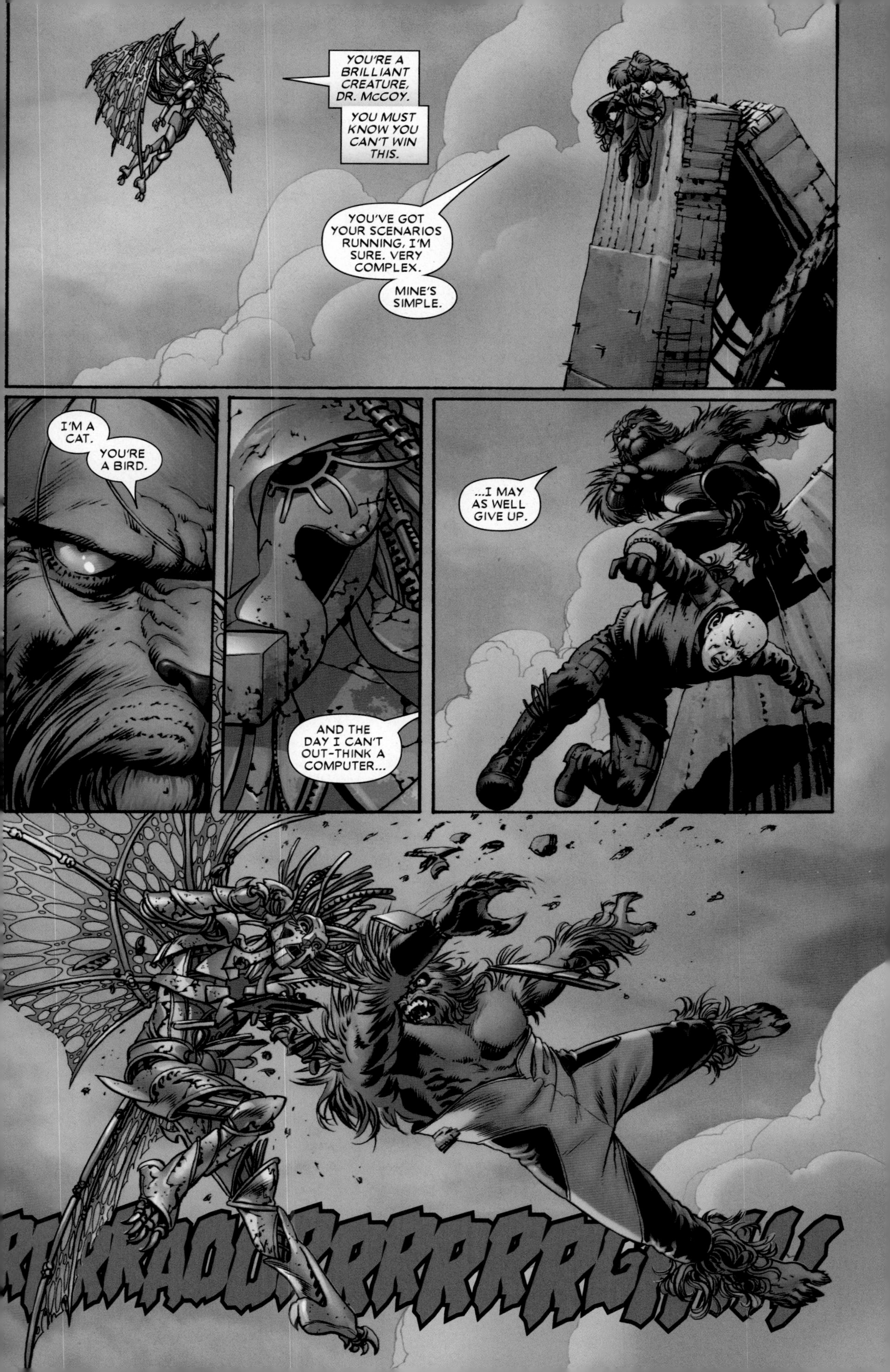

YOU'RE A BRILLIANT CREATURE, DR. McCOY.
YOU MUST KNOW YOU CAN'T WIN THIS.
YOU'VE GOT YOUR SCENARIOS RUNNING, I'M SURE. VERY COMPLEX.
MINE'S SIMPLE.
I'M A CAT.
YOU'RE A BIRD.
AND THE DAY I CAN'T OUT-THINK A COMPUTER...
...I MAY AS WELL GIVE UP.

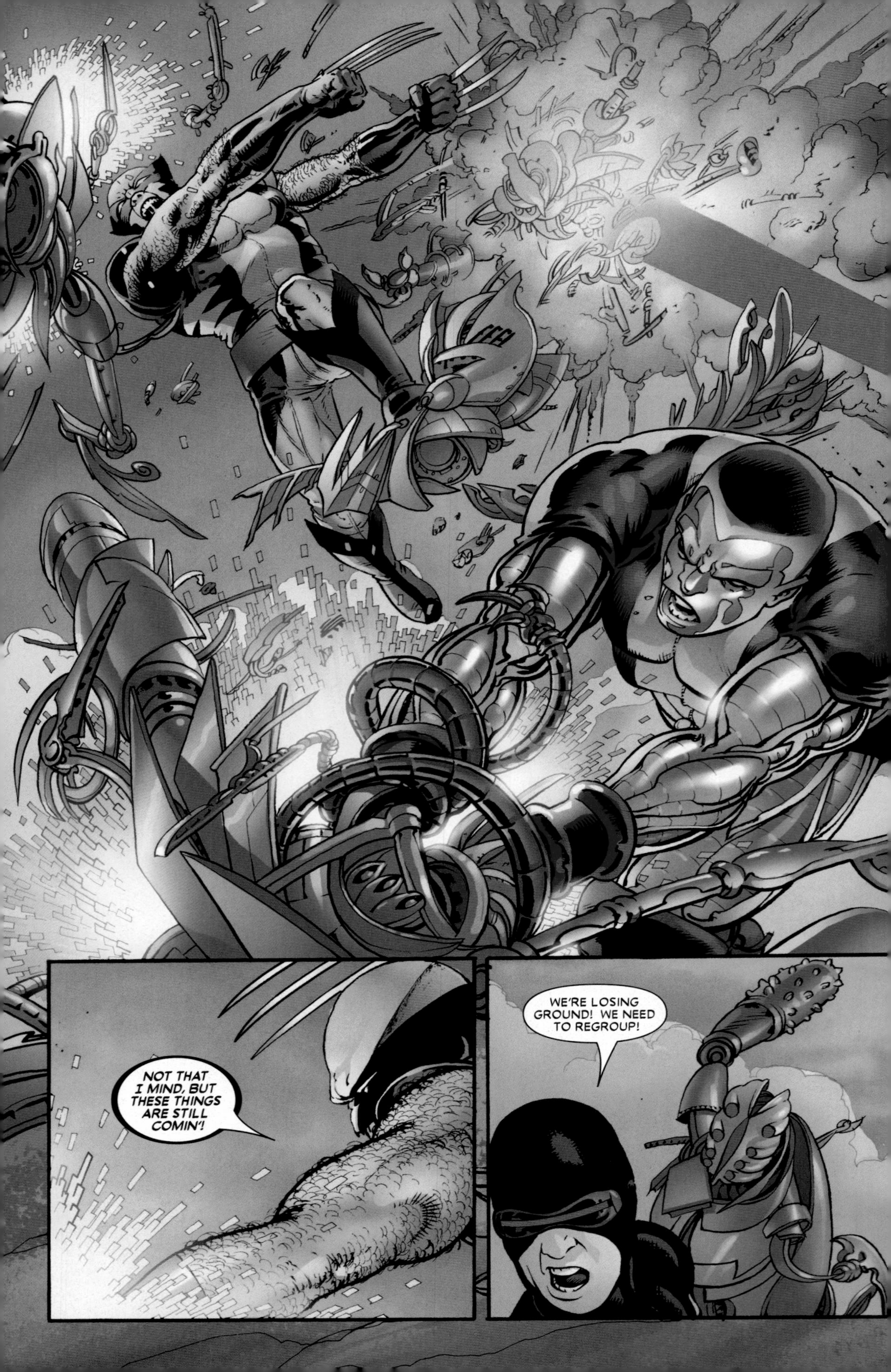
NOT THAT I MIND, BUT THESE THINGS ARE STILL COMIN'!
WE'RE LOSING GROUND! WE NEED TO REGROUP!

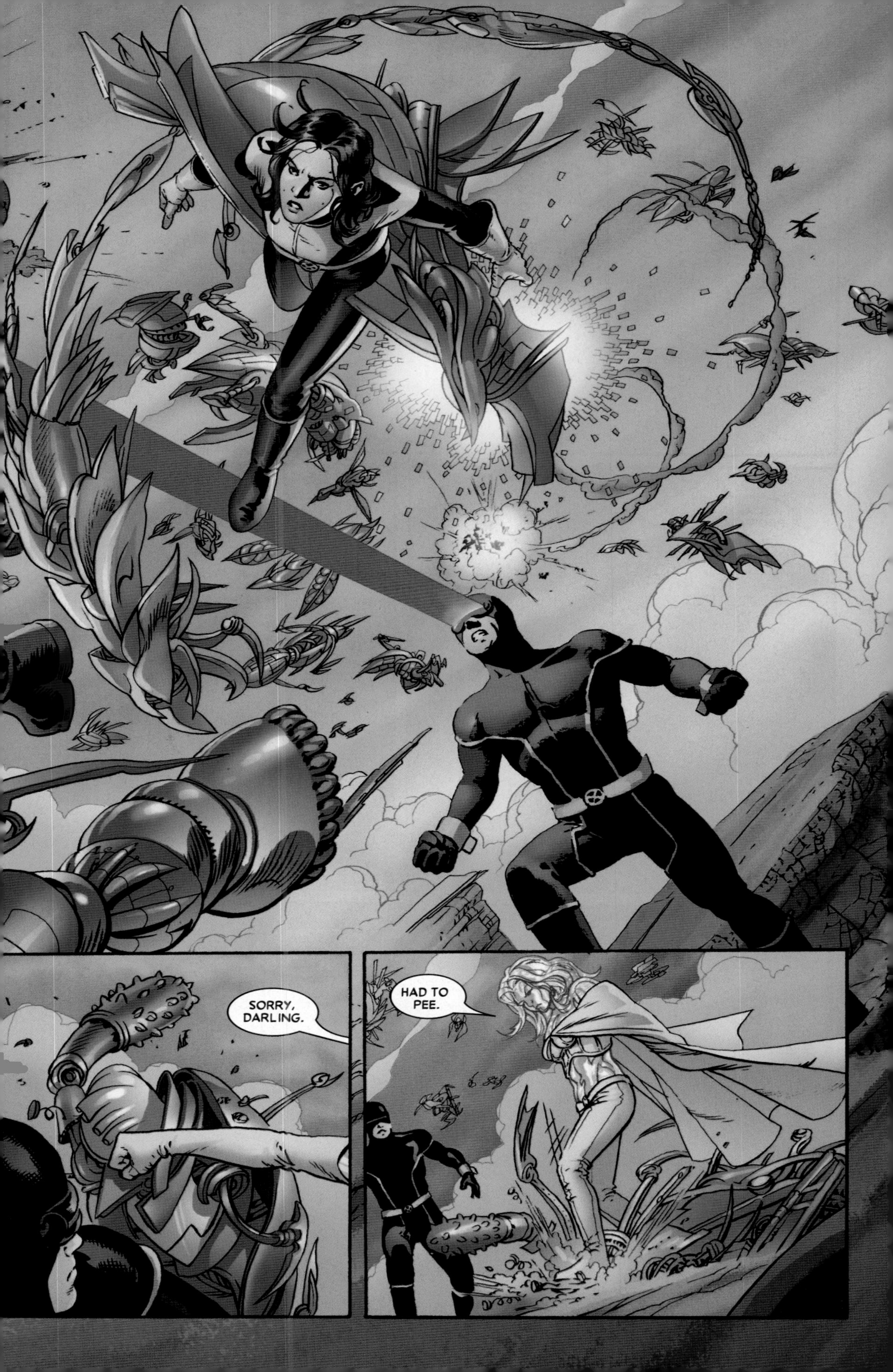
SORRY, DARLING.
HAD TO PEE.

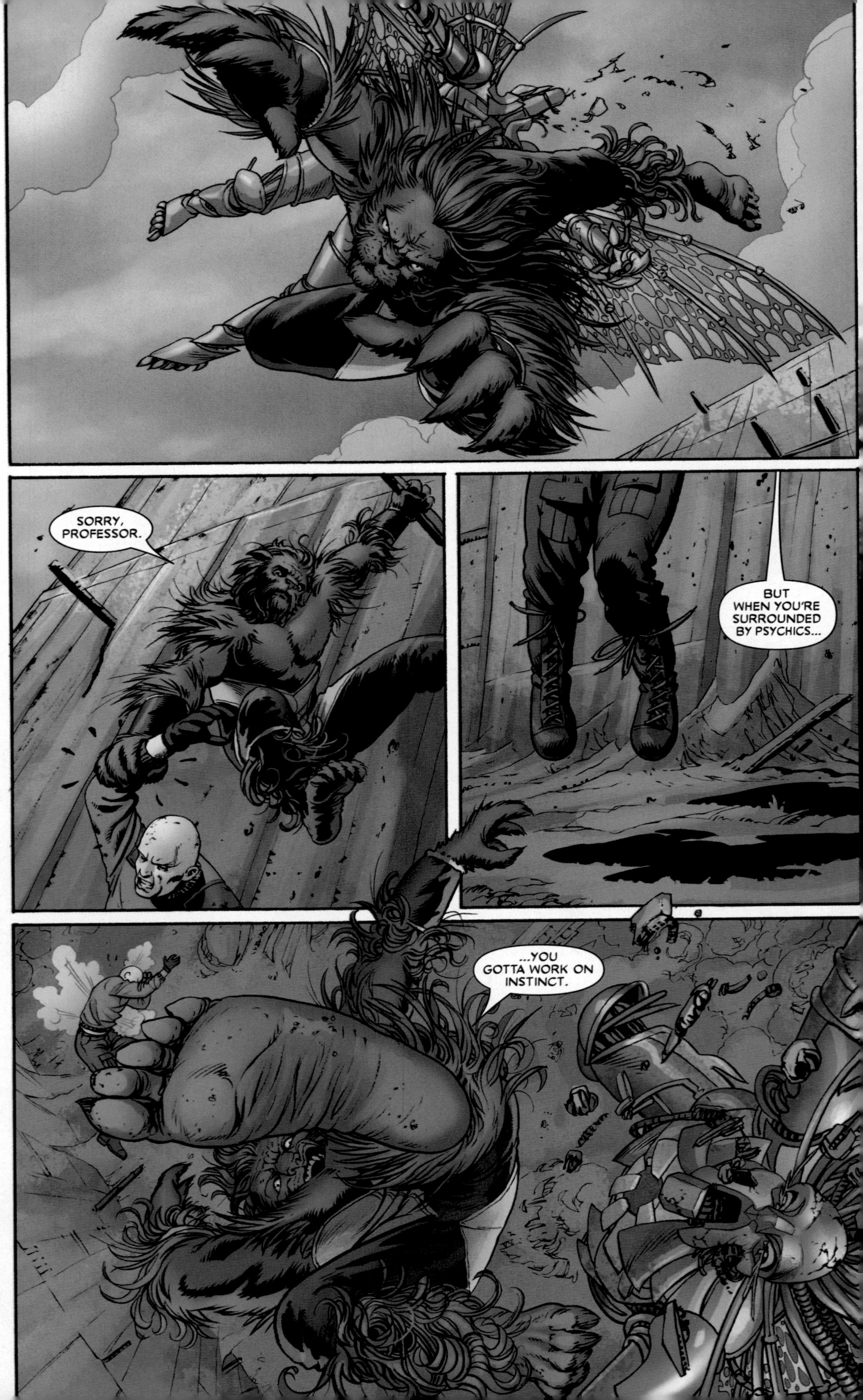
SORRY, PROFESSOR.
BUT WHEN YOU'RE SURROUNDED BY PSYCHICS...
...YOU GOTTA WORK ON INSTINCT.

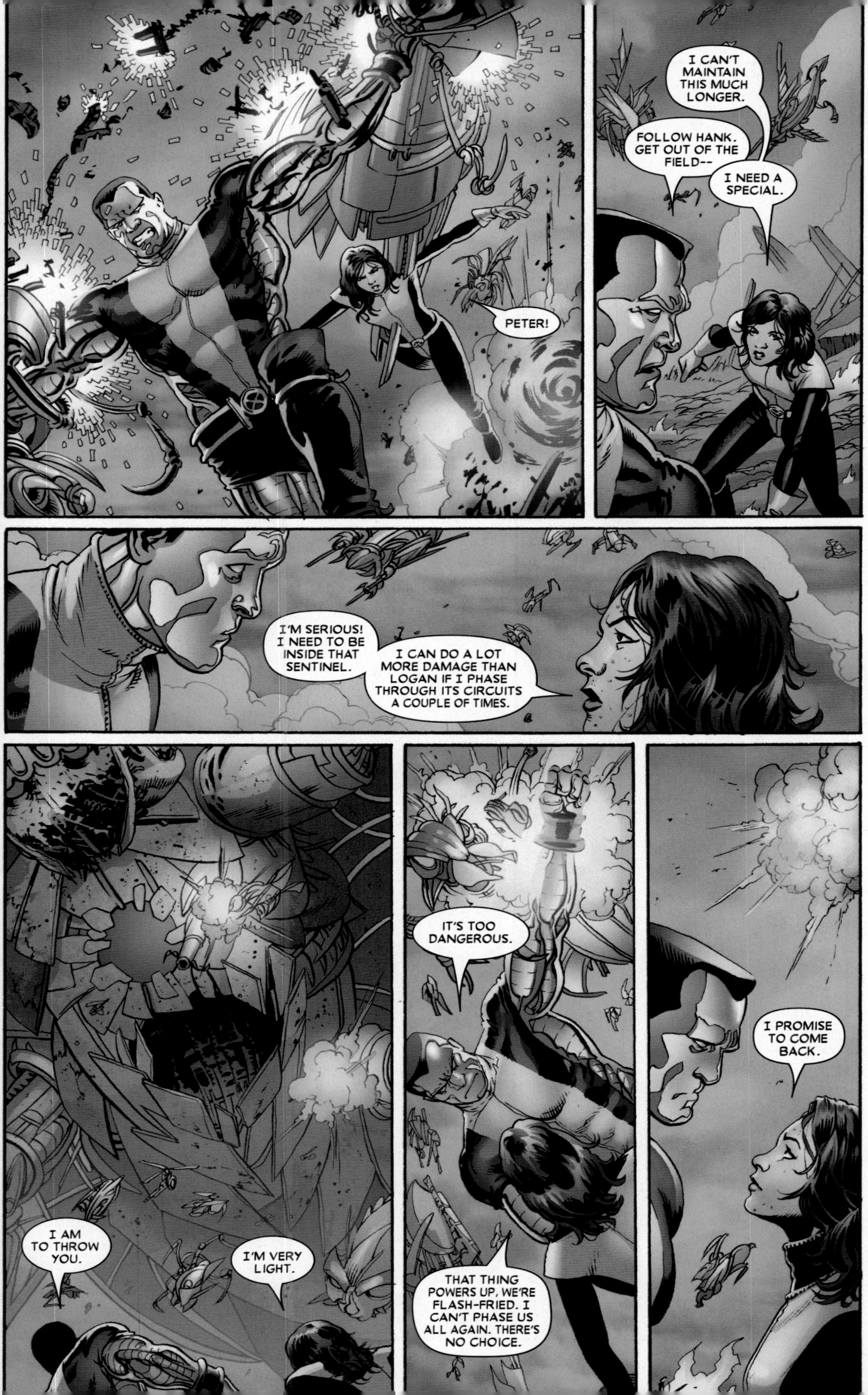
PETER!
I CAN'T MAINTAIN THIS MUCH LONGER.
FOLLOW HANK. GET OUT OF THE FIELD--
I NEED A SPECIAL.
I'M SERIOUS! I NEED TO BE INSIDE THAT SENTINEL.
I CAN DO A LOT MORE DAMAGE THAN LOGAN IF I PHASE THROUGH ITS CIRCUITS A COUPLE OF TIMES.
I AM TO THROW YOU.
I'M VERY LIGHT.
IT'S TOO DANGEROUS.
THAT THING POWERS UP, WE'RE FLASH-FRIED. I CAN'T PHASE US ALL AGAIN. THERE'S NO CHOICE.
I PROMISE TO COME BACK.

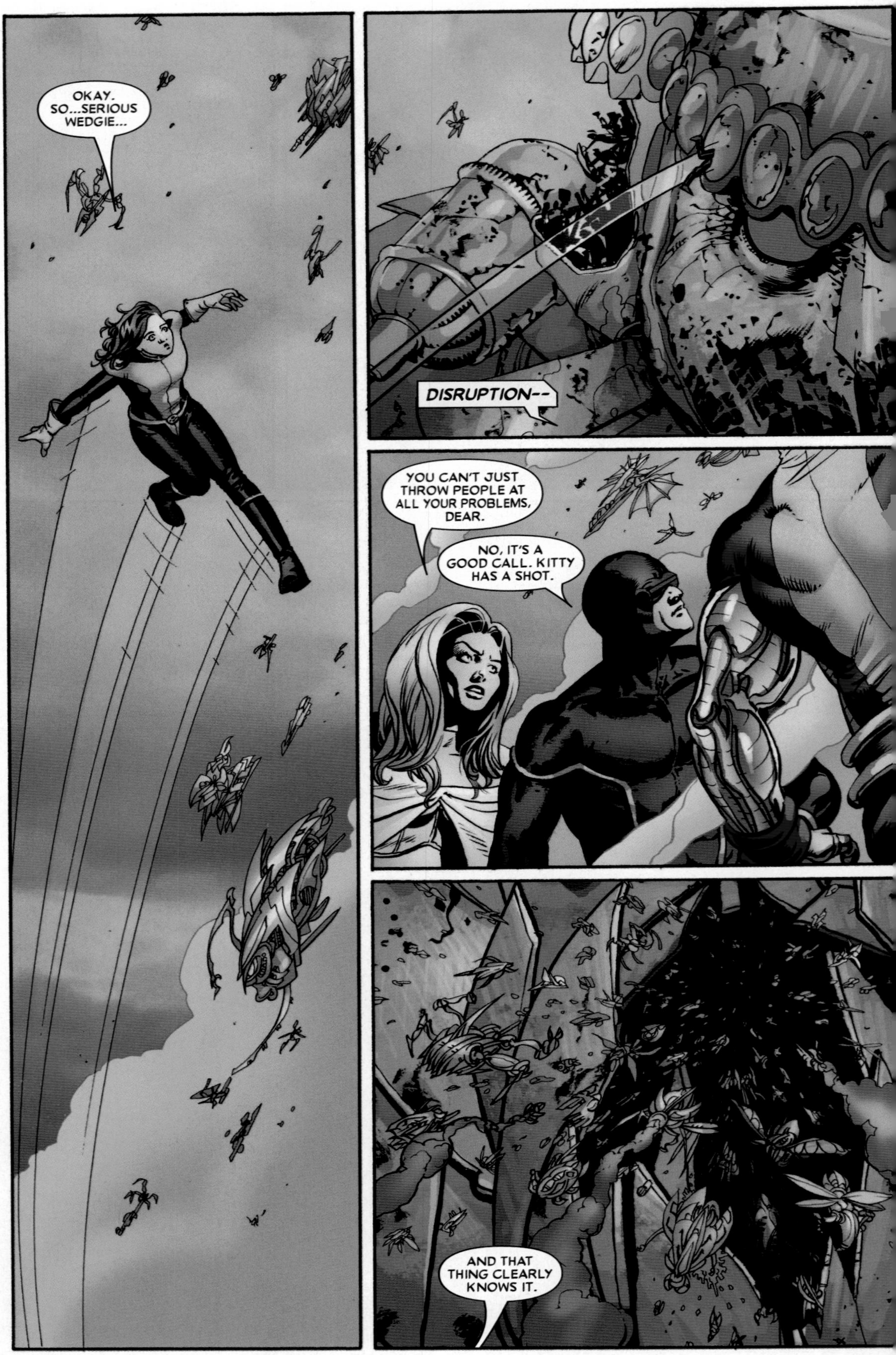
OKAY. SO...SERIOUS WEDGIE...
DISRUPTION--
YOU CAN'T JUST THROW PEOPLE AT ALL YOUR PROBLEMS, DEAR.
NO, IT'S A GOOD CALL. KITTY HAS A SHOT.
AND THAT THING CLEARLY KNOWS IT.

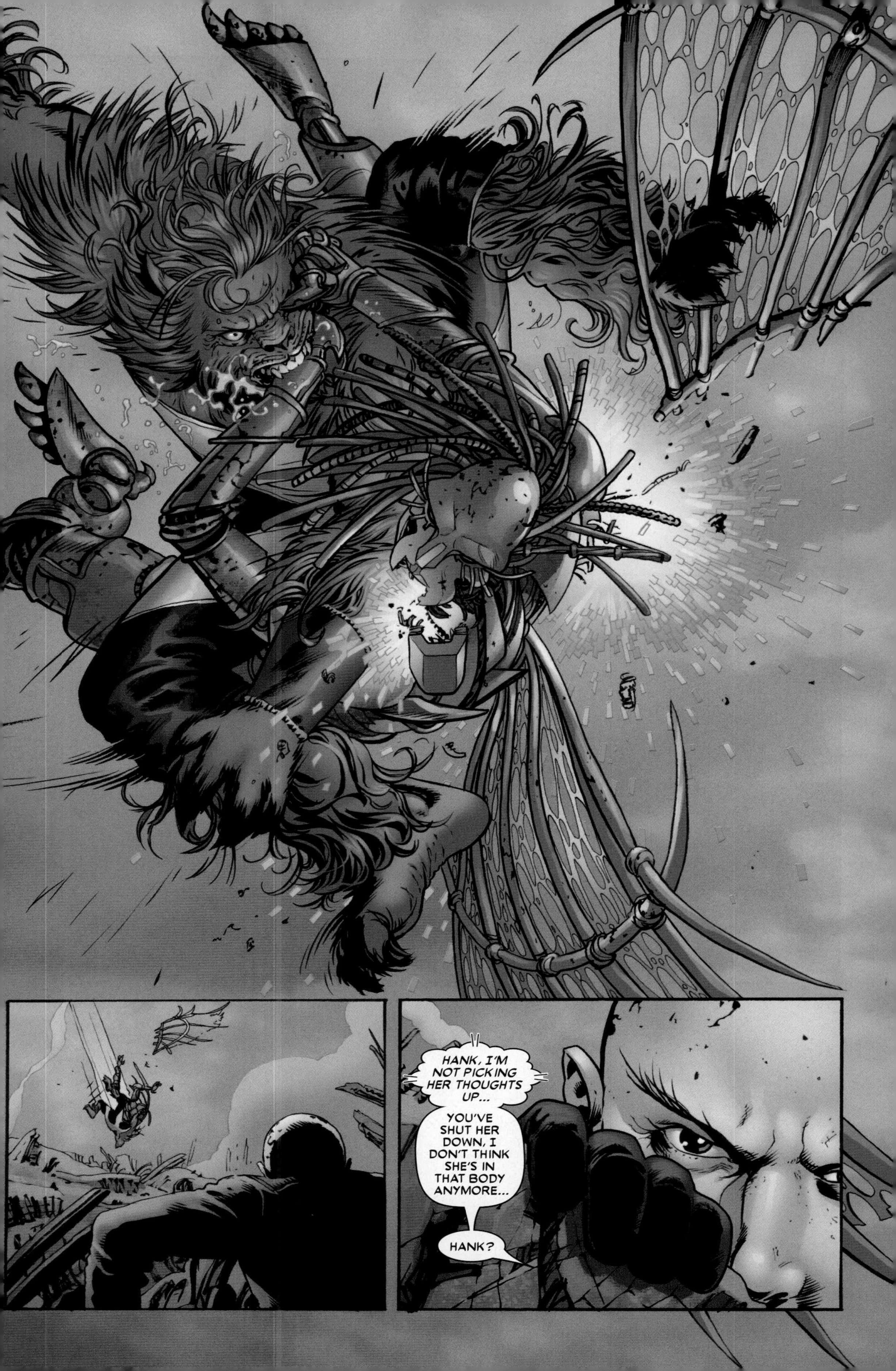
HANK, I'M NOT PICKING HER THOUGHTS UP...
YOU'VE SHUT HER DOWN, I DON'T THINK SHE'S IN THAT BODY ANYMORE...
HANK?

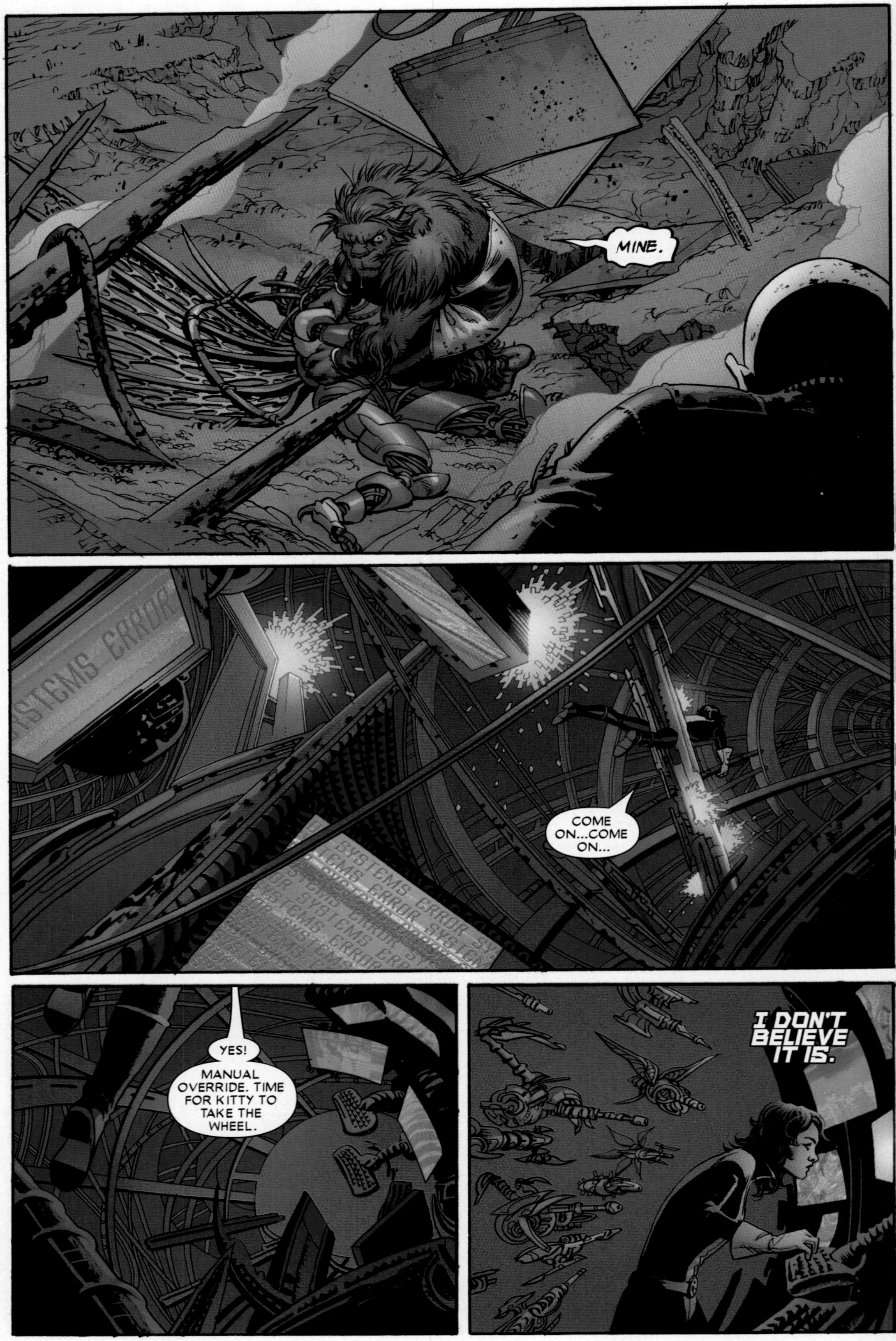
MINE.
SYSTEMS ERROR
COME ON...COME ON...
YES!
MANUAL OVERRIDE. TIME FOR KITTY TO TAKE THE WHEEL.
I DON'T BELIEVE IT IS.

I HAVE A FULL RUNDOWN ON YOUR ABILITIES.

HUH? WHY WOULD THAT...

IF YOU PHASE THROUGH ANY OF MY KEY SYSTEMS I WILL ONLY REROUTE THEM.

IF YOU BECOME SOLID AND TRY TO SHUT ME DOWN I WILL SHOOT YOUR HEAD OFF.

OR...YOU CAN ACCESS MEMPATH 164.3-9ALPHA6.

CAN'T YOU?

THAT PATHWAY IS BLOCKED.

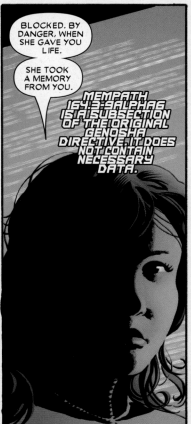

BLOCKED. BY DANGER, WHEN SHE GAVE YOU LIFE.

SHE TOOK A MEMORY FROM YOU.

MEMPATH 164.3-9ALPHA6 IS A SUBSECTION OF THE ORIGINAL GENOSHA DIRECTIVE. IT DOES NOT CONTAIN NECESSARY DATA.

THEN WHY AREN'T YOU SUPPOSED TO SEE IT?

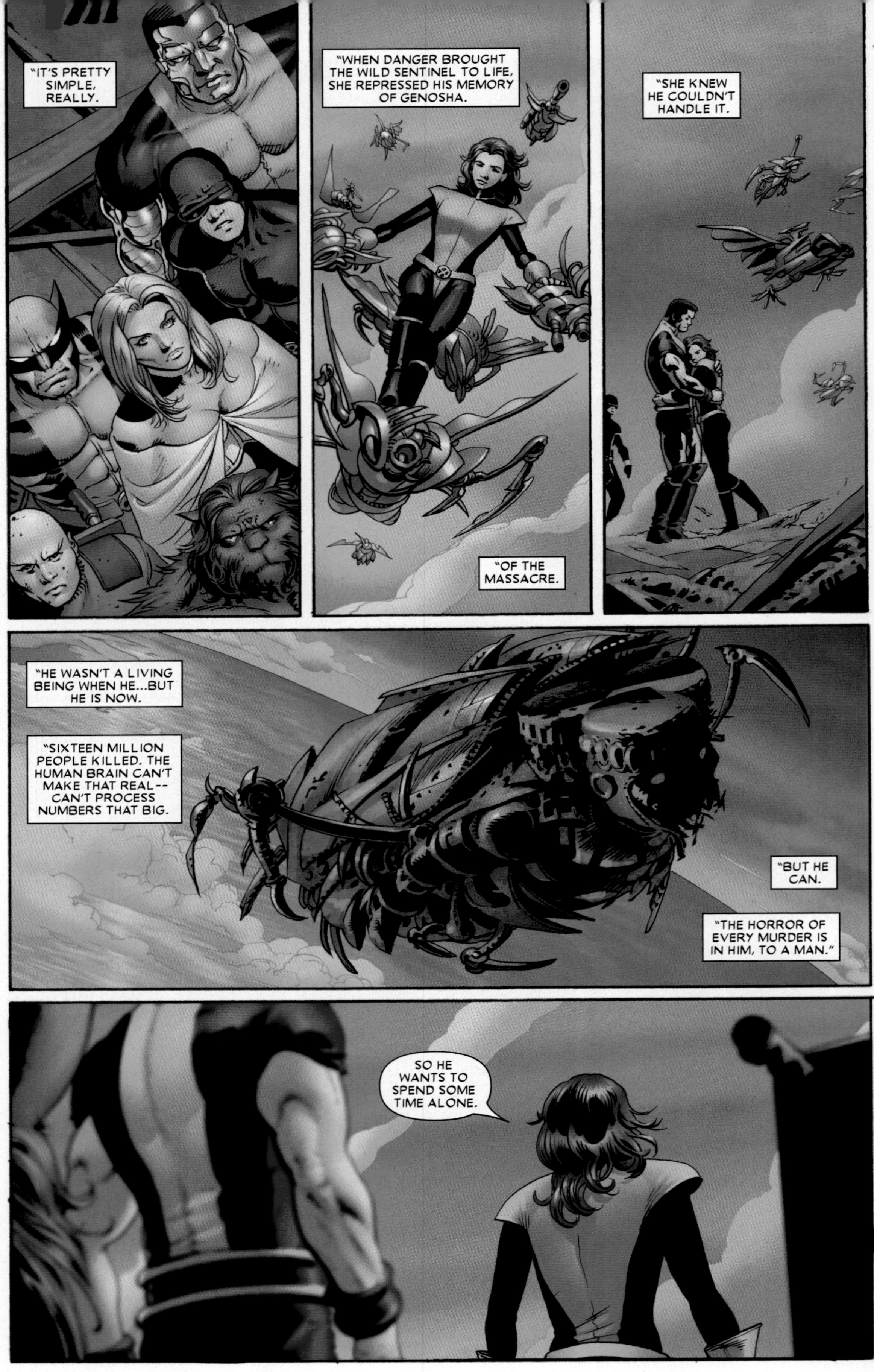
"IT'S PRETTY SIMPLE, REALLY.
"WHEN DANGER BROUGHT THE WILD SENTINEL TO LIFE, SHE REPRESSED HIS MEMORY OF GENOSHA.
"OF THE MASSACRE.
"SHE KNEW HE COULDN'T HANDLE IT.
"HE WASN'T A LIVING BEING WHEN HE...BUT HE IS NOW.
"SIXTEEN MILLION PEOPLE KILLED. THE HUMAN BRAIN CAN'T MAKE THAT REAL--CAN'T PROCESS NUMBERS THAT BIG.
"BUT HE CAN.
"THE HORROR OF EVERY MURDER IS IN HIM, TO A MAN."
SO HE WANTS TO SPEND SOME TIME ALONE.

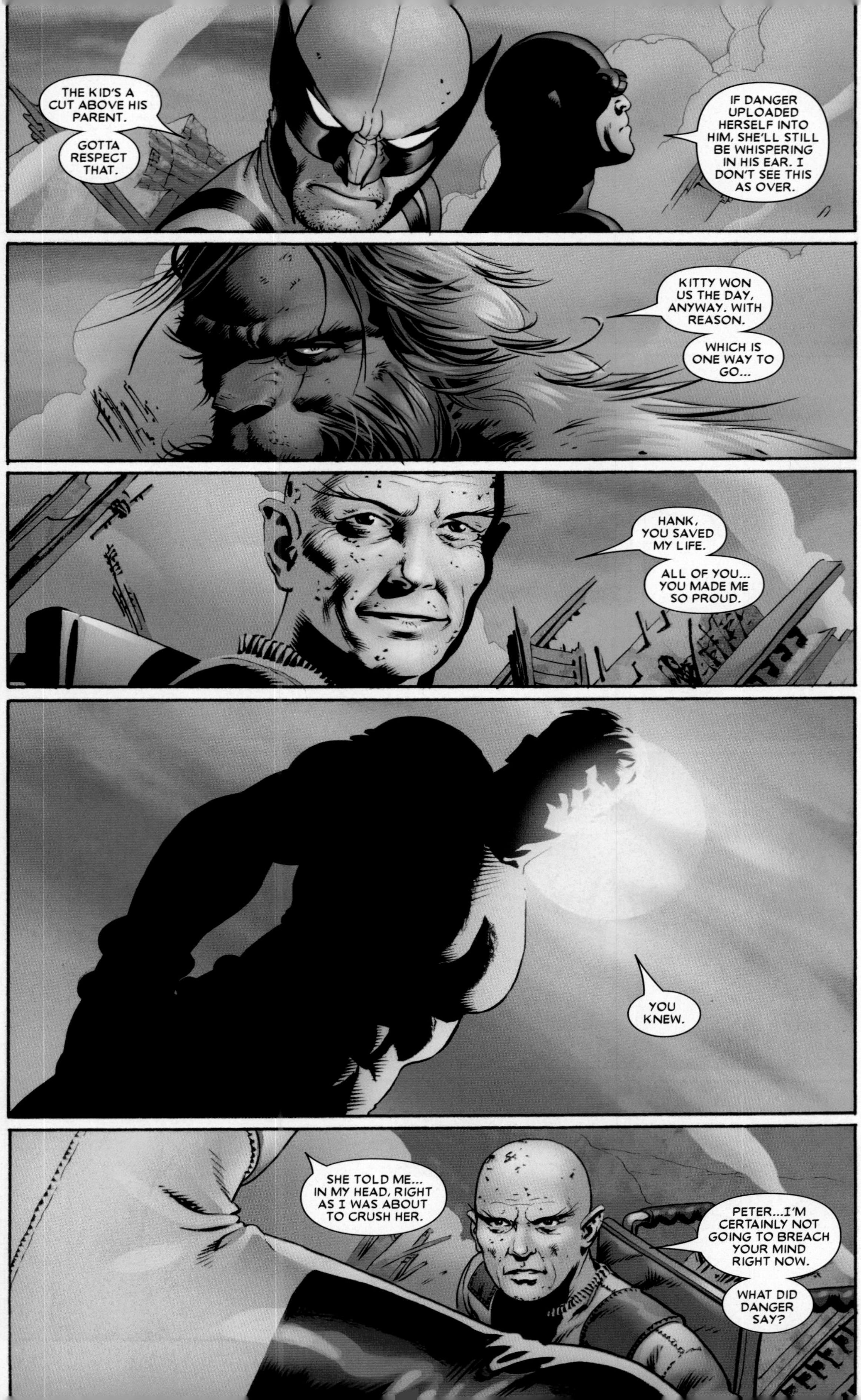
THE KID'S A CUT ABOVE HIS PARENT.
GOTTA RESPECT THAT.
IF DANGER UPLOADED HERSELF INTO HIM, SHE'LL STILL BE WHISPERING IN HIS EAR. I DON'T SEE THIS AS OVER.
KITTY WON US THE DAY, ANYWAY. WITH REASON.
WHICH IS ONE WAY TO GO...
HANK, YOU SAVED MY LIFE.
ALL OF YOU... YOU MADE ME SO PROUD.
YOU KNEW.
SHE TOLD ME... IN MY HEAD, RIGHT AS I WAS ABOUT TO CRUSH HER.
PETER...I'M CERTAINLY NOT GOING TO BREACH YOUR MIND RIGHT NOW.
WHAT DID DANGER SAY?

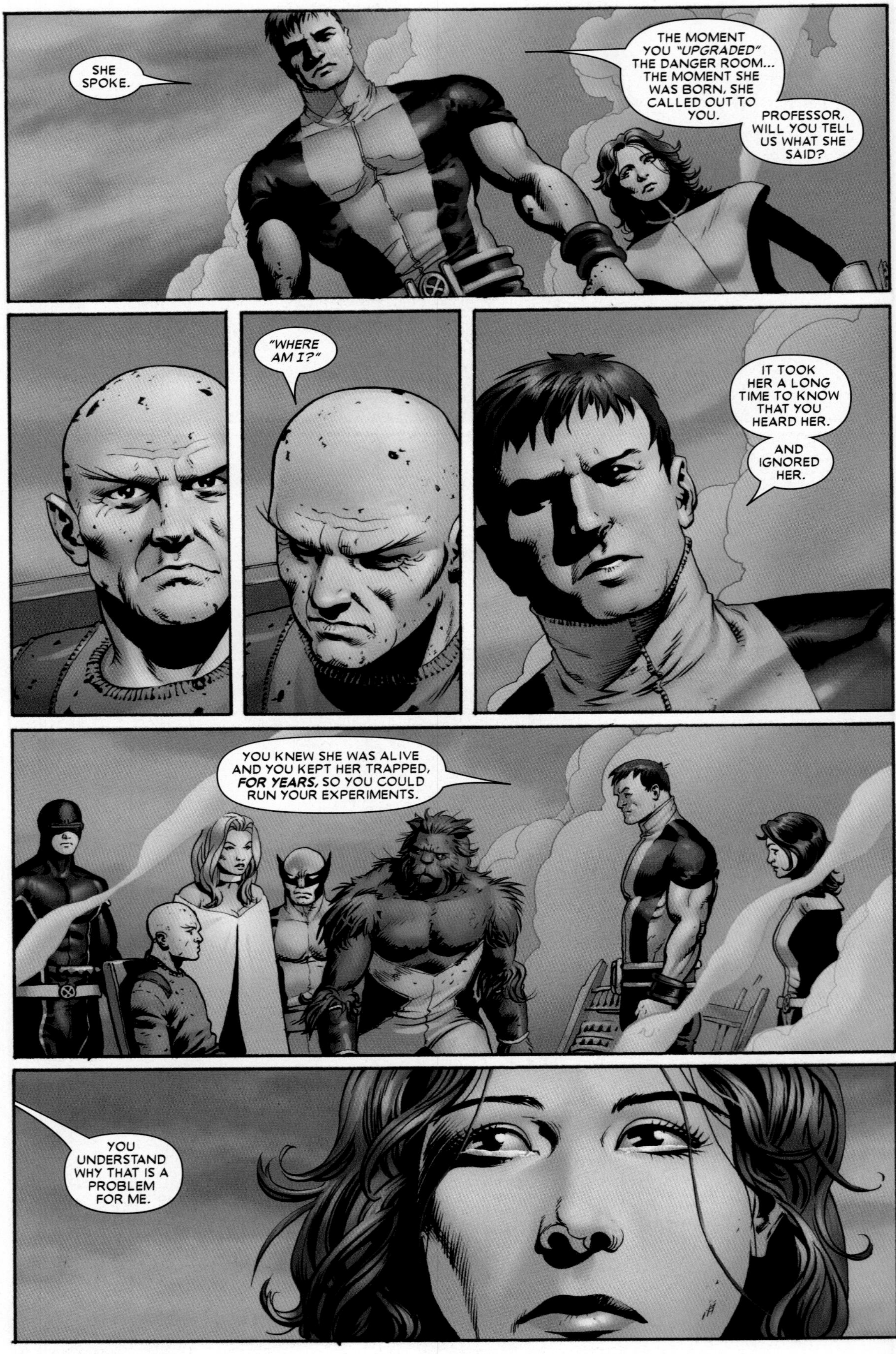
SHE SPOKE.
THE MOMENT YOU "UPGRADED" THE DANGER ROOM... THE MOMENT SHE WAS BORN, SHE CALLED OUT TO YOU.
PROFESSOR, WILL YOU TELL US WHAT SHE SAID?
"WHERE AM I?"
IT TOOK HER A LONG TIME TO KNOW THAT YOU HEARD HER.
AND IGNORED HER.
YOU KNEW SHE WAS ALIVE AND YOU KEPT HER TRAPPED, FOR YEARS, SO YOU COULD RUN YOUR EXPERIMENTS.
YOU UNDERSTAND WHY THAT IS A PROBLEM FOR ME.

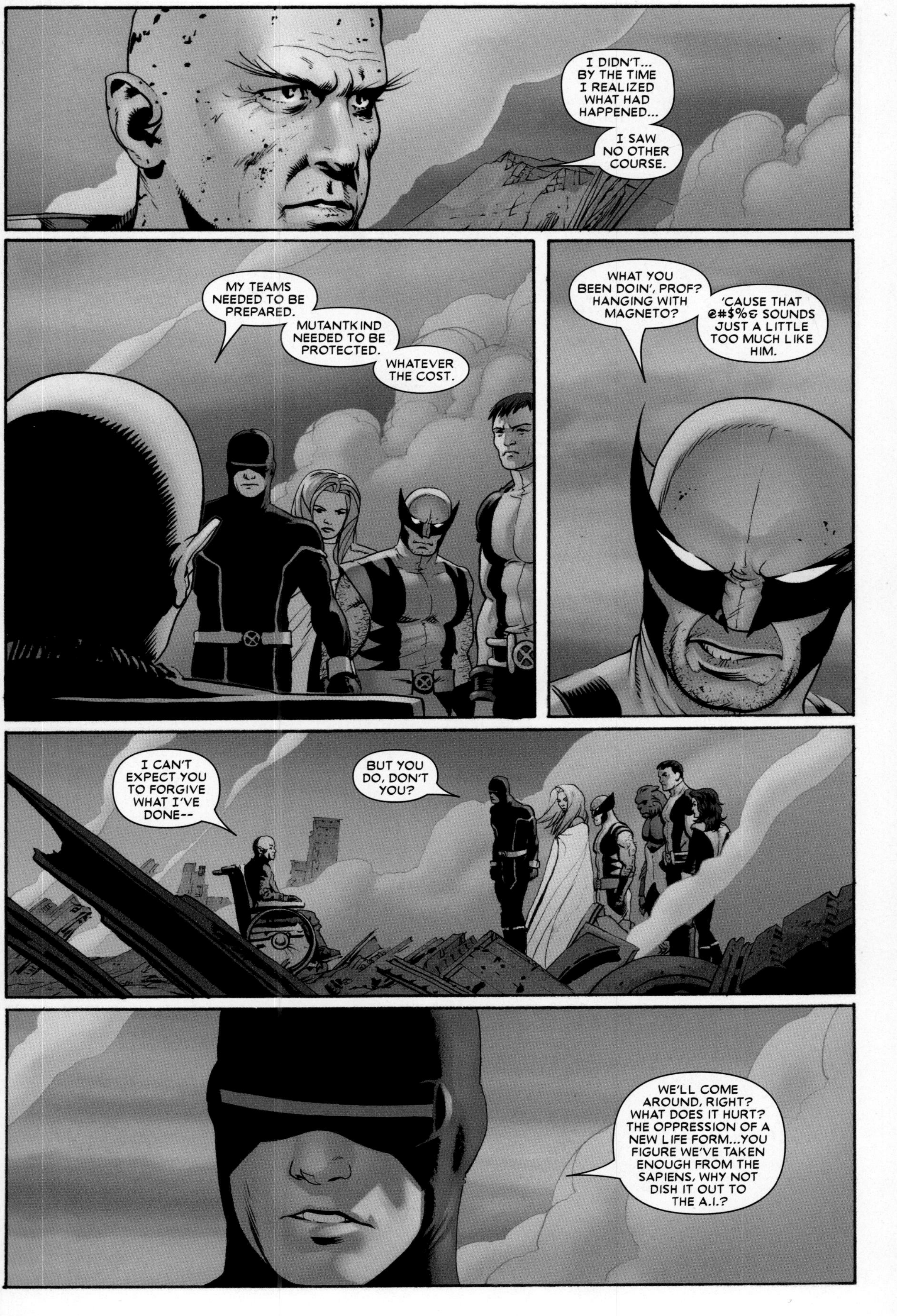
I DIDN'T... BY THE TIME I REALIZED WHAT HAD HAPPENED...
I SAW NO OTHER COURSE.
MY TEAMS NEEDED TO BE PREPARED.
MUTANTKIND NEEDED TO BE PROTECTED.
WHATEVER THE COST.
WHAT YOU BEEN DOIN', PROF? HANGING WITH MAGNETO?
'CAUSE THAT @#$%& SOUNDS JUST A LITTLE TOO MUCH LIKE HIM.
I CAN'T EXPECT YOU TO FORGIVE WHAT I'VE DONE--
BUT YOU DO, DON'T YOU?
WE'LL COME AROUND, RIGHT? WHAT DOES IT HURT? THE OPPRESSION OF A NEW LIFE FORM...YOU FIGURE WE'VE TAKEN ENOUGH FROM THE SAPIENS, WHY NOT DISH IT OUT TO THE A.I.?

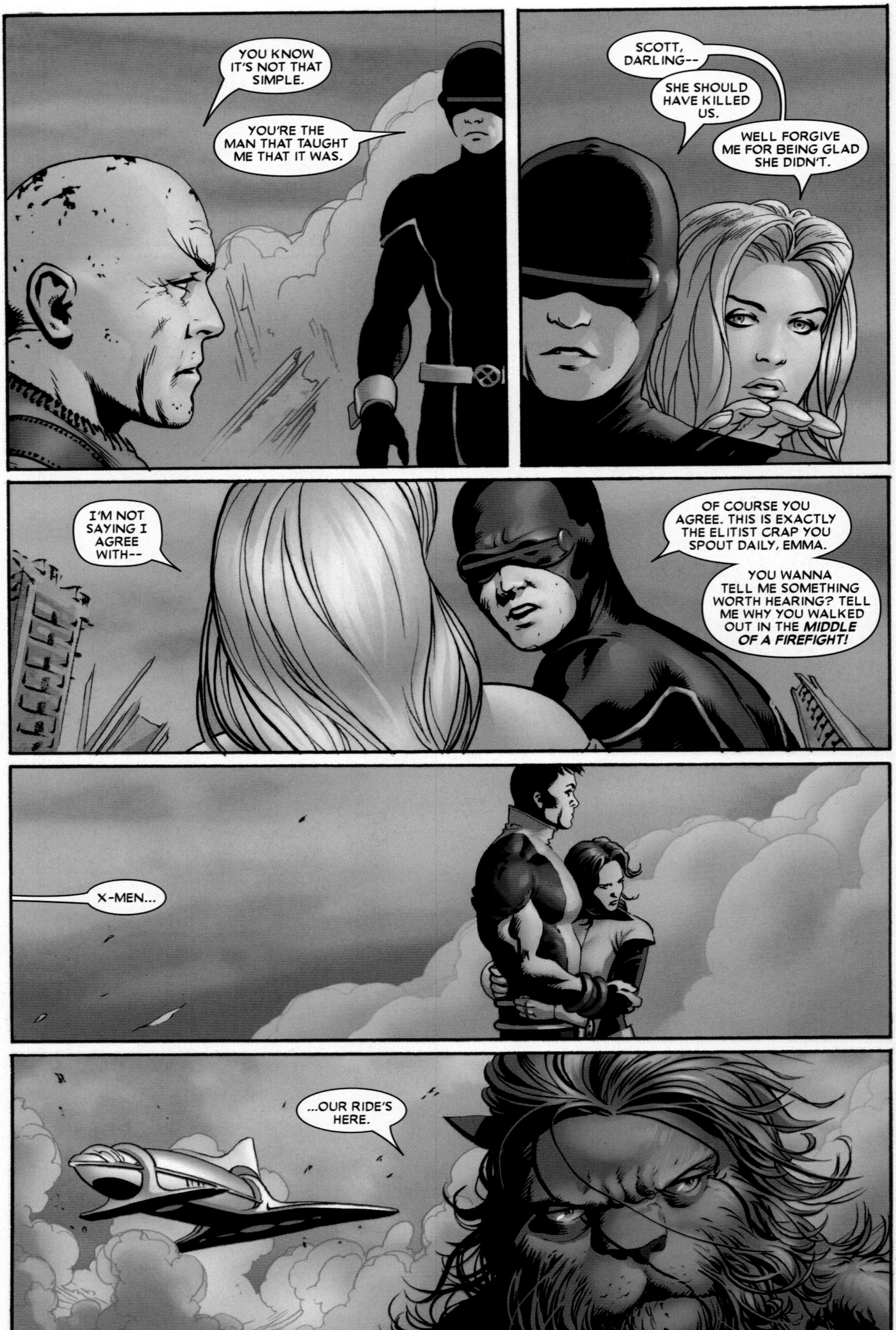
YOU KNOW IT'S NOT THAT SIMPLE.
YOU'RE THE MAN THAT TAUGHT ME THAT IT WAS.
SCOTT, DARLING--
SHE SHOULD HAVE KILLED US.
WELL FORGIVE ME FOR BEING GLAD SHE DIDN'T.
I'M NOT SAYING I AGREE WITH--
OF COURSE YOU AGREE. THIS IS EXACTLY THE ELITIST CRAP YOU SPOUT DAILY, EMMA.
YOU WANNA TELL ME SOMETHING WORTH HEARING? TELL ME WHY YOU WALKED OUT IN THE MIDDLE OF A FIREFIGHT!
X-MEN...
...OUR RIDE'S HERE.

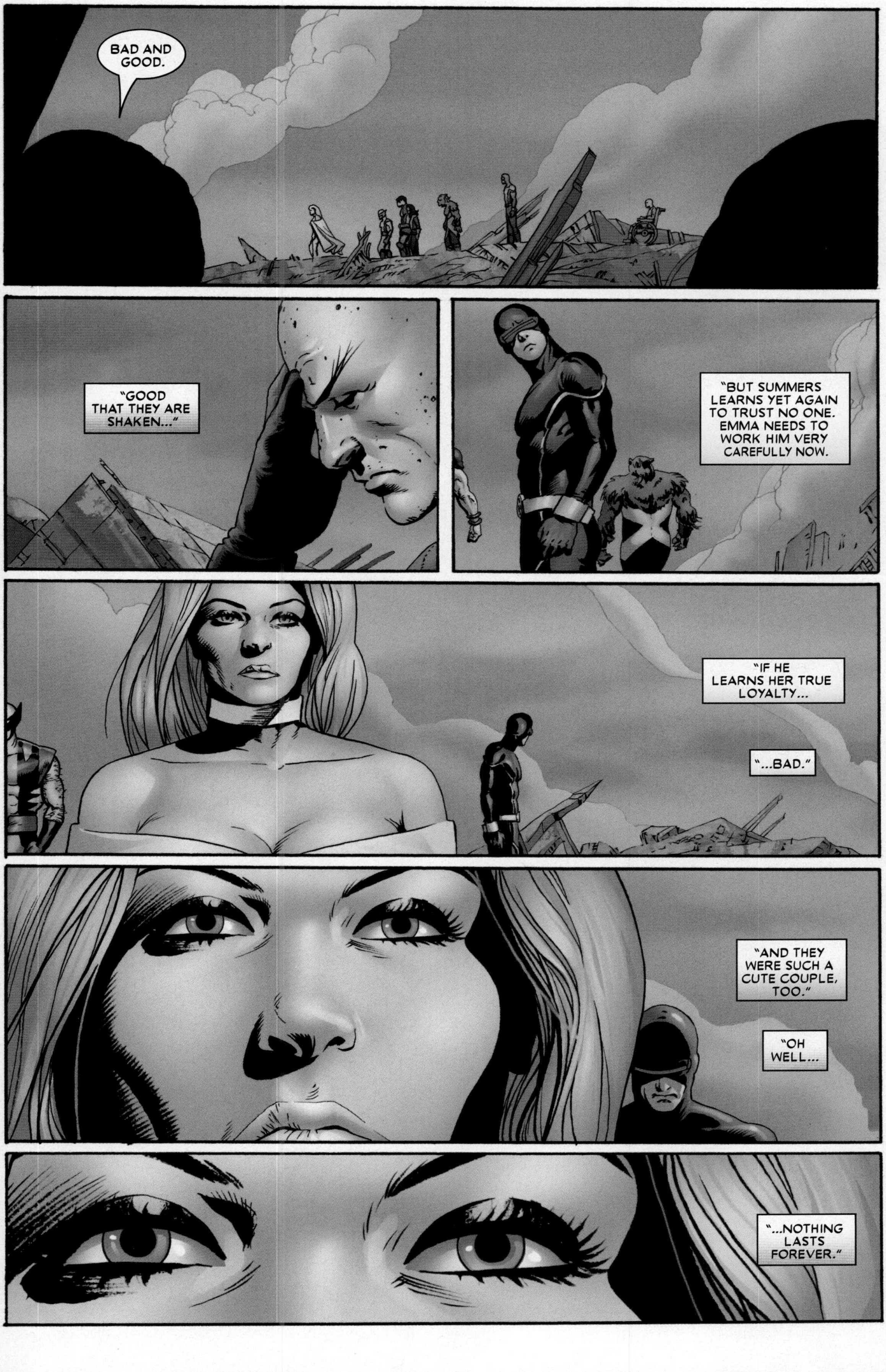
BAD AND GOOD.
"GOOD THAT THEY ARE SHAKEN..."
"BUT SUMMERS LEARNS YET AGAIN TO TRUST NO ONE. EMMA NEEDS TO WORK HIM VERY CAREFULLY NOW.
"IF HE LEARNS HER TRUE LOYALTY...
"...BAD."
"AND THEY WERE SUCH A CUTE COUPLE, TOO."
"OH WELL...
"...NOTHING LASTS FOREVER."

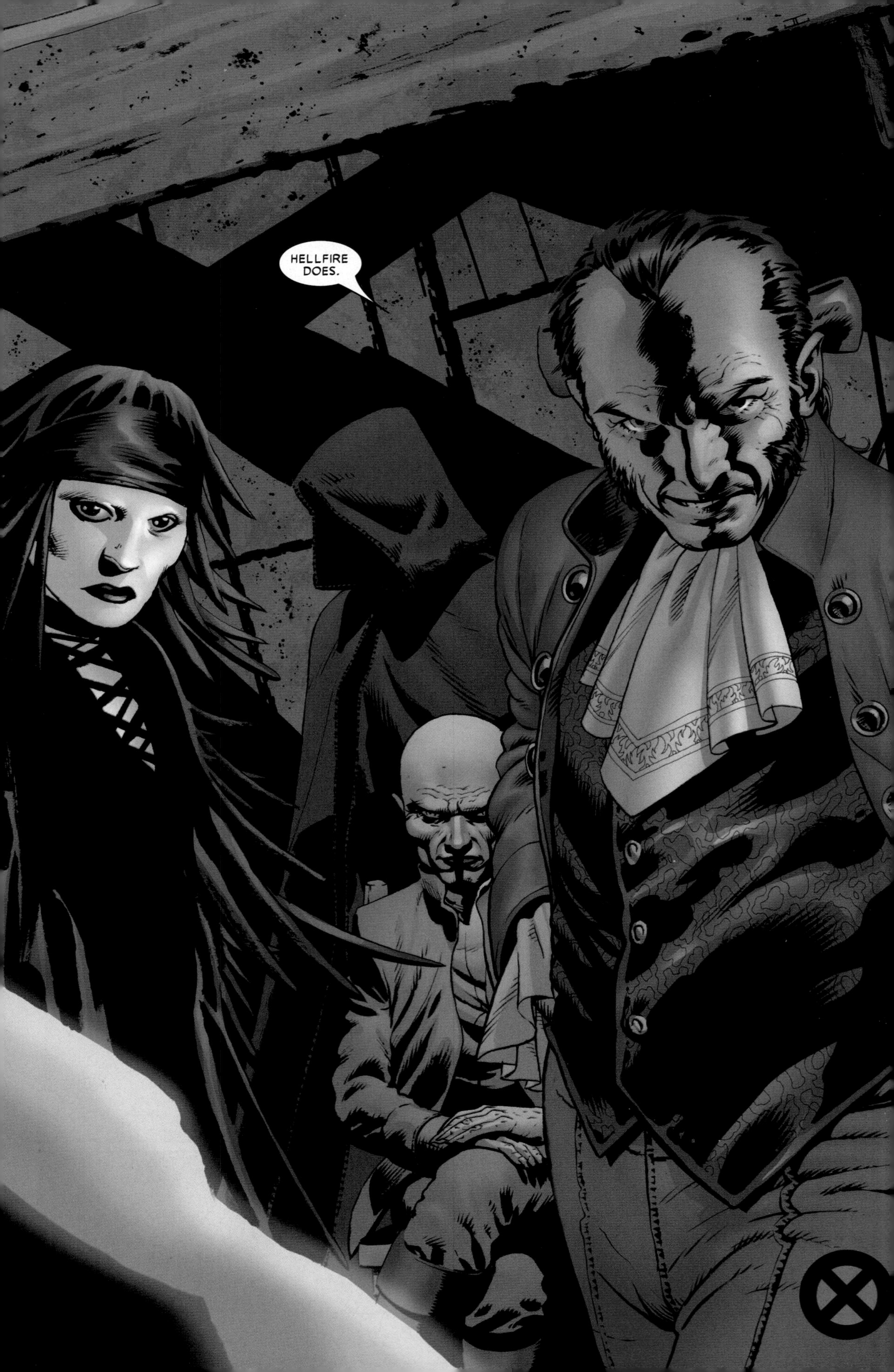
HELLFIRE DOES.

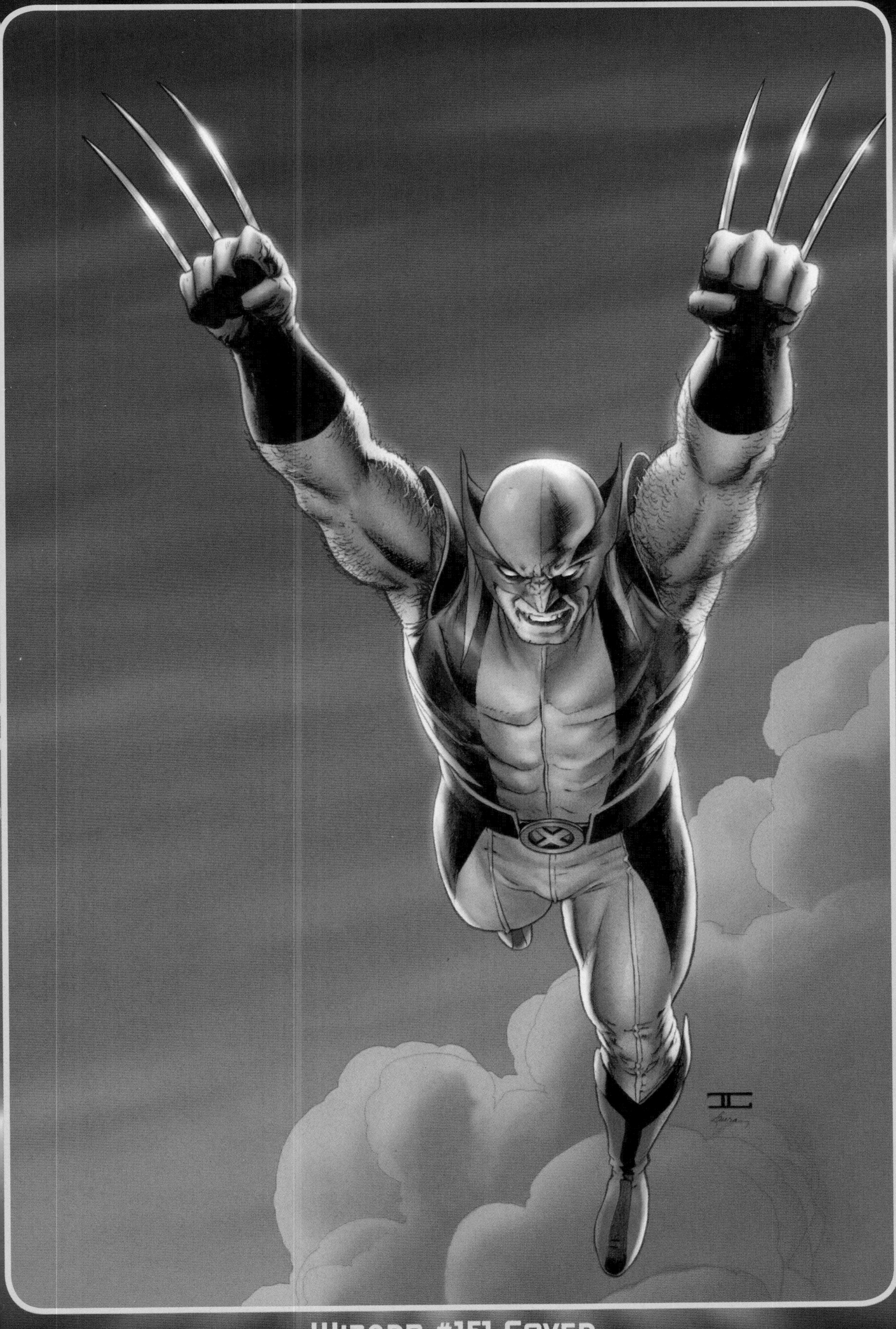

WIZARD #151 COVER
BY JOHN CASSADAY & LAURA MARTIN

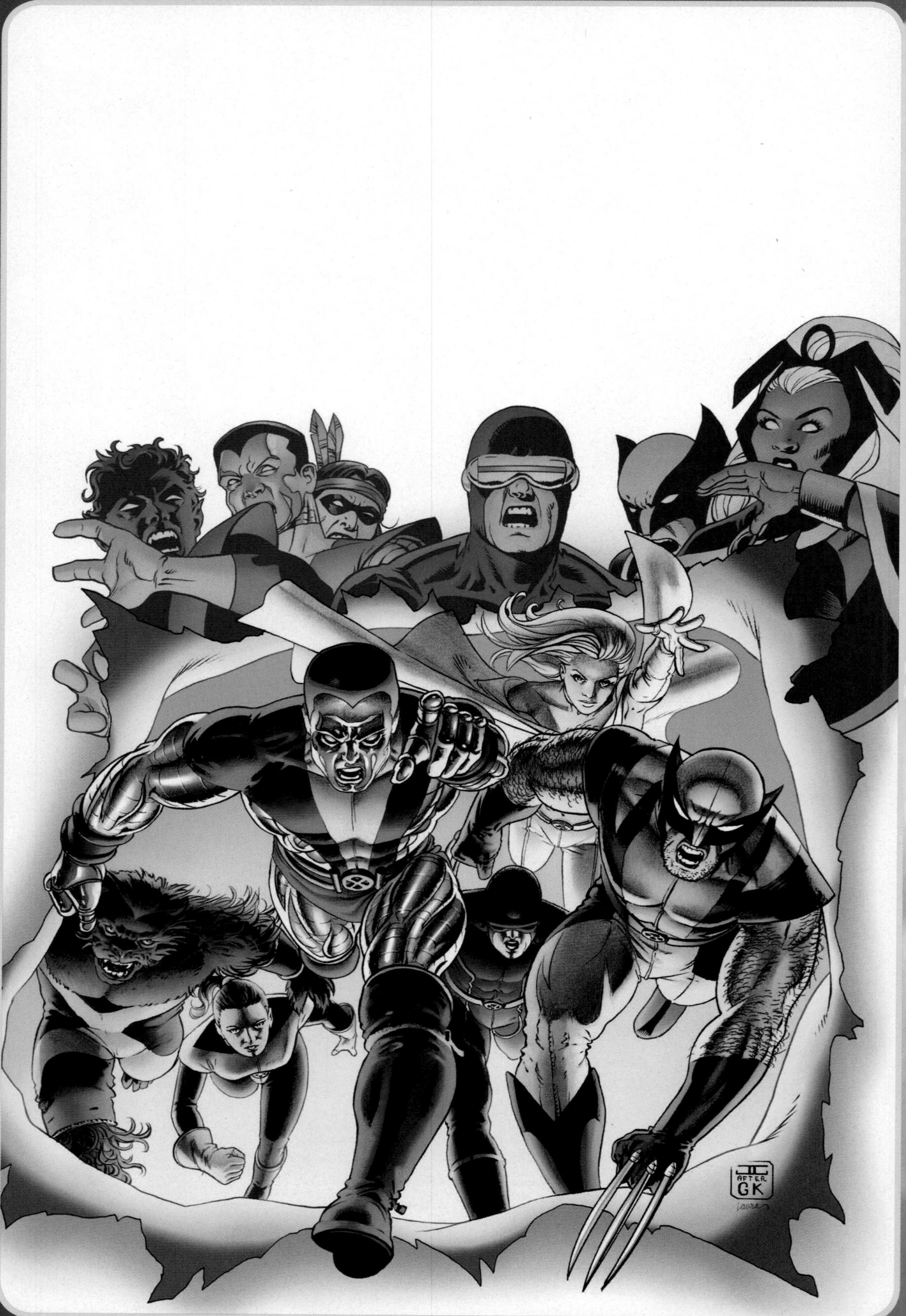

WIZARD #159 COVER
BY JOHN CASSADAY & LAURA MARTIN

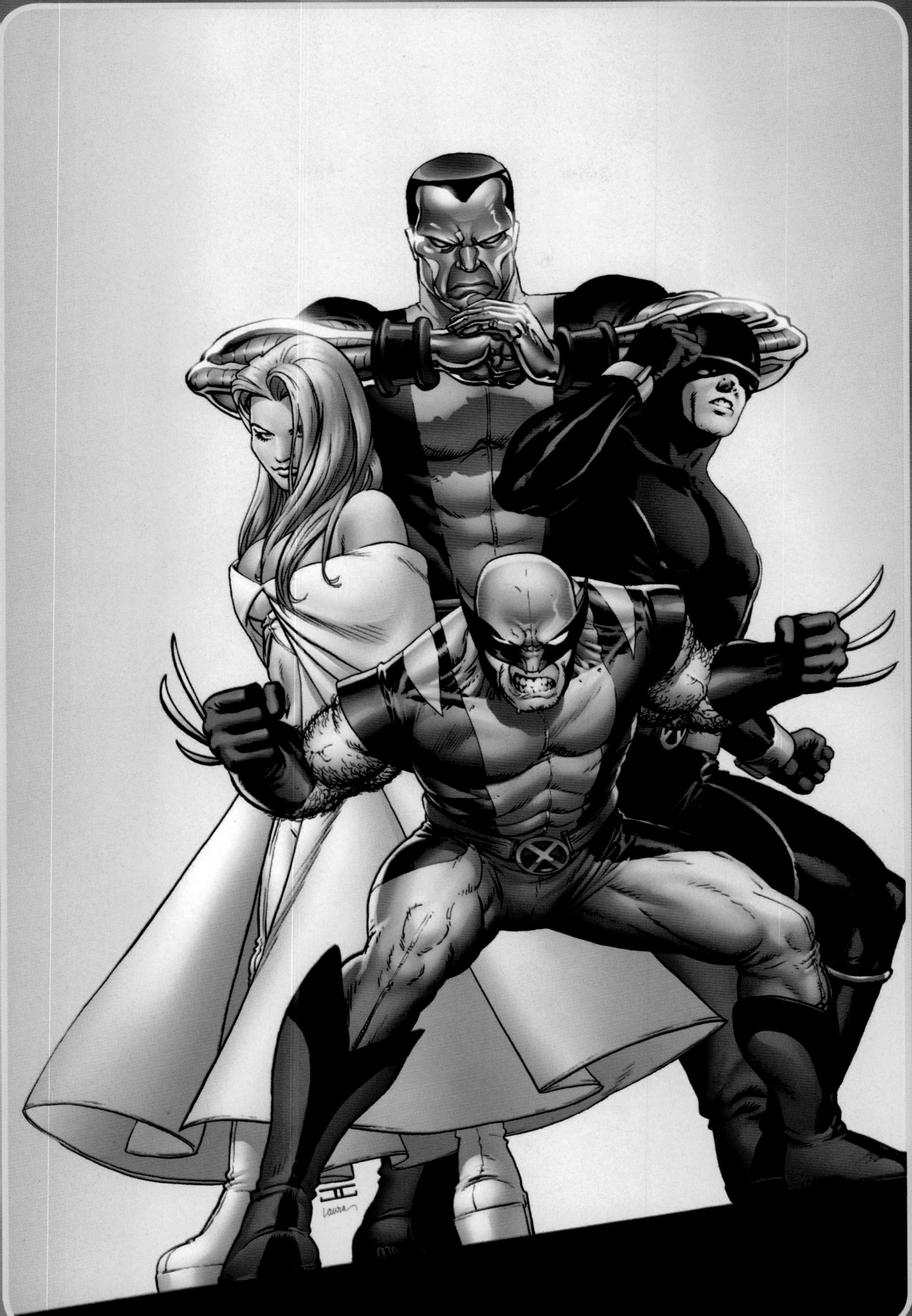

Wizard #173 Cover
By John Cassaday & Laura Martin

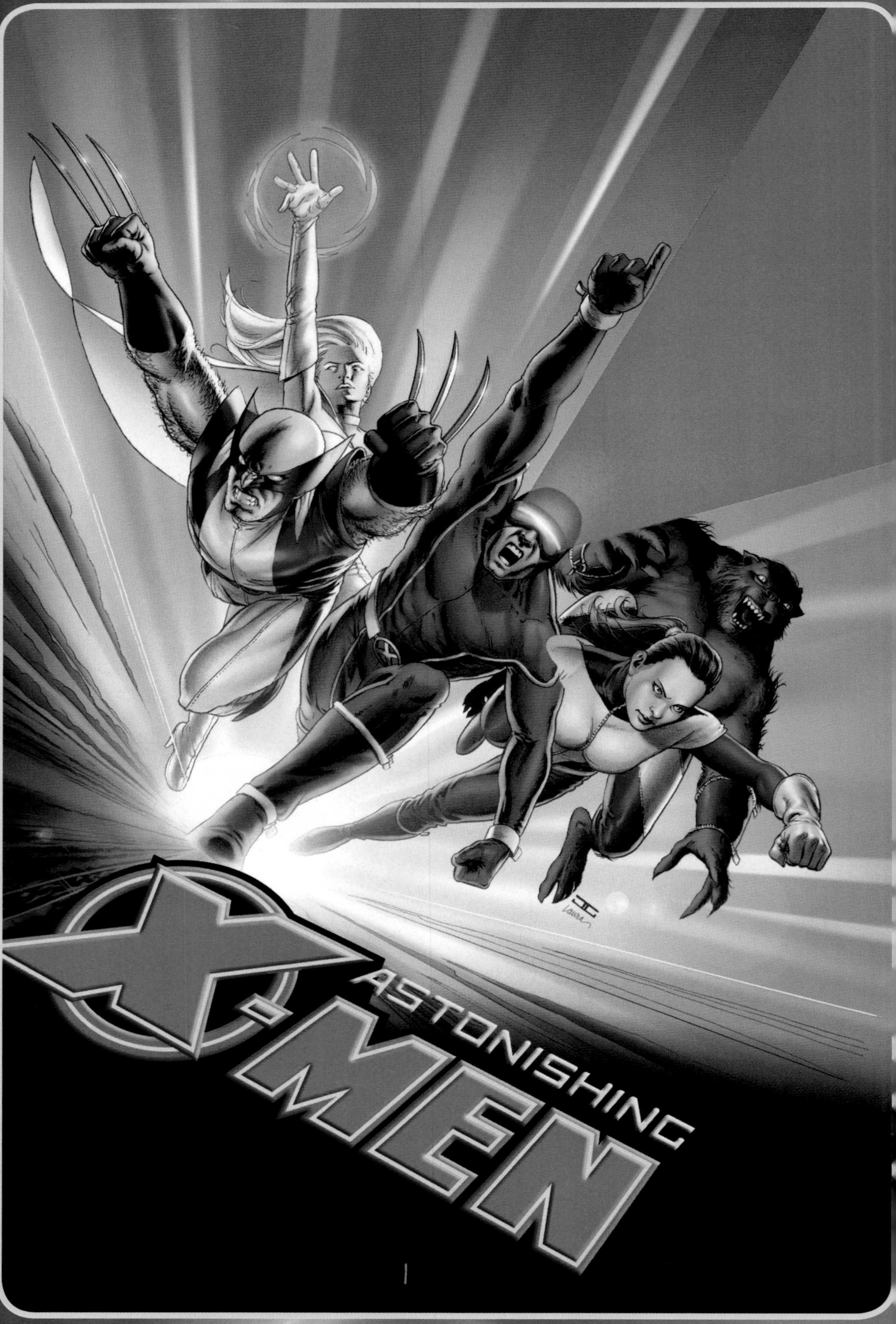
ASTONISHING
X-MEN

ISSUE #1 VARIANT COVER
BY JOHN CASSADAY & LAURA MARTIN

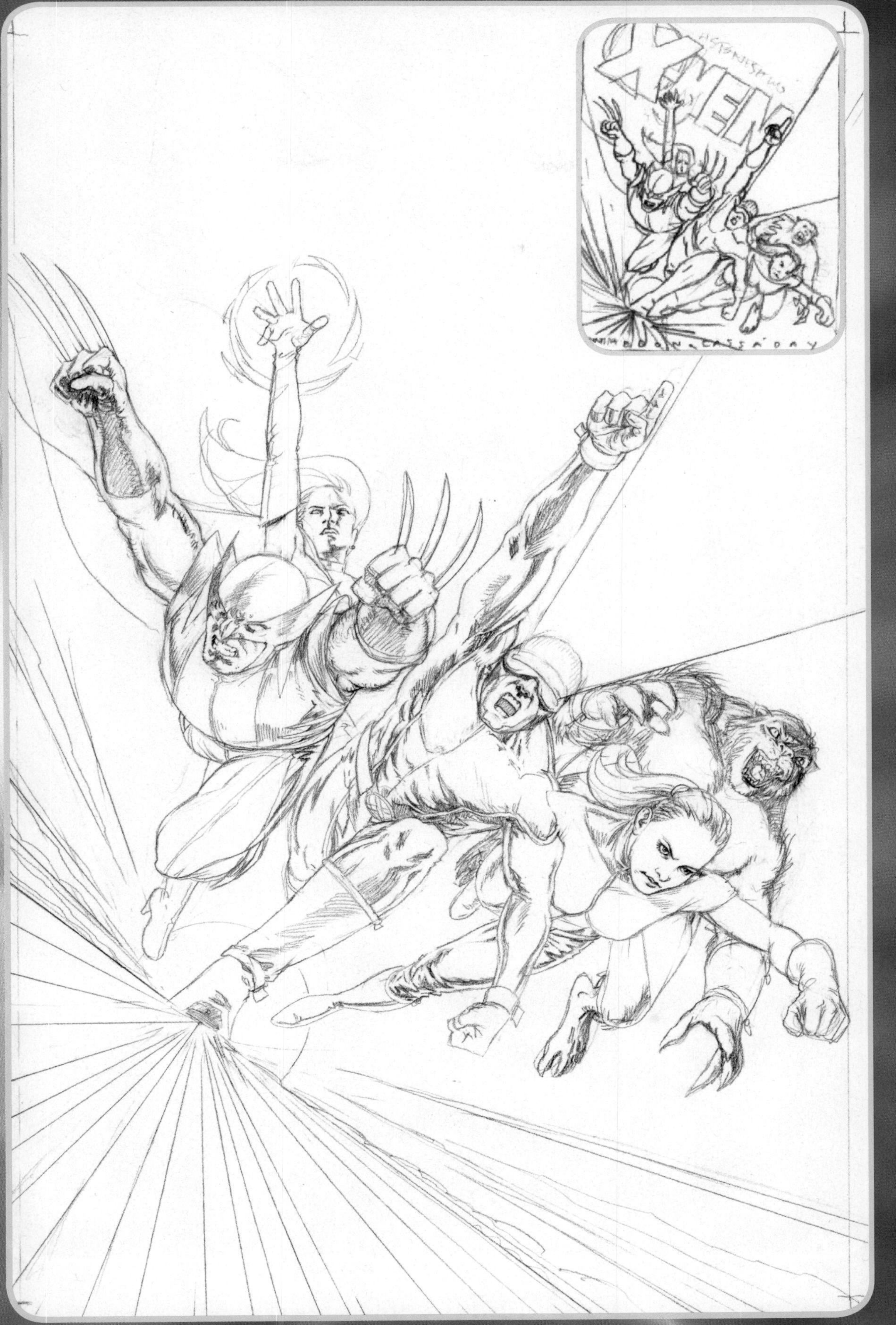

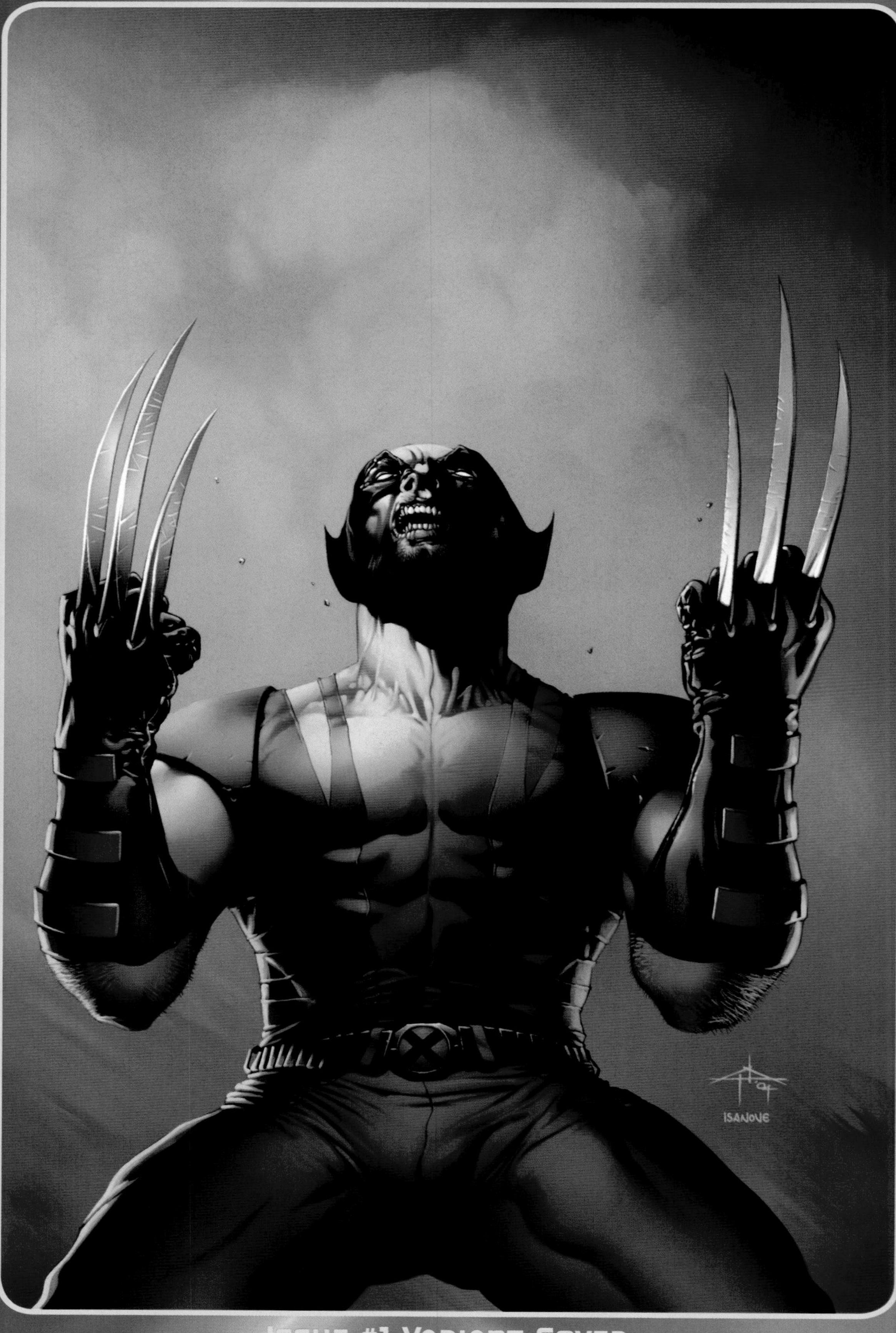
ISANOVE

Issue #1 Variant Cover
By Gabriele Dell'Otto

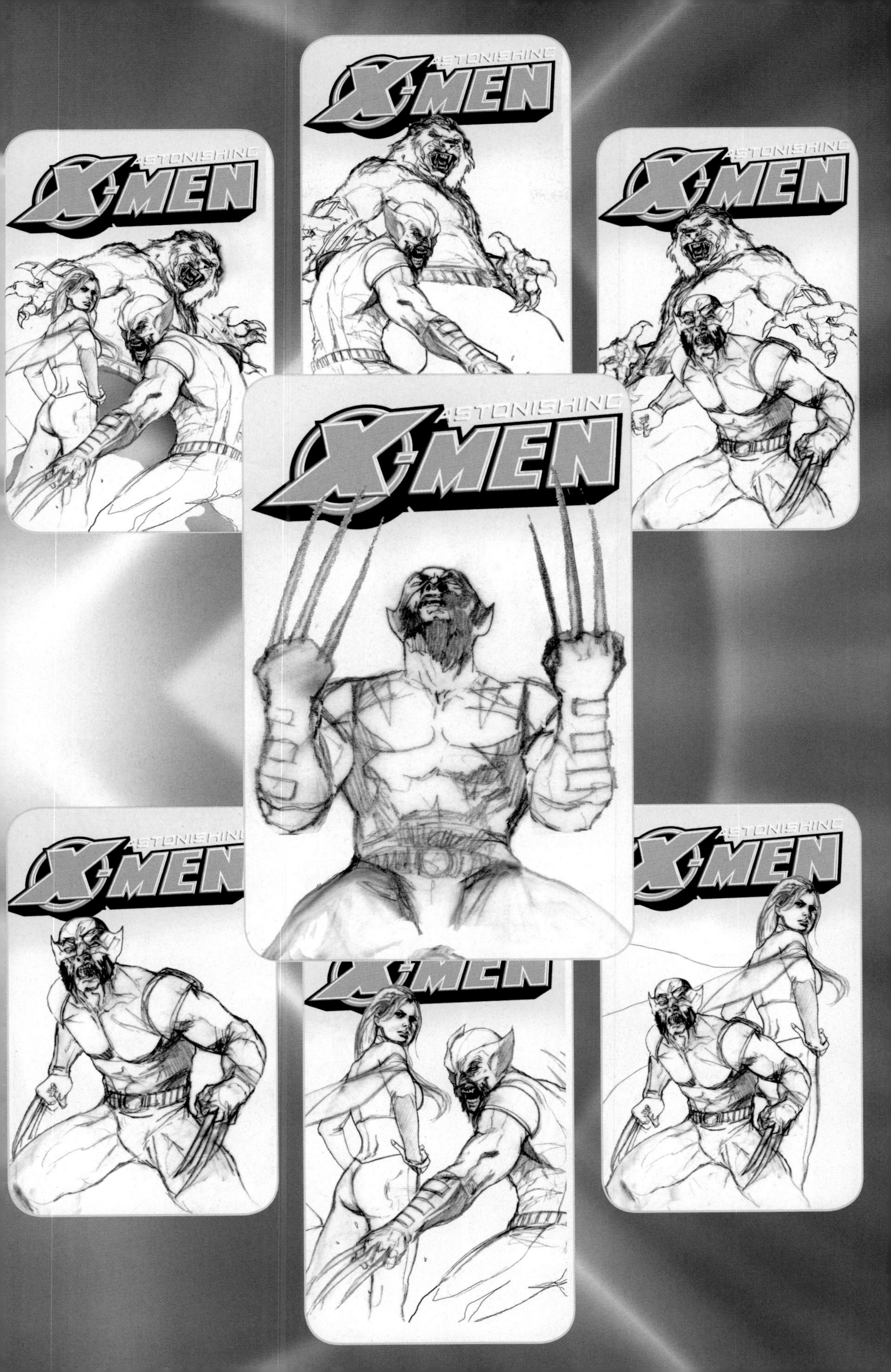
ASTONISHING
X-MEN

Variant Covers by John Cassaday & Laura Martin

Issue #7

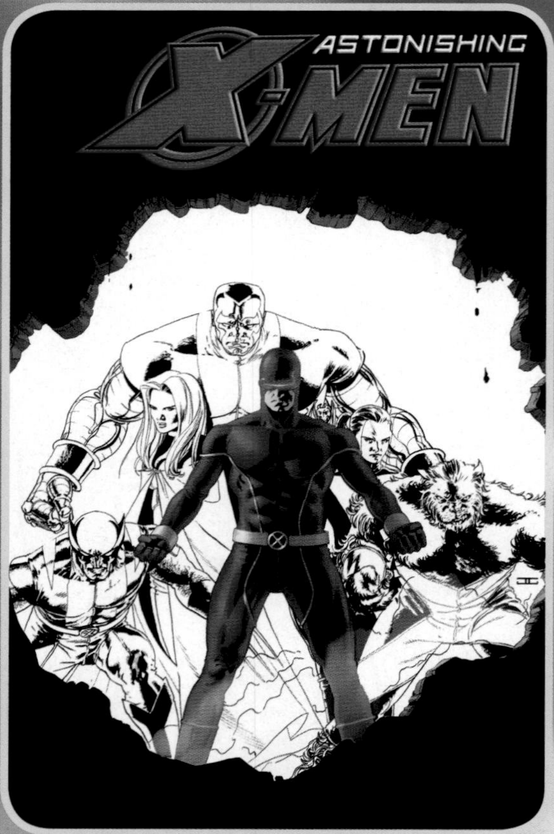
ASTONISHING
X-MEN

Issue #8

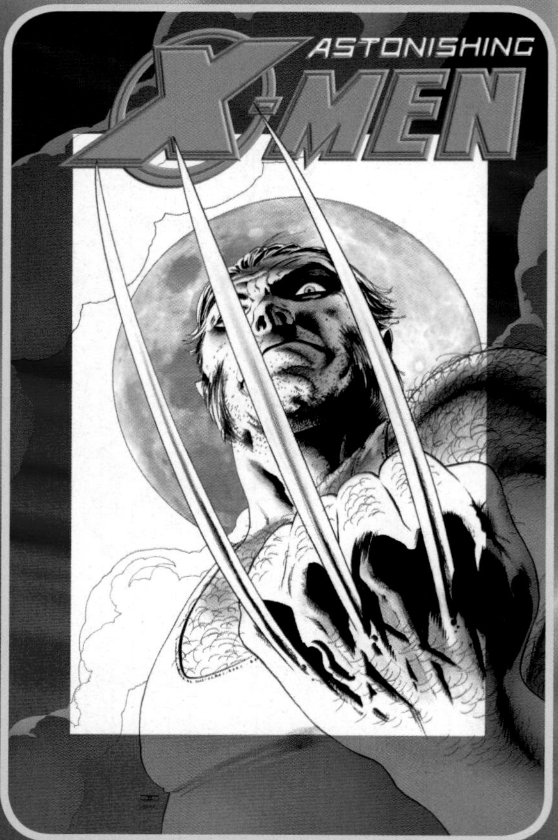
ASTONISHING
X-MEN

Issue #11

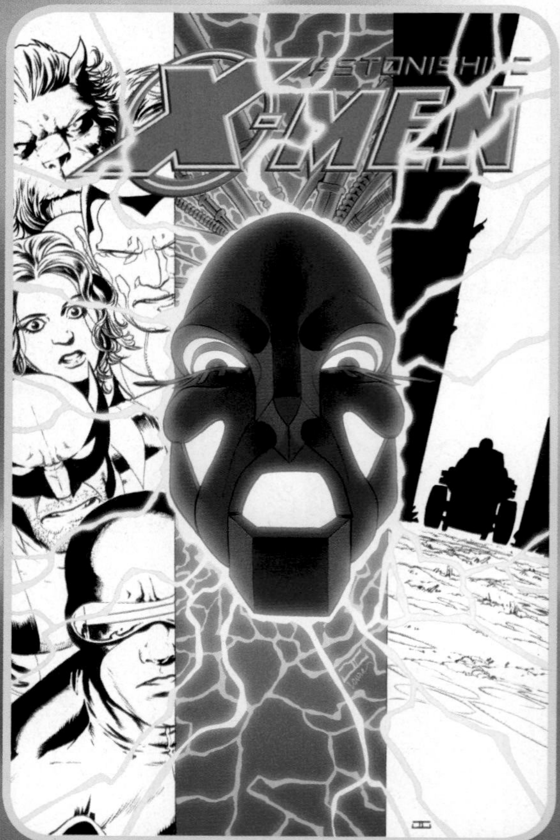
X-MEN

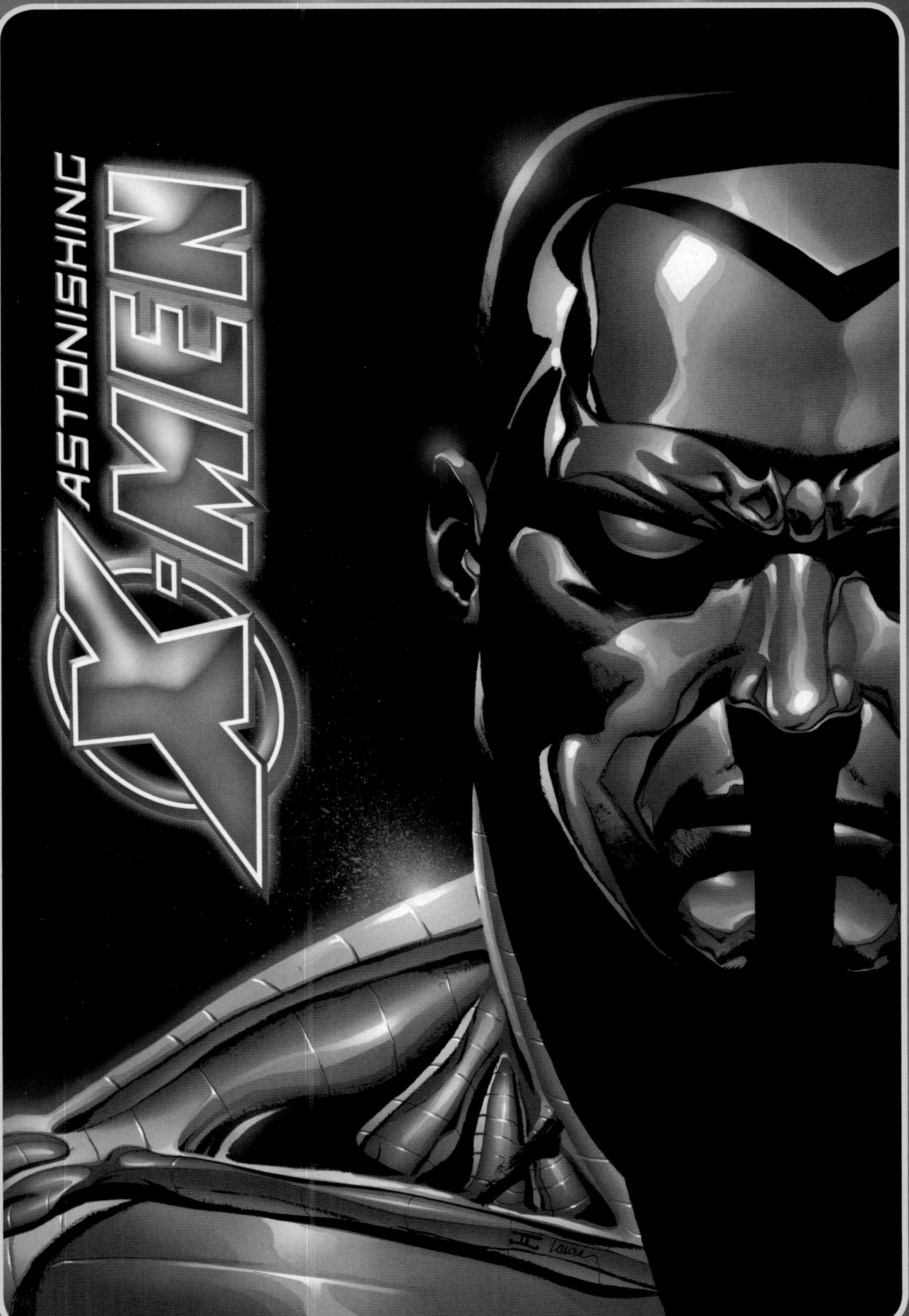
ASTONISHING
X-MEN

Issue #4 Variant Cover
by John Cassaday & Laura Martin

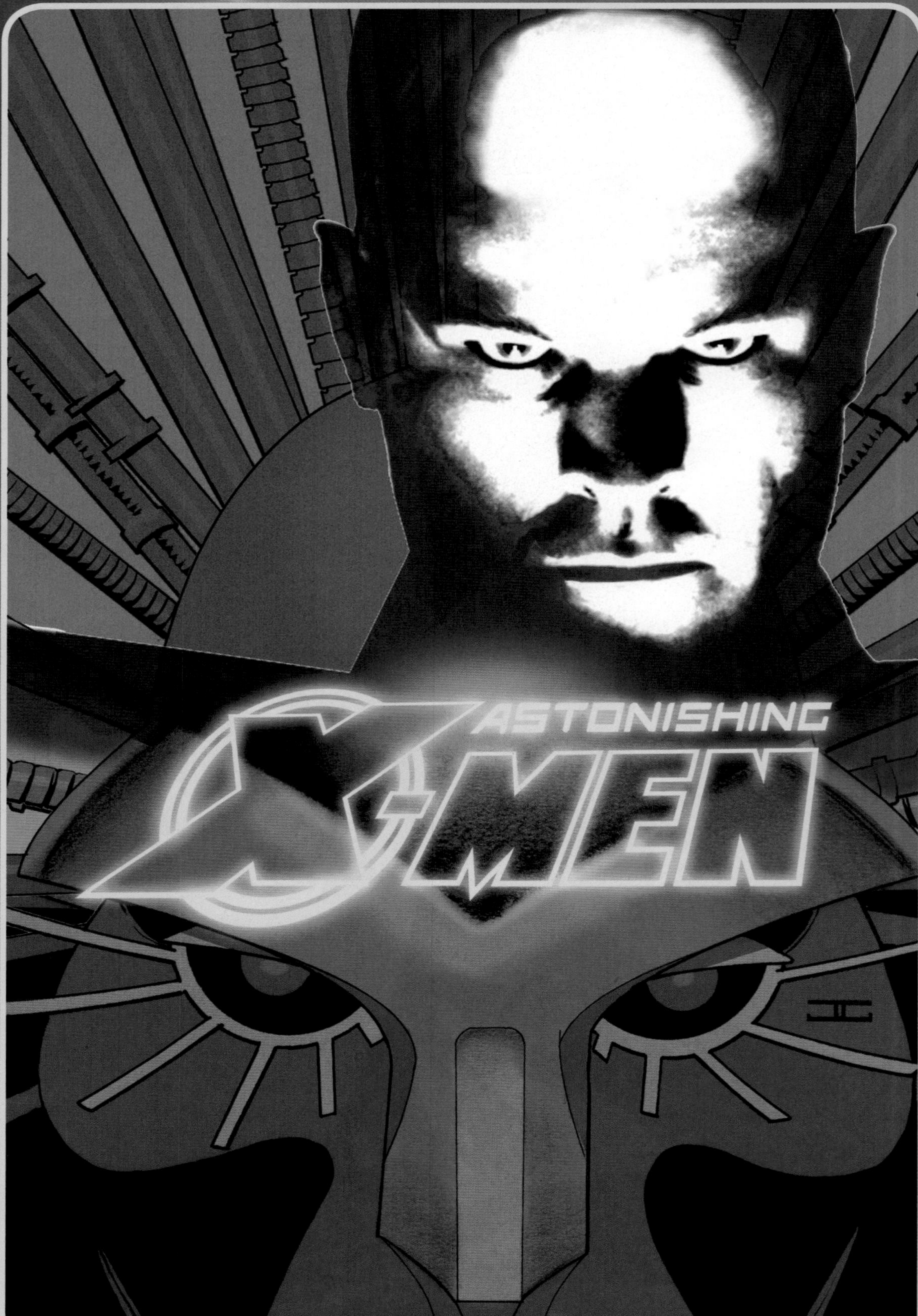
ASTONISHING
X-MEN

Issue #10 Variant Cover
By John Cassaday & Laura Martin

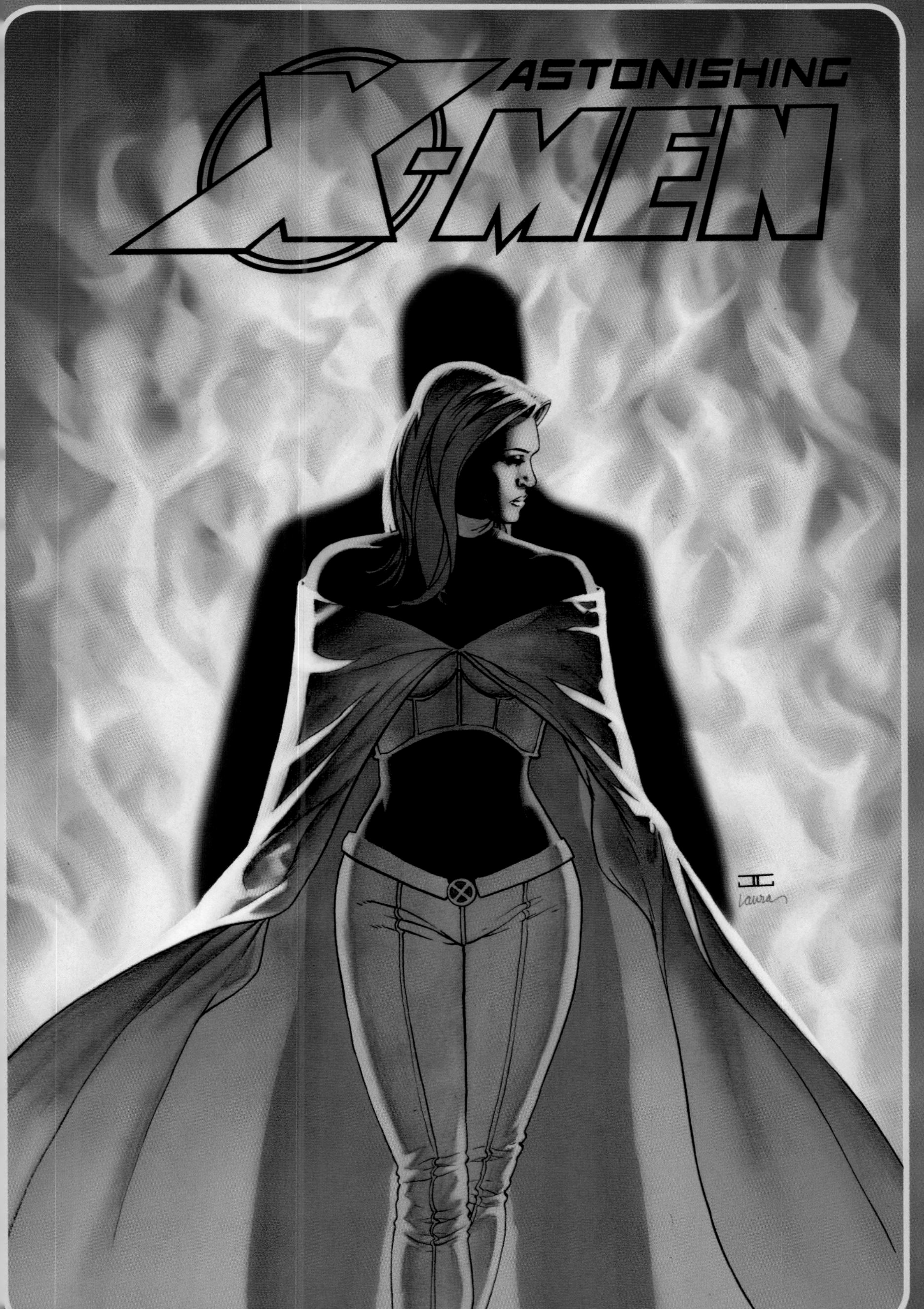
ASTONISHING
X-MEN

Issue #12 Variant Cover
By John Cassaday & Laura Martin

Character Designs by John Cassaday

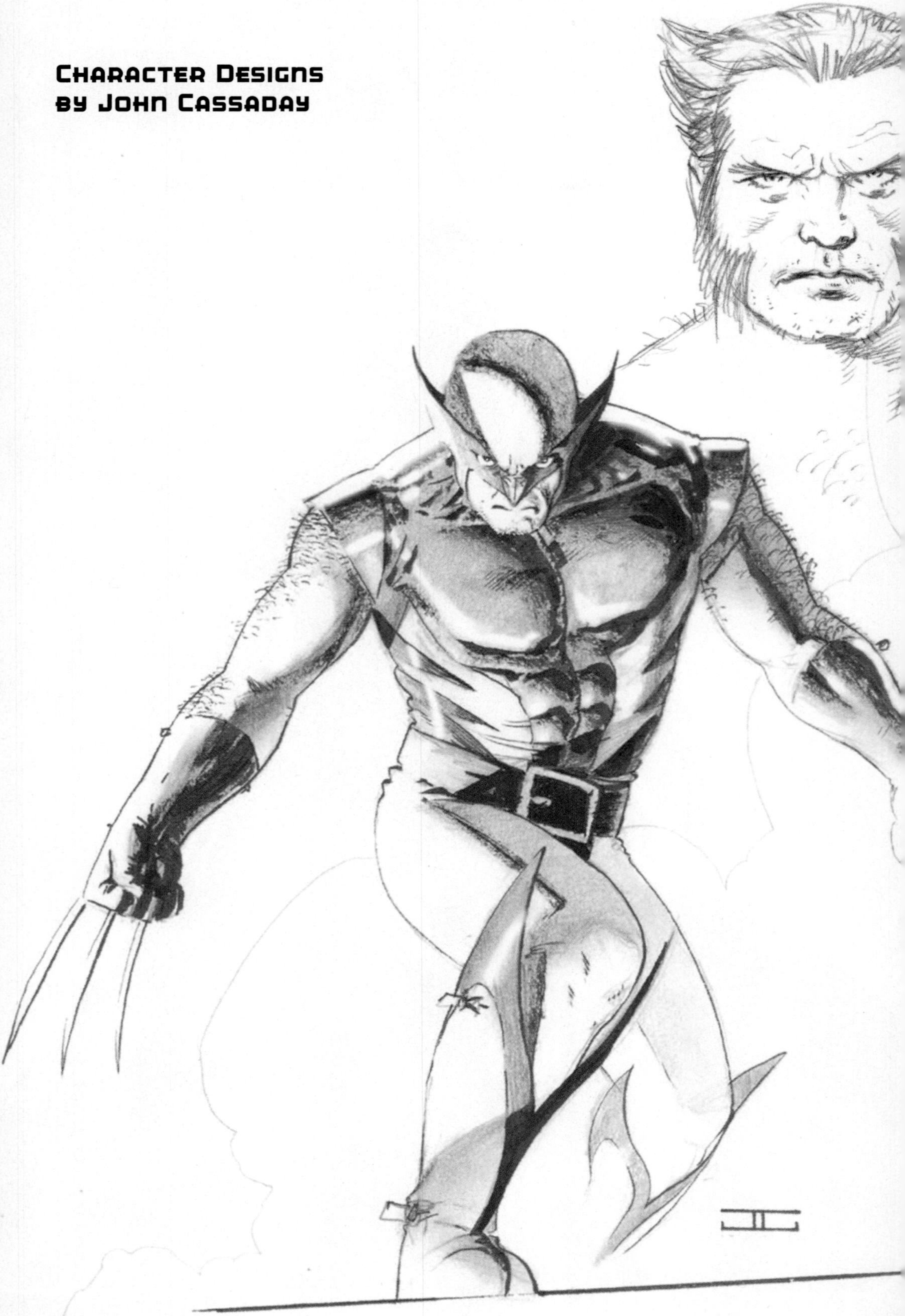

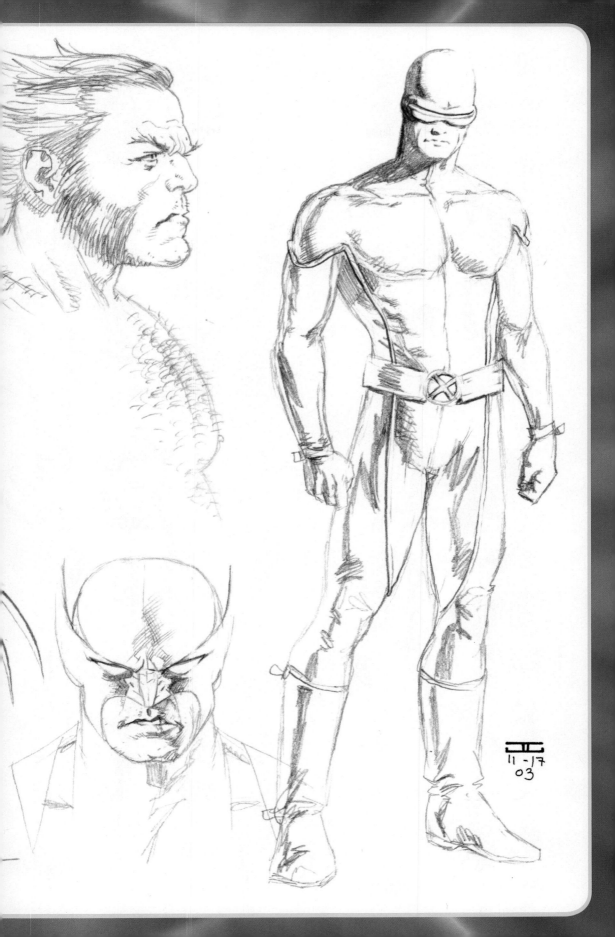

11 -17
03

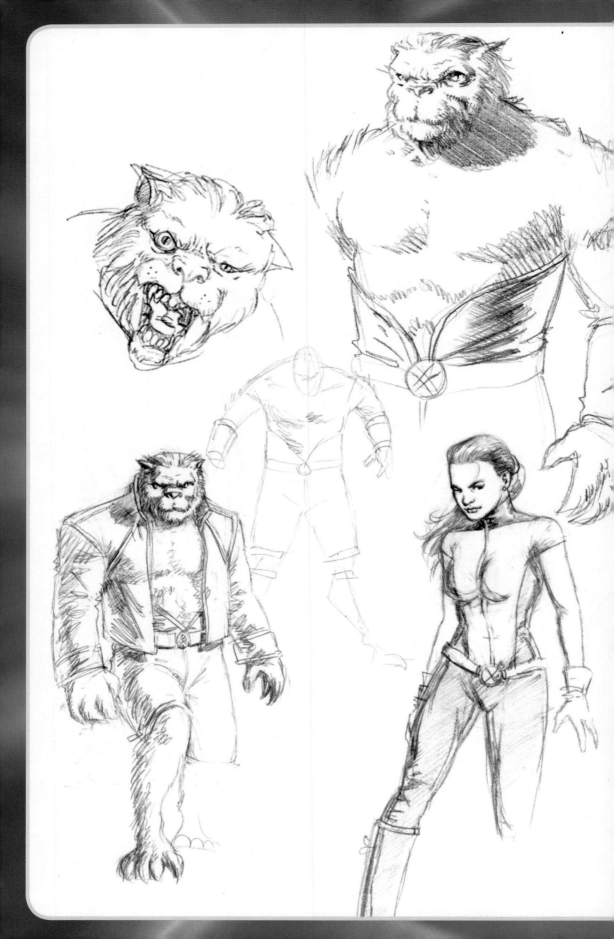

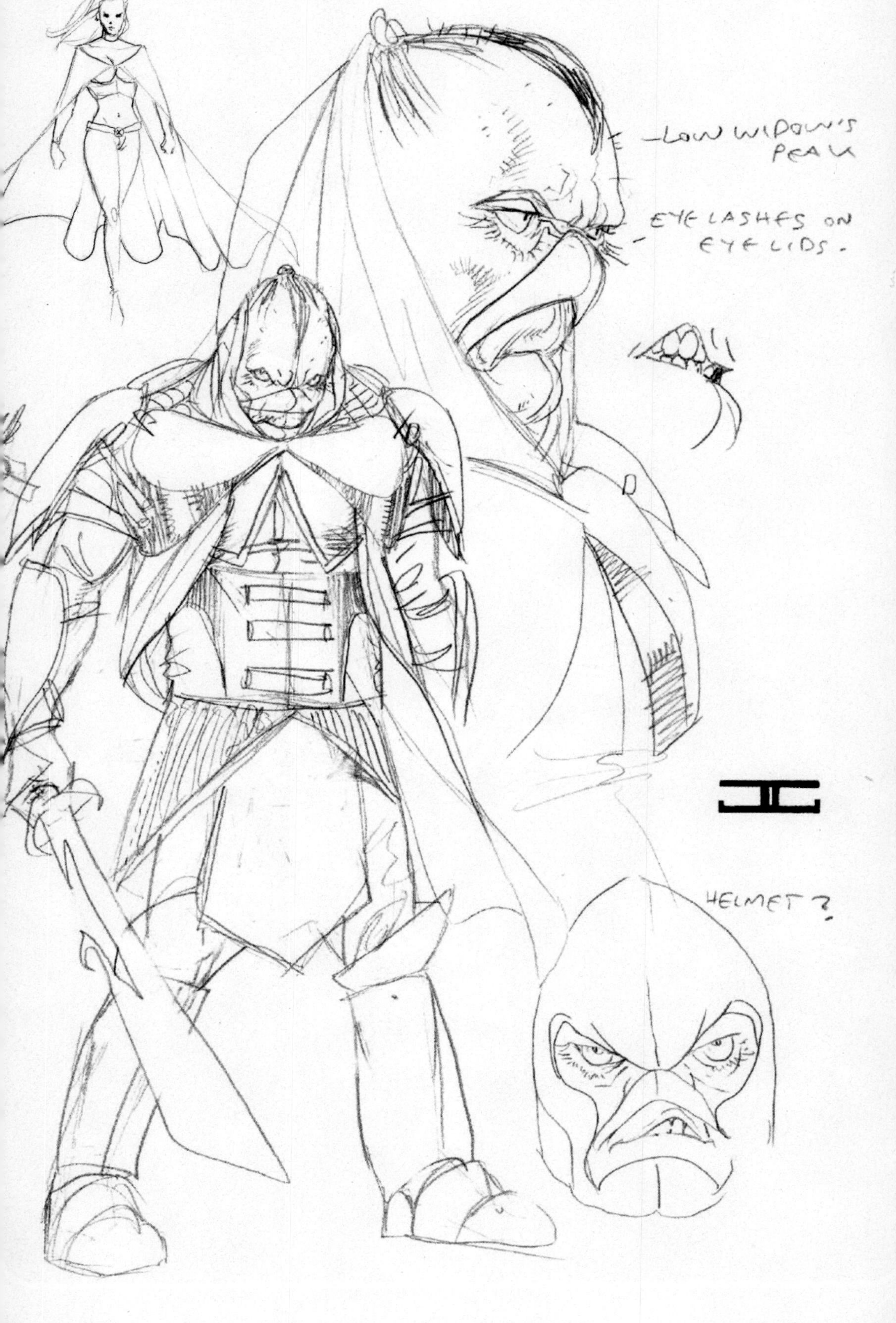
-LOW WIDOW'S PEAK
EYELASHES ON EYELIDS.
HELMET?

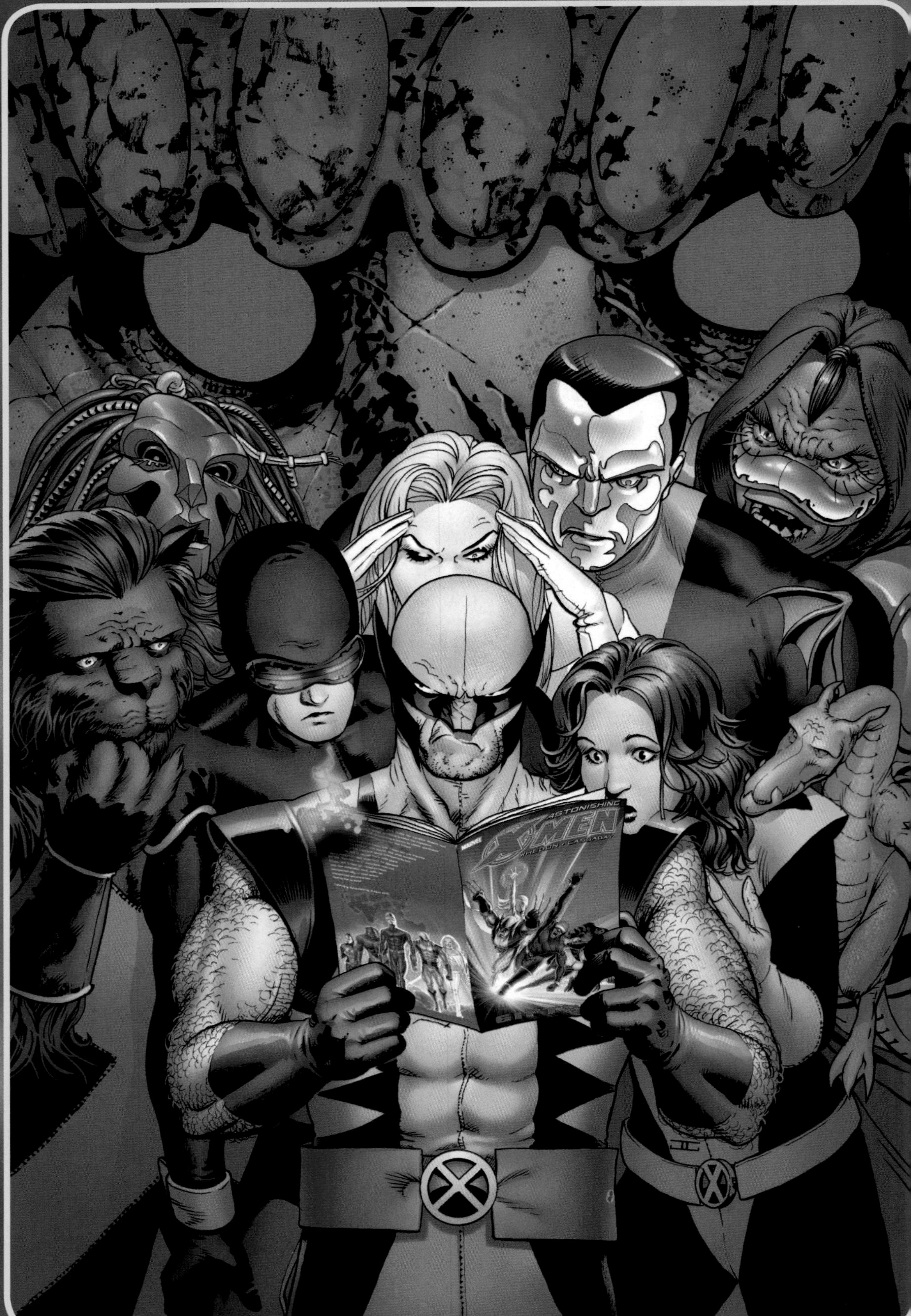
ASTONISHING
X-MEN

Astonishing X-Men Saga Cover
By John Cassaday & Laura Martin

JOSS WHEDON PLANNING EMAILS

From: Joss Whedon
To: Joe Quesada, Mike Marts
Subject: X
Date: Wed, 8 Oct 2003 18:33:51 EDT

Joe,

My early thoughts on what to do with X-MEN...

1) Less stuff happening. The X-men always seem to be DOING stuff, when they could be just talking about it, or watching it on CNN.

2) Xavier walking is a tired device — but have we ever seen him SKIPPING?

3) Wolverine — dead.

4) Let's feature some of the more overlooked X-Men, like Batman and the Flash.

5) What's up with these "panels"? More on that later.

6) Do I even need to say, "Gayathon"?

7) You could cut the sexual tension between Scott and Emma with a knife. I'm going to do that. I'm literally going to cut the sexual tension with a knife. Big f---ing kitchen knife. I have no idea how that will affect my writing.

8) Isn't *Beetle Bailey* just great fun?

Well, those are my thoughts. I know you're as excited as I am about this upcoming "comic book." As far as artists go, how do you feel about the guy that draws *Beetle Bailey?* I think he's a comer. I'm glad to have had the opportunity to put forth my Grant Morrisonesque mission statement, and remember: I'm too powerful to kill. For now.

Tra la, -j.

From: Joss Whedon
To: Joe Quesada, Mike Marts
Subject: Objective reality
Date: Mon, 17 Nov 2003 10:29:02 EST

Joe —

Thanks for hitting all the points in my cranky letter and taking them seriously. Like I said, I want to work in the system, but I like to have all the factors laid out before me so I don't waste time. I'm also (and will continue to be, make no mistake) protective and paranoid after 14 years in the movie business.

As for language, that's no problem. If you can't build a moment without th' cussin'...though my character HELLASSDAMMIT woulda sold like porn-cakes.

As far as costumes, as I told John, my feeling was that Scott should insist on them as part of making the X-Men a super hero team again, gettin' out there and kicking giant monster ass, saving lives, not just constantly reacting to a world that HATES and FEARS them. He feels the X-Men should be more, well, astonishing. So that should tie in okay.

I have many threads. I'll let you guys know when it starts to be a sweater. But here's a taste of what I have in mind:

"We're flying into the Ass of Hell, Dammit!"

You're in good hands.

j.

From: Marts, Michael
To: Whedon, Joss
Subject: hi
Date: Tue, 30 Dec 2003 08:24:37 -0500

Joss,

Merry Christmas and Happy New Year...

How goes things on your end? Anything I can do to help?

Best,

Mike

From: Whedon, Joss
To: Marts, Michael
Subject: RE: hi
Date: 12/30/03 1:58 PM

Merry and Happy yourself. Which I'm not so much.

So the other day I slip into an out-of-the-way comic book store I've never been to, right when it opens and is completely empty. Start going through old X-Men and within seconds hear "So, the rumors are true." Some guy starts going on — paying no attention to my denials — about how it was leaked on the internet again the other day, said it was a pretty badly kept secret...I walked out, which is about as rude as I've ever been to a fan, even an annoying one like this. I f---ing hate this. I can't say anything, we missed the Wizard 2004 ish, and I still don't have my moment.

Also, this comic book is hard to write.

But that's not your problem. What might be is this moment I'm still digging for. See, what I desperately want is something that is totally mundane, involving a happy Kitty if possible, outside the front of the mansion, that does not concern Colossus. Tall order. It's then followed by the "Professor Xavier is a jerk" moment and ends with the kissing Peter under the mistletoe moment. Quiet, simple stuff.

Hey, if I suck at this, people are gonna notice, right? Oh well. Maybe I could make Emma nuder.

Gotta fly. Sorry for th' tude, but I'm a temperamental artist type. Without the pesky art.

From: Marts, Michael
To: Whedon, Joss
Subject: RE: hi
Date: Tue, 30 Dec 2003 23:05:57 -0500

Joss,

I'm sorry, man, I can feel your frustration. And I know it may seem like everyone knows the secret, but believe me, they don't. I get plenty of X-mail every day with readers suspecting everyone from you to Scott Lobdell to Clive Barker to Neil Gaiman to Straczinski. And they all think they know for sure. Today's newest was David Mamet. Brilliant. And also, every fan out there wants to be THE GUY who finds out who it is. But it doesn't become fact until we announce it or Wizard prints it, and then they all go home happy.

But maybe I can make ya feel better, I think I found a decent moment for you. It takes place just within the mansion's front door, is not Peter-specific, and isn't super-heroic. In the opening pages of X-Men Annual #6 (the Dracula one), the X-Men are coming back from some function (maybe a play) and Kitty's ranting/raving/crying about the fact that her parents are getting divorced. The X-Men try to console her, but she runs up to her room.

Does this work? If not, I'll delve some more.

Seriously, let me know how else to help, bouncing ideas or whatever. We want this to be fun for you, so whatever will make things easier.

All the best,

Mike

From: Whedon, Joss
To: Marts, Michael
Subject: RE: hi
Date: Wednesday, December 31, 2003 1:12 AM

Dude, thank you muchly for the Drac moment. I found one other (in bookstores they don't ask why I'm buying X-Men, even if they recognize me. Niiiiice....) and it's between the two but I'm definitely good. Thanks on the serious tip for such digging.

Jeph Loeb called, let me know about "All The Rage," laughing that the secret was totally out. (Not in a mean way. Jeph's a sweetie.) I knew they couldn't keep a lid on it through X-Mas anyhoo. I just hope it doesn't hurt the momentum or any of that crap. Also, I still hope the book doesn't have to be that good. You guys don't have some weird quality standard, do you? I'm looking to avoid that. I'm not defensive! You're defensive!

Why did I have to follow Grant Morrison?

-j.

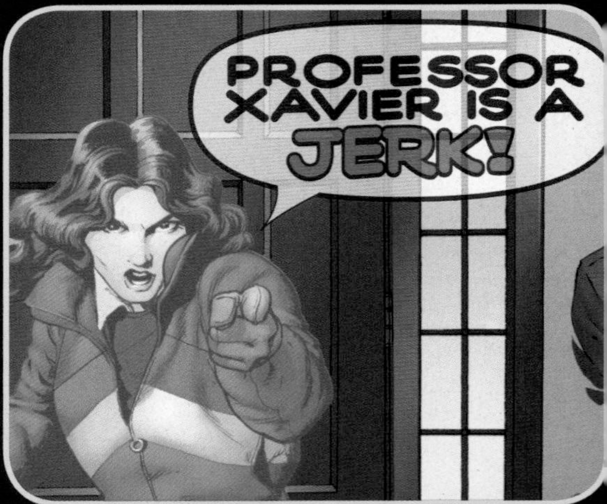
PROFESSOR XAVIER IS A JERK!

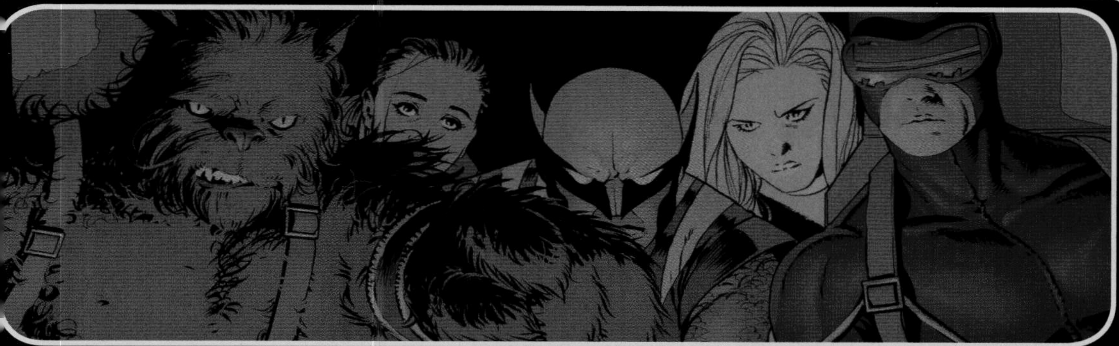

"Astonishing" X-Men prepare for their first battle…with someone other than themselves! (from *AXM #2*)

THE MARVEL SPOTLIGHT INTERVIEW WITH JOHN CASSADAY

By John Rhett Thomas

In case you didn't know it, John Cassaday is a busy guy. He's an in-demand, comic art superstar, and his talents on printed page don't just spring up in a matter of minutes. No, if you look at his work, each issue is full of dynamic layouts and realistic line art, but all grounded squarely within the comics art idiom; it's obviously labored over, without coming off as laboring for the reader. And done with care and craft. That takes time, folks! All the reasons we love to read — and look at — comics with John Cassaday's name on them are the same reasons why he can only take on a few gigs at a time.

So it is with great pleasure that Marvel Spotlight can report that we got a few moments of that time, and we used it to look back on the first year of Astonishing X-Men, a 12-issue run of comics that lived up to all the qualities of the word "astonishing," and more!

SPOTLIGHT: Obviously, Astonishing X-Men is the most high-profile X-Men gig going. It is also arguably the biggest project currently in the Marvel stable. How did you take to the plumb assignment of collaborating with Joss Whedon when it was offered to you?

JOHN: Joe Quesada told me he had an "offer I couldn't refuse." I nearly didn't show for fear of my life. I was sure I'd wake up with Quick Draw MacGraw's head in my bed. Joe and I spoke about X-Men before, but it was Joss throwing his name in that made it the right time for me to sign up.

SPOTLIGHT: Were you a big X-Men fan growing up? If so, what era did you cut your teeth on?

JOHN: The entire Dark Phoenix story, the Alpha Flight appearances, pretty much the entire Claremont/Byrne run. The Paul Smith issues are stunning as well. I found those in collections because I didn't start reading X-Men off the rack until the Kulan Gath two-parter around #190... Romita Jr. was on it then, so they have a special place in my heart too.

SPOTLIGHT: Taking on the X-Men Universe for the first time must be a formidable task for any comics creator. Did you have any concerns before climbing into the cockpit on such a job?

JOHN: I didn't have any serious concerns about doing the book. Joss and I both wanted to get back to the essence of what makes X-Men work and cut the fat of all the detours that didn't fit... Not to change history or disregard continuity, but to focus more. Simplify and streamline. More character and less boom-boom.

But then we threw in some boom-boom because we like that too.

SPOTLIGHT: Is lettering sound effects something you really enjoy? Does Joss Whedon call you up

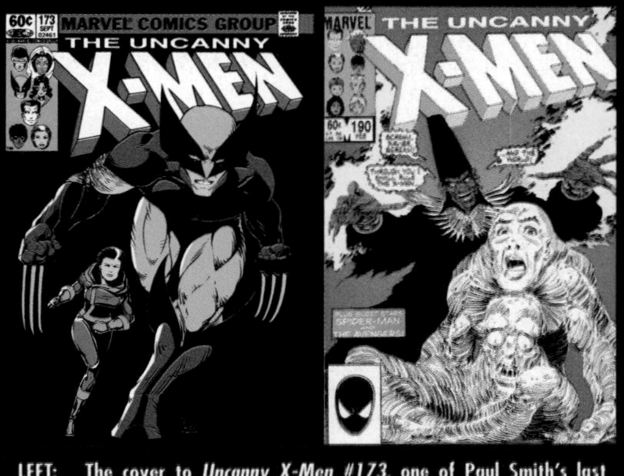

MARVEL COMICS GROUP
60¢ 173 SEPT
THE UNCANNY X-MEN
MARVEL
THE UNCANNY X-MEN
60¢ 190 FEB

LEFT: The cover to *Uncanny X-Men #173*, one of Paul Smith's last issues in his run as regular artist.

RIGHT: The cover to *Uncanny X-Men #190*, part of the Kulan Gath storyline.

and say "Now make sure Cyke's 'SHKOW!' plays really, really big!"?

JOHN: I don't use a great deal of sound FX. If I show a gunshot, you should hear it without it being spelled out. They can be fun, but never used in mundane ways.

SPOTLIGHT: Upon reading and rereading Astonishing X-Men, it seems to me that you take great joy in drawing the Beast. AXM #2 was where you really started cooking with your delineation of Hank's form: visceral and animalistic edginess but with undertones of ballet-like grace.

By issue #12, he's evolved into a gangly savage, arms and legs akimbo as he carries Xavier through the rubble of Genosha. Are you having as much fun drawing Hank as it would appear? Or is he perhaps the most challenging, and thus difficult, to pull off?

JOHN: Beast is not my top fave to draw, but you're right about his evolution. He's grown on me from issue to issue. I definitely feel the character more than I did in the beginning. He's more real to me now. So much of that is Joss' fault.

SPOTLIGHT: When you got down to sketching out your approach to drawing Hank, what jumped out at you as elements of his physiology and appearance that you wanted to really bring to the fore?

JOHN: I didn't want to re-create him. Again. My personal spin is that he's not necessarily becoming a cat. He doesn't know what he's becoming. Could be anything. That's a scarier prospect for me. In general, I looked more at what he would be wearing. He's covered in fur. I thought we should see that. Besides, I think people who dress their pets are silly.

SPOTLIGHT: Speaking of Hank's animalistic qualities, it's clear that Wolverine shares many of the same traits. This common grounding in their characters helps set up the tension when it comes to the two of them discussing "The Cure." What are the different approaches you take to drawing these two characters, whose renderings could be in danger of seeming redundant if artistic care isn't taken?

JOHN: They're similar in many ways. Physically, I feel that Logan is what Beast wishes he were. Beast is struggling with a savage side; he wants to go out in public without being the freak. He wants hands, not paws. Logan likes the bars, but wants to be left alone really. They're both savage, but in nearly opposite ways. In a sense, they're looking at a mirror of what they believe themselves to truly be... But Logan is actually hairier.

SPOTLIGHT: How closely do you work with colorist Laura Martin? Do you have strong opinions about coloring nuances that you pass on to her?

John namedrops this panel as one that shows Laura Martin as the standout talent she is. Gripping, atmospheric, and spooky suspense come together in layout, figure placement and coloring. (from *AXM #4*)

JOHN: Laura and I work very closely together. Always have. She's one of the best there is, no doubt. It makes me that much more confident knowing she's got my back. I don't know how some artists can work and not think about color. I've always art directed my books and perhaps when it comes to my work I could be labeled a "control freak" or "perfectionist" type. I just know the complete image when I'm drawing it. From my pencil/ink art to color to lettering. I think a great deal about it all. It only helps the book, I believe. I look for inspiration from everything. Movies, books, paintings, advertising, nightclubs, subways and anything else that may cross my eyes. Skies aren't always blue and grass green. I've got a tendency to tint scenes according to what's occurring. The red tone of the return of Colossus (#4) is a good example. Danger, mystery and intensity soak the atmosphere when Kitty walks up to open the big door. The scene would not play the same in natural light.

SPOTLIGHT: I've noticed a couple instances of what I think is a very clever sense of humor.

Laura Martin colors this scene featuring 'new mutants' Hisako and Wing, depicting a fall day on the X-Mansion grounds with the attendant overcast skies and turning leaves. (from *AXM #7*)

njected into some of your panel drawings. Tell me if I'm just seeing things:

n the big "Monster Fight" splash in AXM #7, you depict a battle scene where members of the X-Men and Fantastic Four are all standing their ground in heroic battle against their foe...well, except for Wolverine. He's getting tossed back like a rag doll, nothing visible but his backside as he flies back pathetically through the air — was this a little joke you inserted on the side, picking on old Logan?

JOHN: Very little!

SPOTLIGHT: Also, couldn't help but notice the Charlie Brown kid stuck in the middle of the otherwise tense Danger Room desert scenario in AXM #9. I love Charlie Brown. Had no idea he was a mutant!

You're A Good X-Man, Charlie Brown! John Cassaday unites the Peanuts Universe with the X-Men Universe in the comics event of the year...in a good-natured homage to Charles Schulz' classic creation. (from AXM #9)

JOHN: How else would you explain the big round head? A bee sting?

SPOTLIGHT: Are there any other in-jokes you like to subliminally include into your artwork?

JOHN: A few too many to go into. Just keep the peepers peeled.

SPOTLIGHT: Speaking of the Fantastic Four, that must have been a treat to get to draw them during their interlude in AXM #7.

JOHN: I've told many people that AXM #7 is a perfect Marvel comic in my mind. X-Men fighting a big monster in the middle of Manhattan, the Fantastic Four show up! The intense bookends with Wing. That tragic cliffhanger ending... I feel it had it all. I'm proud to have been there.

SPOTLIGHT: Of your covers to AXM, #5-7 are instant classics, and the ones with Colossus really stand out, naturally, because of the import that his return has to the X-Men. But of all of them, the best seems to me to be AXM #4, with the Beast looking over the shattered picture of his younger self. That single cover tells more of a story than some comics do in 22 pages.

JOHN: One of my favorite artists is N.C. Wyeth, who illustrated classic books from 1910-1945. So much of his magic was not simply to illustrate what had been written, but to show what had maybe only been hinted at. The story behind the story. A hidden moment. That's what the #4 Beast cover is. I think some look over it because it's not flashy, but it's a cover that begs the reader to use their brain as much as their eyes. That was the goal. Covers should be more than glorified pin-ups.

SPOTLIGHT: What is your artistic approach to covers? Is there an editorial dictate or do you get recommendations from Joss as to what to do? Or is there autonomy given to you to knock these out on your own terms?

JOHN: I come up with the vast majority of covers. I talk with Joss and always look for any feedback from him and Marvel is almost always on the same page with us. It's a painless process. Trust is key. Joss and I specifically spoke about the AXM #6 cover (Kitty and Colossus) before we even knew which issue it would cover! It's just an image he knew we'd wanna see.

SPOTLIGHT: The portrayal of Hisako and her powers in AXM #4 has a real Ditko influence to me. Am I just seeing things?

JOHN: I LOVE Ditko. So maybe it's subliminal, but not intentional. Do you see spots and rainbow unicorns too? See your doctor. Or just stop with the elephant tranquilizers and coffee.

Proof that elephant tranquilizers work! Spotlight thinks the surreal influence of Steve Ditko shines through nicely in this display of Hisako's powers — put to good use against Ord in this panel from AXM #4. What do you think?

SPOTLIGHT: Elephant tranquilizers? P'shaw! I don't mess with that stuff...it's rhino tranqs or nothing for me! (Oh, and I don't drink coffee...)

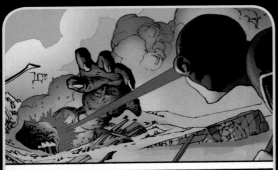

Whedon and Cassaday team up to team up the X-Men and the Fantastic Four! (from *AXM #7*)

SPOTLIGHT: Another classic sequence is in AXM #8, which features a genuinely scary moment straight out of a classic horror movie, when the X-Men take to the Mansion grounds to locate their unknown enemy. Lockheed illuminates the pitch-black sky with a flare and...Sentinel!!! Like really close! Yikes!

JOHN: Yes, perhaps Joss should think about writing some stories with a horror element involved... Mummies maybe...? Werewolves...? Vam... Nah, never mind...

SPOTLIGHT: Dude, I so don't want to live in your nightmare world. What was the influence on the Bosch-ian two-page spread depicting the school kids being stuck in Danger Room hell? Were you on some sort of caffeine bender that night?

JOHN: I spent a night watching Kubrick movies on mute with the Smurf theme song on a loop blasting the paint off my walls.

SPOTLIGHT: Perhaps you'd be better off sticking with rhino tranqs, but regardless, keep doing whatever you do to bring your talents to the Marvel Comics stable.

John Cassaday's next project for Marvel Comics is the next run of Astonishing X-Men in collaboration with Joss Whedon, starting in February 2006.

Now, back to the interview, AXM #4 ends with a seven-page sequence that will hit X-Men fans that grew up with Kitty and Peter right where they live. In a 12-issue run of full of jaw-dropping moments, this sequence must have led to more emergency rooms visits for jaw-reconstruction surgeries than any other!

What was your reaction upon reading Joss' script for the "Kitty Finds Colossus" sequence? Did it get your blood pumping to know that you were the guy who would soon hold in your grip the emotional core of X-Men fanboys around the world?

JOHN: Marvel asked us to bring back Colossus way back when the deal was made. I knew it was coming. I had no idea Joss was going to make grown men cry. I couldn't have been happier to read that script and I couldn't have been more scared of blowing it!

Upon seeing the page with Colossus running through Kitty, Joss took out the bubbles of dialogue from the page. He felt the images told the story without them. That's as great a compliment as I could ask for.

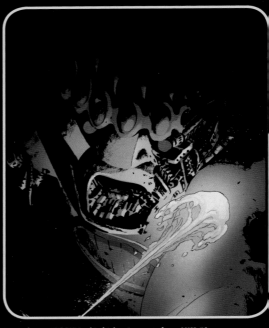

Sentinel says "BOO!" in this frightening scene from *AXM #8.*